Psychopathology: From Science to Clinical Practice

Psychopathology: From Science to Clinical Practice

Editor: Somer Ebert

AMERICAN
MEDICAL PUBLISHERS
www.americanmedicalpublishers.com

AMERICAN
MEDICAL PUBLISHERS
www.americanmedicalpublishers.com

Cataloging-in-Publication Data

Psychopathology : from science to clinical practice / edited by Somer Ebert.
p. cm.
Includes bibliographical references and index.
ISBN 979-8-88740-407-3
1. Psychology, Pathological. 2. Psychiatry. 3. Mental illness--Diagnosis.
4. Mental illness--Treatment. 5. Psychotherapy. I. Ebert, Somer.
RC435 .P794 2023
616.89--dc23

American Medical Publishers,
41 Flatbush Avenue,
1st Floor, New York,
NY 11217, USA

ISBN 979-8-88740-407-3 (Hardback)

Contents

Preface

Over the recent decade, advancements and applications have progressed exponentially. This has led to the increased interest in this field and projects are being conducted to enhance knowledge. The main objective of this book is to present some of the critical challenges and provide insights into possible solutions. This book will answer the varied questions that arise in the field and also provide an increased scope for furthering studies.

Pathology refers to the study of a disease which acts as a connecting link between science and medicine. Psychopathology is the connecting link between the science and clinical practice of psychology. It is the scientific study of abnormal mental states. It has provided a structure for psychiatric diseases and driven clinical and scientific advancement in modern psychiatry. Changes in eating patterns, mood swings, worry or anxiety, distress, irritability or anger, inability to focus, anger, weariness, sleep disturbances, thoughts of self-harm, difficulty coping with daily life, and withdrawal from hobbies and friends are all symptoms studied under psychopathology. Some of the leading causes of mental disorder conditions include genetics, brain chemistry, chronic medical conditions, isolation feeling, lack of social support, alcohol abuse, and traumatic or stressful experiences. The different types of psychopathological disorders include anxiety disorders, bipolar disorders, eating disorders, obsessive-compulsive disorder (OCD), personality disorders, sleep disorders, trauma-related disorder, etc. This book contains some path-breaking studies in the field of psychopathology. It elucidates the concepts and researches with respect to this field. The book is appropriate for students seeking detailed information in this area of psychopathology as well as for experts.

I hope that this book, with its visionary approach, will be a valuable addition and will promote interest among readers. Each of the authors has provided their extraordinary competence in their specific fields by providing different perspectives as they come from diverse nations and regions. I thank them for their contributions.

Editor

1

Bleuler's Psychopathological Perspective on Schizophrenia Delusions: Towards New Tools in Psychotherapy Treatment

Filipe Arantes-Gonçalves[1,2], João Gama Marques[3,4] and Diogo Telles-Correia[3,5]*

[1] *CliniPinel, Lisbon, Portugal,* [2] *Clínica de Saúde Mental do Porto, Porto, Portugal,* [3] *Clínica Universitária de Psiquiatria e Psicologia Médica, Faculdade de Medicina, Universidade de Lisboa, Lisbon, Portugal,* [4] *Consulta de Esquizofrenia Resistente, Centro Hospitalar Psiquiátrico de Lisboa, Lisbon, Portugal,* [5] *Serviço de Psiquiatria e Saúde Mental, Hospital de Santa Maria, Centro Hospitalar de Lisboa Norte, Lisbon, Portugal*

***Correspondence:**
João Gama Marques
joaogamamarques@gmail.com

The authors begin by addressing the historical evolution of the delusion concept and its different approaches, focusing afterwards mainly on the work of Bleuler, who stressed the proximity between delusions and the emotional life of patients with schizophrenia. I Therefore, the present work intends to review the main aspects of the theory of delusion formation in schizophrenia according to Bleuler's psychopathological perspective. For that purpose, first the role of delusions in the psychopathology of schizophrenia is explored in a close relation with the Bleuler's fundamental symptoms (Alogia, Autism, Ambivalence, and Affect Blunting) nowadays known as negative symptoms. Then, persecutory, grandiosity and sexual delusions in schizophrenia are described according to the tension between logic and affects, as well as, internal conflict, schizoid features, and auto-erotism as key psychopathological pathways. Thus, with this subjective perspective, it is intended to highlight Bleuler's psychopathological contribution to the affective and meaningful causality of delusions in schizophrenia. The former might be useful in the integration with other psychopathological phenomena (hallucinations and negative symptoms) and new forms of research and therapeutic approaches in this disorder that are complementary with the contemporary tendencies in psychopathology.

Keywords: affectivity, Bleuler, delusions, schizophrenia, psychopathology

INTRODUCTION

Throughout the history of psychopathology the term delusion had several meanings distant from its current meaning of thought disorder (1). In antiquity and in the eighteenth and nineteenth centuries' French Psychiatry, the term *délire* (delusion), meant general detachment from reality that was not specific of thought impairment (1).

In eighteenth and nineteenth centuries' French Psychiatry, the term delusion included disturbances of thought, perception, emotions and affects and even psychomotricity (2). By contrast, in the twentieth century German and British Psychiatry, the term delusion gradually became synonymous with a false belief, a disorder of the thought content (3). This tendency was generalized in the majority of the European countries and also in the United States of America, with the replacement of the old broader concept by a newer and narrower concept of delusion as a disorder of thought content.

Jaspers defined delusion as a disorder in the content of thought, separating it from other psychopathological disorders such as perception, affect and personality's. He considered primary delusion incomprehensible and in discontinuity with the individual's personality (4).

However, throughout the twentieth century, some authors such as Freud and Bleuler were not satisfied with the Jasperian definition of primary delusion as an isolated and incomprehensible phenomenon, and tried to integrate it in the general psychic life of patients.

For Freud, delusions result from a conflict between the ego and the external world that makes the former lose its contact with reality, mainly because of an intolerable frustration (5). He assumes that delusions might occupy the place left by that loss of contact with reality (6). These efforts to recapture the outside world through delusion occur in continuity with the emotional memories of the patient, previous to reality detachment (5).

Bleuler thought much about delusion in schizophrenia, namely its relation with affect, personality and the proximity with what he called the fundamental symptoms (nowadays known as negative symptoms of schizophrenia). Bleuler was the first author to gather descriptive and analytical perspectives on the psychopathology of schizophrenia. He added comprehensive and interpretative components without forgetting the importance of psychopathological description and systematization. This is an example of how it is possible to integrate different paradigms regarding the same psychopathological phenomenon.

In this article, we intend to review the main aspects related to the theory of the formation of delusion in schizophrenia, according to Bleuler's psychopathological perspective.

THE ROLE OF DELUSIONS IN SCHIZOPHRENIA PSYCHOPATHOLOGY

Bleuler systematizes the clinical presentation of schizophrenias into fundamental, accessory, primary and secondary symptoms. The fundamental symptoms, which are virtually present through all the course of the disorder (7), are also known as the famous Bleuler's four A's: Alogia, Autism, Ambivalence, and Affect blunting (8). Delusion is regarded as one of the accessory symptoms because it is episodic in the course of schizophrenia. Among the primary symptoms one can find alogia that Bleuler claimed to have a neurological etiology. All the remaining symptoms, including delusion, are considered secondary symptoms because they are an attempt of psychogenic compensation of the deficits caused by alogia. Bleuler conceptualized delusion as an accessory and secondary symptom in schizophrenia's psychopathology in very close relation with fundamental symptoms.

In alogia, as the logical thought weakens, affects become predominant and dominate the associations of the thinking processes (9). Based on this hypothesis, Bleuler described a link from alogia to delusion formation, with wishes and fears dominating the association of thoughts, bringing way to autistic thought, withdrawing the patient from external reality, predisposing him to delusion formation (7).

Regarding autism, it can be conceptualized as the predominance of inner life that distances the patient from external reality. In this sense, autism can be seen as a difficulty in contact with others (auto-erotism) but also as social isolation and negativism predisposing the patient to delusion formation (10).

Concerning affect blunting, Bleuler argues that although affects seem to be decreased at superficial psychiatric observation, they are very intense at deeper layers of the psychic life of the patient (11). Affect blunting might predispose patients with schizophrenia to delusion specifically when interpersonal conflicts bring to surface those apparently hidden emotions.

Finally, ambivalence is described as a tendency to be in the presence of contradictory feelings. Bleuler described this ambivalence as much more intense, regarding anxiety, than the one present in neurotic (not psychotic) patients (12). Considering this intense anxiety in schizophrenia's ambivalence, delusions represent a psychopathological way of dealing with these internal and emotional conflicts.

THEORY OF DELUSION FORMATION IN SCHIZOPHRENIA

According to Kraepelin (13), delusions were incorrect ideas created, not by an accidental failure of logic, but by an inner need of the patient (13). And for Bleuler and Brill (9) the most important inner needs are the affective ones. In that sense, delusions always follow a definite direction corresponding to the patients affects, and in the vast majority of cases cannot be corrected by new experience or instructions, as long as the condition which gave origin to them remains (9). Thus, delusions have their origin mainly in belief instead of logic. From Bleuler's point of view, delusions are frequently egocentric and very significant for the personality of the patient (7). By other words we can stress that the delusions thematic is mainly anchored in the patient's biography.

Bleuler acknowledges that the strength of affects (in affect blunting) combined with the weakness of logic (alogia) is the most common feature in delusions formation. When affects are present and strong, patients are more prone to logic errors, which mean that affects have a key-role in the formation of delusions (7). The latter ones might be conceptualized as stemming from unconscious thinking derived from the wide splitting of mental functions (9) where the autonomy of traumatic emotional memories becomes predominant. These traumatic emotional memories belong to the autistic way of thinking, based on the fantasies that are detached from reality. So autistic thinking and affective needs take advantage, over realistic and logical thinking, and patients become vulnerable to delusion formation (10).

PSYCHOPATHOLOGICAL MECHANISMS IN DELUSION FORMATION IN SCHIZOPHRENIA

As previously adressed, Bleuler argued that delusions were a secondary, psychogenic, kind of symptom, involving different specific psychopathological mechanisms: internal conflict, schizoid features, and auto-erotism (12).

In internal conflict we can assume that traumatic emotional memories have influence in realistic thinking, giving rise to conflict between internal and external reality. Moreover, there is a tension because of the imbalance between pleasant and unpleasant affects and delusion formation is the only way allowing traumatic emotional memories to manifest (11).

Regarding schizoid features, Bleuler claimed that these personality traits are essential and in accordance with the autistic way of thinking (11). This kind of thinking, based on fantasies turns the patient away from reality, liberating subjective wishes, but without further adaptation (10). It always seeks pleasure and avoids pain. Freud argued that schizophrenic delusions are not only wish-fulfilling but also the attempt to recapture lost internal objects (6).

Finally, auto-erotism is as a key-feature of autism in schizophrenia as negativism has frequently an erotic side that may be pleasant as flirting, unpleasant as harassment, or both at the same time (12).

PERSECUTORY DELUSIONS

In this kind of delusion, Bleuler considers that there is frustration after a great ambition of the patient is not achieved (11). The patient is kept in an internal conflict between denying and accepting this frustration that may decrease his self-esteem, damaging his narcissism. Many patients in this situation cannot deal with failure and project their guilt feelings in people around them (7). Without this contradiction between ambition (wishes) and reality (possibilities) there would be no delusion of persecution (11). In other words, first patients don't have what they wish, then they don't admit their incompetency and the result is the delusion of persecution, blaming others for their failure (9). Delusion of persecution is the most common type of delusion in schizophrenia (7).

GRANDIOSITY DELUSIONS

Very frequently grandiosity delusion is secondary to persecutory delusion (6, 14, 15). When the projection of guilt (persecutory delusion) fails to balance internal wishes and external reality, delusion of grandiosity may occur as a fulfillment of the repressed wish (11). As the external reality contradicts the guilt projected into the outside world, narcissistic injury to self-esteem grows, leaving the patient with the escape of wish-fulfillment through delusion of grandiosity (7). In other words the patient justifies his persecution delusion with a grandiose explanation, feeling him as an extremely important person, thus restoring his fragile self-esteem (9). Delusion of grandiosity is the second most common type of delusions in schizophrenia (7).

SEXUAL DELUSIONS

This kind of delusions is also very common in schizophrenia. Usually, the patient believes it is forbidden for him to do what he wishes, under threats of danger, or punishment (12). Bleuler conceptualized that sexual thematic memories have a prominent role in schizophrenia as many patients presented sexual delusions of being loved (delusional erotomania), abused (delusional rape), or pregnant (delusional gestation). According to Bleuler, sexual delusions are a combination of persecutory and grandiosity delusions (7) and can also express the traumatic emotional memories that belong to the autistic way of thinking.

DISCUSSION

Nowadays the biological paradigm has monopolized psychopathology's studies, leaving meaning and symbolic causalities behind. This approach brought a reductive and poor view of psychopathology which could and should be enriched with other lines of thought.

For Bleuler, patients' affects are extremely important in the formation of delusions in schizophrenia, and this perspective may be useful in the investigation of new forms of therapeutic approach of this disorder. It also represents humanistic and patient-centered approach regarding the patient with schizophrenia, and reflects what is actually observed in clinical practice.

Bleuler also pointed out that delusions cannot be evaluated and studied separately from the rest of psychopathology. This view is in agreement with several authors of French psychopathologists (e.g., Esquirol and Henry Ey) for whom delusions were very close to other psychopathological phenomena such as hallucinations, an interdependence that has already been approached conceptually and empirically by more recent authors (16–18).

Another important aspect of Bleuler's vision is the proximity between positive and negative symptoms. For Bleuler they are strongly linked, with the negative symptoms preceding the positive symptoms (e.g., delusions).

In sum, with Bleuler, schizophrenia deserves to be approached not only from an objective perspective but also from a subjective perspective (taking into account the affective component, and the symbolic causality) in order to grasp the real picture of what is happening inside the patients.

New research could be based on this line of thought. Namely the study of the role of psychological trauma and emotional memory in schizophrenia patients' psychopathology, trying to add complementary knowledge to genetic studies, building bridges between genetics and environment (nowadays called epigenetics); On the other hand it would be interesting to assess the effectiveness of psychotherapies (which focus on factors related to the affective and the meaningful components of symptoms), alone or in combination with psychopharmacology in the treatment of schizophrenia.

AUTHOR CONTRIBUTIONS

FA-G conceptualized and wrote the first draft of the manuscript. JG contributed with commentaries and suggestions. DT-C reviewed and supervised all the writing process.

REFERENCES

1. Berrios G, Filiberto F. *Historia Conceptual del Delirio Antes del Siglo Vol. 19.* Madrid: Trotta (1996).
2. Pinel PA. *Treatise on Insanity.* Chicago, IL: Classics of Medicine Library (1983).
3. Jaspers K. *General Psychopathology.* Baltimore, MD: The Johns Hopkins University Press (1997).
4. Telles-Correia D, Saraiva S, Gama Marques J. Jaspers' phenomenology. *Folia Med.* (2016) 60:95–102. doi: 10.2478/folmed-2018-0009
5. Freud S. *Neurosis and Psychosis. The Standard Edition of the Complete Psychological Works of Sigmund Freud.* Vol. 19. London: Hogarth Press (1971).
6. Freud S. *Psycho-Analytic Notes on an Autobiographical Account of a Case of Paranoia (Dementia Paranoids).* Worcestershire: Read Books Ltd. (1911).
7. Bleuler E. *Dementia Praecox or the Group of Schizophrenias.* New York, NY: International Universities Press (1950).
8. McNally K. Eugene Bleuler's four As. *Hist Psychol.* (2009) 12:43–59. doi: 10.1037/a0015934
9. Bleuler E, Brill AA. *Textbook of Psychiatry.* Mineola, NY: Dover Publications (1951).
10. Arantes-Gonçalves F. *Autismo de Bleuler: Repensar as Esquizofrenias Pelo "Sintoma Invisível".* Lisboa: Climepsi Editores (2014).
11. Bleuler E. *Affectivity, Suggestibility, Paranoia.* New York, NY: State Hospitals Press (1912).
12. Bleuler E. *The Theory of Schizophrenic Negativism.* London: Forgotten Books (2012).
13. Kraepelin E. *Dementia Praecox and Paraphrenia.* London: Wentworth Press (2016).
14. De Matos JA. *Paranóia, Ensaio Patogénico Sobre os Delírios Sistematizados.* Lisboa: Ulmeiro (2007).
15. Schreber DP. *Memoirs of My Nervous Illness.* New York, NY: New York Review of Books (2000).
16. Telles-Correia D, Moreira AL, and Gonçalves JS. Hallucinations and related concepts-their conceptual background. *Front Psychol.* (2015) 6:991. doi: 10.3389/fpsyg.2015.00991
17. Telles-Correia D, Moreira AL, Gama Marques J, Saraiva S, Moreira CA, Antunes F, et al. The proximity between hallucination and delusions dimensions: an Observational, Analytic, Cross-Sectional, Multicentre Study. *Front Psychol.* (2016) 7:1642. doi: 10.3389/fpsyg.2016.01642
18. Telles-Correia D, Barbosa-Rocha N, Gama-Marques J, Moreira AL, Alves-Moreira C, Saraiva S, et al. Validation of the Portuguese version of the Psychotic Symptom Rating Scales (PSYRATS). *Actas Esp Psiquiatr.* (2017) 45:56–61.

2

New Perspectives in Phenomenological Psychopathology: Its Use in Psychiatric Treatment

Guilherme Messas[1], Melissa Tamelini[2], Milena Mancini[3] and Giovanni Stanghellini[3,4]*

[1] Department of Mental Health, Santa Casa de Sao Paulo School of Medical Sciences, São Paulo, Brazil, [2] Institute of Psychiatry- Hospital das Clínicas de São Paulo, São Paulo, Brazil, [3] Department of Psychological Sciences Humanities and Territory, University of Chieti, Chieti, Italy, [4] Diego Portales University, Santiago, Chile

***Correspondence:**
Guilherme Messas
guilherme.messas@fcmsantacasasp.edu.br

Phenomenological psychopathology is a body of scientific knowledge on which the clinical practice of psychiatry is based since the first decades of the twentieth century, a method to assess the patient's abnormal experiences from their own perspective, and more importantly, a science responsible for delimiting the object of psychiatry. Recently, the frontiers of phenomenological psychopathology have expanded to the productive development of therapeutic strategies that target the whole of existence in their actions. In this article, we present an overview of the current state of this discipline, summing up some of its key concepts, and highlighting its importance to clinical psychiatry today. Phenomenological psychopathology understands mental disorders as modifications of the main dimensions of the life-world: lived time, lived space, lived body, intersubjectivity, and selfhood. Psychopathological symptoms are the expression of a dialectical modification of the proportions of certain domains of the life-world or of the lived experience. The far-reaching relevance of the concepts of proportion and dialectics for the clinical agenda is explored. The article presents two contemporary models for clinical practice based on phenomenological psychopathology: Dialectical-proportional oriented approach and Person-centered dialectic approach (P.H.D. method). The main characteristics of these approaches are considered, as well as the new perspectives they bring to the challenges of psychiatric care in the twentieth-first century.

Keywords: phenomenological psychopathology, psychiatric care, phenomenological approaches, psychotherapy, person-centered approach, life-world, dialectics, anthropological proportion

INTRODUCTION

The association between phenomenology and psychopathology was first postulated by Karl Jaspers, in his seminal work, "General Psychopathology" (1913/1997). Since "General Psychopathology," psychopathology has been understood as a body of scientific knowledge on which the clinical practice of psychiatry is based, a method to assess the patient's abnormal experiences from their own perspective, and more importantly, a science responsible for delimiting the object of psychiatry. Gradually, phenomenological psychopathology started to be understood not just as a description of the subjective experiences of patients suffering mental disorders, but as a search for their conditions of possibilities (1)—the structures of subjectivity that underpin the experience of reality, which, when modified, determine psychopathological life-worlds. Furthermore, phenomenological psychopathology in recent times has become the background knowledge from which "know-how" methods for treatment have developed. In this article, we present an overview of the current state of this discipline, summing up some of its key concepts, and highlighting its importance to clinical psychiatry today.

MAIN DIMENSIONS OF THE LIFE-WORLD

Phenomenological psychopathology assesses the life-worlds of mental disorders. The life-world is the world each of us live by, the original, obvious, and unquestioned foundation of everyday acting and thinking. Next to the common-sense world we all more or less share, there are several frameworks of experience, as for example, fantasy worlds, dream worlds, and psychopathological worlds. In the latter, psychopathological symptoms are the expression of a modification of the framework within which they are generated. In each symptom the change in the framework of experience becomes manifested. The experience of time, space, body, Self, and others are the basic dimensions of the life-world within which each single symptom is situated (2, 3).

Lived Time

Lived time must be distinguished from the time of the clock ("objective" time). Lived time is the way we subjectivey experience time rather than the objective time of the clock (4). Every experience receives its specific significance and value from its temporal profile.

Lived Space

Lived space is the way people live space, that is, the totality of the space that a person prereflexively "lives" and "experiences." This space is based on the relationship of the person to her world as a situated and embodied entity.

Lived Body

The term "lived body" is used to designate the body that is lived by us and distinguish it from the physical body. It is the body experienced from within, the body in the first-person perspective (5). The lived body is the center of three main dimensions of experience (6): (a) self-experience and especially the most primitive form of self-awareness; (b) object-experience and meaning-bestowing; (c) the experience of other people.

Intersubjectivity

Intersubjectivity is a key factor for reality constitution. Pragmatically, it is the capacity to grasp the meaning of the other persons' behavior and expression (7). The majority of everyday relations are grounded on pre-reflexive encounters with other persons. The others' mental states, including emotions, beliefs, and desires are directly expressed in their actions and are typically grasped as meaningful in an emergent, pragmatic context. We are attuned with each other through a direct, prethematic contact with the expressive behavior of the others.

Selfhood

The notion of "Self" comprises at least two different dimensions: the pre-reflexive Self and the reflexive Self (8). By "pre-reflexive Self" we mean the most primitive form of self-consciousness. This primitive experience of oneself, rooted in the lived body, does not arise in reflection and is not inferentiallly or criterially given. It is neither conceptual nor linguistic, but a primordial contact or acquaintance with oneself. Next to this dimension of self-consciousness there is an experience of one' s own Self that implies the possession of a concept of oneself. This is the Self as narrative identity—the Self that tells stories about itself that exists in those stories and conceives its identity in terms of those stories.

THE TWO PSYCHOPATHOLOGICAL GROUPS: THE LIFE-WORLD OF STRUCTURAL DISORDERS AND ANTHROPOLOGICAL DISORDERS

Mental disorders can be divided into two major groups, in consistency with the depth of the alteration of the structure of the life-worlds: structural and anthropological disorders (9). Structural disorders correspond to life-world disturbances in the strict sense, in which the very constitution of reality and the overall ontological framework within which the patient's existence takes place is at stake (10). The prototypical model of structural disorders is schizophrenia. In anthropological disorders, such as non-psychotic ones, e.g., phobias and neurotic obsessions, the overall constitution of reality is not compromised, but the anomalies can be seen as dialectical modifications of the proportions of certain domains of the lived experience. The far-reaching relevance of the concepts of proportion and dialectics for all mental disorders and for the clinical agenda is explored in the following sections.

MODELS FOR CLINICAL PRACTICE BASED ON PHENOMENOLOGICAL PSYCHOPATHOLOGY

Dialectical-Proportional Oriented Approach

Dialectics is a notion that expresses the basic tensions and oppositions that permeate human life. It is the basis for understanding the immanent mobility of existence, the "*source* of constant movement [of existence]" [(11), p. 341]. The introduction of the notion of dialectical proportion into phenomenological psychopathology (12) is indicative of the considerable expansion of their heuristic and technical importance in the discipline at the present time. We will now examine a few of the reasons for this breadth of scope.

The notion of dialectical proportion:

- favors the observation of the complexities inherent to each mode of pathological experience, both structural and anthropological. In structural disorders, it allows psychopathological understanding to be extended to the most complex of clinical situations, in which identifying the

person's relationship with her basic abnormal experience is what matters (13). For instance, schizophrenia can be understood not just from its core elements of delusion, but from the dialectical relationship between the loss of the constitution of reality and its maintenance (14).
- allows the themes of psychic movement and transformation to be introduced to the field of psychopathology (15, 16), offering diagnostic instruments that expand phenomenologically the observation of clinical course beyond a strictly biomedical sense (17).
- enables a conception of phenomenology-based care attuned with the latest needs of psychiatric practice. According to the current-day perceptions of clinical practice, treatment essentially consists of recovering from mental disorders (18). The centrality of the goals of treatment in the notion of recovery is generally in line with the idea of mental disorders having unique features, for which the conceptions of somatic medicine fall short. As such, the most reliable criteria for evaluating the development of a mental disorder have to do with the subject and his/her contexts, not external factors expressed in terms of signs or symptoms. For this reason, it is fundamentally important for the categorized mental disorders to reflect the dialectical aspect of the criteria. And, even more importantly, for these categories to allow a scientific view of the existential movements by which the person is renewed in the process of recovery. As such, offering a framework of psychopathological categories usable in clinical practice means offering categories that identify the movements of psychological transformation and evolution (15) through which recovery can be attained. Clinical practice depends strongly on this conceptual work, not only for setting the right therapeutic course, but also for appraising clinical developments.

There are two main forms of dialectical apprehension, which contributes distinctly to clinical practice.

a. Dialectic of ambiguity
b. Dialectic of anthropological proportions

Dialectic of Ambiguity

This perspective picks up on the ambiguity of human experience (19). The ambiguity inherent to the human being reveals how all experience presents two simultaneous faces. As such, a "melancholic type" of personality (20) curbs the potential for personal expansion as it is too strongly linked to normality and duty in the performance of its social role; meanwhile, for the very same characteristics, a person with this personality structure is seen as someone to be trusted and respected by her family and community. Knowing this inherent ambiguity in existence is key to developing a therapeutic strategy for two reasons. First, understanding the ambiguities inherent to each pathological condition orientates therapeutic strategies, guiding more accurately the clinician's intervention and supporting her choice of certain procedures or conducts to the detriment of others. For instance, a distinctive characteristic of the "melancholic type" is intolerance of ambiguity (21, 22). Such people have almost insurmountable difficulty when they experience situations where any emotional indetermination is present. Faced with such circumstances, they tend toward existential restriction, retreating far from the world and themselves (20) and ultimately descending into a full-blown melancholic state. The clinician, aware of this limitation, should therefore: (i) find out what dilemmas the patient is unable to face; (ii) process and interpret their existential situation in terms that do not imply great existential risks; (iii) understand the extent and importance of these patients' existentially conservative values; (iv) stress the positive features of their potentialities, avoiding increasing the ambiguity in which the pathological state is immersed; (v) guide the pharmacological strategies along the same lines, following the same principles; (vi) select a method of treatment that leads to a resumption of the previous existential plans, as far as possible.

Dialectic of Anthropological Proportions

The dialectic of proportions is interested in a kind of microscope knowledge of *indeterminate* and *dynamic* elements. Elements that are *indeterminate* are so because they seek out something that is not yet known to the clinician or the patient—i.e., the tendency to have some kind of experience, which, emerging on the horizon of the patient's consciousness in the course of treatment, may influence its progress. It is a psychopathology of anticipation (23) or, to put it differently, a psychopathology of the middle ground between "what no longer is" and "what is yet to be." The clinician seeks to incorporate the meaning of this indeterminism to the totality of the patient's existence to better conduct the case. An example of the importance of this indeterminism is the high risk of relapse in patients with substance addiction, even after having managed to abstain, when they are faced with a new challenge. The new challenge puts new demands on the patient in recovery—ones to which his/her consciousness may not yet be accustomed—because their lived time has been restricted to the present for so long (24, 25), making them incapable of opening up to the future. The demands of the future may, then, destabilize their existence, increasing their tension, and ultimately making them more vulnerable to relapse, which would constitute a return to the previous state of complete fusion with the world in the present (26). Such knowledge is extremely valuable for a clinician, because it prepares him/her to observe and monitor the patient closely, even when they are not using any substance, at these moments of anticipation of an experience and, when necessary, to take measures to protect them behaviorally. Thus, understanding the risk of relapsing extrapolates a merely behavioral perspective, expressed in terms of the capacity to resist the urge to use the substance, and takes on a broad existential meaning that is more in line with the profound characteristics of existence.

The *dynamic* aspect in the analysis of anthropological proportions picks up on tensions that are fundamental to existence: the tension between *permanence* and *becoming* and the opposition between *individuality* and *generality*. Throughout our lives, we are and we cease to be at one and the same time. Although we recognize our experiences and our memories as belonging to us, we know we are no longer the same as we once were, for instance, in our childhood. Phenomenological psychopathology examines the different ways existence transits between permanence and transformation (27), offering instruments for clinicians to lead each case through the characteristics and possibilities of each human type and each disorder. Clinical conduct based on examining the forms of the permanence-transformation dialectic focuses on allowing each existence to open up to the future wide enough and long enough for the personal identity to modify and become plural, while respecting the limits of each temperament and each individual.

Meanwhile, when it comes to the tension between individuality and generality, the quest for individualized treatment as part of person-centered care calls for the clinician to assimilate phenomenological observation categories that focus on the dialectics between the mental disorder and the individual meaning they take on for each person (24).

The Person-Centered Dialectic Approach and the P.H.D. Method

In this section we describe the overall framework into which the clinical approach based on dialectical proportions is applied. The aim of such a therapy is re-establish the dialectic between selfhood and otherness that will allow the suffering person to recover a sense of identity. The main principles of this approach can be summed up as follows (3):

- it supports the patient's unfolding his personal experience;
- it helps him to identify a core-meaning in his experiences around which his narrative can become meaningful;
- it incites him to make explicit his personal horizon of meaning, values and beliefs, within which her narrative is set;
- it also incites the clinician to make explicit to the patient her own assumptions, personal experiences, beliefs (at least, that part that is relevant for therapeutic purpose) on which her understanding of the patient's narrative is based;
- it promotes a reciprocal exchange of perspectives between the clinician and her patient;
- this "reciprocity of perspectives" is aimed to co-construct of a new meaningful narrative which includes and, if possible, integrates contributions from both the patient's and the clinician's perspectives;
- the clinician supports the patient to tolerate potential conflicts of values and beliefs and facilitates coexistence in case it is not possible to establish consensus.

The practice of care that derives from this is based on the integration of three basic dispositives, synthesized in the acronym PHD (28, 29):

Phenomenological unfolding (P): The explication of the patient's field of experience. This is done through a dialogue that opens up and lays bare the pleats of the patient's experiences and actions. Unfolding enriches understanding through recovering the implicit (not necessarily rejected), automatic (not censored), forgotten (not forbidden) sources that make phenomena appear as they appear to the patient, his drives, emotions, and habitus—the three emblematic components of the obscure and dissociated spontaneity that make up the involuntary dimension in human existence.

Hermeneutic analysis (H): The explication of the person's position-taking toward her experience. Since psychopathological symptoms, according to clinical hermeneutics, are the outcomes of an active interplay between the person and her basic anomalous, disturbing and dysfunctional experiences, attention is paid to the active role that the person has in taking a position and interacting with them. Rescuing from the implicit the active role that the patient has in shaping his symptoms is the *via regia* to help the patient to recalibrate his miscarried position-taking and, finally, to recover his sense of responsibility and agency.

Dynamic analysis (D): The explication of the life-history in which experiences and position-taking are embedded. The patient's life-history is the personal context within which her experiences may become meaningful. All of any person's life-events (including those that at face value look meaningless) are, according to psychodynamics, lawful and potentially meaningful in a particular way for that person. Also, all psychological events have at least as one of their motivations a psychological one and can thereby become meaningful on a psychological basis.

CONCLUSIONS

Since the first decades of the twentieth century, the phenomenological branch of psychopathology has been developing more in-depth understandings of mental disorders. Recently, the frontiers of phenomenological psychopathology have expanded to the productive development of therapeutic strategies that target the whole of existence in their actions. The way we understand human existence determines how we understand psychopathological experiences and, especially, how we behave toward such patients. Phenomenology offers a radically human way of practicing psychiatry, a way that captures existence in all its determinations and singularities.

AUTHOR CONTRIBUTIONS

GM wrote the manuscript and discussed suggestions from the co-authors. MT contributes to the conception of the work and co-wrote its manuscript. MM helped drafting the work and contributed to its conception. GS contributed to the conception of the manuscript and critically discussed its content.

REFERENCES

1. Fuchs T. Phenomenology and psychopathology. In: Schmicking D, Gallagher S, editors. *Handbook of Phenomenology and Cognitive Science.* Dordrecht: Springer (2010) 546–73.
2. Stanghellini G, Rossi R. Pheno-phenotypes: a holistic approach to the psychopathology of schizophrenia. *Curr Opin Psychiatry* (2014) 27:236–41. doi: 10.1097/YCO.0000000000000059
3. Stanghellini G, Mancini M. *The Therapeutic Interview in Mental Health: A Values-Based and Person-Centered Approach.* Cambridge: Cambridge University Press (2017).
4. Minkowski E. *Lived Time: Phenomenological and Psychopathological Studies.* Evanston, IL: Northwestern University Press (1970).

5. Stanghellini G, Ballerini M, Blasi S, Mancini M, Presenza S, Raballo A, et al. The bodily self: a qualitative study of abnormal bodily phenomena in persons with schizophrenia. *Compreh Psychiatry* (2014) 55:1703–11. doi: 10.1016/j.comppsych.2014.06.013
6. Stanghellini G. Embodiment and schizophrenia. *World Psychiatry* (2009) 8:56–9. doi: 10.1002/j.2051-5545.2009.tb00212.x
7. Stanghellini G, Ballerini M, Mancini M. Other persons: on the phenomenology of interpersonal experience in schizophrenia (ancillary article to EAWE domain 3). *Psychopathology* (2017) 50:75–82. doi: 10.1159/000456037
8. Kyrios M, Nelson B, Ahern C, Parnas J. The self in psychopathology. *Psychopathology* (2015) 48:275–7. doi: 10.1159/000438876
9. Charbonneau G. *Introduction à la Psychopathologie Phénoménologique: Ipséité et Phenomenological Mind, le Délire/l'Expérience Paranoïaque, Dépressions et Pathologies de la Temporalité, les Pathologies de l'Historialité Humaine.* Paris: MJW Fédition (2010).
10. Sass L. *Madness and Modernism: Insanity in the Light of Modern Art, Literature, and Thought (revised edition). (International Perspectives in Philosophy and Psychiatry).* New York, NY: Oxford University Press (2017).
11. Jaspers K. *General Psychopathology, Vol. 1, 2.* Baltimore, MD: Johns Hopkins University Press (1997).
12. Blankenburg W. A dialectical conception of anthropological proportions. In: *de* Koning, AJJ, Jenner, FA, editors. *Phenomenology and Psychiatry.* New York, NY: Grune & Stratton (1982).
13. Stanghellini G, Rosfort R. Disordered selves or persons with schizophrenia? *Curr Opin Psychiatry* (2015) 28:256–63. doi: 10.1097/YCO.0000000000000155
14. Messas G, Tamelini M, Cutting J. A meta-analysis of the core essence of psychopathological entities: an historical exercise in phenomenological psychiatry. *Hist Psychiatry* (2017) 28:473–81. doi: 10.1177/0957154X17715414
15. Messas GP. *Psicopatologia e Transformação: um Esboço.* São Paulo: Casa do Psicólogo (2004).
16. Barthélémy JM. Importance et extension de l'approche qualitative dans la méthode phénoméno-structurale en psychopathologie. *Bull Soc Sci Med.* (2006) 2:249–64. Available online at: http://ssm.lu/wp-content/uploads/2014/09/2006.2.pdf
17. Messas GP. A phenomenological contribution to the approach of biological psychiatry. *J Phenomenol Psychol.* (2010) 41:180–200. doi: 10.1163/156916210X532117
18. Leamy M, Bird V, Le Boutillier C, Williams J, Slade M. Conceptual framework for personal recovery in mental health: systematic review and narrative synthesis. *Br J Psychiatry* (2011) 199, 445–452. doi: 10.1192/bjp.bp.110.083733
19. Merleau-Ponty M. *Phenomenology of Perception.* Abingdon: Routledge (2013).
20. Tellenbach H. *Melancholie: Problemgeschichte Endogenität Typologie Pathogenese Klinik.* Heidelberg: Springer-Verlag (2013).
21. Kraus A. Melancholia from the Perspective of the Self. In: Stanghellini G, Aragona M, editors. *An Experiential Approach to Psychopathology.* Springer (2016). p. 189–219.
22. Ambrosini A, Stanghellini G, Raballo A. Temperament, personality and the vulnerability to mood disorders. The case of the melancholic type of personality. *J Psychopathol.* (2014) 20:393–403. Available online at: http://www.jpsychopathol.it/wp-content/uploads/2015/07/07_raballo1.pdf
23. Sutter J. *L'anticipation. Psychologie et Psychopathologie.* Paris: Presses Universitaires de France (1983).
24. Messas G. *Psicose e Embriaguez. Psicopatologia Fenomenológica da Temporalidade.* São Paulo: Intermeios (2014).
25. Di Petta G. Psychopathology of addictions. *J Psychopathol.* (2014) 20:471–9. Available online at: http://www.jpsychopathol.it/wp-content/uploads/2015/07/15_dipetta1.pdf
26. Kimura B. *Écrits de Psychopathologie Phénoménologique, trad.* Joël Bouderlique, Paris: Psychiatrie ouverte (1992).
27. Messas G. *Ensaio Sobre a Estrutura Vivida.* São Paulo: Roca (2010).
28. Stanghellini G. *Lost in Dialogue: Anthropology, Psychopathology, and Care.* Oxford: Oxford University Press (2016).
29. Stanghellini G. Phenomenological Psychopathology and Care. From Person-Centered Dialectical Psychopathology to the PHD Method for Psychotherapy. In Stanghellini G, Aragona M, editors. *An Experiential Approach to Psychopathology.* Heidelberg: Springer (2016). p.361–78.

3

A Perspective on a Possible Relation Between the Psychopathology of the Schizophrenia/Schizoaffective Spectrum and Unconjugated Bilirubin: A Longitudinal Protocol Study

João Gama Marques[1,2] and Filipe Arantes-Gonçalves[3,4]*

[1] Clínica Universitária de Psiquiatria e Psicologia Médica da Faculdade de Medicina da Universidade de Lisboa, Lisbon, Portugal, [2] Hospital Júlio de Matos, Centro Hospitalar Psiquiátrico de Lisboa, Lisbon, Portugal, [3] Clínica de Saúde Mental do Porto, Porto, Portugal, [4] CliniPinel - Clínica de Psiquiatria, Psicoterapia e Psicanálise, Lisbon, Portugal

***Correspondence:**
João Gama Marques
joaogamamarques@gmail.com

Some authors suggest a relation between Unconjugated Bilirubin (UCB) plasma high levels and schizophrenia, as schizophrenia patients have been showing higher UCB levels when compared with other psychiatric patients and general population. These higher UCB levels have been already correlated with acute psychotic states, positive symptoms, and poor outcome in patients with schizophrenia. Schizophrenia and schizoaffective disorders share common symptoms but there aren't yet accepted biomarkers for their distinction. In our study protocol we propose an observational longitudinal study on a sample composed of two subgroups: patients with schizophrenia and patients with schizoaffective disorder. We will compare the UCB levels between groups, and search for a possible correlation with patient's psychopathology. For that purpose we will use nosological, psychopathological, neuropsychological, and psychosocial instruments. Thus we will be testing two different hypotheses: (1) Is UCB serum level a diagnosis indicator, with categorical distinction potential, between groups of patients with different psychotic disorders? (2) Is UCB serum level a severity indicator, with dimensional distinction potential, among groups of patients with the same psychotic disorder? We believe that UCB mean levels may contribute to some clarification of this controversy, as a potential biological indicator, facilitating the distinction between these two diagnostic categories and\or discriminating the dimensional severity among each of these psychotic conditions. Thus we may be opening a new opportunities for innovative and exciting biological psychiatry research regarding organic aspects in the schizophrenia spectrum.

Keywords: schizophrenia, schizoaffective, psychoses, unconjugated bilirubin, unconjugated hyperbilirubinemia

INTRODUCTION

Schizophrenia and several other psychiatric disorders share the complexity of their etiology, which reflects the interplay of different risk factors at multiple levels of analysis. The impact of psychosocial risk factors is well-established and neurobiological research is trying to define the underlying changes at molecular, cellular, anatomic or physiological levels that can support both the definition and the phenotypic presentation of those disorders, in a more integrative models.

In a recent review about the environment and susceptibility to schizophrenia, the authors stated that, in schizophrenia, the diversity of risk factors probably interacts in complex ways with the macrostructural environment, including the psychological, cultural, and socioeconomic context and he also points to the significant implications of the study of environmental factors to improve the explanatory power of neurodevelopmental models, the identification of causes and prevention of this complex disorder [1].

Schizophrenia is characterized by persistent cognitive, positive and negative symptoms typically beginning in youth, and brain alterations including dopaminergic dysregulation. Several pathophysiological models have been proposed, accumulating knowledge involving a neurodevelopmental imbalance in excitatory/inhibitory neurotransmitters, which could result from a variety of genetic, epigenetic and environmental causes, as well as pathophysiological processes such oxidative stress [2]. A dysregulation of the redox and glutamatergic systems due to genetic and early-life environmental risk factors could contribute to the anomalies of white matter in schizophrenia, ultimately impacting the patient's behavior via abnormal function of neural circuits [3].

UNCONJUGATED BILIRUBIN: AN UNDERESTIMATED NEUROTOXIN?

High levels of UCB (the main product of heme catabolism), sometimes are observed in the newborn, resulting from a decreased erythrocyte survival and a deficient hepatic clearance [4]. A significantly increase in the prevalence of mental disorder among children with neonatal hyperbilirubinemia was found when compared to a control group [5]. Idiopathic unconjugated hyperbilirubinemia (Gilbert's syndrome) is a common genetic deficiency of the enzyme UDP-glucuronosyltransferase-1 that is found in a maximum of 10% of the general population [6], but may have the double of that prevalence among patients with schizophrenia [7].

The Gunn rat (a Wistar strain mutant), has a genetic deficiency in glucuronyl transferase [8] and has already been used as a schizophrenia animal model [9]. Some works showed that microglial activation due to UCB chronic toxicity could be an important causal factor in the behavioral neuropathological abnormalities of these rats [10] (after crossing the blood brain barrier). Other studies showed that the antipsychotic medication (e.g., aripiprazole, risperidone, or haloperidol) effect on the Gunn rats' behavior is quite similar to those verified in humans with schizophrenia, enhancing social behaviors (e.g., isolation) [11]. The physiopathology underneath is related with UCB's insult to glial cells, leading to glutamate secretion and release of pro-inflammatory cytokines that may influence gliogenesis and neurogenesis, with secondary deficit in learning and memory; while glutamate metabolism dysregulation is consistent with schizophrenia neuropathology [12].

UNCONJUGATED BILIRUBIN: A BIOMARKER CANDIDATE FOR ACUTE PSYCHOSIS?

Patients with schizophrenia have already shown a significantly higher frequency of UCB mean levels when compared with patients with bipolar disorder [13, 14]. This kind of evidence suggests that UCB high levels may have a potential role as an indicator in the categorical distinction of among different psychiatric diagnosis.

In the other hand, patients suffering from schizophrenia frequently presented with higher than expected plasma UCB concentration, especially when acutely ill and admitted to the hospital [15]. Some authors suggested that the association of hyperbilirubinemia and schizophrenia disorders is stronger in acute psychosis episodes [16, 17]. Indeed, patients with schizophrenia with higher rates of hyperbilirubinemia presented a positive correlation between bilirubin levels and psychosis severity, namely higher scores on the positive and negative symptoms (PANSS) [18–20]. Besides this correlation with acute psychosis, it might also represent a poor outcome for the schizophrenia patients with idiopathic unconjugated hyperbilirrubinemia [18], an idea that has been strengthened by some neuroimaging findings: with wider frontotemporal sulci, inter-hemispheric fissure, and lateral ventricular sizes in CT brain scan [21]; increased signal intensity in various areas in FLAIR MRI brain scan [22]; and decreased metabolism in various areas in 1H-MRS brain scan [23, 24]. Thus UCB high levels may have a potential role as an indicator in the dimensional assessment of severity and chronicity among patients with schizophrenia.

UNCONJUGATED BILIRUBIN: A TOOL IN THE DISTINCTION BETWEEN SCHIZOPHRENIA AND BIPOLAR DISORDER?

Schizophrenia, schizoaffective and bipolar disorders share some common symptoms but there aren't yet true biomarkers clearly separating those disorders. There is still a lot of controversy regarding schizoaffective disorder as an independent category and its relationship with schizophrenia and bipolar disorders [25]. We are aware at least of four different conceptual possibilities for schizoaffective disorder: a severe form of bipolar disorder in which episode-related psychotic symptoms fail to remit completely between mood episodes; a milder variant of schizophrenia in which mood symptoms are more prominent than usual; the co-occurrence of schizophrenia and bipolar disorder; or is it actually a third and different type of psychosis, completely autonomous from the bipolar and schizophrenia categories? [26].

We believe that UCB mean levels may contribute to some clarification of this controversy, as one of many potential biological markers, facilitating the distinction between these diagnostic categories and\or discriminating the dimensional severity among each of these psychotic conditions. In our perspective, searching for contributing factors in a biological domain and across a spectrum does not reflect a reductionist approach or the denial of the importance of individual vulnerabilities depending on affective, relational and communicational dimensions, which are determinants at a systemic level, in schizophrenia spectrum disorders.

UNCONJUGATED BILIRUBIN: A STUDY PROTOCOL FOR THE PSYCHOSIS SPECTRUM

Our study will be an observational longitudinal study, with two assessments in 1 year time span, in order to achieve a better correlation between variables during the evolution of the patient's disorder and its respective treatment.

Sample

After publishing a case report [17] we got interest in this topic, so we did a retrospective study and found a 0.1 mg\dL significant statistical difference ($p \leq 0.0001$) between the UCB mean values of patients with schizophrenia (0.39 mg\dL with SD 0.16 mg\dL) patients vs. bipolar patients (0.29 mg\dL with SD 0.13 mg\dL) [14]. Using www.openepi.com software, with a confidence interval of 95%, and a beta value of 80%, we calculate a minimum sample size of 34 patients per group. Thus we expect to need no more than 70 individuals, composed by two different groups (35 patients with schizophrenia and 35 patients with schizoaffective disorder).

Inclusion Criteria

Age older than 18 but below 65 years old; understanding and signing informed consent; diagnosis (any type) of schizophrenia or schizoaffective disorder, according to ICD10 criteria [27]. Exclusion criteria: Any substance abuse detected on urine test; any organic brain disorder impairing protocol assessment; any hepatic, hemolytic, or cholestasis related condition detected on blood work. Scientific and Ethical approval: obtained at local Scientific and Ethical Boards.

General Variables

We would like to verify if exists any kind of influence on UCB mean levels by any of the following general variables: age; gender; fasting; exercise; occupation; education years; smoking (pack-year) [28]; use of contraceptive pill; body mass index (weight\height^2); family history of psychiatric disorder; duration of psychiatric disorder (years since first diagnosis); treatment setting (outpatient or inpatient); mean duration of Psychiatric admission (days); metabolic syndrome comorbidity (diabetes, dyslipidemia, and\or hypertension), psychiatric medication (controlled through chlorpromazine [29, 30] and benzodiazepine [31] equivalents).

Biochemistry Study

Calculated UCB serum levels (UCB = Total Bilirubin - Direct Bilirubin); blood sample will be taken and all procedures will be readily made: blood collection: vacuum S-Monovette® Serum Gel Z/4.9 ml (Sarstedt AG&Co); analytic method: 2,4-dicloroanilina (DCA) photometry; laboratory hardware System: ABX Pentra 400® (Horiba Group); laboratory software system: SISLAB® (Glintt); blood work (hemogram, LDH, AST, ALT, GGT, HCV, and HBV); urine drug testing (cannabinoids, amphetamines, cocaine and heroin).

Psychopathological Instruments

Clinical Global Impression (CGI) [32]—for general clinical severity; and Positive and Negative Schizophrenia Scale (PANSS) [33]—for psychosis severity.

Neuropsychological Instruments

We will, for the first time ever, test any kind of correlation between UCB mean levels and the following neuropsychological changes, previously described in patients with schizophrenia [34]; Montreal Cognitive Assessment (MOCA) [35]—general cognitive assessment. Trail Making Test-A (TMT-A)—cognitive processing speed; Trail Making Test-B (TMT-B) [36]—executive functions; and Wechsler Adult Intelligence Scale Digital Span (WAIS-DS) [37]—attention and working memory.

Psychosocial Instruments

We will test, also for the first time, any kind of correlation between UCB mean levels and Personal and Social Performance (PSP) [38]—for social functioning assessment.

For the two patients group (35 patients with schizophrenia and 35 patients with schizoaffective disorder), all study quantitative variables will be summarized through descriptive statistics namely mean, median, standard deviation, range, and proportions. This analysis include: socio-demographics characterization as well psychosocial (PSP), psychopathological (CGI, PANSS), neuropsychological (MOCA, TMT, WAIS-DS), and biological variables (biochemical study including UCB). For a better control of confounding variables patients will be paired regarding their age, gender, and level of education. Regarding statistics we plan to use the Statistical Package for the Social Sciences (SPSS) software.

UNCONJUGATED BILIRUBIN: ANOTHER DIFFERENCE BETWEEN SCHIZOPHRENIA AND SCHIZOAFFECTIVE DISORDER?

In future studies we will try to contribute for a better understanding of biological aspects in patients with psychosis, and particularly the possible role of UCB as an indicator in the distinction among patients with schizophrenia and schizoaffective disease. Thus, as our main objective, we would like to test two different hypotheses:

1. Is UCB serum level a diagnosis indicator, with (diagnostic and nosological) categorical distinction potential, between groups of patients with different psychotic disorders (e.g., between schizophrenia vs. schizoaffective disorder)?
2. Is UCB serum level a severity indicator, with (psychopathological, neuropsychological, and psychosocial) dimensional distinction potential, among groups of patients with the same psychotic disorder (e.g., among patients with schizophrenia)?

We shall highlight that UCB mean levels have never been studied before in patients with schizoaffective disorder, nor have been correlated with neuropsychological and psychosocial variables in any kind of psychiatric patients. Thus our future studies will try to innovate, adding more data to the hypothesis of a categorical but also dimensional spectrum of psychosis: schizophrenia—schizoaffective disorder.

AUTHOR CONTRIBUTIONS

JG: designed the project and wrote the article; FA-G: commented on the manuscript.

ACKNOWLEDGMENTS

The authors would like to thank our dear colleagues at *Associação Portuguesa de Psicopatologia (APPSICO)* for financial support, and Prof. Sílvia Ouakinin at Faculdade de Medicina da Universidade de Lisboa for scientific supervision.

REFERENCES

1. Brown AS. The environment and susceptibility to schizophrenia. *Prog Neurobiol.* (2011) **93**:23–58. doi: 10.1016/j.pneurobio.2010.09.003
2. Keshavan MS, Nasrallah HA, Tandon R. Schizophrenia, "Just the Facts" 6. Moving ahead with the schizophrenia concept: from the elephant to the mouse. *Schizophr Res.* (2011) **127**:3–13. doi: 10.1016/j.schres.2011.01.011
3. Steullet P, Cabungcal JH, Monin A, Dwir D, O'Donnell P, Cuenod M, et al. Redox dysregulation, neuroinflammation, and NMDA receptor hypofunction: a "central hub" in schizophrenia pathophysiology? *Schizophr Res.* (2014) **176**:41–51. doi: 10.1016/j.schres.2014.06.021
4. Dennery PA, Seidman DS, Stevenson DK. Neonatal hyperbilirubinemia. *N Engl J Med.* (2001) **344**:581–90. doi: 10.1056/NEJM200102223440807
5. Dalman C, Cullberg J. Neonatal hyperbilirubinaemia - a vulnerability factor for mental disorder? *Acta Psychiatr Scand.* (1999) **100**:469–71.
6. Bosma PJ, Chowdhury JR, Bakker C, Gantla S, de Boer A, Oostra BA, et al. The genetic basis of the reduced expression of bilirubin UDP-glucuronsyltransferase 1 in Gilbert's syndome. *N Engl J Med.* (1995) **333**:1171–5.
7. Miyaoka T, Seno H, Itoga M, Iijima M, Inagaki T, Horiguchi J. Schizophrenia-associated idiopathic unconjugated hyperbilirubinemia (Gilbert's syndrome). *J Clin Psychiatry* (2000) **61**:868–71.
8. Johnson L, Sarmiento F, Blanc WA, Day R. Kernicterus in rats with an inherited deficiency of glucuronyl transferase. *AMA J Dis Child.* (1959) **97**(5 Pt 1):591–608.
9. Hayashida M, Miyaoka T, Tsuchie K, Yasuda H, Wake R, Nishida A, et al. Hyperbilirubinemia-related behavioral and neuropathological changes in rats: a possible schizophrenia animal model. *Prog Neuropsychopharmacol Biol Psychiatry* (2009) **33**:581–8. doi: 10.1016/j.pnpbp.2009.02.013
10. Liaury K, Miyaoka T, Tsumori T, Furuya M, Wake R, Ieda M, et al. Morphological features of microglial cells in the hippocampal dentate gyrus of Gunn rat: a possible schizophrenia animal model. *J Neuroinflammation* (2012) **9**:56. doi: 10.1186/1742-2094-9-56
11. Tsuchie K, Miyaoka T, Furuya M, Liaury K, Ieda M, Wake R, et al. The effects of antipsychotics on behavioral abnormalities of the Gunn rat (unconjugated hyperbilirubinemia rat), a rat model of schizophrenia. *Asian J Psychiatry* (2013) **6**:119–23. doi: 10.1016/j.ajp.2012.09.007
12. Brites D, Fernandes A, Falcão AS, Gordo AC, Silva RFM, Brito MA. Biological risks for neurological abnormalities associated with hyperbilirubinemia. *J Perinatol.* (2009) **29**:S8–13. doi: 10.1038/jp.2008.214
13. Radhakrishnan R, Kanigere M, Menon J, Calvin S, Janish A, Srinivasan K. Association between unconjugated bilirubin and schizophrenia. *Psychiatry Res.* (2011) **189**:480–2. doi: 10.1016/j.psychres.2011.03.003
14. Gama-Marques J, Tinoco I, Pedro I, Leote F, Silva R, Ouakinin S. Unconjugated bilirubin and acute schizophrenia: a probable correlation? *Actas Esp Psiquiatr.* (2017) **45**:79–88.
15. Miyaoka T, Seno H, Maeda T, Itoga M, Horiguchi J. Schizophrenia-associated idiopathic unconjugated hyperbilirubinemia (Gilbert's syndrome): 3 case reports. *J Clin Psychiatry* (2000) **61**:299–300.
16. Rodriguez R, Roca A, Pineiro B, Conangla G, Enero C, Ramos I, et al. Bilirubin and brief psychotic disorder. *Eur Psychiatry* (2012) **27**:1.
17. Gama Marques J. Mitsuda psychosis and holodysphrenia revisited: An atypical psychosis in a patient with parieto-occipital paroxysmal electroencephalographic activity and high unconjugated bilirubin. *Psychiatry Clin Neurosci.* (2017) **71**:148–9. doi: 10.1111/pcn.12487
18. Miyaoka T, Yasukawa R, Mizuno S, Sukegawa T, Inagaki T, Inagaki T, et al. Clinical features of schizophrenia associated with idiopathic unconjugated hyperbilirubinemia (Gilbert's syndrome). *Int J Psychol Clin Pract.* (2003) **7**:199–203.
19. Powell AJ, Hansen LK. Gilbert's syndrome in a patient with predominantly negative symptoms of schizophrenia. *Int J Psychiatry Clin Prac.* (2007) **11**:239–41. doi: 10.1080/13651500600811735
20. Bardanca SG, Vivanco EF, Gonzalez MJA, Ventoso CV, Vazquez MS. Esquizofrenia y síndrome de Gilbert: a propósito de un caso. *Cad Aten Primaria* (2006) **13**:203–5.
21. Miyaoka T, Seno H, Itoga M, Inagaki T, Horiguchi J. Structural brain changes in schizophrenia associated with idiopathic unconjugated hyperbilirubinemia (Gilbert's syndrome): a planimetric CT study. *Schizophr Res.* (2001) **52**:291–3.
22. Miyaoka T, Yasukawa R, Mihara T, Mizuno S, Yasuda H, Sukegawa T, et al. Fluid-attenuated inversion-recovery MR imaging in schizophrenia-associated with idiopathic unconjugated hyperbilirubinemia (Gilbert's syndrome). *Eur Psychiatry* (2005) **20**:327–31. doi: 10.1007/s0033000 00587
23. Miyaoka T, Yasukawa R, Mizuno S, Sukegawa T, Inagaki T, Horiguchi J, et al. Proton magnetic resonance spectroscopy (1H-MRS) of hippocampus, basal ganglia, and vermis of cerebellum in schizophrenia associated with idiopathic unconjugated hyperbilirubinemia (Gilbert's syndrome). *J Psychiatr Res.* (2005) **39**:29–34. doi: 10.1016/j.jpsychires.2004.05.003
24. Yasukawa R, Miyaoka T, Mizuno S, Inagaki T, Horiguchi J, Oda K, et al. Proton magnetic resonance spectroscopy of the anterior cingulate gyrus, insular cortex and thalamus in schizophrenia associated with idiopathic unconjugated hyperbilirubinemia (Gilbert's syndrome). *J Psychiatry Neurosci.* (2005) **30**:416–22.
25. Du Y, Liu J, Sui J, He H, Pearlson GD, Calhoun VD. Exploring difference and overlap between schizophrenia, schizoaffective and bipolar disorders using resting-state brain functional networks. *Conf Proc IEEE Eng Med Biol Soc.* (2014) **2014**:1517–20. doi: 10.1109/EMBC.2014.6943890
26. Abrams DJ, Rojas DC, Arciniegas DB. Is schizoaffective disorder a distinct categorical diagnosis? A critical review of the literature. *Neuropsychiatr Dis Treat.* (2008) **4**:1089–109.
27. World Health Organisation. *International Statistical Classification of Diseases and Related Health Problems, 10th Revision (ICD-10).* Geneva: World Health Organization (1992).

28. World Health Organization. *WHO Report on the Global Tobacco Epidemic 2008: The MPOWER Package.* Geneva: World Health Organization (2008).
29. Woods SW. Chlorpromazine equivalent doses for the newer atypical antipsychotics. *J Clin Psychiatry* (2003) **64**:663–7.
30. Andreasen NC, Pressler M, Nopoulos P, Miller D, Ho BC. Antipsychotic dose equivalents and dose-years: a standardized method for comparing exposure to different drugs. *Biol Psychiatry* (2010) **67**:255–62. doi: 10.1016/j.biopsych.2009.08.040
31. Hewitt J. *Calculating equivalent doses of oral benzodiazepine.* Drugs & Therapeutics Group, NHS Foundation Trust, Sussex Partnership (2013).
32. Guy W. *Clinical Global Impressions (CGI) Scale.* Washington DC: APA (2000).
33. Kay SR, Fiszbein A, Opler LA. The positive and negative syndrome scale (PANSS) for schizophrenia. *Schizophr Bull.* (1987) **13**:261–76.
34. Fioravanti M, Bianchi V, Cinti ME. Cognitive deficits in schizophrenia: an updated metanalysis of the scientific evidence. *BMC Psychiatry* (2012) **12**:64. doi: 10.1186/1471-244X-12-64
35. Nasreddine ZS, Phillips NA, Bédirian V, Charbonneau S, Whitehead V, Collin I, et al. The montreal cognitive assessment (MoCA): a brief screening tool for mild cognitive impairment. *J Am Geriatr Soc.* (2005) **53**:695–9. doi: 10.1111/j.1532-5415.2005.53221.x
36. Tombaugh TN. Trail making test A and B: normative data stratified by age and education. *Arch Clin Neuropsychol.* (2004) **19**:203–14. doi: 10.1016/S0887-6177(03)00039-8
37. Wechsler D, Stone CP. Wais-R: *Wechsler Adult Intelligence Scale-Revised.* New York, NY: The Psychological Corporation (1981).
38. Brissos S, Palhavã F, Marques JG, Mexia S, Carmo AL, Carvalho M, et al. The Portuguese version of the Personal and Social Performance Scale (PSP): reliability, validity, and relationship with cognitive measures in hospitalized and community schizophrenia patients. *Soc Psychiatry Psychiatr Epidemiol.* (2012) **47**:1077–86. doi: 10.1007/s00127-011-0412-6

4

Formal Thought Disorders – Historical Roots

Joana Jerónimo[1,2], Tiago Queirós[2], Elie Cheniaux[3,4] and Diogo Telles-Correia[1,2]*

[1] Faculdade de Medicina da Universidade de Lisboa, Lisbon, Portugal, [2] Hospital de Santa Maria, Centro Hospitalar Lisboa Norte, Lisbon, Portugal, [3] Faculdade de Ciências Médicas da Universidade do Estado do Rio de Janeiro, Rio de Janeiro, Brazil, [4] Instituto de Psiquiatria da Universidade Federal do Rio de Janeiro, Rio de Janeiro, Brazil

***Correspondence:**
Joana Jerónimo
joana.santos.jeronimo@gmail.com

In this article the authors intend to review in an intelligible and comprehensive way the historical roots of Formal Thought Disorders. Early descriptions of thought disorders date back to the XIX century with Esquirol, but it was in the first half of the XX century that several authors introduced the main features of the actual concept of Formal Thought Disorders. Emil Kraepelin described *akataphasia* (inability to find the appropriate expression for a thought) in patients with *dementia praecox* (a term that some years later was replaced by schizophrenia). Bleuler and Kretschmer also identified in schizophrenic patients a generalized "loosening of associations" and Carl Schneider described several Formal Thought Disorders such as derailment, fusion, omission, suspension and driveling. At the end of the XX century Nancy Andreasen studied the classical descriptions regarding Formal Thought Disorders, reclassified them and also introduced a scale to assess them. Although the specificity of these symptoms in schizophrenia and psychosis has been a source of controversy among the different authors, the importance given to their presence in these mental disorders is universal. We defend that it is crucial that these historical and conceptual elements are grasped in order to assess Formal Thought Disorders for clinical and research purposes.

Keywords: psychopathology, descriptive psychopathology, thought disorders, formal thought disorders, schizophrenia, history of psychiatry

INTRODUCTION

The term psychopathology derives from two Greek words: "psyche" meaning "soul," and "pathos" meaning "suffering." Throughout the evolution of the term, it has been used under two strands: explanatory psychopathology and descriptive psychopathology (DP). While the former includes explanations of symptoms based on specific lines of thought (e.g., psychodynamic, cognitive-behavioral, neuroscientific or biological), the later refers only to the precise description and categorization of psychopathological manifestations (1).

According to Berrios, DP can be defined as a systematic set of general principles, terms and rules of application, used to capture and describe aspects of behavior that are assumed to result from a psychic or organic dysfunction (1).

The DP, as it is today, results from a combination of historical contributions from several centuries of clinical research in psychiatry.

Different kinds of classification of psychopathological symptoms were proposed to guide the development of assessment scales for clinical and research purposes and facilitate peer communication.

As Jaspers stressed, it is impossible to order and classify satisfactorily the phenomenological findings, at least for now, but we must sort the phenomena somehow provisionally and "this is best done by a classification which gives some plastic impression of what the facts will naturally yield" [(2), p60]. He suggested the organization of symptoms into 8 groups: (1) awareness of the objects (anomalies of perception), (2) experience of space and time, (3) awareness of the body, (4) delusion and awareness of reality, (5) feelings and affective states, (6) urge, drive and will, (7) awareness of the self, (8) phenomena of self-reflection (2).

It was based on Jaspers' classification that Fish, in his book *Clinical Psychopathology: Signs and Symptoms in Psychiatry*, presented a psychopathological classification that still guides the classification of psychiatric symptoms in many countries. Fish' classification is based on several categories: (1) disorders of perception, (2) disorders of thought and speech, (3) disorders of memory, (4) disorders of emotion, (5) disorders of the experience of self, (6) disorders of consciousness and (7) motor disorders (3).

According to Fish, thought disorders can be generically divided into (1) disorders of the stream of thought, (2) disorders of the possession of thought, (3) disorders of the content of thinking, (4) disorders of the form of thinking. In formal thought disorders (FTD) the organization and associative process of thinking, mainly the abstract component and conceptualization, are impaired. On the other hand, in content thought disorders the disturbance lies on the content of the patients' thought (e.g., delusions) (3).

Initially this psychopathological category has been introduced as almost specific to schizophrenia. However, it is now accepted that this symptom may also present itself in other situations such as organic cerebral disorders (e.g., in confusional states) and in other psychiatric disorders, such as depression and mania (4).

This article intends to review the evolution of the concept of formal thought disorders (FTD) taking into account the contributions of the various authors who have studied the subject throughout the history of psychiatry.

FTD IN THE XIX CENTURY

Esquirol (5) was the first author to hint at the presence of a primary pathology of the faculty that is in charge of coordinating ideas (5).

Some years later, Prichard uses the term "incoherence" for the situations where there are flaws in the connection between thoughts, which often arise in psychiatric patients (6).

Guislain (7) also uses the term "*incoherence des ideées*" and proposes a distinction between thought (including FTD) and speech disorders (7).

In 1867, Griesinger distinguished for the first time the "formal deviations" (*formale Abweichungen*) from "false contents" (*falscher Inhalt der Gedanken*) (8), nowadays known as formal and content thought disorders, respectively.

The disorders of thought were also reported by Hecker in 1871, who wrote about a peculiar departure from normal logical sentence structure, with frequent changes in direction that may or may not lose the train of thought (9).

Jules Séglas (10) gave an important contribute to the development of thought disorders (including FTD) (10). According to him, all the symptoms with diagnostic value for mental disorders were expressed through language and gesture. In turn, changes in speech could be divided into *dyslogies* (thought disorders), *dysphasies* (language disorders), or *dyslalies* (speech disorders). This author described four types of *dyslogies*: *Tempo* (increased or decreased rate of thought), *Form* (changes in plaintiveness of thought, verbigeration, etc), *Syntax* (e.g., referring to the self in the third person or disintegration of sentence construction), *Content* (including fixation in certain themes, stereotypes and neologisms) (6, 10).

FIRST HALF OF THE XX CENTURY

In the beginning of the twentieth century, Renée Masselon (1902) included in the chapter of *Psychologie des Déments Précoces* the description of some symptoms compatible with the actual definition of FTD that he classified as "language disorders" (11).

In 1910, Emil Kraepelin introduces the term *akataphasia* as one of the linguistic expression disorders frequent in *dementia praecox*. In this case the patients either do not find the appropriate expression to their thoughts and produce words with similar sounds, or they let their speech follow in a totally different direction (12). These changes, which are closely related to the phenomena described by other authors in formal thought disorders, are presented by Kraepelin in the language disorders section.

The difficulty in differentiating thought disorders from language and speech disorders (patent in Masselon, Kraeplin, and several other authors) is very common throughout the history of psychopathology. As already explained by Jaspers, it is related to artificiality and subjectiviy, both present in psychopathology classifications.

In 1914, Kleist described that some patients used words idiosyncratically to cover a greater range of meaning than they mentally encompass. He called these *stock* words or phrases. This psychopathological disorder reflected a poverty of words and syntax and also an active tendency for words to intrude into thoughts, and therefore speech. According to this author, in schizophrenic patients, the constellation of associations between words is also disordered and they often presented apparently irrelevant associations, even though they seem appropriate subjectively to the patient himself (13).

Bleuler (14) studied this subject in much more detail than any author before. He described FTD as a direct consequence of the *"loosening of association"* and a fundamental disturbance in schizophrenia. In his opinion, there would be an inability to associate ideas due to the absence of a central deterministic idea. Thoughts arise linked to each other by means of idiosyncratic causal connections, leading to a production of distorted concepts characterized by condensation, displacement, and symbolism. This way patients present thoughts that are disconnected from reality (autistic) (14).

Kretschmer, similarly to Bleuler also regarded FTD in schizophrenia as a result of a generalized "loosening of association" in mental functions (15). Babcock (1933) also described FTD in the schizophrenic patients but he stressed that they resulted from a slowing of all intellectual processes and not from the "loosening of association" that other authors suggested (16).

The work of Carl Schneider (1930) was also a key contribution in the history of FTD. He described a number of changes in thought that could be regarded as FTD: derailment, fusion, suspension and drivelling (16). According to Schneider, the three components of normal thinking (constancy, organization, and continuity) are disturbed in schizophrenic thinking. *Derailment* (*entgleisen*) consists in the breakdown in association so that the main thought flows into another subsidiary unrelated thought (e.g., "I'm going to take the bus, I go to my parents' house, the president controls my ideas, the cameras are in my room"). In *fusion* (*verschmelzung*) there is some preservation of the normal chain of associations, with juxtaposition of heterogeneous and incomprehensible contents. In other words, several ideas A, B, C are interconnected. (e.g., "I know that the martians have been chasing me since that day on the beach. The shape of my room has changed since I have these supernatural powers and my mother knows it, so the martians will come back to get me and that beach remains blue, but the powers that I have my mother never denied them"). *Suspension* consists in the sudden interruption of a certain thought (e.g., "I am going to take the bus to... today I had lunch and it was fine"). This last phenomenon is very similar to the "block of thought," a disorder of the stream of thought (3). In *drivelling* there is a miscellany of fragments of heterogeneous thoughts, with loss of associations and loss of sense (3). This can occur when there is a high degree of *derailment* and *fusion*, with or without maintenance of the syntactic structure (17).

Goldstein (18) described a special form of concrete thinking that was present in patients with schizophrenia. This *concrete thinking* or abstraction deficit refers to the inability to make the distinction between the symbolic and the concrete, and also to the incapacity to treat internal and external stimuli conceptually and to delimit them in relation to the surrounding environment. The patient is not able to deal with his experiences conceptually, does not perceive the objects as belonging to a class or category and is incapable of understanding abstraction (19).

Norman Cameron (20) emphasized the lack of connections between successive thoughts that could be present in psychiatric patients. He termed this phenomenon as *asyndesis*. Cameron also includes the following as FTD: *over-inclusiveness* when the patient cannot maintain the boundaries of a concept (including in it attributes from other concepts, e.g., the patient may confuse "living room" with "living room chair"), *metonyms* that mean the use of imprecise expressions in which a term of a phrase is used instead of more accurate ones (e.g., "I'm going to eat a plate"), *interpenetration of themes* (difficult to differentiate from C. Schneider's fusion concept) and *thought fragmentation* (bearing many resemblances to C. Schneider's derailment concept) (20).

Hamilton (19), in his main work "*Die beginnende Schizophrenie*," describes in *apophany* several psychopathological phenomena compatible with FTD, such as fusion and drivelling (original concepts from C. Shneider) and alogy (thought without logic) (21).

END OF THE XX CENTURY/BEGINNING OF THE XXI CENTURY

Frank Fish (3) has brought together the classic descriptions of psychiatric symptoms, and based on them he presented a psychopathological classification. It included the FTD, which he described and organized according to several classical authors. Fish also subdivided them into negative or positive: while in the negative FTD the patient loses his capacity to think (even though he doesn't produce abnormal concepts), in the positive FTD the patient produces false concepts resulting from the fusion of several disconnected elements. After Fish' death, the text was revised and updated by Max Hamilton in 1974 and 1985 (19).

Other authors have developed concepts that are very close to the original meaning of FTD. Among them, Arieti points out, in 1969, that while the process of human brain evolution has shown continual rise from the concrete to the abstract, in schizophrenia concrete forms of thought re-emerge. Therefore, not only schizophrenic patients, but also little children tend to show a paleological logic that is progressively replaced by the Aristotelian logic of adults, using second-order cognitive processes compared to those used by normal subjects. In an example cited by Arieti, a schizophrenic patient says she is the Madonna. The paleological reasoning behind this statement can be interpreted thusly. E.g., the patient thinks: the Madonna is a virgin. I am also a virgin, so I am the Madonna. Arieti defines this idea as paleological thought, which is applied by the patient to understand psychic events that are complex and do not respond to a logical linearity (22). The schizophrenic patient abandons Aristotelian logic and adopts paleological logic to escape anguish, because, according to Aristotelian logic reality is interpreted as threatening and unbearable (23). In conclusion, Arieti argues that paleological thought expresses a less integrated and evolved mode of thought (22).

Nancy Andreasen (4) argues that the set of psychiatric symptoms gathered under the name of FTD should be redefined and regrouped into new categories of thought, language and communication disturbances (4). This author criticizes some aspects about the way that FTD have been addressed over the time. Among these, she points out that it is not correct to deal with FTD as if they represented a unitary dimension, when in reality all of these symptoms are conceptually divergent. Another aspect with which Andreasen does not agree is that FTD are traditionally considered to be specific to schizophrenia, and she stresses that it has been concluded in several studies that not only these symptoms may appear in other psychiatric or medical diseases (or even in healthy individuals) but also they aren't present in many patients with schizophrenia.

Therefore, Andreasen created a scale in which the classic FTD are subdivided in three groups (24–26): (1) Communication disturbances—when the speaker does not meet the necessary requirements for the listener's understanding (poverty of content of speech, pressure of speech, distractible speech, tangentiality, derailment, stilted speech, echolalia, self-reference, circumstantiality, loss of goal, perseveration, and blocking); (2) Language disturbances—when the speaker violates the semantic and syntactic conventions (incoherence, clang association (e.g., assonance), neologisms, use of word approximations); (3) Thought disturbances—when only thinking alone seems affected (poverty of thought and illogicality aberrant inferential processes). According to this classification FTD should rather be referred as disorders of thought-language-communication (24). Andreasen demonstrated a good reliability for this classification system and also demonstrated that these psychopathological findings were not specific to schizophrenia and were also common in other mental disorders (e.g., Mania) (27).

Sims, in the first edition of his book, from 1988, defends the use of the expression "disorder of the thinking process" instead of FTD. According to him, abnormalities of thinking process "cannot be easily related to any clearly described, already established notion of what normal processes are"[(28), p129].

With the release of Diagnostic and Statistics Manual IV (DSM-IV) in 1994, the term "disorganized speech" was chosen instead of the classical FTD designation: " Because of the difficulty inherent in developing an objective definition of "thought disorder," and because in a clinical setting inferences about thought are based primarily on the individual's speech" [(29), p276]. It is added in this manual that these symptoms are not specific of schizophrenia.

In the fifth edition of DSM (DSM-5), published in 2013, it was decided that this designation should remain (30).

A lack of consensus regarding a better way to conceptualize and assess these symptoms has remained so far. This situation could be a case for concern since psychiatric research (clinical and neurobiological) should ideally be grounded in unambiguous descriptive psychopathology (30).

DISCUSSION AND CONCLUSIONS

Since Esquirol, there have been reports of certain psychopathological disorders in which the main characteristic is the failure of association between successive thoughts. In the XIX century Griesinger distinguished for the first time the "formal deviations" from "false contents" among thought disorders. But it was in the first half of the twentieth century that the greatest investment was given to this concept. Although several authors such as Kraepelin, Masselo and Kleist had contributed to this cause, Bleuler was the one who invested the most, not only in the description, but also concerning the etiopathogenic basis of the FTD. Other authors such as Carl Schneider, Kurt Goldstein and Norman Cameron have made an essential contribution to the psychopathological semiology of FTD. At the end of the XX century, there was an attempt to bring together and reformulate the historical contributions of the former authors on this subject, notably with Nancy Andreassen.

As we have seen, several concepts related to FTD were created by the great authors of psychiatry and it seems difficult to gather all within the same theoretical model. Phenomenological psychopathology is characterized by a lack of uniformity in relation to its terms and concepts. Thus, it is possible that the same phenomenon has been designated in different terms by different authors.

Accordingly, for example, terms such as "incoherence" by Prichard, "loosening of association" by Bleuler and "derailment" by Carl Schneider, may all represent the same concepts in FTD.

Although the specificity of these symptoms in schizophrenia and psychosis has been a source of controversy among the different authors, the importance given to their presence in these mental disorders is consensual. It was demonstrated in a recent systematic review (which included 120 articles, based on several ways of defining and assessing FTD) that FTD are a common symptom of psychosis and may be considered a marker of illness severity (31).

In recent times there has been a reflection on what are the most important symptoms in schizophrenia and which should base the translational neuroscience research in this area (32). There seems to be no doubt about the importance of FTD in schizophrenia and thus these symptoms seem to be a good candidate to guide research that seeks to find the neurobiological correlates of schizophrenia. Some evidence has already been found in this area, such as several structural and functional changes in the lateral temporal lobes that have been related to FTD (again based on several ways of defining and assessing FTD) (33).

Crow (34) defended the idea that FTD could be derived from an absence of hemispheric asymmetry in language areas. His work supports genetic association between language and schizophrenia, defending that the genetic mutation that allowed the emergence of language in humans, can be responsible for their vulnerability to failures, which may be clinically manifested as schizophrenia (34, 35).

One of the major problems associated with FTD, and psychopathology in general, is the lack of uniformity of concepts and ways of accessing symptoms. As well as there have been several ways of defining FTD, also multiple methods of assessing this symptom have been used.

General psychopathological scales such as the Scale for the Assessment of Positive Symptoms [SAPS] (26), the Scale for the Assessment of Negative Symptoms [SANS] (27), the Positive and Negative Syndrome Scale [PANSS] for schizophrenia (36), the Brief Psychiatric Rating Scale [BPRS] (37), have some items dedicated to FTD. Some specific FTD scales have also been developed such as the Thought and Language Disorder (TALD) scale (38), Thought, Language, and Communication Disorders (TLC) scale (25), The Thought and Language Index (TLI) (39), The Thought Disorder Index (TDI) (40).

This variability in the ways of defining and measuring this psychopathological disorder has important consequences in both clinical and translational research.

In this article we intended to describe in an intelligible and comprehensive way the historical roots of the FTD concept. We defend that it is crucial that these elements are grasped in order to assess FTD for clinical (eg. schizophrenia and psychosis diagnosis) and research (clinical and translational) purposes.

As Andreasen (40) pointed out: "Applying technology without companionship of wise clinicians with specific expertise in psychopathology will be a lonely, sterile and perhaps fruitless enterprise." (41).

AUTHOR CONTRIBUTIONS

DT-C conceived and directed the work. JJ took the lead in writing the manuscript. JJ and TQ wrote the manuscript with input from all authors. All authors provided critical feedback.

REFERENCES

1. Berrios G. Descriptive psychopathology: conceptual and historical aspects. *Psychol Med.* (1984) 14:303–13.
2. Jaspers K. *General Psychopathology (Trans. Hamilton M and Hoenig J). Volume 1.* Manchester: Manchester University Press (1963). p. 60.
3. Fish F. *Clinical Psychopatholgy: Signs and Symptoms in Psychiatry.* Bristol: John Wright & Sons (1967).
4. Andreasen NC. Thought, language, and communication disorders. I. Clinical assessment, definition of terms, and evaluation of their reliability. *Arch Gen Psychiatry* (1979) 36:1315–21.
5. Esquirol E. *Des Maladies Mentales Considérées sous les rapports médical, Hygiénique et Médico-Legal.* Paris: Baillière (1838).
6. Berrios G. *The History of Mental Symptoms - Descriptive Psychopathology Since the Nineteenth Century.* Cambridge: Cambridge University Press (1996). p. 71–84.
7. Guislain J. *Leçons Orales sur les Phrénopathies.* Gand: L. Hebbelynck (1852).
8. Griesinger W. *Mental Pathology and Therapeutics.* New York: Hafner Publishing Company (1867).
9. Hecker E. Die Hebephrenie. (trans. M.L. Schoelly), ed. M.J. Sedler. *Am J Psychiatry* (1985) 142:1265–127.
10. Séglas J. *Les Troubles du Langage chez les Aliénés.* Paris: Ed. Rueff (1892).
11. Masselon R. *La Démence Précoce.* Paris: L. Boyer (1902). p. 87–93.
12. Kraeplin E. *Dementia Praecox and Paraphrenia. 8th Edn.* Edinburgh: Livingstone (1919).
13. Oyebode F. *Sims' Symptoms in the Mind: Textbook of Descriptive Psychopathology.* London: Elsevier Health Sciences (2014). p. 167–8.
14. Bleuler E. Dementia Praecox or the Group of Schizophrenias. In: Zinkin J, editor. *Dementia Praecox or the Group of Schizophrenias* New York, NY: International Universities Press (1950).
15. Eysenck HJ. *Experiments in Personality - Volume II : Psychodiagnostics and Psychodynamics.* London: Routledge & Kean Paul (1960). p. 3.
16. Babcock H. *Dementia Praecox.* New York: Science Press (1933).
17. Sims A. *Symptoms in the Mind: An Introduction to Descriptive Psychopathology.* London: Saunders (1988).
18. Goldstein K. Metodological Approach to the study of Schizophrenic Thought Disorder. In: Kasanin JS, editor. *Language and Thought in Schizophrenia.* New York, NY: The Norton Library (1944). pp. 133–65.
19. Hamilton M. *Fish's Clinical Psychopathology: Signs and Symptoms in Psychiatry.* Bristol: John Wright & Sons (1974).
20. Cameron N. Experimental analysis of schizophrenic thinking. In: Kasanin JS, editor. *Language and Thought in Schizophrenia.* New York, NY: The Norton Library (1944). p. 17–39.
21. Conrad K. *Die beginnende Schizophrenie.* Stuttgart: Thieme Verlag (1958).
22. Scrimali T. *Entropy of Mind and Negative Entropy: A Cognitive and Complex Approach to Schizophrenia and Its Therapy.* London: Karnac Books (2018).
23. Melo JC. O conceito de pensamento paleológico segundo Arieti. *Psilogos* (2005) 2:75–81.
24. Andreasen NC. Scale for the Assessment of Thought, Language, and Communication (TLC). *Schizophr Bull.* (1985) 12:473–82.
25. Andreasen NC. *The Scale for the Assessment of Positive Symptoms (SAPS).* Iowa City: The University of Iowa Press (1983).
26. Andreasen NC. *The Scale for the Assessment of Negative Symptoms (SANS).* Iowa City: The University of Iowa Press (1983).
27. Andreasen NC, Grove WM. Thought, language, and communication in schizophrenia: diagnosis and prognosis. *Schizophr Bull.* (1986) 12:348–59. doi: 10.1093/schbul/12.3.348
28. Schneider C. *Psychologie der Schizophrenen.* Leipzig: Ed. Thieme (1930).
29. Association AP. *Diagnostic and Statistical Manual of Mental Disorders IV. 4th edition.* Washington: American Psychiatric Association (1994). p. 276.
30. Association AP. *Diagnostic and Statistical Manual of Mental Disorders 5. 5th edition.* Washington: American Psychiatric Association (2013).
31. Roche E, Creed L, MacMahon D, Brennan D, Clarke M. The epidemiology and associated phenomenology of formal thought disorder: a systematic review. *Schizophr Bull.* (2015) 41:951–62. doi: 10.1093/schbul/sbu129
32. Parnas J, Henriksen MG. Disordered self in the schizophrenia spectrum: a clinical and research perspective. *Harv Rev Psychiatry* (2014) 22:251–65. doi: 10.1097/HRP.0000000000000040
33. Kircher T, Bröhl H, Meier F, Engelen J. Formal thought disorders: from phenomenology to neurobiology. *Lancet Psychiatry* (2018) 5:515–26. doi: 10.1016/S2215-0366(18)30059-2
34. Crow TJ. Schizophrenia as failure of hemispheric dominance for language. *Trends Neurosci.* (1997) 20:339–43.
35. Crow TJ. The torque defines the four quadrants of the human language circuit and the nuclear symptoms of schizophrenia identify their component functions. In: Stemmer B, Whitaker HA, editors. *Handbook of the Neuroscience of Language.* San Diego, CA: Academic Press (2008). p. 299–307.
36. Kay SR, Fiszbein A, Opler LA. The positive and negative syndrome scale (PANSS) for schizophrenia . *Schizophr Bull.* (1987) 13:261–76.
37. Overall JE, Gorham DR. The brief psychiatric rating scale. *Psychol Rep.* (1962) 10:799–812. doi: 10.2466/pr0.1962.10.3.799
38. Liddle PF, Ngan ETC, Caissie SL, Anderson CM, Bates AT, Quested DJ, et al. Thought and language index: an instrument for assessing thought and language in schizophrenia. *Br J Psychiatry* (2002) 181:326–30. doi: 10.1192/bjp.181.4.326
39. Johnston MH, Holzman PS. *Assessing Schizophrenic Thinking.* San Francisco: Jossey-Bass (1979).
40. Andreasen NC. DSM and the death of phenomenology in america: an example of unintended consequences. *Schizophr Bul.* (2007) 33:108–112. doi: 10.1093/schbul/sbl054
41. Kircher T, Krug A, Stratmann M, Ghazi S, Schales C, Frauenheim M, et al. A rating scale for the assessment of objective and subjective formal thought and language disorder (TALD). *Schizophr Res.* (2014) 160:216–21. doi: 10.1016/j.schres.2014.10.024

5

Seeing Beyond Diseases and Disorders: Symptom Complexes as Manifestations of Mental Constituents

*Maurício V. Daker**

Departamento de Saúde Mental, Universidade Federal de Minas Gerais—UFMG, Belo Horizonte, Brazil

***Correspondence:**
Maurício V. Daker
mauriciodaker@gmail.com

Many psychopathologists have approached symptom complexes without prejudging them as physical deficits or diseases, an approach suitable to connections with normal mind, to a broad dimensional and anthropological view of mental disorders. It contrasts with the prevailing orientation in psychiatry toward the medical model of delimited diseases. Discussions of this order centered on symptom complexes gained special prominence in psychiatry between the early 20th century through Alfred Hoche and World War II through Carl Schneider. Their works, in addition to the work of other authors of that period, are considered. The late Kraepelin conceded the possibility that affective and schizophrenic manifestations do not represent disease processes but rather represent areas of human personality. Seeing mind or persons is a paradigmatic different perspective than seeing diseases. Re-emerge in this comprehensive or integrationist context the notion of unitary psychosis and philosophical questions as the mind-body problem; as background there was a process metaphysics. The possibility of human experience in a phenomenological sense is considered, and a matrix of symptom or function complexes is related to it. Examples of past unitary models of mental disorders with their neurophysiologic explanations are given, as well as an analogy to current biological aspects of the endogenous in chronobiology. The question or hypothesis arises whether mental symptom complexes are manifestations of mind constituents or functions that make human experience and mind possible. The present work is a conceptual analysis that indicates a positive answer to this question. The expectation is to emphasize the perspectives of investigation in psychopathology and sciences of mind fostered by this view of symptom complexes.

Keywords: symptom complexes, dimensional diagnosis, unitary psychosis, personality, psychopathology, history of psychiatry, philosophy and psychiatry, sciences of mind

INTRODUCTION

"Of the madman, we all have a little," is a folk psychological assertion that should hold scientific interest and be considered more seriously. The mainstream notion of disease in psychiatry, aiming to discover specific mental disorders and to demarcate normality from abnormality, may give an artificial impression of simple, detached things, rather than intricately connected factors and causes. There is no unquestionable scientific evidence, however, that major mental diseases or disorders are clearly divided from normal mind, or even divided among themselves. An epistemological clash is embedded here, among the hybrid condition "constituted by the blending of components arising from disparate sources of knowledge ranging from the biological to the semantic in its widest sense" (1), or that "symptoms and signs cannot be properly understood or identified apart from an appreciation of the nature of consciousness or subjectivity, which in turn cannot be treated as a collection of thing-like, mutually independent objects" (2).

Mainstream psychiatry, however, was not always concerned with a strict notion of disease or was epistemologically naive in this way. Apart from the psychodynamic and the phenomenological—anthropological orientations, the history of psychiatry tells of many psychopathologists who saw close relations or a continuum through mental disorders and normality. This was the case in the last century between the 1910s and World War II, a period in which symptom complexes were conceived and investigated more neutrally in relation to possible mental diseases (3).

At that time, the optimism and certainties concerning science in its positivistic contours were shaken at their foundations, as shown by the paradigmatic shifts in physics from atomism to quantum and relativity theories. In psychology and psychiatry, the prime foundation-shaking forces were the phenomenological movement and psychoanalysis. Psychiatry was questioning the previously believed linearity in mental diseases among causes, anatomic pathological findings, and clinical manifestations, as stated in Kraepelin's treatises. In 1920, however, Kraepelin conceded the possibility that "the affective and the schizophrenic manifestation forms of insanity do not represent, in themselves, the expression of certain disease processes, but merely reveal those areas of our personality in which they take place" [(4), p. 27].

Seeing diseases and seeing "areas of our personality" or "a man's character" [(5), p. 549] are totally different conceptions or perspectives. The latter view led those psychopathologists to approach more comprehensively the psychopathological manifestations, to the point of asserting deep relations to normal mind.

STATIC SPECIFIC DISEASES OR CATEGORIES OF DISCRETE SUBSTANCES VS. DYNAMIC WHOLE PERSONS

"Hard" science of positivistic contours aims to isolate the studied object from possible external interferences, including from subjective factors. The isolated object or part is investigated and sometimes elucidated in its own limits, as a reduced unit, which can well be summed to other units in a mosaic form. If we know how the pieces of a clock work, we will know how the clock works, a reasoning usually applied also to cells, organs and the organism in medicine. The problem is how far such reasoning is suitable to investigate persons or mind. In the clock model we deal with more tangible facts and concrete concepts; with persons and mind, with more flowing processes and abstract concepts. There a more static approach is feasible, whereas here a dynamic approach seems to be demanded, including an ongoing dialectic process between the parts and the whole, which can be more relevant than a simple sum of isolated parts. Similarly, it can be said that atoms, molecules, genes, or neurons act not simply mechanistically or deterministically to originate mind in a bottom-up one-way road. Top-down concerns are needed, thinking here in the man-made world that implies agency and beliefs, historical process and culture, and intersubjectivity—that means in cognitive sciences a "top-top process" (6), i.e., a collective top interacting with an individual top. All is integrated in a dynamic, comprehensive and non-reducible real unit: the whole person.

Embedded in these discussions are the ancient contrasting views of static delimited substances vs. dynamic flowing processes, which can be tracked in philosophy as far as Parmenides and Heraclitus. Concerning mental disorders, the categorial vs. dimensional diagnosis or classification reflects these contrasting or complementary views. Importantly, as mentioned by Kendell [(7), p. 136]: "Those whose interest is primarily in the nature of the relationship between different syndromes, and between illness and normality, will probably prefer to think in dimensional terms." Dimensions are prone to dynamic systems in a complex network of internal and external interactions, rather than being based on independent and comparatively discrete substances as are categories. Taken in the sense of a discrete substance, in a dogmatic uncritical one-sided fashion, the medical idea of disease can impose a constraint upon advancement in psychiatry, since isolated units of diseases are self-sufficient and not suitable for dynamic considerations about interrelationships among mental disorders and normal mind. However, if we take the idea of categories less rigidly, e.g., as patterns or prototypes, it allows thinking psychopathology as a matter of degree as opposed to a matter of kind, as shared liability factors conceptualized as continuous dimensions of personality that confer risk for the development of psychopathology (8).

The relation of mental symptom complexes to the whole person indeed allows or, as we will see, demands a more dynamic view in psychiatry that encompasses both the normal mind and the world. Here we are in tune, as alluded above when referring to dynamic flowing processes, with a process metaphysics, which would be more adequate to many scientific fields or approaches than the classical Western metaphysics based on static substances or on an assembly of them (9). Probably not a mere coincidence, the process philosophy was facing a revival in the early 20th century, or turned itself a more distinct branch of philosophy, with Alfred North Whitehead, Henri Bergson, Martin Heidegger, and many others (9).

SYMPTOM COMPLEXES, PERSON, AND MIND

According to Hoche (5), it is due to the occurrence of the special, constant, and largely merging forms of reactions, i.e., psychic dispositions such as hysteric, hypochondriac, neurasthenic, suspicious, querulant, etc., the pressing indication that in the normal psyche certain symptom associations or complexes lie preformed. "In part they make up what we call a person's character. In part, in the case of special illness-inducing influences, determine how the morbid deviant form of reaction of the personality occurs" [(5), p. 549]. Hoche thinks that the same applies word by word to the most named mental disorders, such as the symptom complexes melancholia, mania, chronic paranoia. These symptom complexes are therefore observed in mental disorders that appear to be only a strengthening of certain morbid personal dispositions, or they can also be triggered by organic processes, here with a secondary significance [(5), p. 549]. Hoche is striking against the idea that these symptom complexes might be like disease entities, as conceived in general medicine, comparing the investigation of disease entities in psychiatry to a hopeless and exhausting hunt for ghosts:

> It underlies all these strenuous efforts [to find disease entities], the indestructible belief that it should be possible also in psychiatry to find particularly defined, pure, single forms of disease, a belief that again and again is nourished from the analogy to somatic medicine, without thinking that the nature of the relationships between symptom and anatomical basis, as they are here and there, cannot be compared at all with each other [(5), p. 542].

The psychic, following Hoche, represents an entirely new category, obeying its own laws, not commensurable with material processes, like music is not comparable to the musical instrument. In the same sense, we can say that biology produces the instrument and culture writes the music.

In being more malleable than the previous, rigid Kraepelinean view of disease entity, or because of it, the new approach entails an inevitable anthropological perspective in psychopathology, that is, entails normal aspects of the mind and the person. The late Kraepelin was already contemporaneous to or was anticipating interest by many psychopathologists in the personality of the patient, as would become prominent in mainstream psychiatry of that time through Ernst Kretschmer's work (he achieved a nomination in 1929 to the Nobel Prize), among many others, also those of phenomenological orientation like Minkowski, who emphasized the whole living personality in psychiatry. As far as for dementia praecox or schizophrenia, Kretschmer's work, also Eugen Bleuler's, ended up perceiving, in Oswald Bumke's words, "nothing but a morbid condensation of normal mental reactions" (10), originated in the characteristic personality of the schizophrenic patients. Except in cases of schizophrenia, Bumke himself saw a smooth transition between the endogenous or functional diseases and the manifestations of healthy mental life (11).

Ferdinand Kehrer, commenting on Hoche, welcomed "the displacement of an elementary psychology strange to life through a matter of lived personality within psychiatry" [(12), p. 433], which is also a warning against rigid schematizing. According to him, "preformed" or "to lie ready" should be understood as disposition, which manifests either in the permanent mental constitution or in the readiness for mental disorders. When confronted with a somatic or a psychogenic involvement or etiology, the dispositions act as a "pathogenetic intermediate constituent" between that etiology and the manifestation. Kehrer mentions here Karl Bonhoeffer, who fomented the discussion on the typical syndromic reaction that mediate different etiologies.

Karl Jaspers had already considered the intermediate position of symptom complexes, in this case between the elementary manifestations or symptoms and the disease units, and he advised that "they should be studied in themselves, regardless of disease unit and disease processes, to investigate the regularity and needful togetherness that exist in them" [(13), p. 268]. According to Jaspers [(14), p. 491], Carl Schneider placed symptom complexes at the epicenter of psychiatry. Schneider diverged clearly from Kraepelin's conception of disease entities in psychiatry with its linear correlations among etiology, anatomopathological findings, and clinical manifestation. Importantly, Schneider's "symptom associations" (some of them were empirically investigated by him, concerning schizophrenia) are intimately related to normal "function associations," to the point of saying that the cluster of symptoms in the symptom complexes are already present in normal mind and, for differentiation, are here better named function associations [(15), p. 142]. It is emphasized that the identified associations are not static constructions in the sense of a rigid categorization but rather expressions of an always-fluid process of life with dynamic effects and changeable responsiveness [(15), p. 194]. All reflects his broad concept of "biological" (3).

HUMAN EXPERIENCE AND REALITY: THE ROLE OF SYMPTOM/FUNCTION COMPLEXES

Philosophers have much to say about how human beings access or constitute reality. Following Kraus (16), we can trace a deepening in the subject from Kant to Heidegger, going through Husserl. These philosophers also established the foundations of the phenomenological—anthropological psychiatry. Kant's transcendental categories of mind or consciousness are inherent to and make possible the human experience. Husserl emphasized the new understanding of consciousness as reality-constituting through its intentional acts, mingling subject and object. Heidegger sees a fusion among being human and world by means of the presence or existence, which is prior to consciousness and to the self. Heidegger's term for this presence or existence is *Dasein*, which as human "being-in-the-world," in a constant interplay of existence and the historical world or sedimented meanings, stands open to other beings and to itself, constituting one's world and the self through endowing of meaning. Still following Kraus, the existentials, which are fundamental structures of *Dasein*, act in this sense as Kant's categories: "The existential, or to say it better, the existential a priori, give meaning to and thereby constitute the world of anybody (in the present discussion, the patient). As such, they are one's matrix of possible experience" [(16) p. 101]. Altered "existentials a priori" or pre-objective being interferes with the constitution of the most fundamental ontological components of reality, as space, time, causality, and objecthood, making possible many kinds of strange self-disorders, hallucinations, and delusions (16, 17), that is, making possible or constituting a different reality. Kraus also asserts the need for a dynamic reasoning here: "For psychopathology it is important that being on this level, as these notions already indicate, is by no means something static, but has to be understood as a process of happening" [(15), p. 102].

Maiese (18) considers that one of the aims of phenomenology has been to outline invariant formal structures of consciousness, as the categories or existentials mentioned above, that serve as necessary constraints on human experience. This author points out that a systematic analysis of these structures is central to an enactive conceptualization of subjectivity and self-consciousness and describes five necessary structures of consciousness: spatial, temporal, egocentric (an inner source-point), intentional, and conative affective. They are physically grounded in the endogenous processes and self-organizing neurobiological dynamics of our living animal bodies and constitute a natural matrix of a basic sensorimotor subjectivity to be understood as a system of causal-dynamic relations [(18), p. 9–13].

The point in the present work is whether, on the psychopathology side, the above considerations on symptom complexes would also allow thinking about a matrix that makes human experience or the human mind possible. "Symptom" or "function complexes" also occur within anyone and would act to constitute one's world or the human world. The disconnectedness, the perception becoming "an object of noetic awareness" or a "disembodied spirit" (19) in schizophrenia might not be entirely disadvantageous: It could be necessary for abstraction or for a detachment of an immediate bond with things and the world. It could be an important feature for imagination or creativity, which is found in the relatives of patients, comprising for example divergent thinking and originality (20). This capacity of loose or broad associative thinking and flexibility in schizophrenia might be contrasted or somehow balanced with the over-systematized and rigid pole of paranoia, which in fact also seems to have advantageous aspects—e.g., religions or normal necessary beliefs. Both schizophrenia and paranoia would be intercrossed with the poles of depression and mania responsible for affective attunement, as well as for over-involvement in social situation and commitment to social norms in depression. The pole of obsession expresses part of the rigidity of paranoia and the over-attunement of depression, while hysteria or dissociation might express a mingling of schizophrenic disconnectedness and aspects of mania. Relevant here is that, as well as an ordering of symptoms in each symptom complex, there would be an ordering among the symptom complexes, recalling the tradition in psychopathology of the unitary psychosis (21, 22); ahead are described the unitary psychosis or continuum of symptom complexes by Guislain and Griesinger]. Such dynamic and integrative ordering among the symptom/function complexes is what is meant when thinking about them acting as a matrix in human experience and mind, either in normal as in the considered psychopathological conditions.

Taken in this dynamic configuration, regarding the primary mental disorders, there would be no specific anomalies properly or necessary deficits, but a systemic modification or disequilibrium. As in the ancient Hippocratic humoral theory, whereby humors are not anomalous by themselves, function complexes are necessary to normality when in balance. In other words, there would be a disorder and restriction of quality of life (whether or not it is called "disease" or "symptoms") due to a substantial unbalance of essential human qualities or functions—of the "intermediate constituent" or functional matrix. In such a disproportional and condensed way, it is possible to understand, with Carl Schneider, that symptom complexes can be a clue to the knowledge of normal function associations [(15), p. 237]—that is, the unbalanced pathological disorder highlights the more fluid and thus less accessible connections of normal functions. Again, we need to think about a dynamic process to be able to see possible interrelations in all directions among the complexes, whether deviant (unbalanced) or not. Better to think here in terms of forces, as in electromagnetism, whose physics influenced the process metaphysics and vice versa, and where in a certain sense everything is everywhere at all times (23, 24), rather than thinking on an interaction of discrete detachable substances or parts.

It is probably that the phenomenological-anthropological psychiatry and the theory of symptom complexes are confluent in important aspects, also because they emerged concurrently. Likewise, process philosophy was concurrent, as already mentioned, seemingly underpinning both or being close related to them. Associating these approaches should be promising to (re)opening perspectives in psychopathology in an embracing spectrum: philosophy and medicine, mind and body. For example, it can be conceptualized that the endogenous symptom/function complexes interact early in life with the living body sensations, with human environment and intersubjectivity, from where categories or existentials could emerge, a process that turns out to be like a procedural memory and, hence, a priori or pre-reflexive. Much of that could be suitable to neuroscientific or neurobiological investigations [(25, 26), p. 311–37].

UNITARY PSYCHOSIS AND THE ENDOGENOUS IN A NEUROSCIENTIFIC APPROACH: PAST AND FUTURE

As a branch of medicine, psychiatry has always been concerned with anatomophysiological thinking, usually in the search of specific biological markers. But also, due to the own dynamicity of the mind and its psychopathologies, psychiatry has, since its beginnings, often offered more holistic or systemic conceptions of mental disorders in relation to other branches of medicine. Examples are Joseph Guislain's and Wilhelm Griesinger's unitary views of mental disorders.

Guislain sustained in the first half of the 19th century one general modus of evolution for all mental disorders: from manifestations of sensibility or *Phrenalgie* (*lypérophrenie* or melancholia), followed by reactions (*hyperphrénie* or mania, *paraphrénie* or folly, *hyperplexie* or ecstasy, *hyperspasmie* or convulsion, *idéosynchysie* or delusion and mental aberrance, and *anacoluthie* or mental disintegration), up to an end in annihilation or destruction (*noasthénie* or dementia). The disorders described in each of these three groups would usually mix one after another or at the same time, in such way that he believed to be able to describe over 100 disorders. As Kraepelin (1920) explains it, there would be a great variety of disorders according to the location and intensity of brain impairments. Guislain influenced Wilhelm Griesinger, who among others propagated the usual evolution of mental disorders through continuous stages: melancholia, mania, psychic weakness, and dementia, each of them with typical symptom complexes, and manifold mixed states between them (27).

The clinical observations corroborating those usual stages were convincing enough: think also about general paralysis, which evolves from affective to dementia stages, and was around 30% of the hospitalized patients. Yet Griesinger added an appealing physiological explanation, indeed a "neuropsychophysiological" explanation, to it. He began from an analogy of the normal functioning of the spinal cord with the brain, which would be an evolutional prolongation of the former. The charge of energy or tonus in spinal cord (responsible for the muscle tonus) becomes psychic tonus and (mostly unconscious) idea associations in the brain, and instead of motricity there are aspirations, which are voluntary, with liberty of action, or impulsive. The movement of the psychic tonus and of the ideas results in emotions and affects. Normal mental reflection or deep thinking corresponds to a normal physiological slow-down of the afferent, central and efferent pathways flux. When the flux becomes hampering, however, it results in the state of melancholia, with its manifestation of hypersensitivity to the dammed afferent stimuli, psychic pain, sluggish thinking, no action, and so on. On the other hand, mania emerges from a convulsion-like reaction in spinal cord, bringing immediate action after the afferent stimuli—mania is energy to volition and impulses. All these affective manifestations can return to normality, but if there is damage to this physiology—think of a rubber band that is so stretched and loosened that loses its elasticity or tonus—it results in the secondary clinical manifestations, which are chronic: "a wreckage of a boat after the storm," in Griesinger's words [(27), p. 324], a loss of the psychic tonus and of idea associations—and also of liberty. This "wreckage" can sink further down into dementia.

In his later life, Griesinger assumed a more neuropathological and less physiological and dynamic view of mental disorders, since it became accepted that paranoia would begin without the prior affective stages. This development challenged his physiological conception that had presupposed the presence of primary affective stages (apart from rash brain damage). The neuropathological wave in psychiatry is well known, for there was a time of eminent neuropsychiatrists. Conversely, Karl Kahlbaum, Kraepelin, and colleagues believed that psychiatry should first do its homework by describing the psychiatric diseases; otherwise the neuroanatomists or neuropsychiatrists would fall on their faces, as it indeed happened on the side of psychiatry.

The problem is that the new described diseases, though laborious and judiciously described, were not as such proven, at least in the strict sense of disease as they were supposed to be. Then, the theory of symptom complexes emerged with its connectedness to personality and openness to normal aspects of mind, as we saw above.

This theory was virtually abandoned after World War II, and the strict medical model of disease soon prevailed again in psychiatry, after the psychodynamic and the phenomenological-anthropological waves (3). It is difficult to say to what neuroscientific approach it would correspond nowadays. Here an analogy with the concept of endogenous in chronobiology might be useful in some respects. Decades ago, it was demonstrated that living beings have their own endogenous or internal biological rhythms, which are being elucidated from anatomical structures, genetics, and molecules. The endogenous rhythms are supposed to couple with the external rhythms or *Zeitgebers* ("time givers"), facilitating or making possible the adaptation and survival of living beings. It is vital to adapt to night and day, and in many cases also to tides, moon cycles, and seasons—that is, to the geophysical cycles. What in chronobiology are called endogenous oscillators originated in physics: They synchronize their rhythms as two pendulums attached to a beam tend to synchronize their movements. Such dynamic rhythmicity of several integrated oscillators makes the organism malleable or adaptable to different internal and external conditions (28).

It would similarly succeed with the matrix from which the symptom complexes originate: Past biological conditions in phylogeny concerning the relations between the living being, as well as the human being, with the environment would have been incorporated genetically, leading to the endogenous preformed function complexes that make adaptation and survival possible. Of course, the relation of living beings with geophysical rhythms is much simpler than within the context of mind and its relation to historical, social, cultural, or linguistic aspects. Hereby, the *Zeitgebers* would be better thought as *Sinngebers* ("sense givers" or "meaning givers"). The relation between the historical world as *Sinngeber* and the person, self or existence could be considered here, provided that endogeny is conceived in the latter. William Stern's process of "introception" might also involve such relationship between historical process and person, for it indicates a personal act through which values can be taken up from the cultural milieu by individuals and appropriated or embraced as their own during personality development [(29), p. 329]. Living beings, including human beings, must be prepared, predisposed, or "preformed" for the situations with which they will interact in the world to which they pertain. The synchronization of function complexes with the world or with *Sinngebers* would be a process of "structural coupling" (30), "a phase in the co-temporaneous development of two systems (e.g., organism and environment) where mutual dynamic dependencies unfold across system boundaries" (9). In other words, the multivariate genomic level intersects with the ways in which genetic effects are contingent on environmental moderators (8). The subject of this work is an attempt to glimpse *how* this relation between biology and environment might proceed in the realm of mind.

CONCLUSIONS

Following Jaspers in his introduction to *General Psychopathology*, psychopathology faces a wide, impenetrable continent of which we have knowledge only from its edges, one of body and one of meaning. Indeed, it seems that in the present work we are traveling through a shadowy region in between. Dealing with psychiatry and philosophy, which profoundly influences psychopathology, or dealing with mental disorders, exposes this situation. As a branch of medicine, psychiatry is in relation to philosophy more suitable to the edge of the body, whereas philosophy is prone to meanings without delving much into anatomophysiological or neurobiological concerns. Both should be complementary in the investigation of our continent. It is the case that phenomenological psychopathology already offers accurate descriptions and original conceptions that can aid the neurosciences, but some concepts as existentials or Kantian categories, which make the human experience possible, seem difficult to relate to biology. Psychopathology might contribute to an advance in this puzzle with its theory of symptom or function complexes coming from medicine, even though the knowledge of their anatomophysiological or neuroscientific basis are still incipient. Better it is to say that psychopathology and the function complexes might be indispensable in regarding the mediation between organism, its world, and mind—or, between biology and culture. Symptom/function complexes are manifestations or basic chords of delicate instruments, making possible the human mind symphony.

AUTHOR CONTRIBUTIONS

The author confirms being the sole contributor of this work and has approved it for publication.

REFERENCES

1. Marková I, Berrios G. Epistemology of psychiatry. *Psychopathology* (2012) 45:220–7. doi: 10.1159/000331599
2. Parnas J, Sass LA, Zahavi D. Rediscovering psychopathology: the epistemology and phenomenology of the psychiatric object. *Schizophr Bull.* (2013) 39:270–7. doi: 10.1093/schbul/sbs153
3. Daker MV. The theory of symptom complexes, mind, and madness. *Hist Psychiatry* (in press).
4. Kraepelin E. Die erscheinungsformen des irreseins. *Z ges Neurol Psychiat* (1920) 62:1–29. doi: 10.1007/BF02887354
5. Hoche AE. Die bedeutung der symptomenkomplexe in der psychiatrie. *Z ges Neurol Psychiat* (1912) 12:540–51. doi: 10.1007/BF02866386
6. Roepstorff A, Frith C. What's at the top in the top down control of action? Script sharing and 'top-top' control of action in cognitive experiments. *Psychol Res.* (2001) 68:189–98. doi: 10.1007/s00426-003-0155-4
7. Kendell RE. *The Role of Diagnosis in Psychiatry.* Oxford: Blackwell Scientific Publications (1975).
8. Krueger RF, Goldman D. The need for dimensional approaches in discerning the origins of psychopathology. In: Shrout PE, Keyes KM, Ornstein K, editors. *Causality and Psychopathology.* Oxford; New York, NY: Oxford University Press (2011). p. 338–51.
9. Seibt J. *Process Philosophy. The Stanford Encyclopedia of Philosophy.* Stanford, CA (2018).
10. Bumke O. The dissolution of dementia praecox. Introduction and translation by P. Dalén. *Hist Psychiatry* (1993) 4:129–39.
11. Bumke O. Über die umgrenzung des "manisch-depressiven irreseins. *Zentral Nervenheilkunde Psychiatrie* (1909) 32:381–403.
12. Kehrer F. Die Stellung von Hoches "Syndromenlehre" in der heutigen psychiatrie. *Arch Psychiatrie Nervenkrankheiten* (1925) 74:427–56.
13. Jaspers K. *Allgemeine Psychopathologie.* Berlin: Julius Springer (1913).
14. Jaspers K. *Allgemeine Psychopathologie, 4th ed.* Berlin; Heidelberg: Springer-Verlag (1946).
15. Schneider C. *Die Schizophrenen Symptomverbände.* Berlin: Springer-Verlag (1942).
16. Kraus A. Schizophrenic delusion and hallucination as the expression and consequence of an alteration of the existential a prioris. In: Chung MC, Fulford KWM, Graham G, editors. *Reconceiving Schizophrenia.* Oxford; New York, NY: Oxford University Press (2007). p. 97–111.
17. Wiggins OP, Schwartz MA. Schizophrenia: a phenomenological-anthropological approach. In: Chung MC, Fulford KWM, Graham G, editors. *Reconceiving Schizophrenia.* Oxford; New York, NY: Oxford University Press (2007). p. 113–27.
18. Maiese M. *Embodied Selves and Divided Minds.* Oxford; New York, NY: Oxford University Press (2016).
19. Stanghellini G. Schizophrenia and the sixth sense. In: Chung MC, Fulford KWM, Graham G, editors. *Reconceiving Schizophrenia.* Oxford; New York, NY: Oxford University Press (2007). p. 130–49.
20. Kyaga S, Landén M, Boman M, Hultman CM, Långström N, Lichtenstein P. Mental illness, suicide and creativity: 40-year prospective total population study. *J Psychiatr Res.* (2013) 47:83–90. doi: 10.1016/j.jpsychires.2012.09.010
21. Angst J. Historical aspects of the dichotomy between manic-depressive disorders and schizophrenia. *Schizophr Res.* (2002) 57:5–13. doi: 10.1016/S0920-9964(02)00328-6
22. Kumbier E, Herpertz SC. Helmut Rennert's universal genesis of endogenous psychosis: the historical concept and its significance for today's discussion on unitary psychosis. *Psychopathology* (2010) 43:335–44. doi: 10.1159/000320348
23. Desmet R, Irvine AD. *Alfred North Whitehead. The Stanford Encyclopedia of Philosophy.* Stanford, CA (2018).
24. Gare A. Process philosophy and the emergent theory of mind: whitehead, Lloyd Morgan and schelling. *Concrescence* (2002) 3:1–12. Available online at: https://www.researchgate.net/publication/277064020_Process_Philosophy_and_the_Emergent_Theory_of_Mind_Whitehead_Lloyd_Morgan_and_Schelling
25. Kendler KS. The structure of psychiatric science. *Am J Psychiatry* (2014) 171:931–8. doi: 10.1176/appi.ajp.2014.13111539
26. Sass L. *Madness and Modernism.* Oxford: Oxford University Press (2017).
27. Griesinger W. Die *Pathologie und Therapie der Psychischen Krankheiten, 4th ed.* Braunschweig: Verlag von Friedrich Wreden (1876).
28. Daan S. A history of chronobiological concepts. In: Albrecht U, editor. *The Circadian Clock (Atassi MZ, series editor, Protein Reviews 12).* New York, NY; Dordrecht; Heidelberg; London: Springer (2010). p. 1–35.
29. Lamiell JT. *Beyond Individual and Group Differences. Human Individuality, Scientific Psychology, and William Stern's Critical Personalism.* Thousand Oaks, CA: Sage Publications, Inc (2003).
30. Maturana H. Autopoiesis. Structural coupling and cognition: a history of these and other notions in the biology of cognition. *Cybernet Hum Knowing* (2002) 9:5–34. Available online at: https://pdfs.semanticscholar.org/7881/d48deaffe4c8dc07200b9b5932a7ef74d783.pdf

6

Mental Ill-Health and the Epidemiology of Representations

*Ladislav Kesner**

National Institute of Mental Health, Klecany, Czechia

Correspondence:
Ladislav Kesner
Ladislav.Kesner@nudz.cz

One of major challenges facing contemporary psychiatry is the insufficient grasp of relationship between individual and collective mental pathologies. A long tradition of diagnosing "mental illness" of society—exemplified by Erich Fromm—stands apart from approach of contemporary social psychiatry and is not perceived as relevant for psychiatric discourse. In this Perspective article, I argue that it is possible to uphold the idea of a supra-individual dimension to mental health, while avoiding the obvious pitfalls involved in categorical diagnosing of society as suffering from mental illness. I argue for an extended notion of public mental ill-health, which goes beyond the quantitative understanding of mental health as an aggregate of individual diseased minds captured in statistics, and which can be conceived as a dynamic, emergent property resulting from interactions of individual brains/minds in social space. Such a notion, in turn, presents a challenge of how to account for the interfacing between individual minds/brains and the collective mental phenomena. A suitable theoretical framework is provided by the notion of epidemiology of representations, originally formulated by cognitive anthropologist Dan Sperber. Within this framework, it is possible to highlight the role of public (material) representations in inter-individual transfer of mental representations and mental states. It is a suitable conceptual platform to explain how the troubling experiences with causal or mediating role on mental health, to a significant degree arise through a person's direct interaction with material representations and participation in collective mental states, again generated by material representations.

Keywords: mental ill-health, social psychiatry, epidemiology of representations, images, narratives

INTRODUCTION

In a provocative study devoted to the "pathology of contemporary western society," psychoanalyst, sociologist, and humanist philosopher Erich Fromm presented a sustained argument about why Western society should seriously question its collective sanity (1). Combining psychological erudition with philosophical acumen and the insights of an astute social critic, Fromm paints a bleak picture of the modern human predicament. From today's perspective, the aim of his *The Sane Society*—to diagnose the social mental illness of his time—seems both anachronistic and very timely. It looks anachronistic because, as I shall discuss below, it is removed from the methods and language of contemporary psychiatry. It is nevertheless timely in that most of Fromm's observations about the "pathologies of normalcy" and the "social character of contemporary man" sound all too familiar now, six decades after his book was first published. They strike a chord in our time as the media and public discourse have become increasingly saturated with views like Fromm's, with many thinkers trying to comprehend the great waves of irrationality and negative emotions that are flooding the public space and social media. Fromm's thoughts hit home at a time when it is plainly obvious that people's mental states are being massively manipulated and negative emotions intentionally elicited by media and by groups with vested political and economic interests in achieving particular and in some cases clearly sinister goals. They moreover resonate in a time when psychiatry itself is reassessing its theoretical paradigms, not least of all owing to a sobering realization about the limits of its biological bias (2, 3).

But does diagnosing modern-day society's mental pathologies in the spirit of Fromm have any heuristic value for contemporary psychiatry? I suggest that it might. Recent psychiatry has been taken to task for the decline of the "sociological imagination"—"a decline of theory and interest in the major questions that initially drove early sociological studies of mental disorder" (4). If this charge is taken seriously, then one challenge would be to construct conceptual frameworks for linking individual and collective dimensions of mental health.

Here, Fromm's perspective might provide a useful starting point.

WHAT IS WRONG WITH NOTIONS OF COLLECTIVE MENTAL ILL-HEALTH

Since the publication of his book, Fromm's effort to link social, and mental pathologies at the collective level has found some following in academic writing (5, 6). Within psychiatric discourse, it occasionally echoes in those works that view the current socio-political order of western societies as inherently detrimental to human well-being and psychological health (7, 8) and explicitly focus on "diseases of the collective *esprit de corps* of contemporary civilization" (9). Some social theorists and opinion makers have further extended this line of thought by linking social pathologies to what they perceive to be the pervasive psychological and mental malaise of contemporary society or even "a crisis of Western civilization" (10–12). Such "diagnoses" of collective mental ill-health stand apart from the rigorous science of contemporary psychiatry. A critic would object that they suffer from at least three related problems, each sufficient to render them invalid in the eyes of academic and clinical psychiatrists. First, diagnoses of collective mental ill-health are not reached impartially but in most cases emerge with just a thinly disguised ideological agenda. Almost invariably this involves criticism of capitalism, with global neoliberal capitalism being the usual culprit behind society's illness. Simple causality and correlation between the perception of social and mental pathologies are sought and established, while more nuanced considerations are swept under the carpet. Tellingly, Mark Fisher accuses neo-liberalism of generating a "mental health plague" (10) while political theorist Franco Berardi writes of the "suicidal form of the neoliberal will to win" that is permeating contemporary culture, together with the phenomenology of panic, aggression, and resultant violence, the subjects of his book being heroes "of an age of nihilism and spectacular stupidity: the age of financial capitalism" (11).

Secondly, these views suffer from a negative bias. Diagnoses of collective mental malaises are often based on their authors' interpretation of media representations, which tend to produce a negatively biased picture of the state of the world. Events, possibly caused by an individual mental disorder, all too easily acquire the symptomatic value. Thus, tragic incidents, such as the suicide of the German pilot who crashed his plane, killing all passengers on board (or other mass murders discussed by Berardi), are quickly established as both a symptom and a consequence of the collective psychopathology of an "increasingly anxious and depressed society". Both these problems, and in particular the shortcut from socio-economic order to mental disorder, have plagued even the most serious meditations on collective mental health, such as Karl Jaspers's observations on modern anxiety (13) or Fromm's own book.

Thirdly, and most importantly, notions about collective mental states, which were once popular but are nowadays rather marginalized, even in social sciences, have never gained much traction in psychiatry, and even less so within the realm of biological psychiatry, which is keen on rebranding mental disorders as "brain disorders"(14, 15). After all, there are no collective brains.

TWO COMPLEMENTARY NOTIONS OF COLLECTIVE MENTAL (ILL) HEALTH

Diagnoses of collective mental ill-health, in the tradition of Fromm, thus seem inherently at odds, and impossible to reconcile with the nuanced and sophisticated methods of social psychiatry and psychiatric epidemiology, which provide increasingly accurate assessments of the prevalence of mental disorders and insights into the converging effects of genetic and socio-environmental and socio-economic risk factors and stressors. Public or "global mental health" epidemiology (16, 17) relies on objectifiable measures of mental disease obtained from large-scale mental health surveys and epidemiological studies (18, 19) and, more recently, the use of epidemiological "big data" (20, 21). But it has also been argued that "...much of the recent social epidemiology of mental disorder has been largely atheoretical, seeking simply to document the rates of occurrence of specific mental disorders and their socio-demographic correlates" [(4), p. 57]. The prevailing conceptualization of mental health, which is based on a quantitative approach and nosological categories of psychiatry and thus depending on statistically validated cases of reported mental disorders, is, for all its virtues, clearly limited by the nature of its data. What it cannot capture is the broader, collective dimension, implicit in Fromm's diagnoses. Rethinking the Frommian perspective is thus clearly germane to current debates and contentions about the reliability and validity of measures of mental health and illness (16), as well as to ongoing discussions about the role of the social dimension in the etiology of psychiatric disorders and the view that social factors are not well acknowledged by the dominant model of biological psychiatry (22–24). But it should be possible to uphold the idea of a supra-individual dimension to mental health, while avoiding the pitfalls involved in diagnosing—in Fromm's manner—an entire society as suffering from mental illness. In concrete terms this would involve considering a notion of disordered collective mental state (25) as an entity that at any given moment is composed of all the statistically reported cases of mental illness, as well as (i) instances of (as yet) undiagnosed and untreated cases of "harmful mental dysfunctions" (26, 27) and (ii) individual cases of dysfunctional psychic life, which lie in the gray zone between normalcy and pathology or fluctuate between the two. The latter cases have not (yet) achieved the status of a diagnosis and do not fulfill the nosological criteria of mental disease; therefore, they remaining below the radar of psychiatric epidemiology, but nonetheless manifest in maladaptive, individually and socially harmful behaviors that affect subjects' social interactions and can be readily observed as a sign and symptom of overarching malaise. Such a notion is in line with the view that the boundaries of mental disease are fluctuating (28) and in particular is consistent with the well-established dual-factor or two-continua models of mental health and illness (29–31) and dimensional model of psychopathology (32).

It is a matter of consensus that human minds and brains are not stand-alone fixtures, but are modified in and through interactions with other brains. If this is so, one should make room for the coexistence of two related, yet ontologically distinct, notions of public mental ill-health: (i) the one that is currently circulating in social psychiatry and epidemiology, based on hard epidemiological and statistical data, and (ii) a second notion, which goes beyond and above the quantitative understanding of mental health as an aggregate of individual (diseased) minds/brains captured in statistics, and which can be conceived *as a dynamic, fluctuating emergent property resulting from interactions of individual brains/minds in social space.* This type of inclusive, dynamic notion of mental ill-health creates an immediate theoretical challenge: the central question for the philosophy and theory of psychiatry is not just *how mental states (normal or disordered) are related to brain states* (2, 33, 34). Rather, what is at stake is how we theorize the relationship between *individual minds/brains and the collective mental phenomena* or *individual and collective mental health.* A potentially rewarding framework is provided by the epidemiology of representations, a notion introduced by cognitive anthropologist Dan Sperber to describe the realization and implementation of mental content in the material world (35–37).

THE EPIDEMIOLOGY OF REPRESENTATIONS

In its most basic terms, the epidemiology of representations can be formulated as follows: individual humans have their own subjective mental representations, which are underlined by specific patterns of neural representations—that is to say, by spatiotemporal patterns of neural activity demarcated from the background activity of the brain. Some interactions among individuals in the social space result in the creation and dissemination of collective representations in multiple minds/brains, which recursively shape the structure and content of individual consciousness and probably the functional microstructure of individual brains as well (38, 39). Collective mental representations arise and propagate along two main trajectories. First, through direct "on-line" interactions involving various kinds of exchanges, synchronizations, attunements, and emotional contagions among people. Recent research has provided fascinating new evidence on the interindividual transfer of mental states, such as mass-scale emotional contagions that proceed through social networks (40) or the spread of happiness (41) or depressive symptoms and moods (42) along social networks. Other studies have demonstrated that certain mental states may be underlined by the synchronization of brain activity within a given collective (43). On a broader scale, there are cycles of mutual constitution of individual brains/minds and culture that involve a "looping effect," in which culture shapes the brain by contextualizing behavior, and the brain fits and modifies culture via behavioral influences (44–46).

However, the inter-individual transfer of mental representations and mental states also crucially propagates along a second trajectory, namely through public (material) representations. Some individual mental representations (beliefs, ideas, attitudes, stereotypes, presumptions, memories, etc.) are transformed or "offloaded" into materially instantiated public representations (images, symbols, and texts), which, spreading through social and virtual space, in turn activate, disseminate, and stabilize mental representations among a certain (and often large) number of people. Sperber argued that the ontology of this transfer resembles epidemiology. The epidemiology metaphor appears particularly apt for our purpose, as it captures both the potential of public representations to quickly affect a large population and their viral effect on individual mental states. At the same time, it is compatible with current sociological models of collective subjectivities (47) and models of social cognition or macrocognition (48, 49). Extending Sperber's model appears eminently useful for psychiatry.

As many authors have forcefully argued, the genetic and neurobiological factors of mental disorders are profoundly, if not decisively, shaped by the psychosocial environment and life experiences (4, 50, 51). Indeed, the blind spot of strictly biomedical approaches and neuroimaging of mental disorder may be the failure to consider life experience (51, 52). As Paradiso and Rudrauf recently argued: "..the adequate level of integration is precisely that of a subject with genetic vulnerability and with a history and place assigned or imagined to be assigned by others, living in a world of representations while building a narrative about them, and coping with conflicts and dissonances at multiple levels" [(53), p. 72].What has not been sufficiently recognized and theorized is the fact that a person's real and symbolic relationship with the world, and in particular the troubling and traumatic experiences with causal or mediating role on mental health, to a significant degree arise through a person's direct interaction with material representations.

PATHWAYS AND MECHANISMS

There are a number of challenges involved in specifying the pathways and mechanisms by which the epidemiology of representations impacts mental health. Given the limited space here, I shall briefly focus on the main ones. First, material representations span several hierarchical levels. Humans are affected on a cognitive and neural level by (i) individual images, symbols, or texts. Most of these, however, are embedded and thus perceived within (ii) more complex image-texts and symbolic structures. These, in turn, are often incorporated into and participate in (iii) complex narratives and metanarratives. Marshal McLuhan's famous dictum that the "medium is the message" is pertinent here, for it is not just *content,* but also the *structural features* of the various media platforms that deliver public representations that can exercise a negative impact on mental health. There is, e.g., some evidence that addiction to social media and the Internet is associated with psychiatric comorbidity (54–56). Neuronal and cognitive mechanisms of (mostly autonomic, reactive) response to individual pictorial or verbal stimuli have been extensively studied and specific abnormalities of such responses are routinely associated with specific psychiatric disorders, such as depression, PTSD, alexithymia, and others [e.g., (57–59)]. However, the focus on dysfunction of low-level perceptual and reflexive emotional processes in the psychiatric population may in fact have little bearing on mechanisms of psychiatric illness (53). There is also growing evidence of the role of the media in generating negative mental states—for example, the effects of "media amplification," in which exposure to traumatic disaster news triggers anxiety symptoms, stress disorders, and psychopathology (60–63). In these cases, representations affect their consumers directly.

Much less is known about responses to material representations on the conscious and behavioral levels and particularly about the dynamics of tripartite interaction among individual and collective mental and material representations. What needs to be unraveled are the mechanisms involved in the cyclical effect, whereby individual cognitive and affective mental states determine people's response to and interpretation of public representations, including massive amount of weaponized political messages and targeted disinformations. Consumption of a broad spectrum of these representations, spanning both unconscious/reflexive and conscious/reflective response, then elicits affective, and cognitive responses, which directly impact emotion, and mood states and through them recursively shape the formation and circulation of attitudes, stereotypes, prejudices, ideas, and other mental contents.

Different trajectories are at work: in one, the dissemination of certain public representations generates collective mental representations, with the potential to impact affective mental states in large groups. Thus, e.g., media-inflicted dehumanized stereotypes of an enemy ethnicity have been proven to be potential triggers of collective genocidal rage, manifested in atrocities, such as those observed in Rwanda and the former Yugoslavia. More importantly for out topic here, the effects of media are mostly less extreme and cataclysmic, but all the more pervasive. Public representations are (often in subtle ways) capable of generating and exacerbating negative emotions, anxieties, frustrations, and anhedonia, some of which are transferred into collective mental states and behavioral outcomes. Indeed, influential current models, which single out increasing uncertainty and negative anticipation as a causal factor in the pathogenesis of anxiety (64, 65) and depression (66) should be productively extended by recognizing the critical role that material representations play in these mechanisms, specifically by triggering, and augmenting uncertainty, negative anticipation, and feelings of anhedonia and helplessness.

Furthermore, it is necessary to consider how the epidemiology of representations relates to adverse social risk factors and social stressors, whose impact on mental health has been extensively documented (67–69). Social disorganization, rapid social change, socio-economic disadvantage, and deprivation, increased competition and inequality, and social isolation and loneliness are traumatic experiences that act as facilitators and triggers of mental illness. Remembering that people exist in both a real and a symbolic relationship with the world, it is imperative to fully acknowledge that most of these factors are also mediated and exacerbated by mutually interacting collective mental and material representations. Research needs to focus on analyzing how (epidemiologically-operating) representations disseminate and amplify other social stressors and adversities.

CONCLUSION

One of the major challenges facing psychiatry today is to analyse how specific social contexts and experiences combine with biological and genetic mechanisms in the etiology of mental disorders. To do this, as I have tried to argue here, research needs to account for the dynamics of the tripartite interaction between individual and collective mental representations and public (material) representations. Admittedly, such a perspective may be inherently difficult for the prevailing model of psychiatry today, embedded as it is in an individual-level perspective of brain disease (70). Finally, it bears emphasizing that material representations, while having powerful effects on humans, impacting them across a range of levels, from the neural to the social, have no agency of their own. Rather, they are intentionally created, and disseminated by human actors, often to elicit specific patterns of behavior through their impact on mental states. The task of accounting for the impact of public representations on mental health thus extends to seeking to understand the motives and intentions of these actors. Such a task, admittedly, is beyond the purview of psychiatry alone. But if dialogue between the neurosciences and other (anthropological, social) sciences is required in order to explore the etiopathogenesis of patterns of mental disorders and to elucidate higher-order psychological and cultural factors in mental disorders (71), then the epidemiology of representations constitutes a prime example of a framework within which this kind of dialogue can occur.

AUTHOR CONTRIBUTIONS

The author confirms being the sole contributor of this work and approved it for publication.

ACKNOWLEDGMENTS

This work was supported by the project Nr. LO1611 with financial support from the Ministry of Education, Youth, and Sport under the NPU I program. I am grateful to Jiří Horáček, Cyril Höschl, Tomáš Kašpárek, Petr Winkler, and Yuliya Zaytseva for their thoughtful comments on earlier draft of this paper.

REFERENCES

1. Fromm E. *The Sane Society*. London: Routledge & Kegan Paul Ltd. (1956).
2. Walter H. The third wave of biological psychiatry. *Front Psychol.* (2013) 4:582. doi: 10.3389/fpsyg.2013.00582
3. Davies W, Roache R. *Reassessing biopsychosocial* psychiatry. *Br J Psychiatry* (2017) 210:3–5. doi: 10.1192/bjp.bp.116.182873
4. Morgan C, Kleinman A. Social science perspectives: a failure of the sociological imagination. In: C. Morgan, D. Bhugra editors. *Principles of Social Psychiatry*. London: Wiley-Blackwell (2010). p. 51–64.
5. Ehrenberg A. The *Weariness* of the *Self: Diagnosing* the *History* of *Depression* in the *Contemporary Age*. Montreal, QC: McGill-Queen's University Press (2009).
6. Honneth A. Die Krankheiten der Gesellschaft. Annäherung an einen nahezu unmoglichen Begriff. *WestEnd* (2014) 11:45–60.
7. Kasser T, Cohn S, Kanner AD, Ryan R M. Some costs of American corporate capitalism: a psychological exploration of value and goal conflicts. *Psychol. Inq.* (2007) 18:1–22. doi: 10.1080/104784007013 86579
8. Hidaka B.H. Depression as a disease of modernity. Explanations for increasing prevalence. *J Affect Disord.* (2012) 140:205–14. doi: 10.1016/j.jad.2011.12.036
9. Keohane K, Petersen A. (eds). *The Social Pathologies of Contemporary Civilization*. Farnham: Ashgate (2013).
10. Fisher M. *Capitalist Realism: Is There No Alternative?* Winchester: Zero Books. (2009). p 20.
11. Berardi, F. *Heroes: Mass Murder and Suicide*. London; New York, NY: Verso (2015).
12. Monbiot, G. *Neoliberalism is Creating Loneliness. That's What's Wrenching Society Apart. Guardian*. Available online at: https://www.theguardian.com/commentisfree/2016/oct/12/neoliberalism-creating-loneliness-wrenching-society-apart
13. Jaspers K. *Die Geistige Situation der Zeit*. Berlin; Leipzig: de Gruyter (1931).
14. Kandel E. New intellectual framework for psychiatry. *Am J Psychiatry* (1998) 155:457–69.
15. Insel T, Cuthbert B. Brain disorders? Precisely. *Science* (2015) 348:499–500. doi: 10.1126/science.aab2358
16. Keyes K, Susser E. The expanding scope of psychiatric epidemiology in the 21st century. *Soc Psychiatry Psychiatr Epidemiol.* (2014) 49:1521–24. doi: 10.1007/s00127-014-0938-5
17. Susser E, Patel V. Psychiatric epidemiology and global mental health: joining forces. *Int J Epidemiol.* (2014) 43:287–93. doi: 10.1093/ije/dyu053
18. Steel Z, Marnane C, Iranpour C. Chey T, Jackson JW, Patel V et al. The global prevalence of common mental disorders: a systematic review and meta-analysis 1980–2013. *Int J Epidemiol.* (2014) 43:476–93. doi: 10.1093/ije/dyu038
19. Reininghaus U, Keyes K, Morgan, C. Novel methods in psychiatric epidemiology. *Soc Psychiatry Psychiatr Epidemiol.* (2016) 51:917–19. doi: 10.1007/s00127-016-1251-2
20. Falk EB, Hyde LW, Mitchell C, Faul J, Gonzalez R, Heitzeg M. M. et al. What is a representative brain? Neuroscience meets population science, *Proc Natl Acad Sci USA.* (2013) 110:17615–22. doi: 10.1073/pnas.13101 34110
21. Stewart R, Davis K. 'Big data' in mental health research: current status and emerging possibilities. *Soc Psychiatry Psychiatr Epidemiol.* (2016) 51:1055–72. doi: 10.1007/s00127-016-1266-8
22. Cohen C. Overcoming social amnesia: the role for a social perspective in psychiatric research and practice. *Psychiatric Serv.* (2000) 51:72–78. doi: 10.1176/ps.51.1.72
23. Miller GA. Mistreating psychology in the decades of the brain. *Perspect Psychol Sci.* (2010) 5:716–43. doi: 10.1177/1745691610388774
24. Reininghaus U, Morgan C. Integrated models in psychiatry: the state of the art. *Soc Psychiatry Psychiatr Epidemiol.* (2014) 49:1–2. doi: 10.1007/s00127-013-0807-7
25. Bostock WW, Bostock ECS. Disorders of the collective mental state. *J Psychol Psychotherapy* (2017) 7:6. doi: 10.4172/2161-0487.1000331
26. Wakefield J. The concept of mental disorder. On the boundary between biological facts and social values. *Am Psychol.* (1992) 47:373–88.
27. Wakefield, J. The concept of mental disorder: diagnostic implications of the harmful dysfunction analysis. *World Psychiatry* (2007) 6:149–56.
28. Kendell R. The concept of disease and its implications for psychiatry. *Br J Psychiatry* (1975) 127:305–15.
29. Greenspoon PJ, Saklofske DH. Toward integration of subjective well-being and psychopathology. *Soc Indicat Res.* (2001) 54:81–108. doi: 10.1023/A:1007219227883
30. Keyes CLM. The mental health continuum: from languishing to flourishing in life. *J Health Soc Behav.* (2002) 43:207–22. doi: 10.2307/3090197
31. Westerhof G, Keyes CL. Mental illness and mental health: the two continua model across the lifespan. *J Adult Dev.* (2010) 17:110–19. doi: 10.1007/s10804-009-9082-y
32. Widiger T, Gore W. Dimensional versus categorical models of psychopathology. In: R. Cautin, S. Lilienfeld, editors. *The Encyclopedia of Clinical Psychology*. Wiley Online Library (2015). p. 1–12. doi: 10.1002/9781118625392.wbecp108
33. Eisenberg L. Mindlessness and brainlessness in psychiatry. *Br J Psychiatry* (1986) 148:497–508.
34. Graham G. *The Disordered Mind: An Introduction to Philosophy of Mind and Mental Illness*. London: Routledge (2010).
35. Sperber D. Anthropology and psychology: towards an epidemiology of representations *Man* (1985) 20:73–89.
36. Sperber D. Conceptual tools for a natural science of society and culture. In: *Proceedings of the British Academy* (2001) 111:297–317.
37. Claidière N, Scott-Phillips TC, Sperber D. How Darwinian is cultural evolution? *Philos Trans R Soc Lond B Biol Sci.* (2014) 369:20130368. doi: 10.1098/rstb.2013.0368
38. Li S. Biocultural orchestration of developmental plasticity across levels: the interplay of biology and culture in shaping the mind and behavior across the life span. *Psychol Bull.* (2003) 129:171–94. doi: 10.1037/0033-2909.129.2.171
39. Turner R, Whitehead C. How collective representations can change the structure of the brain. *J Conscious Stud.* (2008) 15:43–57.
40. Kramer A, Guillory J, Hancock J. Experimental evidence of massive -scale emotional contagion through social networks. *Proc Nat Acad Sci USA.* (2014) 111:8788–90. doi: 10.1073/pnas.1320040111
41. Fowler J, Christakis N. Dynamic spread of happiness in a large social network: longitudinal analysis over 20 years in the Framingham Heart Study. *Br Med J.* (2011) 337:a2338. doi: 10.1136/bmj.a2338
42. Rosenquist JN, Fowler JH, Christakis NA. Social network determinants of depression. *Mol Psychiatry* (2011) 16:273–81. doi: 10.1038/mp.2010.13
43. Nummenmaa L, Glerean E, Viinikainen M, Jääskeläinen I, Hari R, Sams M. Emotions promote social interaction by synchronizing activity across individuals. *Proc Natl Acad Sci USA.* (2011) 109:9599–9604. doi: 10.1073/pnas.1206095109

44. Marcus HR, Kitayama S. Cultures and selves: a cycle of mutual constitution. *Perspect Psychol Sci.* (2010) 5:420–30. doi: 10.1177/1745691610375557
45. Han S, Ma Y. A culture-behavior-brain loop model of human development. *Trends Cogn Sci.* (2015) 19:666–76. doi: 10.1016/j.tics.2015.08.010
46. Kirmayer L. Re-visioning psychiatry: toward an ecology of mind in health and illness. In: L. J. Kirmayer, R. Lemelson, C. A. Cummings, editors. *Re-Visioning Psychiatry. Cultural Phenomenology, Critical Neuroscience, and Global Mental Health.* New York, NY: Cambridge University Press (2015): p. 622–60.
47. Vandenberghe F. Avatars of the collective: a realist theory of collective subjectivities. *Sociol Theory* (2007) 25:295–324. doi: 10.1111/j.1467-9558.2007.00311.x
48. Zerubavel E. *Social Mindscapes: An Invitation to Cognitive Sociology.* Cambridge, MA: Harvard University Press (1997).
49. Huebner B. *Bryce Macrocognition: A Theory of Distributed Minds and Collective Intentionality.* Oxford: Oxford University Press (2014).
50. Kendler K. Toward a philosophical structure for psychiatry. *Am J Psychiatry* (2005) 162:433–40. doi: 10.1176/appi.ajp.162.3.433
51. Kirmayer L Crafa D. What kind of science for psychiatry? *Front Hum Neurosci.* (2014) 8:435. doi: 10.3389/fnhum.2014.00435
52. Bentall RP, de Sousa P, Varese F, Wickham S, Sitko K, Haarmans M. From adversity to psychosis: pathways and mechanisms from specific adversities to specific symptoms. *Soc Psychiatry Psychiatr Epidemiol.* (2014) 49:1011–22. doi: 10.1007/s00127-014-0914-0
53. Paradiso S, Rudrauf D. Struggle for life, struggle for love and recognition: the neglected self in social cognitive neuroscience. *Dialog Clin Neurosci* (2012) 14:65–75.
54. Ko CH, Yen JY, Yen CF, Chen CS, Chen CC. The association between Internet addiction and psychiatric disorder: a review of the literature. *Eur Psychiatry* (2012) 27:1–8. doi: 10.1016/j.eurpsy.2010.04.011
55. Weinstein A, Dorani D, Elhadif R, Bukovza Y, Yarmulnik A, Dannon P. Internet addiction is associated with social anxiety in young adults. *Ann. Clin. Psychiatry* (2015) 27:2–7. doi: 10.1093/med/9780199380183.003.0001
56. Starcevic V. The rise of online impulsivity: a public health issue. *Lancet Psychiatry* (2016) 3:1014–15. doi: 10.1016/S2215-0366(16)30231-0
57. Leppänen JM. Emotional information processing in mood disorders: a review of behavioral and neuroimaging findings. *Curr Opin Psychiatry* (2006) 19:34–39. doi: 10.1097/01.yco.0000191500.46411.00
58. Stuhrmann A, Suslow T, Dannlowski U. Facial emotion processing in major depression: a systematic review of neuroimaging findings. *Biol Mood Anxiety Disord.* (2011) 1:10. doi: 10.1186/2045-5380-1-10
59. Joorman J, Quinn ME. Cognitive processes and emotion regulation in depression. *Depress Anxiety* (2014) 31:308–15. doi: 10.1002/da.22264.
60. Ahern J, Galea S, Resnick H, Vlahov D. Television watching and mental health in the general population of New York City after September 11. *J Aggress Maltreat Trauma* (2005) 9:109–24. doi: 10.1521/psyc.65.4.289.20240
61. Alia-Klein N, Wang GJ, Preston-Campbell RN, Moeller SJ, Parvaz MA, Zhu W, et al. Reactions to media violence: it's in the brain of the beholder. *PLoS ONE* (2014) 9:e107260. doi: 10.1371/journal.pone.0107260
62. Holman EA, Garfin DR, Silver RC. Media's role in broadcasting acute stress following the Boston Marathon bombings. *Proc Natl Acad Sci USA.* (2014) 111:93–98. doi: 10.1073/pnas.1316265110
63. Bodas M, Siman-Tov M, Peleg K, Solomon Z. Anxiety-inducing media: the effect of constant news broadcasting on the well-being of Israeli television viewers. *Psychiatry Interpers Biol Process.* (2015) 78:265–76. doi: 10.1080/00332747.2015.1069658
64. Hirsh B, Mar R, Peterson B. Psychological entropy: a framework for understanding uncertainty—related anxiety. *Psychol. Rev.* (2012) 119:304–20. doi: 10.1037/a0026767
65. Grupe D, Nitschke J. Uncertainty and anticipation in anxiety: an integrated neurobiological and psychological perspective. *Nat Rev Neurosci.* (2013) 14:488–501. doi: 10.1038/nrn3524
66. Badcock PB, Davey CG, Whittle S, Allen NB, Friston KJ. The depressed brain: an evolutionary systems theory. *Trends Cogn Sci.* (2017) 21:182–94. doi: 10.1016/j.tics.2017.01.005
67. Lederbogen F, Kirsch P, Haddad L. Streit F, Tost H, Schuch P et al. City living and urban upbringing affect neural social stress processing in humans. *Nature* (2011) 474:498–501. doi: 10.1038/nature10190
68. Gianaros P, Manuck S, Sheu L. Kuan DC, Votruba-Drzal E, Craig AE, et al. Parental education predicts corticostriatal functionality in adulthood. *Cerebral Cortex* (2011) 21:896–910. doi: 10.1093/cercor/bhq160
69. Tost H, Champagne FA, Meyer-Lindenberg A. Environmental influence in the brain, human welfare and mental health. *Nat Neurosci.* (2015) 18:1421–31. doi: 10.1038/nn.4108
70. Van Os J. Mental disorder: a public health problem stuck in an individual -level brain disease perspective? *World Psychiatry* (2015) 14:46–47. doi: 10.1002/wps.20181
71. Maj M. The need for a conceptual framework in psychiatry: acknowledging complexity while avoiding defeatism. *World Psychiatry* (2016) 15:1–2. doi: 10.1002/wps.20291

7

Culture and Psychopathology: New Perspectives on Research, Practice and Clinical Training in a Globalized World

Carla Moleiro *

Instituto Universitário de Lisboa (ISCTE-IUL), CIS, Lisbon, Portugal

Correspondence:
Carla Moleiro
carla.moleiro@iscte-iul.pt

The present paper discusses the role of culture in understanding and treating psychopathology. It describes new perspectives on the conceptualization of psychopathology and on the definition of culture, and how these are intertwined. The impacts of culture, explicit and implicit discrimination, and minority stress on mental health are reviewed, especially in the current era. Culturally-sensitive assessment practices in psychopathology are emphasized, including addressing the multiple cultural identities of the patient, the explanatory models of the experienced distress, specific psychosocial stressors and strengths, and the cultural features of the practitioner-patient relationship in the clinical encounter. The particular case of psychotherapy in working with culturally diverse patients is explored. Finally, mainstreaming of culture in research and clinical training in psychopathology is highlighted, acknowledging that each clinical interaction is a cultural one.

Keywords: psychopathology, culture, explanatory models, cultural competences, psychotherapy

It has never been truer that cultural context has a prominent role in understanding and treating psychopathology. In a globalized world, it is currently widely recognized that it is the cultural context that defines (mal)adjustment of human behavior, which includes how people usually behave, think, feel, and relate in social interactions. It also shapes the threshold of distress, and the range and forms of its expressiveness that are acceptable and adaptive. As with overall health and illness, psychological suffering implies an understanding of a complex, multi-dimensional process of biopsychosocial variables, which is culturally situated. Similarly, most treatments or interventions in face of psychopathology require the recognition of their historical roots in specific cultural perspectives, as culture also shapes psychotherapy models (1) and patient care in psychiatry, influencing every moment and every process in patient narratives of their suffering (2). In addition, culture also determines how credible and/or acceptable are treatment types in the eyes of a patient and his/her family (3), and consequently treatment adherence. Thus, culture is a key, undeniable current perspective on psychopathology and, for many authors, it has moved to the forefront in the study of psychopathology (4), parallel to the emerging impact of social neuroscience (5).

NEW PERSPECTIVES ON THE DEFINITIONS OF PSYCHOPATHOLOGY AND OF CULTURE

The focus on culture when understanding psychopathology has not always been present and it is still not mainstreamed in clinical psychology and psychiatry. In fact, throughout most of its history, psychopathology has neglected to address cultural diversity, as health sciences have easily labeled behaviors, cognitions, emotional, and social functioning as psychopathological for their deviance from social norms—usually defined in a Western, Eurocentric perspective. An illustration of this perspective lies on the tradition of "deviant" or "abnormal psychology" in the literature - attempts to understand and control behavior deemed to be aberrant or deviant from a statistical, functional, or moral standard (6).

Moving away from more traditional conceptions of statistical and social norms as indicators of psychopathological functioning, main psychopathology classification systems (7, 8) currently focus on the role of subjective distress, dysfunction and impairment (6). In other words, the presence of clinically significant subjective distress that is experienced by the patient, and the experience of impairment to one or more of the patient's areas of functioning (i.e., social, occupational or educational functioning) are core elements for conceptualizing psychopathology [see (7)]. In the DSM-5, APA (7) conceptualizes mental disorders as those conditions with clinically significant dysfunction in the individual, underlined by patterns of functioning in cognition, emotional regulation, or behavior that are associated with distress or disability. APA (7) adds that (i) this pattern must not be merely an expected and culturally sanctioned response to a particular event, stressor or situation; and that (ii) deviant behavior (e.g., political, religious, sexual) in relation to society does not represent psychopathology in itself. This definition seeks to acknowledge the interaction of biological and psychological processes, and sociocultural systems.

Even after its expansion in the 80's [see (9)], efforts to mainstream cross-cultural psychiatry were not present until recent years, and its impact on clinical practice and training has been slow to observe. Nonetheless, in recent years we have witnessed a growth in the literature on social and cultural psychiatry, with increasing recognition of the influence of culture as a key factor in the prevalence, clinical manifestation, diagnosis, treatment response and outcomes of mental illnesses for individuals [see (2, 10, 11)]. This has also resulted in a quite novel perspective on the conception of culture itself, in light of critics of group-based definitions of culture (based usually on nationality or racial/ethnic background), mostly arising from social sciences (e.g., anthropology). Two key novel elements in the conception of culture ought to be highlighted. First, current definitions of culture in mental health research and practice acknowledge the role of multiple collective influences that combine to constitute a person's identity. These influences arise from diverse origins, not only nationality, migration status, racial and/or ethnic origin, language, religion, and spirituality, but also age, gender identity, sexual orientation, socioeconomic and educational class, and functional status. These influences overlap in unique or particular ways, resulting in specific experiences of a given individual or group, for instance, with impacts on interdependent systems of discrimination or disadvantage [i.e.. intersectionality—(12, 13)]. In all, these multiple lenses influence how a patient views the world, how he/she experiences it emotionally, and how he/she behaves in relation to other people. Secondly, recent conceptualizations of culture regard it as processual (11). This process of meaning-making is dynamic and interpersonal, as those multiple facets of one's identity become more or less prominent at any given moment, in the presence of some social interactions and contexts, and not others. This includes the clinical encounter. This notion underlies the most recent revision of the DSM [DSM-5, (3)], which recognizes the importance of a cultural case formulation of any patient's presenting complaint and clinical history, and the understanding of culture as a process, rather than synonymous with static group membership.

EXPLAINING PSYCHOPATHOLOGY: THE ROLE OF CULTURE, DISCRIMINATION AND MINORITY STRESS ON MENTAL HEALTH

Culture has a recognized role in not only conceptualizing psychopathology, but also in explaining and accounting for experienced distress, health and illness (14, 15). Certain conditions surrounding minority stress [gender; sexual orientation; e.g., (16)] and migration processes [e.g., (17)] may increase vulnerability, and stigmatized groups may be exposed to a higher number of risk factors for psychological distress [e.g., related to legal status, perceived discrimination, social exclusion, stigmatization, and victimization; (18)]. For instance, lesbian, gay, bisexual and transgender (LGBT) populations have been found to present increased risk for suicide (19, 20), traumatic stress reactions (21), major depression disorders (22, 23), anxiety disorders (24, 25), among others [e.g., (26)]. Also, socio-economic adversities, including poverty and environmental risk factors, have been associated with the onset and maintenance of psychopathological symptoms and low life satisfaction (27). This relationship has been explained through material deprivation but also increased adverse life events (such as unemployment, abuse and neglect), with consequences for treatment outcomes, including among children and adolescents [e.g., (28)]. Given the recent recession period and current socio-economic strain for many individuals, it seems relevant to recognize that people living in poverty are more likely to experience mental health problems (29), less likely to access treatment (30) and less likely to achieve full recovery from emotional psychopathological problems (31).

In addition, contemporary migration has an unprecedented mobility with an estimated number of 232 million international migrants in the world [World Migration Report; (32)]. Forced migration, steadily increasing as a result of armed conflict (both within and between nations), but also political, economic, social, and climate changes, has most recently been discussed in the mental health field, with undeniable impacts on health and psychological functioning (33). The effects of pre-migration and migration-related trauma among refugees have been acknowledged and documented (34).

Recent literature has emphasized the role of not only explicit discrimination, but also implicit attitudes in interpersonal interactions [evaluations automatically activated by the actual or symbolic presence of a social object; (35–38); see Hall et al., (39) for a systematic review]. Micro-aggressions in daily life [continuous experiences of aggression, often invisible to the perpetrator, who unconsciously holds biases and prejudice; (40–42)] have also been investigated, and have been found to have significant effects on an individual's well-being.

In sum, culture and other related socio-contextual factors, such as minority stress, discrimination and exposure to interpersonal violence, influence the development of clinically significant distress and resulting disability.

ON CULTURALLY-SENSITIVE ASSESSMENT OF PSYCHOPATHOLOGY

Assessment bias [called "cultural malpractice" by Dana (43)] has been identified as an issue in a variety of measures of personality and psychopathology among individuals from diverse backgrounds. This construct and method bias has a variety of sources (e.g., including instrument development, standardized test norms that under-represent social minority groups, neglect for language barriers and acculturation processes), and permeate the assessment process and results, and treatment recommendations. For instance, the use of the Minnesota Multiphasic Personality Inventory (MMPI-2; one of the most widely used and researched psychodiagnostic self-report measures in the world) among diverse patients has raised concerns (related to conceptual, metric, and functional equivalence) as it may not be appropriate among those whose worldviews differ from the Euro-American culture (43).

In an effort to strengthen culturally-sensitive assessment practices, aligned with the DSM-5 (7), the Cultural Formulation Interview (3) was developed. This interview represents a proposal for cultural assessment for use in routine clinical care. It presents a conceptual framework for clinicians to identify the role of culture on the patient's clinical presentation and care, in four domains: (1) cultural identity of the individual; (2) cultural explanations of the experienced signs and symptoms (i.e., explanatory models of illness); (3) cultural factors that may be associated with the psychosocial environment and levels of functioning (i.e., protective and risks factors); and (4) cultural features involved in the communication and the clinical relationship between the patient and the psychiatrist or psychologist.

The concept of explanatory models of the experienced distress was introduced in psychiatry by Kleinman (10), highlighting the clinical relevance of eliciting the patient's understanding of his/her own symptoms. These models stressed the predictive value of the patient representations of his/her illness (causes of the problems and its effects over time on different realms of life) on coping and help-seeking behaviors, and consequently treatment adherence and outcome [see (44), for a review]. Addressing the patient's explanatory models may, hence, maximize engagement and adherence; improve therapeutic alliance; strengthen empathy and positive expectations, while decreasing stigma, shame and other catastrophic beliefs [i.e., "weakness," "going mad," (3)].

Even though the evaluation of specific psychosocial stressors has been emphasized, a strength-based approach has also been pointed out as a valuable perspective on culturally-sensitive assessment among patients of stigmatized social groups (3). This includes the evaluation of the social network of the patient (e.g., extended family, migrant and religious communities, LGBT associations), as it may play a pivotal role in both the onset and development of psychopathology, as well as a buffer of the effects of risk or stressful factors and the course and outcomes of mental health conditions (45).

In light of the aforementioned definition of culture, cultural identity is conceptualized in a intersectional perspective, and encompasses (i) aspects related to national, ethnic, and racial background, including language and migration, as well as social economic and educational status; (ii) spirituality, religion, and moral traditions; and (iii) gender, gender identity, and sexual orientation. Hence, a particular example of an important aspect to assess is patient's religiosity and spirituality. Indeed, religion and spirituality represent key dimensions when aiming a complete understanding of an individual [e.g., (46)], as well as having a potential positive impact on both physical and mental health. Purpose, meaning making and connection to others and the transcendent (through religion and spirituality) may influence one's core beliefs, emotions and behaviors (47). Religiosity and spirituality may have different impacts across one's life spam, on mental health outcomes and to the psychological treatment process, with some positive and some negative impacts (46–48). However, religious and spiritual dimensions have been separated from mental health care in the nineteenth century (49) and patients' spiritual experiences oftentimes labeled as "bizarre" and pathologized.

Another particular example of a key dimension to consider in culturally-sensitive assessment is related to gender roles, gender identity and sexual orientation, as culture clearly shapes the roles of women and men in a society, their expressions of distress, and their interpersonal relations (14, 50). Culture also determines the way diversity in gender identities and expressions are understood, as well as diversity in human sexuality (i.e., sexual orientation). In addition, mental health research has mainly treated sexual and ethnic identities separately, focusing on either of these two domains, with a few studies in the field addressing the experiences of individuals whose minority cultural/ethnic identities intersect with non-normative sexuality/gender expression [e.g., coping and resilience among Black lesbians; (51)].

In sum, culturally-sensitive psychopathology assessment will require the clinician to identify the cultural identities of the patient; conceptualizing his/her distress in a cultural lens; evaluate psychosocial stressors and protective factors; and be mindful of the cultural features of the relationship between the patient and the clinician and how the clinical encounter plays a role in the overall evaluation process (52).

PSYCHOTHERAPY: WORKING WITH CULTURAL DIVERSITY

Since the seminal work by Frank and Frank (53), psychotherapy has been compared with diverse healing practices or treatments across different times and different cultures (54). Still, in a globalized world, even though the need for culturally competent mental health services has been well recognized, health and mental health care disparities have been largely documented. While meta-analysis have shown a moderate effect size of culturally adapted interventions (55), studies in psychotherapies across many disorders have concluded that outcomes for minority cultural groups are not as good as for the majority populations and found greater rates of premature termination (1, 52). The sources of these disparities in healthcare are complex and exist in a broader historical and contemporary context of social and economic inequality, prejudice, and systematic bias (18). In fact, the Western biomedical health model has created a professional culture, based on specific values (e.g., power, agency, objectivity, individualism), which may differ from the diverse cultures of those attending health services. Psychotherapeutic theoretical models (e.g., psychoanalytic, psychodynamic, humanistic, cognitive-behavioral, systemic approaches) have also been historically rooted in concepts and developed in contexts that were not sensitive to the current cultural diversity. In other words, the healthcare system itself can be less in accordance with the cultural perspectives of some patients than others. Therefore, clinicians' sense of social responsibility and social justice concerns have arisen as a response to social inequalities in mental health care, and specific culturally-sensitive treatments have been developed [e.g., multicultural counseling; LGBT affirmative psychotherapies; (56)].

A recent special issue of the Journal of Contemporary Psychotherapy critically reviewed the practice and development of psychotherapy in Nigeria (57), China (58), India (59), Saudi Arabia (60), Pakistan (61), and Israel (62). Iwakabe (63) had already done so for the Japanese context. These authors discuss the relevance and applicability of "Western" psychotherapies in different populations, considering distinct cultural, religious, political, social, familial, and individual features, with implications not only for treatment outcomes, but also the clinical therapeutic relationship. Another relevant, recent example is a special issue of Counseling and Psychotherapy Research (27), which brings light to the role of social inequalities in psychotherapy research and practice, acknowledging that, for a long time, psychotherapy was seen as an endeavor for the middle- and upper-class of educated and psychologically minded clients.

Moreover, only recently the impact of cultural diversity on practitioner-patient interactions has been examined, for instance in medicine (64). However, the American Institutes for Research had already acknowledged in 2002 that "*social issues such as stereotyping, institutionalized racism, and dominant-group privilege are as real in the examining room as they are in society at large*" [(65), p. 8]. That is, issues of stereotyping and discrimination may be as real in the clinician-patient relationship as in any other interpersonal relationship. Indeed, social, educational and economic disparities between patients and clinicians are often evident (27). Moreover, there is evidence of stereotyping and bias among healthcare providers [e.g., (39, 66, 67)], and diverse micro-aggressions in the health care systems (42). This is due to the fact that, even though negative explicit attitudes toward stigmatized groups have been declining, substantial implicit negative attitudes still exist and exert influence on behavior, from everyday encounters to clinical interactions (64). Still, blatant examples persist in the practices of many clinicians in helping patients redirect or change same-sex sexual orientation (68).

MAINSTREAMING CULTURE IN RESEARCH ON PSYCHOPATHOLOGY AND IN CLINICAL TRAINING

The present paper argues for mainstreaming culture in research and clinical training in psychopathology, acknowledging that each clinical interaction is a cultural one. As aforementioned, different characteristics of one's identity are salient in different contexts and interactions. In the practitioner-patient interaction, this is no exception and thus clinicians need to be able to be responsive to this cultural encounter—i.e., to be culturally competent.

Cultural competence is generally defined in a tri-dimensional model, as the extent to which clinicians possess appropriate awareness, relevant knowledge, and practical skills in working with individuals from diverse cultural backgrounds (11, 15, 18). The first dimension—awareness—refers to the way the clinicians' attitudes, beliefs, values, assumptions, and self-awareness affect how they interact with those patients who are culturally different from themselves. It involves the exploration of the self as a cultural being, and of one's own cultural preconceptions. The second dimension—knowledge—relates to the informed understanding of cultures that are different from one's culture, including their histories, traditions, values, practices, and so forth. It also involves knowledge about such concepts and processes as cultural impacts on psychosocial development, acculturation models and acculturation stress, social minority stress and identity development, cultural communication styles in the helping relationship, perceived discrimination and socioeconomic adversity as risks factors for well-being, among others. Finally, an important third dimension consists in the ability to engage in effective and meaningful interactions with diverse individuals, including the development of a relationship, by integrating one's awareness and knowledge into practical skills in the clinical relation, assessment and intervention. Cultural competence has been proposed as a strategy to respond to diversity in contemporary societies and make health care services more accessible, acceptable and effective for diverse communities. Initially intended for work with migrants and ethnic minorities, cultural competence has been extended to include other forms of client diversity, such as age, gender, sexual orientation, gender identity, religion, social class, language, and ability status [e.g., (69, 70)]. It has been proposed as a developmental process, both at an individual (i.e., the clinician) and an organizational (i.e., healthcare unit) levels. Despite recent debates and criticisms [cultural safety, cultural sensitivity, cultural responsiveness, and cultural humility; (11)], developing cultural competence in psychopathology is a key process aligned with person-centered care, where patient narratives and meanings are shared and interpreted in the clinical encounter. However, research is still needed on the processes of implementation, clinical effectiveness, clinical communication, wider social impact, and outcomes of culturally competent services and interventions (11, 39). Indeed, Delgadillo (27) argues for a better integration of the literature on social inequalities, power imbalance, and cultural competence into clinical training programmes. The recent aforementioned understandings of culture and of psychopathology in a social and cultural context, rather than an (exclusively) intra-individual process, provide a possible route to develop these clinical competences. While some have reported training pilot studies and their evaluation, and guidelines have been proposed [e.g., (3, 17)], clinical training in individual and cultural diversity is still scarce and unsystematic, both in the educational/academic process and in professional development. Addressing this gap and mainstreaming cultural competence in clinical training seems to be a key future development if we are to enable clinicians to provide support and address mental health concerns in a diverse world.

AUTHOR CONTRIBUTIONS

The author confirms being the sole contributor of this work and approved it for publication.

FUNDING

This work was supported by the national Foundation for Science and Technology (FCT) in Portugal, under the Grant number UID/PSI/03125/2013.

REFERENCES

1. Rathod S. Contemporary psychotherapy and cultural adaptations. *J Contemp Psychother.* (2017) 47:61–3. doi: 10.1007/s10879-016-9344-5
2. Kirmayer LJ. Beyond the 'new cross-cultural psychiatry': cultural biology, discursive psychology and the ironies of globalization. *Transcult Psychiatry* (2006) 43:126–44. doi: 10.1177/1363461506061761
3. Lewis-Fernández R, Aggarwal NK, Hinton L, Hinton DE, Kirmayer LJ. *DSM-5® Handbook on the Cultural Formulation Interview.* Washington, DC: APA (2016).
4. López SR. Guarnaccia PJ. Cultural dimensions of psychopathology: The social world's impact on mental illness. In: Maddux JE, Winstead BA editors. *Psychopathology: Foundations for a Contemporary Understanding.* Mahwah, NJ: Lawrence Erlbaum Associates (2005). p. 19–38.
5. Manes F, Mendez MF editors. *Social Neuroscience of Psychiatric Disorders: A Special Issue of the Journal of Social Neuroscience.* New York, NY: Psychology Press (2013).
6. Maddux JE, Gosselin JT, Winstead BA. Conceptions of psychopathology: a social constructionist perspective. In: Maddux JE, Winstead BA editors. *Psychopathology: Foundations for a Contemporary Understanding.* Mahwah, NJ: Lawrence Erlbaum Associates (2005). p. 3–18.
7. American Psychiatric Association. *Diagnostic and Statistical Manual of Mental Disorders* 5th edn. Arlington, VA: American Psychiatric Publishing (2013).
8. World Health Organization. *International Statistical Classification of Diseases and Related Health Problems* 10th rev. Geneva: Author (1992).
9. Kleinman A. *Rethinking Psychiatry: From Cultural Category to Personal Experience.* New York: Free Press (1988).
10. Kleinman A. *Patients and Healers in the Context of Culture: An Exploration of the Borderland between Anthropology, Medicine, and Psychiatry.* Berkeley: University of California Press (1980).
11. Kirmayer LJ. Rethinking cultural competence. *Transcult Psychiatry* (2012) 49:149–64. doi: 10.1177/1363461512444673
12. Crenshaw K. Mapping the margins: intersectionality, identity politics, and violence against women of color. *Stanf Law Rev.* (1991) 43:1241–99.
13. Iyer A, Sen G, Ostlin P. The intersections of gender and class in health status and health care. *Glob Public Health* (2008) 3:13–24. doi: 10.1080/17441690801892174
14. Eisler RM. Hersen M editors. *Handbook of Gender, Culture and Health.* Mahwah, NJ: Lawrence Erlbaum Associates (2000).
15. Sue DW, Sue D. *Counseling the Culturally Diverse: Theory and Practice* 5th ed. New Jersey: Wiley (2008).
16. Meyer I. Prejudice, social stress, and mental health in lesbian, gay, and bisexual populations: conceptual issues and research evidence. *Psychol Bull.* (2003) 129:674–97. doi: 10.1037/0033-2909.129.5.674
17. Bhugra D, Gupta S, Bhui K, Craig T, Dogra N, Ingleby D, et al. WPA guidance on mental health and mental health care in migrants. *World Psychiatry* (2011) 10:2–10.
18. Sue S, Zane N, Hall GC, Berger LK. The case for cultural competency in psychotherapeutic interventions. *Annu Rev Psychol.* (2009) 60:525–48. doi: 10.1146/annurev.psych.60.110707.163651
19. Maguen S, Shipherd J. Suicide risk among transgender individuals. *Psychol Sex.* (2010) 1:34–43. doi: 10.1080/19419891003634430
20. Mustanski B, Liu RT. A longitudinal study of predictors of suicide attempts among lesbian, gay, bisexual, and transgender youth. *Arch Sex Behav.* (2013) 42:437–48. doi: 10.1007/s10508-012-0013-9
21. D'Augelli AR, Pilkington NW, Hershberger SL. Incidence and mental health impact of sexual orientation victimization of lesbian, gay, and bisexual youths in high school. *School Psychol Q.* (2002) 17:148–67. doi: 10.1080/10538720.2011.561474
22. Cochran SD, Mays VM. Relation between psychiatric syndromes and behaviourally defined sexual orientation in a sample of the U.S. population. *Am J Public Health* (2000) 92:516–23.
23. Nuttbrock L, Hwahng S, Bockting W, Rosenblum A, Mason M, Macri M, et al. Psychiatric impact of gender-related abuse across the life courseofmale-to-female transgenderpersons. *J Sex Res.* (2010) 47:12–23. doi: 10.1080/00224490903062258
24. Bostwick WB, Boyd CJ, Hughes TL, West BT, McCabe SE. Discrimination and mental health among lesbian, gay, and bisexual adults in the United States. *Am J Orthopsychiatry* (2014) 84:35–45. doi: 10.1037/h0098851
25. Mustanski BS, Garofalo R, Emerson EM. Mental health disorders, psychological distress, and suicidality in a diverse sample of lesbian, gay, bisexual, and transgender youths. *Am J Public Health* (2010) 100:2426–32. doi: 10.2105/AJPH.2009.178319
26. King M, Semlyen J, Tai SS, Killaspy H, Osborn D, Popelyuk D, et al. A systematic review of mental disorder, suicide, and deliberate self-harm in lesbian, gay and bisexual people. *BMC Psychiatry* 8:70. doi: 10.1186/1471-244X-8-70
27. Delgadillo J. Worlds apart: social inequalities and psychological care. *Counsel Psychother Res.* (2018) 18:111–3. doi: 10.1002/capr.12168
28. Blackshaw E, Evans C, Cooper M. When life gets in the way: systematic review of life events, socioeconomic deprivation, and their impact on counselling and psychotherapy with children and adolescents. *Counsel Psychother Res.* (2018) 18:143–53. doi: 10.1002/capr.12156

29. Lund C, Breen A, Flisher AJ, Kakuma R, Corrigall J, Joska JA, et al. Poverty and common mental disorders in low and middle income countries: A systematic review. *Soc Sci Med.* (2010) 71:517–28. doi: 10.1016/j.socscimed.2010.04.027
30. Saxon D, Fitzgerald G, Houghton S, Lemme F, Saul C, Warden S. et al. Psychotherapy provision, socioeconomic deprivation, and the inverse care law. *Psychother Res.* (2007) 17:515–21. doi: 10.1080/10503300601063246
31. Delgadillo J, Asaria M, Ali S, Gilbody S. On poverty, politics and psychology: The socioeconomic gradient of mental healthcare utilisation and outcomes. *Br J Psychiatry* (2016) 209:429–30. doi: 10.1192/bjp.bp.115.171017
32. International Organization for Migration. *World Migration Report 2015. Migrants and cities: new partnerships to manage mobility.* Brussels: Author (2015).
33. Ingleby D editor. *Forced Migration and Mental Health: Rethinking the Care of Refugees and Displaced Persons.* New York, NY: Springer (2005).
34. Hollifield M, Warner TD, Krakow B, Westermeyer J. Mental health effects of stress over the life span of refugees. *J Clin Med.* (2018) 7:25. doi: 10.3390/jcm7020025
35. Dovidio JF, Kawakami K, Gaertner SL. Implicit and explicit prejudice and interracial interaction. *J Pers Soc Psychol.* (2002) 82:62–8. doi: 10.1037/0022-3514.82.1.62
36. Dovidio JF, Gaertner SL, Pearson AR. "Racism among the well-intentioned: bias without awareness," In: Miller AG, editors. *The Social Psychology of Good and Evil* (2nd ed.). New York: Guilford Press (2016), p. 95–118.
37. Hebl MR, Foster JB, Mannix LM, Dovidio JF. Formal and interpersonal discrimination: a field study of bias toward homosexual applicants. *Pers Soc Psychol Bull.* (2002) 28:815–25. doi: 10.1177/0146167202289010
38. Kawakami K, Phillis CE, Steele JR, Dovidio JF. (Close) Distance makes the heart grow fonder: Improving implicit racial attitudes and interracial interactions through approach behaviors. *J Pers Soc Psychol.* (2007) 92:957–71. doi: 10.1037/0022-3514.92.6.957
39. Hall WJ, Chapman MV, Lee KM, Merino YM, Thomas TW, Payne BK, et al. Implicit racial/ethnic bias among health care professionals and its influence on health outcomes: a systematic review. *Am J Public Health* (2015) 105:60–76. doi: 10.2105/AJPH.2015.302903
40. Constantine MG. Racial micro aggressions against African American clients in cross-racial counselling relationships. *J Couns Psychol.* (2007) 54:1–16. doi: 10.1037/0022-0167.54.1.1
41. Sheldon K, Delgado-Romero EA. Sexual orientation microaggressions: the experience of lesbian, gay, bisexual, and queer clients in psychotherapy. *J Couns Psychol.* (2011) 58:210–21. doi: 10.1037/a0022251
42. Sue DW. *Microaggressions in Everyday Life: Race, Gender, and Sexual Orientation.* Hoboken, NJ: Wiley (2010).
43. Dana R. *Handbook of Cross-Cultural and Multicultural Personality Assessment.* Mahwah, NJ: Lawrence Erlbaum Associates (2000).
44. Weiss MG, Somma D. Explanatory models in psychiatry. In: Rhugra D, and Bhui K editors. *Textbook of Cultural Psychiatry.* Cambridge: Cambridge University Press (2007). p. 127–40.
45. Cohen S, Underwood LG, Gottlieb BH. *Social Support Measurement and Intervention: A Guide for Health and Social Scientists.* New York, NY: Oxford University Press (2000).
46. Fallot RD. The place of spirituality and religion in mental health services. *New Dir Ment Health Serv.* (1998) 80:3–12.
47. Koenig HG. Religion, spirituality, and health: the research and clinical implications. *ISRN Psychiatry* (2012) 2012:278730. doi: 10.5402/2012/278730
48. Rosmarin DH, Krumrei EJ, Pargament KI. Are gratitude and spirituality protective factors against psychopathology? *Int J Exist Psychol Psychother.* (2010) 3:1–5. Available online at: http://journal.existentialpsychology.org/index.php/ExPsy/article/view/148 (Accessed July 30, 2018).
49. Thielman SB. Spirituality and the care of madness: historical considerations. In: Huguelet P, Koenig HG editors. *Religion and Spirituality in Psychiatry.* Cambridge: Cambridge University Press (2009). p. 6–18.
50. Ussher JM. Diagnosing difficult women and pathologising femininity: gender bias in a psychiatric nosology. *Femin Psychol.* (2013) 23:63–9. doi: 10.1177/0959353512467968
51. Bowleg L, Craig ML, Burkholder G. Rising and surviving: a conceptual model of active coping among Black lesbians. *Cult Divers Ethnic Minor Psychol.* (2004) 10:229–40. doi: 10.1037/1099-9809.10.3.229
52. Fung K, Lo T. An integrative clinical approach to culturally competent psychotherapy. *J Contemp Psychother.* (2017) 47:65–73. doi: 10.1007/s10879-016-9341-8
53. Frank JD, Frank JB. *Persuasion and Healing: A Comparative Study of Psychotherapy* 3rd ed. Baltimore: Johns Hopkins University Press (1993).
54. Tseng W-S. *Handbook of Cultural Psychiatry.* San Diego, CA: Academic Press (2001).
55. Griner D, Smith TB. Culturally adapted mental health intervention: a meta-analytic review. *Psychotherapy* (2006) 43:531–48. doi: 10.1037/0033-3204.43.4.531
56. Ratts MJ, Pedersen PB. *Counseling for Multiculturalism and Social Justice: Integration, Theory, and Application* 4th ed. Alexandria, VA: American Counseling Association (2014).
57. Ebigbo PO, Elekwachi CL, Nweze FC. Cross cutting issues in the practice of psychotherapy in Nigeria. *J Contemp Psychother.* (2017) 47:75–86. doi: 10.1007/s10879-016-9356-1
58. Ng RMK, Lee CK, Liu J, Luo J, Zu S, Mi S. Psychotherapy services in China: current provisions and future development. *J Contemp Psychother.* (2017) 47:87–94. doi: 10.1007/s10879-016-9345-4
59. Bhargava R, Kumar N, Gupta A. Indian perspective on psychotherapy: cultural issues. *J Contemp Psychother.* (2017) 47:95–103. doi: 10.1007/s10879-016-9348-1
60. Algahtani H, Buraik Y, Ad-Dab'bagh Y. Psychotherapy in Saudi Arabia: its history and cultural context. *J Contemp Psychother.* (2017) 47:105–17. doi: 10.1007/s10879-016-9347-2
61. Irfan M, Saeed S, Awan NR, Gui M, Aslam M, Naeem F. Psychological healing in Pakistan: from Sufism to culturally adapted cognitive behaviour therapy. *J Contemp Psychother.* (2017) 47:119–24. doi: 10.1007/s10879-016-9354-3
62. Avisaar N. Israeli psychotherapy, politics and activism: Is there a way out of the trap? *J Contemp Psychother.* (2017) 47:125–34. doi: 10.1007/s10879-016-9346-3
63. Iwakabe S. Psychotherapy integration in Japan. *J Psychother Integr.* (2008) 18:103–25. doi: 10.1037/1053-0479.18.1.103
64. West TV, Schoenthaler A. Color-blind and multicultural strategies in medical settings. *Soc Issues Policy Rev.* (2017) 11:124–58. doi: 10.1111/sipr.12029
65. American Institutes for Research. *Teaching Cultural Competence in Health Care: A review of current concepts, policies and practices.* Report prepared for the Office of Minority Health. Washington, DC: Author (2002).
66. Bieschke KJ, Paul PL, Blasko KA. Review of empirical research focused on the experience of lesbian, gay, and bisexual clients in counseling and psychotherapy. In: Bieschke K, Perez R, DeBord K, editors. *Handbook of Counseling and Psychotherapy With Lesbian, Gay, Bisexual, and Transgender Clients.* Washington, DC: American Psychological Association (2006). p. 293–316.
67. Van Ryn M, Burke J. The effect of patient race and socio-economic status on physicians' perceptions of patients. *Soc Sci Med.* (2000) 50:813–28. doi: 10.1016/S0277-9536(99)00338-X
68. Bartlett A, Smith G, King M. The response of mental health professionals to clients seeking help to change or redirect same-sex sexual orientation. *BMC Psychiatry* (2009) 26:9–11. doi: 10.1186/1471-244X-9-11
69. Israel T, Selvidge M. Contributions of multicultural counseling to counselor competence with lesbian, gay, and bisexual clients. *J Multicult Couns Devel.* (2003) 31:84–98. doi: 10.1002/j.2161-1912.2003.tb00535.x
70. Swartz S. Feminism and psychiatric diagnosis: reflections of a feminist practitioner. *Femin Psychol.* (2013) 23:41–8. doi: 10.1177/0959353512467965

8

Relationship Between Depression and Subtypes of Early Life Stress in Adult Psychiatric Patients

*Camila Maria Severi Martins-Monteverde[1], Cristiane Von Werne Baes[1], Emilene Reisdorfer[2], Thalita Padovan[1], Sandra Marcia de Carvalho Tofoli[1] and Mario Francisco Juruena[1,3]**

[1] Stress and Affective Disorders Programme, University of São Paulo, São Paulo, Brazil, [2] School of Community and Health Studies, Centennial College, Toronto, ON, Canada, [3] Centre for Affective Disorders, Department Psychological Medicine, King's College London, London, United Kingdom

***Correspondence:**
Mario Francisco Juruena
mario.juruena@kcl.ac.uk

Numerous studies have researched the aggravating and maintainer effect of Early Life Stress in patients adults with psychiatric disorders. This study examined the relationship between depression and subtypes of early life stress among 81 psychiatric patients treated at the inpatient Day Hospital Unit of a University General Hospital. Psychiatric diagnosis was confirmed according to the MINI International Neuropsychiatric Interview (MINI). The Childhood Trauma Questionnaire (CTQ) was used for evaluating as retrospective assessment of the presence of ELS on these patients, and we also evaluated the severity of hopelessness with the Beck Hopelessness Scale (BHS). Our results suggested that the occurrence of depression in adulthood is related to situations of emotional abuse, sexual, and physical neglect during childhood. The analysis between depression and childhood emotional abuse was significant after a multiple logistic regression analysis OR (IC 95%): 4.4 (1.7–11.2), even accounting for gender adjusted OR [AOR] 4.0; (IC 1.5–10.5); psychiatry family history AOR 3.8 (1.4–10.5); previous suicide attempted AOR 3.7; (1.4–10.5) and Hopelessness AOR 3.2 (1.11–9.4). Thus, these findings demonstrate emotional abuse as a significant risk factor to be part of the mechanism involved in the pathogenesis of depression related to early life stress.

Keywords: early life stress, subtypes of early life stress, depressive disorder, emotional abuse, neglect, childhood trauma

INTRODUCTION

Recent studies have examined the effect of stress in the early stages of development of the individual demonstrating that when stress occurs early, can lead to "biological scars" lifelong (1). The Early Life Stress (ELS) is a variety of traumatic experiences that can occur during childhood and adolescence, such as abuse, neglect, parental loss, divorce of parents, caregivers with psychiatric disorders, childhood disease involving prolonged hospitalizations, lack of primary care, abandonment, deprivation of food, and adequate shelter, lack of encouragement and support, as well as family violence (2, 3). Numerous studies have studied the aggravating effect and maintainer of the ELS in psychiatric disorders in adults. Recognized studies (4–7) evidence the future impact of various early trauma on mental health. In the systematic review we conducted (8) the data demonstrated that individual exposure to adversities in childhood and adolescence is predictive of psychiatric disorders in adulthood, such as depression and borderline personality disorder. In this same direction, other systematic review evaluated the association between subtypes of ELS with psychiatric disorders in adults, finding that physical abuse, sexual, and unspecified neglect are associated with mood disorder and anxiety disorders, while emotional abuse is associated with personality disorder and schizophrenia and that the physical neglect is related to personality disorders (9). In consonance, some studies (10–12) showed that emotional abuse is associated with depressive symptoms in adults. Furthermore, the literature indicates that it is quite common co-occurrence of abuse or neglect, it is difficult occurs in a single subtype of ELS, so that the incidence may range around 40–95% of the sample (13, 14). The study by Chartier et al. (15), shown that among psychiatric patients with ELS, 37% of them had reports of the occurrence of more than one subtype of ELS. The study of Felitti et al. (16) showed that individuals who have experienced situations of child adversity likely to have experienced more than one subtype ELS varies around approximately 80%. According to Hahm et al. (17), the co-occurrence of ELS subtypes is an essential measure of the severity of psychopathology, since in many studies was associated with increased severity of psychiatric symptoms. In this sense, given the importance of stress in the development of psychiatric disorders, recently the Diagnostic and Statistical Manual of Mental Disorders (DSM-5), included among its ratings a specific category for the diagnosis of Trauma and Stressor-Related Disorders (18). Thus, researchers also point to the need to analyze how stress triggers interact with psychopathology, showing that stress increases the risk for depression, but leave the individual susceptible to the occurrence of different types of stress (10). According to Heim and Nemeroff (19) children exposed to traumatic experiences in early childhood have an increased risk of developing depression. The persistent sensitization of the circuits of the central nervous system, which are integrally involved in the regulation of tension and emotion, may represent the underlying biological substrates to increased vulnerability to subsequent stress, predisposing these individuals to develop a broad range of physical and mental disorders which are known to express or worsen in relation to acute stress. The intense stress starts to play a substantial adverse effect on a person's life, affecting not only the mental health but physical, cognition, and occupational performance in everyday activities. Another important consequence of ELS is related to the increase of suicide attempts in individuals with psychiatric disorders who suffered ELS. Several studies have suggested an association between ELS and increased suicidality in adulthood (7, 20–24). The study by Sfoggia et al. (25) it was shown that adults with a history of severe abuse and neglect had more suicide attempts than those who reported no ELS. Also, in the survey conducted by Brown et al. (26) relevant data found, in which victims of sexual abuse has eight times more likely to suicide. Our previous data (27), demonstrated that among the ELS subtypes, significant association was found only between the emotional abuse subtype and psychiatric diagnoses. Emotional abuse was positively associated with psychopathology in adults, particularly with depressive disorders. The patients with a history of emotional abuse had higher severity in depression, hopelessness, suicidal ideation, anxiety, and impulsivity. Thus, the present study aimed to analyze the relationship between depression and subtypes of ELS among patients with psychiatric disorders, mainly control the analysis of the association between emotional abuse and patients with depression treated at the inpatient Day Hospital Unit of a General University Hospital.

METHODS

Study Sample and Design

The sample was composed of 81 adult psychiatric patients, treated at inpatient Day Hospital Unit of a General University Hospital. The inclusion criteria for this study were patients with psychiatric diagnosis confirmed according to Mini International Neuropsychiatric Interview (MINI) (28, 29), in the follow-up inpatient Day Hospital Unit, aged 18–65 years. We excluded patients with any significant physical illness in acute, mental disorders caused by a general medical condition or resulting from the direct physiological effect of a substance, substance-related disorders, mental retardation, and patients in an acute psychotic episode, cognitive deficits, and neurological progressive and degenerative diseases.

Procedure and Measures

The study was approved by the Research Ethics Committee of the General University Hospital, Faculty of Medicine of Ribeirao Preto, University of Sao Paulo. Participants were informed that the purpose of the study was to investigate the association between early life stress and psychiatric disorders in adult life. Later, written informed consent was obtained from all patients, and the questionnaires included in this study were applied.

Demographic and Clinical Data

Clinical and sociodemographic characteristics (age, gender, religious practice, family history of psychiatric disorder, suicide attempt, among others) were obtained through the administration of a sociodemographic questionnaire developed by researchers. We also evaluated the severity of hopelessness with the Beck Hopelessness Scale [BHS; (30)]. This is a self-report questionnaire with 20 true-false statements developed to assess the extent of positive and negative beliefs about the future. The version in Portuguese was translated and adapted by Cunha (31).

Psychiatric Diagnosis

The assessment of psychiatric diagnosis was conducted using Mini International Neuropsychiatric Interview [MINI; (28)], the version in Portuguese translated and adapted by Amorim (29). The MINI is a brief structured interview designed to assess criteria for the majority of psychiatric disorders classified in DSM-IV and ICD-10. There is a version called MINI PLUS, intended for assessment of the primary psychiatric diagnosis throughout life, in clinical and research psychiatry and systematically explores all the criteria for inclusion and exclusion and chronology (onset and duration of the disorder, number of episodes) (29). All subjects were interviewed by two senior psychiatrists (MFJ; CWB) trained and certified to the use of the standardized interviews. The interviewers had long-standing experience in the administration of standardized interviews. In the total sample, the distribution of psychiatric disorders was as follows: more than 75% had a diagnosis of mood disorders, prevailing depressive disorders ($n = 44$; 54%), followed by bipolar disorder ($n = 17$; 21%). The other diagnoses assessed were anxiety disorders ($n = 10$; 12.3%), eating disorders ($n = 3$; 4%), and others ($n = 7$; 8%). We did not include patients with diagnoses of substance use disorder in the sample because the Day Hospital Unit does not admit patients with this diagnosis.

Subtypes of Early Life Stress

The subtypes of ELS was assessed using the Childhood Trauma Questionnaire [CTQ; (32)]. The CTQ is a retrospective self-report questionnaire that investigates the history of abuse and neglect during childhood and can be applied to adolescents (from 12 years) and adults, where the responder assigns values of frequency to 28 sentences, graduate issues related to situations arising in childhood. The CTQ evaluates five subtypes of early life stress:

- Emotional abuse: verbal assaults on a child's sense of worth or well-being or any humiliating or demeaning behavior directed toward a child by an adult or older person;
- Physical abuse: bodily assaults on a child by an adult or older person that posed a risk of or resulted in injury;
- Sexual abuse: sexual contact or conduct between a child younger than 18 years of age and an adult or older person;
- Emotional neglect: the failure of caretakers to meet children's basic emotional and psychological needs, including love, belonging, nurturance, and support;
- Physical neglect: the failure of caretakers to provide for a child's basic physical needs, including food, shelter, clothing, safety, and healthcare (inadequate parental supervision was also included in this definition if it placed children's security in jeopardy) (3).

The items are rated on a Likert scale ranging from 1 (never) to 5 (very often). Furthermore, the scores range from 5 to 25 for each subtype of ELS. A cut-point for early life stress, and its subtypes (emotional, physical and sexual abuse, and emotional and physical neglect), was defined as when one of these experiences before the age of 18 reached a degree of at least moderate to severe, according to classification in the CTQ (3, 32–34). The version in Portuguese was translated and adapted by Grassi-Oliveira et al. (35).

Statistical Analysis

Logistic multiple regression analysis was conducted in Stata 9 statistical program to test the relationship between depression and emotional abuse when controlled by independent variables. Univariate analysis of depression was performed with each of the analyzed independent variables. We conducted the analysis of association between ELS and all psychiatric disorders. However, according to data presented in **Table 2**, there was no significant difference between the groups with and with- out ELS ($\chi^2 = 8.44$, df = 6.0, $p = 0.188$) in relation to the distribution of psychiatric diagnoses.

In addition, we performed a second statistical analysis, comparing ELS subtypes with psychiatric disorders. Thus, significant association was found only between the emotional abuse subtype and psychiatric diagnoses. Those with $p < 0.30$ or that are relevant in the literature to the Raw Model: Depression Disorder + Emotional Abuse and Model 2 = Raw Model + Gender; Model 3 = Model 2 + Familiar History of Mental Disorders; Model 4 = Model 3 + Suicide Attempt; and Model 5 = Model 4 + Hopelessness; were included in the multiple models using the stepwise forward strategy when the association between depression and emotional abuse in childhood was adjusted for all independent variables. Remained for analysis the variables with $p < 0.20$ or those that adjusted the dependent variables. We also used Chi-square for analysis of the occurrence of subtypes of ELS and the Student t-test for analysis of CTQ scores.

RESULTS

The participants were predominantly women (72.8%), under 40 years of age, reporting religious practice (86.5%) and with a family history of mental disorder (77.0%). Concerning, the psychiatric diagnosis, 54% of patients seen at the hospital had depression, followed by Bipolar disorder (21.0%). The other diagnoses assessed were: Anxiety Disorders (12.3%), Schizophrenia and Other Psychotic Disorders (6.2%), Eating Disorders (3.7%), Dissociative Disorders (1.2%), Impulse Control Disorders not elsewhere classified (1.2%). We do not include patients with diagnoses of Substance Use Disorder in the sample

TABLE 1 | Demographic and clinical characteristics of the sample.

Variable	*N* (%)
GENDER	
Male	22 (27.2)
Female	59 (72.8)
AGE GROUP	
<29 yrs	22 (27.2)
30–39 yrs	22 (27.2)
40–49 yrs	29 (35.8)
>50 yrs	8 (9.8)
RELIGIOUS PRACTICE	
Yes	64 (86.5)
No	10 (13.5)
MARITAL STATUS	
With partner	41 (50.6)
Without partner	40 (49.4)
SUICIDE ATTEMPT	
Yes	54 (66.7)
No	27(33.3)
FAMILY HISTORY OF PSYCHIATRIC DISORDER	
Yes	57 (77.0)
No	17 (23.0)
DEPRESSION DISORDER	
Yes	44 (54.3)
No	37 (45.7)

TABLE 2 | Occurrence and CTQ scores of subtypes of early life stress among the whole sample ($n = 81$).

Variable	N (%)	$p (X^2)$	CTQ score, mean ± SEM	p (t)
Childhood emotional abuse	–	<0.001	–	<0.001
No	35 (43.2)	–	8.26 (±0.40)	–
Yes	46 (56.8)	–	16.7 (±0.68)	–
Childhood physical abuse	–	<0.001	–	<0.001
No	49 (60.5)	–	5.60 (±0.22)	–
Yes	32 (39.5)	–	11.96 (±0.80)	–
Childhood sexual abuse	–	<0.001	–	<0.001
No	59 (72.8)	–	5.04 (±0.04)	–
Yes	22 (27.2)	–	9.25 (±0.84)	–
Childhood emotional neglect	–	<0.001	–	<0.001
No	44 (54.3)	–	9.43 (±0.59)	–
Yes	37 (45.7)	–	16.32 (±0.68)	–
Childhood physical neglect	–	<0.001	–	<0.001
No	42 (51.9)	–	6.43 (±0.31)	–
Yes	39 (48.2)	–	11.79 (±0.53)	–

CTQ subscale, threshold score of each subtype is Emotional Abuse score > 13; Physical Abuse score > 10; Sexual Abuse score > 8; Emotional Neglect > 15; Physical Neglect >10.

TABLE 3 | Relationship between depression and subtypes of early life stress among patients.

Variable	Depression		p-value
	No 37 (45.7%)	Yes 44 (54.3%)	
Childhood emotional abuse			**0.002**
No	53 (65.7)	28 (34.3)	
Yes	25 (30.4)	56 (69.6)	
Childhood physical abuse			0.23
No	41(51.1)	40 (48.9)	
Yes	30 (37.5)	51 (62.5)	
Childhood sexual abuse			**0.01**
No	44 (54.2)	37 (45.8)	
Yes	18 (22.7)	63 (77.3)	
Childhood emotional neglect			0.19
No	42 (52.3)	39 (47.7)	
Yes	31 (37.8)	50 (62.2)	
Childhood physical neglect			0.08
No	44 (54.8)	37 (45.2)	
Yes	29 (35.9)	52 (64.1)	

because the University Day Hospital does not include patients with this diagnosis. Further details can be found in **Table 1**.

The data regarding the subtypes of early life stress are shown in **Table 2**. There has been a higher frequency of childhood emotional abuse among patients, while the sexual abuse had a lower occurrence, see in **Table 3**.

In this population, depression was associated with emotional abuse and sexual abuse, with considerable statistical significance. However, the relationship with physical neglect, demonstrated a trend ($p = 0.08$). These data indicate that the occurrence of depression in adulthood is related to situations of emotional abuse, sexual and physical neglect during childhood.

The analysis of the chances of occurrence of depression according to the epidemiological characteristics showed that women are more exposed compared with men. Moreover, it was also observed an increase of about four times the chance of depression among people who have suffered emotional or sexual abuse in childhood or who reported at least one suicide attempt throughout life. Patients with a high level of hopelessness also showed a higher chance of depression (**Table 4**).

Patients with a history of childhood emotional abuse had a frequency of 4.38 higher of depression compared to those without such a history in the bivariate regression (**Table 5**). In the following models, with adjustments for demographic variables and health conditions, the magnitude of odds ratio decreased, although the adjusted odds ratio was still 3.23 times higher in the group exposed to emotional abuse during childhood (*p*-value 0.031). Multiple Logistic regression analysis between depression and childhood emotional abuse was significant after a multiple logistic regression analysis OR (IC 95%): 4.4 (1.7–11.2), even accounting for gender adjusted OR [AOR] 4.0, (1.5–10.5); psychiatry family history AOR 3.8 (1.4–10.5); previous suicide attempted AOR 3.7; (1.4–10.5) and Hopelessness AOR 3.2 (1.11–9.4).

DISCUSSION

Depression is one of the most common mental disorders, with estimates ranging around 16 % of the population at some point in life. The World Health Organization has recognized that it is one of the psychopathologies that lead to greater commitment and mental suffering, thus being considered a public health problem (36). For this reason, it is a necessary an identification of the etiological factors that could help to minimize the incidence of these conditions and also improve the development of more effective therapeutic approaches to minimize the harmful effects of such a psychopathological condition. The scientific literature has been pointing out that the early stressors in childhood, called

TABLE 4 | Univariate logistic regression between depression and childhood emotional abuse among patients.

Variable	Odds ratio (IC 95%)	*p*-value
Gender		0.14
Male	1	
Female	2.11 (0.78–5.71)	
Age group		
<29 yrs	1	
30–39 yrs	1.73 (0.53–5.82)	0.36
40–49 yrs	2.74 (0.87–8.61)	0.08
>50 yrs	1.44 (0.28–7.34)	0.65
Religious practice		0.31
Yes	1	
No	1.24 (0.32–4.83)	
Marital status		0.90
With partner	1	
Without partner	1.05 (0.44–2.53)	
Family history of mental disorder		0.45
No	1	
Yes	0.65 (0.21–1.99)	
Childhood emotional abuse		**0.002**
No	1	
Yes	4.38 (1.71–11.2)	
Childhood sexual abuse		**0.01**
No	1	
Yes	4.03 (1.31–12.36)	
Suicide attempt		**0.009**
No	1	
Yes	3.68 (1.39–9.77)	
Hopelessness (bhs)		**0.01**
Normal or Suave Hopelessness	1	
Moderate/Severe Hopelessness	3.07 (1.20–7.87)	

TABLE 5 | Multiple Logistic regression analysis between depression and childhood emotional abuse among patients.

Model[a]	Childhood emotional abuse		*p*-value
	No	Yes–OR (IC 95%)	
Raw Model	Reference	4.38 (1.71–11.20)	0.002
Model 2	Reference	4.04 (1.54–10.55)	0.004
Model 3	Reference	3.84 (1.40–10.55)	0.009
Model 4	Reference	3.71 (1.31–10.47)	0.013
Model 5	Reference	3.23 (1.11–9.38)	0.031

[a]Raw Model: Depression Disorder + Emotional Abuse.
Model 2 Raw model + Gender.
Model 3 Model 2 + Familiar History of Mental Disorders.
Model 4 Model 3 + Suicide Attempt.
Model 5 Model 4 + Hopelessness.

early stress, are also closely linked to the onset of psychiatric disorders (4, 37). Among the early stress subtypes, emotional abuse has been studied in several studies, showing that the same appears to be associated with the development of depressive disorders in adulthood (10, 11, 38–40). The study conducted by Pinto et al. (41), with a Portuguese sample also demonstrated, from logistic regression and linear analysis that adversity in childhood and adolescence elucidate around 6% of depressive symptoms and increases the risk of suicide attempts around 1,818 times. In our study evidenced a percentage around 70% of depressive patients with emotional abuse and from the results of the regression analysis was found an odds ratio of 4.38 times of occurrence of depression in patients with emotional abuse in childhood, thus demonstrating the importance of this early stress subtype as a trigger to trigger the depressive disorder. Emotional abuse often becomes unnoticeable by the health and education professionals because of its invisibility and discretion; however, it is imperative to its recognition. Moreover, in our research, we found a predominance of depressive patients were female (72.8%) and from the multiple logistic regression analysis was shown that patients with emotional abuse in childhood and females have an odds ratio of occurrence 4.04 times in developing depression, thus corroborating evidence from the scientific literature. According to studies by Kessler et al. (42), Fleck et al. (43) there is a relationship of two depressed women to a man, from adolescence, prevalence this explained by multifactor, with emphasis neuroendocrine and biological agents. Hormonal changes at different stages of development of women, i.e., premenstrual period, pregnancy and perimenopausal period seem to offer explanations for the association between depression and females (44). Research conducted by Weissman and Klerman (45) pioneered this relationship is particularly important for other researchers to extend understanding of the etiology for the higher prevalence of depression in women compared to men. Furthermore, studies show that men tend to have coping strategies to externalized depression, such as alcohol and drug abuse, while women internalize the symptoms, expressing sadness from social isolation, crying, and emotional withdrawal, more symptoms characteristic of depressive symptomatology (46). Other studies show that adolescent girls have problems related to the sense of well-being, the performance of social roles, as well as physical and sexual abuse in childhood, while men are involved with the abuse of alcohol and drugs, being this behavior a trigger also for attempted suicide (47). Another result of high scientific evidence concerning the association between depression and family history of psychiatric disorder. In our survey, 77% of patients had a family history of psychiatric disorders, and from the regression analysis, patients with a history of emotional abuse, female and mental disorder family history have an odds ratio of 3.84 times more on developing depression. This result corroborates the findings in the literature since the risk of depression increases 2 to 3 times in first-degree relatives of individuals with major depression compared to healthy people (48). Levinson (49) emphasizes that an individual who has a first-degree relative with depression have a higher risk of developing the same disorder, therefore the prevalence of depression in children of depressed parents is 5–12% higher than in the general population. Besides the positive family history is indicative of poor prognosis in psychiatric treatment (24, 50).

In the meta-analysis of Sullivan et al. (51) has seen an odds ratio of 2.84 times in patients with a family history of depression, compared to individuals with no family history. Such genetic influence becomes more evident when analyzing the appearance period of the disease and the number of episodes, as family members of individuals with recurrent depression and early onset present 17.4% rate while the relatives of individuals with single episode late-onset depression and have rates of 3.4% (52). It is worth mentioning that genetic predisposition and interaction with the environment is an individual aspect, therefore will depend on the combination of genetics and environment for the person presenting or not depression (53). Consecrated studies and current also show a potential association between depression and suicide, and impulsive behavior and aggression are important clues in this association (54–57). The study of Isometsa et al. (58) showed that while half of the depressed who committed suicide were receiving psychiatric treatment, few were under proper treatment for depression at the time of suicide, deserving emphasis on male patients, which they receive less frequent diagnosis of depression, thereby receiving less treatment and those who were diagnosed adhere less. Kessler et al. (59) evaluated the ratio between major depression and suicidal ideation, planning, trial and suicidal gestures in the years 1990–1992, and this research repeated after a decade; the findings of this study remained similar, demonstrating the temporal stability of the association between depression and suicide. Our study is in accordance with scientific evidence (24), since more than 70% of the sample had a history of suicide attempt; besides from the statistical analysis it was shown that patients with emotional abuse in childhood, female, with a history of mental illness in the family and attempted suicide have an odds ratio of occurrence of 3.71 times to develop depression. Also, the cohort of 3,017 individuals conducted by Brezo et al. (60) found an odds ratio of 6.8 times between childhood sexual abuse and suicide. Another exciting point identified in this study was the association between depression and hopelessness. According to the theory of Aaron Beck, depression result from thoughts and distorted beliefs where there is a negative view of the future, generating great hopelessness about life itself. Also, the hopelessness is closely associated with suicidal ideation, and the incidence of suicide in depressed people is 15%. Leahy (61) points that stress is a primary source of distorted thoughts in depressed activation in this sense the cognitive restructuring process will work to prevent the presence of depressed mood, apathy, fatigue, and other physiological changes present in depression. In our study, it was clear that patients with emotional abuse in childhood, female, with a history of mental disorders and suicide attempts and hopelessness have the odds ratio of 3.23 times in developing depression. It is important to emphasize that our study presents a methodological limitation regarding the research of early stress with psychiatric disorders in adults, so it would be necessary to evaluate the stress of current life, so further research can help to broaden the understanding of past stress and present, favoring the understanding of depressive illness. Depression is a complex disease, and explained by the interaction of genotype including heredity, the lived-in childhood environment, which can be marked for possible traumas, temperament that gives the individual the ability to deal with the environment and the resilience of some individuals who may explain different response to the same stressful events.

CONCLUSIONS

Our results suggested that the occurrence of depression in adulthood is related to situations of emotional abuse, sexual and physical neglect during childhood. The relationship between depression and childhood emotional abuse in females with psychiatry family history and previous suicide attempted is significant. Thus, these findings contribute to better understanding the mechanism involved in the pathogenesis of depression related to childhood emotional abuse.

AUTHOR CONTRIBUTIONS

MJ conceived and designed the study. CM-M, TP, and CB organized the database. MJ, CM-M, ST, and ER performed the statistical analysis and reviewed the literature. CM-M, ST, and CB dealt with psychometric evaluation. MJ, TP, and CM-M wrote the manuscript. MJ critically reviewed and finalized the paper. All authors contributed to manuscript revision, read, and approved the submitted version.

FUNDING

This work was supported by Academy of Medical Sciences/Royal Society, UK funding to MJ. It also represents independent research part funded by the National Institute for Health Research (NIHR) Biomedical Research Centre at South London and Maudsely NHS Foundation Trust and King's College London. The views expressed are those of the authors and not necessarily those of the NHS, the NIHR or the Department of Health and Social Care.

REFERENCES

1. Juruena MF. Early-life stress and HPA axis trigger recurrent adulthood depression. *Epilepsy Behav.* (2014) 38:148–59. doi: 10.1016/j.yebeh.2013.10.020
2. Zavaschi MLS, Satler F, Poester D, Vargas CF, Piazenski R, Rohde LAP, et al. Association between childhood loss trauma and depression in adulthood. *Rev Bras Psiquiatr.* (2002) 24:189–95. doi: 10.1590/S1516-44462002000400009
3. Bernstein DP, Stein JA, Newcomb MD, Walker E, Pogge D, Ahluvalia T, et al. Development and validation of a brief screening version of the childhood trauma questionnaire. *Child Abuse Negl.* (2003) 27:169–90. doi: 10.1016/S0145-2134(02)00541-0
4. Collishaw S, Pickles A, Messer J, Rutter M, Shearer C, Maughan B. Resilience to adult psychopathology following childhood maltreatment, evidence from a community sample. *Child Abuse Negl.* (2007) 31:211–29. doi: 10.1016/j.chiabu.2007.02.004

5. Edwards VJ, Holden GW, Felitti VJ, Anda RF. Relationship between multiple forms of childhood maltreatment and adult mental health in community respondents. *Am J Psychiatry* (2003) 160:1453–60. doi: 10.1176/appi.ajp.160.8.1453
6. Kessler RC, Davis CG, Kendler KS. Childhood adversity and adult psychiatric disorder in the US National Comorbidity Survey. *Psychol Med.* (1997) 27:1101–19. doi: 10.1017/S0033291797005588
7. Mullen PE, Martin JL, Anderson JC, Romans SE, Herbison GP. The long-term impact of the physical, emotional, and sexual abuse of children, a community study. *Child Abuse Negl.* (1996) 20:7–21. doi: 10.1016/0145-2134(95)00112-3
8. Martins CMS, Tofoli SM, Baes CVW, Juruena MF. Analysis of the occurrence of early life stress in adult psychiatric patients, a systematic review. *Psychol Neurosci.* (2011) 4:219–27. doi: 10.3922/j.psns.2011.2.007
9. Carr CP, Martins CMS, Stingel AM, Lemgruber VB, Juruena MF. The role of early life stress in adult psychiatric disorders. A sistematic review according to childhood trauma subtypes. *J Nerv Mental Dis.* (2013) 201:1007–20. doi: 10.1097/NMD.0000000000000049
10. Wingenfeld K, Schaffrath C, Rulkoetter N, Mensebach C, Schlosser N, Beblo T, et al. Associations of childhood trauma, trauma in adulthood and previous-year stress with psychopathology in patients with major depression and borderline personality disorder. *J Child Abuse Negl.* (2011) 35:647–54. doi: 10.1016/j.chiabu.2011.04.003
11. Gibb BE, Chelminski I, Zimmerman M. Childhood emotional, physical, and sexual abuse, and diagnoses of depressive and anxiety disorders in adult psychiatric outpatients. *Depression Anxiety* (2007) 24:256–63. doi: 10.1002/da.20238
12. Gibb BE, Butler AC, Beck JS. Childhood abuse, depression, and anxiety in adult psychiatric outpatients. *Depression Anxiety* (2003) 17:226–8. doi: 10.1002/da.10111
13. Berzenski SR, Yates TM. Classes and consequences of multiple maltreatment, a person centered analysis. *Child Maltreat.* (2011) 16:250–61. doi: 10.1177/1077559511428353
14. Higgins DJ, McCabe MP. Multi-type maltreatment and the long-term adjustment of adults. *Child Abuse Rev.* (2000) 9:6–18. doi: 10.1002/(SICI)1099-0852(200001/02)9:1<6::AID-CAR579>3.0.CO;2-W
15. Chartier MJ, Walker JR, Naimark B. Separate and cumulative effects of adverse childhood experiences inpredicting adult health and health care utilization. *Child Abuse Negl.* (2010) 34:454-64. doi: 10.1016/j.chiabu.2009.09.020
16. Felitti VJ, Anda RF, Nordenberg D, Williamson DF, Spitz AM, Edwards V. Relationship of childhood abuse and household dysfunctions to many of the leading causes of death in adults, The adverse childhood study. *Am J Prev Med.* (1998) 14:245–58. doi: 10.1016/S0749-3797(98)00017-8
17. Hahm HC, Lee Y, Ozonoff A, Van Wert MJ. The impact of multiple types of child adolescence to young adulthood. *J Youth Adolesc.* (2010) 39:528–40. doi: 10.1007/s10964-009-9490-0
18. Martins CMS, Juruena MF. Trauma-and stressor-related disorders. *Medicina* (2017) 50(Suppl. 1):37–50. doi: 10.11606/issn.2176-7262.v50isupl1.p37-50
19. Heim C, Nemeroff CB. The role of childhood trauma in the neurobiology of mood and anxiety disorders, preclinical and clinical studies. *Biol Psychiatry* (2001) 49:1023–39. doi: 10.1016/S0006-3223(01)01157-X
20. Briere J, Kaltman S, Green BL. Accumulated childhood trauma and symptom complexity. *J Traumatic Stress* (2008) 21:223–6. doi: 10.1002/jts.20317
21. Ford JD, Wasser T, Connor DF. Identifying and determining the symptom severity associated with polyvictimization among psychiatrically impaired children in the outpatient setting. *Child Maltreat.* (2011) 16:216–26. doi: 10.1177/1077559511406109
22. Sesar K, Zivcic-Becirevic I, Sesar D. Multi-type maltreatment in childhood and psychological adjustment in adolescence, questionnaire study among adolescents in western Herzegovina Canton. *Croat Med J.* (2008) 49:243–526. doi: 10.3325/cmj.2008.2.243
23. Arrata CM, Langhinrichsen-Rohling J, Bowers D, O'Brien N. Differential correlates of multitype maltreatment among urban youth. *J Child Abuse Negl.* (2007) 31:393–415. doi: 10.1016/j.chiabu.2006.09.006
24. Tunnard C, Rane LJ, Wooderson SC, Markopoulou K, Poon L, Fekadu A, et al. The impact of childhood adversity on suicidality and clinical course in treatment-resistant depression. *J Affect Disord.* (2014) 152:122–30. doi: 10.1016/j.jad.2013.06.037
25. Sfoggia A, Pacheco MA, Grassi-Oliveira R. History of childhood abuse and neglect and suicidal behavior at hospital admission. *Crisis* (2008) 29:154–8. doi: 10.1027/0227-5910.29.3.154
26. Brown J, Cohen P, Johnson JG, Smailes EM. Childhood abuse and neglect, specificity of effects on adolescent and young adult depression and suicidality. *J Am Acad Child Adolesc Psychiatry* (1999) 38:1490–6. doi: 10.1097/00004583-199912000-00009
27. Martins CM, Baes C, Tofoli S, Juruena MF. Emotional abuse in childhood is differential factor for the development of depression in adults. *J Nerv Mental Dis.* (2014) 202:774–82. doi: 10.1097/NMD.0000000000000202
28. Sheehan DV, Lecrubier Y, Sheehan KH, Amorim P, Janavs J, Weiller E, et al. The Mini International Neuropsychiatric Interview (MINI), the development and validation of a structured diagnostic psychiatric interview for DSM-IV and ICD-10. *J Clin Psychiatry* (1998) 59:22–33.
29. Amorim P. Mini International Neuropsychiatric Interview (MINI), validação de entrevista breve para diagnóstico de transtornos mentais. *Rev Bras Psiquiatr.* (2000) 22:106–15. doi: 10.1590/S1516-44462000000300003
30. Beck AT, Weissman A, Lester D, Trexler L. The measurement of pessimism, the hopelessness scale. *J Consult Clin Psychol.* (1974) 42:861–5. doi: 10.1037/h0037562
31. Cunha JA. *Manual da versão em português das Escalas Beck. Casa do Psicólogo.* São Paulo (2001).
32. Bernstein DP, Fink L, Handelsman L, Foote J, Lovejoy M, Wenzel K, et al. Initial reliability and validity of a new retrospective measure of child abuse and neglect. *Am J Psychiatry* (1994) 151:1132–6. doi: 10.1176/ajp.151.8.1132
33. Carpenter LL, Carvalho JP, Tyrka AR, Wier LM, Mello AF, Mello MF, et al. Decreased adrenocorticotropic hormone and cortisol responses to stress in healthy adults reporting significant childhood maltreatment. *Biol Psychiatry* (2007) 62:1080–7. doi: 10.1016/j.biopsych.2007.05.002
34. Bernstein DP, Ahluvalia T, Pogge D, Handelsman L. Validity of the childhood trauma questionnaire in an adolescent psychiatric population. *J Am Acad Child Adolesc Psychiatry* (1997) 36:340–8. doi: 10.1097/00004583-199703000-00012
35. Grassi-Oliveira RG, Stein LM, Pezzi JC. Tradução e validação de conteúdo da versão em português do Childhood Trauma Questionnaire. *Rev Saúde Públ.* (2006) 40:249–55. doi: 10.1590/S0034-89102006000200010
36. WHO. *Depression and Other Common Mental Disorders. Global Health Estimates.* WHO reference number (2017).
37. McLaughlin KA, Green JG, Gruber MJ, Sampson NA, Zaslavsky AM, Kessler RC. Childhood adversities and adult psychopathology in the national comorbidity survey reapplication (NCS-R) III, associations with functional impairment related to DSM-IV disorders. *Psychol Med.* (2010) 40:847–59. doi: 10.1017/S0033291709991115
38. Norman RE, Byambaa M, De R, Butchart A, Scott J, Vos T. The long-term health consequences of child physical abuse, emotional abuse, and neglect, a systematic review and meta-analysis. *PLoS Med.* (2012) 9:1001349. doi: 10.1371/journal.pmed.1001349
39. Seok J, Lee K, Kim W, Lee S, Kang E, Ham B, et al. Impact of early-life stress and resilience on patients with major depressive disorder. *Yonsei Med J.* (2012) 53:1093–8. doi: 10.3349/ymj.2012.53.6.1093
40. Shapero BG, Black SK, Liu RT, Klugman J, Bender RE, Abramson LY, et al. Stressful life events and depression symptoms, the effect of childhood emotional abuse on stress reactivity. *J Clin Psychol.* (2013) 70:1–15. doi: 10.1002/jclp.22011
41. Pinto VCP, Alvez JFC, Maia AC. Adversity in childhood predicts depressive symptoms and suicide attempts in adult Portuguese women. *Estudos de Psicologia* (2015) 32:617–25. doi: 10.1590/0103-166X2015000400005
42. Kessler RC, Demler O, Frank RG, Olfson M, Pincus HA, Walters EE, et al. Prevalence and treatment of mental disorders, 1990 to 2003. *N Engl J Med.* (2005) 16:2515–23. doi: 10.1056/NEJMsa043266
43. Fleck MP, Berlim MT, Lafer B, Sougey EB, Del Porto JA, Brasil MA, et al. Review of the guidelines of the Brazilian Medical Association for the treatment of depression. *Braz J Psychiatry* (2009) 31(Suppl. 1):S7–17. doi: 10.1590/S1516-44462009000500003
44. Baptista T, Reyes D, Hernández L. Antipsychotic drugs and reproductive hormones: relationship to body weight regulation. *Pharmacol Biochem Behav.* (1999) 62:409–17.

45. Weissman MM, Klerman GL. Sex diferences and the epidemiology of depression. *Arch Gen Psychiatry* (1977) 34:98–111.
46. Windle MA. Longitudinal study of stress buffering for adolescente problem behaviors. *Dev Mental Psychol.* (1992) 522–530. doi: 10.1037/0012-1649.28.3.522
47. Smith DK, Saldana L. Trauma delinquency and substance use: co-occurring problems for adolescent girls in the juvenile justice system. *J Child Adolesc Subst Abuse* (2013) 22:450–65. doi: 10.1080/1067828X.2013.788895
48. Klerman GL, Weissman MM. Increasing rates of depression. *JAMA* (1989) 261:229–35. doi: 10.1001/jama.1989.03420150079041
49. Levinson DF. The genetics of depression: a review. *Biological Psychiatry* (2006) 60:84–92. doi: 10.1016/j.biopsych.2005.08.024
50. Nierenberg AA, Trivedi MH, Fava M, Biggs MM, Shores-Wilson K, Wisniewski SR, et al. Family history of mood disorder and characteristics of major depressive disorder, a STAR*D (sequenced treatment alternatives to relieve depression) study. *J Psychiatr Res.* (2007) 41:214–21. doi: 10.1016/j.jpsychires.2006.02.005
51. Sullivan PF, Neale MC, Kendler KS. Genetic epidemiology of major depression, review and meta-analysis. *Am J Psychiatry* (2000) 157:1552–62. doi: 10.1176/appi.ajp.157.10.1552
52. Bland RC, Newman SC, Orn H. Recurrent and non-recurrent depression. A family study. *Arch Gener Psychiatry* (1986) 43:1085–9. doi: 10.1001/archpsyc.1986.01800110071009
53. Menezes IC, Baes CV, Lacchini R, Juruena MF. Genetic biomarkers for differential diagnosis of major depressive disorder and bipolar disorder, a critical and systematic review. *Behav Brain Res.* (2018) 57–358:29–38. doi: 10.1016/j.bbr.2018.01.008
54. McGirr A, Renaud J, Seguin M, Alda M, Benkelfat C, Lesage A, et al. An examination of DSM-IV depressive symptoms and risk for suicide completion in major depressive disorder, a psychological autopsy study. *J Affect Disord.* (2007) 97:203–9. doi: 10.1016/j.jad.2006.06.016
55. Dumais A, Lesage AD, Alda M, Rouleau G, Dumont M, Chawky N, et al. Risk factors for suicide completion in major depression, a case-control study of impulsive and aggressive behaviors in men. *Am J Psychiatry* (2005) 162:2116–24. doi: 10.1176/appi.ajp.162.11.2116
56. Brent DA, Oquendo M, Birmaher B, Greenhill L, Kolko D, Stanley B, et al. Familial transmission of mood disorders, convergence and divergence with transmission of suicidal behavior. *J Am Acad Child Adolesc Psychiatry* (2004) 43:1259–66. doi: 10.1097/01.chi.0000135619.38392.78
57. Turecki G. Dissecting the suicide phenotype: the role of impulsive-aggressive behaviours. J *Psychiatry Neurosci.* (2005) 30:398–408.
58. Isometsa ET, Henriksson MM, Aro HM, Heikkinen ME, Kuoppasalmi KI, Lonnqvist JK. Suicide in major depression. *Am J Psychiatry* (1994) 151:530–6. doi: 10.1176/ajp.151.4.530
59. Kessler RC, Berglund P, Borges G, Nock M, Wang PS. Trends in suicide ideation, plans, gestures and attempts in the United States, 1990-1992 to 2001-2003. *JAMA* (2005) 293:2487–95. doi: 10.1001/jama.293.20.2487
60. Brezo J, Paris J, Barker ED, Tremblay R, Vitaro F, Zoccolillo M, et al. Natural history of suicidal behaviors in a population-based sample of young adults. *Psychol Med.* (2007) 37:1563–74. doi: 10.1017/S003329170700058X
61. Leahy RL. *Contemporary Cognitive Therapy, Theory, Research, and Practice.* New York, USA: Guilford (2006).

9

Mental Disorder—The Need for an Accurate Definition

Diogo Telles-Correia[1], Sérgio Saraiva[1] and Jorge Gonçalves[2]*

[1] *Clinica Universitaria de Psiquiatria e Psicologia, Faculty of Medicine, Universidade de Lisboa, Lisbon, Portugal,*
[2] *Faculty of Social and Human Sciences, IFILNOVA, Universidade Nova de Lisboa, Lisbon, Portugal*

***Correspondence:**
Sérgio Saraiva
sergiomotasaraiva@gmail.com

There are several reasons why a definition for mental disorder is essential. Among these are not only reasons linked to psychiatry itself as a science (nosology, research) but also to ethical, legal, and financial issues. The first formal definition of mental disorder resulted from a deep conceptual analysis led by Robert Spitzer. It emerged to address several challenges that psychiatry faced at the time, namely to serve as the starting point for an atheoretical and evidence-based classification of mental disorders, to justify the removal of homosexuality from classifications, and to counter the arguments of antipsychiatry. This definition has been updated, with some conceptual changes that make it depart from the main assumptions of Spitzer's original definition. In this article, we intend to review the factors that substantiated the emergence of the first formal definition of mental disorder that based all its later versions.

Keywords: mental disorders, definition and concepts, antipsychiatry, DSM classification, classification, homosexuality

INTRODUCTION

The existence of a formal definition of mental disorder remains essential for several reasons that include the following: 1) to know which diagnosis should or not be included in the classifications (1–3); 2) to separate areas of responsibility of the medical system from other societal systems; 3) to avoid dangerous medicalization of social problems; 4) to distinguish between pathological and normal; 5) to identify the conditions that, as a result of their negative consequences, implicitly have a call to action to the psychiatrists; 6) to identify the cases that justify societal recognition of the appropriateness of the sick role; 7) to understand which situations may prevent legal imputability; 8) to avoid false positives and other related problems such as overmedicalization, unnecessary labeling, wasted resources; and 9) to define psychiatry's position as a special medical discipline (1–7).

The first formal definition of mental disorder was presented in DSM-III stemming from a deep conceptual review carried out by APA's Committee on Nomenclature, headed by Spitzer. This definition was designed to address various needs psychiatry had at the time, notably to serve as a starting point for an atheoretical and evidence-based classification of mental disorders, to justify the removal of homosexuality from classifications, and to counter the arguments of antipsychiatry (according to which psychiatry was more oriented to social and ethical values rather than medical ones and could constitute a form of social control) (6, 7).

In recent times, this definition has been updated, with conceptual changes insufficiently discussed within psychiatry, and a consequent gradual detachment from Spitzer's original definition. It is essential to reflect on the context in which this first formal definition of mental disorder emerges, and all the considerations that resulted therein, before making any updates to this definition.

This article intends to briefly review the factors that laid the foundations for the establishment of the first formal definition of mental disorder and which formed the basis for all its later versions.

The Need for a Definition of Mental Disorder As a Starting Point for an Atheoretical and Evidence-Based Classification

Prior to the DSM-III, diagnostic classification was "based upon the best clinical judgment and experience of a committee and its consultants" [Ref. (5), p. 57]. The 1970s marked the beginning of a movement aimed at improving the quality of classification in psychiatry with various initiatives, including the development of the "Diagnostic Criteria for Use in Psychiatric Research"—DCPR (5) and the "Research Diagnostic Criteria" (RDC) (8). These initiatives represent the basis for the development of DSM-III nosological classification and criteria (6). The goal was to create systems with better validity for classifying mental disorders that did not depend, as in the past, on theoretical perspectives (psychodynamic, biological, etc). Spitzer believed that the starting point for any psychiatric classification should begin with the most atheoretical and value independent definition of mental disorder. Therefore, in the DSM-III "each of the mental disorders is conceptualized as a clinically significant behavioral or psychological syndrome or pattern that occurs in an individual and that is typically associated with either a painful symptom (distress) or impairment in one or more important areas of functioning (disability). In addition, there is an inference that there is a behavioral, psychological, or biological dysfunction (...)" [Ref. (9), p. 6].

Consistent with a descriptive and atheoretical structure, the DSM-III enhances the importance of the harm criteria (distress and disability) comparatively with the criteria of psychiatric/psychological dysfunction (generally linked to a specific theoretical point of view) (9).

The Issue of Homosexuality and the Concept of Dysfunction

One of the contributing factors for the need to define mental disorder was an attempt not to include situations more related to cultural, moral, and religious values than to medical ones (which define what is harmful to the patient and should be treated) and which long undermined psychiatric classifications. Several such situations have been defined as mental disorders throughout history, such as, "drapetomania" (applied to American slaves who wanted to escape) and "sluggish schizophrenia" (applied to political dissidents in the Soviet Union). The case of homosexuality motivated a deep reflection within the APA on which situations to include as mental disorder or not.

According to Spitzer, the category of homosexuality did not make sense because one could not "insist on a label of sickness for individuals who insist that they are well (i.e., have 'no subjective distress') and who demonstrate no generalized impairment in social effectiveness" [Ref. (10), p. 1216].

In another document he refers "in reviewing the characteristics of the various mental disorders included in DSM-II, Spitzer concluded that, except for homosexuality, and perhaps other 'sexual deviations,' they all regularly caused subjective distress or were associated with generalized impairment in social effectiveness or functioning. It was proposed that the consequences of a condition, and not its etiology determined whether the condition should be considered a disorder" [Ref. (11), p. 16]. These arguments led Spitzer to privilege the criteria of harm (distress and disability) in detriment of criteria such as dysfunction, which was the main criterion for the definition of medical disease at the time.

The most defended model of disease in the 20th century was Boorse's. According to this model, a disease corresponds to a dysfunction—alteration of natural functions resulting in reduced life expectancy and/or reproductive expectations (supposedly a value-free concept), emphasizing the importance of a dysfunction (biological or psychological) for the existence of a disease (12, 13, 14). Later, Wakefield agrees with Boorse's dysfunction concept, arguing that these mechanisms may be physical or mental (12): "mental processes play important species-typical roles in human survival and reproduction, there is no reason to doubt that mental processes were naturally selected and have natural functions as Darwin himself often emphasized" [Ref. (12), p. 375]. But for Wakefield, the presence of dysfunction is insufficient to determine the presence of medical disturbance, the criteria of harm (distress–disability) must also be present, disagreeing with Boorse at this point (for whom biological or mental dysfunction suffices) (7). Both Boorse and Wakefield considered that the concept of dysfunction is independent of values and essential for the definition of any medical or psychiatric disorder.

Numerous criticisms have since arisen to the possibility of classifying certain psychological characteristics such as dysfunctions (7). Wakefield himself assumes this when stating that in some cases, such as homosexuality, it is difficult to assume the criterion of dysfunction (such as psychological alteration that interferes with the reproductive function), "in the contemporary context of overpopulation and widespread birth control among heterosexuals, the highest generally accepted normative goal of sexual-love relationships in our society is not reproduction *per se* but mutual interpersonal and sexual satisfaction" [Ref. (15), p. 676].

Thus, the most appropriate criteria for the definition of mental disorder and depending upon more universal values (than those associated with the definition of psychological dysfunction) would be those of distress and disability (7). As Gert and Culver stated "every society regards death, pain, disability and loss of pleasure as harms" [Ref. (16), p. 421].

Perhaps that is why Spitzer masterfully highlighted the presence of distress and disability criteria as priority in the definition of mental disorder in order to avoid and exclude dubious situations such as homosexuality, and other entities historically considered as mental disorders, alleging a psychological dysfunction assessed according to values (social, moral, and cultural) often masked as science. So Spitzer says about his definition of mental disorder that "these criteria avoid such terms as 'dysfunction'... which themselves beg definition" [Ref. (1), p17]. Though he ends up using it (perhaps to not completely dissociate himself from the definition of medical disease valid at the time) referring "in addition, there is an inference that there is a behavioral, psychological, or biological dysfunction" [Ref. (9), p. 6], the universal criteria of distress and disability undoubtedly take supremacy in this definition.

Antipsychiatry

Although antipsychiatry in the general sense of the term is as old as psychiatry (17), emerging in the 19th century, the movement known as "antipsychiatry" rose in the 1960s and 1970s. Associated with this movement were the names of Foucault, Szasz, Basaglia, Cooper, Laing, and others. Although there are several "antipsychiatries," the common denominator is the fight against the psychiatric institution synthesized in the figure of the doctor and his power (18, 19). Criticism of repressive psychiatric power is the essential point of the movement, being the criticism of the concept of mental disorder and pharmacological therapies derivatives of this fundamental position.

In the book *Madness and Civilization*, Foucault presents the historical genesis of the concept of mental disorder, as we understand it today, which he does not separate from the psychiatric institution. That is to say, no knowledge about mental disorder is separated from its place of formation, the asylum. Asylum, in turn, follows a series of historical experiences that are predominantly of social control. Thus, finally, claiming that the science of psychiatry is essentially a knowledge seeking to justify the moral power of the physician. According to this view, psychiatrists forget this origin of their power and attribute it to objective knowledge obtained scientifically (20).

Szasz also considered the concept of mental disorder to be a myth (21). There is psychological suffering and life problems, but it will be a categorical mistake to consider them as "diseases" (22). Body and mind would belong to two orders of *being* qualitatively different. The body of medicine is explained by a mechanistic causality, and physiological diseases are lesions of organs, perfectly identified. The mind could not be explained by mechanical causes because it is intentionality and rationality. Thus, according to Szasz, one should not speak of mental "disorders" but of deviations from socially accepted norms and values. It would not be a question of the violation of the natural order, but of the social order (21).

Considering all these arguments, psychiatry had no alternative but to strengthen its status with a valid definition of mental disorder that would deviate from social, moral, and religious values. It should therefore be a priority to delimit the activity of psychiatry as a medical specialty, according to the main objective of medicine: the relief of the patient's symptoms linked to distress and disability. Thus, distress and disability became the main criteria of this new definition of mental disorder. Spitzer himself preferred the name of disorder rather than disease highlighting that "there is no assumption that the organismic dysfunction or its negative consequences are of a physical nature," because disease "often denotes a progressive physical disorder with known pathophysiology" [Ref. (1), p. 17], accepting a general basic difference between mental disorders and medical disease.

Conversely, giving a primordial role to the criteria of harm could also divert the focus of mental disorder, from the doctor (his values and power) to the patient and his needs arising from the suffering he bears.

DISCUSSION

The first formal definition of mental disorder appears in DSM-III as a result of a deep conceptual review. This definition emerged to meet various needs of psychiatry at that time, in particular to serve as a starting point for an evidence-based and atheoretical classification of mental disorder and to justify the removal of homosexuality from classifications and counter the arguments of antipsychiatry. A definition was elaborated in which the main condition for a mental disorder to be present was the presence of the criteria of distress and disability (less permeable to theoretical differences and to moral, cultural, and religious values than the concept of psychiatric or psychological dysfunction).

The criteria of harm (distress and disability) remained as paramount in the definition of mental disorder in DSM-IV and the importance of these criteria also led them to make part of the specific diagnostic criteria for most disorders listed in DSM-IV.

Nevertheless, in DSM-5 a major and barely discussed change occurred, the concept of dysfunction takes precedence, appearing at the beginning of the definition, possibly being considered its main criterion:

> A mental disorder is a syndrome characterized by clinically significant disturbance in an individual's cognition, emotion regulation, or behavior that reflects a dysfunction in the psychological, biological, or developmental processes underlying mental functioning. Mental disorders are usually associated with significant distress or disability in social, occupational, or other important activities… [Ref. (23), p. 20].

Harm criteria are no longer a basic requirement, but a frequent occurrence that might or not be present.

This could lead to the inclusion (in psychiatric diagnostic manuals) of situations that are not associated with distress and disability as happened in the past, potentially re-exposing psychiatry to the danger that entities considered psychological or biological dysfunctions, according to certain theoretical currents (easily permeable to moral and social values), may be considered mental disorders.

The problem of considering a mental disorder to be mainly a dysfunction (as in DSM-5) may arise in both perspectives: as a biological dysfunction or as a psychological dysfunction.

Several problems arise regarding the possibility of considering mental disorders as synonymous of biological dysfunction. Psychiatric disorders are not natural kinds directly visualized and discriminated by neuroimaging tests. Psychiatric disorders are "social constructs" that do not exist independently of human effort (6, 24, 25). The evaluation of what is pathological or not in psychiatry is related to 1) comprehensibility (whether or not the mental state/behavior is comprehensible given the sociocultural context of the patient), 2) adaptability (adaptive or non-adaptive in the context of the patient), and 3) connection to distress and disability (whether or not they cause distress or disability) (26). The latter being the most universal criteria (7, 24). The above-mentioned criteria define the presence or absence of mental symptoms or disorder that is primary or secondary to a physical dysfunction. As an example, in the case of a brain tumor that subsequently induces depressive symptoms, clinical depression is assessed through clinical criteria (comprehensibility, adaptability, and harm inducing). Mental manifestations, regardless of the physical or neurological core, only represent a mental disorder if they are regarded as inadequate, non-adaptative, or causing harm (considering the sociocultural background and circumstances of the patient). That cannot mean that we cannot try to find the physical or neurological correlates of these mental manifestations. However, in psychiatry, separation of disordered from non- disordered is not dependent upon neurological biomarkers. This means that clinical concepts are precursors to biological concepts. Thus, mental disorder cannot only be defined by a physical or biological dysfunction (27).

Conversely, it is also controversial to define mental disorder through a psychological dysfunction. As mentioned by Fullford, dysfunction as the concept of failure of a mechanism to determine a natural function is a concept inextricably linked to values. For biological issues and medical values (what is considered useful or not to the organism by specific societies) change over time (28, 29). Additionally, there is much less consensus about the concept of psychological dysfunction than that of biological dysfunction, due to an insufficient knowledge about the psychological processes. Thus, recognizing the dysfunctional aspects of psychological mechanisms is harder (30). Notwithstanding, mental functions are directly bound to a social role that physical functions are not, meaning that the former are much more linked to social and cultural values (30).

Moreover, the definition of dysfunction of psychological mechanisms, as a failure of internal mechanisms to perform their functions as designed by nature, traces an artificial boundary between what is natural (innate), as opposed to social (cultivated) (22). Additionally, "human behavior is also socially designed and the relative contributions of biology and social rules are complex and interwoven, not easy to tease apart" [Ref. (25), p. 124].

Kirmayer adds that: "there is little consensus on what our psychological systems are for and many evolutionary psychologists argue that we have evolved to be able to adapt to situations rather than to have fixed or specific functions. Any change in culture will change the fitness of specific psychological, traits, give new meaning and purpose to biological functions, and change their boundaries and interdependence. Beyond relatively simple physiological functions it is impossible to identify what psychological systems or functions are for in any universal sense" [Ref. (31), pp. 18–19].

Furthermore, psychiatric disorders could be caused by distinct situations, instead of disruption function (e.g., defensive/coping strategies, design/environment mismatches, maladaptive-looking phenotypes that may be adaptive; highly evolved learning capacities leading to maladaptive behavior) (25).

CONCLUSION

The difficulties inherent to the use of the concept of dysfunction to define a psychiatric disorder are not only a problem of validity in psychiatry but may also make psychiatry permeable (again) to the typical criticisms of antipsychiatry which claimed that psychiatric disorders were more linked to values associated with culture-specific social and political ideologies rather than medical values (which identify harmful situations to the patient and in need of treatment). Spitzer attempted to circumvent these issues by making distress and disability (revealed at the patients' level) the main defining criteria of mental disorders. These are concepts that are closer to the patient than to the psychiatrist and that are loaded with more universal values (it is consensual that distress and disability are negative for the patient and deserve to be relieved). On the other hand, as mentioned, the determination of biological or even psychological dysfunction in most psychiatric disorders is difficult, controversial, and usually the result of influenceable theoretical currents.

In essence, the first definition of mental disorder resulted from a rigorous conceptual analysis. We should continue to promote critical reviews and conceptual analysis on this topic which can debate the problems that it entails and the dangers that an apparently harmless change to the definition of mental disorders (such as that which was taken in DSM 5) can bring toward psychiatry.

AUTHOR CONTRIBUTIONS

DT-C conceived and designed research. DT-C and SS wrote the first draft of the manuscript. JG did critical revision for important intellectual content. The manuscript has been read and approved by all the authors. There are no other persons who satisfied the criteria for authorship but are not listed. We further confirm that the order of authors listed in the manuscript has been approved by all of us.

REFERENCES

1. Spitzer RL, Endicott I. Medical and mental disorder: proposed definition and criteria. In: Spitzer RL, Klein DF, editors. *Critical Issues in Psychiatric Diagnosis*. New York, NY: Raven Press (1978). p. 15–40.
2. Bolton D. Overdiagnosing problems in the DSM.IV and the new DSM-5: can they be resolved by the distress impairment criterion? *Can Psychiatry* (2013) 58(11):612–7. doi:10.1177/070674371305801106
3. Decker HS. A snapshot in the time: the DSM-III in midstream, 1976. In: Decker HS, editor. *The Making of DSM-III*. New York, NY: Oxford University Press (2013). p. 163–202.
4. Klein DK. A proposed definition of mental disorder. In: Spitzer RL, Klein DF, editors. *Critical Issues in Psychiatric Diagnosis*. New York, NY: Raven Press (1978). p. 41–84.
5. Feighner J, Robins E, Guze S, Woodruff R, Winokur G, Munos R. Diagnostic criteria for use in psychiatric research. *Arch Gen Psychiatry* (1972) 26:57-63. doi:10.1001/archpsyc.1972.01750190059011
6. Telles-Correia D. The concept of validity throughout the history of psychiatry. *J Eval Clin Pract* (2017) 23(5):994–998. doi:10.1111/jep.12750
7. Telles-Correia D. Mental disorder: are we moving away from distress and disability? *J Eval Clin Pract* (2018). doi:10.1111/jep.12871
8. Spitzer RL, Endicott J, Robins E. Research diagnostic criteria: rationale and reliability. *Arch Gen Psychiatry* (1978) 35(6):773–82. doi:10.1093/schbul/8.1.1
9. American Psychiatric Association (APA). *Diagnostic and Statistical Manual of Mental Disorders*. 3rd ed. Washington, DC: APA (1980).
10. Spitzer RL. A Proposal about homosexuality and the APA nomenclature: homosexuality as an irregular form of sexual behavior, and sexual orientation disturbance as a psychiatric disorder: a symposium. Should

homosexuality be in the APA nomenclature? *Am J Psychiatry* (1973) 130:1207–16.
11. Spitzer RL, Williams JB. The definition and diagnosis of mental disorder. In: Grove WR, editor. *Deviance and Mental Illness*. Beverly Hill: SAGE (1982). p. 15–31.
12. Wakefield JC. The concept of mental disorder. On the boundary between biological facts and social values. *Am Psychol* (1992) 47(3):373–88. doi:10.1037/0003-066X.47.3.373
13. Boorse C. On the distinction between disease and illness. *Philos Public Aff* (1975) 5(1):49–68.
14. Kendell RE. The concept of disease and its implications for psychiatry. *Br J Psychiatry* (1975) 127(4):305–15. doi:10.1192/bjp.127.4.305
15. Wakefield JC. The biostatistical theory versus the harmful dysfunction analysis, part 1: is part-dysfunction a sufficient condition for medical disorder? *J Med Philos* (2014) 39(6):648–82. doi:10.1093/jmp/jhu038
16. Gert B, Culver CM. Defining mental disorder. In: Radden J, editor. *The Philosophy of Psychiatry: A Companion*. New York: Oxford University Press (2003). p. 415–25.
17. Quétel C. *Histoire de la Folie – De l' Antiquité à nos jours*. Paris: Éditions Tallandier (2012).
18. Foucault M. La maison des Fous. In: Basaglia F, Basaglia-Ongaro F, editors. *Criminini di Pace*. Turin: Eunadi (1975). p. 151–69.
19. Rose N. Foucault, Laing et le pouvoir psychiatrique. *Social Soc* (2006) 38(2):113–31. doi:10.7202/016375ar
20. Foucault M. Chapter IX (The Birth of Asylum). In: Howard R, editor. *Madness and Civilization: A History of Insanity in the Age of Reason (Abridged Version)*. New York: Random House (1967). p. 241–78.
21. Szasz T. The Myth of mental illness. *Am Psychol* (1960) 15:113–8. doi:10.1037/h0046535
22. Creswell M. Szasz and his interlocutors: reconsidering Thomas Szasz's 'myth of mental illness' thesis. *J Theory Soc Behav* (2008) 38:23–44. doi:10.1111/j.1468-5914.2008.00359.x
23. American Psychiatric Association (APA). *Diagnostic and Statistical Manual of Mental Disorders*. 5th ed. Washington, DC: APA (2013).
24. Bolton D, editor. The sciences on mental order/disorder and related concepts. *What Is Mental Disorder? An Essay in Philosophy, Science, and Values*. Oxford: Oxford University Press (2008). p. 47–101.
25. Bolton D. Mental disorder and human nature. In: Bolton D, editor. *What Is Mental Disorder? An Essay in Philosophy, Science, and Values*. Oxford: Oxford University Press (2008). p. 103–62.
26. Telles-Correia D. The mind-brain gap and the neurosciences-psychiatry gap. *J Eval Clin Pract* (2018). doi:10.1111/jep.12981
27. Jaegwon K, editor. Mental causation and consciousness. *Physicalism, or Something Near Enough*. New Jersey: Princeton University Press (2005). p. 1–29.
28. Fullford KW. Dysfunction and function. In: Fullford KW, editor. *Moral Theory and Medical Practice*. New York, NY: Cambridge University Press (1989). p. 89–108.
29. Moore MS. Discussion of the Spitzer-Endicott and Klein proposed definitions of mental disorder (illness). In: Spitzer RL, Klein DF, editors. *Critical Issues in Psychiatric Diagnosis*. New York, NY: Raven Press (1978). p. 85–108.
30. Spitzer RL, Wakefield JC. DSM-IV diagnostic criterium for clinical significance: does it help solve the false positives problem? *Am J Psychiatry* (1992) 156:1856–64.
31. Kirmayer LJ. Rejoinder to professor Wakefield. Debate on "Is the concept of mental disorder culturally relative?" with JC Wakefield. In: Kirk SA, Einbinder SD, editors. *Controversial Issues in Mental Health*. Boston, MA, London: Allyn and Bacon (1984). p. 17–24.

10

Mental State Examination and its Procedures — Narrative Review of Brazilian Descriptive Psychopathology

Helio Gomes Rocha Neto[1], Carlos Eduardo Estellita-Lins[2], José Luiz Martins Lessa[3] and Maria Tavares Cavalcanti[3]*

[1] Centro Universitario Lusíada, São Paulo, Brazil, [2] Fundação Oswaldo Cruz (Fiocruz), Rio de Janeiro, Brazil, [3] Instituto de Psiquiatria, Universidade Federal do Rio de Janeiro, Rio de Janeiro, Brazil

***Correspondence:**
Helio Gomes Rocha Neto
hgrochaneto@gmail.com

Background: Mental State Examination (MSE) is compared with physical examination as a reliable method of objective data investigation. There is a growing concern with psychiatric clinics, nosology, and the reliability of diagnostic interview methods as a source of valid diagnostic strategy. Efforts to achieve an international diagnosis protocol have been unsuccessful or polemical. This paper focuses on psychopathology, MSE, and mental function development within Brazilian psychiatry over the last few decades.

Methods: Searches, interviews, and narrative reviews were done to look for systematic ways in which to conduct MSE, mental functions, symptom clusters, orientations about data observation and records. Brazilian psychopathology textbooks were examined, if they provided access to consolidated knowledge on psychopathology examination.

Results: Sixteen textbooks were selected from a 49 year span. Descriptive psychopathology with phenomenological orientation was the primary trend in the MSE. Concepts derived from different traditions, most lacking common terminology, suggested some divergence among authors. Recommendations for patient observation and how to collect objective data was clear, but MSE standardization efforts were missing. A detailed description of mental function abnormalities was the main MSE record strategy, without consensus about ways to summarize and record this data. In an examination summary, mental strata was divided into "mental functions," and MSE subsets were frequent. All authors considered the following mental functions: consciousness, perception, thought, memory, attention, orientation, and volition.

Discussion: Psychiatric competence demands MSE proficiency. Official documents are not clear about performance and recording standards. MSE data was usually recorded through descriptive psychopathology. A shift from detailed descriptive findings, to an array of observed pathological elements, described through a mental function checklist was observed over time. Clinical practice and research guidelines should consider the development of reliable MSE practices; however, it has been neglected by modern psychiatry/neuroscience through the excessive emphasis on interview protocols. Better MSE practices, and the improvement of bedside skill in psychiatry are necessary and depend on the recovery of psychopathological debates and semiological reasoning, which will allow the return of phenomenology-oriented "observational" techniques.

Keywords: mental state examination, psychopathology, descriptive psychopathology, history of medicine, psychiatry, diagnosis, diagnosis technics and procedures

INTRODUCTION

In modern clinical medicine, a diagnosis is obtained through the crossover of symptoms, obtained by anamnesis or by a clinical interview, and signs of symptoms, obtained through a physical examination and laboratory or image tests (1). The former is supposed to spark multiple hypotheses which the clinician then further investigates by looking at patient's signs and symptoms. Semiology has been described in many textbooks as Porto (2) or Bates (3), and was over time formalized as the paramount method of clinical examination in internal medicine.

Such standard foundational programs were made possible through Claude Bernard's experimental medicine (4), confirmed by Alvan Feinstein one century later, whereby stating that recent clinical epidemiology belongs to the same epistemological strata (5–7). The same method was implemented in most medical specialties, including psychiatry (8, 9). With regard to general medical practice, physical examination (PE), lab, and image procedures provide the standard method to gather objective information, which is then used to refine the previously elaborated hypothesis through the anamnesis/interview method. The very idea of a PE and semiology was strengthened by the transformations of modern medicine, and was consolidated with the Flexnerian reformation of medical schools (10, 11).

Psychiatry has tried to take part in this agenda and match such standards (12). Clinical interviews as a standard procedure for anamnesis in psychiatry, has been rigorously investigated. An extensive bibliography, concerning how to improve an examiners agreement about symptoms, and a rising consensus about the need for a minimal structure for better clinician reliability, is now evident (13–19). Mental health practice often uses Mental State Examination (MSE) as an equivalent to PE from routine clinical examination and as a reliable method for objective data gathering (13, 20–22), since PE and MSE are logically correlated. However, clinical interview/anamnesis is previous to, and also guides PE procedures and laboratory searches, but it is the core of the mental/psychic examination process and used predominately in most cases. However, the interview is a narrative, history taking method, and not an objective sign gatherer tool.

The interview should be a narrative, recollection method, not an objective investigative tool. PE is consistently mentioned throughout almost all propaedeutical textbooks in medicine, with minimal, if not aesthetical, variations. MSE however has not achieved any international protocol or structured general tool, not even a minimal array of standard techniques and clinical report methods. Although MSEs widespread use as a PE correlative might not be suitable and may also be equivocated (9, 23, 24), it still universally used to gather data, objective information and evidence in mental health practice.

MSE was simultaneously developed in different regions of the world, influenced by philosophically-oriented ideas on psychopathology (25, 26). Many psychopathology textbooks have also been written in different languages, according to different traditions, which have resulted in vast variations in technique and nomenclature (27, 28). Nevertheless, mental semiology has been overlooked in most historiographical efforts, despite the importance of nosological history (29).

In the last 30 years, new trends in the history of psychiatry in Brazil developed, but none has considered mental examination. Estellita-Lins attempted to emphasize the phenomenology of living space (espace vécu) in Jaspers Psychopathology Textbook and its vital role concerning signs, "evidence" and examination (30). Cheniaux (31) reviewed some of the Brazilian, and even foreign textbooks about "descriptive psychopathology," searching for conceptual regularity or terminological "uniformity" among authors, but MSE was not addressed. Viotti Daker worked on the main Brazilian textbook by Nobre de Melo, examining its psychopathological models (32). Again, the MSE was not mentioned, but Melo's emphasis on fully assessing the person, before evaluating the particular functions subdivision, is noteworthy.

There is an increasing concern related to clinics and nosology in psychiatry. This concern might be traced back to Nancy Andreassen's claim concerning the loss of psychopathological knowledge by younger psychiatrists, and to Parnas' Danish group that contested the validity of the schizophrenia nosologic construct in DSM/ICD, further extended to the unreliability of diagnostic interview methods with structured diagnostic questionnaires (33, 34). We should also mention Jacob's questioning of MSE training in India (28), Aragona's interrogation about the collaboration of neuroscience in psychiatric diagnosis, among many others (35). As Rodrigues and Banzato have stated, if a sound agreement concerning the "validity" of a concept in psychiatry had already been achieved, there would not be such confusion around it (36).

We foresee epistemological issues concerning psychiatry and mental health care, that have not yet been resolved, as the importance of examination skills and training in the evidence-based era. These themes are not simply classificatory issues but are fundamental psychopathological efforts demanding a discussion concerning the diagnosis process in mental health and psychiatry.

This study deals with modern psychiatry from a historical perspective but addresses some clinical problems such as MSE, examination reporting, patient records and psychopathology teaching/transmission. A narrow comprehension of what evidence means may have been overlooked such as bedside skills and in particular phenomenological examining tradition (37–39). Maybe ongoing "taxonomic issues" and "classification wars" in psychiatry (40–42) are fair and useful, but we should also pinpoint some relevant matters that concern the examination, clinical reasoning and the diagnostic process itself (43).

Aiming to elucidate the origins, development, and methods of how MSE has been consolidated in Brazil, a review was carried out on the national literature.

METHODS

MSE still lacks proper categorization in MESH and DeCS, and the best results of descriptors or key word searches were related to standard clinical interviews, therefore unsuitable for systematic MSE research purposes. Textbooks are known to be the introductory means to access expert knowledge in the medical field as defined by Ludwig Fleck (44). It was then decided to consider textbooks on psychopathology as a primary reference, following a timeline based on its reference and contents. A backward reference search was carried out at the start of 2017, using the Universidade Federal do Rio de Janeiro Library System, to look for psychopathology textbooks written or edited by Brazilian authors (UFRJ, Rede Minerva).[1] The same search strategy was extended to main bookstore digital systems, and sites specialized in old or out of print editions, and finally to Google and Google Scholar. The main search string used was "psicopatologia" or "psiquiatria."

RESULTS

An initial list of 35 textbooks was selected. Among them were textbooks translated into Portuguese, not edited or written by Brazilian authors, and which were therefore excluded. Other books without any relevant chapters on MSE were also excluded. Twelve textbooks were finally chosen for the present study. The original list of books found and selected are presented in **Tables 1, 2.** Whenever possible, the first and last edition of each book was consulted, and discussions about systematic ways to conduct MSE, the ordering of MSE topics (distinct functions), orientations about data gathering and registration, definitions about "mental functions" and its levels, symptom clusters, groupings and set organization, were studied. Referenced articles and books citations were also checked. In older textbooks, terms and notions that are semantically related to MSE have changed over time. Therefore, any mention of a mental examination that clearly described careful mental observation techniques or descriptions was considered as similar or equivalent to MSE.

A comprehensive review was carried out on Brazilian authors, researchers and literature, focusing on different MSE traditions, describing its various approaches and MSE segmentation around psychic functions. The list of discrete elements assembled into MSE was studied in detail. A structured method to register significant psychopathological abnormalities/anomalies through examinations did show up in the search results. It was identified as "súmula psicopatológica" (psychopathological summary) in some textbooks.

The works examined spanned over the last 49 years. The books were written mostly by psychiatrists with clinical expertise, working as University Professors or lecturers. Most publications were designed to teach psychopathology to medical doctors being trained as a resident/internist in psychiatry. No MSE standard was identified, even though every author confirmed its relevance and consistency.

Most authors provided orientations on how to proceed with a careful patient observation during an interview, aimed at obtaining objective data. The most referred method, to organize and register MSE, consistently cited by some authors, was descriptive psychopathology with a phenomenological orientation. Textbooks agreed and actively encouraged a very detailed description of observed mental functions as the best way to record MSE. Additionally, there was no agreement on how to summarize its components (20–22, 45–54).

Throughout the time span studied, MSE was not the standard term used to refer to psychic examination and was first adopted in 2000 in the Brazilian psychopathology and semiology textbook by Paulo Dalgalarrondo (46), after which it was consistently used. It remains unclear if the term was chosen because of evidence-based efforts on examination, or if it represents a particular tradition. Regardless, Luiz Salvador de Miranda Sá Jr mentioned "mental examination," an expression semantically related (50), and Elias Paim called it "psychic examination" around 1976, as did Leme Lopes in about 1980 (51, 55). The only author that did not use MSE after 2000 was Claudio Lyra Bastos, who still mentioned "Psychic Examination" (47).

All authors used subdivisions to analyze and describe MSE, but each provided a specific set. Even though there was a clear consensus that consciousness could only be artificially fragmented for didactic purposes, no agreement, convergence or discussion about the nature or number of necessary items could be identified. The theoretical basis underlying the operating subdivisions is therefore lacking. It remains unclear how these mental strata turned into a divided set of "mental functions." **Table 2** shows the items that form MSE, according to each author.

A concise examination summary through "súmula psicopatológica" was mentioned by only four authors (21, 22, 45, 47, 48). It was not possible to track the origins of this notion, since the authors did not mentioned or contextualize it. Some hypothesis is developed through discussion.

It is noteworthy that among the initial textbook list, some belonged to a field aimed at researching psychotherapy and psychoanalysis—therefore promoting a broader signification of psychopathology. Although these books were not included, and considering that psychoanalytic psychopathology is different from descriptive psychopathology, it probably suggests that psychoanalysis has had some influence in Brazilian psychiatric practices, perhaps in a slightly different way than what occurred in the United States (33, 56, 57). The term "interview" has widespread use when referring to the diagnostic and therapeutic encounter with patients, including psychoanalytical sessions,

[1] https://minerva.ufrj.br

TABLE 1 | Textbook set with editions, publication years, and the 12 titles (in bold) chosen for investigation of MSE.

Textbook	Author/editor	Edition	Publication year
1. Psychopathology course[a] (Curso de psicopatologia)	Isaías Paim	1st, 11th	1969, 1993
2. Treaty of psychiatry[a] (Tratado de psiquiatria)	Augusto Luiz Nobre de Melo	1st, 3rd	1970, 1981
3. Treaty of clinical psychiatry[a] (Tratado de clínica psiquiátrica)	Isaías Paim	1st	1976
4. Diagnoses in psychiatry[a] (Diagnóstico em psiquiatria)	José Leme Lopes	1st	1980
5. Psychopathology fundamentals[a] (Fundamentos de psicopatologia)	Luiz Salvador de Miranda Sá Jr	1st	1988
6. Psychopathology and semiotics of mental disorders[a] (Psicopatologia e semiologia dos transtornos mentais)	Paulo Dalgalarrondo	1st, 2nd	2000, 2008
7. Basic psychiatry[a] (Psiquiatria básica)	Mario Rodrigues Louzã Neto and Helio Élkis	2nd	2007
8. Manual of psychopathology[a] (Manual de psicopatologia)	Ellie Cheniaux	4th, 5th	2011, 2015
9. Manual of psychic exam: an introduction to psychopathology[a] (Manual do Exame Psíquico uma Introdução a Psicopatologia)	Claudio Lyra Bastos	3rd	2011
10. Compendium psychiatric clinic[a] (Compêndio de Clínica psiquiátrica)	Forlenza and Miguel	1st	2012
11. Basic psychopathology and psychiatry[a] (Psicopatologia e psiquiatria básicas)	Geraldo José Ballone, José Carlos Souza, and Liliana Andolphi M. Guimarães	2nd	2013
12. Manual of descriptive psychopathology and psychiatry semiology[a] (Manual de psicopatologia descritiva e semiologia psiquiátrica)	Leonardo F. Fontenelle and Mauro V. Mendlowicz	1st	2017
13. Psychopathology contributions and psychiatry clinic[a] (Psicopatologia Contribuições a Clínica Psiquiátrica)	Cleto Brasileiro Pontes	1st	2000
14. Abnormal psychology: clinical perspectives on psychological disorders (Psicopatologia)	Susan K. Whitbourne	7th	2015
15. Psychopathology: theory and clinic[a] (Psychologie pathologique: théorique et clinique)	Jean Bergeret	19th	2004
16. Scheduled meeting with madness: teaching and learning psychopathology[a] (Encontro marcado com a loucura: ensinando e aprendendo psicopatologia)	Tania Cocciufo	1st	2008
17. Psychopathology: fundamentals, disorders, and consequences of chemical addiction[a] (Psicopatologias: fundamentos, transtornos e consequencias da dependencia química)	Rita Campos Ferreira	1st	2015
18. Teaching-learning of psychopathology: a colective project[a] (Ensino-aprendizagem de psicopatologia: um projeto coletivo)	Ligia Maria Ananias Cardoso	1st	2004
19. Psychopathology of daily clinic[a] (Psicopatologia da clínica cotidiana)	Gustavo Fernando Julião de Souza	1st	2015
20. Foundations of psychopathology	John C. Nemiah, Kenneth Appel	1st	1981
21. Manual of general psychopathology[a] (Manual de psicopatologia general)	Pedro J. Mesa, Pedro J. Mesa Cid, and Juan F. Rodriguez Testal	1st	2010
22. Manual of psychopathology[a] (Manual de psicopatologia)	Diogo Telles correia	1st	2013
23. Phenomeno-structural psychopathology[a] (Psicopatologia fenomeno estrutural)	Anna Elisa de Villemor Amaral	1st	2010
24. Psychiatry for general doctor[a] (Psiquiatria para o medico generalista)	Gustavo C. Mansur	1st	2013
25. Psychoanalytic clinics of contemporaneous psychopathology[a] (A clinica psicanalitica das psicopatologias contemporâneas)	Gley P. Costa	1st	2007

(Continued)

TABLE 1 | Continued

Textbook	Author/editor	Edition	Publication year
26. Adolescence et psychopathologie[a] (Adolescência e psicopatologia)	Daniel Marcelli and Alain Braconnier	8th	2013
27. Homeopathic practices in psychopathology (Pratique homéopathique en psycho-pathologie)[a]	Jacqueline Barbancey	1st	1981
28. Introduction to psychopatology[a] (Introduction à la psychopathologie)	Jean Ménéchal	1st	2007
29. Lived time: phenomenological and psychopathological studies (Le Temps vécu. Étude Phénoménologique et Psychopathologiques)	Eugéne Minkowski	1st	2013
30. Abnormal psychology: an integrative approach	David H. Barlowe and V. Mark Duran	8th	2018
31. Evolutionary psychopathology[a] (Psicopatologia evolutiva)	Francisco B. Assumpção Jr.	1st	2008
32. Fundamental psychopathology research[a] (Pesquisa em psicopatologia fundamental)	Edilene Freire de Queiroz, Antonio Ricardo Rodrigues da Silva	1st	2002
33. Conceptual psychopathology[a] (Psicopatologia conceitual)	Adriano C.T. Rodrigues, Luis Guilherme Streb, Maurício Viotti Daker, Octavio Domont de Serpa Júnior	1st	2012
34. The black book of contemporary psychopatology[a] (El libro negro de la psicopatologìa contemporánea)	Alfredo Jerusalinsky, Silvia Frendrik	1st	2011
35. Phenomenological contemporary psychopathology[a] (Psicopatologia fenomenológica contemporanea)	Guilherme Peres Messas	1st	2008

[a] *Author translation.*

which may add further confusion when searching for Psychiatric methods of MSE using indexed expressions, and which justifies the frequency of these textbooks in the initial search sample. A better evaluation of such influence would be desirable, but it is out of the scope of this paper.

DISCUSSION

Mental Health as a Brazilian tradition started in the nineteenth-century, after the creation of the hospice, by a Portuguese emperor (58–61). It was not before the beginning of 1900, however, that academic psychiatry began to thrive, particularly after studies published by Juliano Moreira, Ulisses Pernambucano, followed by studies on forensic psychiatry published by Nina Rodrigues and Franco da Rocha psychiatry (62–64).

The first psychopathology textbook edited by a Brazilian author was published by Isaías Paim at the very end of the 1960s (52), as far as we were able to trace. Paim's textbook stresses that psychopathology is not a psychiatric "tool," but an entirely different "science," that could be applied by psychiatrists to comprehend and investigate mental illness (52). Influenced by German and French authors, Paim thoroughly recommended detailed observations and descriptions of subjective reports (52) and behaviors as the best way to register and carry out psychic examination (55). This coupling of observation and description was continually reinforced by most authors analyzed (20–22, 45–55, 65).

The vast majority of textbooks considered MSE with clear subdivisions, except Paim's (55) Psychiatry Treatise. The number of partitions ranged from 6 (49) up to 18 items (45). The first time they are referred to as "Mental Functions" in our textbook sample was in Dalagalarrondo's "Psicopatologia e Semiologia" (46). Despite considerable variations in mental function descriptions and items adopted, all authors have explicitly considered the following mental functions: consciousness, perception, thought (not frequently comprising its 3-fold structure—Flow, Process, and content/Beliefs), memory, attention, orientation, and volition. Paim did not list mental functions in his treatise but had openly used it in his 1969 psychopathology textbook. These conceptual developments in Brazilian psychopathology call for further studies. We considered them as hints at the importance of mental function fragmentation and structure in psychopathology.

It was not possible to identify how subdivisions were adopted or created according to Brazilian textbooks. The lack of theoretical background may be responsible for the significant variation observed. Dividing or stratifying MSE seems to be the best method to analyze and to conveniently engage in description efforts, to evaluate psychic life. A discussion concerning ways to split MSE for adequate observation and educational purposes is out of the scope of the present review, but highly desirable. Since there are no globally standardized guidelines on psychopathology training (66), bedside examination skills must be regarded seriously, as an asset worth further exploring.

This chronologically considered textbook series, suggests that the first Brazilian authors that wrote about psychopathology—Nobre de Melo, (49) and Isaías Paim, (52)—did not aim to or were not used to describe MSE as mental function subdivisions, but were eager to build long and meticulous reports of observed behavior, through a personal interaction with patients. Contemporary Brazilian authors however usually mention clear descriptions of mental function subdivisions, setting standards on how to study MSE and how to describe it. It was not

TABLE 2 | MSE in the investigated textbooks, number of items, how it is named, and their items or assessed functions.

Textbook	N° of items	How MSE is named	Items
Psychopathology Course[a] (Curso de Psicopatologia) Isaías Paim, 1st edition, 1969	12	No term	1. Perception Disturbances—Illusions and basic perception phenomena (Alterações da Percepção) 2. Representations Disturbances—Hallucinations and Imagination (Alterações das Representações) 3. Concepts—Think Process (Alterações dos Conceitos) 4. Judgments—Delusions, but also insight and Reasoning (Alterações do Juízo) 5. Reason—Flow of Thinking, but also Thinking Process and Associative Process (Alterações do Raciocínio) 6. Disturbances of Memory (Alterações da Memória) 7. Disturbances of Attention (Alterações da Atenção) 8. Disturbances of Orientation (Alterações da Orientação) 9. Disturbances of Consciousness (Alterações da Consciência) 10. Disturbances of Affect and Emotions (Alterações da Afetividade) 11. Disturbances of Volition and Execution (Alterações da Atividade Voluntária) 12. Disturbances of Speech and Language (Alterações da Linguagem)
Treatise of Psychiatry[a] (Tratado de Psiquiatria) Augusto Nobre de Melo, 1st edition, 1970	6	No Term	1 Consciousness and Its Abnormalities: Attention, Orientation—Self Experience, Time Experience, Temporal Experience (Da Consciência e suas Perturbações: Atenção, Orientação—Consciência do Eu, Vivências Temporais e Espaciais) 2 Intelligence and Its Abnormalities (Da Inteligência e suas Anormalidades) 3 Elementary Intellectual Activity: Perception and Memory (Atividades Intelectuais Elementares: Percepção e Memória) 4 Superior Intellectual Activity: Comprehension, Ideation, Imagination, Association, Thinking, Judgment, Reasoning, Expression (Atividades Intelectuais Superiores: Compreensão, Ideação, Imaginação, Associações, Pensamento, Juízo, Raciocínio e Expressão) 5 Psychopathology Affect: Emotions and Feelings (Psicopatologia da Afetividade: Emoções e Sentimentos) 5.1 Primary Emotions (Emoções Primárias): Shock (Choque), Choleric Affect (Emoção Colérica), Affectionate Affect (Emoção Afetuosa); 5.2 Secondary Emotions (Emoções Secundárias): Sensorial Affective State (Estados Afetivos Sensoriais),Vital Affective State (Estados Afetivos Vitais); Derivative Emotions (Emoções Derivadas e Mistas), Soul and Spiritual Feelings (Sentimentos Anímicos e Espirituais); Passion and Tendencies (Inclinações e Paixões) 6 Volition and Execution Psychopathology (Psicopatologia da Vontade): 6.1 Elementary Automatism: Acquired Automatism, Voluntary and Involuntary Activity (Automatismos Elementares: Adquiridos, Voluntárias e Involuntárias) 6.2 Volition Nature (Natureza da Vontade) 6.3 Volition Anomalies (Perturbações da Vontade): Pathological Impulse (Impulsos Patológicos), Perversions and Compulsions (Compulsões e Perversões), Alterations of Psychomotricity (Alterações da Psicomotricidade)
Treatise of Clinical Psychiatry[a] (Tratado de Clínica Psiquiátrica) Paim, 1st edition, 1976	14	Psychic exam	Does not establish a clear division between mental functions, but describe 14 segments to analyze
Diagnoses in Psychiatry[a] (Diagnóstico em Psiquiatria) Leme Lopes, 1st edition, 1980	9	Psychic Exam	1. Presentation (Apresentação) 2. Consciousness - Dimensions; Orientation: Time, Space and Person; Attention (Consciência—Nível; Orientação: Autopsíquica, Alopsíquica e somatopsíquica; Atenção) 3. Disturbance of Memory (Memória) 4. Disorders of Perception (Percepção) 5. Affect and Emotional Disorders (Afetividade) 6. Thinking—Process and Beliefs (Pensar—Forma e Conteúdo) 7. Psychomotricity—Motricity, Volition (Psicomotricidade—Motricidade, Volição) 8. Personality (Personalidade) 9. Insight
Psychopathology Fundamentals[a] (Fundamentos de Psicopatologia) Miranda Sá Jr, 1st edition, 1988	9	Mental Exam	1. Ambient description and Personal Presentation (Descrição do Paciente e Condições Ambientais) 2. Appearance and Behavior (Aspecto Geral e Comportamento Espontâneo) 3. Attitude and Cooperation (Atitude Frente ao Exame)

(Continued)

TABLE 2 | Continued

Textbook	N° of items	How MSE is named	Items
			4. Cognition: Perception, Attention, Thinking, Imagination (Estado da Cognição: Sensopercepção, Atenção, Pensamento, Imaginação) 5. Affect: Volition,Affect and Emotions (Afetividade: Pulsões, Emoções e Sentimentos) 6. Psychomotricity: Motor Activity and Language (Estado da Motricidade: Psicomotricidade, Expressão e Linguagem) 7. Consciousness—Vigilance (Estado da Consciência—Vigilância) 8. Memory (Estado da Memória) 9. Orientation (Estado da Orientação)
Psychopathology Course[a] (Curso de Psicopatologia) Isaías Paim, 11th edition, 1993	13	No term	1. Perception—Illusions and basic perception phenomena (Alterações da Percepção) 2. Representations—Hallucinations and Imagination (Alterações das Representações) 3. Concepts—Thinking Process (Alterações dos Conceitos) 4. Judgments—Beliefs, but also insight and Reasoning (Alterações do Juízo) 5. Reason—Think Flow, but also Thinking and Associative Process (Alterações do Raciocínio) 6. Disturbances of Memory (Alterações da Memória) 7. Disturbances of Attention (Alterações da Atenção) 8. Disturbances of Orientation (Alterações da Orientação) 9. Dimensins of Consciousness (Alterações da Consciência) 10. Affect and Emotions (Alterações da Afetividade) 11. Volition and Execution (Alterações da Atividade Voluntária) 12. Life Tendencies—Volitional Instincts (Alterações das Tendências Vitais) 13. Language and Speech (Alterações da Linguagem)
Psychopathology and Semiotics of Mental Disorders[a] (Psicopatologia e Semiologia dos Transtornos Mentais) Paulo Dalagalarrondo 1st edition, 2000; 2nd edition 2008	14	Psychic exam/MSE	1. Consciousness and its Disturbances (A Consciência e suas Alterações) 2. Attention and its Disturbances (A Atenção e suas Alterações) 3. Orientation and its Disturbances (A orientação e suas Alterações) 4. Disturbances of Memory (Memória) 5. Intelligence (Inteligência) 6. Language and Speech (Linguagem) 7. Affect and Emotions (Afetividade) 8. Volition (Vontade) 9. Execution (Psicomotricidade) 10. Personality (Personalidade) 11. Perception (Sensopercepção) 12. Thinking—Flow, Process and Beliefs (Pensamento) 13. Insight (Juízo de Realidade) 14. Self-awareness (Vivência do Eu)
Manual of Psychopathology[a] (Manual de Psicopatologia) Elie Chenieux, 1st edition, 2002; 3rd edition, 2005; 4th edition, 2008;4th edition, 2011; 5th edition, 2015	18	Psychic exam/MSE "Súmula psicopatológica"	1. Appearance (Aparência) 2. Attitude (Atitude) 3. Consciousness—Vigilance and Dimensions (Consciência—Vigilância) 4. Attention (Atenção) 5. Perception (Sensopercepção) 6. Memory (Memória) 7. Language (Linguagem) 8. Thinking—Flow, Process and Beliefs (Pensamento) 9. Intelligence (Inteligência) 10. Imagination (Imaginação) 11. Volition (Conação) 12. Pragmatism (Pragmatismo) 13. Psychomotricity (Psicomotricidade) 14. Affectivity—Emotions and Affect (Afetividade) 15. Time, Space and Personal Orientation (Orientação Alopsíquica) 16. Self-awareness (Consciência do Eu) 17. Future Projects (Prospecção) 18. Insight (Consciência de Morbidade)
Basic Psychiatry[a] (Psiquiatria Básica) Louzã Neto and Helio Élkis, 2nd edition, 2007	15	Psychic exam/ MSE "Súmula psicopatológica"	1. Appearance (Aspecto Geral) 2. Dimensions of Consciousness (Nível de Consciência) 3. Time, Space and Personal Orientation (Orientação) 4. Attention (Atenção)

(Continued)

TABLE 2 | Continued

Textbook	N° of items	How MSE is named	Items
			5. Memory (Memória) 6. Perception (Percepção Sensorial) 7. Thinking—Flow, Process, and Beliefs (Pensamento) 8. Language and Speech (Linguagem) 9. Reality Reasoning (Juízo da Realidade) 10. Affect and Emotions (Vida Afetiva) 11. Volition (Volição) 12. Psychomotricity (Psicomotricidade) 13. Intelligence (Inteligência) 14. Personality (Personalidade) 15. Transference (Sentimentos Contra Transferenciais) 16. Insight (Crítica em Relação aos Sintomas e Desejo de Ajuda)
Manual of Psychic Exam: An Introduction to Psychopathology[a] (Manual do Exame Psíquico uma Introdução a Psicopatologia) Lyra Bastos, 3rd edition, 2011	13	Psychic exam "Súmula psicopatológica"	1. Dimensions of Consciousness (Estado de Consciência) 2. Attention (Atenção—Vigilância e Tenacidade) 3. Appearance/Presentation (Aspecto Geral) 4. Attitude and Cooperation (Atitude em Relação ao Entrevistador) 5. Psychomotricity and Behavior (Comportamento e Psicomotricidade) 6. Language and Speech (Linguagem) 7. Time, Space and Personal Orientation (Orientação) 8. Affect and Emotions (Afetividade) 9. Volition and Pragmatism (Vontade e Pragmatismo) 10. Thinking—Flow, Process, and Beliefs (Pensamento) 11. Perception (Sensopercepção) 12. Memory (Memória) 13. Intelligence (Inteligência)
Compendium of Psychiatric clinic[a] (Compêndio de Clínica Psiquiátrica) Forlenza and Miguel, 1st edition, 2012	9	MSE	1. Consciousness and Attention (Consciência e Atenção) 1.1 Self-awareness (Consciência do eu) 1.2 Dimension of Consciousness (Vigília) 1.3 Time, Space and Personal Orientation (Orientação) 1.4 Cognition (Cognição) 1.5 Awareness (Apercepção) 1.6 Responsiveness (Responsividade) 1.7 Alertness (Alerta) 1.8 Attention (Atenção) 1.9 Mental Activity Course (Curso da Atividade Mental) 2. Memory (Memória) 3. Inteligence (Inteligência) 4. Perception (Alterações da Sensopercepção) 4.1 Imagination (Imaginação) 4.2 Representation (Alterações da Representação) 4.3 Temporal and Spatial Experience (Tempo e Espaço: Vivência e Rendimento) 5. Thought and Language (Pensamento e Linguagem) 6. Reasoning (Juízo) 7. Affect (Afetividade) 8. Volition: Impulse, Instinct and Will (Volição: Impulso, Instinto e Vontade) 9. Movement (Movimento)
Basic Psychopathology and Psychiatry[a] (Psicopatologia e Psiquiatria Básicas) Geraldo José Ballone, José Carlos Souza, and Liliana Andolphi M. Guimarães, 2nd edition, 2013	11	MSE	1. Appearance and General Behavior (Aparência e Comportamento Durante o Exame) 2. Relationship with Interviewer (Relação com o Entrevistador) 3. Attention and Consciousness (Consciência e Atenção) 4. Time, Space and Personal Orientation (Orientação) 5. Thinking—Flow and Beliefs (Pensamento) 6. Memory (Memória) 7. Affect and Emotions (Afetividade) 8. Perception (Sensopercepção) 9. Volition (Vontade) 10. Psychomotricity (Psicomotricidade) 11. Intelligence (Inteligência)

(Continued)

TABLE 2 | Continued

Textbook	N° of items	How MSE is named	Items
Manual of Descriptive Psychopathology and Psychiatry Semiology[a] (Manual de Psicopatologia Descritiva e Semiologia Psiquiátrica) Leonardo F. Fontenelle and Mauro V. Mendlowicz, 1st edition, 2017	16	MSE "Súmula psicopatológica"	1. Appearance (Aparência) 2. Nonverbal Communication (Comunicação Não Verbal) 3. Verbal Communication (Comunicação Verbal) 4. Consciousness (Consciência) 5. Attention (Atenção) 6. Time, Space and Personal Orientation (Orientação) 7. Self-consciousness (Consciência do Eu) 8. Intelligence (Inteligência) 9. Memory (Memória) 10. Thinking—Reasoning, Process and Flow (Pensamento) 11. Language and Speech (Linguagem) 12. Perception (Sensopercepção) 13. Imagination (Imaginação) 14. Needs/Volition (Necessidades) 15. Affect and Emotions (Afetividade) 16. Psychomotricity (Psicomotricidade)

[a]Authors translation.
Mental functions translated by the author.

possible to identify a "standard" MSE organization, although a written description of all that is observed is consistent in both older and recent textbooks (20–22, 45–48, 50, 51, 53–55, 65). We could not identify any efforts aimed toward comparative clinical psychopathology.

The origins of the clinical resume called "súmula psicopatológica" could not be identified. It may have a forensic and juridical background, as its etymology suggests. Besides lawsuit writing rights, there were many other compulsory examination practices that the Brazilian and then the eugenics Constitution (1937) recommended. Psychiatrists were accountable for defining a person's state of mental health in many common judiciary cases such as criminal subjects, couples before marriage, institutionalized children, among others. For instance, forensic demands synthesis during a long diagnostic process and extensive judicial records.

Some leading psychiatrists, such as Franco da Rocha were very fond of this reporting procedure after clinical examination. A historiographic article, reviewing old patient files, depicts an explicit use of "súmula" by psychiatrists (67–69) when writing down their patient's observations around 1929. It is then possible to affirm that the use of "súmula" as the name given to the set of observed signs and symptoms in psychiatric interview was already widespread in Brazilian psychiatry by the early twenties.

Within the textbook set investigated, the first register of the word "súmula"—as a concise list of mental function subdivisions, containing psychopathological disturbances, observed through MSE—appears in Dalgalarrondo's textbook (46). The term "súmula psicopatológica" was also mentioned in Cheniaux psychopathology treatise (70). Cheniaux's communication, however, admitted that this precise notion had been in colloquial use since the early 90s, and declared that he was first introduced to it by prof Dr. Miguel Chalub, who also introduced him to categorized lists of mental functions with descriptive purposes[2].

Chalub, in turn, declared that he learned this exact expression from Professor José Leme Lopes, the chairman of UFRJ Psychiatric Institute in the seventies.[2] However, Leme Lopes' "Diagnoses in Psychiatry," published in 1980 does not contain any mention of it (51). Neither Chalub nor Cheniaux needed to trace its roots but acknowledged its common use in bedside practices. Both authors hypothesized that it was borrowed from international psychopathological tradition, and that it become mainstream through everyday use in many institutional facilities in Brazil. The same inference about the expression "mental function" might therefore be adopted.

Efforts to standardize medical examinations have been at the core of scientific experimental medicine. These attempts have branched alongside psychopathology developments. The systematization of diagnostic psychiatric interview has been considered a significant step toward the improvement of clinician reliability. However, doubts about the best way to use it clinically, still remains (15, 71, 72). Countries, like Denmark, have already regulated the use of at least one standard interview in clinical practice, for any diagnosis in psychiatry (73) and others such as Australia use diagnostic tools in a mental health triage (74, 75). These are anamnesis/interview standardized methods however, not MSE.

ICD and DSM contain examining tools (Schedules for Clinical Assessment in Neuropsychiatry—SCAN, Structured Clinical Interview for DSM-5 Disorders—SCID-5, Mini International Neuropsychiatric Interview—MINI) (76–78). OPCRIT is supposedly useful to organize MSE, although it seems vastly different from what is usually accepted in descriptive psychopathology, since it provides neither mental function subdivisions nor any coordinated step care to enhance MSE observation and description (79). Nevertheless, the entire MSE procedure demands more than a structured interview, since it is not analogous to anamnesis, but correlated to the PE procedure. We suppose that MSE is not entirely congruent or wholly embedded in semi-structured interview protocols. Attempting to

[2]Personal Communication.

turn personal experiences into objective data is probably a source of unreliability between examiners, as previously described (19, 80–84). As far as we know, there is no standard method or procedure for MSE.

Parnas argues that DSM-V and ICD-10 were constructed to avoid subjectivity, but its developers have not accomplished such intent (23). He emphasizes that it is easy to find objective, observable signs inside many diagnostic criteria, such as "blunt affect" in schizophrenia or "fast speech" in mania. Such categories should have been avoided in a categorial diagnostic system based on a standard interview, that was developed to eliminate examiner opinion as a source of unreliability. In a standard interview, all diagnostic emphasis relies on a "yes" and "no" type series of questions, directed at the patient, who decides if a symptom is or is not present. If MSE categories were to be used in a categorial diagnostic system, it should provide a template MSE method to be followed by the examiner during practice. A list of valid abnormal psychopathological categories for classificatory issues should also be provided.

In Brazil, at least one recent official report, demands a careful description of MSE subdivisions into patient record files (85). The official document on psychiatric training in Brazil states that all candidates must be proficient on MSE skills (apply and record). Despite that, a standard MSE is not explicitly provided, and it is not clear how it should be done or registered (86). The Brazilian Association of Psychiatry (ABP), the professional body responsible for education, training, setting and raising standards in Brazilian Psychiatry, did not mention or provide any statements concerning MSE, until now (4th of May 2018).[3]

Since 2014, doctors that have experience in psychiatry or that have attended a psychiatry internship and desire to obtain a certificate in psychiatry must be submitted to a practical clinical examination test, in which they are observed while interviewing and examining a patient.[3] It is not evident in the documentation how the MSE, or even the clinical interview, would be assessed and what they are expected to perform during a practical examination test (87). The only clue provided is from Dalgalarrondo's textbook inclusion of bibliographic references, which suggests that a detailed descriptive MSE and "súmula psicopatológica" is expected from candidates.

CONCLUSION

Our research suggests that descriptive psychopathology seems to be the usual MSE method used to observe and record data, not much different from the European schools or other parts of the world (80). Seven mental functions were consistently identified in the selected textbooks (consciousness, perception, thought, memory, attention, orientation, and volition), however no standard MSE and mental functions set was found. It was possible to identify a shift from the semiological discussion in Brazil during the last 50 years, from a detailed descriptive routine observed during the patient interaction to an array of observed pathological elements described through a mental function checklist. The "súmula psicopatológica" appears to be one pattern of examination, which could be improved or updated. Ethnopsychiatry or transcultural psychiatry research is needed regarding MSE, to achieve a regional attunement with patients and to comprehend the MSE practice in general.

MSE altogether, with anamnesis or a clinical interview, provides the basis for psychiatric clinics and research. Good clinical exercise and research guidelines in psychiatry must include the development of reliable MSE practice; however, it seems to have been neglected by modern psychiatry and neuroscience. Stressing interview protocols might flatten examination skills and impoverish MSE abilities. Development of better MSE practices and the improvement of bedside skills in psychiatry rely on reviving the psychopathological debate and semiologic reasoning of a vibrant tradition, and allowing for the return to a phenomenology-oriented "observational" technique.

Since we are now dealing with knowledge that has almost become lost, the recovery of the history of psychiatry and of national/regional practices plays a paramount role in bringing previous experiences to the foreground, that could assist in the pursuit of this everlasting objective. In other words, the history of psychiatry plays a critical and hermeneutical role, and particular national attempts and enterprises in psychopathology should be re-evaluated. Practice standardization is now an international goal, but should not lead to one-way, top-down unification from high-tech oriented research centers, as global mental health policies have already advised. A call for diverse, multiple and manifold cultural experiences in MSE is necessary for the future development and improvement in Psychiatric practice and research.

LIMITATIONS

This is a comprehensive review about Psychopathology Textbooks in Brazil and, although rigorous work has been done, it is possible that some critical publication is lacking due to methodological bias. Furthermore, because we dealt with vintage books, which have not yet been cataloged by electronic repositories, it is possible that old Brazilian Textbooks with some contradictory information were not found. Mainstream psychiatry has neglected psychiatric semiology, Mental State Examination, Mental Functions and its role in psychopathology standards and clinical practice, so it is possible that other authors have already answered the questions presented here, which was not picked up by our search strategy. This is a very complicated issue that needs to be addressed by a multi-professional team of linguists, anthropologist, science and medicine historians, and psychiatry practitioners. Further work may clarify and better elucidate these questions and issues.

AUTHOR CONTRIBUTIONS

HR elaborated the search strategy, compiled the main data, and written the text. CE-L reviewed the compiled data, added most of historical data, and reviewed the main text. JL contributed for the elaboration of search strategy, delineated the main objective, and reviewed the final version of the text. MC contributed as main reviewer of data gathering, text writing, and conclusion.

[3]http://www.abp.org.br/portal/

REFERENCES

1. Kasper DL, Braunwald E, Hauser S, Longo D, Jameson JL, Fauci AS. *Harrison's Principles of Internal Medicine*. 16th ed. New York, NY: McGraw-Hill Professional (2006).
2. Porto CC, Lemos PA. *Semiologia Médica*. Rio de Janeiro: Guanabara Koogan (2005). p. 1356.
3. Bickley LS, Bates B, Hoekelman RA. *Bates' Guide to Physical Examination and History Taking*. Philadelphia, PA: Lippincott Williams and Wilkins (1999). p. 789.
4. Bernard C. *Introduction à L'étude de la Médecine Expérimentale Parm*. Baillière: Claude Bernard (1865).
5. Feinstein AR. Boolean algebra and clinical taxonomy. *N Engl J Med*. (1963) 269:929–38. doi: 10.1056/NEJM196310312691801
6. Feinstein AR. Scientific methodology in clinical medicine. *Ann Intern Med*. (1964) 61:1162. doi: 10.7326/0003-4819-61-6-1162
7. Feinstein AR. An additional basic science for clinical medicine: IV. The development of clinimetrics. *Ann Intern Med*. (1983) 99:843. doi: 10.7326/0003-4819-99-6-843
8. Weisz G. The emergence of medical specialization in the nineteenth century. *Bull Hist Med*. (2003) 77:536–75. doi: 10.1353/bhm.2003.0150
9. Ramos Gorostiza P, Adan Manes J. Misunderstanding psychopathology as medical semiology: an epistemological enquiry. *Psychopathology*. (2011) 44:205–15. doi: 10.1159/000322692
10. Flexner A. *Medical Education in the United States and Canada Bulletin Number Four*. The Flexner Report. Carnegie Bulletin (1910). p. 364.
11. Rodrigues AMM, de Freitas CHA, Guerreiro M das G da S, Jorge MSB. Preceptorship in the perspective of comprehensive care: conversations with nurses. *Rev Gaúcha Enferm*. (2014) 35:106–12. doi: 10.1590/1983-1447.2014.02.43946
12. Foucault M, Gros F, Ewald F, Fontana A. *Le Gouvernement de Soi et Des Autres: Cours au Collège de France, 1973-1974*. Paris: Gallimard (2003).
13. Zuardi AW, Loureiro SR. Semiologia psiquiátrica. *Med Ribeirão Preto*. (1996) 29:44–53.
14. Taggart C, O'Grady J, Stevenson M, Hand E, Mc Clelland R, Kelly C. Accuracy of diagnosis at routine psychiatric assessment in patients presenting to an accident and emergency department. *Gen Hosp Psychiatry*. (2006) 28:330–5. doi: 10.1016/j.genhosppsych.2006.05.002
15. Sartorius N, Janca A. Psychiatric assessment instruments developed by the World Health Organization. *Soc Psychiatry Psychiatr Epidemiol*. (1996) 31:55–69. doi: 10.1007/BF00801901
16. Helzer JE. The use of a structured diagnostic interview for routine psychiatric evaluations. *J Nerv Ment Dis*. (1981) 169:45–9. doi: 10.1097/00005053-198101000-00006
17. Chen Y, Li H, Li Y, Xie D, Wang Z, Yang F, et al. Resemblance of symptoms for major depression assessed at interview versus from hospital record review. *PLoS ONE*. (2012) 7:e28734. doi: 10.1371/journal.pone.0028734
18. Martin DC. The mental status examination. In: Walker HK, Hall WD, Hurst JW, editors. *Clinical Methods: The History, Physical, and Laboratory Examinations*. Boston, MA: Butterworths (1990). p. 1087.
19. Aboraya A, First MB. Point/counterpoint: the reliability of psychiatric diagnosis. *Psychiatry*. (2007) 4:22–5.
20. Souza JC, Guimarães LAM, Ballone GJ. *Psicopatologia e Psiquiatria Básicas*. 2nd ed. São Paulo: Vetor (2013). p. 314.
21. Cheniaux EJ. *Manual de Psicopatologia*. 4th edição. Rio de Janeiro: Guanabara Koogan (2011). p. 218.
22. Elkis H, Dalgalarrondo P. Exame psíquico. In: Louzã Neto MR, Elkis H, editors. *Psiquiatria Básica*. Porto Alegre: Artmed (2007). p. 712.
23. Parnas J, Sass LA, Zahavi D. Rediscovering psychopathology: the epistemology and phenomenology of the psychiatric object. *Schizophr Bull*. (2013) 39:270–7. doi: 10.1093/schbul/sbs153
24. Kendler KS, Parnas J. *Philosophical Issues in Psychiatry III : The Nature and Sources of Historical Change*. New York, NY: Oxford University press (2015).
25. Ionescu S. *Quatorze Abordagens de Psicopatologia*. 2ª. Porto Alegre: Artmed (1997). p. 256.
26. Kendler KS, Parnas J. *Philosophical Issues in Psychiatry: Explanation, Phenomenology, and Nosology*. Baltimore, MD: Johns Hopkins University Press (2008). p. 424.
27. Tilley DH, Hoffman JA. Mental status examination: myth or method. *Compr Psychiatry*. (1981) 22:562–4. doi: 10.1016/0010-440X(81)90004-3
28. Jacob KS. Mental state examination: the elicitation of symptoms. *Psychopathology*. (2003) 36:1–5. doi: 10.1159/000069653
29. Blashfield RK. *The Classification of Psychopathology : Neo-Kraepelinian and Quantitative Approaches*. New York, NY: Plenum Press (1984). p. 354.
30. Estellita-lins C. Visibilidade e conhecimento: investigando a semiologia psiquiátrica. In: Rodrigues ACT, Streb LG, Viotti Daker M, Domont De Serpa Junior O, editors. *Psicopatologia Conceitual*. 1st ed. São Paulo: Roca (2012). p. 73–102.
31. Cheniaux E. Psicopatologia descritiva: existe uma linguagem comum? *Rev Bras Psiquiatr*. (2005) 27:157–62. doi: 10.1590/S1516-44462005000200017
32. Viotti Daker M. Revisitando nobre de melo: conceitos em psiquiatria. In: Rodrigues ACT, Streb LG, Viotti Daker M, Serpa Junior OD, editors. *Psicopatologia Conceitual*. 1st ed. São Paulo: Roca (2012) 31–50.
33. Andreasen NC. DSM and the death of phenomenology in america: an example of unintended consequences. *Schizophr Bull*. (2007) 33:108–12. doi: 10.1093/schbul/sbl054
34. Parnas J. A disappearing heritage: the clinical core of schizophrenia. *Schizophr Bull*. (2011) 37:1121–30. doi: 10.1093/schbul/sbr081
35. Aragona M. The impact of translational neuroscience on revisiting psychiatric diagnosis: state of the art and conceptual analysis. *Balkan Med J*. (2017) 34:487–92. doi: 10.4274/balkanmedj.2017.1190
36. Rodrigues ACT, Banzato CEM. Validade: um exame de seu significado na nosologia psiquiátrica. In: Rodrigues ACT, Streb LG, Daker MV, Serpa Junior OD, editors. *Psicopatologia Conceitual*. São Paulo: Roca (2012). p. 115–30.
37. Flegel KM. Does the physical examination have a future? *CMAJ*. (1999) 161:1117–8.
38. Peixoto AJ. Birth, death, and resurrection of the physical examination: clinical and academic perspectives on bedside diagnosis. *Yale J Biol Med*. (2001) 74:221–8.
39. American Psychiatric Association. *The American Psychiatric Association Practice Guidelines for the Psychiatric Evaluation of Adults. Practice Guidelines*. Arlington, TX: American Psychiatric Association (2015).
40. American Psychiatric Association. *In: Diagnostic and Statistical Manual of Mental Disorders*. 4th Edition. *Text Revision (DSM-IV-TR)*. Arlington, TX: American Psychiatric Association (2000). p. 943.
41. Pan American Health Organization. *ClassificaÇão Estatística Internacional de DoenÇas e Problemas Relacionados à Saúde : Décima Revisão*. 7th ed. São Paulo: Edusp (1999).
42. American Psychiatric Association. DSM-5 Task Force. In: *Diagnostic and Statistical Manual of Mental Disorders : DSM-5*. 5th ed. Arlington, VA; Washington, DC: American Psychiatric Association (2013). p. 947.
43. Banzato CEM. Assigning things to their proper class: taxonomic issues and trends in psychiatry. *Rev Latinoam Psicopatol Fundam*. (2002) 5:11–9. doi: 10.1590/1415-47142002001002
44. Ludwik F. *Genesis and Development of a Scientific Fact*. Chicago, IL: The University of Chicago Press (1979).
45. Cheniaux EJ. *Manual de Psicopatologia*. 5th ed. Rio de Janeiro: Guanabara Koogan (2015). p. 230.
46. Dalgalarrondo P. *Psicopatologia e Semiologia dos Transtornos Mentais*. Porto Alegre: Artes Medicas (2000).
47. Bastos CL. *Manual do Exame Psíquico*. 3rd ed. Rio de Janeiro: Revinter (2011). p. 351.
48. Fontenelle LF, Mendlowicz MV. *Manual de Psicopatologia Descritiva e Semiologia Psiquiátrica*. 1st ed. Rio de Janeiro: Revinter (2017). p. 123.
49. Nobre de Melo AL. *Psiquiatria*. 1ª. São Paulo: Atheneu Editora (1970). p. 585.
50. de Miranda-Sá LS Jr. *Fundamentos de Psicopatologia*. 1st ed. Rio de Janeiro: Atheneu Editora (1988). p. 352.
51. Leme Lopes J. *Diagnóstico em Psiquiatria*. 1st ed. Rio de Janeiro: Cultura Médica (1980). p. 235.
52. Paim I. *Curso de Psicopatologia*. 1ª. São Paulo: Editora Fundo de Cultura (1969). p. 136.
53. Paim I. *Curso de Psicopatologia*. 11th ed. São Paulo: Editora Pedagógica e Universitária (1993). p. 285.

54. Del Sant R, Marchetti RL, Tavares H, Wang Y-P, Cordás TA. Avaliação psicopatológica ao longo da vida. In: Forlenza OV, Miguel EC, editors. *Compêndio de Clínica Psiquiátrica.* 1ª. Barueri: Manole (2012). p. 708.
55. Paim I. *Tratado de Clínica Psiquiátrica.* 1ª. São Paulo: Editora Grijalbo (1976). p. 647.
56. Aboraya A, Nasrallah H, Muvvala S, El-Missiry A, Mansour H, Hill C, et al. The standard for clinicians' interview in psychiatry (SCIP): a clinician-administered tool with categorical, dimensional, and numeric output-conceptual development, design, and description of the SCIP. *Innov Clin Neurosci.* (2016) 13:31–77.
57. Wilson M. DSM-III and the transformation of American psychiatry: a history. *Am J Psychiatry.* (1993) 150:399–410. doi: 10.1176/ajp.150.3.399
58. Moreira J. Notícia sobre a evolução da assistência a alienados no Brasil (1905). *Rev Latinoam Psicopatol Fundam.* (2011) 14:728–68. doi: 10.1590/S1415-47142011000400012
59. Galdini AM, Oda R, Dalgalarrondo P. O início da assistência aos alienados no Brasil ou importância e necessidade de estudar a história da psiquiatria. *Rev Latinoam Psicopat Fund.* (2004) 7:128–41. doi: 10.1590/1415-47142004001012
60. Venacio ATA. *As Fases de Juliano Moreira: luzes e Sombras Sobre seu Acervo Pessoal e Suas Publicações.* Rio de Janeiro: Estudos Históricos (2005). Available online at: http://bibliotecadigital.fgv.br/ojs/index.php/reh/article/viewFile/2241/1380
61. Coelho Edler F, Edler FC. A medicina brasileira no século XIX: um balanço historiográfico. *Asclepio.* (1998) 50:169–86.
62. Oda A, Dalgalarrondo P. Juliano Moreira : um psiquiatra negro frente ao racismo científico. *Rev Bras Psiquiatr.* (2000) 22:178–9. doi: 10.1590/S1516-44462000000400007
63. Ana Teresa A. Venancio. Doença mental, raça e sexualidade nas teorias psiquiátricas de Juliano Moreira. *Physis Rev Saúde Coletiva.* (1991) 14:283–305.
64. Assumpção FB Jr. *Psiquiatria Infantil Brasileira: Um Esboço Histórico.* Lemos (1995).
65. Dalgalarrondo P. *Psicopatologia e Semiologia dos Transtornos Mentais.* 2ª edição. Porto Alegre: Artmed (2008). p. 440.
66. Stanghellini G, Fiorillo A. Five reasons for teaching psychopathology. *World Psychiatry.* (2015) 14:107–8. doi: 10.1002/wps.20200
67. Mota A, da Marinho MGSM. *História da Psiquiatria: Ciência, Práticas e Tecnologias de Uma Especialidade Médica.* São Paulo: USP; Faculdade de Medicina: UFABC; Universidade federal do ABC: CD.G Casa de Soluções e Editora (2012).
68. Monarcha C. Escola "Pacheco e Silva" anexada ao Hospital de Juqueri (1929-1940). *Bol Acad Paul Psicol.* (2010) 30:7–20. Available online at: http://pepsic.bvsalud.org/scielo.php?script=sci_arttext&pid=S1415-711X2010000100002
69. Ribeiro PS. *Um Médico, Uma Ideia e um Hospital: Dr. Franco da Rocha e a Concepção do Juqueri. História da Psiquiatria: Ciência, Práticas e Tecnologias Uma Especialidade Médica.* São Paulo: USP (2012). p. 145–58.
70. Cheniaux E. *Manual de Psicopatologia.* 1st ed. Rio de Janeiro: Grupo Gen - Guanabara Koogan (2000). p. 235.
71. Kawa S, Giordano J. A brief historicity of the Diagnostic and Statistical Manual of Mental Disorders: Issues and implications for the future of psychiatric canon and practice. *Philos Ethics Human Med.* (2012) 7:2. doi: 10.1186/1747-5341-7-2
72. Rosenberger P, Lewine R. Conceptual issues in the choice of a structured psychiatric interview. *Compr Psychiatry.* (1982) 23:116–23. doi: 10.1016/0010-440X(82)90056-6
73. Danske Regioner. *Kvalitet i Psykiatrien.* Danske Regioner. (2011). 36 p.
74. Broadbent M, Moxham L, Dwyer T. The development and use of mental health triage scales in Australia. *Int J Ment Health Nurs.* (2007) 16:413–21. doi: 10.1111/j.1447-0349.2007.00496.x
75. Broadbent M, Creaton A, Moxham L, Dwyer T. Review of triage reform: the case for national consensus on a single triage scale for clients with a mental illness in Australian emergency departments. *J Clin Nurs.* (2010) 19:712–5. doi: 10.1111/j.1365-2702.2009.02988.x
76. Wing JK. SCAN: Schedules fonr Clinical Assessment in Neuropsychiatry. *Arch Gen Psychiatry.* (1990) 47:589–93. doi: 10.1001/archpsyc.1990.01810180089012
77. Sheehan DV, Lecrubier Y, Sheehan KH, Amorim P, Janavs J, Weiller E, et al. The Mini-International Neuropsychiatric Interview (M.I.N.I.): the development and validation of a structured diagnostic psychiatric interview for DSM-IV and ICD-10. *J Clin Psychiatry.* (1998) 59(Suppl. 2):22–33; quiz: 34–57.
78. First MB, Williams JBW. *SCID-5-CV: Structured Clinical Interview for DSM-5 Disorders: Clinician Version.* Arlington, TX: American Psychiatric Association Publishing (2016).
79. Brittain PJ, Lobo SEM, Rucker J, Amarasinghe M, Anilkumar APP, Baggaley M, et al. Harnessing clinical psychiatric data with an electronic assessment tool (opcrit+): the utility of symptom dimensions. *PLoS ONE.* (2013) 8:e58790. doi: 10.1371/journal.pone.0058790
80. Häfner H. Descriptive psychopathology, phenomenology, and the legacy of Karl Jaspers. *Dialogues Clin Neurosci.* (2015) 17:19–29.
81. Aboraya A, Rankin E, France C, El-Missiry A, John C. The reliability of psychiatric diagnosis revisited: the clinician's guide to improve the reliability of psychiatric diagnosis. *Psychiatry.* (2006) 3:41–50.
82. Bongiovi-Garcia ME, Merville J, Almeida MG, Burke A, Ellis S, Stanley BH, et al. Comparison of clinical and research assessments of diagnosis, suicide attempt history and suicidal ideation in major depression. *J Affect Disord.* (2009) 115:183–8. doi: 10.1016/j.jad.2008.07.026
83. Gabriel A. Problem-solving strategies in psychiatry: differences between experts and novices in diagnostic accuracy and reasoning. *Adv Med Educ Pract.* (2013) 4:11. doi: 10.2147/AMEP.S38372
84. Kreitman N, Sainsbury P, Morrissey J, Towers J, Scrivener J. The reliability of psychiatric assessment: an analysis. *Br J Psychiatry.* (1961) 107:887–908. doi: 10.1192/bjp.107.450.887
85. Conselho Federal de Medicina. *Resolução N° 2.153, de 30 de Setembro de 2016.* Brasilia (2017). p. 87–8.
86. Comissão Nacional de Residência Médica. *Resolução CNRM N° 02 /2006, de 17 de maio de 2006.* Diário Oficial da União (2006).
87. Abdo CHN. *Edital no 1 de 30 de Junho de 2017 Prova Para Obtenção de Título de Especialista em Psiquiatria (TEP).* Rio de Janeiro: Associação Brasileira de Psiquiatria (2017). p. 23.

11

Processing of Emotion in Functional Neurological Disorder

Petr Sojka[1], Martin Bareš[1,2], Tomáš Kašpárek[1,2] and Miroslav Světlák[1,3]*

[1] *Department of Neurology, Faculty of Medicine, Masaryk University and St Anne's University Hospital Brno, Brno, Czechia,* [2] *Department of Psychiatry, Faculty of Medicine, Masaryk University and University Hospital Brno, Brno, Czechia,*
[3] *Department of Psychology and Psychosomatics, Faculty of Medicine, Masaryk University and University Hospital Brno, Brno, Czechia*

***Correspondence:**
Petr Sojka
sojka5tr@gmail.com

Emotions have traditionally been considered crucial in the development of functional neurological disorder, but the evidence underpinning this association is not clear. We aimed to summarize evidence for association between functional neurological disorder and emotions as formulated by Breuer and Freud in their conception of hysterical conversion. Based on a systematic literature search, we identified 34 controlled studies and categorized them into four groups: (i) autonomic arousal, (ii) emotion-motion interactions, (iii) social modulation of symptoms, and (iv) bodily awareness in FND. We found evidence for autonomic dysregulation in FND; convergent neuroimaging findings implicate abnormal limbic-motor interactions in response to emotional stimuli in FND. Our results do not provide enough empirical evidence for social modulation of the symptoms, but there is a clinical support for the role of suggestion and placebo in FND. Our results provide evidence for abnormal bodily awareness in FND. Based on these findings, we propose that functional neurological symptoms are forms of emotional reactions shaped into symptoms by previous experience with illness and possibly reinforced by actual social contexts. Additional research should investigate the effect of social context on the intensity of functional neurological symptoms and associated brain regions.

Keywords: functional neurological disorder, interoception, emotion, emotional abuse, predictive coding

INTRODUCTION

Functional neurological disorders (FND) refer to patients with neurological symptoms in the absence of neurological disease. These symptoms have also been labeled as "hysterical," "psychogenic," "non-organic," or "medically unexplained." FND are common in neurology wards with the levels of disability similar to epilepsy or multiple sclerosis (1). Despite the long-standing interest in FND and the growing body of neuroimaging research in the last decade, the etiology of FND remains elusive.

Several etiological models of the disorder have been proposed throughout the history with varying degree of suggested psychological function of the symptoms (2). Whereas in the original formulation of hysterical conversion by Breuer and Freud (3) and in the following psychodynamic theories of FND (4, 5), psychological factors, notably emotions, played a crucial role in the etiology of functional neurological disorders, cognitive and later neurobiological models emphasized other than emotional factors and framed FND as defense behaviors (6, 7), and attention and expectation abnormalities (8).

Some authors question the importance of emotions in the etiology of the disorder, because psychological stressors and emotional dysregulation are not always apparent in FND (8). The change in the clinical focus can be seen in the current revision of DSM-V where association of motor or sensory symptoms with psychological cause has been left out from diagnostic criteria for the disorder (as also reflected in the name change from "psychogenic" to "functional neurological disorder"; APA (9). However, recent experimental studies provide some evidence for abnormal limbic-motor interactions in FND and point to the relevance of emotions in the etiology of the disorder.

In this review, we aim to summarize evidence for the hypothesis that functional neurological symptoms are emotional expressions of distress. We build on the original idea of connection between emotions and physical symptoms formulated in *Studies on Hysteria*. In their seminal work, Breuer and Freud (3) suggest that "the excitation arising from the affective idea is 'converted' into a somatic phenomenon" (p.206). The authors claim that FND patients have higher levels of affective (cerebral) excitation and that ideation has greater effect on nervous apparatuses of organs in FND. Following Pierre Janet, the authors of *Studies on Hysteria* also document altered bodily awareness in conversion hysteria.

To address the conversion hypothesis in a manageable way, we break it into the following four questions: (1) Is there evidence for higher sensitivity to emotional distress in FND? (2) Is there a relationship between processing of emotion and motor behavior in FND? (3) Are functional neurological symptoms modulated by social context in a similar way as emotional expressions? (4) Is bodily awareness reduced in FND?

In the review, we focus on the two most prevalent subtypes of FND: psychogenic non-epileptic seizures (PNES) and functional movement disorders (FMD). Even though there is a debate on whether these two classes of symptoms constitute separate disorders (they differ in a few respects such as age at symptom onset and comorbidities) the functional neurological symptoms commonly co-occur and unifying pathophysiology is therefore likely (10).

We aim to bring together biomedical and psychosocial perspectives on FND. While the biomedical perspective highlights abnormalities in a person's psychological and brain functioning, the psychosocial perspective stresses that the illness occurs in individuals with a personal history within an interactional matrix including their family, health care system, and cultural context such that the symptoms may have meaning other than as signs of underlying psychological or brain pathology (11). These two broad perspectives have already been suggested in the Freudian theory of conversion hysteria, in which repression and conversion constituted intrapsychic primary gains in alleviating internal conflict, with the external motivator of illness allowing the individual to escape from difficult social tasks providing secondary gains (12). Even though recent cognitive and brain-based models largely divert from this mechanistic theory, they continue to describe conversion symptoms as a result of intrapsychic or neural process without addressing their possible meanings or social functions. We aim to bridge these two accounts by showing that FND may have a social signaling function rooted in individual pathophysiology.

EMOTION AND INTEROCEPTION

We use recently developed Bayesian predictive coding framework applied to emotion and interoception (13–15) to integrate and understand the research findings presented in the review. A predictive account of interoception provides neurobiologically sound theory that integrates interoceptive, motor and social aspects of emotion. This approach is highly relevant for somatic disorders with hypothesized emotional etiological factors because it places emotional and bodily information within one conception thereby escaping mind-body dualism. Moreover, this framework makes it possible to show how social factors, such as secondary gains, may influence the processing of information about one's body. Predictive coding perspective has been already applied to sensorimotor aspects of FND (16) and to medically unexplained symptoms generally (17). Van den Bergh (17) describe a comprehensive model of symptom perception in medically unexplained symptoms with use of interoceptive predictive coding paradigm. However, none of the Bayesian models focus on interpersonal and social contexts that may shape the intensity of the functional neurological symptoms.

The predictive coding model of brain function is a powerful neurobiological framework postulating that the brain uses its generative model of the world to make predictions about causes of sensory data (18). The predictions are constructed from previous experiences that together constitute brain's internal models of the world. The difference between prediction (also named prior belief or expectation) and sensory data constitutes a prediction error that is used by the brain to refine predictions. By minimizing mismatches between expectations and experience, the brain tries to maximize evidence for its models of the world. Perceptual inference describes a process in which prediction error is minimized by changing the expectation. Alternatively, the brain can change the sampling of sensory data (e.g., change of perspective by head movement) to make them fit the prediction. This process is described as an active inference in a predictive coding framework (19). Whether prediction or sensory sampling is modified depends on the relative precision of the sensory data. If the sensory information is precise, the prediction is likely to change. On the other hand, if sensory input is noisy relative to precise prediction, the brain uses action to minimize prediction error.

The predictive coding framework applied to interoception puts the homeostatic regulation and sensory consequences of the regulation, i.e. interoception, at the core of the mind and brain architecture (15). In this theory, the brain is assumed to regulate homeostasis by issuing predictions about future physiological demands, e.g., the brain predicts oxygen expenditure due to movement, and fulfills these predictions by bodily adjustments, e.g. by increasing the heart rate (15). Successful energy regulation is not possible without building a proper interoceptive model of the body that generates interoceptive predictions.

Agranular visceromotor cortices, including cingulate cortex, and posterior parts of the ventromedial and orbitofrontal cortex, are hypothesized to estimate predicted body requirements based on past experience (13). Interoceptive signals, such as cardiac and respiratory signals, glucose levels, and temperature, are represented in the posterior and mid insula, which serve as the primary interoceptive cortex. The anterior insular cortex is assumed to be a central region in interoceptive pathways that both detect and cause changes of the physiological condition; is also implicated in self-awareness and the salience of exteroceptive information based on personal significance (20, 21).

In humans, social interaction serves in the regulation of homeostasis (22). Because of the late maturation of the human motor system, the homeostatic regulation of infants is highly dependent on the infant's ability to signal needs and the caregiver's ability to perceive these signals and react accordingly. In other words, in infants, the regulation of homeostasis is partially "outsourced" to a caregiver and is therefore an inherently interactional process. An infant's emotional expressions, linked to its internal state (hunger, irritation, anger, etc.) elicit behavioral responses in others, and the detection of these emotional expressions by a caregiver serves as a validation of the internal state and facilitates the proper development of interoception in an infant. Interoception develops early in childhood (23) and its development is influenced by environmental factors (24); notably, childhood abuse has been shown to alter nodes within the interoceptive network (25). Altered interoceptive processing has been associated with alexithymia (26), emotional regulation (27) and development of somatic symptoms (28), all of which are implied in FND.

METHODS

Search Strategy and Selection Criteria

We searched the databases PubMed and Web of Knowledge from 2007 to June 2018. Search terms were ("conversion disorder" OR "functional neurological disorder" OR "psychogenic") AND (emotion* OR affect*). Reference lists of relevant articles were also searched. The results were assessed for inclusion using the publication title and abstract. Studies were included if they conformed to the following inclusion and exclusion criteria. Studies were included if (i) they reported on patients with functional neurological disorder described as functional, non-organic, psychogenic, hysterical, or conversion disorder; (ii) they reported data comparing cases with at least one control group; (iii) we included studies in adult as well as pediatric populations; (iv) we focused our review on experimental studies so we excluded studies that used only self-reports with exception of studies on life events where self-reporting cannot be avoided. The exclusion of self-reports is motivated by the assumption that self-reports targeting emotional processing demand certain capacity for introspection which may be diminished in the studied population of FND patients; (v) neuroimaging studies were only included if they also yielded behavioral or physiological data.

Organization of Studies

The search yielded 622 results. We selected 34 articles which met the above inclusion criteria. A summary of selected studies is presented in **Table 1**. The studies were categorized with respect to the four questions formulated in the introduction and their findings are summarized in the following sections.

Sensitivity to Distress in FND

A number of reviewed studies have provided evidence for higher autonomic sensitivity to emotional stimuli, especially threat signals in FND patients. Seignourel et al. (54) found increased startle reactions to positive and negative pictures in FND patients with no effect of depression or anxiety scores on startle modulation. Yalcin et al. (55) reported increased orienting responses in PNES patients but no difference in auditory startle reaction as compared to healthy participants. The orienting response facilitates attention to a stimulus and the response was shown to be associated with cortical processing, especialy in ventromedial prefrontal cortex and anterior cingulate cortex (62). Bakvis (44) found PNES patients to be more vigilant for social threat stimuli; this increased threat vigilance was related to self-reported trauma. Bakvis (46) also demonstrated a positive correlation between baseline cortisol levels and attentional bias scores for threat stimuli that was specific only to PNES patients and was absent in epilepsy patients and healthy subjects. PNES patients also showed increased avoidance tendencies to social threat cues (47) but other study showed that avoidance learning is impaired in heterogenous FND group (38). In a pediatric FND patients, Kozlowska et al. (37) found increased cortical arousal during an auditory oddball task and the same research group also demonstrated high autonomic arousal at baseline and in response to emotional faces in children with FND (49).

High sensitivity to threat signals and motor mobilization in FND have led several authors to hypothesize that functional neurological symptoms represent forms of human defensive behavior in response to threat (31, 63). However, several studies showed that increased autonomic arousal found in FND is not specific to threat signals (fear and anger faces used mostly in research studies); it has also been reported in perceptions of positive emotional displays (40, 45, 51, 54) suggesting a generalized state of hyperarousal in FND.

With regard to predisposing factors associated with FND, theoretical models and research have traditionally focused on traumatic events such as sexual or physical abuse (64). Dramatic presentations such as nonepileptic seizures or functional gait disorders may motivate a search for equally traumatic triggers. However, the role of trauma in the etiology of FND remains controversial. The presence of traumatic events in the patient's personal history was left out of the main DSM criteria for FND because it is difficult to prove a causal link between life events and symptom onset. Furthermore, some studies question the relevance of traumatic events in the etiology of the disorder because not all patients report a history of traumatic or adverse life events (57, 58, 64).

On the other hand, not all adverse events reported by patients may conform to the definition of trauma as described in the DSM and in the definitions derived from the DSM used in research

TABLE 1 | Processing of emotion in FND: a summary of studies.

Reference	Symptoms	Illness duration	FND (*n*)	Control (*n*)	Stimuli	Task	Outcome measure
(29)	Motor FND	2 years<	12	14 healthy	Sad and fearful Ekman faces	Incidental affective task	Reaction times, BOLD
(30)	Motor FND	13.5 months	12	13 healthy	Personal narratives	Event recall	Reaction times, BOLD
(31)	Motor FND	31 months	10	10 healthy	Pleasant/unpleasant IAPS pictures	Emotional-force control task	Grip force, BOLD
(32)	Functional dystonia	3.5 years	12	12 organic dystonia, 25 healthy	Emotional faces, IAPS	Incidental affective task, oddball task	BOLD
(33)	Functional tremor	4.8 years	27	16 essential tremor, 25 healthy	Emotional faces, IAPS	Incidental affective task, oddball task	BOLD
(34)	Motor FND	Unspecified	20	20 healthy	Neutral/negative IAPS	Emotion regulation task	MEG
(35)	Functional weakness	12 months	21	21 healthy	Neutral/negative IAPS	Passive watching	MEG
(36)	Functional paresis	83 weeks	13	19 healthy	Sad or calm faces	Sensorimotor stimulation	BOLD
(37)	Acute FND	1.5 months (younger), 12 months (older)	57	57 healthy	Tones	Auditory oddball	EEG
(38)	Motor FND	Unspecified	25	20 healthy	IAPS and aversive sounds	Negative conditioning	BOLD
(39)	PNES	4 years	12	12 temporal epilepsy, 24 healthy	Happy, fearful, sad, neutral faces	Incidental affective task	BOLD
(40)	Motor FND	6.4 years	16	16 healthy	Fearful, happy and neutral faces stimuli	Incidental affective task	BOLD
(41)	Motor FND	Unspecified	11	11 healthy	N/A	Action selection task	BOLD
(42)	Motor FND	4.9 years	35	35 healthy	N/A	CTQ, HAMD, HAMA, SCID, BDI, rsfMRI	BOLD, subjective rating
(43)	Motor FND	73 months	16	15 healthy	N/A	Trier social stress task	Salivary cortisol and alpha amylase
(44)	PNES	6.5 years	19	20 healthy	Backwardly masked angry, neutral, and happy faces	Masked emotional Stroop test, Trier Social Stress Test	Color-naming latencies, HRV, cortisol
(45)	PNES	6.5 years	19	20 healthy	Angry, happy and neutral faces	n-back task, cold pressor task	Working memory performance, cortisol
(46)	PNES	6.5 years	19	17 epilepsy, 20 healthy	Angry, happy and neutral faces	Emotional stroop task	Attentional bias, cortisol
(47)	PNES	Unspecified	12	20 healthy	Angry faces	Approach and avoidance task, cold pressor task	Cortisol, action tendencies
(48)	Motor FND	1.5m (younger), 12 m (older)	57	57 healthy	Six facial expressions of emotion	Emotion-identification task	Reaction time
(49)	Motor FND	1.5m (younger), 12 m (older)	57	57 healthy	Emotional faces	Oddball task, the Go/No-Go task, and the facial emotion-perception task	HRV
(50)	Motor FND	Unspecified	25	24 healthy	Facial expressions of emotion	Emotion-identification task	Reaction time, brain volume

(Continued)

TABLE 1 | Continued

Reference	Symptoms	Illness duration	FND (*n*)	Control (*n*)	Stimuli	Task	Outcome measure
(51)	PNES	60 m	39	42 healthy	IAPS pictures	Valence/arousal rating	SCR, SCL, subjective rating
(51)	PNES	54 m	38	43 healthy	Angry, happy, neutral faces	Pictorial emotional Stroop test	Color-naming errors, RT, attentional bias score
(52)	PNES	Unspecified	18	18 PTSD-high, 18 PTSD-low	IAPS pictures	Valence/arousal rating	Subjective rating, cardiac interbeat interval (IBI) and respiratory sinus arrhythmia (RSA)
(53)	Motor FND	7 years	16	17 healthy	N/A	HB detection task	HB accuracy
(54)	Motor FND	37.44 m	12	12 healthy	neg, pos, neu IAPS pictures	Modulation of the startle eyeblink reflex	EMG, subjective rating
(55)	PNES	Unspecified	22	22 healthy	Auditory bursts	Auditory startle response	EMG
(56)	PNES, motor FND, fibromyalgia	Unspecified	41	41 organic neurological disorder	N/A	CTQ, LEC, DERS, PLC-5, HADS	Subjective rating
(57)	Motor and sensory FND	Unspecified	60	39 PTSD, 40 healthy	N/A	SDQ-20, DES, PDS, MACE, TAS-26	Subjective rating
(58)	Motor FND	6 years	64	39 focal hand dystonia, 38 healthy	N/A	CTQ, TLEQ, SRS, PBI, NEO PI-R, BAI, BDI, DES	Subjective rating
(59)	PNES	Unspecified	56	59 healthy	N/A	CTQ, DIS-Q	Subjective rating
(60)	Motor and sensory FND	Unspecified	45	45 healthy	N/A	CTQ, TLEQ, SRS, PBI, NEO PI-R, bal, BDI, DES	Subjective rating
(61)	FND	Unspecified	34 studies with 1405 FND		N/A	Meta-analysis	N/A

studies. The DSM-5 definition of trauma requires "actual or threatened death, serious injury, or sexual violence" (9). Stressful events not involving an immediate threat to life or physical injury, such as psychosocial stressors (divorce, job loss, illness in the family) are not considered trauma by this definition (65). However, more subtle and chronic traumatization such as emotional abuse and the presence of physical or mental illness in family have been shown to have a great impact on the subsequent levels of an individual's psychological functioning (66).

Several reviewed studies suggest relevance of adverse interpersonal relating, such as emotional abuse and neglect in FND. Emotional abuse includes verbal abuse, constant criticism, intimidation, or manipulation over a prolonged period of time (67). Emotional neglect can be considered a subtype of emotional abuse and represents a parent's failure to respond enough to a child's emotional needs and failure to provide touch, affection, nurturance, and attention (68). One recent study showed that the frequency of emotional abuse, but not physical or sexual abuse, significantly differed between FND and healthy controls (60). Karatzias et al. (56) found that childhood physical neglect was significantly associated with FND. Another research group found emotional neglect had a stronger association with the development of FND than physical or sexual abuse (61). Specifically in PNES, Ozcetin et al. (59) found emotional abuse and emotional neglect to be significantly more frequent than in healthy controls. Kruger and Fletcher (69) showed that childhood emotional neglect by the biological parents and later emotional abuse by intimate partners predict the development of dissociative disorders. Importantly, emotional abuse has been associated with insular volume (70) and abnormal connectivity between the right TPJ and left insula (42) in FND patients. The right TPJ has been associated with body-related attentional processes and social cognition (71), and the insular cortex has been repeatedly implicated in processing interoceptive information and emotional awareness (15). Negative childhood experiences modulate the prefrontal-insular-motor cortical network (72) and cumulative adversity alters connectivity and the gray matter volume of nodes within the interoceptive network, even in healthy adults (25, 73). Even if subtle forms of traumatization such as emotional abuse are prevalent in the general population and may not be specific to FND, these experiences may induce significant biological changes and, thus, influence the physiological response to stress in adult life.

Emotion-Motion Interactions in FND

We summarize the body of neuroimaging evidence addressing motor activation during the processing of emotional information in FND patients and further provide an explanatory framework for the reviewed evidence. Several recent studies found distinct patterns of connectivity between limbic regions and motor areas in FND. In an fMRI study, Voon et al. (40) found patients with functional motor disorders having higher functional connectivity between the amygdala and supplementary motor area (SMA) during processing of both positive and negative emotional stimuli. Similarly, in a study by Aybek et al. (29), FND patients showed higher amygdalar activity in response to fearful faces, accompanied by increased activity in the SMA and periaqueductal gray matter, than healthy controls did. In a different paradigm Aybek et al. (30) also found increased activity of the SMA and temporo-parietal junction (TPJ) during recall of emotional memory in FND patients as well as increased functional connectivity between the SMA and amygdala. Specifically in PNES patients, Szaflarski et al. (39) found altered facial emotion processing, as compared with epilepsy patients, which was associated with abnormal motor (putamen) and limbic (parahippocampal gyrus) activations. Abnormal activation in motor areas during emotional tasks was demonstrated also in functional dystonia patients who showed decreased activity in motor cortex bilaterally when compared with patients with primary organic dystonia (32).

Two recent neuroimaging studies investigated the relationship between emotional processing and motor activity directly by manipulating both motor inputs and the emotional valence of the presented stimuli. The finding of increased SMA-amygdala connectivity was replicated by Hassa et al. (36) in patients with functional paresis during passive movement of the paretic hand while patients were watching negative emotional pictures. Blakemore et al. (31) found that FND patients maintained higher force during hand-grip while exposed to negative (but not positive) emotional stimuli relative to healthy participants. The higher force production in patients was associated with activation in the cerebellar vermis, hippocampus, and posterior cingulate cortex; healthy participants engaged the medial prefrontal cortex and inferior frontal cortex, areas associated with motor control.

In a magnetoencephalography (MEG) study, Fiess et al. (34) found that motor FND patients activated areas corresponding to the sensorimotor cortex during emotion regulation but lacked the frontocortical activity seen in healthy controls. During the rapid visual presentation of emotionally salient stimuli with the use of MEG, Fiess et al. (35) found that the automatic detection of emotional salience is unchanged in patients with FND, but involves an emotion-processing network spanning the posterior and sensorimotor areas. Interestingly, a more pronounced involvement of the sensorimotor areas during emotional stimulation was found in participants with high alexithymia scores, i.e., in participants with reduced emotional awareness.

Even during action generated without emotional stimulus, Voon et al. (41) reported lower SMA and higher amygdala, anterior insula, and posterior cingulate activity in conversion motor patients relative to controls in a purely motor task. Bryant and Das (74) reported a case study of functional (conversion) mutism with abnormal connectivity between the amygdala and motor speech center that diminished after the successful treatment of the patient. In concordance with task-based studies, van der Kruijs et al. (75) reported increased functional connectivity between regions involved in emotion and self-perception (insula) and motor preparation (precentral sulcus) in a resting-state fMRI study with PNES patients. Recently, Kozlowska (50) found greater SMA gray matter volume in children with FND associated with faster reaction times in an emotion-recognition task.

The reviewed articles revealed task-based co-activations between limbic structures and motor areas, especially the SMA, in FND. The SMA is activated by a range of tasks that require motor planning (76); it has also been implicated in the processing of emotional information. Oliveri et al. (77) stimulated the SMA with transcranial magnetic stimulation (TMS) during emotional and non-emotional visually cued movements and found increased motor readiness specifically in emotional contexts after SMA stimulation. The involvement of the SMA in emotional processing was replicated by Rodigari and Oliveri (78), who found that rTMS trains over the SMA increased skin conductance and perceived valence of emotionally negative visual stimuli. The authors concluded that the SMA could interface the limbic and motor systems in the transformation of emotional experiences into motor actions (77). Specific SMA connectivity changes have been also shown after listening to dismissive attachment narratives (79) and in affective empathy research (80).

Beyond the known subcortical-motor pathways that mediate automatic and stereotypical motor behaviors in animals and humans in reaction to threat (81, 82), there are several studies documenting limbic system connections to cortical motor-related areas that may mediate complex emotional behaviors. Specific amygdala-motor interactions have been implicated in generating facial expressions in monkeys (83). Similar to animal neuronal tracing studies (84, 85), a few studies suggest the existence of an amygdala-motor pathway in humans. Grezes et al. (86) found direct tracts between the amygdala and cortical motor-related areas including the SMA using diffusion tensor imaging on a large data sample from the Human Connectome Project. Recently, Toschi et al. (87) reported the existence of a distinct amygdala-motor functional network at rest in a large sample of healthy subjects. In humans, the amygdala and motor-related areas have consistently shown coactivation and functional connectivity during the perception of threatening emotional expressions (88). But connectivity between the amygdala and premotor areas may have a more general meaning. In a recent study, Diano et al. (89) examined patterns of activations during the observation of different classes of emotional expressions and found increased functional connectivity between the amygdala and premotor cortices across all observed classes of emotions, suggesting that observing emotional stimuli increases motor excitability and may reflect approach and avoidance preparation, motor mimicry, or emotional contagion.

Although the motor system has been thus far studied mostly apart from the limbic system, and there is a lack of evidence for a specific meaning of limbic-SMA interactions, a few reviewed studies suggested a possible role of the SMA in transforming emotional experience into motor actions. In their FND research, Voon et al. (41) proposed that in an arousing context, abnormal SMA-amygdala connectivity "may facilitate the expression of salient previously learned and mapped conversion motor representations" (s. 2402). The question remains of the context in which such a behavior is learned and motivated. Interestingly, increased resting-state amygdala-SMA connectivity has been reported in adolescents with nonsuicidal self-harm tendencies (90) which are viewed as habitual behaviors influenced by negative affect. These forms of behavior have been shown to be greatly influenced by social conditioning, i.e. by attention or by avoiding stressful social situations (91). The selection of adaptive behavioral responses in specific social contexts, such as signaling approach or avoidance may be relevant for FND.

Social Modulation of Functional Neurological Symptoms

Two inherent features of emotional expressions are that they influence the behavior of others and are also influenced by social context (92). For example, the intensity of a smile or a pained expression is dependent on social attention and the perceived approval of others (93, 94). If functional neurological symptoms are shaped by social context, it may be concluded that they are similar to expressive behaviors such as emotions. However, in contrast to social modulation of pain, the experimental research of social modulation of FNS is almost non-existent in the reviewed literature and the provided evidence for social shaping of functional neurological symptoms is only indirect.

Serious "escape events" preceding FND onset (95) and increased motor activations in FND when reading "escape event" scripts reported by Aybek et al. (30) provide important evidence that the development of functional neurological symptoms may be sensitive to social context. An escape event is a situation in which signaling symptoms influence social context in favorable way. For example, a patient developing functional paralysis can prevent his partner from ending their relationship. Aybek et al. (30) showed that exposure to an escape event description is associated with distinct activations in the right SMA and the right TPJ; brain regions implicated in motor planning and self-consciousness. Similarly, Bryant and Das (74) report that functional (conversion) mutism together with abnormal amygdala-motor connectivity diminished after treatment that targeted motivational factors; in the reported case, it was a motive to remain distant from stressful work duties.

We draw another support for the social modulation of functional neurological symptoms from placebo effect and hypnotic suggestibility research in FND. Recent evolutionary accounts of animal signaling propose that symptoms of illness may have a signaling function with the goal of shaping the behaviors of conspecifics (96). In this perspective, signaling illness can elicit social support and nurturance from others and also reduce aggression and hostility (97). Illness or injury signaling has been documented in animals (98) and as a cultural phenomenon (99). Fotopoulou and Tsakiris (22) noted that the first thing children do after scraping a knee or incurring a similar mild injury is turn to the parent and await their reaction before proceeding with their own behavioral reaction. Reaction to pain has been shown to be modulated to a great extent by expected or perceived social attention and reaction (94). Behaviors similar to FND symptoms, such as abnormalities in posture, temporally uncoordinated movements, movement stereotypes, freezing behaviors, and staring expressions have been observed in children with "disorganized" attachment whose caregivers may exhibit frightening or frightened behavior, be psychologically unavailable to the child, or themselves have unresolved traumatic experiences (100). Such salient behaviors may play a twofold role in child-parent interactions. First, they heighten the likelihood of mobilizing help and treatment even in the dismissive caregiver. Second, they may represent an exaggerated appeasement display or a feigned helpless strategy (101) that functions as a means of reducing aggression from a person upon whom the child depends.

Cultural anthropology research has repeatedly documented that people use physical symptoms to communicate distress in socially acceptable ways (11, 99). For example, *ataques de nervios* is a phenomenon similar to PNES that is common in Latin American societies; it includes fainting, trembling, or convulsions that people use to communicate distress as a way to elicit social support (102). Generally, people with lower levels of social support and low social capital report greater levels of psychosomatic symptoms (103).

The high responsiveness to placebo and nocebo interventions common in various subtypes of FND may also be evidence of the signaling function of functional neurological symptoms. A placebo is defined as a set of behaviors suggesting a clinical benefit (such as inert substance administration and sham physical treatment) or a set of behaviors provoking symptoms in the case of nocebo (104). These medical rituals may elicit or attenuate functional neurological symptoms as appropriate reactions to offered help or attention in a way similar to how social situations elicit or repress certain behaviors. Responsiveness to symptom provocation has been documented in PNES, with a seizure provoked by a saline injection or a mere verbal suggestion (105), and in functional tremor, which can be provoked by applying a tuning fork to a limb (106). Symptom decline after placebo administration has been documented in functional movement disorders (107). Ricciardi and Edwards (108) reported immediate response to botulotoxin in functional dystonia patients even though it takes botulotoxin a few days to take action.

Higher hypnotic suggestibility reported in FND and strikingly similar neural correlates in experiments matching functional symptoms with clinical analogs created by suggestion (109) are in the same line of evidence. Hypnosis can be conceptualized as a non-deceptive placebo (110)—it is a ritualized set of behaviors aiming to elicit a desired response from a hypnotized subject. A higher hypnotic suggestibility in FND patients thus indicates the propensity of patients to react in the desired direction and fulfill the expectations created by a social context.

Body Awareness in FND

Several reviewed studies provide evidence for abnormal interoceptive awareness in FND. Ricciardi et al. (53) reported decreased cardiac interoceptive accuracy in patients with motor FND; this is assumed to reflect trait awareness of interoceptive sensations. Interestingly, the same authors also showed that lower interoceptive sensitivity predicted the tendency of patients with FND to focus on external aspects of the body (53). A marked difference in subjective and objective symptom reports in FND has also been observed; FND patients tend to over-report somatic symptoms, while clinical assessment (111) or actigraphy specifically in functional tremor (112), show low symptom frequency. Similar dissociation was also found between biological and perceived stress in FND (43). In functional tremor patients, Espay et al. (33) found increased activation in paracingulate gyrus which is associated with externally oriented cognitive style, one of the alexithymia dimensions (113). In two recent meta-analyses, Perez et al. (114) and Boeckle et al. (115) summarized consistent patterns of abnormal activations in the ACC and insula in motor FND patients, i.e., in two principal brain regions within the interoceptive network. Cingulo-insular structural alteration has been reported in female FND patients (70). Specifically, reduced left insular volume was shown to be correlated with subjective symptom severity in FND (70).

Synthesis and Discussion of the Findings

The present review sought to summarize support for the hypothesis that functional neurological symptoms are emotional expressions of distress. We derived our hypothesis from the conception of conversion hysteria postulated by Freud and Breuer (116) and selected four areas of interest we now discuss further.

Affective Excitation in FND

The reviewed experimental research studies provide evidence for higher levels of affective excitation in FND postulated by Breuer and Freud (3). Such excitation seems to be generalized for various emotions and it was shown to be present on the level of cortical and autonomic arousal. Moreover, there is also growing body of evidence supporting presence of impaired child-caregiver bonds in FND such as emotional abuse or neglect. Taken together, we propose that due to adverse family environment, FND patients may fail to learn self-regulation strategies when faced with arousing stimuli. The notion that child-caregiver bonds facilitate development of the brain's major self-regulatory mechanisms has considerable empirical support (117). The ability to regulate arousal in infants has been associated with the quality of caregiving they receive (118) and children with poorer quality maternal-child relationships display poorer vagal regulation and lower heart rate acceleration (119). The impaired arousal regulation in FND thus may be partially caused by impaired close social bonds (such as emotional neglect) and not necessarily by repeated exposure to threat.

From the developmental point of view, emotional abuse and neglect, evidenced in FND by several studies, is potentially harmful also for the proper development of interoceptive brain networks. Lack of attunement between child and dismissive caregiver may cause models of internal bodily processes to be inefficient in predicting sensory inputs. Interoceptive signals then become imprecise and orient child more to external aspect of the body in the state of higher arousal. Later on, when primed by experience with illness or injury, the higher precision of exteroceptive inputs relative to interoceptive inputs may lead to symptom onset as falsely inferred cause of emotional distress.

Processing of Emotion and Motor Behavior in FND

The finding of abnormal limbic-motor interactions in a reaction to emotional stimuli seems to be consistent in the reviewed literature. However, there is a debate about the meaning of the limbic-motor interactions among researchers. Two main hypotheses for the finding have been suggested in the reviewed literature: (i) defense mechanism akin to freezing behavior in animals (30, 31), and (ii) previously learned motor conversion representation (Voon). We shortly discuss the proposed explanatory frameworks respectively.

Blakemore et al. (31) interpret their finding of higher grip force in reaction to negative stimuli in FND as giving evidence for similarity between animal defense mechanisms and functional neurological symptoms—similarity already postulated by Kretchmer and Nijenhuis. However, clinical evidence shows that functional neurological symptoms are oftentimes pronounced in the presence of another person in the context of receiving help and attention, e.g., in the context of medical care that is not necessarily threatening. Moreover, defensive behaviors are highly stereotyped reactions (120), on the other hand conversion motor symptoms vary greatly among patients spanning convulsions, paralysis, dystonias, gait and speech abnormalities, and other motor impairments so symptoms do not always appear to have analogs in defense behaviors. Individuals with a history of adverse life events, which is a common factor in many psychopathologies, show pronounced freeze reactions (121). Increased motor mobilization and autonomic sensitivity to emotional stimuli may therefore represent a common feature in multiple psychiatric disorders. Kozlowska (122) proposed that an impaired prefrontal cortex function due to prolonged exposure to stress may lead to impaired motor-executive functions and strengthened affect-driven motor reactions. This can be the case especially in PNES patients whose convulsions are precipitated by a higher state of arousal and followed by a parasympathetic state, suggesting a role of abnormal movement in the regulation of accumulated arousal (123). Future FND studies should include patients with anxiety, depression and other psychiatric disorders as control groups to disentangle general motor mobilization and autonomic sensitivity from limbic-motor interactions specific to FND.

Voon et al. (41) propose that functional neurological symptoms represent a pattern of movement established perhaps by a previous triggering event. This proposal is based on the observation that physical precipitating factors such as injury or illness are often present at symptom onset. Such an event may provide an explanation for bodily noise caused by chronically increased arousal (e.g., muscle tension, trembling, etc.) and gradually develop into an illness prior belief. Voon et al. (41) suggest that in the arousing situation, amygdala-SMA complex is aberrantly engaged and may facilitate expression of previously learned conversion motor representations. According to Edward et al. (16), abnormal self-directed attention may increase precision of the conversion representation and may cause movement or percepts in keeping with this prior belief. Although this theoretical account explains several clinical features of FND, the postulated association between symptoms and limbic-motor activations are only indirect because most of the reviewed studies focused either on motor or emotional variables. Moreover, to our knowledge, there is no research that would examine association between illness beliefs and limbic-motor interactions in FND.

We can only suggest that the proposed explanatory models for the FND are not mutually exclusive and further speculate that the symptoms serve as protective mechanisms patients use to cope with arousing situations (e.g., avoidance tendencies) and these mechanisms are shaped by previous experience with illness or injury. We also propose that the onset of functional neurological symptoms may be motivated by perceived or expected social reactions (e.g., avoiding unpleasant tasks, obtaining care and attention, lowering demands, more control over difficult situation etc.).

Social Modulation of Functional Neurological Symptoms

In our review, we identified only two studies that indirectly examined social modulation of functional neurological symptoms. However, there is (mostly clinical) evidence for the influence of suggestion and placebo on the intensity of functional neurological symptoms. Functional neurological symptoms seem to be sensitive to motivational factors that a patient receive from his immediate environment. As illness or injury is embedded in social system (family, healthcare), illness behavior may be shaped by behavior of others. In childhood, abnormal behaviors similar to the symptoms of a disease may be one of the limited ways how to elicit nurturance in a psychologically absent caregiver. Bowlby (124) suggested that the attachment relationship generates internal working models of self with other through repeated iterations that come to act as templates on which further relationships are build. In the terms of predictive coding account, prior experience with others' reactions to illness influences subsequent predictions of social outcome related to illness. Anticipated or offered help provided to patients by caregivers may evoke previously learned mental models of social relating—if a patient is inclined by prior experiences to expect potential help from others only during bodily threat (during illness, disease), the patient may experience and react to body-related prediction errors differently than when others' support is available. We therefore hypothesize that the emergence of symptoms may be motivated by their predicted social outcome. In 1986, Taylor proposed that hysteria is inseparable from medical care where it gains its validity by repeated examinations and attention from medical professionals (125). Repeated medical examinations may also increase the precision of prior illness beliefs by nocebo conditioning, consequently affecting active inferential processes and ultimately facilitating the development of symptoms.

Body Awareness in FND

Several reviewed studies showed evidence for impaired interoceptive awareness in FND. Edwards et al. (16) has already postulated abnormal body-centered attention as a potential mechanism behind functional neurological symptoms. Although we are sympathetic to this Bayesian framework, the authors focus mainly on sensorimotor system in FND without addressing emergent evidence of impaired interoceptive awareness in FND. The presented research findings suggest abnormal bodily perception in FND in a way that external aspects of the body are given more weight than internal inputs. If interoceptive signals are viewed as highly ambiguous prediction errors, they are more prone to misinterpretations when integrated with more precise external inputs. The ventriloquist effect is an example of the Bayesian integration of two sensory inputs, where an auditory input is bound to a visual input, such that they appear, falsely, to co-occur spatiotemporally (126). The precision of each input is estimated and weighted relative to the other; imprecise auditory input is given less weight than a more precise visual input. Their co-location is determined accordingly, forming the illusion of a sound located in the mouth of a puppet. In an analogy to the ventriloquist effect, ambiguous interoceptive signals (visceral discomfort) are weighted less than precise tactile signals (hand sweating, dry mouth), proprioceptive sensations, and visual (body trembling) information, causing a state of anxiety to be misinterpreted as a bodily symptom instead of a complex emotion. This effect can be pronounced, especially in the context in which prior expectation is primed by preceding experience with unrelated illness or injury. The weight of exteroceptive inputs relative to interoceptive signals may also be amplified by abnormal attentional resources directed toward external aspects of the body commonly observed in FND patients (8). Functional neurological symptoms then arise as a falsely inferred cause of emotional distress resulting from the Bayesian integration of imprecise interoceptive information with relatively precise exteroceptive information. These symptoms may become new forms of emotional reactions in stressful situations and also subjects of reinforcement by actual social contexts or predicted social outcomes as described above.

CONCLUSION AND FUTURE DIRECTIONS

In the review, we showed that emotional processing is an important factor in the etiology of FND. Taken together, we conclude that limbic-motor interactions evidenced in FND may reflect learned emotional behaviors of an individual with low interoceptive (and emotional) awareness and we interpret functional neurological symptoms as forms of complex affective reactions to stress similar to emotional expressions. Future studies should focused on examining brain activations in FND patients in response to stimuli relevant for the disorder, such as attachment narratives or autobiographical information. Moreover, exploring an effect of social context on the intensity of functional neurological symptoms could provide new information about the function of the symptoms.

AUTHOR CONTRIBUTIONS

The literature search for the study was managed by PS. The first draft of the review was written by PS and MB. TK and MS critically revised and commented on the manuscript and figures. All the authors substantially contributed to and have approved the final manuscript.

FUNDING

This study is supported by Ministry of Health of the Czech Republic, grant no. 16-31457A.

REFERENCES

1. Stone J, Warlow C, Sharpe M. The symptom of functional weakness: a controlled study of 107 patients. *Brain* (2010) 133(Pt 5):1537–51. doi: 10.1093/brain/awq068
2. Brown RJ, Reuber M. Psychological and psychiatric aspects of psychogenic non-epileptic seizures (PNES): a systematic review. *Clin Psychol Rev.* (2016) 45:157–82. doi: 10.1016/j.cpr.2016.01.003
3. Breuer J, Freud S. *Studies on Hysteria* (1957). Oxford: Basic Books.
4. Szasz T. *The Myth of Mental Illness.* London:Secker and Warburg (1962).
5. Shoenberg PJ. The symptom as stigma or communication in hysteria. *Int J Psychoanal Psyhother.* (1975) 4:507–17.
6. Kretschmer E. *Hysteria: Reflex and Instinct.* London: Peter Owen. (1948).
7. Nijenhuis ERS, Vanderlinden J, Spinhoven P, Vanderlinden J, van DyckR, van der HartO. Somatoform dissociative symptoms as related to animal defensive reactions to predatory imminence and injury. *J Abnorm Psychol.* (1998) 107:63–73. doi: 10.1037/0021-843X.107.1.63
8. Edwards MJ, Fotopoulou A, Pareés I. Neurobiology of functional (psychogenic) movement disorders. *Curr Opin Neurol.* (2013) 26:442–7. doi: 10.1097/WCO.0b013e3283633953
9. American Psychiatric Association. *Diagnostic and Statistical Manual of Mental Disorders.* Washington, DC: American Psychiatric Association (2013).
10. Edwards MJ. Neurobiologic theories of functional neurologic disorders. *Handb Clin Neurol.* (2017) 139:131–7. doi: 10.1016/B978-0-12-801772-2.00012-6
11. Kirmayer LJ, Santhanam R. The anthropology of hysteria. In: Halligan PW, Bass C, and Marshall JC, editors. *Contemporary Approaches to the Study of Hysteria: Clinical and Theoretical Perspectives.* Oxford: Oxford University Press (2001), p. 251–70.
12. Kanaan RAA. Freud's hysteria and its legacy. *Handb Clin Neurol.* (2016) 139:37–44. doi: 10.1016/B978-0-12-801772-2.00004-7
13. Barrett LF, Simmons WK. Interoceptive predictions in the brain. *Nat Rev Neurosci.* (2015) 16:419–29. doi: 10.1038/nrn3950
14. Chanes L, Barrett LF. Redefining the role of limbic areas in cortical processing. *Trends Cogn Sci.* (2015) 20:96–106. doi: 10.1016/j.tics.2015.11.005
15. Barrett L, Quigley KS, Hamilton P. An active inference theory of allostasis and interoception in depression. *Philos Trans R Soc Lond B Biol Sci.* (2016) 371:20160011. doi: 10.1098/rstb.2016.0011
16. Edwards MJ, Adams RA, Brown H, Pareés I, Friston KJ. A Bayesian account of "hysteria". *Brain* (2012) 135(Pt 11):3495–512. doi: 10.1093/brain/aws129
17. Van den Bergh O, Witthöft M, Petersen S, Brown R. Symptoms and the body: taking the inferential leap. *Neurosci Biobehav Rev.* (2017) 74:185–203. doi: 10.1016/j.neubiorev.2017.01.015
18. Friston K. The free-energy principle: a unified brain theory? *Nat Rev Neurosci.* (2010) 11:127–38. doi: 10.1038/nrn2787
19. den Ouden HEM, Kok P, de Lange FP. How prediction errors shape perception, attention, and motivation. *Front Psychol.* (2012) 3:548. doi: 10.3389/fpsyg.2012.00548
20. Craig ADB. How do you feel–now? The anterior insula and human awareness. *Nat Rev Neurosci.* (2009) 10:59–70. doi: 10.1038/nrn2555
21. Gu X, Hof PR, Friston KJ, Fan J. Anterior insular cortex and emotional awareness. *J Compar Neurol.* (2013) 521:3371–88. doi: 10.1002/cne.23368
22. Fotopoulou A, Tsakiris M. Mentalizing homeostasis: the social origins of interoceptive inference. *Neuropsychoanalysis* (2017) 19:3–28. doi: 10.1080/15294145.2017.1294031
23. Koch A, Pollatos O. Cardiac sensitivity in children: sex differences and its relationship to parameters of emotional processing. *Psychophysiology* (2014) 51:932–41. doi: 10.1111/psyp.12233

24. Ambrosecchia M, Ardizzi M, Russo E, Ditaranto F, Speciale M, Vinai P, et al. Interoception and autonomic correlates during social interactions. implications for anorexia. *Front Hum Neurosci.* (2017) 11:219. doi: 10.3389/fnhum.2017.00219
25. Teicher MH, Anderson CM, Ohashi K, Polcari A. Childhood maltreatment: altered network centrality of cingulate, precuneus, temporal pole and insula. *Biol Psychiatry* (2014) 76:297–305. doi: 10.1016/j.biopsych.2013.09.016
26. Brewer R, Cook R, Bird G. Alexithymia: a general deficit of interoception. *R Soc Open Sci.* (2016) 3:150664. doi: 10.1098/rsos.150664
27. Füstös J, Gramann K, Herbert BM, Pollatos O. On the embodiment of emotion regulation: interoceptive awareness facilitates reappraisal. *Soc Cogn Affect Neurosci.* (2013) 8:911–7. doi: 10.1093/scan/nss089
28. Schaefer M, Egloff B, Witthöft M. Is interoceptive awareness really altered in somatoform disorders? Testing competing theories with two paradigms of heartbeat perception. *J Abnorm Psychol.* (2012) 121:719–24. doi: 10.1037/a0028509
29. Aybek S, Nicholson TR, O'Daly O, Zelaya F, Kanaan RA, David AS. Emotion-motion interactions in conversion disorder: an FMRI study. *PloS ONE* (2015) 10:e0123273. doi: 10.1371/journal.pone.0123273
30. Aybek S, Nicholson TR, Zelaya F, O'Daly OG, Craig TJ, David AS, et al. Neural correlates of recall of life events in conversion disorder. *JAMA Psychiatry* (2014) 71:52–60. doi: 10.1001/jamapsychiatry.2013.2842
31. Blakemore RL, Sinanaj I, Galli S, Aybek S, Vuilleumier P. Aversive stimuli exacerbate defensive motor behaviour in motor conversion disorder. *Neuropsychologia* (2016) 93(Pt A):229–41. doi: 10.1016/j.neuropsychologia.2016.11.005
32. Espay AJ, Maloney T, Vannest J, Norris MM, Eliassen JC, Neefus E, et al. Dysfunction in emotion processing underlies functional (psychogenic) dystonia. *Move Disord.* (2018) 33:136–45. doi: 10.1002/mds.27217
33. Espay AJ, Maloney T, Vannest J, Norris MM, Eliassen JC, Neefus E, et al. Impaired emotion processing in functional (psychogenic) tremor: a functional magnetic resonance imaging study. *NeuroImage Clin.* (2018) 17:179–87. doi: 10.1016/j.nicl.2017.10.020
34. Fiess J, Rockstroh B, Schmidt R, Steffen A. Emotion regulation and functional neurological symptoms: does emotion processing convert into sensorimotor activity? *J Psychosomat Res.* (2015) 79:477–83. doi: 10.1016/j.jpsychores.2015.10.009
35. Fiess J, Rockstroh B, Schmidt R, Wienbruch C, Steffen A. Functional neurological symptoms modulate processing of emotionally salient stimuli. *J Psychosomat Res.* (2016) 91:61–7. doi: 10.1016/j.jpsychores.2016.10.007
36. Hassa T, Sebastian A, Liepert J, Weiller C, Schmidt R, Tüscher O. Symptom-specific amygdala hyperactivity modulates motor control network in conversion disorder. *NeuroImage Clin.* (2017) 15:143–50. doi: 10.1016/j.nicl.2017.04.004
37. Kozlowska K, Melkonian D, Spooner CJ, Scher S, Meares R. Cortical arousal in children and adolescents with functional neurological symptoms during the auditory oddball task. *NeuroImage Clin.* (2017) 13:228–36. doi: 10.1016/j.nicl.2016.10.016
38. Morris LS, To B, Baek K, Chang-Webb Y-C, Mitchell S, Strelchuk D, et al. Disrupted avoidance learning in functional neurological disorder: implications for harm avoidance theories. *NeuroImage Clin.* (2017) 16:286–94. doi: 10.1016/j.nicl.2017.08.007
39. Szaflarski JP, Allendorfer JB, Nenert R, LaFrance WC, Barkan HI, DeWolfe J, et al. Facial emotion processing in patients with seizure disorders. *Epilepsy Behav.* (2018) 79:193–204. doi: 10.1016/j.yebeh.2017.12.004
40. Voon V, Brezing C, Gallea C, Ameli R, Roelofs K, LaFrance WC, et al. Emotional stimuli and motor conversion disorder. *Brain* (2010) 133(Pt 5):1526–36. doi: 10.1093/brain/awq054
41. Voon V, Brezing C, Gallea C, Hallett M. Aberrant supplementary motor complex and limbic activity during motor preparation in motor conversion disorder. *Move Disord.* (2011) 26:2396–403. doi: 10.1002/mds.23890
42. Maurer CW, LaFaver K, Ameli R, Epstein SA, Hallett M, Horovitz SG. Impaired self-agency in functional movement disorders. *Neurology* (2016) 87:564–70. doi: 10.1212/WNL.0000000000002940
43. Apazoglou. Biological and perceived stress in motor functional neurological disorders. *Psychoneuroendocrinology* (2017) 85:142–50. doi: 10.1016/j.psyneuen.2017.08.023
44. Bakvis P, Roelofs K, Kuyk J, Edelbroek PM, Swinkels WAM, Spinhoven P. Trauma, stress, and preconscious threat processing in patients with psychogenic nonepileptic seizures. *Epilepsia* (2009) 50:1001–11. doi: 10.1111/j.1528-1167.2008.01862.x
45. Bakvis P, Spinhoven P, Putman P, Zitman FG, Roelofs K. The effect of stress induction on working memory in patients with psychogenic nonepileptic seizures. *Epilepsy Behav.* (2010) 19:448–54. doi: 10.1016/j.yebeh.2010.08.026
46. Bakvis P, Spinhoven P, Roelofs K. Basal cortisol is positively correlated to threat vigilance in patients with psychogenic nonepileptic seizures. *Epilepsy Behav.* (2009) 16:558–60. doi: 10.1016/j.yebeh.2009.09.006
47. Bakvis P, Spinhoven P, Zitman FG, Roelofs K. Automatic avoidance tendencies in patients with Psychogenic Non Epileptic Seizures. *Seizure* (2011) 20:628–34. doi: 10.1016/j.seizure.2011.06.006
48. Kozlowska K, Brown KJ, Palmer DM, Williams LM. Specific biases for identifying facial expression of emotion in children and adolescents with conversion disorders. *Psychosom Med.* (2013) 75:272–80. doi: 10.1097/PSY.0b013e318286be43
49. Kozlowska K, Palmer DM, Brown KJ, McLean L, Scher S, Gevirtz R, et al. Reduction of autonomic regulation in children and adolescents with conversion disorders. *Psychosomat Med.* (2015) 77:356–70. doi: 10.1097/PSY.0000000000000184
50. Kozlowska K, Griffiths KR, Foster SL, Linton J, Williams LM, Korgaonkar MS. Grey matter abnormalities in children and adolescents with functional neurological symptom disorder. *Neuroimage Clin.* (2017) 15:306–14. doi: 10.1016/j.nicl.2017.04.028
51. Pick S, Mellers JDC, Goldstein LH. Autonomic and subjective responsivity to emotional images in people with dissociative seizures. *J Neuropsychol.* (2018) 12:341–55. doi: 10.1111/jnp.12144
52. Roberts NA, Burleson MH, Weber DJ, Larson A, Sergeant K, Devine MJ, et al. Emotion in psychogenic nonepileptic seizures: responses to affective pictures. *Epilepsy Behav.* (2012) 24:107–15. doi: 10.1016/j.yebeh.2012.03.018
53. Ricciardi L, Demartini B, Crucianelli L, Krahé C, Edwards MJ, Fotopoulou A. Interoceptive awareness in patients with functional neurological symptoms. *Biol Psychol.* (2016) 113:68–74. doi: 10.1016/j.biopsycho.2015.10.009
54. Seignourel PJ, Miller K, Kellison I, Rodriguez R, Fernandez HH, Bauer RM, et al. Abnormal affective startle modulation in individuals with psychogenic [corrected] movement disorder. *Move Disord.* (2007) 22:1265–71. doi: 10.1002/mds.21451
55. Yalçin M, Tellioglu E, Gündüz A, Özmen M, Yeni N, Özkara Ç, et al. Orienting reaction may help recognition of patients with psychogenic nonepileptic seizures. *Neurophysiol Clin Clin Neurophysiol.* (2017) 47:231–7. doi: 10.1016/j.neucli.2017.02.005
56. Karatzias T, Howard R, Power K, Socherel F, Heath C, Livingstone A. Organic vs. functional neurological disorders: the role of childhood psychological trauma. *Child Abuse Negl.* (2017) 63:1–6. doi: 10.1016/j.chiabu.2016.11.011
57. Kienle J, Rockstroh B, Bohus M, Fiess J, Huffziger S, Steffen-Klatt A. Somatoform dissociation and posttraumatic stress syndrome - two sides of the same medal? A comparison of symptom profiles, trauma history and altered affect regulation between patients with functional neurological symptoms and patients with PTSD. *BMC Psychiatry* (2017) 17:248. doi: 10.1186/s12888-017-1414-z
58. Kranick S, Ekanayake V, Martinez V, Ameli R, Hallett M, Voon V. Psychopathology and psychogenic movement disorders. *Move Disord.* (2011) 26:1844–50. doi: 10.1002/mds.23830
59. Ozcetin A, Belli H, Ertem U, Bahcebasi T, Ataoglu A, Canan F. Childhood trauma and dissociation in women with pseudoseizure-type conversion disorder. *Nordic J Psychiatry* (2009) 63:462–8. doi: 10.3109/08039480903029728
60. Steffen A, Fiess J, Schmidt R, Rockstroh B. "That pulled the rug out from under my feet!" - adverse experiences and altered emotion processing in patients with functional neurological symptoms compared to healthy comparison subjects. *BMC Psychiatry* (2015) 15:133. doi: 10.1186/s12888-015-0514-x
61. Ludwig L, Pasman JA, Nicholson T, Aybek S, David AS, Tuck S, et al. Stressful life events and maltreatment in conversion (functional neurological) disorder: systematic review and meta-analysis of case-control studies. *Lancet Psychiatry* (2018) 5:307–20. doi: 10.1016/S2215-0366(18)30051-8

62. Williams LM, Brammer MJ, Skerrett D, Lagopolous J, Rennie C, Kozek K, et al. The neural correlates of orienting: an integration of fMRI and skin conductance orienting. *Neuroreport* (2000) 11:3011–5. doi: 10.1097/00001756-200009110-00037
63. Vuilleumier P. Hysterical conversion and brain function. *Prog Brain Res.* (2005) 150:309–29. doi: 10.1016/S0079-6123(05)50023-2
64. Roelofs K, Pasman J. Stress, childhood trauma, and cognitive functions in functional neurologic disorders. *Handb Clin Neurol.* (2016) 139:139–55. doi: 10.1016/B978-0-12-801772-2.00013-8
65. Pai A, Suris AM, North CS. Posttraumatic stress disorder in the DSM-5: controversy, change, and conceptual considerations. *Behav Sci.* (2017) 7:7. doi: 10.3390/bs7010007
66. Dvir Y, Ford JD, Hill M, Frazier JA. Childhood maltreatment, emotional dysregulation, and psychiatric comorbidities. *Harvard Rev Psychiatry* (2014) 22:149–61. doi: 10.1097/HRP.0000000000000014
67. Glaser, D. Emotional abuse and neglect (psychological maltreatment): a conceptual framework. *Child Abuse Negl.* (2002) 26:697–714. doi: 10.1016/S0145-213(02)00342-3
68. Naughton AM, Maguire SA, Mann MK, Lumb RC, Tempest V, Gracias S, et al. Emotional, behavioral, and developmental features indicative of neglect or emotional abuse in preschool children. *JAMA Pediatr.* (2013) 167:769. doi: 10.1001/jamapediatrics.2013.192
69. Krüger C, Fletcher L. Predicting a dissociative disorder from type of childhood maltreatment and abuser-abused relational tie. *J Trauma Dissociation* (2017) 18:356–72. doi: 10.1080/15299732.2017.1295420
70. Perez DL, MatinN, Barsky A, Costumero-Ramos V, Makaretz SJ, Young SS, et al. Cingulo-insular structural alterations associated with psychogenic symptoms, childhood abuse and PTSD in functional neurological disorders. *J Neurol Neurosurg Psychiatry* (2017) 88:491–7. doi: 10.1136/jnnp-2016-314998
71. Krall SC, Rottschy C, Oberwelland E, Bzdok D, Fox PT, Eickhoff SB, et al. The role of the right temporoparietal junction in attention and social interaction as revealed by ALE meta-analysis. *Brain Struct Funct.* (2015) 220:587–604. doi: 10.1007/s00429-014-0803-z
72. Duncan NW, Hayes DJ, Wiebking C, Tiret B, Pietruska K, Chen DQ, et al. Negative childhood experiences alter a prefrontal-insular-motor cortical network in healthy adults: a preliminary multimodal rsfMRI-fMRI-MRS-dMRI study. *Hum Brain Mapp.* (2015) 36:4622–37. doi: 10.1002/hbm.22941
73. Ansell EB, Rando K, Tuit K, Guarnaccia J, Sinha R. Cumulative adversity and smaller gray matter volume in medial prefrontal, anterior cingulate, and insula regions. *Biol Psychiatry* (2012) 72:57–64. doi: 10.1016/j.biopsych.2011.11.022
74. Bryant RA, Das P. The neural circuitry of conversion disorder and its recovery. *J Abnor Psychol.* (2012) 121:289–96. doi: 10.1037/a0025076
75. van der Kruijs SJM, Bodde NMG, Vaessen MJ, Lazeron RHC, Vonck K, Boon P, et al. Functional connectivity of dissociation in patients with psychogenic non-epileptic seizures. *J Neurol Neurosurg Psychiatry* (2012) 83:239–47. doi: 10.1136/jnnp-2011-300776
76. Nachev P, Kennard C, Husain M. Functional role of the supplementary and pre-supplementary motor areas. *Nat Rev Neurosci.* (2008) 9:856–69. doi: 10.1038/nrn2478
77. Oliveri M, Babiloni C, Filippi MM, Caltagirone C, Babiloni F, Cicinelli P, et al. Influence of the supplementary motor area on primary motor cortex excitability during movements triggered by neutral or emotionally unpleasant visual cues. *Exp Brain Res.* (2003) 149:214–21. doi: 10.1007/s00221-002-1346-8
78. Rodigari A, Oliveri M. Disrupting SMA activity modulates explicit and implicit emotional responses: an rTMS study. *Neurosci Lett.* (2014) 579:30–4. doi: 10.1016/j.neulet.2014.07.012
79. Borchardt V, Krause AL, Li M, van Tol MJ, Demenescu LR, Buchheim A, et al. Dynamic disconnection of the supplementary motor area after processing of dismissive biographic narratives. *Brain Behav.* (2015) 5:e00377. doi: 10.1002/brb3.377
80. Fan Y, Duncan NW, de Greck M, Northoff G. Is there a core neural network in empathy? An fMRI based quantitative meta-analysis. *Neurosci Biobehav Rev.* (2011) 35:903–11. doi: 10.1016/j.neubiorev.2010.10.009
81. Grèzes J, Dezecache G. How do shared-representations and emotional processes cooperate in response to social threat signals? *Neuropsychologia* (2014) 55:105–14. doi: 10.1016/j.neuropsychologia.2013.09.019
82. Holstege G. Chapter 14 Descending motor pathways and the spinal motor system: limbic and non-limbic components. *Prog Brain Res.* (1991) 87:307–421. doi: 10.1016/S0079-6123(08)63057-5
83. Gothard KM. The amygdalo-motor pathways and the control of facial expressions. *Front Neurosci.* (2014) 8:43. doi: 10.3389/fnins.2014.00043
84. Ghashghaei HT, Hilgetag CC, Barbas H. Sequence of information processing for emotions based on the anatomic dialogue between prefrontal cortex and amygdala. *NeuroImage* (2007) 34:905–23. doi: 10.1016/j.neuroimage.2006.09.046
85. Morecraft RJ, McNeal DW, Stilwell-Morecraft KS, Gedney M, Ge J, Schroeder CM, et al. Amygdala interconnections with the cingulate motor cortex in the rhesus monkey. *J Compar Neurol.* (2007) 500:134–65. doi: 10.1002/cne.21165
86. Grèzes J, Valabrègue R, Gholipour B, Chevallier C. A direct amygdala-motor pathway for emotional displays to influence action: a diffusion tensor imaging study. *Hum Brain Mapp.* (2014) 35:5974–83. doi: 10.1002/hbm.22598
87. Toschi N, Duggento A, Passamonti L. Functional connectivity in amygdalar-sensory/(pre)motor networks at rest: new evidence from the human connectome project. *Eur J Neurosci.* (2017) 45:1224–9. doi: 10.1111/ejn.13544
88. Grèzes J, Dezecache G, Eskenazi T. Limbic to motor interactions during social perception. In: Toga, AW editor. *Brain Mapping.* Cambridge, MA: Elsevier (2015). p. 1027–30.
89. Diano M, Tamietto M, Celeghin A, Weiskrantz L, Tatu M-K, Bagnis A, et al. Dynamic changes in amygdala psychophysiological connectivity reveal distinct neural networks for facial expressions of basic emotions. *Sci Rep.* (2017) 7:45260. doi: 10.1038/srep45260
90. Westlund Schreiner M, Klimes-Dougan B, Mueller BA, Eberly LE, Reigstad KM, Carstedt PA, et al. Multi-modal neuroimaging of adolescents with non-suicidal self-injury: Amygdala functional connectivity. *J Affect Disord.* (2017) 221:47–55. doi: 10.1016/j.jad.2017.06.004
91. Nock MK, Prinstein MJ. A functional approach to the assessment of self-mutilative behavior. *J Consult Clin Psychol.* (2004) 72:885–90. doi: 10.1037/0022-006X.72.5.885
92. Buck R, Losow JI, Murphy MM, Costanzo P. Social facilitation and inhibition of emotional expression and communication. *J Pers Soc Psychol.* (1992) 63:962–8. doi: 10.1037/0022-3514.63.6.962
93. Fernandez-Dols JM, Ruiz-Belda M-A., Mandler G. Spontaneous facial behavior during intense emotional episodes: artistic truth and optical truth. In: Russell JA, Fernandez-Dols JM, editors. *The Psychology of Facial Expression.* Cambridge: Cambridge University Press (1997). p. 255–74.
94. Krahé C, Springer A, Weinman JA, Fotopoulou A. The social modulation of pain: others as predictive signals of salience - a systematic review. *Front Hum Neurosci.* (2013) 7:386. doi: 10.3389/fnhum.2013.00386
95. Nicholson TR, Aybek S, Craig T, Harris T, Wojcik W, David AS, et al. Life events and escape in conversion disorder. *Psychol Med.* (2016) 46:2617–26. doi: 10.1017/S0033291716000714
96. Steinkopf L. The signaling theory of symptoms: an evolutionary explanation of the placebo effect. *Evol Psychol.* (2015) 13:1474704915600559. doi: 10.1177/1474704915600559
97. Tiokhin L. Do symptoms of illness serve signaling functions? (Hint: Yes). *Q Rev Biol.* (2016) 91:177–95. doi: 10.1086/686811
98. Burghardt GM. Cognitive ethology and critical anthropomorphism: a snake with two heads and hognose snakes that play dead. In: Ristau CA, editor. *Comparative Cognition and Neuroscience. Cognitive Ethology: The Minds of Other Animals: Essays in Honor of Donald, R. Griffin.* Hillsdale, NJ: Lawrence Erlbaum Associates (1991). p. 53–90.
99. Wenegrat B. *Theater of Disorder : Patients, Doctors, and the Construction of Illness.* Oxford University Press (2001). Available online at: https://global.oup.com/academic/product/theater-of-disorder-9780195140873?cc=cz&lang=en&
100. Crittenden PM. Attachment and risk for psychopathology. *J Dev Behav Pediatr.* (1995) 16(Supp. 3):S12–6. doi: 10.1097/00004703-199506001-00004

101. Kozlowska K. The developmental origins of conversion disorders. *Clin Child Psychol Psychiatry* (2007) 12:487–510. doi: 10.1177/13591045070 80977
102. Lewis-Fernández R, Gorritz M, Raggio GA, Peláez C, Chen H, Guarnaccia PJ. Association of trauma-related disorders and dissociation with four idioms of distress among Latino psychiatric outpatients. *Culture Med Psychiatry* (2010) 34:219–43. doi: 10.1007/s11013-010-9177-8
103. Åslund C, Starrin B, Nilsson KW. Social capital in relation to depression, musculoskeletal pain, and psychosomatic symptoms: a cross-sectional study of a large population-based cohort of Swedish adolescents. *BMC Public Health* (2010) 10:715. doi: 10.1186/1471-2458-10-715
104. Benedetti F. Placebo and the new physiology of the doctor-patient relationship. *Physiol Rev.* (2013) 93:1207–46. doi: 10.1152/physrev.00043.2012
105. Goyal G, Kalita J, Misra UK. Utility of different seizure induction protocols in psychogenic nonepileptic seizures. *Epilepsy Res.* (2014) 108:1120–7. doi: 10.1016/j.eplepsyres.2014.02.015
106. Thenganatt MA, Jankovic J. Psychogenic tremor: a video guide to its distinguishing features. *Tremor Other Hyperkinet Move* (2014) 4:253. doi: 10.7916/D8FJ2F0Q
107. Peckham EL, Hallett M. Psychogenic movement disorders. *Neurol Clin* (2009) 27:801–19, vii. doi: 10.1016/j.ncl.2009.04.008
108. Ricciardi L, Edwards MJ. Treatment of functional (psychogenic) movement disorders. *Neurotherapeutics* (2014) 11:201–7. doi: 10.1007/s13311-013-0246-x
109. Deeley, Q. Hypnosis as a model of functional neurologic disorders. *Handb Clin Neurol.* (2016) 139:95–103. doi: 10.1016/B978-0-12-801772-2.00009-6
110. Terhune DB, Cleeremans A, Raz A, Lynn SJ. Hypnosis and top-down regulation of consciousness. *Neurosci Biobehav Rev.* (2017) 81(Pt A):59–74. doi: 10.1016/j.neubiorev.2017.02.002
111. Ricciardi L, Demartini B, Morgante F, Parees I, Nielsen G, Edwards MJ. Symptom severity in patients with functional motor symptoms: patient's perception and doctor's clinical assessment. *Parkinsonism Relat Disord.* (2015) 21:529–32. doi: 10.1016/j.parkreldis.2015.02.022
112. Pareés I, Saifee TA, Kassavetis P, Kojovic M, Rubio-Agusti I, Rothwell JC, et al. Believing is perceiving: mismatch between self-report and actigraphy in psychogenic tremor. *Brain* (2012) 135:117–23. doi: 10.1093/brain/awr292
113. Lemche E, Brammer MJ, David AS, Surguladze SA, Phillips ML, Sierra M, et al. Interoceptive–reflective regions differentiate alexithymia traits in depersonalization disorder. *Psychiatry Res.* (2013) 214:66–72. doi: 10.1016/j.pscychresns.2013.05.006
114. Perez DL, Dworetzky BA, Dickerson BC, Leung L, Cohn R, Baslet G, et al. An integrative neurocircuit perspective on psychogenic nonepileptic seizures and functional movement disorders : neural functional unawareness. *Clin EEG Neurosci.* (2014) 46:4–15. doi: 10.1177/15500594145 55905
115. Boeckle M, Liegl G, Jank R, Pieh C. Neural correlates of conversion disorder: overview and meta-analysis of neuroimaging studies on motor conversion disorder. *BMC Psychiatry* (2017). 16:195. doi: 10.1186/s12888-016-0890-x
116. Freud S, Breuer J. *Studies on Hysteria (Basic Books Classics).* New York, NY: Hogarth Press (1895/1955).
117. Newman L, Sivaratnam C, Komiti A. Attachment and early brain development – neuroprotective interventions in infant–caregiver therapy. *Transl Dev Psychiatry* (2015) 3:28647. doi: 10.3402/tdp.v3.28647
118. McLaughlin KA, Sheridan MA, Tibu F, Fox NA, Zeanah CH, Nelson CA. Causal effects of the early caregiving environment on development of stress response systems in children. *Proc Natl Acad Sci USA.* (2015) 112:5637–42. doi: 10.1073/pnas.1423363112
119. Calkins SD, Graziano PA, Berdan LE, Keane SP, Degnan KA. Predicting cardiac vagal regulation in early childhood from maternal-child relationship quality during toddlerhood. *Dev Psychobiol.* (2008) 50:751–66. doi: 10.1002/dev.20344
120. Kozlowska K, Walker P, McLean L, Carrive P. Fear and the defense cascade: clinical implications and management. *Harvard Rev Psychiatry* (2014) 23:263–87. doi: 10.1097/HRP.0000000000000065
121. Hagenaars MA, Stins JF, Roelofs K. Aversive life events enhance human freezing responses. *J Exp Psychol.* (2012) 141:98–105. doi: 10.1037/a0024211
122. Kozlowska K, Palmer DM, Brown KJ, Scher S, Chudleigh C, Davies F, et al. Conversion disorder in children and adolescents: a disorder of cognitive control. *J Neuropsychol.* (2015) 9:87–108. doi: 10.1111/jnp.12037
123. van der Kruijs SJM, Vonck KEJ, Langereis GR, Feijs LMG, Bodde NMG, Lazeron RHC, et al. Autonomic nervous system functioning associated with psychogenic nonepileptic seizures: analysis of heart rate variability. *Epilepsy Behav.* (2016) 54:14–9. doi: 10.1016/j.yebeh.2015.10.014
124. Bowlby J. The nature of the child's tie to his mother. *Int J Psychoanal.* (1958) 39:350–73.
125. Taylor DC. Hysteria, play-acting and courage. *Br J Psychiatry* (1986) 149:37–41. doi: 10.1192/bjp.149.1.37
126. Hohwy J. Delusions, illusions and inference under uncertainty. *Mind Lang.* (2013) 28:57–71. doi: 10.1111/mila.12008

12

Eating Disorders Impact on Vigilance and Decision Making of a Community Sample of Treatment Naive Attention-Deficit/Hyperactivity Disorder in Young Adults

Bruno Palazzo Nazar[1,2], Amanda Pompeu Trindade[1], Monica Leslie[2], Leandro Fernandes Malloy-Diniz[3], Joseph Sergeant[4], Janet Treasure[2] and Paulo Mattos[1,5]*

[1] Institute of Psychiatry, Federal University of Rio de Janeiro, Rio de Janeiro, Brazil, [2] Institute of Psychiatry, Psychology and Neuroscience, King's College London, London, United Kingdom, [3] Departamento de Saúde Mental, Universidade Federal de Minas Gerais, Belo Horizonte, Brazil, [4] VU University Amsterdam, Amsterdam, Netherlands, [5] D'Or Institute for Education and Research, Rio de Janeiro, Brazil

***Correspondence:**
Bruno Palazzo Nazar
bruno.nazar@gmail.com

Although impulsivity is suggested as a possible link to explain the association of Attention-Deficit/Hyperactivity Disorder (ADHD) with an Eating Disorder (ED), there is little research on how clinical and cognitive/neuropsychological functioning might change when this comorbidity occurs. ADHD individuals are at a higher of developing ED and also obesity. Some research has described the impact of ADHD in clinical treatment-seeking samples of ED patients. Consequently, we investigated how ED impacted on clinical and cognitive variables of a community sample of treatment-naive ADHD individuals. Ninety college students arranged in three groups (ADHD+ED, ADHD only and Controls) were analyzed using semi-structured interviews for ADHD (K-SADS), the Iowa Gambling Task, the Conner's Continuous Performance Test, Digit and Visual span, as well as rating scales for anxiety (STAI), depression (BDI) and impulsivity (BIS-11), and binge eating (BES). We found that ADHD+ED individuals significantly differed from both groups, presenting with a higher body mass index; more hyperactivity-impulsivity symptoms; higher binge eating scores; more omission errors on the Continuous Performance Test; disadvantageous choices on the Iowa Gambling Task. Also, we demonstrated through a moderation/mediation analysis that a greater level of binge eating mediated the increases in body mass index on our sample. There were no significant paths to explain binge-eating severity through changes on any of the neuropsychological tests used. The presence of an ED in normal weight in a community sample of ADHD individuals is associated with higher body mass index and a worse cognitive functioning.

Keywords: ADHD, eating disorders, comorbidity, neuropsychology, bulimia, binge eating, obesity, decision making

INTRODUCTION

A recent meta-analysis found that the risk of diagnosing an Eating Disorder (ED) in patients with Attention-Deficit/Hyperactivity Disorder (ADHD) is 3.82 times greater when compared to the general population (1). The heightened risk remains significant after controlling for age and gender, and holds true for all eating disorders syndromes [Anorexia Nervosa (AN), Bulimia Nervosa (BN), and Binge eating Disorder (BED)]. Furthermore, even though EDs are 10 times more prevalent in females, the association is significant for both sexes (2). Interestingly, even before full ED syndromes have developed at adolescence, eating disorder symptoms (e.g., loss of control eating) have also been significantly associated with ADHD (3, 4).

The comorbidity of ADHD with ED is of interest as it defines a subgroup of patients who have greater disordered eating habits (5) and might respond differently to current standard treatments for EDs (6). These patients are also at risk of presenting with a more disrupted mental functioning, exemplified by higher rates of other psychiatric comorbidities, especially greater rates of substance abuse (5, 7). ADHD symptoms can also indicate a higher severity of eating disorder symptoms and personality psychopathology in ED patients (8). Although this has been demonstrated in clinical samples (5, 9), there is scarce evidence to generalize the same phenomenon for community samples. Eating disorders respond poorly to treatment after a 1 year follow up if ADHD symptoms are present at baseline, especially if they present with high inattention symptoms (10).

Of note, the recent approval of lisdexamphetamine for the treatment of Binge Eating Disorder in the United States (11) suggests that psychostimulant medication might have a direct effect on eating behavior regardless of ADHD status. However, this is still poorly understood and concern may arise that populations at-risk for developing an eating disorder might misuse psychostimulants seeking weight regulation or as a compensatory behavior to their disordered eating habits (12, 13).

Results from studies evaluating how comorbid mental disorders influence cognitive functioning of ADHD have had varying results for children (14, 15) and adults (16, 17). Also, most studies have focused on anxiety and mood disorders. The diverse cognitive domains investigated and the varying results for different comorbid disorders prevent us from defining a specific profile of how a comorbid disorder impairs cognitive functioning in ADHD.

Two previous studies explored neuropsychological differences of ADHD individuals comorbid with an eating disorder. Seitz et al. (18) compared a sample of adult women with BN and a past history of ADHD ($n = 12$) to those without a history of ADHD ($n = 45$). They found that women comorbid for BN with ADHD presented more pronounced inattention and impulsivity when compared to those with BN only. This study also found that inattention was significantly more associated with these deficits than hyperactivity/impulsivity. One other study investigated if neuropsychological measures could explain the association of ADHD symptoms with BED symptoms. Steadman et al. (19) assessed 44 individuals and reported that impulsivity measured through a Continuous Performance Test (CPT) didn't moderate the correlation of ADHD and Binge Eating symptoms. The scarce literature on the causal pathways to explain this comorbidity have pointed toward impulse regulation deficits but further studies are necessary to corroborate this hypothesis (20).

In the present work, we aimed to test whether the presence of an ED was associated with poorer attentional function and decision-making in individuals with ADHD. Also, as a secondary aim, we tried to replicate findings from studies that evaluated the clinical profile across these disorders, in a community and treatment-naive sample.

MATERIALS AND METHODS

Sample

The present study was an analysis of a larger protocol presented in detail elsewhere in an open access manuscript (21), hereon summarized. A sectional study was conducted using a convenience sample from the fifth year of the medical course from the Federal University of Rio de Janeiro (UFRJ), over four consecutive years (2010–2014 with 8 recruitment waves in total). All students were invited to participate protocol when they initiated the fifth year, during the first class of psychiatry. The protocol was approved by the Institute of Psychiatry—UFRJ Ethics Committee.

All participants provided informed consent to take part, and the Institute of Psychiatry of the Federal University of Rio de Janeiro (IPUB-UFRJ) Ethics Committee approved this study. The exclusion criteria for the present analysis were: Presence of any psychiatric diagnosis other than ADHD or ADHD+ED, epilepsy, and current use of any psychotropic medication.

Procedures

Screening

Participants were screened for participating in the research with:

- Adult Self-Rating Scale (ASRS-18) (22): an 18-item self-report questionnaire used as a screening tool for ADHD.
- *Binge Eating Scale* (BES) (23): a 16-item self-report questionnaire used as a screening tool for binge eating, which also evaluates the severity of binge eating.

Clinical Assessment

All participants were evaluated through semi-structured interviews using DSM-5 criteria. These evaluations were completed by board certified psychiatrists with more than 10 years of clinical experience in adult ADHD and ED (BPN and PM). All diagnosis were discussed using history, self-report, and semi-structured interviews.

The K-SADS interview adapted for adults with ADHD (24) was used to diagnose ADHD. The participant received a diagnosis of ADHD if they met DSM-5 criteria for at least 5 *current* inattention *or* hyperactivity/impulsivity symptoms, associated with at least 5 *past* inattention *or* hyperactivity/impulsivity symptoms, with onset before the age of 12 and occurring in at least 2 life-time domains with significant impairment. All ADHD assessments were done blind to the participant's self-report status, and all students with more than 5 current symptoms of inattention or hyperactivity/impulsivity were discussed with the other rater for consideration of a diagnosis.

- SCID-P module for ED.
- MINI-Plus: for all other psychiatric diagnosis.

Participants completed the following questionnaires:

- *Beck Depression Inventory* (BDI) (25, 26) developed for assessing the severity of depressive symptoms. The BDI contains 21 questions, which are rated on a Likert scale ranging from 0 to 3.
- *State-Trait Anxiety Inventory* (STAI) (27) is composed of two 20-item scales that measure trait and situational anxiety.
- *Barrat-Impusivity Scale* (BIS-11) (28): This scale measures impulsivity in life situations. The original BIS-11 uses three subscales but the Brazillian transcultural adaptation studies validated two subescales—which were used for the present analysis—in two domains: attentional/planning (BIS-ATPLAN), cognitive and motor inhibition (BIS-CINI) impulsivity.
- All the mentioned rating scales have been translated and adapted to Brazilian Portuguese [ASRS-18 (29), BES (30), BDI (26), STAI (27) and BIS-11(31)].

Neuropsychological Assessment

Neuropsychological evaluation comprised:

- **IQ**, calculated with the four-subtest form of the Wechsler Abbreviated Intelligence Scale (WASI) (32), from which the blocks, vocabulary, matrix, and similarities tests were administered.
- The **Digit Span** and the **Visual Span**: Both these tests are used to assess executive functioning. In the verbal Digit Span task the subject has to recall forward and reverse orders of digit sequences. It uses the phonological loop to measure working memory, attention, and inhibition. The Visual Span is a visuospatial version of the verbal span in which the subject has to recall forwards and reverse sequences of a visual task (tapping on cubes).
- The **Conner's Continuous Performance Task II (CPT-II)** (33): Continuous performance tests are the most commonly used attention tasks in clinical practice (34) and give the opportunity to evaluate the ability of a subject to maintain consistent responses over time and speed of stimuli presentation (35). Variables of interest in the present study were: number of omission errors (OMI), commission errors (COM), hit reaction time (HRT), HRT block change (HRT BL CHANGE), reaction time by inter-stimulus interval (Hit RT ISI CHANGE), and attentiveness (d′). OMI errors occur when subjects fail to respond on trials containing target letters (all non-"X" letters), COM errors occur when they respond on trials with letters "X." HRT is the mean response time for all non-X responses over all six time blocks and represents the subject's easier discrimination of the target. HRT BL CHANGE (a vigilance measure) is the slope of change in the reaction time over the six time blocks; a positive slope indicates a slowing RT, and a negative slope indicates a quicker RT as the test progresses. Hit RT ISI CHANGE (capacity to adjust to presentation speed) is calculated by computing the slope of change in RT over the three ISIs (1, 2, and 4 s). The ISIs are block-randomized so that all three ISI conditions occur every block but in a different order; by varying the inter-stimulus intervals (1, 2, and 4 s), it is possible to assess the ability to adjust to changing *tempo* and task demand. The index d′ reflects the subject's perceptual sensitivity to targets as a measure of how well the individual discriminates between targets (signals) and non-targets (noise). Higher d′-values indicate greater sensitivity and better discrimination between targets and non-targets.
- The **Iowa Gambling Task (IGT)** (36): We used a computerized version of the IGT, in which subjects had to choose a card from four decks. They were told that in order to win the largest sum of money some decks were advantageous while others were disadvantageous. Two decks brought large immediate gains with large future losses (decks A and B), while two decks lead to small wins but also small future losses (Decks C and D). After 100 trials, a net score was calculated using the equation [(Decks C+D) − (Decks A+B)], which produces a measure of the total number of advantageous decks minus the total number of disadvantageous decks. This was also calculated for 5 blocks of 20 trials, which enables the assessment of learning over the test. This test measures decision making and non-planning impulsivity.

Sample

A total of 726 students were eligible for the study but only 662 (91.1%) were screened using the ASRS-18 and BES as some students were not present during research presentation and screening procedures. From the 662 screened students, board certified psychiatrists using the semi-structured interviews interviewed a total of 344 students for mental disorders. All students with positive ASRS-18 or BES were interviewed as well as a random equal proportion of negative screenings. The final sample analyzed in the present study final sample consisted of 90 students. There were no statistically significant differences between the age and gender profile of protocol completers and non-completers.

Statistical Analysis

Statistical tests were performed using SPSS v.20. Subjects were classified into one of three diagnostic groups (Control, ADHD only, ADHD+ED). We have included subjects in the "Control" group that didn't have any psychiatric diagnosis assessed using the MINI-Plus and didn't fulfill criteria for either ADHD or ED. In the ADHD group we included subjects that fulfilled criteria for ADHD but didn't have ED. For the ADHD+ED group we included patients presenting the comorbidity with both diagnoses. The differences between groups were considered significant if $p < 0.05$. The demographic characteristics were tested across groups using a one-way analysis of variance (ANOVA). Afterwards, pairwise contrasts were obtained using independent-samples *t*-tests. *Post-hoc* with Fisher's LSD correction was used.

For the mediation analysis we used the *paramed* command from STATA (37). The significance of the indirect and total effects was tested via bias-corrected bootstrapping, which is robust to violations of the assumption of homoscedasticity.

RESULTS

Sample Characteristics

The sociodemographic characteristics for the final sample are detailed in **Table 1**. The three diagnostic groups were proportional and had non-significant differences regarding gender distribution ($p = 0.215$), socioeconomic status ($p = 0.976$), and global IQ ($p = 0.46$). None of the ADHD subjects from the ADHD-only or from the ADHD+ED groups were currently taking any medication.

The ADHD+ED group consisted of five participants with bulimia Nervosa; three participants with BEDs; three participants with subclinical Bulimia Nervosa (didn't fulfill the frequency criteria for binge and purging episodes); and five participants with subclinical BED (didn't fulfill the frequency criteria for binge episodes).

The proportion of obese and overweight participants in the ADHD+ED group was significantly higher when compared to both the ADHD only and to the Control groups ($p = 0.004$). Also, the mean BMI in this group was significantly greater than the other two groups: 4.1 points higher than the control group and 3.9 points higher than ADHD-only group. The ADHD+ED group was 13 kg (28.6 lbs) heavier than the control group and 12.7 kg (28 lbs) heavier than ADHD-only group on average (**Table 1**).

The analysis of ADHD symptoms revealed that the ADHD+ED group had significantly greater current Hyperactivity/Impulsivity than the ADHD only group. All other comparisons were non-significant between the ADHD+ED and the ADHD only group, with a trend for greater past Inattention symptoms in the ADHD+ED group (**Table 2**).

Self-Report Psychopathology Scales

Regarding anxiety symptoms, there were no significant differences on state anxiety ($p = 0.23$) and there was a significant difference on trait anxiety between controls and ADHD only ($p = 0.01$) or between controls and ADHD+ED ($p = 0.05$). The ADHD only and ADHD+ED groups didn't present significant differences on state ($p = 0.69$) or trait ($p = 0.89$) anxiety. The same occurred with depressive symptoms. Although controls had significantly lower BDI score than ADHD only ($p = 0.02$) and than ADHD+ED ($p = 0.03$), the last two groups didn't differed significantly among themselves ($p = 0.75$). In the analysis of self-report impulsivity, only the BIS-Total ($p < 0.001$) and BIS-CINI ($p < 0.001$) scores presented significant differences with ADHD only and ADHD+ED groups having higher scores than the control group.

Neuropsychological Assessment

Results are reported by means and standard deviations for each group and total, for each test, in the **Supplementary Materials**. Hereon are reported mean differences and group comparisons with *post-hoc* tests. The neuropsychological assessment of verbal and non-verbal IQ (**Table 1**), Digit and Visual Span (**Table 3**), and the IGT (**Table 4**) did not show significant differences across groups. However, there was a trend for the ADHD+ED group having more disadvantageous choices than the other two groups across block 2 and in the net score of the IGT (**Figure 1**). Of note, only the deck B measure from the IGT was found to be to be significantly different in the ADHD+ED vs. Controls ($p = 0.05$).

TABLE 1 | Subjects sociodemographic and clinical characteristics.

	Total Sample ($n = 90$)	Controls ($n = 39$)	ADHD ($n = 35$)	ADHD+E ($n = 16$)	*p*-value[a]	Effect-Size (Partial Eta^2)[a]
Age	23.71 (±1.9)	23.3 (1 ± 0.2)	24 (±2.3)	24 (±1.6)	0.215	0.035
Gender: % (*n*)					0.976	0.001
Female	81% (68)	81.8% (27)	80% (28)	81.3% (13)		
Weight, kgs	62.6 (±12.2)	60.2 (±9)	60.5 (±9.7)	73.2 (±17.5)	<0.0001[b]	0.167
B.M.I.	22.37 (±3.4)	21.6 (±2.7)	21.8 (±2.8)	25.7 (±4.3)	<0.0001[c]	0.205
Overweight	13% ($n = 11$)	10.4% (4)	8.7% (3)	37.8% (6)		
Obese	2.3% ($n = 2$)	0% (0)	2.9% (1)	6.3% (1)		
SES: % (*n*)					0.184	0.038
≥ 32,500 $/y (A1)	6.7% ($n = 6$)	7.7% (3)	8.6% (3)	0% (0)		
≥ 21,900 $/y (A2)	11.1% (10)	2.6% (1)	20% (7)	12.5% (2)		
≥ 6,800 $/y (B 1 e 2)	30% (27)	28.2% (11)	28.6% (10)	37.5% (6)		
≥ 2,500 $/y (C e D)	52.2% ($n = 47$)	61.5% (24)	42.9% (15)	50% (8)		
Global IQ	113 (9)	112 (10)	113 (8)	116 (8.2)	0.46	0.021

[a] *Univariate Analysis. Omnibus p-values and effect sizes. LSD post-hoc correction.*
[b] *Control = ADHD, p = 0.889; Control < ADHD + ED and ADHD < ADHD + ED, p < 0.001.*
[c] *Control = ADHD, p = 0.786; Control < ADHD + ED and ADHD < ADHD + ED, p < 0.001.*

TABLE 2 | ADHD symptoms and self-report psychopathological measures.

	Total Sample ($n = 90$)	Controls ($n = 39$)	ADHD ($n = 35$)	ADHD+ED ($n = 16$)	*Omnibus* p-value[a]	Contrasts	*Omnibus* Effect-Size (Partial Eta^2)[a]
Current Inatt	N.A.	1.5 (±1.9)	5.9 (±1.5)	6.8 (±1.3)	<0.001	1<2=3[b]	0.657
Current H/I	N.A.	1.2 (±1.2)	4 (±2.2)	5.6 (±2.7)	<0.001	1<2<3[c]	0.433
Past Inatt	N.A.	1.1 (±1.3)	5 (±1.9)	6.1 (±1.9)	<0.001	1<2=3[d]	0.607
Past H/I	N.A.	1.1 (±1.4)	4.2 (±2.4)	4.4 (±2.8)	<0.001	1<2=3[e]	0.349
BIS - Total	66.6 (±12)	58.9 (±8.8)	71.8 (±10.3)	71.4 (±15.8)	<0.001	1<2=3[f]	0.256
BIS-ATTPL	18.3 (±4.1)	17.9 (±4.7)	18.8 (±3.9)	18 (±3.6)	0.73	1=2=3	0.010
BIS-CINI	43.5 (±8.4)	36 (±4.8)	48 (±6.6)	50 (±5.2)	<0.001	1<2=3[g]	0.547
STAI-T	41.7 (±9.9)	38.4 (±9.4)	44.2 (±9.6)	44.6 (±9.8)	0.032	1<2[h]	0.089
STAI-S	42.2 (±10.4)	38 (±8.7)	45.3 (±11.5)	44.5 (±8.1)	0.23	1<2[i]	0.087
BES	8.7 (6.3)	6,22 (5.3)	8.82 (6)	15 (5.3)	<0.001	1=2<3[j]	0.234
BDI	7 (±6.9)	4.5 (±4.5)	8.8 (±7.2)	8.5 (±9.1)	0.03	1<2=3[l]	0.092

Mean (SD). N.A, Not Applicable; Current Inatt, KSADS Current Inattention symptoms; Current H/I, KSADS.Current Hyperactivity/Impulsivity symptoms; Past Inatt, KSADS Past Inattention symptoms; Past H/I KSADS Past Hyperactivity/Impulsivity symptoms; BIS, Barrat Impulsivity Scale; BIS-ATTPLAN, Attention and Planning BIS subscale; BIS-CINI, Inhibitory Control BIS subscale; STAI-T and –S, State-Trait Anxiety Inventory – Trait and –State; BES, Binge Eating Scale; BDI, Beck depression inventory.

1= Controls; 2= ADHD; 3= ADHD+ED.

[a]*Univariate Analysis. Omnibus p-values. LSD post hoc correction.*

[b]*1 < 2, p < 0.001; 1 < 3, p < 0.001; 2 = 3, p = 0.11.*

[c]*1 < 2, p <0.001; 1 < 3, p < 0.001; 2 < 3, p = 0.007.*

[d]*1 < 2, p <0.001; 1 < 3, p < 0.001; 2 = 3, p = 0.53.*

[e]*1 < 2, p < 0.001; 1 < 3, p < 0.001; 2 = 3, p = 0.75.*

[f]*1 < 2, p < 0.001; 1 < 3, p = 0.002; 2 = 3, p = 0.92.*

[g]*1 < 2, p <0.001; 1 < 3, p <0.001; 2 = 3, p =0.34.*

[h]*1 < 2, p = 0.01; 1 = 3, p = 0.052; 2 = 3, p = 0.89.*

[i]*1 = 2, p = 0.059; 1 = 3, p = 0.065; 2 = 3, p = 0.69.*

[j]*1 = 2, p = 0.07; 1 < 3, p < 0.001; 2 < 3, p = 0.002.*

[l]*1 < 2, p = 0.025; 1 < 3, p =0.031; 2 = 3, p = 0.757.*

TABLE 3 | Interactions among groups for digit and visual span.

		Omnibus F (Eta^2), p-value[a]	ADHD vs. Control Mean Difference (Cohen's d)	ADHD+ED vs. Control Mean Difference (Cohen's d)	ADHD+ED vs. ADHD Mean Difference (Cohen's d)
Digit span	Raw score	0.93 (0.02), $p = 0.39$	−1.38 (1.87)	0.19 (−0.20)	1.19 (−1.24)
	Straight sequence	0.83 (0.02), $p = 0.44$	−0.72 (1.75)	−0.05 (0.09)	0.67 (1.24)
	Higher straight sequence	0.57 (0.01), $p = 0.56$	−0.19 (.82)	0.27 (−0.93)	0.46 (−1.53)
	Reverse sequence	0.63 (0.01), $p = 0.53$	−0.65 (1.56)	−0.13 (0.26)	0.51 (−0.93)
	Higher reverse sequence	0.73 (0.02), $p = 0.48$	−0.31 (1.33)	0.19 (−0.58)	0.50 (−1.58)
Visual span	Raw score	0.13 (0.004), $p = 0.87$	−0.36 (0.74)	−1.42 (0.22)	0.22 (−0.34)
	Straight sequence	0.004 (0.000), $p = 0.99$	0.93 (0.13)	0.00 (0)	0.03 (0.10)
	Higher straight sequence	0.17 (0.005), p =0.83	0.09 (−0.46)	−0.12(.47)	−0.21 (0.82)
	Reverse sequence	0.30 (0.009), $p = 0.73$	−0.32 (1.13)	−0.14 (.37)	0.18 (0.49)
	Higher reverse sequence	0.56 (0.01), $p = 0.57$	−0.26 (1.52)	−0.09 (.41)	0.16 (−0.76)

Mean difference (Cohen's d).

[a]*Univariate Analysis. Omnibus p-values. LSD post-hoc correction.*

In terms of vigilance testing, measures from the CPT (**Table 5**) yielded significant differences only for the Omission errors. There were significant differences when analyzing ADHD+ED vs. Controls ($p =$ 0.031) and the ADHD+ED vs. ADHD only ($p = 0.042$). This difference was of a moderate effect size in both contrasts. All other CPT measures were non-significantly different in all comparisons (**Table 5**).

Correlations Between BMI, BES, BDI, and ADHD Symptoms

Pearson correlations between BMI, BES, BDI, and ADHD symptoms (current KSADS inattention + current KSADS hyperactivity/ impulsivity as a single composite score) revealed that binge eating was positively correlated with depression ($r = 0.025$; $p < 0.05$) and ADHD ($r = 0.43$; $p < 0.001$) with a moderate effect size. Binge eating was positively correlated with

TABLE 4 | Interactions among groups for Iowa gambling task.

[-10pt]	*Omnibus F (Eta²), p-value*[a]	ADHD vs. Control Mean Difference (Cohen's d)	ADHD+ED vs. Control Mean Difference (Cohen's d)	ADHD+ED vs. ADHD Mean Difference (Cohen's d)
IGT deck A	0.32 (0.009), $p = 0.727$	0.049 (−0.75)	1.63 (−0.29)	1.13 (−0.20)
IGT deck B	2.50 (0.067), $p = 0.089$	2.8 (−0.37)	5 (−0.71)*	2.25 (−0.33)
IGT deck C	1.65 (0.045), $p = 0.19$	−2.46 (0.34)	−3.8 (0.34)	−1.33 (0.19)
IGT deck D	0.48 (0.014), $p = 0.61$	−0.61 (0.07)	−2.67 (0.35)	−2.05 (0.26)
IGT Block 1	0.90 (0.025), $p = 0.41$	−0.53 (0.08)	2.31 (−0.41)	2.83 (−0.44)
IGT Block 2	2 (0.054), $p = 0.14$	0.14 (−0.02)	−3.48 (0.69)	−3.62 (0.66)[a]
IGT Block 3	0.98 (0.027), $p = 0.37$	−1.6 (0.22)	−3.09 (0.41)	−1.49 (0.23)
IGT Block 4	2.12 (0.057), $p = 0.12$	−3.15 (0.35)	−5.19 (0.70)	−2.03 (0.29)
IGT Block 5	1.07 (0.03), $p = 0.34$	−0.76 (0.09)	−3.67 (0.53)	−2.91 (0.42)
Net score	2.12 (0.057), $p = 0.12$	−6.98 (0.30)	−13.77 (0.73)	−6.79 (0.37)[b]

*Mean difference (Cohen's d). *$p < 0.05$; [a]$p = 0.068$; [b]$p = 0.053$.*
Univariate Analysis. Omnibus p-values. LSD post-hoc correction.
Decks A and B = disadvantageous; Decks C and D = advantegeous; Net score for all 100 trials = [(Decks C+D) – (Decks A+B)]; Block refers to Net score of only 20 trials.

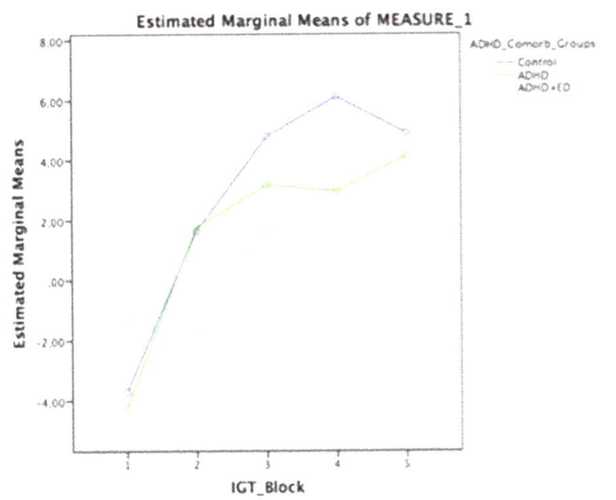

FIGURE 1 | Iowa Gambling Task across groups over time-in-task.

BMI with a strong effect size ($r = 0.48$; $p < 0.001$). ADHD was positively correlated with depression ($r = 0.33$; $p < 0.01$) with a moderate effect size and didn't correlate with BMI ($r = 0.23$, $p = 0.062$). None of the correlations were so high as to suggestion redundancy (all correlations < |0.8|).

Mediational Analysis

The data were first analyzed for missing cases, outliers, and assumptions of normality. Seventeen cases were missing from the BES variable and eight cases were missing from the BDI variable. Cases with missing data on one or more variable were excluded from relevant analyses. One univariate outlier ($Z > |3.00|$) was observed in the BMI variable and one outlier was observed in the BDI variable. These cases were also excluded listwise from all further analyses. No univariate outliers were observed in the ADHD or BES variables. All variables were normally distributed (skew < |2.00|, kurtosis < |9.00|). The descriptive statistics associated with BES, BMI, BDI, and ADHD symptoms are reported in **Table 6**.

Pearson correlations between BES, BMI, BDI, and ADHD symptoms are presented in **Table 7**. Binge eating was positively correlated with depression and ADHD (moderate effect size). Binge eating was positively correlated with BMI with a strong effect size. ADHD was positively correlated with depression (moderate effect size). None of the correlations were so high as to suggestion redundancy (all correlations < |0.8|).

Mediation model 1: Binge eating mediates the relationship between ED diagnostic status and BMI, after controlling for depression.

In the first mediation model we tested, we tested the hypothesis that binge eating mediates the effects of ADHD/ED comorbidity on BMI. This was investigated with a mediation analysis was conducted using the paramed command (37) in STATA (StataCorp, 2015). Assumptions of the mediation analysis for H1 were tested using two regression analyses in SPSS (IBM Corp., 2013): one bivariate regression of BES on eating disorder status and BDI (path a) and a multiple regression of BMI on BES, BDI, and eating disorder status (paths b′ and c′, respectively). Visual inspection of histograms of the standardized residuals revealed that they were approximately normally distributed for both regressions. Visual inspection of a scatterplot of standardized residuals plotted against standardized predicted values revealed that the assumption of homoscedasticity was violated for both regressions. A dummy regression did not reveal any multivariate outliers (Mahalanobis distance > 13.82, $df = 2$, $p < 0.001$) among the ED and BDI variables. A second dummy regression did not reveal any multivariate outliers (Mahalanobis distance > 16.27, $df = 3$, $p < 0.001$) among the ED, BDI, and BES variables. Neither regression was associated with excessive multicollinearity (tolerance > 0.10 for all predictor variables and covariates).

The mediation analysis was then conducted in STATA using the paramed command. The significance of the indirect and total effects was tested via bias-corrected bootstrapping, which is robust to violations of the assumption of homoscedasticity.

TABLE 5 | Interactions among groups for Conner's continuous performance test.

	Omnibus *F (Eta²), p-value*[a]	ADHD vs. Control Mean Difference (Cohen's d)	ADHD+ED vs. Control Mean Difference (Cohen's d)	ADHD+ED vs. ADHD Mean Difference (Cohen's d)
Omission	2.65 (0.072), $p = 0.07$	−0.02 (0.009)	9.05 (−0.42)[b]	9.07 (−0.42)[c]
Comission	1.45 (0.040), $p = 0.24$	2.56 (−0.31)	4.26 (−0.50)	1.69 (−0.19)
Standard error	0.85 (0.024), $p = 0.43$	0.24 (−0.002)	70.36 (−0.33)	70.11 (−0.32)
D Prime	1.74 (0.048), $p = 0.18$	−12.72 (0.29)	−25.41 (0.60)	−12.68 (0.29)
Variability	1.61 (0.045), $p = 0.20$	−85 (−0.89)	−304 (−2.54)	−218 (−1.76)
HRT	0.01 (0), $p = 0.98$	−285.13 (0.04)	−130.20 (0.02)	154.92 (−0.02)
HRT Block change	0.56 (0.016), $p = 0.74$	0.26(−0.29)	0.27(−0.21)	0.01 (−0.01)
HRT ISI change	0.29 (0.009), $p = 0.74$	0.26 (−0.09)	0.69 (−0.24)	0.42 (−0.09)

Mean difference (Cohen's d). HRT, Hit Reaction time; HRT ISI Change, HRT Inter Stimulus Interval Change.
[a]*Univariate Analysis. Omnibus p-values. LSD post-hoc correction.*
[b]*$p = 0.035$.*
[c]*$p = 0.041$.*

Both path a (coefficient = 7.86, SE = 1.76, 95% CI [4.34, 11.38] and path b′ (coefficient = 0.13, 0.05, 95% CI [0.04, 0.23]) were associated with significant but small positive effects. The analysis revealed that having an eating disorder was significantly positively associated with higher BMI (total effect = 3.31, bootstrap standard error = 0.63, 95% CI [2.06, 4.52]). Binge eating significantly mediated this effect (indirect effect = 1.04, bootstrap standard error = 0.58, 95% CI [0.09, 2.30]).

Mediation model 2: Impulsivity mediates the relationship between ADHD and binge eating, after controlling for depression.

For this mediation, we first sought to establish the existence of significant relationships between the predictor, mediator, and dependent variables. We therefore carried out a regression in which BES was entered as the dependent variable and the BDI, BIS, current KSADS inattention, and current KSADS hyperactivity/impulsivity were entered using the forced entry method. This model predicting binge eating from ADHD symptoms and impulsivity was significant, $R^2 = 0.21$, Adj. $R^2 = 0.16$, $SE = 5.88$, $\Delta F_{(4,60)} = 9.64$, $p = 0.006$. However, none of the included variables significantly predicted binge eating. The regression was not affected by multicollinearity (tolerance > 0.1 for all variables).

Therefore, given that a relationship between the mediator and dependent variable could not be established after controlling for the independent variable, the current model did not meet Baron and Kenny's necessary assumptions for a mediated model (38). While modern research has indicated that not all of Baron and Kenny's assumptions are necessary to establish a significant indirect effect (39), we concluded that an indirect effect in the absence of a significant effect between the mediator and dependent variable was not of theoretical interest in the current model.

TABLE 6 | Descriptive Statistics associated with binge eating, body mass index, depression, and ADHD symptoms.

	M	*SD*	Min	Max	Skew	Kurtosis
BES	8.86	6.42	0.00	22.00	0.38	−0.89
BMI	22.23	2.57	16.49	29.59	0.77	0.66
BDI	7.06	6.82	0.00	27.00	1.29	0.85
ADHD	7.19	4.86	0.00	17.00	0.18	−0.93

BES, binge eating specific score; BMI, body mass index; BDI, Beck Depression Inventory; ADHD, current composite score of inattentive and hyperactive/impulsive symptoms. N = 69.

TABLE 7 | Correlations between binge eating, body mass index, depression, and ADHD symptoms.

	BDI	BES	ADHD
BES			0.43***
BDI		0.25*	0.33**
BMI	0.06	0.48***	0.23

*BES, binge eating specific score; BMI, body mass index; BDI, Beck Depression Inventory; ADHD, current composite score of inattentive and hyperactive/impulsive symptoms. N = 69. *$p < 0.05$; **$p < 0.01$; ***$p < 0.001$.*

DISCUSSION

In the present research we have demonstrated that individuals comorbid for ADHD and ED presented greater omission errors in the CPT and a tendency for impaired decision-making using the IGT. Also, these patients presented higher number of current Hyperactivity/Impulsivity symptoms than the ADHD-only group. Furthermore, we demonstrated that comorbid individuals had a higher BMI and that a greater level of binge eating mediated this relationship.

Previous research in the field of ADHD and Obesity has suggested that weight gain in individuals with ADHD might be due to a sleep disorder (e.g., sleep apnea) in obese patients mimicking ADHD (40), a genetic variant with impaired reward processing or altered eating habits due to impulsivity (41). We have presented evidence that the presence of a comorbid ED might contribute to weight gain in ADHD subjects. Even in the presence of mild eating binges, as measured by the BES, our ADHD+ED subjects had a significantly higher BMI than ADHD only. This falls in line with findings from clinical samples, where obese subjects presenting for weight loss comorbid with ADHD had higher BMI (5, 42–44).

The higher number of current HI symptoms in the ADHD+ED group cannot be regarded as an indication of higher impulsive traits or higher anxiety levels since these measures didn't differ from the other groups in self-report questionnaires. This contradicts the findings that ADHD-ED comorbid individuals had higher anxiety levels found in clinical samples of obese (5). ADHD individuals usually change their clinical presentation over time (45) with waning of HI behaviors to more socially age appropriate presentations.

Two previous studies have investigated cognitive function in participants with ADHD+ED. Reinblatt et al. (46), has investigated if children comorbid for Loss of Control Eating (a subclinical form of BED) differed from ADHD-only or Control participants using a Continuous Performance Test (The GNG neurobehavioural task) and a motor inhibition task. They didn't find any differences between groups. Furthermore, Seitz et al. (18) compared a sample of women with current bulimia nervosa with a history of childhood ADHD to a separate sample without a childhood history of ADHD on a continuous performance test, a task for divided attention, and a task for executive functioning. Although they didn't find significant results on the neuropsychological tests, there was a trend greater for omission errors in the comorbid group.

In accordance with the results found by Seitz et al. (18), our ADHD+ED group presented significantly higher omission errors on the CPT. Although this would indicate inattention, distractibility the number of current inattention symptoms didn't differ from ADHD only. Also, this index can denote a slower motor response. Apparently, the presence of an ED further impairs attentional systems in ADHD individuals.

The findings in the IGT suggest that ADHD+ED subjects have their decision-making skills impaired, when compared to ADHD only subjects. This might be explained by the presence of an ED. The IGT could be representative of an information processing mediated by the insula (47). A triadic model of impulse control postulates that abnormal functioning in different parts of the brain impairs this function. These cognitive systems control habitual and salient behaviors processed by the amygdala-striatum; self-regulation modulated by the prefrontal cortex; and translation of interoceptive states to feelings (urges, cravings) by the insula. It might be that ED impairs decision-making of ADHD individuals by the well-documented deficits of ED individuals in insular function (48, 49).

Binge eating was not significantly predicted by depression, impulsivity as measured by the BIS, inattention, or hyperactivity/impulsivity measured by the KSADS. Perhaps low sample size prevented the model from uncovering significant results. This effect might also reflect the poor ecological validity of these self-report measures, given the well-cited associated between impulsivity and binge eating (5, 18).

LIMITATIONS

Our findings are limited by the small sample size, relatively mild-moderate severity of eating behavior disturbances. The high cognitive functioning of all samples, as they are college students, could interfere with cognitive testing as it could induce a ceiling effect of results. Differences could be more pronounced in a clinical sample with severe symptoms and a poorer cognitive functioning. On the other hand, our study has several strengths, exemplified by the control group without any mental disorder, and the use of a treatment-naive sample, as medication could be a factor that could interfere with cognitive testing.

AUTHOR CONTRIBUTIONS

All authors listed have made a substantial, direct and intellectual contribution to the work, and approved it for publication.

FUNDING

BN has been funded with a scholarship from CAPES-PDSE (Comissão de Aperfeiçoamento de Pessoal do Nível Superior - Programa de Doutorado Sanduiche no Exterior).

REFERENCES

1. Nazar BP, Bernardes C, Peachey G, Sergeant J, Mattos P, Treasure J. The risk of eating disorders comorbid with attention-deficit/hyperactivity disorder: a systematic review and meta-analysis. *Int J Eat Disord.* (2016) 49:1045–57. doi: 10.1002/eat.22643
2. Brewerton TD, Duncan AE. Associations between attention deficit hyperactivity disorder and eating disorders by gender: results from the national comorbidity survey replication. *Eur Eat Disord Rev.* (2016) 24:536–40. doi: 10.1002/erv.2468
3. Egbert AH, Wilfley DE, Eddy KT, Boutelle KN, Zucker N, Peterson CB, et al. Attention-deficit/hyperactivity disorder symptoms are associated with overeating with and without loss of control in youth with overweight/obesity. *Child Obes.* (2018) 14:50–7. doi: 10.1089/chi.2017.0114
4. Reinblatt SP, Leoutsakos J-MS, Mahone EM, Forrester S, Wilcox HC, Riddle MA. Association between binge eating and attention-deficit/hyperactivity disorder in two pediatric community mental health clinics. *Int J Eat Disord.* (2015) 48:505–11. doi: 10.1002/eat.22342
5. Nazar BP, Suwwan R, de Sousa Pinna CM, Duchesne M, Freitas SR, Sergeant J, et al. Influence of attention-deficit/hyperactivity disorder on binge eating behaviors and psychiatric comorbidity profile of obese women. *Compr Psychiatry* (2014) 55:572–8. doi: 10.1016/j.comppsych.2013.09.015
6. Levy LD, Fleming JP, Klar D. Treatment of refractory obesity in severely obese adults following management of newly diagnosed attention deficit hyperactivity disorder. *Int J Obes.* (2009) 33:326–34. doi: 10.1038/ijo.2009.5
7. Alfonsson S, Parling T, Ghaderi A. Self-reported symptoms of adult attention deficit hyperactivity disorder among obese patients seeking bariatric surgery and its relation to alcohol consumption, disordered eating and gender. *Clin Obes.* (2013) 3:124–31. doi: 10.1111/cob.12025
8. Fernández-Aranda F, Agüera Z, Castro R, Jiménez-Murcia S, Ramos-Quiroga JA, Bosch R, et al. ADHD symptomatology in eating disorders: a secondary psychopathological measure of severity? *BMC Psychiatry* (2013) 13:166. doi: 10.1186/1471-244X-13-166

9. Nazar BP, de Sousa Pinna CM, Suwwan R, Duchesne M, Freitas SR, Sergeant J, et al. ADHD rate in obese women with binge eating and bulimic behaviors from a weight-loss clinic. *J Atten Disord.* (2016) 20:610–6. doi: 10.1177/1087054712455503
10. Svedlund NE, Norring C, Ginsberg Y, von Hausswolff-Juhlin Y. Are treatment results for eating disorders affected by ADHD symptoms? A one-year follow-up of adult females *Eur Eat Disord Rev.* (2018) 26:337–45. doi: 10.1002/erv.2598
11. McElroy SL, Hudson JI, Mitchell JE, Wilfley D, Ferreira-Cornwell MC, Gao J, et al. Efficacy and safety of lisdexamfetamine for treatment of adults with moderate to severe binge-eating disorder: a randomized clinical trial. *JAMA Psychiatry* (2015) 72:235–46. doi: 10.1001/jamapsychiatry.2014.2162
12. Gibbs EL, Kass AE, Eichen DM, Fitzsimmons-Craft EE, Trockel M, Wilfley DE. Attention-deficit/hyperactivity disorder-specific stimulant misuse, mood, anxiety, and stress in college-age women at high risk for or with eating disorders. *J Am Coll Health* (2016) 64:300–8. doi: 10.1080/07448481.2016.1138477
13. Wilens TE, Adler LA, Adams J, Sgambati S, Rotrosen J, Sawtelle R, et al. Misuse and diversion of stimulants prescribed for ADHD: a systematic review of the literature. *J Am Acad Child Adolesc Psychiatry* (2008) 47:21–31. doi: 10.1097/chi.0b013e31815a56f1
14. Garon N. Decision making in children with ADHD only, ADHD-anxious/depressed, and control children using a child version of the Iowa Gambling Task. *J Atten Disord.* (2006) 9:607–19. doi: 10.1177/1087054705284501
15. Narvaez JC, Zeni CP, Coelho RP, Wagner F, Pheula GF, Ketzer CR, et al. Does comorbid bipolar disorder increase neuropsychological impairment in children and adolescents with ADHD? *Rev Bras Psiquiatr.* (2014) 36:53–9. doi: 10.1590/1516-4446-2013-1085
16. Crunelle CL, Veltman DJ, van Emmerik-van Oortmerssen K, Booij J, van den Brink, W. Impulsivity in adult ADHD patients with and without cocaine dependence. *Drug Alcohol Depend.* (2013) 129:18–24. doi: 10.1016/j.drugalcdep.2012.09.006
17. Silva KL, Rovaris DL, Guimarães-da-Silva PO, Victor MM, Salgado CA, Vitola ES, et al. Could comorbid bipolar disorder account for a significant share of executive function deficits in adults with attention-deficit hyperactivity disorder? *Bipolar Disord.* (2014) 16:270–6. doi: 10.1111/bdi.12158
18. Seitz J, Kahraman-Lanzerath B, Legenbauer T, Sarrar L, Herpertz S, Salbach-Andrae H, et al. The role of impulsivity, inattention and comorbid ADHD in patients with bulimia nervosa. *PLoS ONE* (2013) 8:e63891. doi: 10.1371/journal.pone.0063891
19. Steadman KM, Knouse LE. Is the relationship between ADHD symptoms and binge eating mediated by impulsivity? *J Atten Disord.* (2014) 20:907–12. doi: 10.1177/1087054714530779
20. Reinblatt SP. are eating disorders related to attention deficit/hyperactivity disorder? *Curr Treat Options Psychiatry* (2015) 2:402–12. doi: 10.1007/s40501-015-0060-7
21. Mattos P, Nazar BP, Tannock R. By the book: ADHD prevalence in medical students varies with analogous methods of addressing DSM items. *Rev Bras Psiquiatr.* (2018) 40:382–7. doi: 10.1590/1516-4446-2017-2429
22. Kessler RC, Adler L, Ames M, Demler O, Faraone S, Hiripi E, et al. The world health organization adult ADHD Self-Report Scale (ASRS): a short screening scale for use in the general population. *Psychol Med.* (2005) 35:245–56. doi: 10.1017/S0033291704002892
23. Gormally J, Black S, Daston S, Rardin D. The assessment of binge eating severity among obese persons. *Addict Behav.* (1982) 7:47–5. doi: 10.1016/0306-4603(82) 90024-7
24. Kaufman J, Birmaher B, Brent D, Rao U, Flynn C, Moreci P, et al. Schedule for Affective disorders and schizophrenia for school-age children-present and lifetime version (K-SADS-PL): initial reliability and validity data. *J Am Acad Child Adolesc Psychiatry* (1997) 36:980–8. doi: 10.1097/00004583-199707000-00021
25. Beck AT, Beamesderfer A. Assessment of depression: the depression inventory. *Mod. Probl Pharmacopsychiatry* (1974) 7:151–69. doi: 10.1159/000395074
26. Gorenstein C, Andrade L, Vieira Filho AH, Tung TC, Artes R. Psychometric properties of the portuguese version of the beck depression inventory on Brazilian college students. *J Clin Psychol.* (1999) 55, 553–62.
27. Andrade L, Gorenstein C, Vieira Filho AH, Tung TC, Artes R. Psychometric properties of the Portuguese version of the state-trait anxiety inventory applied to college students: factor analysis and relation to the beck depression inventory. *Braz J Med Biol Res.* (2001) 34:367–74. doi: 10.1590/S0100-879X2001000300011
28. Patton JH, Stanford MS, Barratt ES. Factor structure of the Barratt impulsiveness scale. *J Clin Psychol.* (1995) 51:768–74.
29. Mattos P, Segenreich D, Saboya E, Louzã, M, Dias G, Romano M. Adaptação transcultural para o português da escala Adult Self-Report Scale para avaliação do transtorno de déficit de atenção/hiperatividade (TDAH) em adultos. *Arch Clin Psychiatry* (2006) 33:188–94. doi: 10.1590/S0101-60832006000400004
30. Freitas S, Lopes CS, Coutinho W, Appolinario JC. Tradução e adaptação para o português da escala de compulsão alimentar periódica translation and adaptation into Portuguese of the Binge-Eating Scale. *Rev Bras Psiquiatr.* (2001) 23:215–20. doi: 10.1590/S1516-44462001000400008
31. Malloy-diniz LF, Mattos P, Leite WB, Abreu N, Paula JJ, De Tavares H, et al. Tradução e adaptação cultural da Barratt Impulsiveness Scale (BIS-11) para aplicação em adultos brasileiros. *J Bras Psiquiatr.* (2010) 59:99–105. doi: 10.1590/S0047-20852010000200004
32. Heck VS, Yates DB, Poggere LC, Tosi SMVD, Bandeira DR, Trentini, CM. Validação dos subtestes verbais da versão de adaptação da WASI. *Aval Psicol.* (2009) 8:33–42.
33. Conners BCK. *Conners ' Continuous Performance Test II (CPT II V. 5)* (2004)
34. Rabin LA, Barr WB, Burton LA. Assessment practices of clinical neuropsychologists in the United States and Canada: a survey of INS, NAN, and APA Division 40 members. *Arch Clin Neuropsychol.* (2005) 20:33–65. doi: 10.1016/j.acn.2004.02.005
35. Robertson IH, Manly T, Andrade J, Baddeley BT, Yiend J. "Oops!": performance correlates of everyday attentional failures in traumatic brain injured and normal subjects. *Neuropsychologia* (1997) 35:747–58.
36. Bechara A. *Iowa Gambling Task Professional Manual.* Lutz, FL: Psychological Assessment Resources (2007).
37. Liu H, Emsley R, Dunn G, VanderWeele T, Valeri L. Paramed: a command to perform causal mediation analysis using parametric models. *Unkn J.* (2014).
38. Baron RM, Kenny DA. The moderator-mediator variable distinction in social psychological research: conceptual, strategic, and statistical considerations. *J Pers Soc Psychol.* (1986) 51:1173–82. doi: 10.1037/0022-3514.51.6.1173
39. Hayes AF, Matthes J. Computational procedures for probing interactions in OLS and logistic regression: SPSS and SAS implementations. *Behav Res Methods* (2009) 41:924–36. doi: 10.3758/BRM.41.3.924
40. Cortese S, Morcillo Peñalver C. Comorbidity between ADHD and obesity: exploring shared mechanisms and clinical implications. *Postgrad Med.* (2010) 122:88–96. doi: 10.3810/pgm.2010.09.2205
41. Blum K, Chen ALC, Braverman ER, Comings DE, Chen TJ, Arcuri V. et al. Attention-deficit-hyperactivity disorder and reward deficiency syndrome. *Neuropsychiatr Dis Treat.* (2008) 4:893–918.
42. Altfas JR. Prevalence of attention deficit/hyperactivity disorder among adults in obesity treatment. *BMC Psychiatry* (2002) 2:9. doi: 10.1186/1471-244X-2-9
43. Cortese S, Moreira-Maia CR, St Fleur D, Morcillo-Peñalver C, Rohde LA, Faraone SV. Association between ADHD and obesity: a systematic review and meta-analysis. *Am J Psychiatry* (2016) 173:34–43. doi: 10.1176/appi.ajp.2015.15020266
44. Nigg JT, Johnstone JM, Musser ED, Long HG, Willoughby MT, Shannon J. Attention-deficit/hyperactivity disorder (ADHD) and being overweight/obesity: new data and meta-analysis. *Clin Psychol Rev.* (2016) 43:67–79. doi: 10.1016/j.cpr.2015.11.005
45. Volkow ND, Swanson JM. Clinical practice: adult attention deficit – hyperactivity disorder. *N Engl J Med.* (2013) 369:1935–44. doi: 10.1056/NEJMcp1212625
46. Reinblatt SP, Mahone EM, Tanofsky-Kraff M, Lee-Winn AE, Yenokyan G, Leoutsakos J-MS, et al. Pediatric loss of control eating syndrome: association

with attention-deficit/hyperactivity disorder and impulsivity. *Int J Eat Disord.* (2015) 48:580–8. doi: 10.1002/eat.22404

47. Noël X, Brevers D, Bechara A. A triadic neurocognitive approach to addiction for clinical interventions. *Front Psychiatry* (2013) 4:179. doi: 10.3389/fpsyt.2013.00179
48. Esposito R, Cieri F, di Giannantonio M, Tartaro A. The role of body image and self-perception in anorexia nervosa: the neuroimaging perspective. *J Neuropsychol.* (2018) 12:41–52. doi: 10.1111/jnp.12106
49. Frank GKW, Kaye WH. Current status of functional imaging in eating disorders. *Int J Eat Disord.* (2012) 45:723–36. doi: 10.1002/eat.22016

13

The Effect of Enumeration of Self-Relevant Words on Self-Focused Attention and Repetitive Negative Thoughts

Seiji Muranaka and Jun Sasaki*

Department of Clinical Psychology, Graduate School of Human Sciences, Osaka University, Suita, Japan

Correspondence:
Seiji Muranaka
s.muranaka624@gmail.com

Self-focused attention refers to awareness of self-referent, internally generated information. It can be categorized into dysfunctional (i.e., self-rumination) and functional (self-reflection) aspects. According to theory on cognitive resource limitations (e.g., Moreno, 2006), there is a difference in cognitive resource allocation between these two aspects of self-focused attention. We propose a new task, self-relevant word (SRW) enumeration, that can aid in behaviorally identifying individuals' use of self-rumination and self-reflection. The present study has two purposes: to determine the association between self-focus and SRW enumeration, and to examine the effect of dysfunctional SRW enumeration on repetitive negative thinking. One hundred forty-six undergraduate students participated in this study. They completed a measure of state anxiety twice, before and after imagining a social failure situation. They also completed the SRW enumeration task, Repetitive Thinking Questionnaire, Short Fear of Negative Evaluation Scale, and Rumination-Reflection Questionnaire. A correlational analysis indicated a significant positive correlation between self-reflection and the number of SRWs. Furthermore, individuals high in self-reflection had a tendency to pay more attention to problems than did those high in self-rumination. A significant positive correlation was found between self-rumination and the strength of self-relevance of negative SRWs. Through a path analysis, we found a significant positive effect of the self-relevance of negative SRWs on repetitive negative thinking. Notably, however, the model that excluded self-rumination as an explanatory variable showed a better fit to the data than did the model that included it. In summary, SRW enumeration might enable selective and independent detection of the degree of self-reflection and self-rumination, and therefore should be examined in future research in order to design new behavioral procedures.

Keywords: self-focused attention, repetitive negative thinking, self-control, limited resources, self-relevant word

INTRODUCTION

Self-focused attention refers to an awareness of self-referent, internally generated information (Ingram, 1990). Self-focused attention has a strong influence over internal information, more so than external information; as such, if the contents of self-focused thoughts are negative, self-focused attention can generate negative affect. For this reason, self-focused attention is considered to play an important role in the development and maintenance of various psychopathological conditions, such as depression, anxiety disorder, and schizophrenia (Spurr and Stopa, 2002). Self-focused attention comprises both functional (self-reflection) and dysfunctional (self-rumination) aspects (Trapnell and Campbell, 1999). Self-rumination refers to self-focused attention motivated by perceived threats, losses, or injustices against the self. When an individual is threatened, they experience anxiety, which in turn causes individuals to pay attention to the enfolding events, their own negative affect, and the consequences of the events. As a result, anxiety can be maintained (e.g., Clark and Wells, 1995). In contrast, self-reflection is self-focused attention motivated by curiosity or an epistemic interest in the self; it reduces depressive mood through encouraging problem-solving behavior during intensely stressful events, which suggests that it facilitates self-regulation to solve problems adaptively (e.g., Mori et al., 2015). Thus, it is clinically important to investigate how to switch from a dysfunctional style to a functional one (e.g., Takano et al., 2012).

However, some studies have shown a significant positive correlation between self-rumination and self-reflection (e.g., Takano et al., 2012; Mori et al., 2015). This finding means that heightening the functional self-focus style ironically results in a similar heightening of the dysfunctional style. Accordingly, methods that independently affect these self-focus styles are needed.

Individuals' motivation for focusing on the self and limitations in their cognitive resources potentially determine whether they adopt a functional or dysfunctional self-focus style. Sweller (1988) proposed cognitive load theory (CLT) to explain how limited cognitive resources influence selective attention. According to CLT, depletion of limited cognitive resources decreases performance on certain tasks (in terms of achievements such as number of errors and time spent on the task) (Paas et al., 2003). High ruminator depletes attentional resources for problem solving, and has difficulty in discarding no-longer-relevant negative words from working memory (Koster et al., 2011; Zetsche et al., 2012). The degree to which one allocates these limited cognitive resources to the self in turn may define the style of self-focused attention (Whitmer and Gotlib, 2013). Labor motivation, which orient "have to" goal lead to depleted limited cognitive resources. It need to switch to leisure motivation, which orient "want to" goal (Inzlicht et al., 2014).

Self-regulation and motivation appear to mediate the selection, organization, and integration of information in working memory, as well as retrieval from long-term memory. Motivation also appears to mediate selective attention of information (Moreno, 2006), which may lead to a difference in the allocation of resources between the functional and dysfunctional self-focus style. A ruminative self-focus makes individuals narrowly focus on negative information when negative affects occur (Whitmer and Gotlib, 2013), whereas a self-reflective focus is associated with distancing oneself from problems and paying greater attention to the more positive aspects of the self because self-reflection tends to lead to calmer responses to negative experiences (Ayduk and Kross, 2010). Self-regulation is also a relevant factor; it refers to the capacity to override one's thoughts, feelings, and habitual patterns of behavior. High self-regulation can control negative thoughts such as death related thoughts (Galliot et al., 2006). Baumeister and Vohs (2007) noted that motivation can be helpful in overcoming ego depletion (i.e., a state of depleted cognitive resources), although it must be restrained in order to maintain self-regulation. Thus, motivation is an important influencing factor of self-regulation and how people control intensive negative thoughts. Furthermore, it is crucial in learning to utilize limited cognitive resources for functional self-focused attention.

According to Muraven et al. (1998), cognitive resources can be measured using the time spent engaging in a behavioral task—particularly, how long an individual attends to self-relevant information in such a task. We strove to develop a behavioral task in order to assess self-focused attention through the enumeration of words that individuals use to describe themselves. This task, called self-relevant word (SRW) enumeration, was designed to enable identification of a current process of self- rumination and self-reflection. As mentioned above, negative emotions narrow the attentional scope and maintain rumination (Whitmer and Gotlib, 2013). Furthermore, Gaebler et al. (2014) found a correlation between self-relatedness and the intensity of negative emotion among patients with social anxiety disorder who were looking at aversive pictures, and they reacted more strongly to negative information when the intensity of their negative emotions was high. Accordingly, we expected that individuals with higher self-rumination might better retain negative words. In other words, the strength of the relationship with negative SRWs might be usable as an index of self-rumination. We predicted that self-rumination is associated with the strength of the relevance of negative SRWs (negative SRWstr). On the other hand, individuals higher in self-reflection were expected to have more comprehensive self-perceptions, which means that they would produce a higher number of SRWs overall (SRWnum). This is based on the findings of Ayduk and Kross (2010), who noted that individuals higher in self-reflection tend to adopt a broader perspective on themselves.

Numerous studies have begun focusing on the function of repetitive negative thinking (RNT) in order to understand emotional upsets and persistent emotional disorders (Kashdan and Roberts, 2007; Ehring and Watkins, 2008). RNT refer to iterative thinking about negative content. We assume that SRW enumeration is related to RNT. Confirming the effect of a dysfunctional SRW enumeration style on RNT can help in developing techniques to decrease RNT in emotional disorders.

The present study had two purposes: to determine the association between self-focus and SRW enumeration, and to confirm the effect of dysfunctional SRW enumeration on RNT. We formulated and tested three hypotheses in relation to these purposes. First, there is a positive correlation between self-reflection and the SRWnum. Second, there is a positive correlation between self-rumination and the negative SRWstr. Finally, based on the idea that rumination is maintained by narrowing the attentional scope to the self (Whitmer and Gotlib, 2013), negative SRWstr is expected to have a direct effect on RNT.

MATERIALS AND METHODS

Participants

A total of 146 undergraduate students participated (49 males and 97 females) in this study. Their mean age was 20.92 years [standard deviation (SD) = 3.30].

Measures

State-Trait Anxiety Inventory (Japanese Version; Shimizu and Imae, 1981)

Participants completed the Japanese version of the state scale of the State-Trait Anxiety Inventory (STAI-S) before and after imaging a situation (see below). The STAI-S measures the degree of state anxiety; it contains 20 items and participants are required to answer each item on a 4-point Likert-type scale from 1 (not at all) to 4 (very much). A Cronbach's alpha of 0.87 was reported, indicating high validity (Shimizu and Imae, 1981). We termed scores on the STAI-S before and after the imagining a social failure situation as pre-STAI-S and post-STAI-S scores, respectively. We also calculated the extent to which anxiety increased, denoted as the increment in STAI-S score.

Short Fear of Negative Evaluation (Japanese Version; Sasagawa et al., 2004)

Participants completed the short fear of negative evaluation (SFNE), which measures the degree to which individuals fear negative evaluations. This questionnaire contains 12 items, each rated on a 5-point Likert-type scale ranging from 1 (strongly disagree) to 5 (strongly agree). Sasagawa et al. (2004) confirmed that this scale has high measurement precision according to item response theory. In this study, we increased participants' level of state anxiety by having them imagine a social failure situation. Thus, the SFNE was used to confirm whether fear of negative evaluation (also called social trait anxiety) affected the increase in state anxiety after the imagination task.

Repetitive Thinking Questionnaire (Japanese Edition; Tanaka and Sugiura, 2014)

Participants completed the Japanese version of the Repetitive Thinking Questionnaire (RTQ), which measures their degree of RNT. This questionnaire contains 10 items, each rated on a 5-point Likert-type scale ranging from 1 (strongly disagree) to 5 (strongly agree). The scale had a Cronbach' s alpha value of 0.91, indicating high reliability (Tanaka and Sugiura, 2014).

Rumination-Reflection Questionnaire (Japanese Edition; Takano and Tanno, 2008)

We used the Rumination-Reflection Questionnaire (RRQ) to assess participants' self-rumination and self-reflection tendencies. This questionnaire contains 24 items (two subscales with 12 items each), each rated on a 5-point Likert-type scale ranging from 1 (strongly disagree) to 5 (strongly agree). Takano and Tanno (2008) found that the scale had good internal consistency ($\alpha = 0.89$ for self-rumination; $\alpha = 0.89$ for self-reflection).

Situation Imagination Task

Participants were asked to imagine a social failure situation after reading text in Japanese taken from a study by Fujii (2013): "You have broken some dishes in front of a large number of guests in a restaurant." Participants were asked to report the total number of guests and the number of guests who noticed the sound of the breaking dishes.

SRW Enumeration Task

In this task, participants were asked to enumerate and describe as many SRWs as they could, as outlined in the following instructions (in Japanese): "Please write as many words that you can use to describe yourself as you can." After enumerating the words, participants had to indicate the emotional valence and self-relevance of each word. Emotional valence was measured using a 5-point Likert-type scale, ranging from 1 (negative) to 5 (positive). Therefore, SRWs with an emotional valence scored 1 or 2 were regarded as negative. Self-relevance was also evaluated using a 5-point Likert-type scale, ranging from 1 (strongly disagree) to 5 (strongly agree). In this study, participants could write down a maximum of 16 SRWs because of the limited available space on the page. Examples of SRWs written by participants include "ashamed," "anxious," "impatient," and so on. We calculated two scores from the SRWs: the number of SRWs (SRWnum) and the strength of their self-relevance (SRWstr).

Procedure

All participants were recruited from introductory psychology classes. With the lecturer's cooperation, a researcher distributed the questionnaires and written instructions about this study to participants. Participants completed the STAI-S twice, before and after the situation imagination task. Next, they completed the SRW enumeration task and the RTQ, SFNE, and RRQ. Participants spent approximately 10 min in total. No incentive was given to any participants.

The study protocol was approved by the institutional review board of an author's affiliated institution and this study was carried out in accordance with the recommendations of the ethics committee of the Graduate School of Human Sciences, Osaka University. Written informed consent was obtained from all subjects in accordance with the Declaration of Helsinki.

Statistical Analysis

The normality of each variable was tested before any further analysis. A skewness of over 2.0 and a kurtosis of over 7.0 were considered to reflect a moderately non-normal distribution (Curran et al., 1996). Our analysis consisted of three parts. First, the discrepancies between pre- and post-STAI-S scores were examined with a paired *t*-test. Second, hypotheses 1 and 2 were investigated via correlational analyses between self-reflection scores and SRWnum, as well as between self-rumination scores and negative SRWstr. The correlational analysis required a sample size of at least 80 for a middle effect size and sufficiently high power [$\rho = 0.3$, degree of power $(1-\beta) = 0.80$]. Therefore, this study had a sufficiently large sample. Finally, hypothesis 3 was examined via a path analysis to confirm the relationship between

SRW enumeration and RNT. The effect of self-rumination was nested if hypothesis 1 was followed. Moreover, the effect of the degree of increase in anxiety was nested because negative emotional intensity has a positive effect on self-relatedness (Gaebler et al., 2014).

RESULTS

Descriptive Statistics and Manipulation Check

Descriptive statistics are shown in **Table 1**. The SRWnum ranged from 0 to 16, while the negative SRWnum ranged from 0 to 11. The overall and negative SRWstr ranged from 0 to 5. A normality test revealed that the kurtosis of SRWnum was over 7.0. Thus, it was regarded as having a non-normal distribution.

As a manipulation check, a paired t-test was used to examine the discrepancy between pre-STAI-S and post-STAI-S scores. We found that the post-STAI-S score was significantly higher than was the pre-STAI score [$t(284.35) = 3.32$, $p < 0.001$; *ES: Cohen's* $d = 0.70$, $1-\beta > 0.99$]. The results of the correlational analysis (shown below) indicated significant correlations between scores for the SFNE and each administration of the STAI-S. This finding indicates that fear of negative evaluation could be influenced by the increment in anxiety. Thus, a correlation was calculated between the increment in STAI-S scores and the SFNE scores. This was not significant ($r = 0.09$, n.s.).

Correlation Matrix

Table 2 shows the correlation matrix. Significant positive correlations were found between the pre-STAI-S scores and the post-STAI-S ($r = 0.58$, $p < 0.001$), RTQ ($r = 0.38$, $p < 0.001$), SFNE ($r = 0.35$, $p < 0.001$), and self-rumination scores ($r = 0.39$, $p < 0.001$). Post-STAI-S scores were also significantly and positively correlated with all other variables ($rs = 0.17–0.46$, $ps < 0.05$).

The increment in STAI-S score was significantly and positively correlated with SRWstr ($r = 0.20$, $p < 0.05$) and negative SRWstr ($r = 0.22$, $p < 0.01$). There was also a significant positive correlation between SRWstr and negative SRWstr ($r = 0.78$, $p < 0.01$). Negative SRWstr was significantly and positively correlated with RTQ ($r = 0.21$, $p < 0.05$) and self-rumination scores ($r = 0.21$, $p < 0.05$). Positive correlations were observed between RTQ scores and SFNE ($r = 0.39$, $p < 0.001$) and self-rumination scores ($r = 0.48$, $p < 0.001$). SFNE scores were positively correlated with self-rumination ($r = 0.66$, $p < 0.001$) and self-reflection scores ($r = 0.21$, $p < 0.05$). A significant positive correlation was also found between self-rumination and self-reflection ($r = 0.39$, $p < 0.001$).

As the SRWnum had a non-normal distribution, we evaluated its correlations with each variable via Spearman's coefficient. SRWnum had positive correlations with negative SRWnum ($\rho = 0.71$, $p < 0.001$) and self-reflection scores ($\rho = 0.20$, $p < 0.05$), and negative correlations with SRWstr ($\rho = -0.16$, $p < 0.05$). Thus, hypothesis 1 (i.e., self-reflection has a positive correlation with SRWnum) was partially supported by our results. There was no correlation between self-rumination and negative SRWnum. This finding, coupled with the above results concerning the positive relation between negative SRWstr and self-rumination, was supportive of hypothesis 2 (i.e., there is a positive correlation between self-rumination and the strength of self-relevance of negative SRWs). Moreover, the correlation between self-rumination and self-reflection ($r = 0.39$) was significantly stronger than was the correlation between SRWnum and negative SRWstr ($\rho = -0.01$; $z = 3.39$, $p < 0.001$). Therefore, negative SRWstr might reflect the degree of self-rumination.

The Effect of SRW Enumeration on RNT (Figure 1)

A path analysis was used to examine the statistical effect of negative SRWstr on RNT. The above correlational results indicate positive correlations of negative SRWstr with self-rumination and the increment in anxiety. Thus, Model 1 focused on the path from self-rumination to increment in STAI-S scores, negative SRWstr, and RTQ scores. Model 1 did not show a good fit to the data, as the goodness-of-fit indices did not meet the required standards: $\chi^2(3) = 37.50$, $p < 0.001$; goodness of fit index [GFI] = 0.89; adjusted GFI [AGFI] = 0.64, root mean square error of approximation [RMSEA] = 0.28, Akaike information criterion [AIC] = 51.50. Because the effect of self-rumination on negative SRWstr was somewhat weaker than was the effect of the increment in anxiety, self-rumination was removed from Model 1 (thereby creating Model 2). The results for Model 2 indicated a good fit to the data based on the following fit indices: $\chi^2(1) = 1.89$, n.s.; GFI = 0.99, AGFI = 0.95, RMSEA = 0.08, and AIC = 11.89.

DISCUSSION

This study aimed to determine (1) the association between self-focus and SRW enumeration, and (2) the effect of dysfunctional SRW enumeration on RNT. The hypotheses were as follows: (1) self-reflection is positively correlated with SRWnum; (2) self-rumination is positively correlated with negative SRWstr; and (3) negative SRWstr has a significant effect on RNT.

The increase in STAI-S scores revealed that our anxiety manipulation was effective. Moreover, there was no significant correlation between increment in STAI-S scores and SFNE scores, indicating that the situation imagination task led to an increase in anxiety independent of participants' social trait anxiety.

The correlational analysis revealed a significant positive correlation between self-reflection and SRWnum. However, we cannot conclude that this result fully supports hypothesis 1 because SRWnum had a non-normal distribution. Individuals with high self-reflection have a tendency to pay greater attention to their own problems than do those with high self-rumination (Ayduk and Kross, 2010), which potentially explains their greater SRW enumeration. Moreover, there was a significant negative correlation between SRWnum and SRWstr. This finding suggests that paying greater attention to the self might lower the self-relevance of each piece of information. However, this association between SRW enumeration and attention to the self cannot be explained by the current results, and

TABLE 1 | Descriptive statistics and internal consistency.

	Mean	*SD*	*Chronbach's α*	*Skewness*	*Kurtosis*
Pre-STAI-S	2.12	0.29	0.92	0.60	2.92
Post-STAI-S	2.35	0.39	0.94	0.47	2.59
Increment in STAI-S	0.23	0.53	–	1.21	6.16
SRWnum	4.08	8.07	–	2.17	9.75
Negative SRWnum	2.86	2.00	–	1.46	5.79
SRWstr	4.07	0.77	–	−1.06	4.14
Negative SRWstr	4.09	0.85	–	−1.07	3.86
Repetitive Thinking Questionnaire	2.84	0.82	0.90	−0.04	2.24
Shot fear of negative evaluation scale	3.61	0.80	0.93	−0.53	2.24
Self-rumination	3.61	0.64	0.91	−0.45	2.61
Self-reflection	3.37	0.57	0.88	0.11	2.34

STAI-S, State-Trait Anxiety Inventory – State; pre, measurement before situation imagination; post, measurement after situation imagination; SRW, self-relevance word.

TABLE 2 | Correlation matrix.

	1	2	3	4	5	6	7	8	9	10
1. Pre-STAI-S	–									
2. Post-STAI-S	0.58***	–								
3. Increment in STAI-S	−0.33***	0.57***	–							
4. SRWstr	0.03	0.19*	0.20	–						
5. Negative SRWnum	0.09	0.20*	0.14	−0.10	–					
6. Negative SRWstr	0.09	0.27*	0.22**	0.78***	0.06	–				
7. Repetitive Thinking Questionnaire	0.38***	0.46***	0.16	0.13	0.05	0.21*	–			
8. Short fear of negative evaluation	0.35***	0.38***	0.09	0.04	0.12	0.16	0.39***	–		
9. Self-rumination	0.39***	0.46***	0.13	0.12	0.07	0.21*	0.48***	0.66***	–	
10. Self-reflection	0.03	0.17*	0.17	−0.06	0.13	0.04	0.15	0.21*	0.39***	–
11. SRWnum	0.12	0.06	−0.02	−0.16*	0.71***	−0.01	0.04	0.02	0.02	0.20*

**p < 0.05, **p < 0.01, ***p < 0.001; STAI-S, State - Trait Anxiety Inventory – State; pre, measurement before situation imagination; post, measurement after situation imagination; SRW, self-relevant word. The correlation between each variable and SRWnum calculated with Spearman's method (ρ).*

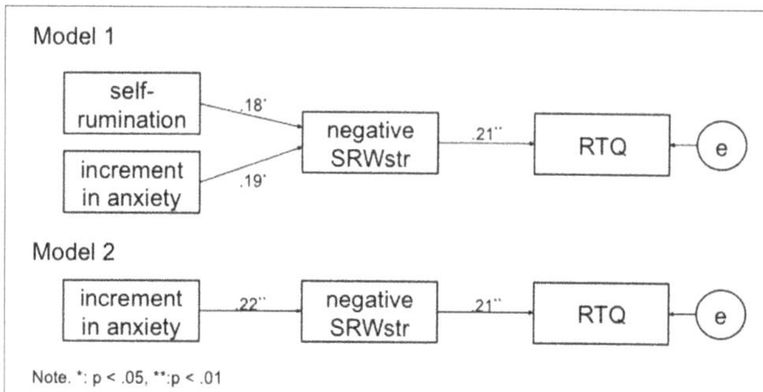

FIGURE 1 | Two models of the effects on RTQ.

thus should be investigated further. As noted in section 1, motivation is a mediating factor underlying the integration of self-information in working memory and retrieving self-information from long-term memory (Moreno, 2006). Therefore, the number of SRW refer to easiness accessing to self-information in long-term memory. It is assumed that the association between SRW enumeration and processing of self-information can be investigated in future research, and that understanding this connection would clarify why self-reflection is functional.

On the other hand, we observed a significant positive correlation between self-rumination and negative SRWstr, which supports hypothesis 2. Trait ruminators have difficulty in discarding no-longer-relevant negative words from working memory (Zetsche et al., 2012). This tendency is considered to reflect a difficulty in switching attention away from negative information, and is the reason for the narrowed attentional scope among ruminators (Whitmer and Gotlib, 2013). Koster et al. (2011) pointed out that trait ruminators have fewer attentional resources for information that is not negative. Based on our findings, we can assume that trait ruminators allocate their limited attentional resources primarily to negative information about themselves, which increased their negative SRWstr. Negative SRWstr was also positively correlated with the increment in state anxiety. A previous study indicated that the intensity of negative emotion influences self-relatedness (Gaebler et al., 2014). Although this study used SRWs enumerated by the participants, whereas Gaebler et al. (2014) measured the intensity of negative emotion and self-relatedness using pictures, increasing negative emotion induce linking with negative information. Thus, we can conclude that increased negative emotion to some degree correlates with the strength of the self-relevance of information.

Additionally, we examined whether the correlation between self-rumination and self-reflection was stronger than was the correlation between SRWnum and negative SRWstr to confirm the reliability of the SRW enumeration task. Some reports have shown a significant positive correlation between self-rumination and self-reflection (e.g., Takano et al., 2012; Mori et al., 2015). Our results indicate individuality between SRWnum and negative SRWstr. Therefore, investigating self-focus using SRW enumeration may allow us to find ways of selectively increasing only self-reflection.

In addition to Trapnell and Campbell's (1999) approach to classifying self-focus (which is based on motivation for self-focus, i.e., self-rumination vs. self-reflection), Teasdale (1999) has attempted to classify self-focus by style of focus: experiential self-focus and analytical thinking. Experiential self-focus is functional, and is induced by focusing on the experience of internal feelings. Analytical thinking refers to a dysfunctional form of self-focus that is produced by excessive thinking about the causes, consequences, and the meaning of internal feelings. Based on this theory, we assume that the tendency in experiential self-focusing to concentrate on self-information exploration without evaluation is associated with the positive correlation found between self-reflection and SRWnum, and with the lack of correlation between SRWnum and SRWstr in this study. On the other hand, the tendency in analytical thinking to focus on self-information while making evaluations perhaps underlies the positive correlation between self-rumination and negative SRWstr.

The results of our study indicate that SRW enumeration might support both of the theories of self-focus—Teasdale's (1999) or Trapnell and Campbell's (1999)—and help integrate them. To some extent, however, the practical implications of our results might differ according to the theory. If Teasdale's (1999) theory is supported, interventions by clinicians might need to address self-focus according to experiential style. On the other hand, if Trapnell and Campbell's (1999) theory is supported, interventions for self-focus need to focus on curiosity and motivation.

The results of the path analysis indicate a significant positive effect of negative SRWstr on RNT, which supports hypothesis 3. However, the model that excludes self-rumination as an explanatory variable demonstrated a better fit to the data than did the model that included it. This result may reflect how, because self-rumination is a trait, it does not respond to changes in state measurements. Retrospective assessments, such as those measuring traits, tend to show negative bias (Moberly and Watkins, 2008). SRW enumeration is regarded as a real-time state measurement; hence, it might respond to self-related statements more than trait measurements. Therefore, it is noted that the association between self-rumination and effect of negative SRWstr on RNT is needed to examine with the process of self-rumination measurement. Our result reveals that increasing anxiety has a positive effect on negative SRWstr, which is in turn connected with the positive effect on RNT. It is expected that a method of investigating negative SRWstr would decrease negative thinking when anxiety occurs.

In summary, SRW enumeration might enable selective detection of the degree of self-reflection and self-rumination. Moreover, the model indicated that increasing anxiety influenced negative SRWstr and RNT. This model suggests that it is enable to decrease RNT to investigate whether negative SRWstr is lower when anxiety is higher. In contrast, to improve self-reflection, it might be necessary to devise ways of enhancing SRWnum; this could lead to more adaptive problem-solving behavior and decreased depression. (Mori et al., 2015). These associations should be examined in future research, as they might enable new procedures using SRW enumeration.

This study has four main limitations. First, we did not include a group that did not experience the anxiety manipulation. This was because the purpose of this study was to determine how SRW enumeration helps in identifying different categories of self-focus. However, because the effect of the increment in anxiety was associated with SRW measurements, future studies should incorporate a control group with no anxiety manipulation. Second, although the manipulation of anxiety by situation imagination was valid, future research should use a method more closely resembling daily life. Third, we measured SRWs using a questionnaire because we could not control the time spent on SRW enumeration, and there were some individual differences in response time. This suggests there were some discrepancies in meaning among participants, even when they had the same number of SRWs; this difference might have affected the results. Thus, response time should be controlled experimentally in future studies. Finally, we could not identify any factors that were negatively correlated with SRW enumeration and self-focused attention. Examining the factors related to decreased ruminative self-focus or RNT is important for future studies, particularly in terms of the treatment of mental disease such as depression and anxiety disorder.

AUTHOR CONTRIBUTIONS

SM contributed to the conception and design of the study, analysis and interpretation of the results, and writing the manuscript. JS contributed to the conception of the study and revising the manuscript.

REFERENCES

1. Ayduk, Ö., and Kross, E. (2010). Analyzing negative experiences without ruminating: the role of self-distancing in enabling adaptive self-reflection. *Soc. Personal. Psychol.* 4, 841–854. doi: 10.1111/j.1751-9004.2010.00301.x
2. Baumeister, R. F., and Vohs, K. D. (2007). Self- regulation, ego depletion, and motivation. *Soc. Personal. Psychol. Compass.* 1, 115–128. doi: 10.1111/j.1751- 9004.2007.00001.x
3. Clark, D. M., and Wells, A. (1995). "A cognitive model of social phobia," in *Social Phobia: Diagnosis, Assessment, and Treatment*, eds R. G. Heimberg, M. R.

4. Liebowitz, D. A. Hope, and F. R. Schneier (New York, NY: Guilford Press), 69–93.
5. Curran, P. J., West, S. G., Finch, J. F., Aiken, L., Bentler, P., and Kaplan, D. (1996). The robustness of test statistics to nonnormality and specification error in confirmatory factor analysis. *Psychol. Methods* 1, 16–29. doi: 10.1037/1082- 989X.1.1.16
6. Ehring, T., and Watkins, E. R. (2008). Repetitive negative thinking as a transdiagnostic process. *Int. J. Cog. Ther.* 1, 192–205. doi: 10.1521/ ijct.2008.1. 3.192
7. Fujii, T. (2013). Development, validity, and reliability of the Social Anxiety IAT. *Jpn. J. Personal.* 22, 23–36. doi: 10.2132/personality.22.23
8. Gaebler, M., Daniels, J. K., Lamke, J., Fydrich, T., and Walter, H. (2014). Behavioural and neural correlates of self-focused emotion regulation in social anxiety disorder. *J. Psychiatry Neurosci.* 39, 249–258. doi: 10.1503/ jpn. 130080
9. Galliot, M. T., Schmeichel, B. J., and Baumeister, R. F. (2006). Self-regulatory processes defend against the threat of death: effects of self-control depletion and trait self-control on thoughts and fears of dying. *J. Personal. Soc. Psychol.* 91, 49–62. doi: 10.1037/0022-3514.91.1.49
10. Ingram, R. E. (1990). Self-focused attention in clinical disorders: review and a conceptual model. *Psychol. Bull.* 107, 156–176. doi: 10.1037/0033-2909. 107.2.156
11. Inzlicht, M., Schmeichel, B. J., and Macrae, C. N. (2014). Why self-control seems (but may not be) limited. *Trends Cogn. Sci.* 18, 127–133. doi: 10.1016/j.tics.2013. 12.009
12. Kashdan, T. B., and Roberts, J. E. (2007). Social anxiety, depressive symptoms, and post-event rumination: affective consequences and social contextual influences. *J. Anxiety Disord.* 21, 284–301. doi: 10.1016/j. janxdis.2006.05.009
13. Koster, E. H. W., De Lissnyder, E., Derakshan, N., and De Raedt, R. (2011). Understanding depressive rumination from a cognitive science perspective: the impaired disengagement hypothesis. *Clin. Psychol. Rev.* 31, 138–145. doi: 10.1016/j.cpr.2010.08.005
14. Moberly, N. J., and Watkins, E. R. (2008). Ruminative self-focus and negative affect: an experience sampling study. *J. Abnorm. Psychol.* 117, 314–323. doi: 10.1037/0021-843X.117.2.314
15. Moreno, R. (2006). Does the modality principle hold for different media? A test of the method-affects-learning hypothesis. *J. Comput. Assist. Learn.* 22, 149–158. doi: 10.1111/j.1365-2729.2006.00170.x
16. Mori, M., Takano, K., and Tanno, Y. (2015). Role of self-focus in the relationship between depressed mood and problem solving. *Motiv. Emot.* 39, 827–838. doi: 10.1007/s11031-015-9486-x
17. Muraven, M., Tice, D. M., and Baumeister, R. F. (1998). Self-control as limited resource: regulatory depletion patterns. *J. Personal. Soc. Psychol.* 74, 774–789. doi: 10.1037/0022-3514.74.3.774
18. Paas, F. G., Tuovinen, J. E., Tabbers, H., and Van Gerven, P. W. M. (2003). Cognitive load measurement as a means to advance cognitive load theory. *Educ. Psychol.* 38, 63–71. doi: 10.1207/S15326985EP3801_8
19. Sasagawa, T., Kanai, Y., Muranaka, Y., Suzuki, S., Shimada, H., and Sakano, Y. (2004). Development of a short fear of negative evaluation scale for Japanese using item response theory. *Jpn. J. Behav. Ther.* 30, 87–98.
20. Shimizu, H., and Imae, K. (1981). State-Trait Anxiety Inventory no nihongoban (daigakuseiyou) no sakusei (development of state-trait anxiety inventory for Japanese college students). *Jpn. J. Educ. Psychol.* 29, 348–353. doi: 10.5926/ jjep1953.29.4_348
21. Spurr, J. M., and Stopa, L. (2002). Self-focused attention in social phobia and social anxiety. *Clin. Psychol. Rev.* 22, 947–975. doi: 10.1016/S0272-7358(02)00107-1
22. Sweller, J. (1988). Cognitive load during problem solving: effects on learning. *Cogn. Sci.* 12, 257–285. doi: 10.1207/s15516709cog1202_4
23. Takano, K., Sakamoto, S., and Tanno, Y. (2012). Functional and dysfunctional self-focus, self-acceptance, and self-disclosure. *Jpn. J. Personal.* 21, 12–22. doi: 10.2132/personality.21.12
24. Takano, K., and Tanno, Y. (2008). Development of Japanese-version rumination- reflection questionnaire. *Jpn. J. Personal.* 16, 259–261. doi: 10.2132/personality. 16.259
25. Tanaka, K., and Sugiura, Y. (2014). Development of Japanese version of repetitive thinking questionnaire. *Jpn. J. Res. Emot.* 21, 62–71. doi: 10.4092/jsre.21.65 Teasdale, J. D. (1999). Emotional processing, three modes of mind and the prevention of relapse in depression. *Behav. Res. Ther.* 37, S53–S77. doi: 10.1016/ S0005-7967(99)00050-9
26. Trapnell, P. D., and Campbell, J. D. (1999). Private self-consciousness and the five-factor model of personality: distinguishing rumination from reflection. *J. Personal. Soc. Psychol.* 76, 284–304. doi: 10.1037/0022-3514.76.2.284
27. Whitmer, A. J., and Gotlib, I. H. (2013). An attentional scope model of rumination. *Psychol. Bull.* 139, 1036–1061. doi: 10.1037/a0030923
28. Zetsche, U., D'Avanzato, C., and Joormann, J. (2012). Depression and rumination: relation to components of inhibition. *Cogn. Emot.* 26, 758–767. doi: 10.1080/ 02699931.2011.613919

14

Altered Resting State Effective Connectivity of Anterior Insula in Depression

Sevdalina Kandilarova[1,2], Drozdstoy Stoyanov[1,2], Stefan Kostianev[1,3] and Karsten Specht[4,5]*

[1] Research Complex for Translational Neuroscience, Medical University of Plovdiv (MUP), Plovdiv, Bulgaria, [2] Department of Psychiatry and Medical Psychology, Medical University of Plovdiv (MUP), Plovdiv, Bulgaria, [3] Department of Pathophysiology, Medical University of Plovdiv (MUP), Plovdiv, Bulgaria, [4] Department of Biological and Medical Psychology, University of Bergen, Bergen, Norway, [5] Department of Education, The Arctic University of Norway (UiT), Tromsø, Norway

***Correspondence:**
Drozdstoy Stoyanov
dstoyanov@meduniversity-plovdiv.bg

Depression has been associated with changes in both functional and effective connectivity of large scale brain networks, including the default mode network, executive network, and salience network. However, studies of effective connectivity by means of spectral dynamic causal modeling (spDCM) are still rare and the interaction between the different resting state networks has not been investigated in detail. Thus, we aimed at exploring differences in effective connectivity among eight right hemisphere brain areas—anterior insula, inferior frontal gyrus, middle frontal gyrus (MFG), frontal eye field, anterior cingulate cortex, superior parietal lobe, amygdala, and hippocampus, between a group of healthy controls (N = 20) and medicated depressed patients (N = 20). We found that patients not only had significantly reduced strength of the connection from the anterior insula to the MFG (i.e., dorsolateral prefrontal cortex) but also a significant connection between the amygdala and the anterior insula. Moreover, depression severity correlated with connectivity of the hippocampal node. In conclusion, the results from this resting state spDCM study support and enrich previous data on the role of the right anterior insula in the pathophysiology of depression. Furthermore, our findings add to the growing evidence of an association between depression severity and disturbances of the hippocampal function in terms of impaired connectivity with other brain regions.

Keywords: depression, brain networks, effective connectivity, resting state functional MRI, spectral dynamic causal modeling, hippocampus, anterior insula, dorsolateral prefrontal cortex

INTRODUCTION

Depression is recognized as one of the most common and disabling psychiatric disorders with increasing prevalence and huge social and economic burden in terms of increased health-care costs, decreased productivity, and absenteeism (1). Symptoms of depressive disorders span across a range of psychopathological domains with major disturbances in affect (increased negative and reduced positive affect) and cognition (concentration, memory, executive function) (2). Accordingly, functional neuroimaging has been concentrated mainly on these domains with a variety of task-related research revealing disrupted activity in specific brain areas (reflecting functional segregation) though not always with consistent results (3).

However, in the last years, the use of functional magnetic resonance imaging (fMRI) in depression as well as in other research areas has been slowly moving away from activity studies with more and more focus on connectivity (functional integration) instead. Two main approaches exist—functional connectivity which is inferred on the basis of correlations of neuronal activity and effective connectivity that refers to the influence one neural system exerts over another, e.g., reflecting direct causal influence (4). The dynamic causal modeling (DCM) has been largely used for the assessment of effective connectivity in task-related but also to an increasing extent in resting state fMRI (5, 6). With respect to resting state fMRI, spectral DCM has been found to be more accurate and more sensitive to group differences compared to stochastic DCM (7).

Functional connectivity studies focused on depressive disorder have revealed disturbances in several of the resting state networks such as the default mode network (DMN), central executive network, salience network (SN), and the affective network (AN) (8–11). Apart from the disturbances of the intrinsic connectivity within those networks evidence is accumulating as well on disrupted connectivity between different networks (12–15). A recent meta-analysis by Kaiser et al. (16) confirms the findings of hyperconnectivity of the DMN, hypoconnectivity within the frontoparietal network (FN)—involved in cognitive control of attention and emotion, as well as hyperconnectivity between the DMN and the FN, and hypoconnectivity between the FN and regions of the AN. It is important to underline that observed disturbances of functional connectivity have been found to correlate with depression severity, diagnostic categories, specific depressive symptoms, and treatment response (17–20).

On the other hand, the majority of the effective connectivity studies in depressed patients have focused on task-related fMRI probing cognitive and emotional processing (21–23) with only a few reports on resting state fMRI (24, 25). By means of spectral DCM, Li et al. (24) investigated the DMN in a sample of healthy controls and depressed patients before and after treatment. The unmedicated patients had significantly lower coupling parameters from left parietal cortex to medial frontal cortex (MFC) and from posterior cingulate cortex (PCC) to right parietal cortex while they also exhibited higher coupling parameters from PCC to MFC compared to the control group but those differences were not significant following treatment.

A stochastic DCM was used by Hyett et al. (25) to investigate the connectivity between resting state networks with a focus on DMN, executive control (EXC), bilateral insula (INS), left frontoparietal, and right frontoparietal (RFP) attention modes in healthy subjects and depressed patients with and without prominent melancholic features. Significant differences between the non-melancholic and the control group were not found but melancholic patients demonstrated weaker connectivity from INS to EXC when compared to the healthy subjects and from INS to RFP mode in comparison with the non-melancholic group.

Those few effective connectivity studies, however, are not allowing scientists to fully understand how depression affects the causal influences between the nodes of the resting state brain networks. The advantages provided by the spectral DCM and the identified lack of sufficient data on effective connectivity in depressive disorder motivated us to investigate the causal influences among several brain regions already outlined by previous research as having a role in the underlying neuronal mechanisms of this highly prevalent psychiatric disorder. We decided to focus on areas mostly belonging to the SN and the EXC network and to see how depression and its severity relates to the connectivity of those regions. Thus, we aimed at exploring differences in effective connectivity among eight brain areas [anterior insula, inferior frontal gyrus (IFG), middle frontal gyrus (MFG), frontal eye field (FEF), anterior cingulate cortex (ACC), superior parietal lobe (SPL), amygdala, and hippocampus] as assessed by spectral DCM between a group of healthy controls and medicated depressed patients. Moreover, built on the abovementioned findings of Hyett et al., our main hypothesis was that patients will demonstrate disturbed causal influences of the insular cortex.

MATERIALS AND METHODS

Subjects

Twenty adult subjects (mean age 46.1 ± 13.9, six males) complying with the DSM-IV-TR criteria for depressive episode (single or recurrent) in the context of major depressive disorder ($n = 16$) or bipolar affective disorder ($n = 4$) were recruited for the present study as well as 20 age- and sex-matched healthy controls (mean age 43.5 ± 12.9 years, six males). All participants were assessed by general clinical interview and the structured Mini International Neuropsychiatric Interview (M.I.N.I. 6.0) (26).

For the patient group, severity of current episode was assessed by means of Montgomery–Åsberg Depression Rating Scale (MADRS) (27) and a total score of at least 20 was the cutoff for inclusion. Subjects were excluded if they had a second axis-I diagnosis (psychotic, anxiety, substance-related disorder), severe decompensated somatic disorder, neurological disorder, history of head trauma with loss of consciousness, severe suicidal risk (10th item of MADRS ≥ 2). All patients have been on a stable medication with various antidepressants and mood stabilizers (including escitalopram, sertraline, venlafaxine, duloxetine, lamotrigine, olanzapine) for at least 3 weeks prior to inclusion. The mean duration of illness was 10.3 years with a SD of 9.8 years.

Healthy controls did not comply with any of the DSM-IV-TR diagnoses included in the M.I.N.I., had no history of any psychiatric or neurological disorder nor head trauma with loss of consciousness. All participants provided a written informed consent complying with the Declaration of Helsinki and the study was approved by the University's Ethics Committee.

MR Scanning

The scanning of the participants was performed on a 3-T MRI system (GE Discovery 750w) and included a high resolution structural scan (Sag 3D T1 FSPGR, slice thickness 1 mm, matrix 256 × 256, TR (relaxation time)—7.2 ms, TE (echo time)—2.3, flip angle 12°,), and a functional scan [2D Echo Planar Imaging (EPI), slice thickness 3 mm, 36 slices, matrix 64 × 64, TR—2,000 ms, TE—30 ms, flip angle 90°, 192 volumes]. Before the EPI sequence subjects were instructed to remain as still as possible with eyes closed and not to think of anything in particular.

fMRI Data Analysis

Data were analyzed using the SPM 12 (Statistical Parametric Mapping, http://www.fil.ion.ucl.ac.uk/spm/) software running on MATLAB R2015 for Windows. The functional images were realigned, co-registered with the structural images, normalized to Montreal Neurological Institute (MNI) space, and smoothed with a 6-mm full-width-at-half-maximum Gaussian kernel.

First-level, resting state analysis was conducted using a general linear model applied to the time series. Nuisance covariates included the six rigid body motion parameters, average white matter and cerebrospinal fluid signal time series. BOLD timeseries were extracted for eight predefined regions of interest of 6-mm radius spheres, which were all located in the right hemisphere. These were the following regions with their MNI coordinates: anterior insula (AI) [38, 22, 3], IFG [50, 26, 16], MFG [36, 42, 28], FEF [31, −5, 58], ACC [5, 45, 12], SPL [24, −54, 68], amygdala (AMY) [24, 3, −16] and hippocampus (HPC) [30, −11, −17]. BOLD signal from some of the ROIs (amygdala) was lacking in one patient and two control subjects which lead to their exclusion from further analysis.

Dynamic Causal Modeling

Dynamic causal modeling was performed as spectral DCM (spDCM) with these eight regions of interest. The spDCM model was a fully connected model where each node was connected to each other node. In contrast to a stochastic DCM on resting state fMRI data, a spectral DCM estimates effective connectivity from the cross spectra of the fluctuations in neuronal states rather from their time courses directly (7). Further, the individual spDCM models were not separately but jointly estimated, using the Parametric Empirical Bayes framework, implemented in SPM12.2. This was followed by Bayesian model reduction to restrict the number of parameters. Finally, connectivity strengths (A-matrix) were extracted from the estimated spDCM models.

Statistical Analysis

Statistical analysis of the demographic and clinical characteristics of the participants as well as of the connectivity strengths of the spDCM model were performed by means of SPSS 22.0 for Windows. The level of significance was set to $p < 0.05$ for all tests. Student's t-test was employed for continuous variables and Chi-square test—for categorical ones. In addition, we used non-parametric correlation analysis on MADRS scores and connectivity strengths in the patient group.

RESULTS

Demographic and Clinical Characteristics

There were no statistically significant differences in age, sex, and education level between the patients and the healthy controls. Expectedly, patients had significantly higher MADRS scores (see **Table 1**).

Effective Connectivity in Healthy Controls

One sample t-test was employed to identify the connections that were significantly different from 0 in the group of healthy controls. As it can be seen in **Table 2**, the main nodes involved were ACC, FEF, hippocampus, and IFG. In addition, all eight nodes demonstrated significant self-inhibitory connections.

TABLE 1 | Demographic and clinical characteristics.

	Healthy controls (n = 20)	Patients (n = 20)	Significance
Age (mean, SD)	43.5 ± 12.9	46.1 ± 13.9	0.308[a]
Sex (M/F)	7/13	7/13	1.00[b]
Education (secondary/higher)	7/13	11/9	0.204[b]
MADRS score (mean, SD)	1.1 ± 2	32 ± 6.1	*0.000[a]

[a]*Independent samples t-test.*
[b]*χ^2 test.*
MADRS, Montgomery–Åsberg Depression Rating Scale.
$^*p < 0.05$.

TABLE 2 | Connections significantly different from 0 in healthy controls.

Nodes	Mean	SD	Significance[a]
ACC⊃	−0.594	0.355	0.000**
ACC → FEF	0.054	0.076	0.008
ACC → HPC	0.106	0.159	0.012
AI⊃	−0.298	0.481	0.018
AI → MFG	0.507	0.379	0.000**
AMY⊃	−0.338	0.504	0.011
FEF → ACC	−0.224	0.398	0.029
FEF → AMY	0.222	0.402	0.031
FEF⊃	−0.268	0.447	0.021
FEF → MFG	0.405	0.267	0.000**
FEF → SPL	0.275	0.397	0.009
MFG⊃	−0.325	0.362	0.001
HPC → ACC	−0.488	0.534	0.001
HPC⊃	−0.234	0.352	0.012
HPC → IFG	−0.402	0.483	0.003
IFG → ACC	0.285	0.387	0.006
IFG → HPC	0.123	0.211	0.024
IFG⊃	−0.214	0.389	0.032
SPL⊃	−0.348	0.414	0.002

[a]*One sample t-test.*
$p < 0.05$, $^{**}p < 0.001$.
⊃, self-inhibitory connection, AI, anterior insula, IFG, inferior frontal gyrus, MFG, middle frontal gyrus, FEF, frontal eye field, ACC, anterior cingulate cortex, SPL, superior parietal lobe, AMY, amygdala, HPC, hippocampus.

Differences Between Patients and Control Subjects

In order to explore the differences between the two groups, independent samples t-tests comparing the mean connectivity strengths were performed. The coupling strengths of six pairs of nodes had significantly different means (ACC → IFG, AI → MFG, AMY → AI, MFG → AI, MFG → SPL, SPL → FEF) but four of them were not significantly different than 0 in either group (see **Table 3** for details). The AI → MFG connectivity strength was significantly higher in healthy subjects than in depressed patients while the AMY → AI connectivity was higher in depressed patients but not significantly different than 0 in control subjects. An illustration of these results is presented in **Figure 1**.

Correlations Between Connectivity Strengths and MADRS Scores

The non-parametric correlation analysis of the MADRS scores and the connectivity strengths in the patient group identified two

TABLE 3 | Connections demonstrating significant difference between the groups.

Nodes	Mean Cs ± SD	Mean Ps ± SD	Significance[a]
ACC → IFG	−0.051 ± 0.169[b]	0.044 ± 0.108[b]	0.048
AI → MFG	0.507 ± 0.379	0.183 ± 0.316	0.008
AMY → AI	0.004 ± 0.151[b]	0.164 ± 0.283	0.040
MFG → AI	−0.067 ± 0.200[b]	0.067 ± 0.194[b]	0.047
MFG → SPL	−0.063 ± 0.182[b]	0.111 ± 0.290[b]	0.036
SPL → FEF	0.105 ± 0.360[b]	−0.111 ± 0.255[b]	0.049

Mean Cs, mean values in healthy controls, mean Ps, mean values in patients.
[a]Independent samples t-test $p < 0.05$.
[b]Not significantly different than 0.
AI, anterior insula, IFG, inferior frontal gyrus, MFG, middle frontal gyrus, FEF, frontal eye field, ACC, anterior cingulate cortex, SPL, superior parietal lobe, AMY, amygdala.

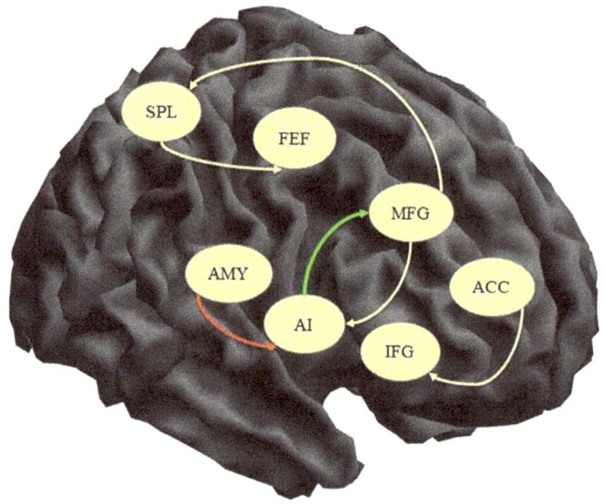

FIGURE 1 | Connections with significant difference between patients and healthy controls. Yellow arrow, connection significantly different between the groups but not significantly different than 0; green arrow, connection significantly higher in controls; red arrow, connection significantly higher in patients; AI, anterior insula; IFG, inferior frontal gyrus; MFG, middle frontal gyrus; FEF, frontal eye field; ACC, anterior cingulate cortex; SPL, superior parietal lobe; AMY, amygdala.

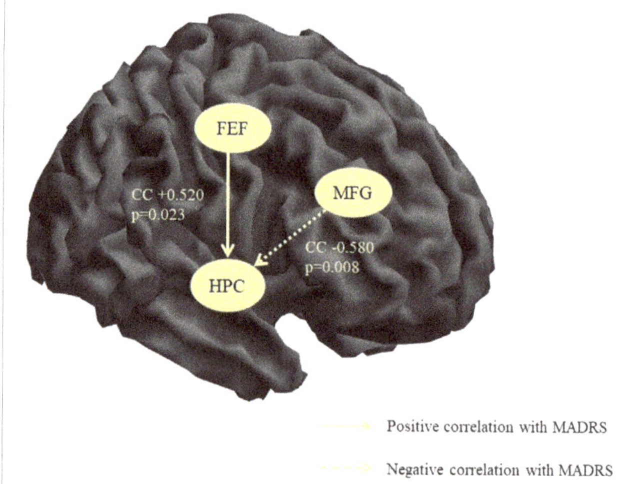

FIGURE 2 | Significant correlations between connectivity strengths and depression severity. MFG, middle frontal gyrus, HPC, hippocampus, CC, correlation coefficient, *p*, significance, MADRS, Montgomery–Åsberg Depression Rating Scale.

significant correlations both of which included the hippocampal node. There was one positive correlation of the MADRS score with the FEF → HPC connectivity (i.e., increasing depression severity correlated with increasing strength of the influence of FEF over HPC) and one negative correlation with the MFG → HPC (i.e., increasing depression severity correlated with decreasing causal influence of MFG on HPC). These results are illustrated in **Figure 2**.

DISCUSSION

In the present study, we found that during resting state fMRI in healthy subjects significant effective connectivity, i.e., causal interaction in terms of excitatory influence was exerted by the ACC on HPC and FEF, by the IFG on ACC and HPC, by the FEF on AMY, SPL, and MFG, and by AI on MFG while inhibitory influences were executed by HPC on IFG and ACC and by FEF on ACC. All eight nodes were found to have significant self-inhibitory connections. The direct comparison of the two groups yielded significant difference in the AI → MFG connection that was higher in the control group and the AMY → AI connection that was only significant in the patient group thus confirming our hypothesis of disturbed causal influences of the insular cortex in depressive disorder. In addition, MADRS scores correlated positively with FEF → HPC and negatively with MFG → HPC connectivity strengths. The results will be discussed below in light of current knowledge about the above-mentioned brain areas and recent research on functional and effective connectivity.

The most prominent finding in the present study was the significantly reduced effective connectivity of the AI → MFG (i.e., dorsolateral prefrontal cortex—DLPFC) in the depressive group compared to the healthy subjects. Both the SN and the ventral frontoparietal network have nodes located in the anterior insular cortex with the distinction that the SN is bilateral while the FN engages the right AI (28). Since all regions of interest in our study were derived from the right hemisphere we have to consider both options: (1) that the AI → MFG connection is part of the ventral FN which is implicated in stimulus driven bottom-up attention control as opposed to the dorsal FPN involved in top-down attention regulation (29) and (2) that this connection is part of the SN. Some authors actually accept this high level of overlap between the two systems as evidence that this is just one network (30). Whatever the case, our results are supported by several lines of previous research.

In major depressive disorder, for instance, decreased functional connectivity within the SN (right AI in particular) was demonstrated by Manoliu et al. (31) along with an association of the coupling parameters with symptom severity. Decreased functional connectivity between DLPFC and insula was found in subjects with subthreshold depression compared to healthy controls (32). We suggest that our results add to this evidence by revealing the directionality of this disturbed influence, namely from the insular cortex to the DLPFC. Moreover, stochastic DCM in melancholic depressed patients identified weaker effective connectivity from the insula to the RFP mode (25) and again our finding might be interpreted as both replicating and refining this result by outlining the specific connection to the frontal part of the ventral attention system.

The weaker causal influence of the insular cortex on the DLPFC might be an aspect of the pathophysiological mechanism underlying the disturbances of some cognitive domains in depression such as attention and decision-making given the role of these two brain areas. According to recent research, the right dorsal anterior insular cortex generates signals that causally influence the DMN (internally directed cognition) and the EXC network (externally directed cognition), thus supporting the dynamic switching between the two major brain networks (33, 34). We can speculate that when the influence toward one of the systems is disturbed (as in our sample of depressed patients) this balance could be easily lost and this would lead to a prevalence of the other system (e.g., hyperactivity of the DMN—evidenced in previous studies). Further research will be needed in order to explore in detail this hypothesis.

The other significant difference between the healthy controls and the patients in our study was related to the AMY → AI connection that was only significant in the patient group. The role of the amygdala in depression has been implied by several lines of neuroimaging research with most of the studies demonstrating increased amygdala reactivity primarily to negative stimuli (35–37) and disturbed connectivity with frontal regions (38–40). The effective connectivity of various prefrontal regions (orbitofrontal cortex, dorsolateral prefrontal cortex) toward the amygdala was found to be reduced in depressed patients with some of the disruptions persisting in remission (40, 41). Since both amygdala and anterior insula are considered to be part of the SN, our finding might be reflecting the increased activity of this network in depression (28). Moreover, we might speculate that this increased effective influence of the amygdala over the anterior insula could be the cause of the reduced AI → MFG connection found in our patient sample.

The other compelling findings of the present study were the significant correlations between the severity of depression (as assessed by MADRS) and the connectivity of the hippocampal area. The role of this region has been long implicated in the neurobiological mechanisms underlying depression through the links with stress and its effects on the hypothalamus–pituitary–adrenal axis and the hippocampus (42). Lower hippocampal volumes have been found in depressed patients (43) and the reductions were associated with the duration of the untreated illness and the severity of depressive symptoms (44, 45). In terms of function, the hippocampal area is crucial to both cognitive and affective processing and impairments in depression are evident on multiple levels from basic neuropsychological assessment (46, 47) to advanced functional neuroimaging of activity and connectivity (38, 48). Thus, our findings can be interpreted as an additional evidence of the disrupted hippocampal function in depressive disorders.

In first episode medication naïve patients, depression severity correlated negatively with hippocampal connectivity, i.e., the more severe the patient's illness, the fewer the connections of the right hippocampus (49). In our patient sample, the increasing depression severity correlated with increasing strength of the influence of FEF over HPC and with decreasing causal influence of MFG on HPC. One possible explanation might be that the first correlation is related to the increased activity of the SN or the AN (as the frontal eye filed is part of the visual attention network) while the second reflects the reduced top-down cognitive regulation in depression exerted by the DLPFC as part of the EXC network (50).

In conclusion, the results from this effective connectivity study support and enrich previous data on the role of the right anterior insula in the pathophysiology of depression by shedding some more light on the possible neurobiological mechanisms underlying specific clinical symptoms related to affect and cognition. Furthermore, our findings add to the growing evidence of an association between depression severity and disturbances of hippocampal function in terms of impaired connectivity with other brain regions. We suggest that future research should try not only to replicate the results but also to extend them with for example additional behavioral data on the severity of specific symptoms (related to affect and cognition) thus allowing for direct testing of the abovementioned hypotheses.

Several limitations of the present study must be admitted. First, the relatively small sample size and the heterogeneity of the patient group in terms of diagnosis (major depressive and bipolar disorder) may have influenced the results since both common and distinct activity and connectivity patterns in those psychiatric disorders have been reported (51, 52). Second, the fact that all patients have been on a stable antidepressant medication prior to inclusion might have contributed to our findings as evidence of "normalization" of the disturbed connectivity patterns following successful treatment has been reported (53). Future research should address those limitations by increasing the study sample and including non-medicated patients.

AUTHOR CONTRIBUTIONS

SKandilarova performed the empirical field study and original draft of the paper; DS contributed to the concept, the interpretation of the results, and revisions of the manuscript; SKostianev contributed to the overall management and supervision of the project; KS delivered the statistical data analysis and contributed to the editing of the paper.

REFERENCES

1. Sartorius N. The economic and social burden of depression. *J Clin Psychiatry* (2001) 62(Suppl 15):8–11.
2. Joormann J, Quinn ME. Cognitive processes and emotion regulation in depression. *Depress Anxiety* (2014) 31(4):308–15. doi:10.1002/da.22264
3. Muller VI, Cieslik EC, Serbanescu I, Laird AR, Fox PT, Eickhoff SB. Altered brain activity in unipolar depression revisited: meta-analyses of neuroimaging studies. *JAMA Psychiatry* (2017) 74(1):47–55. doi:10.1001/jamapsychiatry.2016.2783
4. Friston KJ. Functional and effective connectivity: a review. *Brain Connect* (2011) 1(1):13–36. doi:10.1089/brain.2011.0008
5. Friston KJ, Harrison L, Penny W. Dynamic causal modelling. *Neuroimage* (2003) 19(4):1273–302. doi:10.1016/S1053-8119(03)00202-7
6. Friston KJ, Kahan J, Biswal B, Razi A. A DCM for resting state fMRI. *Neuroimage* (2014) 94:396–407. doi:10.1016/j.neuroimage.2013.12.009
7. Razi A, Kahan J, Rees G, Friston KJ. Construct validation of a DCM for resting state fMRI. *Neuroimage* (2015) 106:1–14. doi:10.1016/j.neuroimage.2014.11.027
8. Sambataro F, Wolf ND, Pennuto M, Vasic N, Wolf RC. Revisiting default mode network function in major depression: evidence for disrupted subsystem connectivity. *Psychol Med* (2014) 44(10):2041–51. doi:10.1017/S0033291713002596
9. Chen Y, Wang C, Zhu X, Tan Y, Zhong Y. Aberrant connectivity within the default mode network in first-episode, treatment-naive major depressive disorder. *J Affect Disord* (2015) 183:49–56. doi:10.1016/j.jad.2015.04.052
10. Guo W, Liu F, Dai Y, Jiang M, Zhang J, Yu L, et al. Decreased interhemispheric resting-state functional connectivity in first-episode, drug-naive major depressive disorder. *Prog Neuropsychopharmacol Biol Psychiatry* (2013) 41:24–9. doi:10.1016/j.pnpbp.2012.11.003
11. Iwabuchi SJ, Krishnadas R, Li C, Auer DP, Radua J, Palaniyappan L. Localized connectivity in depression: a meta-analysis of resting state functional imaging studies. *Neurosci Biobehav Rev* (2015) 51:77–86. doi:10.1016/j.neubiorev.2015.01.006
12. Sheline YI, Price JL, Yan Z, Mintun MA. Resting-state functional MRI in depression unmasks increased connectivity between networks via the dorsal nexus. *Proc Natl Acad Sci U S A* (2010) 107(24):11020–5. doi:10.1073/pnas.1000446107
13. Mulders PC, van Eijndhoven PF, Schene AH, Beckmann CF, Tendolkar I. Resting-state functional connectivity in major depressive disorder: a review. *Neurosci Biobehav Rev* (2015) 56:330–44. doi:10.1016/j.neubiorev.2015.07.014
14. Wang YL, Yang SZ, Sun WL, Shi YZ, Duan HF. Altered functional interaction hub between affective network and cognitive control network in patients with major depressive disorder. *Behav Brain Res* (2016) 298(Pt B):301–9. doi:10.1016/j.bbr.2015.10.040
15. Hamilton JP, Farmer M, Fogelman P, Gotlib IH. Depressive rumination, the default-mode network, and the dark matter of clinical neuroscience. *Biol Psychiatry* (2015) 78(4):224–30. doi:10.1016/j.biopsych.2015.02.020
16. Kaiser RH, Andrews-Hanna JR, Wager TD, Pizzagalli DA. Large-scale network dysfunction in major depressive disorder: a meta-analysis of resting-state functional connectivity. *JAMA Psychiatry* (2015) 72(6):603–11. doi:10.1001/jamapsychiatry.2015.0071
17. Dichter GS, Gibbs D, Smoski MJ. A systematic review of relations between resting-state functional-MRI and treatment response in major depressive disorder. *J Affect Disord* (2014) 172c:8–17. doi:10.1016/j.jad.2014.09.028
18. Brakowski J, Spinelli S, Dorig N, Bosch OG, Manoliu A, Holtforth MG, et al. Resting state brain network function in major depression – depression symptomatology, antidepressant treatment effects, future research. *J Psychiatr Res* (2017) 92:147–59. doi:10.1016/j.jpsychires.2017.04.007
19. Goya-Maldonado R, Brodmann K, Keil M, Trost S, Dechent P, Gruber O. Differentiating unipolar and bipolar depression by alterations in large-scale brain networks. *Hum Brain Mapp* (2016) 37(2):808–18. doi:10.1002/hbm.23070
20. Drysdale AT, Grosenick L, Downar J, Dunlop K, Mansouri F, Meng Y, et al. Resting-state connectivity biomarkers define neurophysiological subtypes of depression. *Nat Med* (2017) 23(1):28–38. doi:10.1038/nm.4246
21. Schlosser RG, Wagner G, Koch K, Dahnke R, Reichenbach JR, Sauer H. Fronto-cingulate effective connectivity in major depression: a study with fMRI and dynamic causal modeling. *Neuroimage* (2008) 43(3):645–55. doi:10.1016/j.neuroimage.2008.08.002
22. Desseilles M, Schwartz S, Dang-Vu TT, Sterpenich V, Ansseau M, Maquet P, et al. Depression alters "top-down" visual attention: a dynamic causal modeling comparison between depressed and healthy subjects. *Neuroimage* (2011) 54(2):1662–8. doi:10.1016/j.neuroimage.2010.08.061
23. O'Nions EJ, Dolan RJ, Roiser JP. Serotonin transporter genotype modulates subgenual response to fearful faces using an incidental task. *J Cogn Neurosci* (2011) 23(11):3681–93. doi:10.1162/jocn_a_00055
24. Li L, Li B, Bai Y, Liu W, Wang H, Leung HC, et al. Abnormal resting state effective connectivity within the default mode network in major depressive disorder: a spectral dynamic causal modeling study. *Brain Behav* (2017) 7(7):e00732. doi:10.1002/brb3.732
25. Hyett MP, Breakspear MJ, Friston KJ, Guo CC, Parker GB. Disrupted effective connectivity of cortical systems supporting attention and interoception in melancholia. *JAMA Psychiatry* (2015) 72(4):350–8. doi:10.1001/jamapsychiatry.2014.2490
26. Sheehan DV, Lecrubier Y, Sheehan KH, Amorim P, Janavs J, Weiller E, et al. The Mini-International Neuropsychiatric Interview (M.I.N.I.): the development and validation of a structured diagnostic psychiatric interview for DSM-IV and ICD-10. *J Clin Psychiatry* (1998) 59(Suppl 20):22–33; quiz 4–57.
27. Montgomery SA, Asberg M. A new depression scale designed to be sensitive to change. *Br J Psychiatry* (1979) 134:382–9. doi:10.1192/bjp.134.4.382
28. Uddin LQ. Salience processing and insular cortical function and dysfunction. *Nat Rev Neurosci* (2015) 16:55–61. doi:10.1038/nrn3857
29. Vossel S, Geng JJ, Fink GR. Dorsal and ventral attention systems: distinct neural circuits but collaborative roles. *Neuroscientist* (2014) 20:150–9. doi:10.1177/1073858413494269
30. Power JD, Cohen AL, Nelson SM, Wig GS, Barnes KA, Church JA, et al. Functional network organization of the human brain. *Neuron* (2011) 72(4):665–78. doi:10.1016/j.neuron.2011.09.006
31. Manoliu A, Meng C, Brandl F, Doll A, Tahmasian M, Scherr M, et al. Insular dysfunction within the salience network is associated with severity of symptoms and aberrant inter-network connectivity in major depressive disorder. *Front Hum Neurosci* (2013) 7:930. doi:10.3389/fnhum.2013.00930.
32. Hwang JW, Egorova N, Yang XQ, Zhang WY, Chen J, Yang XY, et al. Subthreshold depression is associated with impaired resting-state functional connectivity of the cognitive control network. *Transl Psychiatry* (2015) 5:e683. doi:10.1038/tp.2015.174
33. Sridharan D, Levitin DJ, Menon V. A critical role for the right fronto-insular cortex in switching between central-executive and default-mode networks. *Proc Natl Acad Sci U S A* (2008) 105(34):12569–74. doi:10.1073/pnas.0800005105
34. Uddin LQ, Supekar KS, Ryali S, Menon V. Dynamic reconfiguration of structural and functional connectivity across core neurocognitive brain networks with development. *J Neurosci* (2011) 31(50):18578–89. doi:10.1523/JNEUROSCI.4465-11.2011
35. Abler B, Erk S, Herwig U, Walter H. Anticipation of aversive stimuli activates extended amygdala in unipolar depression. *J Psychiatr Res* (2007) 41(6):511–22. doi:10.1016/j.jpsychires.2006.07.020
36. Groenewold NA, Opmeer EM, de Jonge P, Aleman A, Costafreda SG. Emotional valence modulates brain functional abnormalities in depression: evidence from a meta-analysis of fMRI studies. *Neurosci Biobehav Rev* (2013) 37(2):152–63. doi:10.1016/j.neubiorev.2012.11.015
37. Siegle GJ, Thompson W, Carter CS, Steinhauer SR, Thase ME. Increased amygdala and decreased dorsolateral prefrontal BOLD responses in unipolar depression: related and independent features. *Biol Psychiatry* (2007) 61(2):198–209. doi:10.1016/j.biopsych.2006.05.048
38. Anand A, Li Y, Wang Y, Wu J, Gao S, Bukhari L, et al. Activity and connectivity of brain mood regulating circuit in depression: a functional magnetic resonance study. *Biol Psychiatry* (2005) 57(10):1079–88. doi:10.1016/j.biopsych.2005.02.021
39. Kong L, Chen K, Tang Y, Wu F, Driesen N, Womer F, et al. Functional connectivity between the amygdala and prefrontal cortex in medication-naive individuals with major depressive disorder. *J Psychiatry Neurosci* (2013) 38(6):417–22. doi:10.1503/jpn.120117
40. Lu Q, Li H, Luo G, Wang Y, Tang H, Han L, et al. Impaired prefrontal-amygdala effective connectivity is responsible for the dysfunction of emotion

process in major depressive disorder: a dynamic causal modeling study on MEG. *Neurosci Lett* (2012) 523(2):125–30. doi:10.1016/j.neulet.2012.06.058

41. Goulden N, McKie S, Thomas EJ, Downey D, Juhasz G, Williams SR, et al. Reversed frontotemporal connectivity during emotional face processing in remitted depression. *Biol Psychiatry* (2012) 72(7):604–11. doi:10.1016/j.biopsych.2012.04.031
42. Willner P, Scheel-Kruger J, Belzung C. The neurobiology of depression and antidepressant action. *Neurosci Biobehav Rev* (2013) 37(10 Pt 1):2331–71. doi:10.1016/j.neubiorev.2012.12.007
43. Campbell S, Marriott M, Nahmias C, MacQueen GM. Lower hippocampal volume in patients suffering from depression: a meta-analysis. *Am J Psychiatry* (2004) 161(4):598–607. doi:10.1176/appi.ajp.161.4.598
44. Sheline YI, Gado MH, Kraemer HC. Untreated depression and hippocampal volume loss. *Am J Psychiatry* (2003) 160(8):1516–8. doi:10.1176/appi.ajp.160.8.1516
45. Brown ES, Hughes CW, McColl R, Peshock R, King KS, Rush AJ. Association of depressive symptoms with hippocampal volume in 1936 adults. *Neuropsychopharmacology* (2014) 39(3):770–9. doi:10.1038/npp.2013.271
46. Bortolato B, Carvalho AF, McIntyre RS. Cognitive dysfunction in major depressive disorder: a state-of-the-art clinical review. *CNS Neurol Disord Drug Targets* (2014) 13(10):1804–18. doi:10.2174/1871527313666141130203823
47. Delle-Vigne D, Wang W, Kornreich C, Verbanck P, Campanella S. Emotional facial expression processing in depression: data from behavioral and event-related potential studies. *Neurophysiol Clin* (2014) 44(2):169–87. doi:10.1016/j.neucli.2014.03.003
48. Wang L, Hermens DF, Hickie IB, Lagopoulos J. A systematic review of resting-state functional-MRI studies in major depression. *J Affect Disord* (2012) 142(1–3):6–12. doi:10.1016/j.jad.2012.04.013
49. Guo H, Cheng C, Cao X, Xiang J, Chen J, Zhang K. Resting-state functional connectivity abnormalities in first-onset unmedicated depression. *Neural Regen Res* (2014) 9(2):153–63. doi:10.4103/1673-5374.125344
50. Hamilton JP, Chen MC, Gotlib IH. Neural systems approaches to understanding major depressive disorder: an intrinsic functional organization perspective. *Neurobiol Dis* (2013) 52C:4–11. doi:10.1016/j.nbd.2012.01.015
51. Delvecchio G, Fossati P, Boyer P, Brambilla P, Falkai P, Gruber O, et al. Common and distinct neural correlates of emotional processing in bipolar disorder and major depressive disorder: a voxel-based meta-analysis of functional magnetic resonance imaging studies. *Eur Neuropsychopharmacol* (2012) 22(2):100–13. doi:10.1016/j.euroneuro.2011.07.003
52. Cardoso de Almeida JR, Phillips ML. Distinguishing between unipolar depression and bipolar depression: current and future clinical and neuroimaging perspectives. *Biol Psychiatry* (2013) 73(2):111–8. doi:10.1016/j.biopsych.2012.06.010
53. Wang L, Xia M, Li K, Zeng Y, Su Y, Dai W, et al. The effects of antidepressant treatment on resting-state functional brain networks in patients with major depressive disorder. *Hum Brain Mapp* (2015) 36(2):768–78. doi:10.1002/hbm.22663

15

Psychological Distress Symptoms Associated with Life Events in Patients with Bipolar Disorder

Aiko Sato[1], *Tasuku Hashimoto*[1,2]*, *Atsushi Kimura*[1], *Tomihisa Niitsu*[1] *and Masaomi Iyo*[1]

[1] *Department of Psychiatry, Chiba University Graduate School of Medicine, Chuo-ku, Japan,* [2] *Department of Psychiatry, Sodegaura Satsukidai Hospital, Sodegaura, Japan*

Correspondence:
Tasuku Hashimoto
t.hashimoto1109@gmail.com

Stressful life events, although less serious than traumatic experiences, affect the clinical course of patients with bipolar disorder. We previously found that bipolarity in patients with major depression is related to the severity of psychological distress symptoms associated with onset-related events. Here, we investigated whether, and to what extent, bipolar patients perceive stressful events as psychological distress symptoms, specifically, intrusion, avoidance, and hyperarousal. Further, we investigated the relationship between the clinical features and the severity of psychological distress symptoms associated with stressful life events, according to mood states. We recruited 79 bipolar patients (depression group, $n = 32$; mania, $n = 22$; euthymia, $n = 25$) in this cross-sectional study. We adopted the Impact of Event Scale-Revised (IES-R) to assess the severity of psychological distress symptoms associated with past stressful events. We also evaluated the Hamilton Depression Rating Scale (HDRS) and the Young Mania Rating Scale (YMRS). The mean (standard deviation) IES-R scores of bipolar patients with a depressive episode (38.06 [16.56], $p = 0.0005$) and of those with a manic/hypomanic episode (44.56 [24.14], $p = 0.004$) were significantly higher than of those with euthymia (19.81 [12.86]). The HDRS, but not the YMRS, scores showed significant correlations with the IES-R scores, regardless of mood episodes (depression group, $r = 0.42$; mania, $r = 0.64$; euthymia, $r = 0.70$). This study demonstrates that bipolar patients with a manic/hypomanic or depressive episode perceive stressful life events as more severe psychological distress symptoms than do euthymic patients. Moreover, in patients with bipolar disorder, the severity of depressive symptoms, but not of manic symptoms, is positively correlated with that of the psychological distress symptoms, regardless of their mood episodes or euthymic state. Therefore, depressive symptoms may be closely related to the psychological distress symptoms associated with stressful past events in patients with bipolar disorder.

Keywords: bipolar disorder, depression, life events, mania, psychological distress

---

Abbreviations: DSM, Diagnostic and Statistical Manual of Mental Disorders; HDRS, Hamilton Depression Rating Scale; IES-R, Impact of Event Scale-Revised; PDSs, psychological distress symptoms; PTSD, posttraumatic stress disorder; YMRS, Young Mania Rating Scale.

INTRODUCTION

It is well-recognized that stressful life events affect vulnerability, onset, and relapse or recurrence of bipolar disorder (1–4). A previous study has reported that the prevalence of stressful life events in patients with bipolar disorder is higher than that in healthy people (5). Further, social problems, such as a protracted stressful life events, disturb symptomatic remission or recovery of patients with bipolar disorder (3). Although the stressful life events severely affect onset; clinical exacerbation, including relapse; and prognosis of bipolar disorder, only a few studies have investigated how the patients are distressed by them, and to what extent they experience psychological symptoms with intrusive or unpleasant memories of such events. Therefore, it is necessary to investigate clinical features associated with stressful life events in patients with bipolar disorder in the context of psychiatric symptomatology, to develop a better understanding and management strategy against bipolar disorder.

Stressful life events, which occur more frequently, and are less serious than traumatic experiences meeting the diagnostic criteria for posttraumatic stress disorder (PTSD), cause symptoms of intrusion, avoidance, and hyperarousal, which are similar to those observed in PTSD, in adults and adolescents (6, 7). Our previous study reported that patients with treatment-refractory or non-remitting depression suffered from psychological distress symptoms (PDSs), such as intrusion and avoidance, associated with onset-related life events, which alone did not lead to fatal outcomes, compared to PDS combined with remitted depression (8). This study also examined the association between the severity of PDSs that were associated with onset-related life events and depressed patients' bipolarity; bipolarity was defined as patients satisfying the criteria of either "bipolar spectrum disorder" (9) or "bipolar specifier" (10, 11), as described previously (8). Our previous findings indicated that patients with depression and bipolarity are more likely to suffer from PDSs associated with onset-related life events than those without bipolarity (8). Based on this knowledge, we hypothesized that patients with bipolar disorder experience PDSs associated with stressful life events as much as patients with treatment-resistant or non-remitted unipolar depression. Given that many patients with bipolar disorder, without comorbidity of PTSD or experience of traumatic events meeting the diagnostic criteria of PTSD, experience more stressful life events than healthy people (5); recognition of PDSs associated with such cases is important for understanding the pathophysiology of the clinical features of bipolar disorder.

The purpose of this study was to identify PDSs in patients with bipolar disorder. In the present study, we defined PDSs as consisting of intrusions, avoidance, and hyperarousal, associated with the past stressful events experienced by the patients that are more mundane and less serious than those satisfying the PTSD diagnostic criteria A in the fifth edition of the Diagnostic and Statistical Manual of Mental Disorders (DSM-5) (12), objectively. We also investigated the relationships between the clinical features of bipolar disorder and the severity of PDSs associated with stressful life events according to mood states (depression, mania or hypomania, and euthymia).

MATERIALS AND METHODS

Study Design

This study employed a cross-sectional design.

Ethics Statement

This study was approved by the ethics committees of Chiba University Graduate School of Medicine, Kisarazu Hospital, and Sodegaura Satsukidai Hospital. All subjects provided written informed consent for their participation in this study after the protocol had been fully explained to them. All experiments were performed in accordance with the Helsinki Declaration.

Participants and Procedures

This study was conducted between July 2016 and July 2017. Participants were recruited from among patients commuting to or hospitalized in Chiba University Hospital, Kisarazu Hospital, or Sodegaura Satsukidai Hospital. The patients' ages ranged from 20 to 65 years, and they were diagnosed with bipolar disorder according to the DSM-5 criteria (12) using the Japanese version of the Mini International Neuropsychiatric Interview (13, 14). We excluded patients under 20 or over 65 years of age, patients with PTSD, schizophrenia, major depressive disorder, comorbid dementia, organic mental disorder, neurodevelopmental disorders, or impending suicide attempt.

We selected the target sample size of the present study based on our previous study (8). Consequently, a total of 210 outpatients and 17 inpatients underwent eligibility screening for this study. Of these, 118 patients did not meet the criteria for eligibility, and 109 patients were eligible to participate. Of these, 30 patients declined an interview. Finally, 79 patients were included in this study. We classified these patients into 3 groups, according to mood state: depression, mania or hypomania, and euthymia.

Assessment of Depression and Mania

We assessed the severity of depression using the Structured Interview Guide for the 17-item Hamilton Depression Rating Scale (HDRS) (15, 16), and evaluated the severity of mania using the Young Mania Rating Scale (YMRS) (17). Euthymia was defined by an HDRS score ≤ 7 and a YMRS score ≤ 7. We categorized mixed state patients with HDRS and YMRS scores >7 into a depressive or manic state, according to the DSM-5.

Assessment of Clinical Characteristics

We assessed demographic data, such as age, sex, comorbidity, physical disease, family history of psychiatric disorders in first-degree relatives, years of education, employment history, current employment, marital history, history of smoking, history of alcohol drinking, history of substance use, present medication, disease and therapy duration, type of bipolar disorder (bipolar I disorder or bipolar II disorder), and clinical features of the current or past episodes (with anxious distress, mixed features, rapid cycling, melancholic features, atypical features, psychotic features, catatonia, peripartum onset, and seasonal pattern), according to the DSM-5 definition. In the current study, physical diseases included patients under treatment for hypertension, diabetes, hyperlipidemia, reflux esophagitis, gastric ulcer, hypoferric anemia, asthma, gout, lumbar disc hernia, premenstrual syndrome, and sleep apnea syndrome.

Assessment of Stressful Life Events

Interview Procedure for Assessing Stressful Life Events

We had already excluded patients with PTSD, as this was one of the study exclusion criteria. Moreover, we directly asked patients whether they suffered from PTSD according to the Japanese version of the Mini International Neuropsychiatric Interview and the Japanese version of the Structured Clinical Interview for DSM-IV (18).

After excluding patients with PTSD, as described above, we assessed whether patients experienced "life events related to PDSs" (here, referred to as "stressful life events") by asking the following question, "Did you experience life events resulting in nightmares, flashbacks, involuntary and intrusive memories, or persistent effortful avoidance, excluding life events matching PTSD criteria?" We also asked whether patients experienced onset-related events; these events were regarded as general events that the patients themselves recognized as events that could trigger the onset, irrespective of the presence or absence of current PDSs.

Categorizing Life Events

We classified the patients' life events into 10 groups by referring to the list of threatening experiences in a questionnaire that is frequently used to assess stressful events (19) as follows: family problems without abuse, separation from a close person, interpersonal-related events, health-related events, money-related events, sex-related events, change of living conditions, job-related events, bullying or neglect, and other events.

Measure of the Severity of PDSs Associated With Stressful Life Events

The impact of event scale-revised (IES-R) is a self-reported questionnaire for assessing the severity of psychological symptoms related to stressful life events (20). The IES-R has been developed to assess trauma-related symptoms in patients with PTSD. It consists of 22 items, including 8 for intrusion symptoms, 8 for avoidance, and 6 for hyperarousal, which are the 3 major sub-categories of PTSD symptoms. Each of the items is scored from a scale of 0–4, with the higher scores implying greater severity of traumatic symptoms. Therefore, the total score for the IES-R ranges from 0 to 88. The IES-R has been validated, with ensuring internal consistency worldwide (21), and the Japanese version has also been developed and is available (22).

As noted above, we hypothesized that patients with bipolar disorder could perceive PDSs associated with their life events in a manner similar to patients with PTSD and patients with unipolar depression, as reported in our previous study (8). Therefore, we adopted the IES-R to evaluate PDSs in this study. We instructed the patients to write their stressful life events into the blank space of the introductory document of the IES-R, and to answer each item of the IES-R regarding their life event, as described above. In addition, we also instructed the patients to write down their onset-related event, and to answer each item in terms of their onset-related event.

Primary and Secondary Endpoints

The primary endpoint was the prevalence of subjects with PDSs associated with life events among the patients with bipolar disorder. The secondary endpoints were the comparison of the IES-R scores in each group, as classified by mood states, and the relationships between the IES-R scores and clinical features.

Statistical Analysis

We analyzed the data separately for the 3 groups (depression, mania or hypomania, and euthymia groups). We performed all analyses using SPSS for Windows, Version 19 (IBM Corp., Armonk, NY, USA). The chi-square or Fisher's exact test was used for categorical variables, and Student's t-test or one-way analysis of variance (one-way ANOVA) for the other variables. We performed one-way ANOVA for total and sub-category scores of the IES-R, HDRS, and YMRS, followed by Games Howell test for multiple comparisons. We also tested the correlation between IES-R and HDRS scores, and between IES-R and YMRS scores using Pearson's product moment correlation analysis. The level of significance was set at $p < 0.05$, and the power was set at 0.80.

RESULTS

Patients' Characteristics

Table 1 shows the characteristics of the participants included in the analysis. The 79 patients with bipolar disorder were categorized into 3 groups: the depression group ($n = 32$), mania or hypomania group ($n = 22$), and euthymia group ($n = 25$). There were no significant differences in age, sex, and years of education among the 3 groups. Further, there were no significant differences in employment history, current employment, marital history, physical diseases, and first-degree relatives with psychiatric disorders among the 3 groups. However, there were significant differences in the proportion of inpatients and outpatients, and psychiatric comorbidity. **Table 2** shows the categorization of psychiatric comorbidities. In all groups, the most common comorbidity was panic disorder. Three patients in the depression and mania group exhibited 2 psychiatric comorbidities, and 1 patient in the depression group exhibited 3 psychiatric comorbidities. In the euthymia group, no patient exhibited more than 1 comorbidity. There were significant differences in the mixed and the melancholic features, and no significant differences in other clinical features (**Table 1**).

Table 3 shows the prevalence of subjects experiencing life events. Fifty-six subjects (70.9% of all subjects) experienced both a stressful life event and an onset-related event. Eleven out of the 56 subjects answered that their stressful life event and onset-related event was the same event. A further 23 subjects (29.1%) experienced either a stressful life event or an onset-related event. All subjects experienced at least one of these events (**Table 3**).

Table 4 shows the classification of life events for all patients. In terms of stressful life events, there were differences in the events most commonly experienced by patients among the 3

TABLE 1 | Patient characteristics, based on patient groups (depression group, mania or hypomania group, and euthymia group).

	Depression ($n = 32$)	Mania[a] ($n = 22$)	Euthymia ($n = 25$)	*p*-value
Age, years (SD)	45.0 (10.0)	43.4 (12.2)	47.8 (11.1)	NS
[Age range] (years)	[24-63]	[20-64]	[26-64]	
Sex, male/female	16/16	13/9	11/14	NS
Outpatient/In-patient	27/5	14/8	24/1	0.01[d]
Education, years (SD)	13.8 (2.2)	13.2 (2.6)	13.6 (2.0)	NS
Employment history (%)	29 (90.4)	21 (95.5)	24 (96.0)	NS
Current employment (%)	15 (46.9)	7 (31.8)	13 (52.0)	NS
Marital history (%)	16 (50.0)	8 (36.4)	14 (56.0)	NS
Smoking (%)	8 (25.0)	9 (40.9)	8 (32.0)	NS
Alcohol intake (%)	8 (25.0)	6 (27.3)	5 (20.0)	NS
Substance use (%)	0 (0.0)	1 (4.5)	2 (8.0)	NS
Physical disease (%)	14 (43.8)	13 (59.1)	11 (44.0)	NS
Psychiatric comorbidity (%)	21 (65.6)	13 (59.1)	5 (20.0)	0.001[d]
Family psychiatric history[b] (%)	9 (28.1)	9 (40.9)	9 (36.0)	NS
Type, Bipolar I/II	11/21	13/9	10/15	NS
Clinical features[c]				
With anxious distress (%)	0 (0.0)	0 (0.0)	1 (4.0)	NS
With mixed features (%)	2 (6.3)	9 (40.9)	3 (12.0)	0.003[d]
With rapid cycling (%)	0 (0.0)	0 (0.0)	0 (0.0)	NS
With melancholic features (%)	14 (43.8)	3 (13.6)	5 (20.0)	0.03[d]
With atypical features (%)	2 (6.3)	0 (0.0)	0 (0.0)	NS
With psychotic features (%)	8 (25.0)	7 (31.8)	9 (36.0)	NS
With catatonia (%)	0 (0.0)	0 (0.0)	0 (0.0)	NS
With peripartum onset (%)	0 (0.0)	0 (0.0)	1 (4.0)	NS
With seasonal pattern (%)	2 (6.3)	0 (0.0)	0 (0.0)	NS
Disease duration, years (SD)	16.0 (7.9)	18.9 (10.5)	16.2 (10.9)	NS
Therapy duration, years (SD)	12.8 (7.7)	12.7 (8.6)	13.1 (10.3)	NS
HDRS, points (SD)	14.6 (4.9)	7.9 (4.9)	3.2 (2.0)	4.0×10^{-15}[d]
YMRS, points (SD)	1.9 (1.9)	13.7 (5.0)	1.2 (1.7)	1.0×10^{-14}[d]

Variables represent mean (standard deviation: SD).
HDRS, Hamilton Depression Rating Scale; YMRS, Young Mania Rating Scale; NS, not significant.
[a] *Including mania and hypomania patients.*
[b] *Family history of psychiatric disorder in a first-degree relative.*
[c] *Clinical features include current or past episode and may overlap.*
[d] *The data for the three groups were analyzed using one-way ANOVA, followed by the Games–Howell test for multiple comparisons.*

TABLE 2 | Psychiatric comorbidities, based on patient groups.

	Depression ($n = 32$)	Mania[a] ($n = 22$)	Euthymia ($n = 25$)	All ($n = 79$)
Psychiatric comorbidity (%)	21 (65.6)	13 (59.1)	5 (20.0)	39 (49.4)
Panic disorder (%)	9 (28.1)	5 (22.7)	2 (8.0)	16 (20.3)
Social anxiety disorder (%)	7 (21.9)	3 (13.6)	1 (4.0)	11 (14.0)
Obsessive-compulsive disorder (%)	4 (12.5)	2 (9.1)	0 (0)	6 (7.6)
Alcohol dependence (%)	2 (6.3)	3 (13.6)	1 (4.0)	6 (7.6)
Bulimia nervosa (%)	2 (6.3)	1 (4.5)	0 (0)	3 (3.8)
Anorexia nervosa (%)	0 (0)	1 (4.5)	0 (0)	1 (1.3)
2 psychiatric comorbidities (%)	3 (9.4)	3 (13.6)	0 (0)	6 (7.6)
3 psychiatric comorbidities (%)	1 (3.1)	0 (0)	0 (0)	1 (1.3)

[a] *Including mania and hypomania patients.*

TABLE 3 | The prevalence of subjects with life events.

Stressful life events	Onset-related events	Depression ($n = 32$)	Mania[a] ($n = 22$)	Euthymia ($n = 25$)	All ($n = 79$)
Yes	Yes	28 [87.5%]	14 [63.6%]	14 [56.0%]	56 [70.9%]
Yes	No	3 [9.4%]	2 [9.1%]	2 [8.0%]	7 [8.9%]
No	Yes	1 [3.1%]	6 [27.3%]	9 [36.0%]	16 [20.3%]
No	No	0 [0.0%]	0 [0.0%]	0 [0.0%]	0 [0.0%]

[a] *Including mania and hypomania patients.*

groups. Conversely, for onset-related events, the events most commonly experienced by patients were job-related events in the depression and euthymia group, while many patients experienced interpersonal-related events, changes in living conditions, or job-related events. For onset-related events, 30.6% of all patients reported experiencing overlapping events.

Table 5 shows the medication profiles for all participants. The predominant profile for all groups (34.4% in depression, 59.1% in mania or hypomania, and 48.0% in euthymia group) was a combination of mood stabilizers and antipsychotics. The highest proportion of patients treated with a combination of mood stabilizers, antipsychotics, and antidepressants was observed in the depression group (21.9%). Only 1 patient in the euthymia group was drug-free.

TABLE 4 | Classification of life events.

	Stressful life events			Onset-related events		
	Depression (n = 31)	Mania[a] (n = 16)	Euthymia (n = 16)	Depression (n = 29)	Mania[a] (n = 20)	Euthymia (n = 23)
Family problems with no abuse	1	4	1	1	1	0
Separation from close person	3	4	5	3	2	1
Interpersonal-related events	7	3	3	8	4	8
Health-related events	8	0	4	4	2	5
Money-related events	1	0	0	2	0	0
Sex-related events	2	1	0	0	0	0
Change of living conditions	0	0	0	2	7	7
Job-related events	2	0	2	9	5	11
Bullying, neglect	6	3	0	4	4	0
Other events	2	1	1	1	2	1
Overlapping events	1	1	0	4	8	10

[a]*Including mania and hypomania patients.*

IES-R Scores for Life Events Among the 3 Groups

IES-R Scores for Stressful Life Events

Figure 1A shows the IES-R results for stressful life events among the 3 groups. There were significant differences in the total IES-R scores (α = 0.92) observed among the 3 groups (F = 8.40, p = 0.001, power = 0.96). Post-hoc analysis showed significant differences between the groups; the IES-R total scores for the depression group (mean = 38.06, standard deviation [SD] = 16.56) and those for the mania group (mean 44.56, SD = 24.14) were significantly higher than those in the euthymia group (mean = 19.81, SD = 12.86; 95% confidence interval [CI] 7.57–28.94, p = 0.0005; 95% CI 7.62–41.88, p = 0.004, respectively). There were no significant differences in the total IES-R scores between the depression and the mania groups.

As shown in **Figure 1A**, in terms of the IES-R score sub-categories (intrusion, α = 0.89; avoidance, α = 0.84; and hyperarousal, α = 0.82), there were significant differences among the 3 groups for intrusion (F = 6.01, p = 0.004, power = 0.88) and hyperarousal (F = 9.42, p = 0.004, power = 0.98). For avoidance, the IES-R scores were significantly different among the 3 groups; however, the power did not reach 0.80 (F = 4.54, p = 0.015, power = 0.77). Each sub-category score, except for avoidance, was significantly higher in the depression and mania groups than in the euthymia group. For intrusion, the mean scores were as follows: depression group, 14.10 (SD = 7.37); mania group, 16.94 (SD = 9.89); and euthymia group, 7.56 (SD = 6.73). For avoidance, the mean scores were as follows: depression group, 14.74 (SD = 7.07); euthymia group, 8.25 (SD = 6.11); and mania group, 15.25 (SD = 9.88). For hyperarousal, the mean score of the depression group was 9.35 (SD = 4.99), and that of the mania group was 12.38 (SD = 7.99), while it was lower for the euthymia group (mean = 4.00, SD = 3.16).

IES-R Scores for Onset-Related Events

Figure 1B shows the IES-R scores for onset-related events among the 3 groups. There was a significant difference among the 3 groups in terms of the total IES-R scores (α = 0.94) as well as stressful life events scores (F = 10.59, p = 0.0001, power = 0.99). Post-hoc analysis showed significant differences between the groups: the total IES-R scores in the depression group (mean = 32.07, SD = 18.03) and those in the mania group (mean = 35.85, SD = 24.67) were significantly higher than those in the euthymia group (mean = 12.17, SD = 12.30; 95% CI 9.70–30.09, p = 0.0001; 95% CI 8.60–38.76, p = 0.002, respectively). There was no significant difference in the total scores between the depression and mania groups.

As shown in **Figure 1B**, for each sub-category of the IES-R score (intrusion, α = 0.90; avoidance, α = 0.88; and hyperarousal, α = 0.87), there were significant differences among the 3 groups: intrusion (F = 6.97, p = 0.002, power = 0.93), avoidance (F = 8.01, p = 0.001, power = 0.96), and hyperarousal (F = 9.53, p = 0.0002, power = 0.98). Each sub-category score of the depression and mania groups was significantly higher than that of the euthymia group. For intrusion, the mean score was as follows: depression group, 10.24 (SD = 7.38); mania group, 12.85 (SD = 9.86); euthymia group, 4.48 (SD = 5.38). For avoidance, the mean score of the depression group was 13.14 (SD = 7.53) and that of the mania group was 13.50 (SD = 10.25), while it was lower for euthymia (mean = 5.13, SD = 6.43). For hyperarousal, the mean score was as follows: depression group, 8.69 (SD = 5.39) and mania group, 9.50 (SD = 8.59), while it was lower for the euthymia group (mean = 2.57, SD = 2.79).

Correlations of the IES-R Score With the HDRS and YMRS Scores

Figures 2A–C show the correlations between the total IES-R scores for stressful life events or onset-related events and the HDRS scores for the 3 groups. Although some patients experienced both stressful life events and onset-related events, we adopted the higher IES-R score for each patient. There were significant positive correlations between the total IES-R score and the HDRS score for each group (depression group: r = 0.42, p = 0.018; mania group: r = 0.64, p = 0.001; euthymia group: r=

TABLE 5 | Medication profiles of the three patient groups.

Class of medication	Depression ($n = 32$)	Mania[a] ($n = 22$)	Euthymia ($n = 25$)	All ($n = 79$)
MOOD STABILIZERS (MS)				
Lithium	11	12	12	35
Sodium valproate	6	11	5	22
Lamotrigine	18	7	7	32
Topiramate	1	0	0	1
Gabapentin	0	1	0	1
Total (MS)	36	31	24	91
ANTIPSYCHOTICS (AP)				
Olanzapine	3	3	2	8
Quetiapine	8	6	5	19
Aripiprazole	10	6	8	24
Other	4	6	2	12
Total (AP)	25	21	17	63
ANTIDEPRESSANTS (AD)				
SSRI	8	3	1	12
SNRI	5	0	2	7
NaSSA	1	0	1	2
Trazodone	1	0	1	2
Other	1	0	0	1
Total (AD)	16	3	5	24
Benzodiazepine (BZ)	27	24	15	66
MEDICATION COMBINATION				
MS	6	4	5	15
AP	2	1	2	5
AD	0	0	0	0
MS + AP	11	13	12	36
MS + AD	3	1	2	6
AP + AD	3	1	1	5
MS + AP + AD	7	2	2	11
Drug-free	0	0	1	1

MS, Mood stabilizers; AP, Antipsychotics; AD, Antidepressants; SSRI, Selective Serotonin Reuptake Inhibitor; SNRI, Serotonin and Noradrenaline Reuptake Inhibitor; NaSSA, Noradrenergic and Specific Serotonergic Antidepressant; BZ, Benzodiazepine.
[a]Including mania and hypomania patients.

0.70, $p = 0.0001$). In terms of the intrusion score of the IES-R, there were significant positive correlations between the IES-R scores and the HDRS scores for each group (depression group: $r = 0.43$, $p = 0.013$; mania group: $r = 0.63$, $p = 0.002$; euthymia group: $r = 0.55$, $p = 0.005$). For avoidance, there were significant positive correlations between the IES-R scores and the HDRS scores in the mania and euthymia groups (mania group: $r = 0.43$, $p = 0.044$; euthymia group: $r = 0.62$, $p = 0.001$), while there was no significant correlation for the depression group. For hyperarousal, there were significant positive correlations between the IES-R scores and the HDRS scores for each group (depression group: $r = 0.47$, $p = 0.006$; mania group: $r = 0.69$, $p = 0.0004$; euthymia group: $r = 0.61$, $p = 0.001$).

There were significant positive correlations between the total IES-R scores and YMRS scores ($r = 0.40$, $p = 0.05$), and the hyperarousal score of the IES-R and YMRS ($r = 0.41$, $p = 0.04$) in the euthymia group, while no other significant correlations were observed in the other groups.

DISCUSSION

This study yielded two important findings. Firstly, even though stressful life events occur more frequently, and are less serious than traumatic experiences that meet the diagnostic criteria for PTSD, bipolar patients with a manic/hypomanic episode or a depressive episode perceived their experience of such stressful life events, including their onset-related events, as more severe PDSs than those in a euthymic state. Secondly, the severity of depressive symptoms, but not of manic symptoms, was positively correlated with the severity of the PDSs in patients with bipolar disorder, regardless of their mood episodes or euthymic state.

The first finding supports our hypothesis that patients with bipolar disorder experience PDSs associated with stressful life events similar to patients with unipolar major depression (8). Interestingly, this study shows that bipolar patients with a current manic or hypomanic episode also perceive their past stressful events as severe PDSs, similar to patients undergoing a current depressive episode. This study also demonstrates that patients with bipolar disorder in a euthymic state suffer less than those with any mood episode. In terms of depressive episodes, this finding supports those of our previous study, indicating that patients with treatment-refractory or unremitted unipolar major depression perceive their onset-related life events as serious PDSs (8). The finding that manic or hypomanic patients with bipolar disorder also experience PDSs associated with stressful past events was unexpected, as mood in a manic episode is often described as euphoric, cheerful, and high (23). However, considering that labile mood, which includes elevation, expansiveness, or irritability, is a clinical feature of bipolar mania (23), any mood episode may cause PDSs associated with stressful past events in patients with bipolar disorder. In addition, in terms of the psychoanalytic perspective, the hypothesis of manic defense that has been described by Klein (24), may help understand severe PDSs in bipolar patients with manic or hypomanic episode. When patients with bipolar disorder encounter stressful life events, they might exhibit manic symptoms as a defense against depression.

Our results demonstrated that the severity of depressive symptoms, but not that of manic symptoms, correlated positively with the severity of the PDSs in bipolar patients with any mood episodes and a euthymic state. According to the findings of this and our previous study (8), these results indicate that the PDSs associated with stressful past events may be related to depression in mood disorders, such as bipolar disorder and major depression. Experimental studies on human psychology, regarding the relationship between emotion and memory, provide clues to understand the association between depression and PDSs. Bower has advocated his network theory of affect which states that memories of emotional events are stored, connecting the places or situations related to them (25, 26). Therefore, people who feel certain emotions, such as happy or sad ones, are likely to recall the past events during which

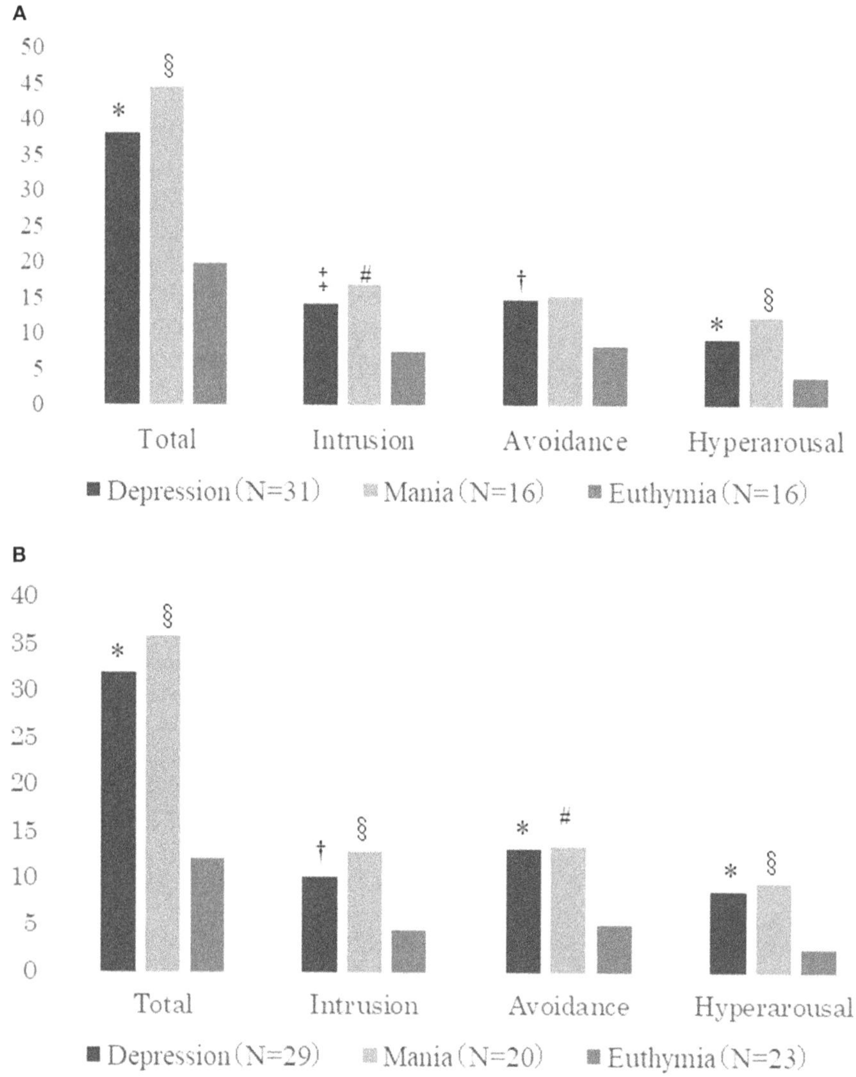

FIGURE 1 | (A) IES-R scores for life events related to PDSs (total and sub-categories: intrusion, avoidance, and hyperarousal) for the depression, mania, and euthymia groups. *Comparison between the depression and euthymia groups ($p < 0.001$); †comparison between the depression and euthymia groups ($p < 0.01$); ‡comparison between the depression and euthymia groups ($p < 0.05$); §comparison between the mania and euthymia groups ($p < 0.01$); #comparison between the mania and euthymia groups ($p < 0.05$). **(B)** IES-R scores for onset-related events (total and sub-categories: intrusion, avoidance, and hyperarousal) for the depression, mania, and euthymia groups. *Comparison between the depression and euthymia groups ($p < 0.001$); †comparison between the depression and euthymia groups ($p < 0.01$); §comparison between the mania and euthymia groups ($p < 0.01$); #comparison between the mania and euthymia groups ($p < 0.05$).

they had experienced the same emotions. This phenomenon is called mood-state-dependent memory (25, 26). Further, in terms of neural mechanisms of retrieval of memories, Anderson and colleagues, using functional magnetic resonance imaging (fMRI) studies, have reported that the suppression of intrusive or unwanted memories is regulated by inhibitory control through the connectivity between frontal cortices, involved in the prefrontal cortex and both the hippocampus and amygdala (27, 28). Considering these neural network theories, bipolar and unipolar depression patients with depressive symptoms might be predisposed to recall and ruminate past stressful events associated with a negative or sad emotion, and to perceive them as the PDSs.

To further investigate the association between depression and PDSs in patients with bipolar and unipolar disorders, experimental studies on biased autobiographical memory may contribute to understanding of the present findings. Such studies show an association of stressful past events with mood disorders, and accumulating evidence points toward negative recall bias in autobiographical memory. Autobiographical memory is thought to be the memory concerned with the recollection of personally experienced past events (29). It is thought that patients with depression recall and ruminate their past life events as negatively biased memories, based on impaired cognitive processing, and that these cognitive distortions and dysfunctions maintain the depressive mood (30, 31). Young et al. have reported abnormal

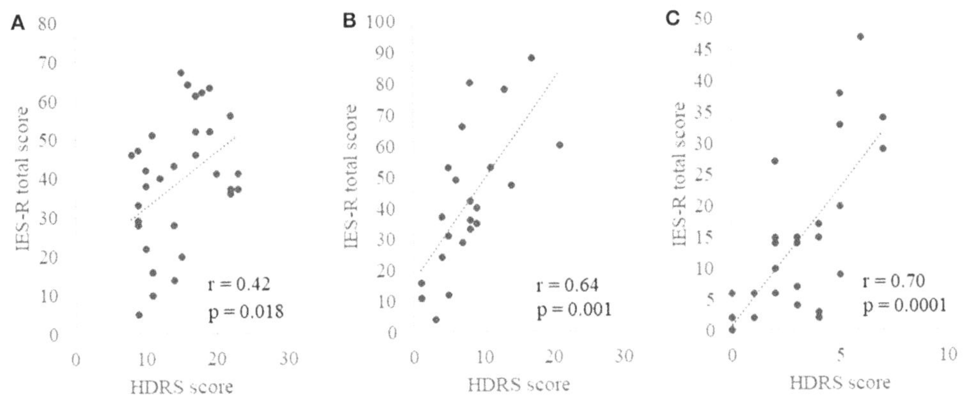

FIGURE 2 | The correlation between the total score of the IES-R for life events related to PDSs or onset-related events and the HDRS for the 3 groups (**A**, depression group; **B**, mania group; and **C**, euthymia group).

activity of the amygdala and its related network, based on fMRI (32), and have demonstrated the effectiveness of real-time fMRI amygdala neurofeedback against major depression, based on the theory of biased autobiographical memory in patients with depression (33). As bipolar patients with any mood episodes also perceive stressful life events as PDSs, such as intrusive memories, future studies should investigate the association between bipolar disorder and biased autobiographical memory, in order to understand the pathophysiology of bipolar disorder.

Further, the severity of manic symptoms positively correlated with the severity of the PDSs associated with stressful life events in bipolar patients with euthymia, but not in those with manic or hypomanic or depressive episodes. It is difficult to interpret this finding, because the severities of manic symptoms and of PDSs associated with stressful events in euthymic patients with bipolar disorder are markedly less severe than those of patients with a manic or hypomanic episode. To address this issue, further detailed questionnaires or structural interviews regarding subthreshold manic symptoms should be conducted for euthymic patients with bipolar disorder.

This study has some limitations. Firstly, this study could not assess whether PDSs become more intense because of severe mood states or whether mood states were more severe because of more intense PDSs, due to its cross-sectional design. Prospective cohort studies are required to investigate this issue. In addition, this study could not exclude confounding factors. Secondly, the application of IES-R to assess PDSs in patients with bipolar disorder remains methodologically limited. Although PDSs associated with stressful life events were sufficiently covered by the items of the IES-R, the IES-R was originally developed as a tool for rating severity of PTSD. Further studies are required to develop and validate a reliable original tool for the assessment of PDSs. Thirdly, this study has been influenced by recall bias, because each participant was requested to recall past stressful events.

In conclusion, this study demonstrates that bipolar patients with a manic or hypomanic episode or a depressive episode perceive their experiences of stressful life events as more severe PDSs than do euthymic patients. Moreover, the severity of depressive symptoms, but not that of manic symptoms, positively correlates with the severity of the PDSs in bipolar patients with any mood episode and those in a euthymic state. These findings indicate that depression may closely correlate with PDSs associated with stressful past events in bipolar disorder.

AUTHOR CONTRIBUTIONS

AS, TH, AK, and MI designed this study. AS and TH acquired data. AS, TH, and TN analyzed the data, and AS, TH, TN, and MI interpreted the results. AS and TH drafted the manuscript, and AK, TN, and MI revised the manuscript. MI supervised the study. All authors approved the final manuscript.

FUNDING

Our department received the endowment from Kusaka Clinic for mood disorders research project at Chiba University.

ACKNOWLEDGMENTS

We would like to thank Editage (www.editage.jp) for English language editing. We would like to thank all the patients and doctors who participated in this study. We are particularly grateful to the doctors and medical staff of the Department of Psychiatry, Chiba University Hospital (Akihiro Shiina, Nobuhisa Kanahara, Masatomo Ishikawa, Tadashi Hasegawa, and Hideki Komatsu), at Kisarazu Hospital (Hiroshi Sekine, Keijiro Koseki, Keisuke Kobayashi, Misaki Takase, Taisuke Yoshida, Kiyotoshi Sakashita, and Daiji Sakurai), and at Sodegaura Satsukidai Hospital (Shuichi Kikuchi, Minoru Ishige, and Makoto Kimura) for cooperating with this study. We also thank the research assistants at the Department of Psychiatry, Chiba University Hospital (Kaoru Ikeda, Komako Ito, Chisako Fujishiro, and Chiharu Fujita).

REFERENCES

1. Hammen C, Gitlin M. Stress reactivity in bipolar patients and its relation to prior history of disorder. *Am J Psychiatry* (1997) **154:**856–57. doi: 10.1176/ajp.154.6.856
2. Horesh N, Iancu I. A comparison of life events in patients with unipolar disorder or bipolar disorder and controls. *Compr Psychiatry* (2010) **51:**157–64. doi: 10.1016/j.comppsych.2009.05.005
3. Johnson SL, Miller I. Negative life events and time to recovery from episodes of bipolar disorder. *J. Abnormal Psychol.* (1997) **106:**449–57. doi: 10.1037/0021-843X.106.3.449
4. Johnson L, Andersson-Lundman G, Aberg-Wistedt A, Mathe AA. Age of onset in affective disorder: its correlation with hereditary and psychosocial factors. *J Affect Disord.* (2000) **59:**139–48. doi: 10.1016/S0165-0327(99)00146-9
5. Hosang GM, Korszun A, Jones L, Jones I, Gray JM, Gunasinghe CM. Adverse life event reporting and worst illness episodes in unipolar and bipolar affective disorders: measuring environmental risk for genetic research. *Psychol Med.* (2010) **40:**1829–37. doi: 10.1017/S003329170999225X
6. Meiser-Stedman R, Dalgleish T, Yule W, Smith P. Intrusive memories and depression following recent non-traumatic negative life events in adolescents. *J Affect Disord.* (2012) **137:**70–8. doi: 10.1016/j.jad.2011.12.020
7. Mol SS, Arntz A, Metsemakers JF, Dinant GJ, Vilters-van Montfort PA, Knottnerus JA. Symptoms of post-traumatic stress disorder after non-traumatic events: evidence from an open population study. *Br. J. Psychiatry* (2005) **186:**494–99. doi: 10.1192/bjp.186.6.494
8. Kimura A, Hashimoto T, Niitsu T, Iyo M. Presence of psychological distress symptoms associated with onset-related life events in patients with treatment-refractory depression. *J Affect Disord.* (2015) **175:**303–9. doi: 10.1016/j.jad.2015.01.027
9. Ghaemi SN, Ko JY, Goodwin FK. "Cade's disease" and beyond: misdiagnosis, antidepressant use, and a proposed definition for bipolar spectrum disorder. *Can J Psychiatry* (2002) **47:**125–34. doi: 10.1177/0706743702047 00202
10. Angst J, Gamma A, Benazzi F, Ajdacic V, Eich D, Rossler W. Diagnostic issues in bipolar disorder. *Eur Neuropsychopharmacol.* (2003) **13**(Suppl. 2):S43–50. doi: 10.1016/S0924-977X(03)00077-4
11. Angst J, Gamma A, Benazzi F, Ajdacic V, Eich D, Rossler W. Toward a re-definition of subthreshold bipolarity: epidemiology and proposed criteria for bipolar-II, minor bipolar disorders and hypomania. *J Affect Disord.* (2003) **73:**133–46. doi: 10.1016/S0165-0327(02)00322-1
12. American Psychiatric Association. *Diagnostic and Statistical Manual of Mental Disorders, 4th Edn.* Washington, DC: American Psychiatric Publishing (2013).
13. Otsubo T, Tanaka K, Koda R, Shinoda J, Sano N, Tanaka S. Reliability and validity of Japanese version of the Mini-International Neuropsychiatric Interview. *Psychiatry Clin Neurosci.* (2005) **59:**517–26. doi: 10.1111/j.1440-1819.2005.01408.x
14. Sheehan DV, Lecrubier Y, Sheehan KH, Amorim P, Janavs J, Weiller E. The Mini-International Neuropsychiatric Interview (M.I.N.I.): the development and validation of a structured diagnostic psychiatric interview for DSM-IV and ICD-10. *J Clin Psychiatry* (1998) **59**(Suppl. 20): 22–33; quiz 34–57.
15. Hamilton M. Development of a rating scale for primary depressive illness. *Br J Soc Clin Psychol.* (1967) **6:**278–96. doi: 10.1111/j.2044-8260.1967.tb00530.x
16. Williams JB. A structured interview guide for the Hamilton Depression Rating Scale. Archives of general psychiatry (1988) **45:**742–7. doi: 10.1001/archpsyc.1988.01800320058007
17. Young RC, Biggs JT, Ziegler VE, Meyer DA. A rating scale for mania: reliability, validity and sensitivity. *Br J Psychiatry* (1978) **133:**429–35. doi: 10.1192/bjp.133.5.429
18. First MB. *Structured Clinical Interview for DSM-IV Axis I Disorders: SCID - I: Clinician Version: Administration Booklet.* Washington, DC: American Psychiatric Press (1997).
19. Brugha TS, Cragg D. The List of Threatening Experiences: the reliability and validity of a brief life events questionnaire. *Acta Psychiatr Scand.* (1990) **82:**77–81. doi: 10.1111/j.1600-0447.1990.tb01360.x
20. Weiss DS, Marmar CR. *The Impact of Event Scale-Revised.* New York, NY: Guilford Press (1997).
21. Baumert J, Simon H, Gundel H, Schmitt C, Ladwig KH. The Impact of Event Scale–Revised: evaluation of the subscales and correlations to psychophysiological startle response patterns in survivors of a life-threatening cardiac event: an analysis of 129 patients with an implanted cardioverter defibrillator. *J Affect Disord.* (2004) **82:**29–41. doi: 10.1016/j.jad.2003.09.006
22. Asukai N, Kato H, Kawamura N, Kim Y, Yamamoto K, Kishimoto J. Reliability and validity of the Japanese-language version of the impact of event scale-revised (IES-R-J): 4 studies of different traumatic events. *J. Nerv. Ment. Dis.* (2002) **190:**175–82. doi: 10.1097/00005053-200203000-00006
23. Cowen P, Harrison P, Burns T. *Shorter Oxford Textbook of Psychiatry, 6th Edn.* Oxford University Press (2012). p. 210–2.
24. Klein M. A contribution to the psychogenesis of manic-depressive states. *Int J Psychoanal.* (1935) **16:**145–74.
25. Bower GH. Mood and memory. American Psychologist (1981) **36:**129–48. doi: 10.1037/0003-066X.36.2.129
26. Bower GH. How might emotions affect learning? In: Christianson S-Å editor. *The Handbook of Emotion and Memory: Research and Theory.* Hillsdale, NJ: Lawrence Erlbaum Associates (1992). p. 3–31.
27. Anderson MC, Ochsner KN, Kuhl B, Cooper J, Robertson E, Gabrieli SW, et al. Neural systems underlying the suppression of unwanted memories. *Science* (2004) **303:**232–5. doi: 10.1126/science.1089504
28. Gagnepain P, Hulbert J, Anderson MC. Parallel regulation of memory and emotion supports the suppression of intrusive memories. *J Neurosci.* (2017) **37:**6423–41. doi: 10.1523/JNEUROSCI.2732-16.2017
29. Williams JM, Barnhofer T, Crane C, Herman D, Raes F, Watkins E, et al. Autobiographical memory specificity and emotional disorder. *Psychol Bull.* (2007) **133:**122–48. doi: 10.1037/0033-2909.133.1.122
30. Gotlib IH, Joormann J. Cognition and depression: current status and future directions. *Annu Rev Clin Psychol.* (2010) **6:**285–312. doi: 10.1146/annurev.clinpsy.121208.131305
31. Ahmadpanah M, Astinsadaf S, Akhondi A, Haghighi M, Sadeghi Bahmani D, Nazaribadie M, et al. Early maladaptive schemas of emotional deprivation, social isolation, shame and abandonment are related to a history of suicide attempts among patients with major depressive disorders. *Compr Psychiatry* (2017) **77:**71–9. doi: 10.1016/j.comppsych.2017.05.008
32. Young KD, Siegle GJ, Bodurka J, Drevets WC. Amygdala activity during autobiographical memory recall in depressed and vulnerable individuals: association with symptom severity and autobiographical overgenerality. *Am J Psychiatry* (2016) **173:**78–89. doi: 10.1176/appi.ajp.2015.15010119
33. Young KD, Siegle GJ, Zotev V, Phillips R, Misaki M, Yuan H. Randomized clinical trial of real-time fMRI amygdala neurofeedback for major depressive disorder: effects on symptoms and autobiographical memory recall. *Am J Psychiatry* (2017) **174:**748–55. doi: 10.1176/appi.ajp.2017.16060637

16

Criterion Validity of the Yale-Brown Obsessive-Compulsive Scale Second Edition for Diagnosis of Obsessive-Compulsive Disorder in Adults

Pedro Castro-Rodrigues[1,2,3,4†], Marta Camacho[1†‡], Sílvia Almeida[1,2], Mónica Marinho[1,4], Catarina Soares[3], J. Bernardo Barahona-Corrêa[1,2,3,5] and Albino J. Oliveira-Maia[1,2,3,5]*

[1] Champalimaud Clinical Centre, Champalimaud Centre for the Unknown, Lisbon, Portugal, [2] Champalimaud Research, Champalimaud Centre for the Unknown, Lisbon, Portugal, [3] NOVA Medical School, Faculdade de Ciências Médicas, Universidade Nova de Lisboa, Lisbon, Portugal, [4] Centro Hospitalar Psiquiátrico de Lisboa, Lisbon, Portugal, [5] Department of Psychiatry and Mental Health, Centro Hospitalar de Lisboa Ocidental, Lisbon, Portugal

***Correspondence:**
Albino J. Oliveira-Maia
albino.maia@neuro.fchampalimaud.org

† These authors have contributed equally to this work

***‡Present Address:**
Marta Camacho,
Jon Van Geest Center for Brain Repair, University of Cambridge, Cambridge, United Kingdom

Background: While the Yale-Brown Obsessive-Compulsive Scale Second Edition (Y-BOCS-II) is the gold-standard for measurement of obsessive-compulsive (OC) symptom severity, its factor structure is still a matter of debate and, most importantly, criterion validity for diagnosis of OC disorder (OCD) has not been tested. This study aimed to clarify factor structure and criterion validity of the Y-BOCS-II.

Methods: We first validated and quantified the psychometric properties of a culturally adapted Portuguese translation of the Y-BOCS-II (PY-BOCS-II). The PY-BOCS-II and other psychometric instruments, including the OCD subscale of the Structured Clinical Interview for the DSM-IV, used to define OCD diagnosis, were administered to 187 participants (52 patients with OCD, 18 with other mood and anxiety disorders and 117 healthy subjects). In a subsample of 20 OCD patients and the 18 patients with other diagnoses, PY-BOCS-II was applied by clinicians blinded to diagnosis.

Results: PY-BOCS-II had excellent internal consistency (Cronbach's $\alpha = 0.96$) and very good test-retest reliability (Pearson's $r = 0.94$). Exploratory factor analysis revealed a two-factor structure with loadings consistent with the Obsessions and Compulsions subscales, and there was good to acceptable convergent and divergent validity. Importantly, the area under the curve (AUC) of the receiver operating characteristic (ROC) curve suggested elevated accuracy in discriminating between patients with OCD and control subjects (AUC = 0.96; 95% confidence interval [CI]: 0.92–0.99), that was retained in comparisons with age, gender and education matched controls (AUC = 0.95; 95% CI: 0.91–0.99), as well as with patients with other mood and anxiety disorders (AUC = 0.93; 95% CI: 0.84–1). Additionally, a cut-off score of 13 had optimal discriminatory ability for the diagnosis of OCD, with sensitivity ranging between 85 and 90%, and specificity between 94 and 97%, respectively when all samples or only the clinical samples were considered.

Conclusion: The PY-BOCS-II has excellent psychometric properties to assess the severity of obsessive-compulsive symptoms, reflecting obsessive, and compulsive dimensions, compatible with currently defined subscales. Furthermore, we found that a cut-off of 13 for the Y-BOCS-II total score has good to excellent sensitivity and specificity for the diagnosis of OCD.

Keywords: Yale-Brown Obsessive-Compulsive Scale—Second Edition (Y-BOCS-II), obsessive-compulsive disorder, psychometric properties, criterion validity, Portuguese language

INTRODUCTION

Obsessive-compulsive disorder (OCD) is a chronic and incapacitating neuropsychiatric condition, with a lifetime prevalence of 2.3% in the United States and an estimated prevalence of 5.3% in Portugal (1–3). It is characterized by the presence of obsessions (recurrent and persistent thoughts, experienced as intrusive or inappropriate and causing marked anxiety or distress) and/or compulsions (repetitive behaviors or mental acts that the person feels driven to perform, typically to reduce the anxiety caused by the obsessions) (4–7). Accurate assessment of OCD is critical due to its under-diagnosis, difficulty in establishing accurate diagnosis and need for careful and specific treatment planning and evaluation (8).

The Yale-Brown Obsessive-Compulsive Scale (Y-BOCS) is a clinician-administered instrument, developed in 1989 to assess the presence and severity of obsessive-compulsive symptoms (9, 10). It is divided into a symptom checklist and a severity scale. The symptom checklist comprises 54 dichotomous items assessing current or prior presence of specific obsessions and compulsions. The severity scale consists of 10 items that quantify the impact of obsessions and compulsions identified using the symptom checklist. These 10 items are 5-point Likert-type scales characterizing the time spent on compulsions (item 1), interference from obsessions (item 2), distress associated with obsessions (item 3), resistance to obsessions (item 4), subject's control over obsessions (item 5) and equivalent items for compulsions (items 6–10). The Y-BOCS has shown good psychometric properties and sensitivity to the therapeutic effects of medication and psychotherapy (9–14). However, several problems have been identified for this scale, including a poor conceptual fit of the "resistance to obsessions" item, possibly contributing toward inconsistent factor structure, with some studies finding a two-factor (obsessions and compulsions) and others a three-factor structure (obsessions, compulsions, and resistance to obsessions), as well as low sensitivity to change in severe cases and poor divergent validity relative to depressive symptoms (15–20).

To address some of these problems, a revised version, the Y-BOCS-II, was published in 2000 (20), with several differences relative to the original scale. Specifically, the obsessions and compulsions checklists are not formally subdivided into different symptom groups, some items in the symptom checklist were reworded and expanded, and a new checklist for avoidance was created. Additionally, in the severity scale, the item assessing "resistance against obsessions" was replaced by an item of "obsessions-free interval," the scoring for each item was revised from 0–4 to 0–5, and the order of assessment of items was changed. Furthermore, avoidance was considered in the definition of severity, namely for the items of interference from obsessions and interference from compulsions. Finally, the definitions of obsessions and compulsions were rephrased and several ancillary items removed from the text. Y-BOCS-II has excellent psychometric properties, with strong internal consistency, high test-retest and interrater reliabilities, and strong correlations with other clinician-rated measures of obsessive-compulsive symptom severity, namely the National Institute of Mental Health Global Obsessive Compulsive Scale (NIMH-GOCS), and only moderate correlations with measures of worry and depressive symptoms (20). The authors of the original scale also conducted an exploratory factor analysis, the results of which were consistent with the obsession and compulsion severity subscales (20). Thus, the Y-BOCS scales are typically considered the gold-standard instrument in assessing severity of obsessive-compulsive symptoms (8, 21), with the Y-BOCS-II translated and validated for other languages in addition to English (22, 23).

Further exploration of the psychometric properties of the Y-BOCS-II is pertinent for several reasons. In fact, criterion validity of this scale has not been tested, namely through comparisons between OCD patients and control samples, such as healthy subjects or, most importantly, other patients with similar disorders. Such comparisons would be important to define a cut-off value, allowing clinicians to establish that obsessive or compulsive symptoms may reflect an OCD diagnosis, rather than symptoms of a mood or anxiety disorder (e.g., rumination in depressive disorders and fear or worries in anxiety disorders) (24). Furthermore, the underlying factor structure of the Y-BOCS-II is still a matter of debate (21), with the original American and the Thai versions showing a two-factor structure, as described above, while the Italian version has a different factor structure, with distinct dimensions (20, 22, 23). Finally, the temporal stability of the Y-BOCS-II, while clinically relevant to understand temporal stability for longer periods (20, 22, 25), has only been tested in short intervals, no longer than 2 weeks.

Here, we explored the psychometric properties of a culturally adapted Portuguese translation of the Y-BOCS-II (PY-BOCS-II), including internal consistency, factor structure, test-retest reliability, convergent validity, and divergent validity. Importantly, we focused on the scale's criterion validity, through comparisons of total scores between patients with OCD and control subjects, including both healthy volunteers and patients with other mood and anxiety disorders, as defined by a gold-standard instrument for diagnosis of OCD.

MATERIALS AND METHODS

Participants

Eligibility was assessed in 223 participants, recruited either at the Champalimaud Clinical Centre or Centro Hospitalar Psiquiátrico de Lisboa. Patients with a clinical diagnosis of OCD ($n = 60$) were referred to the study by attending psychiatrists and psychologists, while control patients with other psychiatric diagnoses ($n = 35$) were selected randomly from the institutional databases at each institution. A convenience sample of 128 healthy community dwelling subjects was also recruited at each of the two institutions. Exclusion criteria for all samples were: acute medical illness; active neurological disease or clinically significant focal structural lesion of the central nervous system; acute episode of neuropsychiatric disease requiring hospitalization; history or clinical evidence of chronic psychosis, dementia, developmental disorders with low intelligence quotient or any other form of cognitive impairment; current substance or alcohol abuse or dependence; and illiteracy or otherwise not understanding the study's instructions. For all participants except those in the OCD sample, current diagnosis of OCD, as assessed by structured diagnostic interviews (OCD subscale of the Structured Clinical Interview for the DSM-IV and MINI Neuropsychiatry Interview), was also an exclusion criterion. For the healthy volunteers sample, current or past history of any psychiatric disorder, as assessed by the MINI Neuropsychiatry Interview, was an additional exclusion criterion. Among the 223 participants that were assessed, 52 OCD patients, 18 patients with non-OCD mood or anxiety disorders and 117 healthy participants were eligible for the study.

Measures

Y-BOCS-II

The Y-BOCS-II consists of two main components: a 67-item Symptom Checklist and a 10-item Severity Scale (20). In the Symptom Checklist, 29 items assess the presence of specific obsessions, another 29 items assess the presence of specific compulsions, and the remaining 9 items assess the presence of avoidance. Each item is dichotomously rated for current (i.e., within the past month) and past presence. In the Severity Scale, items assess, for the previous week, time spent with either obsessions or compulsions (items 1 and 6, respectively), obsession-free interval (item 2), resistance to compulsions (item 7), degree of control over either obsessions or compulsions (items 3 and 8, respectively), distress associated either with obsessions or with the impossibility of performing compulsions (items 4 and 9, respectively), and interference from either obsessions or compulsions (items 5 and 10, respectively). Items 5 and 10 also assess severity of avoidance related with obsessions or compulsions, respectively. Each of the 10 items is rated in a 6-point scale (0–5) and 2 subscales are typically considered: an Obsessions subscale (items 1–5) and a Compulsions subscale (items 6–10). A more detailed description of the scale is given in the Introduction.

The Y-BOCS-II was not previously validated for use in adult populations speaking European Portuguese. To guarantee that linguistic and semantic equivalence of the Y-BOCS-II was preserved for use in such populations, we used a 3-step translation/back-translation method to obtain a Portuguese Y-BOCS-II (PY-BOCS-II). For the first step, multiple independent translations from US English into European Portuguese, performed separately by four bilingual experts in Psychology or Psychiatry of Portuguese dominant language, were obtained, and then joined into a single consensus translation by the 4 translators. In the second step, back-translation of the consensus Portuguese translation into English was performed by two bilingual translators, of English dominant language, that were not involved in the original translation. This was followed by comparison of the back-translated versions by the original translation team, for creation of a consensus back-translation. In the last step, the consensus back-translation was compared with the original version by the initial translation team, and also sent for review and comments by the original authors of the Y-BOCS-II. This allowed for adjustments of the consensus Portuguese translation, to obtain a refined consensus Portuguese translation of the Y-BOCS-II. This version was then discussed among a panel of Portuguese-speaking experts in the fields of Psychiatry or Psychology, including but not limited to the original translation team, for assessment of face validity and proposal of additional adjustments for cultural adaptation. Finally, the scale was applied to a group of 10 patients suffering from OCD, followed by interviews for qualitative assessment of duration, cognitive effort, and adequate comprehension of items. Considering the input from these patients, the translation was further adapted, and the final version of the PY-BOCS was defined.

Structured Clinical Interview for the DSM-IV, OCD Subscale (SCID-OCD)

The OCD Subscale of the SCID-IV is a semi-structured interview that allows for the diagnosis of current OCD according to DSM-IV criteria (26). It has been validated for Brazilian Portuguese by Del-Ben et al. (27) and we adapted this version for European Portuguese. The SCID-OCD was used to discriminate between participants with and without OCD, for the purpose of criterion validity assessment.

MINI Neuropsychiatric Interview

The MINI is a brief structured clinical interview divided into 15 modules (28). It allows for detection of major depressive disorder (MDD), dysthymia, suicide risk, manic and hypomanic episodes, panic disorder, agoraphobia, social phobia, generalized anxiety disorder (GAD), OCD, post-traumatic stress-disorder, alcohol abuse or dependence, substance abuse or dependence, psychotic disorders, anorexia nervosa and bulimia nervosa, based on the rapid screening of DSM-IV diagnostic criteria. The interview has been translated to European Portuguese by Guterres, Levy and Amorim (29). We used this version of the MINI to assess comorbidity and identify exclusion criteria.

Beck Depression Inventory II (BDI-II)

The BDI-II is a 21-item self-report screening instrument that assesses the presence of depressive symptoms in the previous 15 days (30). Responses are scored from 0 ("absent") to 3 ("severe"). It was validated to the Portuguese adult population by Campos and Gonçalves (31). We used the BDI-II results to assess divergent validity with the PY-BOCS-II.

State-Trait Anxiety Inventory (STAI)

The STAI is a widely-used 40 item self-report screening instrument that assesses the presence of anxiety symptoms (32). It is composed of two subscales: the STAI-state and the STAI-trait. Trait anxiety corresponds to feelings of tension, apprehension and increased autonomic activity and is a relatively stable personality trait (32, 33). People with high trait anxiety have a tendency to perceive more situations as dangerous or threatening than people who have lower trait anxiety scores. State anxiety, on the other hand, fluctuates over time according to the presence of stressors. Individuals with high trait anxiety scores also tend to have higher state anxiety scores (32, 33). The scale was validated for use in Portuguese-speaking adults by Santos and Silva (34).

Coimbra Obsessive Inventory (COI—Inventário Obsessivo de Coimbra)

The COI is a self-report scale, developed for the Portuguese population, that assesses obsessive and compulsive symptoms through 12 dimensions, namely doubt and indecision, intrusive thoughts and covert rituals, magical thinking, slowness and repetition, need for control, need for order and symmetry, collection and hoarding, religious obsessions and compulsions, somatic obsessions, and obsessive and aggressive impulses (35). It is subdivided in "frequency" and "emotional distress" subscales. The COI score was used to assess convergent validity for the PY-BOCS-II.

Procedures

Study procedures and protocol were reviewed and approved by the Ethics Committees of the Champalimaud Centre for the Unknown and of Centro Hospitalar Psiquiátrico de Lisboa. All subjects gave written informed consent in accordance with the Declaration of Helsinki. In the non-blinded sample, after participants had responded to a global clinical questionnaire, instruments were applied in the following order: MINI, SCID-IV, PY-BOCS-II, BDI-II, STAI, COI. In the blinded sample, in a first session participants responded to the clinical questionnaire and the following instruments were applied, in the same order: MINI, SCID-IV, BDI-II, STAI, COI. In a second session, conducted by another researcher who did not have access to the first set of results, PY-BOCS-II was applied. Temporal stability was tested in a subsample of 27 OCD patients and 72 healthy participants by applying PY-BOCS-II a second time, 4 weeks after initial testing.

Data Analysis

Descriptive statistics were calculated for sociodemographic and psychometric data, including means and standard deviations, minimum and maximum absolute values and percentage. We used independent samples *t*-tests to compare means between groups, except for gender (in which chi-squared was used), with two-tailed significance values and the alpha-level was set to 0.05. We assessed several psychometric properties of the PY-BOCS-II. To estimate reliability, we analyzed internal consistency using Cronbach's α and temporal stability using Pearson's correlation coefficient. To assess dimensionality, exploratory factor analysis with principal axis factoring and oblique rotation was performed in the Severity Scale. Factor analysis of the Symptom Checklist was not performed due to insufficient sample size of the OCD sample (a sample size of 5–10 participants per item is generally recommended—for 67 items a much larger sample size would be needed) (36). To assess construct validity, we used Pearson's correlation coefficient of PY-BOCS-II scores with COI scores for convergent validity, and with BDI-II scores and STAI scores for divergent validity. Finally, criterion validity was analyzed by studying the relationship between PY-BOCS-II scores and SCID-OCD classification using receiving operating characteristic (ROC) curves. Such curves are obtained by plotting the true positive rate (i.e., sensitivity) in function of the false positive rate (1-specificity), with each point in the curve representing a sensitivity/specificity pair corresponding to each possible decision threshold. Here, the area under the curve (AUC) of the ROC curve reflects the probability that a randomly chosen individual with OCD had a higher PY-BOCS-II score than a randomly chosen individual without OCD diagnosis (with diagnosis defined by the SCID-OCD) The decision threshold, or cut-off value, for OCD diagnosis was then chosen according to the ROC curve, as the total score that maximized sensitivity and specificity over all possible values.

RESULTS

Descriptive Statistics

Sociodemographic data and mean scores of all psychometric instruments are presented in **Table 1**. While the non-OCD sample was slightly younger than the OCD sample, there were no significant differences in gender or education. A more detailed subgroup analysis revealed a more complex pattern of differences between subgroups (see **Table S1**). In the OCD sample, the most common comorbid diagnoses were MDD (38%), GAD (17%), prior MDD (15%), panic disorder (15%), and social phobia (12%). For the mood and anxiety disorders sample, a full description of diagnoses is listed in **Table S2** and included MDD, dysthymia, Bipolar Disorder (BD), GAD, and panic disorder. Descriptive statistics of individual PY-BOCS-II Severity Scale items in the OCD sample are presented in **Table 2**. The PY-BOCS-II total score had a weak positive correlation with age ($r = 0.28$) when considering all participants, but in OCD patients this correlation was non-significant. Also, across all participants, there were no statistically significant differences between genders in any of the psychometric measures ($t < 1.23$; $p > 0.21$), and the correlations with education were either non-significant (for the PY-BOCS-II total score) or weak ($r < 0.3$ for all other psychometric measures).

TABLE 1 | Sociodemographic and psychometric data from each sample.

	OCD Sample (n = 52)		Non-OCD Sample (n = 135)		
	Range	Mean (SD)	Range	Mean (SD)	*p*-value
Gender (% male)	42.3%		30%		0.1
Age (years)	19–62	40.0 (10.0)	20–64	32.9 (9.5)	<0.001
Education (years)	7–23	14.7 (3.4)	4–23	15.4 (3.3)	0.2
Y-BOCS-II total score	0–45	22.7 (10.4)	0–25	1.8 (3.9)	<0.001
BDI-II total score	1–45	22.2 (13.6)	0–42	6.2 (9.1)	<0.001
STAI-state score	22–75	47.9 (14.9)	20–75	33.8 (10.8)	<0.001
STAI-trait score	26–77	56.9 (14.4)	20–74	32.8 (10.7)	<0.001
COI total score	18–332	137.9 (82.7)	0–290	31.9 (40.0)	<0.001

For all variables, mean and standard deviation are shown, except for gender (presented as percentage of males). Differences were tested using chi-square for gender and independent samples t-test for the other variables (p-values displayed). OCD, Obsessive-compulsive disorder; Y-BOCS-II, Yale-Brown Obsessive-Compulsive Scale-II; BDI-II, Beck Depression Inventory-II; STAI, State-Trait Anxiety Inventory; COI, Coimbra Obsessive Inventory.

TABLE 2 | Individual Y-BOCS-II item summaries for the OCD sample.

Items	Statistics			Percentage of endorsement							Reliability	
	Mean (SD)	Sk	Ku	0	1	2	3	4	5	Total	Item-total corr.	α if deleted
1	2.0 (1.3)	0.7	0.2	9.6	30.8	30.8	17.3	3.8	7.7	100	0.65	0.87
2	2.4 (1.5)	0.0	−1.0	11.5	21.2	21.2	19.2	23.1	5.8	100	0.58	0.87
3	2.6 (1.6)	−0.3	−1.0	15.4	11.5	15.4	23.1	23.1	11.5	100	0.63	0.87
4	2.2 (1.3)	0.2	−0.3	9.6	21.2	26.9	28.8	7.7	5.8	100	0.50	0.88
5	1.8 (1.4)	0.5	−0.5	19.2	26.9	26.9	11.5	11.5	3.8	100	0.64	0.87
6	1.9 (1.3)	0.5	−0.1	13.5	30.8	25.0	23.1	3.8	3.8	100	0.64	0.87
7	2.5 (1.7)	−0.2	−1.3	21.2	11.5	11.5	19.2	25.0	11.5	100	0.53	0.88
8	2.8 (1.6)	−0.5	−0.7	13.5	5.8	19.2	19.2	30.8	11.5	100	0.68	0.87
9	2.7 (1.4)	−0.1	−0.7	7.7	13.5	25.0	25.0	17.3	11.5	100	0.69	0.87
10	1.8 (1.5)	0.2	−1.1	26.9	19.2	17.3	23.1	11.5	1.9	100	0.65	0.87

For each item of the Y-BOCS-II, the mean, standard deviation and the percentage of endorsement for each possible item score (range 0-5) is displayed. OCD, Obsessive-compulsive disorder; Y-BOCS-II, Yale-Brown Obsessive-Compulsive Scale-II; SD, Standard deviation; comp, compulsions; Sk, Skewness; Ku, Kurtosis; Item-total corr, Item-total correlation; α if deleted, Cronbach's α if item is deleted.

Reliability

A Cronbach's alpha of 0.96 was obtained for the PY-BOCS-II severity scale when data from all participants were considered, demonstrating robust internal consistency. A slightly lower value (0.94) was found for both the Obsessive and Compulsive subscales, when tested separately. Furthermore, Cronbach's alpha remained stable with removal of any item from the scale (0.96 for all items), and corrected item-total correlations ranged between 0.8 and 0.87. Reliability measures when considering only data from the OCD sample are presented in **Table 2**.

Regarding temporal stability, assessed in 99 participants in the global sample, a Pearson's r of 0.94 ($p < 0.001$) was obtained for the correlation of PY-BOCS-II total score at the first application and 30 days later. When considering only the OCD sample ($n =$ 27), test-retest reliability was slightly higher ($r = 0.95$, $p <$ 0.001). Finally, the temporal stability of the Obsessions subscale was higher than the temporal stability of the Compulsions subscale, both when considering all participants ($r = 0.94$ vs. $r = 0.89$, respectively) and OCD patients only ($r = 0.92$ vs. $r = 0.84$, respectively).

Dimensionality

We conducted exploratory factor analysis using principal axis factoring with promax rotation in the OCD sample. The Kaiser-Meier-Olkin measure of sample adequacy was 0.836, above the recommended value of 0.6, and the Bartlett's test of sphericity was significant [$X^2_{(45)} = 265.75$, $p < 0.001$]. Two factors with eigenvalues >1 were obtained (eigenvalues of 5.05 for the first factor and 1.47 for the second factor) and this two-factor solution was consistent with the deflection of the scree plot (**Figure 1**). The pattern matrix revealed that items 6–10 had higher loadings on factor 1 (all >0.4) and items 1–5 on factor 2. Item 3 had relatively small loadings on both factors, although with slightly higher loading on factor 2. The correlation between factor 1 and factor 2 was 0.55.

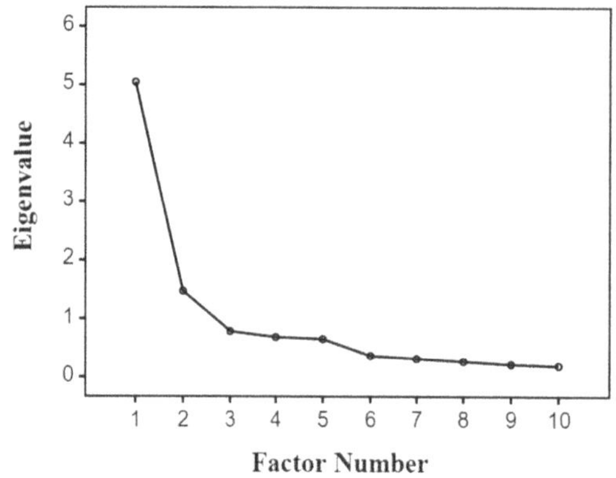

Y-BOCS-II	Factor 1	Factor 2
Item 1	0.06	**0.76**
Item 2	0.1	**0.61**
Item 3	0.36	**0.39**
Item 4	-0.27	**0.98**
Item 5	0.28	**0.5**
Item 6	**0.51**	0.25
Item 7	**0.92**	-0.19
Item 8	**0.84**	-0.01
Item 9	**0.81**	0.01
Item 10	**0.48**	0.33

FIGURE 1 | Scree plot (exploratory factor analysis) and pattern matrix for Y-BOCS-II factors in the OCD sample. In the pattern matrix, standardized weights of a regression analysis in which item responses are predicted from their levels of the underlying factors are represented. Factor loadings above 0.4 or highest factor loading shown in bold.

TABLE 3 | Correlations between psychometric measures and Y-BOCS-II partial and total score in all participants.

All participants	Y-BOCS-II obsessions	Y-BOCS-II compulsions	Y-BOCS-II total
COI total	0.67	0.64	0.67
BDI-II total	0.61	0.48	0.57
STAI-state	0.46	0.37	0.43
STAI-trait	0.73	0.58	0.68

Pearson's product moment correlation coefficient used as correlation measure. All correlations are highly significant (p's < 0.001). Y-BOCS-II, Yale-Brown Obsessive-Compulsive Scale-II; COI, Coimbra Obsessive Inventory; BDI-II, Beck Depression Inventory-II; STAI, State-Trait Anxiety Inventory.

Construct Validity

Measures of construct validity, using correlations between the PY-BOCS-II and several self-report psychometric measures, are shown in **Table 3**. For convergent validity, we found a significant and strong correlation between the PY-BOCS-II total score and the score for a self-report obsessive-compulsive inventory (COI) ($r = 0.67$, $p < 0.001$), with similar correlations with each of the COI subscales ($r = 0.67$ for the frequency subscale and $r = 0.66$ for the emotional distress subscale, both with $p < 0.001$). For divergent validity, the correlations between the Y-BOCS-II total score and the STAI-state scores was only moderate ($r = 0.43$, $p < 0.001$), higher, but still moderate, for the BDI-II score ($r = 0.57$, $p < 0.001$), and strong for the STAI-trait ($r = 0.68$, $p < 0.001$). Furthermore, the PY-BOCS-II Compulsions subscale had lower correlation with BDI-II and both STAI scores than the Obsessions subscale (**Table 3**) suggesting a better divergent validity for the Compulsions subscale. **Table S3** shows the correlation matrix for all psychometric measures in all participants.

Criterion Validity

To assess criterion validity, we created receiver operating characteristic (ROC) curves (**Figure 2**), using the SCID-OCD as the discriminator between participants with OCD ($n = 35$) and controls ($n = 135$; **Figure 2** left panel). An area under the curve (AUC) of 0.96 (95% Confidence interval [95% CI]: 0.92, 0.99) was obtained, and further analyses of the ROC curve values showed that a PY-BOCS-II total score of 13 points, when used as a cut-off for diagnosis, correctly identifies OCD with a sensitivity of 85% and a specificity of 97% (**Table 4**). To further explore the discriminatory capacity of the Y-BOCS-II, a similar analysis was performed comparing the OCD sample with a group of age-, gender- ,and education-matched controls (frequency-matched balanced mixture of healthy subjects and patients with mood and anxiety disorders; **Figure 2** middle panel). The AUC was similar (AUC = 0.95; 95% CI: 0.91, 0.99) and a total score cut-off of 13 points remained optimal, with sensitivity of 85% and specificity of 96%. Importantly, the same analyses were repeated in data from a subgroup of patients with either OCD ($n = 20$) or other mood and anxiety disorders ($n = 18$), for whom PY-BOCS-II was applied by a researcher blinded to diagnosis and to the results of other psychometric tests. In this group (**Figure 2** right panel), AUC was only slightly lower (AUC = 0.93; 95% CI: 0.84, 1) and the 13-point cut-off resulted in sensitivity of 90% and specificity of 94% for diagnosis of OCD.

DISCUSSION

Here, we have translated and successfully validated the Y-BOCS-II for the Portuguese adult population. A translated and culturally adapted version of the scale had excellent reliability and was valid for assessment of the severity of obsessive-compulsive symptoms. Our results further supported a two-factor structure for the scale, consistent with the Obsessions and Compulsions subscales proposed by the original authors. Importantly, and addressing the main objective of this study, we have demonstrated, to the best of our knowledge for the first time, that the Y-BOCS-II adequately discriminates patients with OCD, and that a cut-off of 13 points for the Y-BOCS-II total score has excellent sensitivity and specificity for that diagnosis.

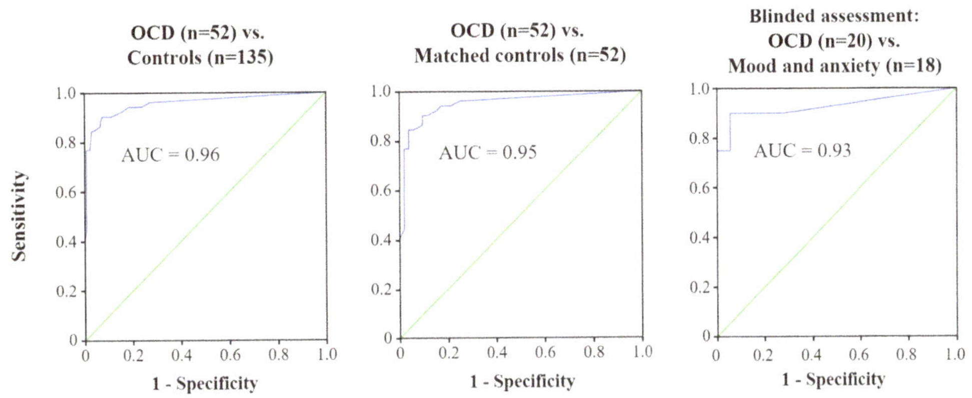

FIGURE 2 | ROC curves for use of the Y-BOCS-II to identify OCD. Plot of the true positive rate (1 −specificity) against the false positive rate (sensitivity) for the different possible cut-offs of the Y-BOCS-II using the SCID-OCD as the diagnostic instrument. In the left panel, all participants were considered. In the middle panel, OCD and age-, gender-, and education-matched controls (balanced mixture of healthy subjects and patients with mood and anxiety disorders) are considered. In the right panel, patients who completed a blinded assessment are considered. ROC, Receiver operating characteristic; Y-BOCS-II, Yale-Brown Obsessive-Compulsive Scale-II; OCD, Obsessive-compulsive disorder; AUC, Area under the curve.

Our results on reliability of the PY-BOCS-II are in line with the studies that have previously assessed the psychometric properties of this scale. Storch and colleagues found strong internal consistency (Cronbach's alpha = 0.89), similar to what was described later for the Thai (0.94) and Italian (0.83) versions of the scale (20, 22, 23). Regarding test-retest reliability, high values were reported in the original description of the psychometric properties of the scale (Intraclass correlation [ICC] > 0.85), as well as for the Italian version (ICC = 0.74), while the Thai version did not assess this psychometric dimension (20, 22, 23). Recently, psychometric properties of the original American version of the Y-BOCS-II were retested, with findings of good internal consistency (Cronbach's alpha = 0.86), acceptable test-retest reliability (r = 0.64–0.81) and excellent inter-rater reliability (ICC = 0.97–0.99) (25). Our findings for internal consistency (Cronbach's alpha = 0.96) and test-retest reliability (r = 0.94–0.95) are in the upper range of prior studies, suggesting that the process of translation and cultural adaptation was successful. Furthermore, other authors have suggested that temporal stability be tested with longer test-retest intervals than 2 weeks (20, 22, 25). Ours is, to our knowledge, the first study to demonstrate stability of test scores after 4 weeks.

Regarding dimensionality, and due to lack of consensus regarding the factor structure of the Y-BOCS-II, we decided to perform an exploratory factor analysis rather than a confirmatory factory analysis, as was common practice in previous studies. While, in general terms, our results replicate previous findings of a two-factor solution corresponding to obsessions and compulsions, there a few subtle but noteworthy differences (20, 23). Specifically, for the original and Thai versions of the task, interference from obsessions (item 5) had high loadings (>0.4) on both factors, with the authors of the Thai version also reporting higher loadings of distress associated with obsessions (item 4) on the compulsions factor than the obsessions factor (23). Loadings in our data were more clearly distributed between the two factors, with the first five items mainly loading on a factor that is consistent with an Obsessive dimension, and the last five items loading mainly on the second factor, consistent with a Compulsive dimension. Unexpectedly, item 3 ("control over obsessions") loaded similarly on both factors, possibly because a subset of patients may feel that their level of control over obsessions is dependent on the frequency and severity of compulsions. Importantly, our results are in marked contrast with those for the Italian version of the scale, which revealed a "symptom severity" factor (items 1–4 and 6–9) and "interference from symptoms in daily life" factor (items 5 and 10) (22). It is unclear whether these differences in factor structure reflect true cultural differences across different countries with respect to the presentation of OCD, or are merely due to methodological differences, namely regarding sample size.

With regards to convergent validity, the PY-BOCS-II showed a correlation of 0.67 with self-reported obsessive-compulsive symptom scores in the COI. This correlation was observed even though a high score in the COI reflects a high number of different symptoms causing distress, but not necessarily the severity of individual symptoms (9, 37), while the Y-BOCS-II measures severity of OCD symptoms regardless of the number of different symptoms. Other authors have found low to moderate correlations between Y-BOCS-II scores and scores on self-reported OCD symptom assessment tools such as the Obsessive-Compulsive Inventory-Revised (OCI-R), while correlations with clinician-rated obsessive-compulsive symptom scales such as the National Institute of Mental Health Global Obsessive Compulsive Scale are stronger (e.g., r = 0.85) (20). Assessing convergent validity against a clinician-rated scale would thus, in all likelihood, have yielded a more robust correlation for the PY-BOCS-II. For divergent validity, the PY-BOCS-II total score showed a moderate correlation with both depression and state-anxiety scores, and a strong correlation with trait-anxiety scores. This observation replicates the findings of previous studies on the psychometric properties of the Y-BOCS, that also found weak correlations with self-reported measures of

TABLE 4 | Coordinates for the ROC curve of the Y-BOCS-II using all participants.

Y-BOCS-II cut-off score	Sensitivity (%)	Specificity (%)
0.50	96.2	72.6
1.50	94.2	76.3
2.50	94.2	78.5
3.50	94.2	81.5
4.50	92.3	84.4
5.50	90.4	88.9
6.50	90.4	91.1
7.50	90.4	91.9
8.50	90.4	92.6
9.50	88.5	93.3
10.50	86.5	93.3
11.50	84.6	96.3
13.00	**84.6**	**97.0**
14.50	76.9	97.8
15.50	76.9	98.5
16.50	76.9	99.3
17.50	75.0	99.3
18.50	73.1	99.3
19.50	67.3	99.3
20.50	63.5	99.3
21.50	59.6	99.3
22.50	55.8	99.3
23.50	50.0	99.3
24.50	44.2	99.3
25.50	40.4	100.0

For each coordinate (Y-BOCS-II total score), its sensitivity and specificity in identifying OCD are shown. The total score with the best sensitivity and specificity for diagnosis of OCD is shown in bold. ROC, Receiver operating characteristic; Y-BOCS-II, Yale-Brown Obsessive-Compulsive Scale-II; OCD, Obsessive-compulsive disorder.

anxiety and moderate to strong correlations with self-reported measures of depression such as the Inventory of Depressive Symptomatology—Self-Report ($r = 0.35$) (20), the Patient Healthy Questionnaire ($r = 0.45$) (23), the BDI ($r = 0.40$) (22), or the Depression Anxiety Stress Scale—Depression subscale ($r = 0.41$) (25). Together, the currently available data suggests that divergent validity regarding depression symptoms is, at best, only moderate. This was also a problem with the first version of the Y-BOCS, and may be related to the high co-morbidity between OCD and major depressive disorder (MDD), which may be as high as 50% (38–40). As to the robust correlation between the PY-BOCS-II and STAI-trait anxiety, it may simply reflect the fact that patients with more severe OCD tend to have higher levels of longstanding comorbid anxiety, rather than a true limitation in the scale's ability to discriminate between these two dimensions.

Our findings of higher correlations with self-reported depression and anxiety symptoms in the Obsessions subscale than in the Compulsions subscale suggest that the latter may have better divergent validity. This finding is in line with the results from Storch and colleagues. In their study, the Y-BOCS-II Compulsion subscale had higher correlations with the NIMH-GOCS and with the OCI-R and lower correlations with the PSWQ and with the IDS-SR when compared with the Obsessions subscale (20). For the Thai version of the Y-BOCS-II, the correlations of subscales with depressive symptoms were non-significant and in the Italian version they were not presented (22, 23). This finding is particularly interesting because it could suggest higher tendency for obsessions than for compulsions in patients with comorbid OCD and MDD and higher tendency for compulsions in patients with OCD only.

The main objective of this project, however, was to clarify criterion validity for this scale. AUC of the ROC curves demonstrated that the Y-BOCS is accurate in discriminating between patients with OCD and others without the disorder. To our knowledge, this is the first study exploring criterion-related validity of the Y-BOCS-II in OCD patients, healthy controls and patients with other psychiatric disorders. The cut-off value that we propose (Y-BOCS total score = 13) is in line with previous findings using the first edition of the Y-BOCS (14). Using that version, Farris and colleagues have shown that a posttreatment YBOCS score of 14 or lower was the best predictor of symptom remission and that a posttreatment YBOCS score of 12 or lower was the best predictor of wellness (defined as symptom remission, good quality of life and high level of adaptive functioning) (14). However, it is important to note that this study focused on treatment response and that while the first edition of the YBOCS has an upper limit of 40 points, the upper limit of Y-BOCS-II is 50 points. In any case, the cut-off we propose here can be useful from a diagnostic perspective, because clinicians often assess patients with obsession-like ideas or compulsive-like behaviors, who may or may not suffer from OCD.

Nevertheless, our study is not free of limitations. Regarding validation of the PY-BOCS-II, information about inter-rater reliability would be reassuring. However, all previous studies of psychometric measures of the Y-BOCS-II which have performed this analysis have found excellent inter-rater reliability (20, 22, 25). Furthermore, it would have been desirable to have larger sample sizes, namely in the non-OCD clinical control group, as well as to have a control group without significant differences in demographic characteristics, especially considering the weak positive correlations with age across all psychometric instruments used. However, the Y-BOCS-II had the weakest correlations with age and, in the OCD group, the correlation between Y-BOCS-II and age was non-significant. Nevertheless, to eliminate any potential effects of such differences in the ROC curves, we selected a sample of age-, gender- and education-matched controls and repeated our main analysis only with this group, obtaining confirmation of our previous results. Also, in a subsample of individuals (32 OCD participants), raters were not blind to diagnosis, which could lead to criterion contamination. To account for this potential limitation, we also created ROC curves using only the subset of OCD and non-OCD patients that were assessed in a blinded fashion. While the number of participants included in this analysis was lower, the results obtained were very similar to the remaining ROC curves, thus validating our findings. In the future it could be important to repeat this specific analysis using larger OCD and non-OCD clinical samples. The use of the SCID-OCD as a diagnostic instrument can also be considered a limitation because it has never been validated for the Portuguese population. However, it has been validated for Brazilian Portuguese and the adaptation to European Portuguese was very straightforward. Furthermore, it must be noted that the version of SCID used here was according to DSM-IV, and thus includes hoarding symptoms, which are considered a separate disorder in DSM-5 (Hoarding Disorder). However, we do not believe that this had a significant impact in our results, since none of the participants included in the study presented exclusively hoarding symptoms, as assessed by the Y-BOCS-II Symptom Checklist (items 26 and 46). Finally, future studies could address the properties of the Y-BOCS-II regarding classification of treatment sensitivity, as has been done for the first version of the scale.

In conclusion, we have successfully translated and validated the Y-BOCS-II for use in the Portuguese adult population, showing that the Portuguese version of the Y-BOCS-II maintains the psychometric properties of the original version in evaluating the severity of obsessive-compulsive symptoms. Using this version of the task we have also, for the first time, assessed criterion validity of the Y-BOCS-II, by exploring its capacity to distinguish between patients with OCD and subjects in several clinical and non-clinical groups, using both a blinded and a non-blinded design. Our results suggest that a Y-BOCS-II total score cut-off of 13 has good sensitivity and excellent specificity in identifying OCD. Although a replication in a larger sample, with a blinded study design, would be important to confirm our findings, these results are useful given the importance of correctly assessing obsessive-compulsive symptoms to establish an adequate diagnosis and a thorough treatment plan.

AUTHOR CONTRIBUTIONS

PC-R, MC, JB-C, and AO-M conceived and designed the study. PC-R, MC, JB-C, and AO-M participated in the translation procedures. PC-R, MC, SA, MM, and CS collected data. PC-R and MC organized the database and performed the statistical analysis. PC-R wrote the first draft of the manuscript that was critically read, revised, and approved by all authors.

FUNDING

PC-R, JB-C, and AO-M are supported by grant 030302, funded by national funds from Fundação para a Ciência e Tecnologia (FCT/MCTES) and co-funded by FEDER, under the Partnership Agreement Lisboa 2020-Programa Operacional Regional de Lisboa. PC-R was supported by a doctoral fellowship (SFRH/SINTD/94350/2013) from FCT and a Fullbright Research Grant. FCT/MCTES, FEDER and Fullbright Portugal did not have a role in the design and conduct of the study, in the collection, management, analysis, and interpretation of the data, in the preparation, review, or approval of the manuscript, nor in the decision to submit the manuscript for publication.

ACKNOWLEDGMENTS

The authors would like to thank the original authors of the Y-BOCS-II for providing access to the scale, and Sofia Santos and Soraia Salgueiro for contributions in the translation procedures.

REFERENCES

1. Kessler RC, Berglund P, Demler O, Jin R, Merikangas KR, Walters EE. Lifetime prevalence and age-of-onset distributions of. *Arch Gen Psychiatry* (2005) 62:593–602. doi: 10.1001/archpsyc.62.6.593
2. Ruscio AM, Stein DJ, Chiu WT, Kessler RC. The epidemiology of obsessive-compulsive disorder in the National Comorbidity Survey Replication. *Mol Psychiatry* (2010) 15:53–63. doi: 10.1038/mp.2008.94
3. Caldas de Almeida J, Xavier M, Cardoso G, Pereira M, Gusmão R, Corrêa B, et al. *Estudo Epidemiológico Nacional de Saúde Mental - 1.o Relatório.* Lisboa Fac Ciências Médicas (2013).
4. American Psychiatric Association. Diagnostic and Statistical Manual of Mental Disorders, 5th Edition (DSM-5). Diagnostic Stat Man Ment Disord 4th Ed TR. (2013) 280.
5. Stein DJ, Craske MA, Friedman MJ, Phillips KA. Anxiety disorders, obsessive-compulsive and related disorders, trauma- and stressor-related disorders, and dissociative disorders in DSM-5. *Am J Psychiatry* (2014) 171:611–3. doi: 10.1176/appi.ajp.2014.14010003
6. Van Ameringen M, Patterson B, Simpson W. DSM-5 obsessive-compulsive and related disorders: clinical implications of new criteria. *Depress Anxiety.* (2014) 31:487–93. doi: 10.1002/da.22259
7. Bernardo Barahona-Corrêa J, Camacho M, Castro-Rodrigues P, Costa R, Oliveira-Maia AJ. From thought to action: how the interplay between neuroscience and phenomenology changed our understanding of obsessive-compulsive disorder. *Front Psychol.* (2015) 6:1798. doi: 10.3389/fpsyg.2015.01798
8. Benito K, Storch EA. Assessment of obsessive–compulsive disorder: review and future directions. *Expert Rev Neurother.* (2011) 11:287–98. doi: 10.1586/ern.10.195
9. Goodman WK, Price LH, Rasmussen SA, Mazure C, Fleischmann RL, Hill CL, et al. The yale-brown obsessive compulsive scale: I. development, use, and reliability. *Arch Gen Psychiatry* (1989) 46:1006–11. doi: 10.1001/archpsyc.1989.01810110048007
10. Goodman WK, Price LH, Rasmussen SA, Mazure C, Delgado P, Heninger GR, et al. The yale-brown obsessive compulsive scale: II. validity. *Arch Gen Psychiatry* (1989) 46:1012–6. doi: 10.1001/archpsyc.1989.01810110054008
11. Storch EA, Lewin AB, De Nadai AS, Murphy TK. Defining treatment response and remission in obsessive-compulsive disorder: a signal detection analysis of the children's yale-brown obsessive compulsive scale. *J Am Acad Child Adolesc Psychiatry* (2010) 49:708–17. doi: 10.1016/j.jaac.2010.04.005
12. Lewin AB, De Nadai AS, Park J, Goodman WK, Murphy TK, Storch EA. Refining clinical judgment of treatment outcome in obsessive-compulsive disorder. *Psychiatry Res.* (2011) 185:394–401. doi: 10.1016/j.psychres.2010.08.021
13. Simpson HB, Huppert JD, Petkova E, Foa EB, Liebowitz MR. Response versus remission in obsessive-compulsive disorder. *J Clin Psychiatry* (2006) 67:269–76. doi: 10.4088/JCP.v67n0214

14. Farris SG, McLean CP, Van Meter PE, Simpson HB, Foa EB. Treatment response, symptom remission, and wellness in obsessive-compulsive disorder. *J Clin Psychiatry* (2013) 74:685–90. doi: 10.4088/JCP.12m07789
15. McKay D, Danyko S, Neziroglu F, Yaryura-Tobias JA. Factor structure of the yale-brown obsessive-compulsive scale: a two dimensional measure. *Behav Res Ther.* (1995) 33:865–9. doi: 10.1016/0005-7967(95)00014-O
16. McKay D, Neziroglu F, Stevens K, Yaryura-Tobias JA. The yale-brown obsessive-compulsive scale: confirmatory factor analytic findings. *J Psychopathol Behav Assess.* (1998) 20:265–7. doi: 10.1023/A:1023019419065
17. Amir N, Foa EB, Coles ME. Factor structure of the yale-brown obsessive compulsive scale. *Psychol Assess.* (1997) 9:312–6. doi: 10.1037/1040-3590.9.3.312
18. Nestadt G, Samuels J, Riddle MA, Liang KY, Bienvenu OJ, Hoehn-Saric R, et al. The relationship between obsessive-compulsive disorder and anxiety and affective disorders: results from the Johns Hopkins OCD Family Study. *Psychol Med.* (2001) 31:481–7. doi: 10.1017/S0033291701003579
19. Moritz S, Meier B, Kloss M, Jacobsen D, Wein C, Fricke S, et al. Dimensional structure of the yale-brown obsessive-compulsive scale (Y-BOCS). *Psychiatry Res.* (2002) 109:193–9. doi: 10.1016/S0165-1781(02)00012-4
20. Storch EA, Rasmussen SA, Price LH, Larson MJ, Murphy TK, Goodman WK. Development and psychometric evaluation of the yale-brown obsessive-compulsive scale-second edition. *Psychol Assess.* (2010) 22:223–32. doi: 10.1037/a0018492
21. Rapp AM, Bergman RL, Piacentini J, McGuire JF. Evidence-based assessment of obsessive-compulsive disorder. *J Cent Nerv Syst Dis.* (2016) 8:13–29. doi: 10.4137/JCNSD.S38359
22. Melli G, Avallone E, Moulding R, Pinto A, Micheli E, Carraresi C. Validation of the Italian version of the yale-brown obsessive compulsive scale-second edition (Y-BOCS-II) in a clinical sample. *Compr Psychiatry* (2015) 60:86–92. doi: 10.1016/j.comppsych.2015.03.005
23. Hiranyatheb T, Saipanish R, Lotrakul M. Reliability and validity of the Thai version of the yale-brown obsessive compulsive scale - second edition in clinical samples. *Neuropsychiatr Dis Treat.* (2014) 10:471–7. doi: 10.2147/NDT.S56971
24. Stein DJ. Obsessive-compulsive disorder. *Lancet* (2002) 360:397–405. doi: 10.1016/S0140-6736(02)09620-4
25. Wu MS, McGuire JF, Horng B, Storch EA. Further psychometric properties of the Yale-Brown Obsessive Compulsive Scale - Second Edition. *Compr Psychiatry* (2016) 66:96–103. doi: 10.1016/j.comppsych.2016.01.007
26. First MB, Spitzer RL, Gibbon M, Williams JBW. *Structured Clinical Interview for DSM-IV-TR Axis I Disorders, Research Version, Non-patient Edition.* New York, NY: DSMIV (2002).
27. Del-Ben CM, Vilela JA, de S.Crippa JA, Hallak JE, Labate CM, Zuardi AW. Reliability of the structured clinical interview for DSM-IV–clinical version translated into portuguese. *Rev Bras Psiquiatr.* (2001) 23:159. doi: 10.1590/S1516-44462001000300008
28. Sheehan DV, Lecrubier Y, Sheehan KH, Janavs J, Weiller E, Keskiner A, et al. The validity of the mini international neuropsychiatric interview (MINI) according to the SCID-P and its reliability. *Eur Psychiatry* (1997) 12:232–41. doi: 10.1016/S0924-9338(97)83297-X
29. Amorim P. Mini International Neuropsychiatric Interview (MINI): validação de entrevista breve para o diagnóstico de transtornos mentais. *Revista Brasileira de Psiquiatria* (2000) 22:106–15. doi: 10.1590/S1516-44462000000300003
30. Beck AT, Steer RA, Brown GK. *Manual for the Beck Depression Inventory-II.* San Antonio, TX: Psychol Corp. (1996).
31. Campos R, Gonçalves B. The Portuguese Version of the Beck Depression Inventory-II (BDI-II). *Eur J Psychol Assess.* (2011) 27:258–64. doi: 10.1027/1015-5759/a000072
32. Spielberger C. *Manual for the State-Trait Anxiety Inventory (STAI).* Palo Alto, CA: Consult Psychol Press (1983). p. 4–26.
33. Barnes LLB, Harp D, Jung WS. Reliability generalization of scores on the spielberger state-trait anxiety inventory. *Educ Psychol Meas.* (2002) 62:603–18. doi: 10.1177/0013164402062004005
34. Santos S, Silva D. Adaptação do State-Trait Anxiety Inventory (STAI)- Forma Y para a população portuguesa: primeiros dados. *Rev Port Psicol.* (1997) 32:85–98.
35. Galhardo A, Pinto-Gouveia J. Inventário Obsessivo de Coimbra: avaliação de Obsessões e Compulsões. *Psychologica* (2008) 48:101–24. Available online at: http://repositorio.ismt.pt/handle/123456789/825
36. Furr M, Bacharach V. *Psychometrics: An Introduction. 2nd edn.* Newbury Park, CA: SAGE Publications (2013).
37. Frost RO, Steketee G, Krause MS, Trepanier KL. The Relationship of the Yale-Brown Obsessive Compulsive Scale (YBOCS) to Other Measures of Obsessive Compulsive Symptoms in a Nonclinical Population. *J Pers Assess.* (1995) 65:158–68. doi: 10.1207/s15327752jpa6501_12
38. Jin PH, Samuels J, Bienvenu OJ, Cannistraro P, Grados M, Riddle MA, et al. Clinical correlates of recurrent major depression in obsessive-compulsive disorder. *Depress Anxiety* (2004) 20:86–91. doi: 10.1002/da.20024
39. Kolada JL, Bland RC, Newman SC. Obsessive-compulsive disorder. *Acta Psychiatr Scand.* (1994) 89:24–35. doi: 10.1111/j.1600-0447.1994.tb05788.x
40. Rasmussen SA, Tsuang MT. Clinical characteristics and family history in DSM-III obsessive-compulsive disorder. *Am J Psychiatry* (1986) 143:317–22. doi: 10.1176/ajp.143.3.317

17

Hypomania Symptoms across Psychiatric Disorders: Screening Use of the Hypomania Check-List 32 at Admission to an Outpatient Psychiatry Clinic

Marta Camacho[1†‡], Sílvia Almeida[1,2†], Ana Rita Moura[1,3], Ana B. Fernandes[1,2,4], Gabriela Ribeiro[1,2,5], Joaquim Alves da Silva[1,2,4], J. Bernardo Barahona-Corrêa[1,2,3,4] and Albino J. Oliveira-Maia[1,2,3,4]*

[1] Champalimaud Clinical Centre, Champalimaud Centre for the Unknown, Lisbon, Portugal, [2] Champalimaud Research, Champalimaud Centre for the Unknown, Lisbon, Portugal, [3] Department of Psychiatry and Mental Health, Centro Hospitalar de Lisboa Ocidental, Lisbon, Portugal, [4] NOVA Medical School/Faculdade de Ciências Médicas, Universidade Nova de Lisboa, Lisbon, Portugal, [5] Lisbon Academic Medical Center PhD Program, Faculdade de Medicina, Universidade de Lisboa, Lisbon, Portugal

***Correspondence:**
Albino J. Oliveira-Maia
albino.maia@neuro.fchampalimaud.org*

† These authors have contributed equally to this work

***‡ Present Address:**
Marta Camacho,
John Van Geest Centre for Brain Repair, University of Cambridge, Cambridge, United Kingdom*

Introduction: Hypomania symptoms are best described as a continuum, ranging beyond Bipolar Spectrum Disorders (BSD). Other nosological entities, such as major depressive disorder, schizoaffective disorder, or borderline personality disorder, may also share symptoms with BSD, raising challenges for differential diagnosis. While the Hypomania Checklist-32 is one of the most widely used tools for screening hypomania, there is limited evidence describing its use in a real-world outpatient psychiatric clinical setting.

Methods: Here we tested the psychometric properties of a European Portuguese adaptation of the HCL-32, establishing its factor structure, reliability and construct validity. Furthermore, we analyzed differences in hypomanic symptoms among several clinical groups and in a non-clinical sample. Data was obtained retrospectively in an ecological setting from a clinical sample of an outpatient psychiatry and psychology clinic, comprising 463 Portuguese individuals, 326 of whom had a psychiatric diagnosis, namely BSD ($n = 66$), major depressive disorder ($n = 116$), or other psychiatric disorders ($n = 144$). A separate non-clinical sample was also collected among healthy volunteers ($n = 62$). A battery of self-report measures of affective symptoms was applied, and in a subset of patients, diagnosis was established using a structured diagnostic interview.

Results: Psychometric properties of the HCL-32 were adequate, with good internal consistency (Cronbach's $\alpha = 0.86$) and test-retest stability (ICC = 0.86), and two subscores ("active/elated" and "risk-taking/irritable") defined by Principal Component Analysis. Receiver Operating Characteristic curve analysis demonstrated that the test score discriminated moderately between patients with BSD and other clinical samples as well as healthy volunteers, with a cut-off score of 17 for the total score of the HCL-32 rendering the best combination of sensitivity and specificity. When compared to the

HCL-32 total score, the risk-taking/irritable subscore seems to provide additional benefit in discriminating between different clinical groups, namely regarding specificity in the discrimination from patients with a diagnosis of major depressive disorder that was low for the full scale and the alternate subscale.

Conclusions: HCL-32 can be used as a screening tool for BSD among adult patients presenting in an outpatient psychiatric clinical setting.

Keywords: hypomania, bipolar spectrum disorders, HCL-32, adaptation, European Portuguese

INTRODUCTION

The World Health Organization (1) estimates that 2.4% of people worldwide may suffer from Bipolar Spectrum Disorders (BSD), which have been proposed as one of the leading causes of years lost due to disability (2). In Portugal, where this study was conducted, the National Health Observatory, estimated a prevalence of medically confirmed Bipolar Disorder of 0.4% (3), highlighting the problems with unrecognized and misdiagnosed BSD in clinical practice. It is widely accepted that Bipolar Disorder, rather than a categorical condition, is best conceived as a continuum of disorders, varying in severity as well as other characteristics. The continuum ranges from bipolar disorder types I (BD-I) and II (BD-II), to cyclothymia and bipolar disorder not otherwise specified (2), that are clustered as BSDs. Hypomanic episodes are distinct periods of 4 or more days, with elevated, expansive or irritable mood, among other symptoms, that are observable by others (4), but of insufficient severity or compromise of functionality to meet criteria for full-fledged mania episodes (5, 6). While mania is more distinctive and easier to identify than hypomania, manic episodes are significantly less frequent than hypomania, and occur only in a specific subtype of BSD (BD-I) (4, 7). Thus, accurately identifying a current or prior episode of hypomania is decisive for the differential diagnosis of BSD.

Identifying a past history of hypomania can be difficult (8) and, as a result, BSDs are frequently misdiagnosed as unipolar major depressive disorder (5), borderline personality disorder (9), or other disorders. Consequences of such misdiagnosis include inadequate treatment and worsening of the disorder, inappropriate use of antidepressants, litigation and increased risk of suicide (10). To address these difficulties, several psychometric instruments have been developed to screen for hypomanic episodes and assess their severity. The Hypomania Checklist-32 (11) (HCL-32) is one of such self-report questionnaires, designed to screen for hypomania symptoms in patients with major depressive disorder. It is currently available in many languages and has been extensively studied (12–27). While the HCL-32 does not provide a formal diagnosis of BSD, it has been proposed as a valuable screening tool (28), with adequate psychometric properties, allowing for the assessment of BSD symptoms in an integral and standardized fashion. However, there is limited research exploring use of this instrument as a screening tool in an ecological context. One study, using the Italian version of the scale, tested the performance of the HCL-32 as a screening tool in a naturalistic psychiatric outpatient setting, demonstrating good screening accuracy of the scale, albeit in a relatively small sample of BSD patients (20). In more recent work conducted in a larger sample from both outpatient and inpatient settings in Korea, full and shortened versions of the scale had a similar screening performance to that described in previous work, but analyses were restricted to discrimination between BSD and major depressive disorder (29). Here, we focused on the profiles of hypomania symptoms in patients with BSD, when compared with patients with other psychiatric diagnoses, using the HCL-32 as a screening tool at admission to an outpatient psychiatry clinic. Specifically, after analyzing psychometric properties of a European Portuguese version of the HCL-32, including internal consistency, factor structure, test-retest reliability, convergent validity and divergent validity, we analyzed discriminant and criterion validity of the HCL-32 total score and subscores, to assess screening efficacy.

MATERIALS AND METHODS

Participants

We conducted a retrospective study with data collected at the Neuropsychiatry Unit of the Champalimaud Clinical Center, an outpatient psychiatric clinic, between April 2013 and May 2018. Clinical protocol at admission to the Unit involved the application of a battery of self-report instruments, followed by an interview with a clinical psychologist that included a structured diagnostic interview (see section on ‘Other Instruments’ for details), or a clinical assessment by a psychiatrist. While a psychiatrist saw the majority of patients assessed by the psychologist on the same day or a few days later, a subgroup had been referred for psychological and cognitive assessment only. For research purposes, data was also collected from a separate non-clinical sample, recruited using a non-probabilistic sampling technique. For both samples, only adults, 18 years or older, were eligible. Patients with active medical disease, current substance or alcohol dependence, history or clinical evidence of neurological disorders, dementia, illiteracy, or who otherwise did not understand instructions for the study, were excluded. The clinical status of the non-clinical sample was ascertained through a customized questionnaire about medical history and current medication, with a particular focus on psychiatric or neurological history and medication.

HCL-32

Hypomania Check-List 32 (11) is a screening instrument for lifetime hypomanic episodes. It consists of 32 questions investigating the presence or absence of a variety of symptoms, including inflated self-esteem, decreased need for sleep, augmented communication or pressure to keep talking, subjective experience of racing thoughts, distractibility, increase in goal-directed social or occupational activities, psychomotor agitation and excessive involvement in pleasurable activities (e.g., shopping, hypersexuality, careless driving). Respondents are requested to focus on a given period of "high mood," and then to indicate whether specific thoughts, emotions and behaviors were present during this period, including low-threshold symptoms such as "making jokes" or "I am less shy and inhibited." In addition, the HCL-32 includes 8 severity and functional impact items related to the duration of the episodes and to positive and negative consequences across different areas that are not included in the total score. The total score, reflects the sum of one point for each positive response to the 32 questions investigating specific symptoms. Several studies have performed factor analysis of the original HCL-32 or its many translations (11–13, 15, 16, 30) and identified two subscales: "active/elated" and "risk-taking/irritable." The "active/elated" subscale included items relate to mood elation and improved thinking, self-confidence and sexual activity. The "risk-taking/irritable" subscale includes symptoms of irritable and impatient mood, anger, and risk taking behavior.

Other Instruments

A self-report clinical questionnaire, used as standard clinical protocol at the Neuropsychiatry Unit, was used to collect sociodemographic data and medical history. The Beck Depression Inventory-II (BDI-II) (31, 32) was used to assess severity of depressive symptoms occurring in the last 15 days, while the State-Trait Anxiety Inventory STAI (Form Y, STAI-Y) (33, 34) measured the severity of anxiety symptoms. STAI-Y (State) assesses a transient anxious emotional state while STAI-Y (Trait) assesses a relatively stable predisposition to anxious posture. In a subset of patients Mini International Neuropsychiatric Interview (MINI) (35) was also applied. This is a brief structured diagnostic interview, based on DSM-IV criteria and comprising 15 modules that allow for the clinical diagnosis of several psychiatric disorders and conditions, namely major depressive disorder, dysthymia, suicide risk, manic and hypomanic episode, panic disorder, agoraphobia, social phobia, generalized anxiety disorder, obsessive-compulsive disorder, post-traumatic stress disorder, alcohol abuse or dependence, psychotic disorders, anorexia nervosa, and bulimia nervosa. For this study, we used the European Portuguese translation by Guterres et al. (30).

Procedures

Permission to use and adapt the HCL-32 to European Portuguese was granted by a member of the team that developed the original scale (11) (Rolf Adolfsson) and authors of the Brazilian Portuguese version (18) (Ricardo Moreno). A team of Portuguese-English bilingual mental health experts, with European Portuguese as the native language, performed several independent adaptations of the validated Brazilian HCL-32 to European Portuguese. According to comparisons with the original English version, minor adjustments were resolved and the research team reached a consensus version of the adaptation to European Portuguese. As mentioned previously, data collection in the clinical sample was part of the routine clinical protocol of the Champalimaud Clinical Center Neuropsychiatry Unit, with patients completing the BDI-II, STAI, and HCL-32 while waiting for the psychology and/or psychiatry appointment, using a pen-and-paper format. In a subset of the patients assessed in a psychology appointment, the MINI was applied. Our local Ethics Committee granted approval for retrospective analysis of fully anonymous and de-identified data from this patient population. Data from a non-clinical sample was collected exclusively for research purposes, in healthy volunteers for whom BDI-II and HCL-32 were applied. The Champalimaud Foundation Ethics Committee also approved procedures for data collection in this group.

Data Analysis

Data analyses were performed using SPSS version 25.0. Results are presented as mean (M) ± standard deviation (SD). All analyses were two-tailed, with significance considered at $p < 0.05$. Continuous measurements were normally distributed according to analysis of kurtosis, skewness, and comparison between mean and median. We performed independent samples *t*-tests to compare age, education and the scores for BDI-II, STAI, and HCL-32 across groups, and Chi-square (χ^2) analysis for comparisons of sex. Pearson's correlation coefficient (*r*) was used to assess the relationship between HCL-32 and self-report measures of anxiety and depression. Internal consistency of the European Portuguese HCL-32 was assessed using Cronbach's alpha (α) and, based on the two-factor model found in previous studies (11, 18), a Principal Component Analysis (PCA) with varimax orthogonal rotation was conducted to assess factorial structure. To test temporal stability of HCL-32 in the clinical sample, single measures intra-class correlation coefficient (ICC) was employed. Finally, to estimate a cut-off score for screening of BSDs, we used Receiver Operating Characteristic (ROC) curve analysis, using diagnosis of mania/hypomania by MINI as the reference for diagnosis. ROC curves are obtained by plotting the true positive rate (i.e., sensitivity) in function of the false positive rate (1-specificity), with each point in the curve representing a sensitivity/specificity pair corresponding to a decision threshold. Area under the curve (AUC) of these ROC curves reflects the probability that a randomly chosen individual with BSD had a higher HCL-32 score than a randomly chosen individual without BSD, as defined by MINI. The cut-off score was then chosen according to the ROC curve, as the score that maximized sensitivity and specificity. ROC curves using BSD clinical diagnosis by the psychiatrist as the reference standard diagnosis were also obtained.

RESULTS

Sample Characteristics

Demographic, clinical and psychometric data of the study samples are summarized in **Table 1**. At the Champalimaud Clinical Center Neuropsychiatry Unit, 463 patients were eligible and had a valid HCL-32 (i.e., with no missing items) collected at the first psychiatry or psychology appointment. A valid HCL-32 was also collected in 62 healthy controls (HC), comprising the non-clinical sample. Among the clinical sample, 382 had a psychiatry appointment, resulting in a diagnosis of bipolar spectrum disorder (BSD, i.e., BD-I, BD-II, or BD-not otherwise specified; $n = 66$), major depressive disorder or major depressive episode (MDD; $n = 116$), or another psychiatric disorder (OPD; $n = 144$)—these groups were considered for further comparisons, as shown in **Table 1**. In 56 patients, a psychiatric diagnosis was not defined or diagnostic criteria were not met. Among the 181 patients who completed the MINI, 26 fulfilled diagnosis criteria for BSD, 83 for MDD and 31 for OPD, while 41 did not meet diagnostic criteria (DMC). The non-clinical sample was significantly younger compared to the three psychiatric diagnostic groups, with ages ranging from 18 to 47 years. In the three clinical groups, ages ranged from 18 to 83 years, with slightly older participants in the MDD sample. Predominance of female participants was similar across all the samples (54.5–66.4%). The four samples did not differ in terms of formal years of schooling, with the great majority of the participants (86.5%) with 12 or more years of formal education. As expected, BDI-II total scores and anxiety symptoms were higher in the clinical samples, particularly in the MDD group. Following the same pattern, anxiety trait scores differed in the clinical groups, with OPD having the lowest anxiety trait scores. **Table 2** summarizes the main psychiatric comorbidities of the clinical groups.

General Psychometric Properties

To assess the factorial structure of HCL-32, we performed a PCA of the 32 HCL items for the patient population (**Table 3**). PCA

TABLE 2 | Main psychiatric co-morbidities of the clinical samples.

	BSD (n = 66) (%)	Depressive disorders (n = 116) (%)	OPD (n = 144) (%)
BD-I	(28) 42.4	(0) 0.0	(0) 0.0
BD-II	(9) 13.6	(0) 0.0	(0) 0.0
Other BSD	(29) 43.9	(0) 0.0	(0) 0.0
Anxiety disorders	(4) 6.1	(13) 11.2	(67) 46.5
OCD	(3) 4.5	(5) 4.3	(20) 13.8
Other comorbidities	(1) 1.5	(1) 0.9	(3) 2.1

Diagnosis were established by a psychiatrist after clinical assessment. Number of patients and percentages are displayed respectively. BSD, bipolar spectrum disorders; Depressive Disorders, major depressive disorder and major depressive episode; OPD, other psychiatric disorders (e.g., schizophrenia, anxiety disorders, dysthymia, adjustment disorder); BDI-I, Bipolar type 1; BDI-II, Bipolar type II; Other BSD, non-specified BSD; Anxiety Disorders, generalized anxiety disorder, panic disorder, agorafobia, social anxiety disorder, fobias, unspecified anxiety disorder; OCD, obsessive-compulsive disorder; Other comorbidities, other psychiatric diagnosis.

TABLE 1 | Demographic and clinical information of the bipolar spectrum disorders sample (BSD), major depressive disorder (MDD), other psychiatric disorders (OPD) and healthy controls (HC).

	BSD (n = 66)		MDD (n = 116)		OPD (n = 144)		HC (n = 62)		
	Range	Mean ± SD	Range	Mean ± SD	Range	Mean ± SD	Range	Mean ± SD	p
Sex (% male)	45.5%		33.6%		36.8%		38.6%		0.180
Age (years)	20–81	46.0 ± 14.8	18–83	50.6 ± 14.3	18–78	47.4 ± 14.8	18–47	27.9± 6.7	0.041[a] 0.521[b] 0.081[c] <0.0001[d] <0.0001[e] <0.0001[f]
Education (years)	6–22	14.9 ± 3.4	4–20	14.3 ±3.5	4–25	14.7 ±3.5	9–19	14.0 ± 2.6	0.216[a] 0.639[b] 0.346[c] 0.094[d] 0.650[e] 0.187[f]
BDI	3–53	27.3 ± 13.4	10–56	30.4 ± 9.9	2–53	22.6 ± 11.8	0–22	4.6 ± 4.4	0.088[a] 0.015[b] <0.0001[c] <0.0001[d] <0.0001[e] <0.0001[f]
STAI-State	23–78	53.3 ± 12.3	23–80	58.9 ±12.3	20–80	52.6 ± 12.0		–	0.004[a] 0.696[b] <0.0001[c]
STAY-Trait	25–78	56.0 ± 12.5	33–78	59.4 ± 9.3	24–79	53.5 ± 11.7		–	0.045[a] 0.146[b] <0.0001[c]

Independent samples T-tests were performed for statistical comparison between groups: [a]BSD vs. MDD; [b]BSD vs. OPD; [c]MDD vs. OPD; d BSD vs. HC; [e]MDD vs. HC; [f]OPD vs. HC. SD, Standard Deviation. Chi-square (X^2) test were performed for sex.

TABLE 3 | Factor structure of HCL-32 after Principal Component Analysis with orthogonal varimax rotation for all the study samples combined ($n = 525$).

Item	Factor loadings	
	Factor 1 "Active/elated"	Factor 2 "Risk-taking/irritable"
HCL-1. I need more sleep	0.32	
HCL-2. I feel more energetic and more active	0.41	
HCL-3. I am more self-confident	0.52	
HCL-4. I enjoy my work more	0.54	
HCL-5. I am more sociable (make more phone calls, go out more)	0.54	
HCL-6. I want to travel and do travel more	0.55	
HCL-7. I tend to drive faster and take more risks when driving	0.37	0.40
HCL-8. I spend more money/too much money	0.32	0.37
HCL-9. I take more risks in my daily life (in my work and/or other activities)	0.51	
HCL-10. I am physically more active (sports, etc.)	0.35	
HCL-11. I plan more activities or projects	0.54	
HCL-12. I have more ideas, I am more creative	0.54	
HCL-13. I am less shy or inhibited	0.46	
HCL-14. I wear more colorful and more extravagant clothes/make-up	0.42	
HCL-15. I want to meet or actually do meet more people	0.57	
HCL-16. I am more interested in sex, and/or have increased sexual desire	0.51	
HCL-17. I am more flirtatious and/or am sexually more active	0.54	
HCL-18. I talk more	0.51	
HCL-19. I think faster	0.55	
HCL-20. I make more jokes or puns when I am talking	0.49	
HCL-21. I am more easily distracted	0.44	
HCL-22. I engage in lots of new things	0.52	
HCL-23. My thoughts jump from topic to topic	0.44	
HCL-24. I do think more quickly and/or more easily	0.54	
HCL-25. I am more impatient and/or get irritable more easily		0.54
HCL-26. I can be exhausting or irritating for others		0.55
HCL-27. I get into more quarrels		0.53
HCL-28. My mood is higher, more optimistic	0.40	
HCL-29. I drink more coffee	0.32	0.44
HCL-30. I smoke more cigarettes		0.48
HCL-31. I drink more alcohol		0.43
HCL-32. I take more drugs		0.43

Small coefficients with values below 0.3 were excluded.

with data from the BSD group alone was not possible due to factor invariance of some HCL-32 items. The PCA yielded 32 factors, the first 8 of which with an Eigenvalue of 1 or more. The Kaiser–Meyer–Olkin measure of sampling adequacy was 0.85, indicating the model's adequacy for the factor analysis, while the Bartlett's test of sphericity was statistically significant ($p < 0.0001$), suggesting the data was factorizable. A 2-factor solution, consistent with the deflection of the scree plot and in accordance with Angst et al. (11), was preferred. While the first factor accounted for 19.4%, and the second factor for 8.1% of the total variance of the HCL-32 items, the remaining factors accounted for 5% or less of the total variance. The first factor (Factor 1) included 26 items relating to the previously described "active/elated" factor, while the second factor (Factor 2) had 9 items corresponding to the "risk-taking/irritable" factor, also identified by Angst et al. (11). Internal consistency for the HCL-32 total score was good, with a Cronbach's α coefficient of 0.86. Inter-item correlations were low, ranging between 0.04 and 0.45, but item-total correlations were all significant, ranging between $r = 0.20$ and $r = 0.53$, $p < 0.001$, for items 32 and 15, respectively. The removal of any of the 32 items resulted in an equivalent or lower Cronbach's α. Internal consistency for the HCL-32 "Active/Elated" and "Risk-Taking/Irritable subscores was also adequate with Cronbach's α coefficients of 0.86 and 0.71, respectively.

Across the patient sample ($n = 463$), the HCL-32 total score showed a moderate positive correlation with depressive symptoms as measured by the BDI-II ($r = 0.38$, $p < 0.0001$), as did the "active/elated" subscore ($r = 0.40$ $p < 0.0001$) but not the "risk-taking/Irritable" subscore. State anxiety symptoms were weakly correlated with the HCL-32 total score ($r = 0.30$, $p < 0.0001$) and "active/elated" subscore ($r = 0.33$, $p < 0.0001$) but

TABLE 4 | Mean and standard deviation of HCL-32 total score, HCL-32 "Active/Elated" subscore and "Risk Taking" subscore in the bipolar spectrum disorders sample (BSD), major depressive disorder (MDD), other psychiatric disorders (OPD), and healthy controls (HC).

	BSD ($n = 66$)	MDD ($n = 116$)	OPD ($n = 144$)	HC ($n = 62$)	p
HCL-32 Total Score	23.0 ± 4.9	19.9 ± 4.0	17.6 ± 5.6	14.6 ± 5.9	<0.0001[a] <0.0001[b] <0.0001[c] <0.0001[d] <0.0001[e] 0.001[f]
HCL-32 "Active/Elated" subscore	20.7 ± 3.8	19.0 ± 3.8	16.6 ± 5.3	13.8 ± 5.4	0.003[a] <0.0001[b] <0.0001[c] <0.0001[d] <0.0001[e] 0.001[f]
HCL-32 "Risk-Taking/Irritable" subscore	3.9 ± 2.5	1.9 ±1.6	1.8 ±1.8	1.2 ± 1.6	<0.0001[a] <0.0001[b] 0.614[c] <0.0001[d] 0.005[e] 0.023[f]

Independent T-tests were performed for statistical comparison between groups: [a]BSD vs. MDD; [b]BSD vs. OPD; [c]MDD vs. OPD; [d]BSD vs. HC; [e]MDD vs. HC; [f]OPD vs. HC.

not the "risk-taking/irritable" subscore. Anxiety traits followed a similar pattern, correlating moderately only with the HCL-32 total score ($r = 0.37$, $p < 0.0001$) and the "active/elated" subscore ($r = 0.39$, $p < 0.0001$). Given the differences in age across study subsamples we also investigated correlations between age and HCL-32 scores (total and both subscores), but did not find significant associations between age and HCL-32 scores in any of the sample groups (data not shown). Across the three groups, correlations with age were significant but very weak, and with p-values that would not survive corrections for multiple comparisons (HCL-32 total score, $r = 0.15$, $p < 0.05$; "active/elated" subscore, $r = 0.15$, $p < 0.05$; "risk-taking/irritable" subscore, $r = 0.1$, $p < 0.05$).

Temporal stability of the scale was analyzed by re-administration of the HCL-32 in a subgroup of 78 patients (13 patients with BSD, 10 patients with MDD and 55 patients with OPD; this patient subsample did not differ significantly from the remaining study participants regarding sex, age, education, as well as baseline BDI-II, STAI and HCL-32 scores—data not shown) at follow-up clinical appointments, for comparisons with the first assessment. Test-retest reliability was found to be moderate for this sample (single measures ICC = 0.69), despite the long average interval between assessments (average interval of 175.2 ± 299.0 days).

Criterion Validity

Table 4 summarizes the mean scores of the Portuguese HCL-32 total score, and the "active/elated" and "risk-taking/irritable" subscores of all four-sample groups. As expected, HCL-32 scores differed significantly between all groups, with the BSD group having the higher scores and the HC group the lowest scores. The HCL-32 "Active/Elated" and HCL-32 "Risk-Taking/Irritable" subscore followed the same pattern, except for the lack of difference in risk-taking/irritability scores between the MDD and the OPD sample.

To explore criterion validity of the HCL-32 total score in screening for BPD, we performed a ROC analysis to estimate the optimal cut-off score to discriminate between patients with and without BSD diagnoses, as established by the MINI. The ROC curve in **Figure 1**, with an area under the curve (AUC) of 0.69, suggests that a cut-off point of 17 yields the best combination of sensitivity (80.7%) and specificity (35.5%) for the HCL-32 total score to distinguish between BSD and non-BSD cases. The ROC curve of the "active/elated" subscale suggested a cut-off score of 14 (sensitivity = 80.8%; specificity = 23.9%; AUC = 0.65). The "risk-taking/irritable" subscale showed particular advantage over the total scores in distinguishing between BSD and non-BSD cases (sensitivity = 84.6%; specificity = 58.1%; AUC = 0.76), with a cut-off score of 2. The same cut-off of 17 for the HCL-32 total score was suggested for ROC curves between patients with BSD and MDD (sensitivity = 80.8%; specificity = 31.3%; AUC = 0.65), OPD (sensitivity = 80.8%; specificity = 22.6%; AUC = 0.68) or DMC (sensitivity = 80.8%; specificity = 53.7%; AUC = 0.78; **Figure 2A**). The AUC obtained in these subgroup analyses for the HCL-32 subscores ranged from 0.60 to 0.76 for the "active/elated" subscore (Factor 1; **Figure 2B**) and 0.70 to 0.78 for the "risk-taking/irritable" subscore (Factor 2; **Figure 2C**). Optimal cut-off scores of the two subscores were also calculated based on the comparison between BSD and non-BSD patients.

ROC curve analyses were also performed using psychiatric diagnoses, rather than diagnoses established by the MINI, in order to confirm HCL-32 sensitivity and specificity in a more ecological context. **Figure 3** shows that HCL-32 total scale and both of the subscales have similarly good discriminative properties in a more ecological assessment context. Sensitivity

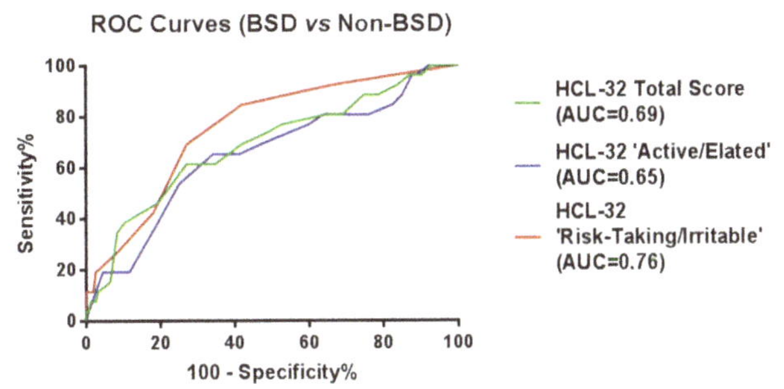

FIGURE 1 | ROC curves showing the power of the HCL-32 scores to discriminate between BSD and MDD, OPD and DMC according to the MINI.

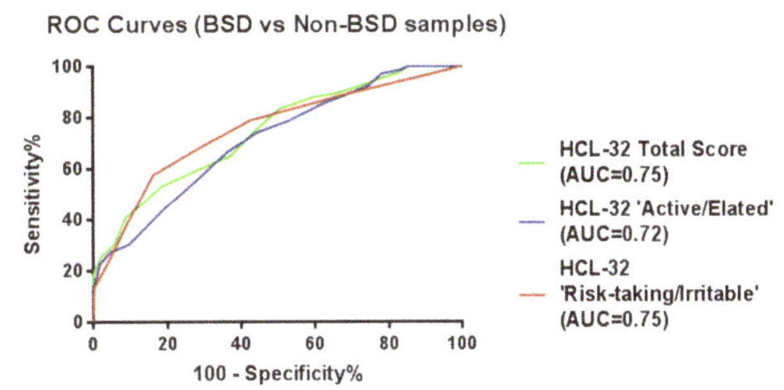

FIGURE 3 | ROC curves showing the power of the HCL-32 scores to discriminate between BSD and non-BSD samples according to a psychiatrist diagnosis.

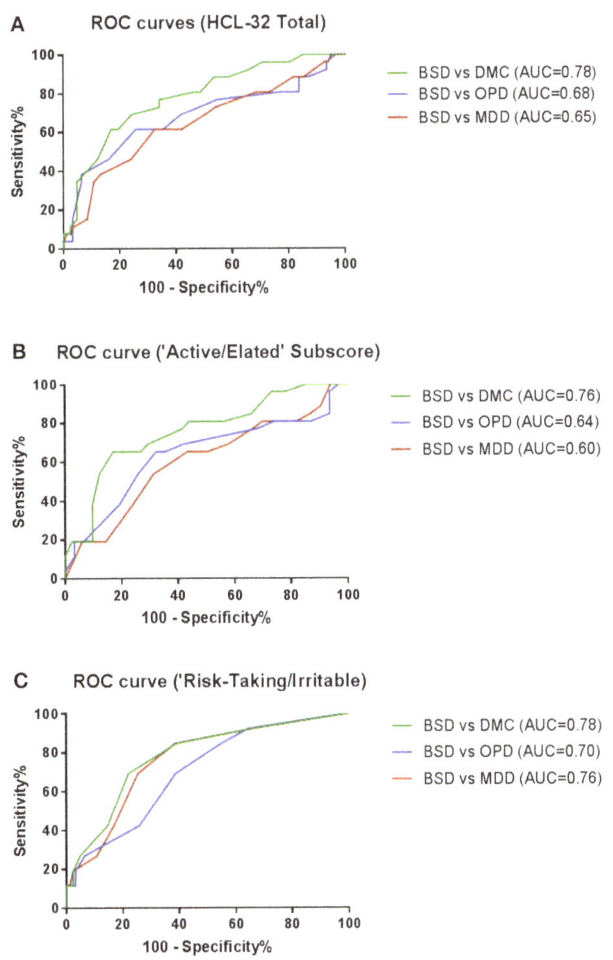

FIGURE 2 | ROC curves showing the ability of the HCL-32 total score **(A)**, the "Active/Elated" subscore **(B)** and the "Risk-Taking/Irritable" subscore **(C)** to discriminate between BSD and MDD, OPD and DMC diagnosis established according to the MINI.

and specificity of the cut-off points defined above in comparisons between groups defined according to psychiatric diagnoses are summarized in **Table 5**.

DISCUSSION

In this study we formally adapted the HCL-32 for the Portuguese adult population and assessed its psychometric properties in a first-visit setting, where the intervening clinicians were first establishing a clinical diagnosis, thus providing the best scenario to test the performance of a screening tool. To date, no psychometric instrument for assessment of hypomania has been validated for use among patients who speak European Portuguese. While the scale was found to have adequate psychometric properties, we further demonstrated that the scale is a valid tool to screen adults who have BSD and distinguish them from others, including MDD patients, at admission to an outpatient psychiatry clinic. Similarly to previous research, we also found a dual-factor structure of the scale, namely with "active/elated" and "risk-taking/irritable" subscales. Importantly, we found that the HCL "risk-taking/irritable" subscale may provide advantages for the discrimination between BSD and non-BSD patients.

Regarding the general psychometric properties of the European Portuguese adaptation of the HCL-32, we found that the scale has good internal consistency (Cronbach's $\alpha = 0.86$), equivalent to that found for the original versions of the scale (0.82 in an Italian sample and 0.86 in a Swedish sample) (11) and higher than the Brazilian Portuguese version of HCL-32 (0.79) (18). Furthermore, a PCA supported a two-factor solution ("active/elated" with 26 items and "risk-taking/irritable" with 9 items) already verified in the original HCL-32 and most other versions (11–13, 15, 16, 36), with only a few studies proposing 3-factor or 4-factor solutions (37), most likely due to sample differences such as size or clinical status. We also performed a test-retest reliability analysis and found it to be adequate, thus supporting the use of the HCL-32 in prospective studies and clinical monitoring. Previous studies reported adequate test–retest reliability over a time interval of 4 weeks (12, 24), whilst in our study, performed in an ecological setting within customary follow-up visits, the time interval was much longer. At the same time, this results could also suggests that HCL-32 is a reliable tool independently on the patient's bipolar disorder stage. Finally, and regarding associations with scores in other instruments, while Forty et al. (38) found no correlation between HCL-32

TABLE 5 | Cut-off scores and sensitivity and specificity values for the HCL-32 and its subscores, derived from patients with a MINI interview (left) and those with a psychiatric diagnosis (right).

	MINI				Psychiatric diagnosis				
BSD vs. NON-BSD (MDD+OPD+CONTROLS)									
	Cut-off	**Sensitivity**	**Specificity**	**AUC**		**Cut-off**	**Sensitivity**	**Specificity**	**AUC**
HCL-32	17	80.7	35.5	0.69	HCL-32	17	89.4	34.2	0.75
FACTOR 1	14	80.8	23.9	0.65	FACTOR 1	14	97.0	22.1	0.72
FACTOR 2	2	84.6	58.1	0.76	FACTOR 2	2	78.8	57.6	0.75
BSD vs. MDD									
HCL-32	17	80.8	31.3	0.65	HCL-32	17	89.4	15.5	0.68
FACTOR 1	14	80.8	18.1	0.60	FACTOR 1	14	97.0	8.62	0.63
FACTOR 2	2	84.6	61.5	0.76	FACTOR 2	2	78.8	53.5	0.73
BSD vs. OPD									
HCL-32	17	80.8	22.6	0.68	HCL-32	17	89.4	36.2	0.75
FACTOR 1	14	80.8	12.9	0.64	FACTOR 1	14	97.0	25.7	0.73
FACTOR 2	2	84.6	45.2	0.70	FACTOR 2	2	78.8	56.6	0.74
BSD vs. CONTROLS									
HCL-32	17	80.8	53.7	0.78	HCL-32	17	89.4	64.5	0.86
FACTOR 1	14	80.8	43.9	0.76	FACTOR 1	14	97.0	38.7	0.85
FACTOR 2	2	84.6	61.0	0.78	FACTOR 2	2	78.8	67.7	0.82

AUC, Area under the curve.

and BDI-II in a large sample of patients with Bipolar disorder type I ($n = 230$), we found a moderate positive correlation, supporting the presence of pervasive depressive symptoms in BSD patients, possibly because patients tend to seek care during depressive episodes (28). We also found a moderate positive correlation for anxiety symptoms as well as anxiety traits, which is in agreement with Fornaro et al. (39) who found similar correlations in a sample of 280 patients with Major Depressive Episode (STAI-State, $r = 0.26$ and STAI-Trait, $r = 0.25$). Although anxiety disorders are known co-morbidities of BSD (2, 13), our results may also reinforce the proposal that STAI scales don't strictly assess anxiety but also negative affect, resulting in similar correlations with anxiety and depressive symptoms (40).

In addition to symptom severity, the nature of hypomanic symptoms are also related to impairment and prognosis (16), stressing the importance of identifying the structure of the HCL-32. In a Chinese validation of the HCL-32, Wu et al. (13) proposed two subscales based on the same two-factor model found here, that were able to discriminate between patients with MDD, BP-I, and BP-II. The small sample size of our BSD sample did not allow for the assessment of whether these 2 factors could also discriminate between types of Bipolar Disorder.

However, the primary goal of this study was to assess the utility of HCL-32 for screening individuals with BSD, in order to avoid missing a diagnosis of BSD. As expected, total score and subscores of the HCL-32 revealed higher mean hypomania symptom severity scores in the BSD group, followed by the MDD, OPD, and HC groups. Furthermore, we found the scale has good criterion validity to identify patients with BSD, namely when diagnosis was defined formally using the MINI, based on DSM-IV diagnosis criteria. Moreover, criterion validity was conserved when assessed according to psychiatric diagnosis. This finding is particularly interesting, not only because it validates the initial findings based on the MINI, but also because it demonstrates that the scale could be useful as a screening tool in a non-research context. Regarding criterion validity, while most studies proposed a cut-off of 14 (28), in our study a score of 17 was the best cut-off point for the HCL-32 total score to discriminate between BSD patients and the full non-BSD sample, as well as MDD and OPD patients, and HC. In an outpatient clinical screening setting, where it is important to identify high-risk cases for a more comprehensive clinical assessment of BSD, it is preferable to avoid false-negative cases. A cut-off score with high sensitivity may obtain such an effect, while typically at a cost of a lower specificity (14). The cut-off point of 17 for the Portuguese HCL-32 could thus allow for greater accuracy in a two-stage investigation for BSD, as well as potentially reduce unnecessary extensive clinical interviews by correctly identifying patients without BSD. On the other hand, in studies performed in settings in which the proportion of psychiatric disorders is lower than that observed in a clinical sample (i.e., general population, college students, primary care), a higher specificity would be needed (24). Nevertheless, the same cut-off point of 17 performed equally well in distinguishing patients with BSD and healthy volunteers.

Furthermore, when using the HCL-32 subscales, AUC of the ROC curves demonstrated that the two HCL factors (Factor 1: "active/elated," Factor 2: "risk-taking/irritable") have differential screening ability to distinguish BSD patients against all samples (MDD, OPD, DMC). Our results suggest that Factor 2 ($AUC = 0.76$) has better screening ability than both Factor 1 ($AUC = 0.65$) and the HCL-32 total score ($AUC = 0.69$). Thus, a shortened 9-item HCL subscale (risk-taking/irritable) may present advantages as a screening tool for BSD relative to both the alternate "active/elated" subscale and the HCL-32 total score. In the original study by Angst et al. (11) these two subscales were similarly defined, but screening benefits were not identified. Soares (18), on the other hand, using the Brazilian Portuguese version of HCL-32, found that factor 2 ("risk-taking/irritable") rendered good specificity and sensitivity, suggesting the possibility of language or cultural specificities for Portuguese-speaking patients. However, these authors did not propose its use as a subscale due to concerns regarding the presence of irritability and risk taking behaviors in other psychiatric disorders. However, our data for the "risk-taking/irritable" subscale suggests that, with a cut-off point of 2, it performs better not only in the discrimination of BSD and MDD or HC, but also OPD, suggesting that concerns regarding the presence of irritability and risk taking behaviors in other psychiatric disorders may be unwarranted. Furthermore, the advantageous properties of this subscale are mostly reflected in enhanced specificity, rather than sensitivity, also suggesting that false positives may not be a problem for this shortened 9-item HCL subscale. Nevertheless, our sample groups did not include specific groups of psychiatric disorders with a prominent feature of risky behaviors, such as substance abuse, borderline disorder or antisocial disorders, and the items composing factor 2 were administered within the total HCL-32 scale. Thus, further studies regarding the potential use of Factor 2 as a stand-alone screening scale for BSD, namely in clinical populations including patients diagnosed with disorders characterized by risky behaviors, are in need.

Limitations of the present study must also be acknowledged. In fact, the HCL-32 was not validated from the original scale using standard translation and back-translation procedures. However, our adaption of the Brazilian version showed robust psychometric properties that are in complete agreement to previous validation studies and support the use of this version of the HCL-32 in the Portuguese adult population. Another caveat is that the sample size of BSD patients did not allow for detailed subgroup analyses, namely between distinct diagnoses (BD-I, BD-II, etc.) that should be explored in future research. Also, a significant difference in age mean between the control group and the clinical samples may have had an impact in the HCL-32 differences observed in further analyses. However, we did not find significant associations between age and HCL-32 scores in any of the sample groups and significant correlations across the 3 groups were weak and not robust. Furthermore, a previous study (11) described a negative association between age and HCL-32 scores, that was not shown to affect the differences in HCL-32 scores between diagnostic groups. Finally, while data from an ecological context are advantageous with regards to implementing and generalizing findings, there are inherent limitations to retrospective analyses that apply here, for example regarding variability in test-retest reliability testing, and in the definition of a clinical diagnosis by the patient's psychiatrist, in the absence of a formal diagnostic interview.

In conclusion, we have successfully adapted the HCL-32 for use in the Portuguese adult population, and found that it is a useful tool to discriminate between BSD and MDD patients, as well as patients with other psychiatric diagnoses. While a cut-off of 17 was found to have the optimal combination of sensitivity and specificity for the full scale, we also found that a briefer version of HCL, namely the "risk-taking/irritable" subscale, demonstrated adequate, and possibly even enhanced screening properties, supporting potential use of that subscale in a clinical outpatient setting, pending confirmation of these findings. Overall, we thus believe this study makes important contributions to research and clinical activity in BSD in Portugal, while providing support, beyond the Portuguese context, for use of full and reduced versions of the HCL-32 in a real-world outpatient psychiatric clinical setting.

AUTHOR CONTRIBUTIONS

MC, AM, and AO-M conceived and designed the study. MC, SA, AF, GR, JB-C, JdS, and AO-M collected data. MC, SA, and AM created and organized the study database. MC performed statistical analysis. MC, SA, and AO-M wrote the manuscript that was critically reviewed and approved by the remaining authors.

FUNDING

AO-M was supported by grant PTDC/MED-NEU/31331/2017 funded by national funds from Fundação para a Ciência e Tecnologia (FCT/MCTES) and co-funded by FEDER, under the Partnership Agreement Lisboa 2020-Programa Operacional Regional de Lisboa. FCT/MCTES and FEDER did not have a role in the design and conduct of the study, in the collection, management, analysis, and interpretation of the data, in the preparation, review, or approval of the manuscript, nor in the decision to submit the manuscript for publication.

ACKNOWLEDGMENTS

The authors would like to thank Ricardo Moreno and Rolf Adolfsson for providing access to the HCL-32 and the administrative team of the Champalimaud Clinical Center Neuropsychiatry Unit, in particular Rute Fonseca.

REFERENCES

1. The WHO World Mental Health Survey Consortium. *Prevalence, Severity, and Unmet Need for Treatment of Mental Disorders in The World Health Organization World Mental Health Surveys.* WHO (2004).
2. Merikangas KR, Jin R, He JP, Kessler RC, Lee S, Sampson NA, et al. Prevalence and correlates of bipolar spectrum disorder in the world mental health survey initiative. *Arch Gen Psychiatr.* (2011) 68:241–51. doi: 10.1001/archgenpsychiatry.2011.12.Prevalence
3. Branco M, Nogueira P, Contreiras T. *Uma Observação Sobre Estimativas Da Prevalência de Algumas Doenças Crónicas, Em Portugal Continental* (2005).
4. American Psychiatric Association. *Diagnostic and Statistical Manual of Mental Disorders.* 5th ed. (2013). Available online at: https://www.google.pt/books?hl=pt-PT&lr=&id=-JivBAAAQBAJ&pgis=1 (Accessed March 19, 2015).
5. Angst J. The bipolar spectrum. *Br J Psychiatr.* (2007) 190:189–91. doi: 10.1192/92bjp.bp106.036.030957
6. Scott J, Grunze H, Meyer TD, Nendick J, Watkins H, Ferrier N. A bipolar II cohort (ABC): the association of functional disability with gender and rapid cycling. *J Affect Disord.* (2015) 185:204–8. doi: 10.1016/j.jad.2015.06.050
7. Kakiskal H. Mood disorders. In: Sadock B, Sadock V, Ruiz P, editors. *Kaplan and Sadock's Comprehensive Textbook of Psychiatry.* Vol I. 9th ed. Philadelphia, PA: Lippincott Williams & Wilkins (2009). p. 1693–733.
8. Hirschfeld RM, Lewis L, Vornik LA. Perceptions and impact of bipolar disorder: how far have we really come? Results of the national depressive and

manic-depressive association 2000 survey of individuals with bipolar disorder. *J Clin Psychiatr.* (2003) 64:161–74. doi: 10.4088/jcp.v64n0209
9. Henry C, Mitropoulou V, New AS, Koenigsberg HW, Silverman J, Siever LJ. Affective instability and impulsivity in borderline personality and bipolar II disorders: similarities and differences. *J Psychiatr Res.* (2001) 35:307–12. doi: 10.1016/S0022-3956(01)00038-3
10. Dunner DL. Clinical consequences of under-recognized bipolar spectrum disorder. *Bipolar Disord.* (2003) 5:456–63. doi: 10.1046/j.1399-5618.2003.00073.x
11. Angst J, Adolfsson R, Benazzi F, Gamma A, Hantouche E, Meyer TD, et al. The HCL-32: towards a self-assessment tool for hypomanic symptoms in outpatients. *J Affect Disord.* (2005) 88:217–33. doi: 10.1016/j.jad.2005.05.011
12. Vieta E, Sanchez-Moreno J, Bulbena A, Chamorro L, Ramos JL, Artal J, et al. Cross validation with the mood disorder questionnaire (MDQ) of an instrument for the detection of hypomania in Spanish: the 32 item hypomania symptom check-list. *J Affect Disord.* (2007) 101:43–55. doi: 10.1016/j.jad.2006.09.040
13. Wu YS, Angst J, Ou CS, Chen HC, Lu RB. Validation of the Chinese version of the Hypomania Checklist (HCL-32) as an instrument for detecting hypo(mania) in patients with mood disorders. *J Affect Disord.* (2008) 106:133–43. doi: 10.1016/j.jad.2007.06.004
14. Carta MG, Hardoy MC, Cadeddu M, Murru A, Campus A, Morosini PL, et al. The accuracy of the Italian version of the Hypomania Checklist (HCL-32) for the screening of bipolar disorders and comparison with the Mood Disorder Questionnaire (MDQ) in a clinical sample. *Clin Pract Epidemiol Ment Health* (2006) 2:2. doi: 10.1186/1745-0179-2-2
15. Holtmann M, Pörtner F, Duketis E, Flechtner HH, Angst J, Lehmkuhl G. Validation of the Hypomania Checklist (HCL-32) in a nonclinical sample of German adolescents. *J Adolesc.* (2009) 32:1075–88. doi: 10.1016/j.adolescence.2009.03.004
16. Meyer TD, Hammelstein P, Nilsson LG, Skeppar P, Adolfsson R, Angst J. The Hypomania Checklist (HCL-32): its factorial structure and association to indices of impairment in German and Swedish nonclinical samples. *Compr Psychiatr.* (2007) 48:79–87. doi: 10.1016/j.comppsych.2006.07.001
17. Poon Y, Chung KF, Tso KC, Chang CL, Tang D. The use of Mood Disorder Questionnaire, Hypomania Checklist-32 and clinical predictors for screening previously unrecognised bipolar disorder in a general psychiatric setting. *Psychiatr Res.* (2012) 195:111–7. doi: 10.1016/j.psychres.2011.07.014
18. Soares OT. *Avaliação da Confiabilidade e Validação da Versão em Português de uma Escala de Auto-Avaliação de Hipomania (HCL-32: Hypomania Checklist)* Ph.D. dissertations, Universidade de São Paulo (2010).
19. Yang H, Yuan C, Liu T, Li L, Peng H, Liao C, et al. Validity of the 32-item Hypomania Checklist (HCL-32) in a clinical sample with mood disorders in China. *BMC Psychiatr.* (2011) 11:84. doi: 10.1186/1471-244X-11-84
20. Bech P, Christensen EM, Vinberg M, Bech-Andersen G, Kessing LV. From items to syndromes in the Hypomania Checklist (HCL-32): psychometric validation and clinical validity analysis. *J Affect Disord.* (2011) 132:48–54. doi: 10.1016/j.jad.2011.01.017
21. Mosolov SN, Ushkalova AV, Kostukova EG, Shafarenko AA, Alfimov PV, Kostyukova AB, et al. Validation of the russian version of the hypomania checklist (HCL-32) for the detection of bipolar II disorder in patients with a current diagnosis of recurrent depression. *J Affect Disord.* (2014) 155:90–5. doi: 10.1016/j.jad.2013.10.029
22. Haghighi M, Bajoghli H, Angst J, Holsboer-Trachsler E, Brand S. The Farsi version of the Hypomania Check-List 32 (HCL-32): applicability and indication of a four-factorial solution. *BMC Psychiatr.* (2011) 11:14. doi: 10.1186/1471-244X-11-14
23. Fornaro M, Elassy M, Mounir M, Abd-Elmoneim N, Ashour H, Hamed R, et al. Factor structure and reliability of the Arabic adaptation of the Hypomania Check List-32, second revision (HCL-32-R2). *Compr Psychiatr.* (2015) 59:141–50. doi: 10.1016/j.comppsych.2015.02.015
24. Leão IAT, Del Porto JA. Cross validation with the mood disorder questionnaire (MDQ) of an instrument for the detection of hypomania in Brazil: the 32 item hypomania symptom check-list, first revision (HCI-32-R1). *J Affect Disord.* (2012) 140:215–21. doi: 10.1016/j.jad.2011.12.033
25. Rybakowski JK, Angst J, Dudek D, Pawlowski T, Lojko D, Siwek M, et al. Polish version of the Hypomania Checklist (HCL-32) scale: the results in treatment-resistant depression. *Eur Arch Psychiatry Clin Neurosci.* (2010) 260:139–44. doi: 10.1007/s00406-009-0030-4
26. Fornaro M, Elassy M, Mounir M, Abd-Elmoneim N, Ashour H, Hamed R, et al. Factor structure and reliability of the Italian adaptation of the Hypomania Check List-32, second revision (HCL-32-R2). *J Affect Disord.* (2015) 178:112–20. doi: 10.1016/j.jad.2015.03.001
27. Meyer TD, Bernhard B, Born C, Fuhr K, Gerber S, Schaerer L, et al. The Hypomania Checklist-32 and the Mood Disorder Questionnaire as screening tools—Going beyond samples of purely mood-disordered patients. *J Affect Disord.* (2011) 128:291–8. doi: 10.1016/j.jad.2010.07.003
28. Meyer TD, Schrader J, Ridley M, Lex C. The Hypomania Checklist (HCL) - Systematic review of its properties to screen for bipolar disorders. *Compr Psychiatr.* (2014) 55:1310–21. doi: 10.1016/j.comppsych.2014.03.002
29. Kim BN, Lee EH, Kim HJ, Kim JH. Comparing the screening property of the shortened versions of the Hypomania Checklist-32 (HCL-32): cross-validation in Korean patients with bipolar disorder and major depressive disorder. *J Affect Disord.* (2018) 227:384–90. doi: 10.1016/j.jad.2017.11.008
30. Guterres T, Levy P, Amorim P. *Mini International Neuropsychiatric Interview: Versão Português (Portugal) 5.0.0* (1999).
31. Beck AT, Steer RA, Brown GK. *Manual for the Beck Depression Inventory-II.* San Antonio, TX: Psychological Corporation (1996).
32. Campos RC, Gonçalves B. The portuguese version of the beck depression inventory-II (BDI-II) preliminary psychometric data with two nonclinical samples. *Eur J Psychol Assess.* (2011) 27:258–64. doi: 10.1027/1015-5759/a000072
33. Spielberger CD. *Manual for the State-Trait Anxiety Inventory STAI (Form Y)("Self-Evaluation Questionnaire").* Palo Alto, CA: Consulting Psychologists Press (1983).
34. Silva DR, Campos R. Alguns dados normativos do Inventário de Estado-Traço de Ansiedade–Forma Y (STAI-Y) de Spielberger para a população portuguesa. *Rev Port Psicol.* (1998) 33:71–89.
35. Sheehan DV, Lecrubier Y, Harnett-Sheehan K, Amorim P, Janavs J, Weiller E, et al. The Mini International Neuropsychiatric Interview (M.I.N.I.): the development and validation of a structured diagnostic psychiatric interview. *J Clin Psychiatr.* (1998) 59:22–33.
36. Meyer TD, Castelao E, Gholamrezaee M, Angst J, Preisig M. Hypomania Checklist-32–cross-validation of shorter versions screening for bipolar disorders in an epidemiological study. *Acta Psychiatr Scand.* (2017) 135:539–47. doi: 10.1111/acps.12715
37. Glaus J, Van Meter A, Cui L, Marangoni C, Merikangas KR. Factorial structure and familial aggregation of the Hypomania Checklist-32 (HCL-32): results of the NIMH family study of affective spectrum disorders. *Compr Psychiatr.* (2018) 84:7–14. doi: 10.1016/j.comppsych.2018.03.010
38. Forty L, Smith D, Jones L, Jones I, Caesar S, Fraser C, et al. Identifying hypomanic features in major depressive disorder using the hypomania checklist (HCL-32). *J Affect Disord.* (2009) 114:68–73. doi: 10.1016/j.jad.2008.07.017
39. Fornaro M, Ventriglio A, De Pasquale C, Pistorio ML, De Berardis D, Cattaneo CI, et al. Sensation seeking in major depressive patients: relationship to sub-threshold bipolarity and cyclothymic temperament. *J Affect Disord.* (2013) 148:375–83. doi: 10.1016/j.jad.2013.01.002
40. Bados A, Gómez-Benito J, Balaguer G. The state-trait anxiety inventory, trait version: does it really measure anxiety? *J Pers Assess.* (2010) 92:560–7. doi: 10.1080/00223891.2010.513295

18

Associative Memory Impairments are Associated with Functional Alterations within the Memory Network in Schizophrenia Patients and their Unaffected First-Degree Relatives: An fMRI Study

Viola Oertel[1], Dominik Kraft[1,2], Gilberto Alves[3], Christian Knöchel[1], Denisa Ghinea[1,2], Helena Storchak[1,2], Silke Matura[1], David Prvulovic[1], Robert A. Bittner[1], David E. J. Linden[4], Andreas Reif[1] and Michael Stäblein[1]*

[1] Laboratory for Neuroimaging, Department of Psychiatry, Psychosomatic Medicine and Psychotherapy, Goethe University, Frankfurt am Main, Germany, [2] Brain Imaging Centre, Goethe University, Frankfurt am Main, Germany, [3] Post Graduation in Psychiatry and Mental Health, Federal University of Rio de Janeiro, Rio de Janeiro, Brazil, [4] MRC Centre for Neuropsychiatric Genetics and Genomics, School of Medicine, Institute of Psychological Medicine and Clinical Neurosciences, Cardiff University, Cardiff, United Kingdom

***Correspondence:**
Viola Oertel
Viola.Oertel@kgu.de

Memory impairments are a major characteristic of schizophrenia (SZ). In the current study, we used an associative memory task to test the hypothesis that SZ patients and first-degree relatives have altered functional patterns in comparison to healthy controls. We analyzed the fMRI activation pattern during the presentation of a face-name task in 27 SZ patients, 23 first-degree relatives, and 27 healthy controls. In addition, we performed correlation analyses between individual psychopathology, accuracy and reaction time of the task and the beta scores of the functional brain activations. We observed a lower response accuracy and increased reaction time during the retrieval of face-name pairs in SZ patients compared with controls. Deficient performance was accompanied by abnormal functional activation patterns predominantly in DMN regions during encoding and retrieval. No significant correlation between individual psychopathology and neuronal activation during encoding or retrieval of face-name pairs was observed. Findings of first-degree relatives indicated slightly different functional pattern within brain networks in contrast to controls without significant differences in the behavioral task. Both the accuracy of memory performance as well as the functional activation pattern during retrieval revealed alterations in SZ patients, and, to a lesser degree, in relatives. The results are of potential relevance for integration within a comprehensive model of memory function in SZ. The development of a neurophysiological model of cognition in psychosis may help to clarify and improve therapeutic options to improve memory and functioning in the illness.

Keywords: face-name association task, associative memory, schizophrenia, schizophrenia spectrum, fMRI

INTRODUCTION

Schizophrenia (SZ) is a severe mental disease, with patients not only suffering from "positive" (e.g., delusions, hallucinations, disturbances of thoughts) and "negative" symptoms (e.g., loss of energy, flattened affect) (1), but also from various cognitive deficits. For instance, associative memory deficits are commonly observed in SZ (2–6). The underlying functional network of associative memory processes includes the prefrontal cortex (PFC), the hippocampus (HC), the medial temporal cortex (MTL), the parahippocampal and fusiform gyrus, as well as other cerebral structures (parietal-temporal-occipital association cortex, cerebellum, cingular cortex, thalamus) (7–11). The formation of complex cross-modal associations, such as face–name pairs, is mainly related to the HC (12). According to Sperling et al. (13) and Kirwan and Stark (14), activation of the anterior HC is particularly closely associated with successful memory encoding.

According to a meta-analysis by Achim and Lepage (2). during encoding, schizophrenia patients showed decreased activation of the left inferior PFC, the right middle frontal gyrus, the right medial frontal gyrus, and the right posterior HC. During retrieval, they identified lower activation in SZ compared with controls in several frontal regions, in the right subgenual region, in the thalamus bilaterally, in the left anterior HC, in the right fusiform gyrus and in the cerebellum bilaterally. In contrast, the authors identified higher functional activation in the right anterior MTL in SZ patients compared to controls.

There is also evidence of subtle memory impairments in first-degree relatives of SZ patients (15–17). Stolz et al. (18) reported the intermediate performance of relatives—between SZ patients and controls—in associative memory performance. This was in line with their fMRI findings, indicating no differences between relatives and controls in the functional activation pattern during encoding, but a difference in the PFC, the thalamus and the insula during retrieval in the relatives group compared to controls. Di Giorgio et al. (19) observed hippocampus-parahippocampal abnormalities during the encoding of a memory task in SZ patients and relatives compared to the controls. Pirnia et al. (16) used a face-name associative memory task and a region-of-interest (ROI)-analysis of HC and MTL to explore the fMRI pattern during successful vs. unsuccessful encoding in SZ patients, first-degree relatives and healthy controls. They observed similar hippocampal hypo-activations during successful vs. unsuccessful encoding in SZ patients and their unaffected relatives, although hippocampal volume reductions and hyper-activations in temporo-occipital and parietal regions were restricted to the patient group.

In summary, the few studies which exist show inconsistent results that elucidate the importance of the investigation of patients as well as first-degree relatives with regard to their memory performance and underlying functional activation patterns. This line of research is important because it helps clarify neural systems underlying cognitive deficits in schizophrenia and potential endophenotypes, which is crucial for an integration of associative memory paradigms in translational research and the development of new cognitive markers of disease progression and treatment effects. We tested patients with SZ, first degree relatives, and controls without a family history of schizophrenia with an associative memory paradigm during fMRI. We expected impaired performance and recruitment of memory-relevant brain regions in the patient compared to relatives and controls, but also more subtle impairments in the relatives group.

METHODS AND MATERIALS

Participants

We included 27 healthy control subjects (CON) {M_{age}(mean) = 34.22 years (SD[standard deviation] = ±11.38)}, 27 patients (SZ) (M_{age} = 37.22 years [SD = ±9.14]) with the diagnosis of SZ according to DSM IV (20) and 23 first-degree relatives of SZ patients with no history of psychiatric disorders (REL) (M_{age} = 43.56 years [SD = ±14.25]). All imaging data were controlled for any neuroanatomical abnormality. The subsamples were matched for age, gender, and years of education (see **Table 1** for details). Only right-handed [EHI; (21)] subjects were included.

To verify the diagnosis or exclude possible psychiatric disorders, the German version of the Structured Clinical Interview (SCID-I and -II) for DSM-IV (22) was applied. Revised Hallucinations Scale [RHS; (23)] was used to screen for hallucinatory predisposition. Premorbid intelligence was measured by the German version of the Multiple-Choice-Word-Comprehension Test [MWT-B; (24)] and psychomotor speed was measured with the Trail-Making-Test A [TMT A; (25)]. All subjects were caucasian. They provided written informed consent according to experimental procedures approved by the ethical board of the medical school of the Goethe-University, Frankfurt, Germany.

Patients were under current treatment at the Department of Psychiatry, Goethe-University, Frankfurt, Germany, and in a non-acute, stable clinical condition (see **Table 1**). None of them had any comorbid axis-I or -II disorders according to the DSM-IV criteria (20) or current drug abuse during the last three months preceding the study. We assessed the duration of illness, age of onset and any psychiatric medication taken. The current extent of psychopathological symptoms in patients was assessed using the German version of the Positive and Negative Syndrome Scale (PANSS; (26)). We ensured that SZ patients did not fulfill the criteria for severe acute symptoms in the PANSS (all scores < 85 points) (27). A stable psychopharmacological medication (for at least 4 weeks prior to assessment date) and not receiving benzodiazepine for a month were necessary for patients to be enrolled. All patients were currently treated with antipsychotics either in monotherapy or in combination with other antipsychotics. Antipsychotic medication doses were converted into chlorpromazine equivalents (28) for further analyses (see **Table S1**).

Experimental Procedure

All subjects underwent functional and structural imaging at the Frankfurt University Brain Imaging Center, Frankfurt, Germany. MR images were acquired using a Trio 3-T scanner (Siemens Medical Systems, Erlangen, Germany), with a standard head coil for radiofrequency transmission and signal reception.

TABLE 1 | Group comparisons of sociodemographic and cognitive data across groups (corrected for multiple comparisons using the Bonferroni correction).

	SZ *M (SD)*	**REL *M (SD)***	**CON *M(SD)***	**Significance $F_{(df)}$**
Number	27	23	27	
Gender *(f/m)*	9/20	19/5	17/13	$\chi^2 = 0.57, p = 0.44$
Age *(years)*	37.22 (9.14)	43.56 (14.25)	34.22 (11.38)	$F_{(75)} = 1.96, p = 0.14$
Education *(years)*	14.94 (3.11)	15.63 (2.31)	16.55 (1.75)	$F_{(75)} = 2.93, p = 0.06$
Education mother *(years)*	13.09 (2.59)	13.20 (3.89)	16.71 (1.54)	$F_{(75)} = 2.05, p = 0.14$
Education father *(years)*	14.13 (2.69)	13.42 (3.34)	15.68 (1.38)	$F_{(75)} = 2.91, p = 0.06$
RHS *(points)*	33.92 (7.88)	26.53 (4.92)	23.85 (3.67)	$F_{(75)} = 18.57, p < 0.001^{**}$ SZ/CON, $p < 0.001^{**}$ SZ/REL, $p < 0.001^{**}$
PANSS *(only patients)*	Pos: 17.08 (4.85), Neg: 16.24 (6.09), Gen: 32.32 (7.38), Total: 65.64 (15.22)			
MWT-B *(t-score)*	51.80 (9.51)	58.62 (10.82)	62.50 (8.18)	$F_{(75)} = 8.60, p < 0.001^{**}$ SZ/CON, $p = 0.01^{*}$ REL/CON, $p = 0.03^{*}$
TMT A *(t-score)*	40.92 (13.99)	49.19 (10.96)	47.00 (8.89)	$F_{(75)} = 2.42, p = 0.09$
Associative memory	Time (IR–DR): $F_{(73)} = 43.41, p < 0.001^{**}$ group: $F_{(73)} = 10.65, p < 0.001^{**}$ Interaction group*IR–DR: $F_{(73)} = 0.44, p = 0.647$			
IR *(points)*	18.54 (5.32)	23.80 (4.53)	23.46 (4.68)	$t_{(75)} = 6.24, p = 0.001^{**}$ SZ/CON $p = 0.004^{**}$ SZ/REL $p = 0.004^{**}$
DR *(points)*	14.95 (6.16)	21.30 (5.40)	20.28 (6.43)	$t_{(75)} = 5.03, p = 0.003^{**}$ SZ/CON $p = 0.01^{*}$ SZ/REL $p = 0.006^{**}$
RT *(ms)*	4568.59 (703.86)	4103.72 (696.79)	4013.62 (725.18)	$t_{(75)} = 2.96, p = 0.03^{*}$ SZ/CON, $p = 0.02^{*}$

SZ, SZ patients; REL, relatives; CON, controls; M, mean; SD, standard deviation; RHS, Revised Hallucination Scale; MWT-B, Multiple-Choice-Word-Comprehension-Test; TMT, Trail-Making Test; IR, associative memory immediate retrieval; DR, associative memory delayed retrieval (post-scanning); RT, associative memory reaction time. $^{*}p < 0.05$, $^{**}p < 0.01$. *MWT-B scores were included as covariates into the associative memory analyses.*

For T1-weighted structural imaging, an optimized 3D modified driven equilibrium Fourier transform sequence [3D MDEFT; 176 slices, 1.0mm slice thickness; (29)] was applied. During the acquisition of three functional runs (T2* weighted Echo-Planar-Imaging (EPI) sequence, a face–name association paradigm developed by Sperling et al. (11) was presented. All stimuli were presented and answers logged via the Presentation© Software (Version 10.3 Neurobehavorial Systems Inc.). Stimuli were projected on a frosted screen using a projector, which was visible for all subjects via a mirror mounted on top of the head coil inside the scanner. See **Figure 1** for an illustration of the experimental procedure and **Supplementary Material** for a detailed task and sequences description.

Thirty minutes after MRI scans, subjects underwent post-scanning face–name retrieval. Participants received a questionnaire with the same face–name pairs (with three distractor names) and were instructed to mark the correct names. This task was introduced to assess delayed recall memory functioning. We created a self-constructed questionnaire to explore memory strategies at the end of assessment. The participants were asked whether they used the following potential memory strategies to remember the items: pronouncing names in a low voice, visualization, recollection of striking features, remembering the names by constructing a story, and association of the faces/names with known persons (answer: yes/no). In addition, participants were also asked to rate their attention and concentration during the scan on a 5-point Likert scale (0 = low, 5 = high).

Statistical Analysis

Neuropsychological and Clinical Data

All cognitive and clinical test results were analyzed using SPSS® 22.0 (Statistical Package for Social Sciences, SPSS Inc., USA). After differentiating between parametric and non-parametric data by applying the Kolmogorov-Smirnov test, appropriate statistical tests were conducted. Bonferroni correction ($\alpha = 0.05$) was applied to correct for multiple comparisons. We performed group comparisons (ANOVAs) with group being a fixed factor with three levels (CON, REL, SZ) and the test scores of the cognitive and clinical tests (TMT A, MWT-B, RHS) as dependent variables.

Associative Memory Performance

Regarding the face-name-association paradigm, the mean accuracy of immediate retrieval (IR), delayed retrieval (DR; post-scanning) and the overall mean reaction time (RT) during the immediate retrieval of each participant was computed. We performed group comparisons with repeated measures ANOVA with IR, DR and group being fixed factors with three levels (CON, REL, SZ). We also computed an ANOVA with RT as a dependent variable and group as a fixed factor. Memory strategies were analyzed using adequate statistical tests to compare results between groups (see **Table S2**).

Imaging Data

For (f)MRI data a standard preprocessing pipeline was applied (see **Supplementary Material**). Two general linear models (GLM) were computed separately for encoding and retrieval, with each containing 230 time courses (77 participants × 3

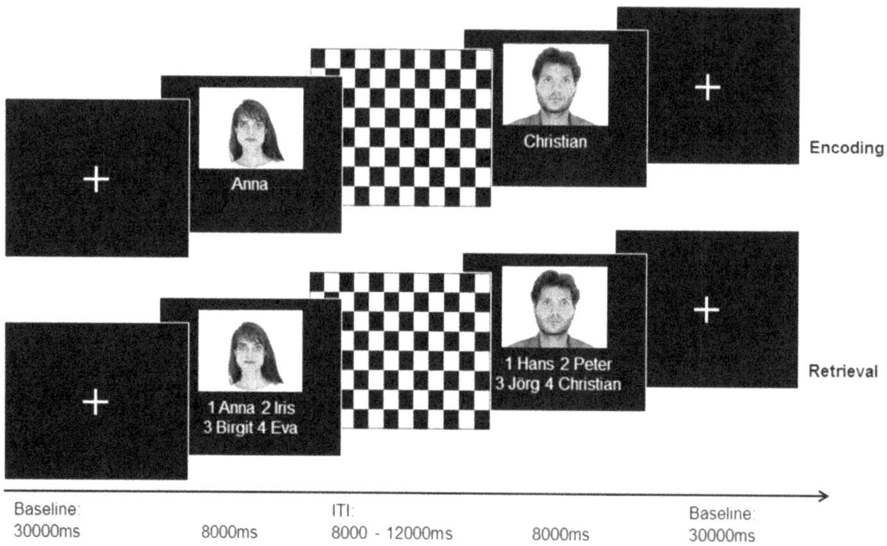

FIGURE 1 | Illustration of the experimental paradigm (face-name-association task) according to Sperling et al. (11) during the acquisition of an fMRI sequence. A total of 30 photographs of emotionally neutral, gray-scaled faces taken from the "AR" face database (30) were randomly assigned to 30 popular German forenames taken from an online database with popular German names (www.beliebtevornamen.de).

runs; we excluded 1 run due to no correct logged responses). Successful or unsuccessful encoding was defined as hits or misses in the respective retrieval trials. The GLM for encoding included two task phases/conditions as separate predictors (successful encoding, ITI) and seven confounding predictors (six z-transformed motion parameters obtained during fMRI preprocessing, unsuccessful encoding). The GLM for the retrieval run also included two predictors (successful retrieval, ITI) and the respective confounders. Since the majority of participants did not make any mistakes during retrieval, we added the "unsuccessful" predictor as a confounder to maximize the explained variability. Event-related fMRI activity was modeled by convolving the predictors with a canonical hemodynamic response function (HFR). In the first level of random effect analysis, condition effects for each subject (beta-values) were estimated.

Obtained beta-values were used to calculate statistical comparisons (F-statistics) between experimental conditions (encoding, ITI; retrieval, ITI). Activations associated with successful encoding (successful encoding>ITI) and successful retrieval (successful retrieval>ITI) were computed for the whole sample using linear contrasts (t-statistics). To correct for multiple comparisons, FDR correction (31) with a threshold of $p < 0.001$ (minimum cluster size > 100 mm^3) was applied.

Random effects analysis was conducted to test for differences in activation between groups (ANOVA). Planned comparisons between groups were conducted within memory conditions (encoding, retrieval), resulting in three between group comparisons each. For the group comparisons, an initial voxel level threshold was set to $p = 0.001$ uncorrected. To correct for multiple comparisons, the Cluster Threshold Estimator Plugin (Monte Carlo Simulation: 1,000 iterations, $p < 0.05$) implemented in BrainVoyager QX 2.8 (Brain Innovation Maastricht, the Netherlands) was applied.

Furthermore, we computed regions-of-interest (ROI)-analyses of anatomically defined brain regions: bilateral prefrontal cortices (PFC), bilateral hippocampus (HC) and bilateral medial temporal lobe (MTL). Activation patterns of ROIs were thresholded at an initial level of $p < 0.05$ uncorrected, cluster-level corrected (Monte Carlo Simulation: 1,000 iterations, $p < 0.05$). The anatomically defined regions were based on the automated anatomical labeling atlas in WFU PickAtlas v2.0 (32) and included the following clusters: {hippocampus:; PFC: −40, 20, 22 [3,583 voxels]; 41, 10, 33 (3393); see **Figure S1** for a ROI mask}.

Correlation Analysis

Correlation analyses were performed to investigate the relationship of between-group differences with clinical and cognitive variables, all corrected for multiple comparisons using Bonferroni correction. Clusters displaying significant between-group differences during encoding and retrieval were targeted for beta-value extraction from spheres with a 44 mm radius around the peak voxel using the BrainVoyager VOI function. These beta values were correlated using bivariate correlation analyses (Spearman product-moment correlation or Pearson correlation coefficient, two-tailed) with associative memory performance (IR, DR, RT) and clinical scores (RHS) for each group individually. In the patient group, we controlled for the potential influence of medication performing bivariate correlation analyses (Spearman product-moment correlation, two-tailed) between the beta scores of significant regions and medication dosage using chlorpromazine equivalents. Accordingly, correlation analyses between the performance in

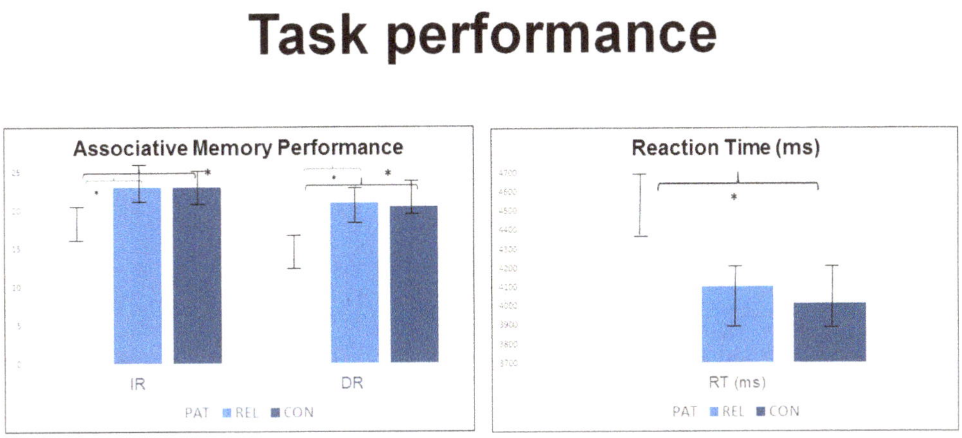

FIGURE 2 | Group comparison in $n = 27$ controls, $n = 23$ first-degree relatives and $n = 27$ SZ patients regarding accuracy and reaction time of the face-name-association-task during the acquisition of an fMRI sequence and during post-scanning debriefing. *M*, mean; *SD*, standard deviation. *Indicates statistial significance.

the face-name task (IR, DR, RT) and acute symptomatology (PANSS) were conducted.

RESULTS

Neuropsychological and Clinical Data

There were significant group differences in predisposition toward hallucinations (RHS), indicating higher values in the patient group compared to REL and CON [$F_{(75)} = 18.57$, $p < 0.001$], and slightly higher values in REL in contrast to CON without reaching statistical significance.

For crystallized intelligence (MWT-B) significant group differences [$F_{(75)} = 8.60$, $p < 0.001$] were observed, with significant differences between patients and controls ($p = 0.01$) and relatives and controls ($p = 0.03$). Due to group differences, we included MWT-B scores as a covariate into the following analyses. There was no difference in psychomotor speed (TMT A) between groups [$F_{(75)} = 2.42$, *ns*]. Effect sizes calculation (Cohens d) indicated for TMT A an effect size of $d = 0.64$ and for MWT-B $d = 1.29$.

Associative Memory Performance

For associative memory a significant effect of time [immediate vs. delayed; $F_{(73)} = 43.40$, $p < 0.001$] and group [$F_{(73)} = 10.65$, $p < 0.001$] was observed, but no interaction group*IR–DR [$F_{(73)} = 0.44$, $p = 0.647$].

We observed significant group effects in immediate [$t_{(75)} = 6.24$, $p = 0.001$] and in delayed [$t_{(75)} = 5.03$, $p = 0.003$] retrieval. Group differences in immediate retrieval were caused by significantly lower correct responses in SZ compared to REL and CON. A comparable pattern was displayed for delayed retrieval indicating differences in performance between SZ and CON and SZ and REL during the retrieval of face-name-pairs (all $p < 0.05$). SZ had significantly higher reaction time compared to CON [$t_{(75)} = 2.96$, $p = 0.03$]. REL showed intermediate values between SZ and CON without reaching statistical significance in *post-hoc* group contrasts (see **Table 1** and **Figure 2**). Immediate retrieval had an effect size of $d = 1.10$, delayed retrieval an effect size of $d = 1.03$ and the reaction time had an effect size of $d = 0.70$.

The memory strategies, self-rated attention and concentration showed significant variance between groups (all $p > 0.05$; see **Table S2**).

Imaging Results

Main Effect

During encoding, we observed the main effect of encoding vs. ITI in the right superior temporal gyrus, left cuneus, right inferior occipital gyrus, right caudate, left inferior frontal gyrus and left fusiform gyrus. The main effect of retrieval vs. ITI was detected in the left inferior parietal lobule, left inferior occipital gyrus, right precentral gyrus (more activated), right cuneus and left medial frontal gyrus (all $p < 0.001$, FDR corrected) (see **Table 2**).

Second Level Analyses: Between-Group Comparisons

Group contrast encoding

We observed significant lower activation in SZ compared to CON in right middle occipital gyrus, left lingual gyrus, left cuneus and right cingulate gyrus (see **Table 3** and **Figure 3**). SZ showed significant lower activation compared to REL in right cingulate gyrus, left lingual gyrus, and left superior frontal gyrus. Significant lower activation in REL compared to CON were observed in the right inferior frontal gyrus and bilateral middle occipital gyrus.

Group contrast retrieval

SZ showed significantly lower activation compared to CON in the right cingulate gyrus). No significant group differences between CON and REL or between SZ and REL were found (see **Table 3**).

TABLE 2 | Main effect for successful encoding (>ITI) and successful retrieval (>ITI) for the whole sample using linear contrasts (*t*-statistics).

Anatomical region	R/L	BA	Talairach coordinates			Cluster size	$t_{(76)}$
			x	y	z	(voxels/mm^3)	
Encoding>ITI							
Superior temporal gyrus	R	13	54	−40	19	4581	−7.3987
Inferior occipital gyrus	R	18	27	−88	−8	18442	10.8565
Cuneus	L	18	0	−79	7	95712	−16.4915
Caudate (Body)	R	*	15	−4	19	2946	7.7406
Inferior frontal Gyrus	L	47	−48	23	1	26134	8.1440
Fusiform gyrus	L	19	−30	−82	−14	18516	9.9319
RETRIEVAL>ITI							
Inferior parietal lobule	L	40	−42	−37	52	188875	13.1462
Inferior occipital gyrus	L	18	−27	−85	−14	95021	13.2546
Precentral gyrus	R	6	30	−13	64	2998	7.1636
Cuneus	R	18	9	−85	25	61462	−10.7883
Medial frontal gyrus	L	10	0	56	10	4274	−6.8900

*To correct for multiple comparisons, FDR correction (31) with a threshold of p < 0.001 (minimum cluster size>100 mm^3) was applied. R/L, Right/Left; BA, Brodmann area; *, no Brodmann area. Talairach coordinates, anatomical regions and Brodmann areas refer to peak voxel of cluster. PAT, SZ patients; REL, relatives; CON, controls.*

TABLE 3 | Statistical group comparisons of functional brain activation differences between groups for successful encoding and retrieval (>ITI).

Anatomical region	R/L	BA	Talairach coordinates			Cluster Size	$t_{(76)}$
			x	y	z	(voxels/mm^3)	
ENCODING							
CON>SZ							
Middle occipital gyrus	R	19	33	−85	7	398	2.2548
Lingual gyrus	L	18	−15	−76	7	346	−3.2746
Cuneus	L	17	−16	−76	7	2110	−3.2971
Cingulate gyrus	R	24	25	−17	40	280	−1.728
SZ>REL							
Cingulate gyrus	R	24	24	−19	50	139	1.6457
Lingual gyrus	L	18	−15	−76	7	260	−3.2746
Superior frontal gyrus	L	6	−18	11	65	181	−1.7561
CON>REL							
Inferior frontal gyrus	R	9	51	17	22	130	−3.4613
Middle occipital gyrus	R	19	33	−85	13	559	2.7364
	L	19	−27	−80	10	109	1.6380
RETRIEVAL							
CON>SZ							
Cingulate gyrus	R	31	18	−37	30	184	2.1345

*SZ, schizophrenia patients; REL, schizophrenia relatives; CON, controls; L, left; R, right; BA, Broadman area, *, no Brodmann area; p < 0.05, corrected using cluster thresholding approach with initial single-voxel threshold of p < 0.001 (uncorrected); Talairach coordinates, anatomical regions and Brodmann areas refer to peak voxel of cluster.*

Post-hoc ROI analysis: hippocampus-related group contrasts

ROI analysis of HC brain activation during encoding (>ITI) revealed significant group differences in the left HC in all computed contrasts (SZ<CON, REL<CON, SZ>REL) and a significant contrast in the right HC between CON and SZ. Lower activations during retrieval were found in the HC bilaterally in SZ compared to CON, whereas higher activation was observed in the parahippocampal gyrus bilaterally ($p < 0.05$). REL showed compared to CON lower activation in left HC and higher activation in parahippocampal gyrus (all p's < 0.05; see **Table S3**, **Figure 3**). We did not observe any differences between SZ and REL ($p > 0.05$).

Post-hoc ROI analysis: prefrontal gyrus-related group contrasts

During encoding (> ITI), we observed significantly lower left PFC activation in SZ compared to CON and REL. We observed bilateral PFC group differences during retrieval. During retrieval, REL and SZ presented significantly lower left and PFC activation in comparison to CON (all $p < 0.05$). REL and SZ showed no significant group contrasts.

Influence of associative memory performance

We computed additional covariate analyses, using the immediate retrieval, delayed retrieval and reaction time scores as covariates and the main imaging scores during encoding and retrieval as dependent variables. However, these analyses revealed no significant influence of cognitive performance on the imaging results ($p > 0.05$).

Correlation Analyses

Across groups, immediate retrieval, delayed retrieval and reaction time was mutually associated ($r = -0.376, p < 0.001$). In CON, the higher the RHS scores, the lower the delayed retrieval performance (rho $= -0.18$, $p = 0.03$); and the lower the RHS scores, the lower the reaction time (rho $= 0.42$, $p = 0.02$). All other computed correlation analyses between clinical scores and cognitive performance or fMRI pattern did not show any significant differences between groups.

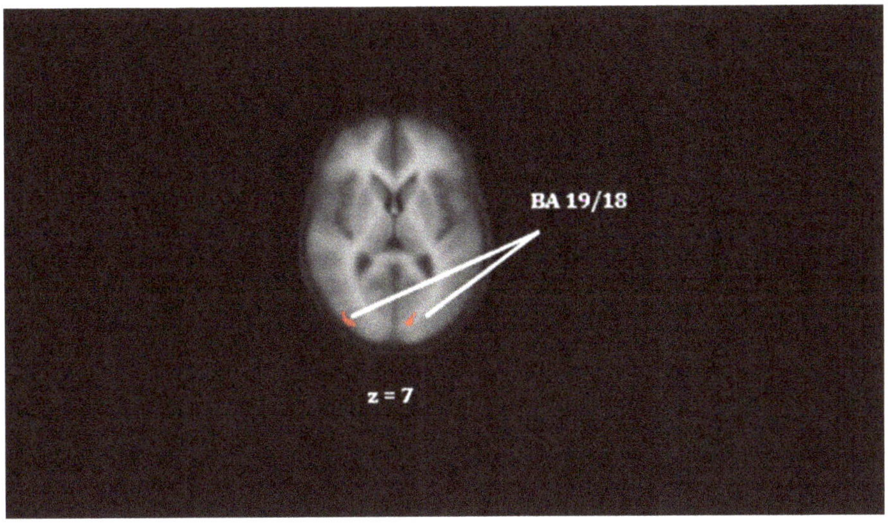

FIGURE 3 | Differences in activation in the right middle occipital gyrus and the left lingual gyrus between CON and SZ (CON > SZ) for successful encoding. The color red indicate lower activation in the reference group. Colors do not represent statistical values and are for visual purposes only, for statistical information please see **Table 3**. Clusters on an anatomical image averaged over all participants in the Talairach standard space, according to the radiological convention. BA indicate the Brodmann area.

Influence of Psychiatric Medication

None of the associative memory scores (IR, DR, RT), clinical scores (PANSS, RHS) or fMRI findings were significantly associated with chlorpromazine equivalents in the patient group (all $p > 0.05$).

DISCUSSION

SZ patients showed significantly lower accuracy in immediate recall (during fMRI) and delayed recall (after fMRI) of face-name-pairs compared to relatives and controls. This was accompanied by higher reaction times in patients compared to controls during immediate recall. Relatives showed slightly higher reaction times and slightly lower accuracy compared to controls. fMRI pattern indicated a network related to cognition (mainly DMN regions) and visual perception/(occipital lobe) to be active during the association of faces to names.

Our results confirm the previous findings which indicated deficits in SZ patients in various tasks exploring associative memory, including verbal and non-verbal associative tasks (6), tasks using free recall vs. recognition of memory items (33, 34), tasks involving different difficulty levels of processing (i.e., perception vs. categorization; (35) and tasks with trained vs. non-trained recall (36). Our results of slightly impaired associative memory in relatives supports the previous findings of subtle memory impairments in first-degree relatives (15–17).

One assumption is that SZ patients have deficits to use any memorization strategy if they are not directly instructed (37, 38). In the present study, we did not find any variance in the use of memory strategies or attention or concentration differences across groups during post scanning debriefing. However, none of the other clinical scores were significantly associated with cognitive performance or the fMRI pattern across groups. Therefore, task performance does not seem to be affected by these parameters or by medication in the patient group. Furthermore, we controlled for the potential influence of crystallized intelligence. Therefore, we postulate that impairments in associative memory in SZ patients are not directly related to illness state, psychiatric treatment or general intelligence.

The canonical memory network activated by the task confirms previous knowledge about functional patterns underlying associative memory tasks (7–9, 11, 39, 40); we observed functional activation in DMN regions (medial frontal gyrus, inferior parietal lobe) and in occipital lobe regions (cuneus, inferior occipital gyrus, fusiform gyrus) during the task.

Beside differences in the visual cortex, the pattern of differences between controls and SZ patients included parts of the DMN during encoding and during retrieval (encoding: cingulate gyrus, cuneus; retrieval: cingulate gyrus); a finding that confirms results from other studies investigating functional patterns during episodic/associative memory tasks (41–43). Accordingly, the few studies investigating the functional activation pattern in memory-related brain regions indicate disconnected (higher activated) brain regions within the default mode network (DMN) (44–47). The aberrant pattern in SZ patients in the DMN if associating faces to names may indicate an attentional deficit to focus on the relevant task and ignore irrelevant stimuli (41, 47). Nevertheless, the direction of the abnormal pattern within the DMN in SZ patients—reduced or increased activation—is yet to be investigated (41, 43, 47, 48). Other abnormal activations—encoding: middle frontal gyrus, middle and superior temporal gyrus, thalamus and occipital gyrus; retrieval: superior frontal gyrus and caudate—may be interpreted as compensatory mechanisms.

During ROI analyses, we observed significant group differences in left and right HC activation, driven during encoding by lower activation in HC bilaterally in patients compared to controls, and a continuum of activation pattern in the left HC, with the lowest activation in patients, followed by relatives and controls. During retrieval, lower activation was found in the HC bilaterally in patients compared to controls, and higher activation in the parahippocampal gyrus bilaterally. Controls showed higher activation in the left HC and lower activation in the right parahippocampal gyrus compared to relatives. This is in line with the meta-analysis by Achim and Lepage (2), as previously stated. They reported deactivated hippocampi during retrieval and increased activation of the parahippocampal gyrus. Activation in the HC may be related to the ability to build associations between faces and names (11). The hippocampus is involved in conscious recall whereas the parahippocampal gyrus is involved in familiarity with the recalled items (49). Previous studies suggested that SZ patients predominantly use familiarity with memorized items as strategy than consciously recall the items (2).

During ROI analyses, lower left PFC activation in SZ patients compared to controls and relatives during encoding, as well as lower PFC activation bilaterally during retrieval, in patients and relatives compared to controls was observed. There was no significant correlation between PFC activation with any clinical score across groups. Decreased activation within the PFC has been frequently reported in SZ (50). The PFC is known to be involved in the selection of items during recall (51); aberrant function during retrieval in SZ may indicate a failure in using efficient strategies (52, 53) leading to lower behavioral performance. This confirms the suggestion of a left-lateralized activation of the left PFC during encoding and a right-lateralized PFC activation during retrieval (9). Accordingly, Sperling et al. (11) reported a predominantly left-sided activation during the encoding of face-name pairs. Regarding our finding of mainly left-sided deactivation during encoding and bilateral deactivation during retrieval in SZ patients, this may be interpreted as a failure in normal left-lateralized encoding which may result in inferior task performance.

Regarding the activation pattern in the relatives group, we observed significant group contrasts in the right middle frontal gyrus, right superior parietal lobule, left lingual gyrus, left precuneus, left insula and in the right claustrum during encoding in contrast to controls. The observation of slight memory deficits, combined with minor functional abnormalities confirms the current knowledge from fMRI studies including first-degree relatives of SZ patients. For instance, Stolz et al. (18) reported the intermediate performance of relatives in episodic memory performance; they observed significant differences in the accuracy during retrieval exclusively. Accordingly, Skelley et al. (54) revealed deficits in first-degree relatives solely in verbal but not in visual episodic memory performance. This is in line with fMRI findings by Stolz et al. (18), who detected differences between relatives and controls during retrieval in the PFC, the thalamus and the insula (but not during encoding). Taken together, current knowledge leads to the assumption that relatives have subtle deficits in parts of the memory domain; underlined by minor fMRI differences; however, they may be able to compensate those alterations during certain conditions.

STRENGTH AND LIMITATIONS

Regarding the patient sample, a widely discussed problem is the heterogeneity of symptoms and illness episodes in patients with psychotic disorders which may influence the results. We attempted to control for these potential characteristics and included only patients in a non-acute, stable condition and limited the patient sample to the paranoid-hallucinatory subtype. Furthermore, patients, first-degree relatives and healthy controls were well-matched regarding age, gender and years of education, which ensured a high level of comparability across groups in sociodemographic variables. Another important source of bias in studies with patients receiving pharmacological treatment is the potential influence of medication on functional imaging findings that has been discussed for SZ (55–58). Dazzan et al. (55) investigated how antipsychotic medication influences functional brain patterns based on typical antipsychotics (55), which may not be relevant for our patient sample (because they mainly received atypical antipsychotics). Other authors have discussed potential signal changes in frontal regions between unmedicated and medicated patients, as well as between patients receiving atypical vs. typical antipsychotics. The current knowledge indicates that antipsychotics may confound the functional activation pattern, and that atypical vs. typical medication might have different influence (55–58). However, most fMRI studies investigated medicated patients, and the authors attempt to solve this issue in controlling for equivalent doses of chlorpromazine. In our current study, we attempted to control these potential biases by only including patients who had been in a stable dosage for at least 4 weeks prior to testing. Furthermore, we computed medication equivalent doses according to the method of Wood (28) and performed correlation analyses to exclude potential associations between medication and imaging data. Moreover, none of the patients received benzodiazepines or tricyclic antidepressants at the time of testing. We also tested first-degree relatives who represent a medication-free sample and found several subtle changes that fit the findings of SZ patients. Furthermore, our results are congruent with findings from task-related fMRI studies, which increases confidence in the validity of our findings.

CONCLUSIONS

Overall, the existing studies that investigate associative memory in SZ and SZ relatives showed inconsistent results. The number of studies that involved not only SZ patients but also their first-degree relatives is limited. Furthermore, only a few studies examined both—encoding and retrieval through behavioral and neuronal measurements. Therefore, we attempted to integrate several measures (behavioral, functional activation) and an additional subject group (unaffected first-degree relatives) into this study. To sum, we detected two major findings: the first one is that SZ patients have deficits in encoding and retrieval of face-name pairs; they have an expanded reaction time accompanied by lower performance. We assume that impairments in encoding and retrieval of face-name pairs are associated with deficient learning strategies (37, 38). This behavioral abnormality goes along with aberrant functional activation pattern during encoding and retrieval in SZ patients. As brain abnormalities were found in both task phases we suggest that there are deficits in both processes. The functional differences fit to other studies that observed deviant functional pattern in memory-relevant brain regions. The second major finding is that the group of unaffected SZ relatives showed only slightly differences in both, the functional activation as well as the behavioral performance.

The present results are important for biological models of schizophrenia that allow the investigation of high-risk samples and may thus aid a future biological classification of mental disorders. Accordingly, cognitive impairments influence the daily living of patients, being unfavorable for the outcome and are therefore a focus of current research. A better understanding of the underlying biological causes of persistent cognitive symptoms may help to develop specific therapeutic options, such as the functional remediation introduced by Martinez-Aran et al. (59) or the fMRI-based neurofeedback (60).

AUTHOR CONTRIBUTIONS

VO, DP, RB, CK, and SM developed the study design. Data collection was performed by MS, DG, HS, and DK. Data analysis and interpretation were performed by VO and DK. VO, DK, and MS wrote the present article. AR, GA, and DL provided critical revisions. All the authors approved the final version of the manuscript for submission.

FUNDING

MRI was performed at the Frankfurt Brain Imaging Center, supported by the German Research Council (DFG) and the German Ministry for Education and Research (BMBF; Brain Imaging Center Frankfurt/Main, DLR 01GO0203). All authors report no conflict of interest. AR is supported by European Community's Seventh Framework Program (FP7/2007–2013) under grant agreement n°602805 (AGGRESSOTYPE), and from the European Community's Horizon 2020 Programme (H2020/2014–2020) under grant agreement n° 643051 (MiND) and 667302 (CoCA) as well as the BMBF (BipoLife) and the DFG (CRC 1193, C07 and Z03).

REFERENCES

1. Crow TJ. The two-syndrome concept: origins and current status. *Schizophr Bull.* (1985) 11:471–86. doi: 10.1093/schbul/11.3.471
2. Achim AM, Lepage M. Is associative recognition more impaired than item recognition memory in Schizophrenia? A meta-analysis. *Brain Cogn.* (2003) 53:121–4. doi: 10.1016/S0278-2626(03)00092-7
3. Clare L, McKenna PJ, Mortimer AM, Baddeley AD. Memory in schizophrenia: what is impaired and what is preserved? *Neuropsychologia* (1993) 31:1225–41. doi: 10.1016/0028-3932(93)90070-G
4. Fioravanti M, Carlone O, Vitale B, Cinti ME, Clare L. A meta-analysis of cognitive deficits in adults with a diagnosis of schizophrenia. *Neuropsychol Rev.* (2005) 15:73–95. doi: 10.1007/s11065-005-6254-9
5. Kalkstein S, Hurford I, Gur RC. Neurocognition in schizophrenia. *Curr Topics Behav Neurosci.* (2010) 4:373–90. doi: 10.1007/7854_2010_42
6. Rushe TM, Woodruff PW, Murray RM, Morris RG. Episodic memory and learning in patients with chronic schizophrenia. *Schizophr Res.* (1999) 35:85–96. doi: 10.1016/S0920-9964(98)00117-0
7. Andreasen NC, O'Leary DS, Cizadlo T, Arndt S, Rezai K, Watkins GL, et al. Remembering the past: two facets of episodic memory explored with positron emission tomography. *Am J Psychiatry* (1995) 152:1576–85. doi: 10.1176/ajp.152.11.1576
8. Cabeza R, Kapur S, Craik FI, McIntosh AR, Houle S, Tulving E. Functional neuroanatomy of recall and recognition: a pet study of episodic memory. *J Cogn Neurosci.* (1997) 9:254–65. doi: 10.1162/jocn.1997.9.2.254
9. Desgranges B, Baron JC, Eustache F. The functional neuroanatomy of episodic memory: the role of the frontal lobes, the hippocampal formation, and other areas. *NeuroImage* (1998) 8:198–213. doi: 10.1006/nimg.1998.0359
10. Nyberg L, McIntosh AR, Cabeza R, Habib R, Houle S, Tulving E. General and specific brain regions involved in encoding and retrieval of events: what, where, and when. *Proc Natl Acad Sci USA.* (1996) 93:11280–5. doi: 10.1073/pnas.93.20.11280
11. Sperling RA, Bates JF, Cocchiarella AJ, Schacter DL, Rosen BR, Albert MS. Encoding novel face-name associations: a functional MRI study. *Hum Brain Mapping* (2001) 14:129–39. doi: 10.1002/hbm.1047
12. Vargha-Khadem F, Gadian DG, Watkins KE, Connelly A, Van Paesschen W, Mishkin M. Differential effects of early hippocampal pathology on episodic and semantic memory. *Science* (1997) 277:376–80. doi: 10.1126/science.277.5324.376
13. Sperling R, Chua E, Cocchiarella A, Rand-Giovannetti E, Poldrack R, Schacter DL, et al. Putting names to faces: successful encoding of associative memories activates the anterior hippocampal formation. *NeuroImage* (2003) 20:1400–10. doi: 10.1016/S1053-8119(03)00391-4
14. Kirwan CB, Stark CE. Medial temporal lobe activation during encoding and retrieval of novel face-name pairs. *Hippocampus* (2004) 14:919–30. doi: 10.1002/hipo.20014
15. Calkins ME, Gur RC, Ragland JD, Gur RE. Face recognition memory deficits and visual object memory performance in patients with schizophrenia and their relatives. *Am J Psychiatry* (2005) 162:1963–6. doi: 10.1176/appi.ajp.162.10.1963
16. Pirnia T, Woods RP, Hamilton LS, Lyden H, Joshi SH, Asarnow RF, et al. Hippocampal dysfunction during declarative memory encoding in

schizophrenia and effects of genetic liability. *Schizophr Res.* (2015) 161:357–66. doi: 10.1016/j.schres.2014.11.030
17. Toulopoulou T, Goldberg TE, Mesa IR, Picchioni M, Rijsdijk F, Stahl D, et al. Impaired intellect and memory: a missing link between genetic risk and schizophrenia? *Arch General Psychiatry* (2010) 67:905–13. doi: 10.1001/archgenpsychiatry.2010.99
18. Stolz E, Pancholi KM, Goradia DD, Paul S, Keshavan MS, Nimgaonkar VL, et al. Brain activation patterns during visual episodic memory processing among first-degree relatives of schizophrenia subjects. *NeuroImage* (2012) 63:1154–61. doi: 10.1016/j.neuroimage.2012.08.030
19. Di Giorgio A, Gelao B, Caforio G, Romano R, Andriola I, D'Ambrosio E, et al. Evidence that hippocampal-parahippocampal dysfunction is related to genetic risk for schizophrenia. *Psychol Med.* (2013) 43:1661–71. doi: 10.1017/S0033291712002413
20. American *Psychiatric Association. Diagnostic and Statistical Manual of Mental Disorders: DSM-IV-TR.* 4th ed. text revision ed. Arlington, TX: American Psychiatric Association (2010).
21. Oldfield RC. The assessment and analysis of handedness: the Edinburgh inventory. *Neuropsychologia* (1971) 9:97–113. doi: 10.1016/0028-3932(71)90067-4
22. Wittchen H-U, Zaudig M, Fydrich T. *SKID Strukturiertes Klinisches Interview für DSM-IV Achse I und II Handanweisung.* Göttingen: Hogrefe (1997).
23. Morrison AP, Wells A, Nothard S. Cognitive and emotional predictors of predisposition to hallucinations in non-patients. *Br J Clin Psychol.* (2002) 41:259–270. doi: 10.1348/014466502760379127
24. Lehrl S. *Mehrfachwahl-Wortschatz-Intelligenztest M-W-T B.* Göttingen: Spitta Verlag GmbH (2005).
25. Reed JC, Reed HBC. The Halstead—Reitan Neuropsychological Battery. In: Goldstein G, Incagnoli TM. editors. *Contemporary Approaches to Neuropsychological Assessment.* Boston, MA: Springer US (1997). p. 93–129. doi: 10.1007/978-1-4757-9820-3_4
26. Kay SR, Fiszbein A, Opler LA. The positive and negative syndrome scale (PANSS) for schizophrenia. *Schizophr Bull.* (1987) 13:261–76. doi: 10.1093/schbul/13.2.261
27. Mass R, Schömig T, Hitschfeld K, Wall E, Haasen C. Psychopathological syndromes of schizophrenia. evaluation of the dimensional structure of the positive and negative syndrome scale (PANSS). *Schizophr Bull.* (2000) 26:167–77. doi: 10.1093/oxfordjournals.schbul.a033437
28. Woods SW. Chlorpromazine equivalent doses for the newer atypical antipsychotics. *J Clin Psychiatry* (2003) 64:663–7. doi: 10.4088/JCP.v64n0607
29. Deichmann R, Schwarzbauer C, Turner R. Optimisation of the 3D MDEFT sequence for anatomical brain imaging: technical implications at 1.5 and 3 T. *NeuroImage* (2004) 21:757–67. doi: 10.1016/j.neuroimage.2003.09.062
30. Martinez AM, Benavente R. *The AR Face Database.* CVC Technical Report No. 24. (1998).
31. Benjamini Y, Hochberg Y. Controlling the false discovery rate: a practical and powerful approach to multiple testing. *J Royal Stati Soc Series B.* (1995) 57:289–300. doi: 10.1111/j.2517-6161.1995.tb02031.x
32. Tzourio-Mazoyer N, Landeau B, Papathanassiou D, Crivello F, Etard O, Delcroix N, et al. Automated anatomical labeling of activations in SPM using a macroscopic anatomical parcellation of the MNI MRI single-subject brain. *NeuroImage* (2002) 15:273–89. doi: 10.1006/nimg.2001.0978
33. Heinze S, Sartory G, Muller BW, de Greiff A, Forsting M, Juptner M. Neural activation during successful and unsuccessful verbal learning in schizophrenia. *Schizophr Res.* (2006) 83:121–30. doi: 10.1016/j.schres.2005.12.852
34. Ragland JD, Moelter ST, McGrath C, Hill SK, Gur RE, Bilker WB, et al. Levels-of-processing effect on word recognition in schizophrenia. *Biol Psychiatry* (2003) 54:1154–61. doi: 10.1016/S0006-3223(03)00235-X
35. Paul BM, Elvevag B, Bokat CE, Weinberger DR, Goldberg TE. Levels of processing effects on recognition memory in patients with schizophrenia. *Schizophr Res.* (2005) 74:101–10. doi: 10.1016/j.schres.2004.05.019
36. Andreasen NC, O'Leary DS, Cizadlo T, Arndt S, Rezai K, Ponto LL, et al. Schizophrenia and cognitive dysmetria: a positron-emission tomography study of dysfunctional prefrontal-thalamic-cerebellar circuitry. *Proc Natl Acad Sci USA.* (1996) 93:9985–90. doi: 10.1073/pnas.93.18.9985
37. Brebion G, Amador X, Smith MJ, Gorman JM. Mechanisms underlying memory impairment in schizophrenia. *Psychol Med.* (1997) 27:383–93. doi: 10.1017/S0033291796004448
38. Danion JM, Huron C, Vidailhet P, Berna F. Functional mechanisms of episodic memory impairment in schizophrenia. *Can J Psychiatry Revue* (2007) 52:693–701. doi: 10.1177/070674370705201103
39. Cabeza R, Nyberg L. Imaging cognition II: an empirical review of 275 PET and fMRI studies. *J Cogn Neurosci.* (2000) 12:1–47. doi: 10.1162/08989290051137585
40. Spaniol J, Davidson PS, Kim AS, Han H, Moscovitch M, Grady CL. Event-related fMRI studies of episodic encoding and retrieval: meta-analyses using activation likelihood estimation. *Neuropsychologia* (2009) 47:1765–79. doi: 10.1016/j.neuropsychologia.2009.02.028
41. Garrity AG, Pearlson GD, McKiernan K, Lloyd D, Kiehl KA, Calhoun VD. Aberrant "default mode" functional connectivity in schizophrenia. *Am J Psychiatry* (2007) 164:450–7. doi: 10.1176/ajp.2007.164.3.450
42. Harrison PJ. The hippocampus in schizophrenia: a review of the neuropathological evidence and its pathophysiological implications. *Psychopharmacology* (2004) 174:151–62. doi: 10.1007/s00213-003-1761-y
43. Reske M, Habel U, Kellermann T, Backes V, Jon Shah N, von Wilmsdorff M, et al. Differential brain activation during facial emotion discrimination in first-episode schizophrenia. *J Psychiatric Res.* (2009) 43:592–9. doi: 10.1016/j.jpsychires.2008.10.012
44. Chang X, Shen H, Wang L, Liu Z, Xin W, Hu D, et al. Altered default mode and fronto-parietal network subsystems in patients with schizophrenia and their unaffected siblings. *Brain Res.* (2014) 1562:87–99. doi: 10.1016/j.brainres.2014.03.024
45. Guo W, Liu F, Chen J, Wu R, Li L, Zhang Z, et al. Hyperactivity of the default-mode network in first-episode, drug-naive schizophrenia at rest revealed by family-based case-control and traditional case-control designs. *Medicine* (2017) 96:e6223. doi: 10.1097/MD.0000000000006223
46. van Buuren M, Vink M, Kahn RS. Default-mode network dysfunction and self-referential processing in healthy siblings of schizophrenia patients. *Schizophr Res.* (2012) 142:237–43. doi: 10.1016/j.schres.2012.09.017
47. Whitfield-Gabrieli S, Thermenos HW, Milanovic S, Tsuang MT, Faraone SV, McCarley RW, et al. Hyperactivity and hyperconnectivity of the default network in schizophrenia and in first-degree relatives of persons with schizophrenia. *Proc Natl Acad Sci USA.* (2009) 106:1279–84. doi: 10.1073/pnas.0809141106
48. Harrison BJ, Yucel M, Pujol J, Pantelis C. Task-induced deactivation of midline cortical regions in schizophrenia assessed with fMRI. *Schizophr Res.* (2007) 91:82–6. doi: 10.1016/j.schres.2006.12.027
49. Yonelinas AP. The nature of recollection and familiarity: a review of 30 years of research. *J Memory Language* (2002) 46:441–517. doi: 10.1006/jmla.2002.2864
50. Ragland JD, Laird AR, Ranganath C, Blumenfeld RS, Gonzales SM, Glahn DC. Prefrontal activation deficits during episodic memory in schizophrenia. *Am J Psychiatry* (2009) 166:863–74. doi: 10.1176/appi.ajp.2009.08091307
51. Simons JS, Spiers HJ. Prefrontal and medial temporal lobe interactions in long-term memory. *Nat Rev Neurosci.* (2003) 4:637–48. doi: 10.1038/nrn1178
52. Nohara S, Suzuki M, Kurachi M, Yamashita I, Matsui M, Seto H, et al. Neural correlates of memory organization deficits in schizophrenia. A single photon emission computed tomography study with 99mTc-ethyl-cysteinate dimer during a verbal learning task. *Schizophr Res.* (2000) 42:209–22. doi: 10.1016/S0920-9964(99)00131-0
53. Ragland JD, Gur RC, Valdez J, Turetsky BI, Elliott M, Kohler C, et al. Event-related fMRI of frontotemporal activity during word encoding and recognition in schizophrenia. *Am J Psychiatry* (2004) 161:1004–15. doi: 10.1176/appi.ajp.161.6.1004
54. Skelley SL, Goldberg TE, Egan MF, Weinberger DR, Gold JM. Verbal and visual memory: characterizing the clinical and intermediate phenotype in schizophrenia. *Schizophr Res.* (2008) 105:78–85. doi: 10.1016/j.schres.2008.05.027

55. Dazzan P, Morgan KD, Orr K, Hutchinson G, Chitnis X, Suckling J, et al. Different effects of typical and atypical antipsychotics on grey matter in first episode psychosis: the AESOP study. *Neuropsychopharmacology: official publication of the American College of Neuropsychopharmacology* (2005) 30:765–74. doi: 10.1038/sj.npp.1300603
56. Buchsbaum MS, Haznedar M, Newmark RE, Chu KW, Dusi N, Entis JJ, et al. FDG-PET and MRI imaging of the effects of sertindole and haloperidol in the prefrontal lobe in schizophrenia. *Schizophr Res.* (2009) 114:161–71. doi: 10.1016/j.schres.2009.07.015
57. Abbott C, Juárez M, White T, Gollub RL, Pearlson GD, Bustillo J, et al. Antipsychotic dose and diminished neural modulation: a multi-site fMRI study. *Prog Neuropsychopharmacol Biol Psychiatry* (2011) 35:473–82. doi: 10.1016/j.pnpbp.2010.12.001
58. Honey GD, Bullmore ET, Soni W, Varatheesan M, Williams SC, Sharma T. Differences in frontal cortical activation by a working memory task after substitution of risperidone for typical antipsychotic drugs in patients with schizophrenia. *Proc Natl Acad Sci USA.* (1999) 96:13432–7.
59. Martinez-Aran A, Torrent C, Sole B, Bonnin CM, Rosa AR, Sanchez-Moreno J, et al. Functional remediation for bipolar disorder. *Clin Practice Epidemiol Mental Health* (2011) 7:112–6. doi: 10.2174/1745017901107010112
60. Fovet T, Jardri R, Linden D. Current Issues in the Use of fMRI-Based Neurofeedback to Relieve Psychiatric Symptoms. *Curr Pharmaceutical Design* (2015) 21:3384–94. doi: 10.2174/1381612821666150619092540

19

Altered Gamma-Band Activity as a Potential Biomarker for the Recurrence of Major Depressive Disorder

Tetsuya Yamamoto[1], Nagisa Sugaya[2], Greg J. Siegle[3], Hiroaki Kumano[4], Hironori Shimada[4], Sergio Machado[5], Eric Murillo-Rodriguez[6], Nuno B. Rocha[7], Antonio E. Nardi[8], Masahiro Takamura[9], Yasumasa Okamoto[9] and Shigeto Yamawaki[9]*

[1] *Graduate School of Technology, Industrial and Social Sciences, Tokushima University, Tokushima, Japan,* [2] *Unit of Public Health and Preventive Medicine, School of Medicine, Yokohama City University, Yokohama, Japan,* [3] *Department of Psychiatry, University of Pittsburgh School of Medicine, Pittsburgh, PA, United States,* [4] *Faculty of Human Sciences, Waseda University, Tokorozawa, Japan,* [5] *Physical Activity Neuroscience, Physical Activity Postgraduate Program, Salgado de Oliveira University, Niterói, Brazil,* [6] *Laboratorio de Neurociencias Moleculares e Integrativas, Escuela de Medicina, División Ciencias de la Salud, Universidad Anáhuac Mayab, Mérida, Mexico,* [7] *School of Health, Polytechnic Institute of Porto, Porto, Portugal,* [8] *Panic and Respiration Laboratory, Institute of Psychiatry, Federal University of Rio de Janeiro, Rio de Janeiro, Brazil,*
[9] *Department of Psychiatry and Neurosciences, Institute of Biomedical and Health Sciences, Hiroshima University, Hiroshima, Japan*

Correspondence:
Tetsuya Yamamoto
t.yamamoto@tokushima-u.ac.jp

Background: The neurophysiological mechanisms of cognitive reactivity, the primary vulnerability factor of major depressive disorder (MDD) recurrence, remain unclear in individuals with recovered MDD (rMDD). Because gamma-band responses (GBRs) can be used to measure cognitive processing, they may also be useful for elucidating the mechanisms underlying cognitive reactivity. Identifying these mechanisms may permit the development of an index for predicting and preempting MDD recurrence. Here, to identify the neurophysiological mechanisms of cognitive reactivity, we examined the characteristics of the GBRs evoked/induced by emotional words in participants with and without rMDD after inducing a negative mood.

Methods: Thirty-three healthy control participants and 18 participants with rMDD completed a lexical emotion identification task during electroencephalography along with assessments of cognitive reactivity after negative mood induction.

Results: No between-group differences were identified for the task reaction times; however, the rMDD group had significantly higher cognitive reactivity scores than did the control group. Furthermore, the power of late GBRs to positive words was significantly greater in the rMDD group, with the greater power of late GBRs being related to higher cognitive reactivity.

Limitations: Considering the population studied, our findings cannot be completely generalized to populations other than adolescents, people with rMDD, and those without a history of co-morbid disorders and early life stress.

Conclusions: Our findings indicate that the dysfunction of neural circuits related to higher-order processes like memory and attention might underlie cognitive reactivity. Altered late GBRs to positive information may be persistent biomarkers of the depression recurrence risk.

Keywords: cognitive reactivity, EEG, depression, gamma, mood induction, recovery, biomarker, memory

INTRODUCTION

Major depressive disorder (MDD), which is characterized by a persistently depressed mood and/or anhedonia, shows a high rate of recurrence after recovery. The recurrence rate in a specialized mental healthcare setting is as high as 85% within 15 years (1), while that in a community-based setting it was found to be ~40% during a 30–39-year follow up (2). To prevent MDD recurrence, it is essential that the mechanisms underlying the associated vulnerability factors be identified. Prior research has shown that the primary vulnerability factor for the recurrence of MDD is cognitive reactivity (3, 4), which is a negative information-processing bias that is triggered when a depressive mood is experienced (5).

Numerous previous studies have reported that people with a history of depression are more likely to demonstrate cognitive biases, such as dysfunctional attitudes (6, 7), biased attention (8, 9), biased interpretation (10, 11), and biased memory (12, 13) after the induction of negative mood. While such cognitive reactivity has mainly been assessed using behavioral and subjective measures (14, 15), several findings have highlighted the low sensitivity of these measurements (16, 17). As such, the underlying biological mechanisms of cognitive reactivity are yet to be identified. Elucidating these mechanisms in individuals with recovered MDD (rMDD) is particularly critical, because cognitive reactivity is "latent" (18), meaning that it is only apparent after psychological challenges and not under ordinary circumstances. Thus, developing a sensitive index for identifying cognitive reactivity in individuals with rMDD, as well as establishing adequate experimental paradigms to study cognitive reactivity, such as those that induce negative mood and use emotional stimuli, is essential for not only assessing the mechanisms underlying cognitive reactivity but also for identifying a potential marker that could alert clinicians to the possibility of recurrence, allowing them to employ preventative or therapeutic measures.

Toward this end, several authors proposed using a neurophysiological approach, such as electroencephalography (EEG), to evaluate the vulnerability factors for depression (18, 19). Indeed, EEG has been shown to be a sufficiently sensitive method for observing mechanisms that could potentially moderate the risk factors for depression in individuals at a high risk (20–22). Prior research regarding gamma-band activity has shown that gamma-band responses (GBRs) are associated with the integration of incoming information and related processes, including feature binding (23), attention (24, 25), object perception (26), and memory (27, 28). These findings suggest that GBRs reflect more than simple perceptual processing, and thus may serve as a marker of complex cognitive mechanisms (29) and major depression (30). Indeed, GBRs comprise both an "early" evoked response (phase-locked) that reflects perceptual processing and a "late" induced response (non-phase-locked) that reflects higher-order cognitive processing, including memory and attentional processes (27). Hence, these two response types may provide information regarding the presence of abnormalities in perception and cognition in individuals who are vulnerable to depression.

Studies examining patients with schizophrenia and MDD using EEG have found that these patients exhibit different GBR characteristics compared to healthy individuals in response to a standard passive auditory oddball paradigm (31) and to emotional words (32). In these studies, compared to those in healthy controls, the amplitudes of early evoked GBRs were significantly smaller in patients with schizophrenia, but not in patients with MDD (31), while the mean power of sustained induced GBRs (3–4 s following the offset of the stimulus) was significantly larger in patients with MDD and significantly smaller in patients with schizophrenia (32). Together, these studies indicate that GBRs can be used as a novel sensitive neurophysiological index of cognitive reactivity. However, to our knowledge, no study has investigated the GBR characteristics in individuals with rMDD using mood induction. Evaluating GBR characteristics using this approach may contribute to our understanding of the neurophysiological mechanisms of cognitive reactivity and allow us to identify a biomarker of this vulnerability factor in individuals with rMDD.

Therefore, the aim of the present study was to examine the characteristics of GBRs to emotional words after inducing a negative mood in individuals who had recovered from recurrent or single-episode depression and compare them with the GBRs of individuals who had never experienced MDD.

MATERIALS AND METHODS

Participants

Fifty-four participants were recruited to this study through poster advertisements. All participants were carefully screened by experienced clinical psychologists to determine if they had current and/or a history of psychiatric disorders according to the Diagnostic and Statistical Manual for Mental Disorders, Fourth Edition, Text Revision (DSM-IV-TR) (33). Exclusion criteria were left-handedness or ambidextrousness, as determined by the Edinburgh Inventory (34), and a previous history of head injury, psychiatric disorders other than MDD, or severe or acute medical illnesses. In addition, to control for current psychiatric symptoms, participants who met the DSM-IV-TR criteria for an Axis I disorder including MDD at the time of the examination were excluded. Furthermore, because successful negative mood induction was a prerequisite for examining cognitive reactivity, participants who did not show an increase in negative mood or a decrease in positive mood after negative mood induction were excluded. Participants who did not have a sufficient number of uncontaminated EEG trials (<50%) for analysis after the rejection of artifact-contaminated trials were also excluded. After applying all exclusion criteria, data from a total of 51 participants were included in the final analysis. Of these, 18 participants who met the criteria for previous MDD were assigned to the rMDD group. At the time of the study, participants in the rMDD group had recovered from MDD, meaning that they no longer met the DSM-IV-TR criteria for MDD. The remaining 33 participants were assigned to the control group. The detailed demographic and clinical features of the participants are shown in **Table 1**. There were no between-group differences in age [$t_{(49)} = 1.63$, $p = 0.109$], sex [$\chi^2_{(1)} = 0.04$, $p = 0.850$], education [$t_{(49)} = 0.94$, $p = 0.351$], or presence of current depression [$t_{(49)} = 0.70$, $p = 0.078$].

The study was approved by the Ethics Committee of Waseda University. All participants provided written informed consent and received 1,500 Japanese Yen (nearly 14 USD) in remuneration.

TABLE 1 | Demographic and clinical characteristics and behavioral data.

Measure	rMDD (*n* = 18)		Control (*n* = 33)	
	Mean	*SD*	Mean	*SD*
Age (years)	21.72	5.63	20.03	1.51
Sex (M/F)	5/13		10/23	
Education (years)	14.72	2.02	14.26	1.47
Age of onset of first episode (years)	18.89	5.25	–	
Duration of last episode (months)	7.71	16.68	–	
Single episode/recurrent episode	10/8		–	
No. of persons who experienced an episode in the last year	7		–	
BDI-II	9.72	8.09	6.27	5.55
LEIDS-R total score	47.67	14.62	30.39	14.51
Hopelessness/Suicidality	4.94	3.39	2.36	2.88
Acceptance/Coping	2.33	2.40	2.12	2.22
Aggression	9.44	5.52	6.18	3.26
Control/Perfectionism	5.22	3.04	2.76	2.89
Risk Avoidance	13.00	2.72	9.18	4.82
Rumination	12.72	5.42	7.79	4.11
PROFILE OF MOOD STATES				
Happy, pre-mood induction	56.11	16.14	60.03	15.90
Happy, post-mood induction	43.33	23.76	37.88	18.50
Sad, pre-mood induction	34.44	25.49	24.24	19.20
Sad, post-mood induction	40.00	21.69	34.85	22.38
REACTION TIMES IN THE EVIT (SECONDS)				
Positive words	0.80	0.15	0.86	0.14
Neutral words	0.85	0.14	0.96	0.20
Negative words	0.81	0.15	0.92	0.17

BDI-II, Beck Depression Inventory II; EVIT, Emotional Valence Identification Task; LEIDS-R, Leiden Index of Depression Sensitivity-Revised

Self-Report Measures

Participants completed two questionnaires prior to the experimental task. These were the (i) Japanese version of the Beck Depression Inventory-II (BDI-II) (35, 36) and (ii) Japanese version of the Leiden Index of Depression Sensitivity-Revised (LEIDS-R) (15, 37).

We employed the BDI-II to assess the depression severity at the time of testing. The BDI-II consists of 21 items that are scored on a Likert scale ranging from 0 (no depressive symptoms) to 3 (strong presence of a symptom). The BDI-II shows good reliability and validity (35, 36).

Here, the LEIDS-R was used to assess cognitive reactivity. This index consists of 34 items that are scored on a Likert scale ranging from 0 (not at all) to 4 (very strongly). Participants indicated whether and how their thinking patterns change when they feel down or are experiencing a low mood. The LEIDS-R has favorable psychometric properties, including adequate internal consistency, test-retest reliability, and concurrent and predictive validity (15). The subscales of the LEIDS-R are Hopelessness/Suicidality, Acceptance/Coping, Aggression, Control/Perfectionism, Risk Avoidance, and Rumination. For this study, we utilized both the total score and the subscale scores of the LEIDS-R.

All participants also assessed their mood before and after mood induction using a visual analog scale (VAS). Participants rated their mood on two unipolar VASs measuring happiness and sadness dimensions. The scales ranged from 0 (not at all) to 100 (extremely).

Stimuli and Experimental Procedure

Mood Induction Paradigm

To induce a negative mood, we used the combination of a 20-anagram task with Japanese nouns (20 solvable) and 20 math tasks in which the participant must solve simple equations (8 solvable/12 unsolvable). This paradigm has been found to successfully induce a depressive mood in healthy people (38). To further increase the mood-inducing effects of this paradigm, participants were informed that most participants get almost all of the answers correct, despite the fact that the math equations were sometimes unsolvable.

Emotional Valence Identification Task and Target-Stimulus Materials

We prepared the modified version of the emotional valence identification task (32). First, a fixation cross was displayed for 200 ms at the center of the screen, which was then replaced by an X character string (forward masking stimulus) for a duration of 2,000 ms. Subsequently, the X character string was replaced with a stimulus word (target stimulus), which was displayed for 150 ms. Then, the stimulus word was again replaced with the X character string (backward masking stimulus) for a duration of

8,000 ms, and participants were asked to indicate the emotional valence of the stimulus word by pressing keys corresponding to "positive," "neutral," or "negative." After this initial trial, similar trials were repeated. The stimulus words and masking stimulus were shown in black against a white background. All participants were asked to respond as quickly and accurately as possible. We recorded the reaction time and response type. Notably, the order of stimulus words was randomized, and the keys assigned to the perceived emotional valence determination were counterbalanced.

The 120 stimulus words consisted of 40 depressive, neutral, and positive words, each. Regarding the depressive words, in addition to previously used words (39, 40), we selected words that were closely associated with depression, based on the measurement scales (e.g., BDI-II) and interviews (e.g., the Mini-International Neuropsychiatric Interview) (41) for depressive symptoms that are used in Japan. Regarding neutral and positive words, we selected words according to previous Japanese research findings on emotional words (42). Adjustments were made so that the number of letters and syllables of the words were as similar as possible among the categories.

Procedure

Participants were asked to complete the questionnaires (LEIDS-R, VAS, and BDI-II) in a sealed room. After attaching the EEG cap and electrodes, we implemented the mood induction paradigm, and then asked participants to again complete the VAS. Upon completion, participants performed the emotional valence identification task, during which EEG data were recorded. Once the task was finished, we removed the EEG cap and electrodes. Participants were then debriefed. The experiment lasted ~120 min.

Apparatus and Data Recording

The EEG data were recorded using a Net Amps 200 amplifier, Net Station version 4.2, and a 64-channel HydroCel Geodesic Sensor Net (Electrical Geodesics, Inc., Eugene, OR, USA). All channels were digitized at a sampling rate of 250 Hz and the signal from the electrodes was amplified via the Net Amps 200 amplifier. Recordings were initially referenced to Cz and later converted to an average reference. Impedances were kept below 50 kΩ, which is the recommended impedance threshold for the employed amplifiers (43).

Data Analysis

Behavioral Data

To test the effects of mood induction, we used a three-way repeated measures multivariate analysis of variance (MANOVA), with one between-subjects factor (group: rMDD and control) and two within-subjects factors (mood: happy and sad; time: pre- and post-mood induction). To control for Type I errors across the analyses, we used the Bonferroni correction. The significance level was set at $p < 0.05$ (two-tailed).

Multivariate t-tests were used to examine between-group differences in the harmonic mean reaction times of the emotional valence identification task and cognitive reactivity scores (total score and subscale scores of the LEIDS-R). *Post-hoc* comparisons were applied only if Hotelling's T^2 indicated significance. The significance level was set at $p < 0.05$ (two-tailed).

All behavioral analyses were performed using SPSS version 22.0 (SPSS Japan Inc., Tokyo, Japan).

Electrophysiological Data

The EEG analysis was conducted using the Net Station software (version 4.2; Electrical Geodesics, Inc.). Data were band-pass filtered at 0.02–100 Hz, notch-filtered at around 50 Hz, and noise removal was performed. The data were split into epochs of 1,200 ms (200 ms before to 1,000 ms after stimulus onset). Blinks, eye movements, and other artifacts (with a voltage exceeding ± 120 μV) were detected based on Net Station's eyeblink and movement detection algorithm (43). The data from bad channels were replaced with interpolated data from the remaining channels using the Bad Channel Replacement tool (43), and artifacts were corrected by applying the Gratton procedure (44). Thereafter, all trials were visually inspected for remaining artifacts and rejected as necessary. In addition to trials with no response, trials with reaction times <150 ms were rejected, because it is possible that these responses were made without considering the stimulus (45). No between-group differences were identified in the percentage of remaining epochs after epoch rejection (rMDD = 89.35%; control = 85.05%).

To detect and characterize both evoked and induced GBRs, a time-frequency analysis was performed on each epoch using a continuous wavelet transform (20–70 Hz, in 1.0-Hz steps), with Morlet wavelets as basic functions. The power at each frequency from 200 ms to 0 ms before stimulus onset was subtracted for each trial. We selected electrodes in a fronto-central region of interest (F3, F4, Fz, C3, C4, and Cz) to prevent the loss of statistical power. Given the known individual variability in the frequency of oscillatory activity (46), we used each participant's individual max power in the 30–70 Hz range in the analyses of the two following time windows: early GBRs (50–150 ms after stimulus onset) and late GBRs (300–800 ms after stimulus onset) (27).

Further analyses were performed using SPSS version 22 (SPSS Japan Inc.) and PROCESS (47). To test whether the rMDD group showed distinct power characteristics for early and late GBRs for positive and negative words, a three-way repeated measures MANOVA was conducted with one between-subjects factor (group: rMDD and control) and two within-subjects factors (valence: positive, neutral, and negative words; component: early and late GBRs). Greenhouse-Geisser-corrected probabilities are reported in any instance in which the assumption of sphericity was violated. To control for Type I errors across the analyses, we used the Bonferroni correction. The significance level was set at $p < 0.05$ (two-tailed).

To examine the association of GBRs with cognitive reactivity in the rMDD group, we performed moderated multiple regression, with group (rMDD and control) as a predictor, GBRs to a priori-determined positive and negative words as a moderator, the LEIDS-R total score as a dependent variable, and participants' moods (happiness and sadness) after mood induction as covariates. Furthermore, we confirmed that the data were not obstructed by multicollinearity using the

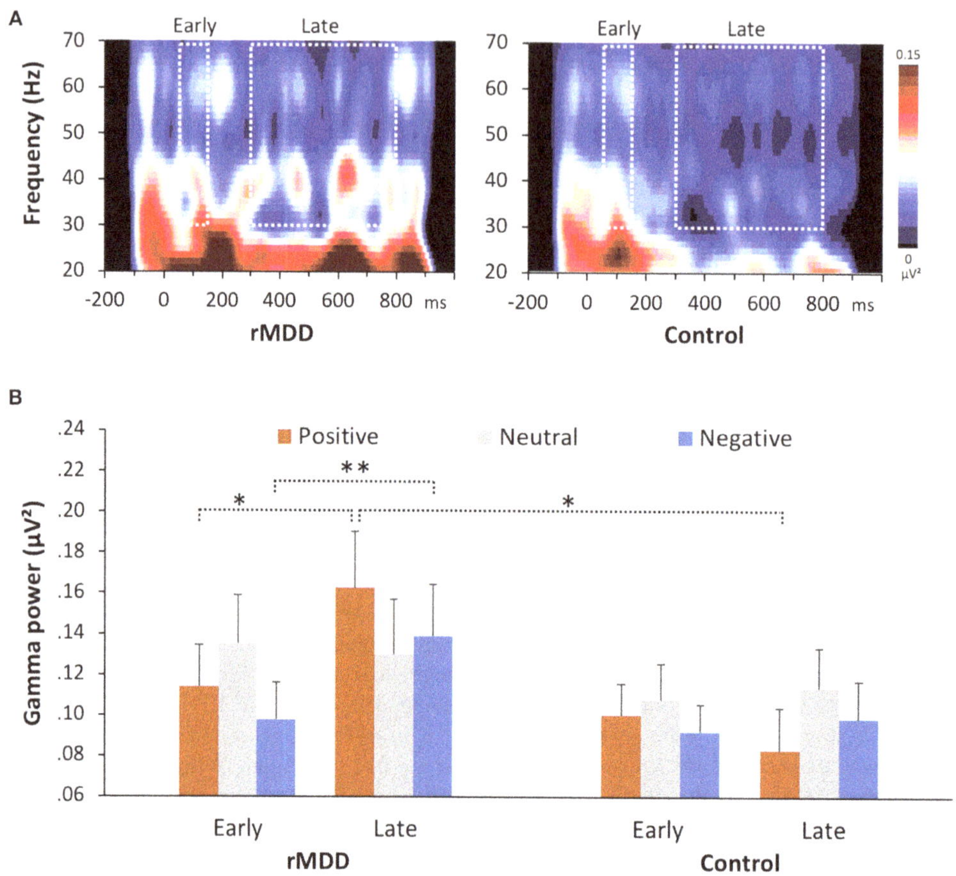

FIGURE 1 | Group differences in gamma-band responses during the emotional valence identification task. **(A)** Wavelet decomposition for both groups showing the response to positive words at all frequencies at electrode F4. **(B)** Early and late gamma powers for all valences in the two groups. Error bars indicate the standard error. *$p < 0.05$, **$p < 0.01$, two-tailed.

variance inflation factor coefficient of independent variables. To demonstrate *post-hoc* probing of moderational effects, the significant interactions were probed by testing the conditional effects of group at three levels of GBRs, including one standard deviation below the mean, at the mean, and one standard deviation above the mean. The significance level was set at $p < 0.05$ (two-tailed).

RESULTS

Confirmation of Mood Induction

The group × mood × time repeated MANOVA revealed a significant interaction between mood and time [$F_{(1,49)} = 30.89$, $p < 0.001$, $\eta p^2 = 0.39$]. After mood induction, participants demonstrated significantly decreased happiness ratings ($p < 0.001$, $\Delta = -1.19$) and significantly increased sadness ratings ($p = 0.024$, $\Delta = 0.40$) (**Table 1**).

Behavioral Data and Cognitive Reactivity

Table 1 shows the harmonic mean reaction times and LEIDS-R scores. The multivariate *t*-test for harmonic mean reaction times did not identify a significant between-group difference [Hotelling's $T^2 = 0.14$, $F_{(3,47)} = 2.19$, $p = 0.10$, $\eta p^2 = 0.12$]. In contrast, a similar analysis performed for LEIDS-R scores revealed a significant between-group difference [Hotelling's $T^2 = 0.40$, $F_{(6,44)} = 2.89$, $p = 0.018$, $\eta p^2 = 0.28$]. Specifically, the rMDD group had a significantly higher total LEIDS-R score ($p < 0.001$, $d = 1.19$), as well as significantly higher scores on most LEIDS-R subscales (Hopelessness/Suicidality: $p = 0.006$, $d = 0.84$; Acceptance/Coping: $p = 0.753$, $d = 0.09$; Aggression: $p = 0.011$, $d = 0.78$; Control/Perfectionism: $p = 0.006$, $d = 0.84$; Risk Avoidance: $p = 0.003$, $d = 0.91$; and Rumination: $p = 0.001$, $d = 1.07$), than did the control group.

Group Differences in Early and Late Gamma-Band Activity

The group × valence × component repeated measures MANOVA revealed a significant interaction between group and component [$F_{(1,49)} = 4.58$, $p = 0.037$, $\eta p^2 = 0.09$] and a significant three-way interaction [Greenhouse-Geisser corrected, $F_{(1.74,85.44)} = 6.49$, $p = 0.004$, $\eta p^2 = 0.12$]. The rMDD group showed significantly greater late-GBR power to positive words than did controls ($p = 0.027$, $d = 0.67$), but not to neutral ($p = 0.623$, $d = 0.14$) or negative words ($p = 0.196$, $d = 0.38$), as shown in **Figure 1**. The rMDD group also showed significantly greater power for late GBRs than for early GBRs to positive ($p = 0.012$, $d = 0.24$) and negative words ($p = 0.003$, $d = 0.26$).

Association of Gamma-Band Activity With Cognitive Reactivity

We confirmed that our data were not obstructed by multicollinearity (variance inflation factor < 6.0). No significant correlations were identified between the LEIDS-R total score and both early and late GBRs: the early GBRs to positive words ($r = 0.13$, $p = 0.367$) or negative words ($r = 0.04$, $p = 0.789$), and the late GBRs to positive words ($r = 0.14$, $p = 0.322$) or negative words ($r = -0.02$, $p = 0.873$). The multiple moderation model was significant when early GBRs were incorporated as a modulator [$F_{(7,43)} = 3.99$, $p = 0.002$, $R^2 = 0.39$] as well as when late GBRs incorporated as a modulator [$F_{(7,43)} = 4.25$, $p = 0.001$, $R^2 = 0.41$]. We also identified significant interactions between group and late GBRs to positive words [$t_{(43)} = 2.26$, $p = 0.029$, $b = 155.09$] and late GBRs to negative words [$t_{(43)} = -2.48$, $p = 0.017$, $b = -168.50$] (**Figure 2**), but not early GBRs to positive words [$t_{(43)} = 2.00$, $p = 0.052$, $b = 202.10$] or negative words [$t_{(43)} = -1.98$, $p = 0.054$, $b = -230.78$]. For late GBRs to positive words, group was significantly related to cognitive reactivity when late GBRs to positive words were one standard deviation above the mean [$t_{(43)} = 3.63$, $p = 0.001$, $b = 36.73$] and at the mean [$t_{(43)} = 3.97$, $p < 0.001$, $b = 17.56$], but not when late GBRs to positive words were one standard deviation below the mean [$t_{(43)} = 0.23$, $p = 0.822$, $b = 1.74$]. For late GBRs to negative words, group was significantly related to cognitive reactivity when late GBRs to negative words were one standard deviation below the mean [$t_{(43)} = 4.17$, $p < 0.001$, $b = 34.79$] and at the mean [$t_{(43)} = 3.97$, $p < 0.001$, $b = 17.56$], but not when late GBRs to negative words were one standard deviation above the mean [$t_{(43)} = -0.04$, $p = 0.967$, $b = -0.35$]. As shown in **Figure 2**, greater late GBRs to positive words and smaller late GBRs to negative words were associated with high predicted cognitive reactivity scores for the rMDD group only.

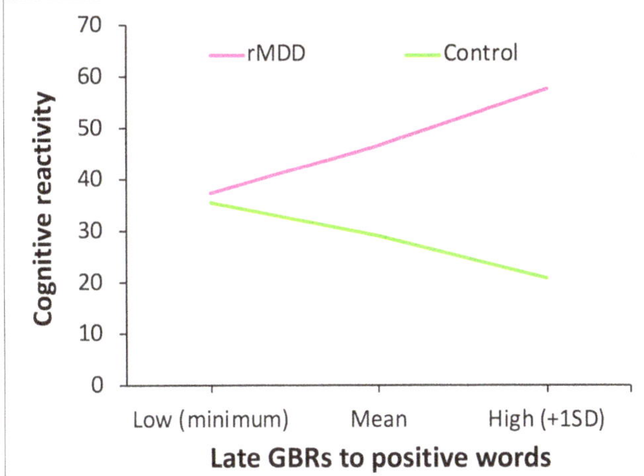

FIGURE 2 | Moderation effects of late gamma-band responses on group and cognitive reactivity. Slope of the relationship between late GBRs to positive words and cognitive reactivity as a function of group.

DISCUSSION

Identification of the neurophysiological mechanisms underlying cognitive reactivity in individuals with rMDD may provide essential clues regarding the prevention of MDD recurrence. To elucidate these mechanisms, we examined the characteristics of GBRs to emotional words in participants with rMDD and healthy controls after negative mood induction. Our results showed that the mood induction elicited decreased happiness and increased sadness, indicating that this paradigm successfully yielded negative mood changes. After mood induction, although no between-group differences in the reaction times of emotional valence identification were found, the power of late GBRs to positive words was greater in the rMDD group than in the control group. In addition, the rMDD group showed greater power for late GBRs to positive and negative words than for early GBRs, while the control group did not. Furthermore, the rMDD group had significantly higher cognitive reactivity, as measured with the LEIDS-R, than did the control group, and we identified moderation effects of the late GBRs on cognitive reactivity in the rMDD group. Collectively, these findings suggest that individuals with rMDD demonstrate abnormal information processing that influences cognitive reactivity.

To the best of our knowledge, the current study is the first to report altered late induced GBRs during the judgment of positive words in people with rMDD. Because late GBRs are related to the modulation of higher-order cognitive processes, including memory and attention, these GBRs may reflect neuronal synchrony involving large-scale coherence across highly distributed brain regions (48). From this perspective, the between-group GBR differences we identified may be interpreted as neural circuit dysfunction related to the top–down processing of emotional information in rMDD.

The present study also identified significant moderation effects of GBRs, suggesting that participants with rMDD who have a greater power of late GBRs to positive words show high predicted cognitive reactivity scores. These findings indicate that altered processing of incoming positive information in individuals with rMDD who are experiencing a negative mood might exacerbate cognitive reactivity. Our findings support those of previous studies showing that formerly depressed participants exhibit several cognitive biases, including impaired retrieval of contextual details for positive compared to negative events (49, 50), difficulty in using positive memories for emotion regulation (51), and less attentional bias for positive stimuli (52), all of which have been proposed as risk factors for the recurrence of MDD (49). Moreover, as noted above, late GBRs are related to higher-order cognitive functions, such as memory and attention, including the updating of memory contents, selection of different behavioral responses, reallocation of attention, or any combination of these (27). Considering these findings, the latent abnormal neural processing of positive information may lead to various cognitive dysfunctions in judgment, memory retrieval, emotion regulation, and attentional orientation, which in turn may underlie cognitive reactivity. Given that the participants with rMDD in this study were fully recovered, it is possible that the late GBRs to positive words reflect the "scars" of depression and serve as persistent markers of the vulnerability to depression recurrence.

While the current study was not designed to determine the cause of the altered late GBRs to positive words in the rMDD group, we can make some speculations based on previous findings of functional changes in the brain. One recent study reported that compared with healthy controls, unmedicated recovered patients with a history of MDD showed attenuated neural responses to pleasant stimuli in the ventral striatum and elevated neural activity in the caudate nucleus in response to aversive stimuli (53). These results indicate that participants with rMDD might have impairments in the neural circuits for reward, and this deficit in the circuits for reward may extend to responses to positive stimuli.

No significant between-group differences in GBRs to negative words were observed in the present study. This conflicts with the findings of Siegle et al. (32), who showed greater sustained gamma activity to negative stimuli in individuals with MDD than in controls. This discrepancy may be explained by differences in the presence of current depressive symptoms. We recruited individuals who had recovered from depression, while Siegle et al. (32) recruited patients in the midst of a current major depressive episode. Some evidence also suggests that individuals with clinical depression show biased attention, memory, and processing for negative stimuli, with specific neural mechanisms that putatively underlie these biases (54). Therefore, rMDD may have led to dysfunctional information processing that differs from that caused by active depression, which may explain these apparently inconsistent results. That said, we focused on two relatively short time windows, that is, early GBRs (50–150 ms) and late GBRs (300–800 ms), whereas Siegle et al. (32) utilized sustained gamma-band activity (0–8000 ms) to evaluate sustained semantic information processing. As our study and that by Siegle et al. (32) examined different neural processes, they cannot be directly compared. Further research is required to more fully investigate the role of late GBRs in people with rMDD vs. MDD.

This study had several limitations. First, we could not determine whether the characteristics of the identified late GBRs were specific to people with rMDD, because we did not directly compare them to those of the late GBRs from different clinical groups, such as individuals with recurrent or single-episode MDD, schizophrenia, or a personality disorder. Future research should aim to identify the neural processes that are specific to rMDD, as this may permit the identification of a neurophysiological biomarker for MDD recurrence. Second, most of the participants with rMDD were young adults (21.72 years old on average), and as a result, they reported a relatively short duration of depressive episodes (7.71 months on average). Considering that the characteristics of cognitive dysfunction in rMDD have been found to vary according to age (55) and the depressive episode duration (56), this may limit the generalizability of our findings to other age ranges and patients with other rMDD severities. Finally, we did not include participants with a history of comorbid disorders and early life stress; however, MDD frequently co-occurs with anxiety (57), and early life stress has been suggested to affect the risk and protective factors of depression (58). Future studies should include more diverse samples to examine whether our findings may be influenced by a previous history of anxiety and early life stress.

CONCLUSIONS

The present study is the first to report altered induced gamma-band activity during the judgment of positive information in people with rMDD. Our findings demonstrate that the greater power of late GBRs to positive words after negative mood elicitation was related to higher cognitive reactivity. This indicates that latent abnormalities in higher-order neural processes, including memory, and attention, might underlie the cognitive reactivity in individuals with rMDD. Overall, these findings suggest that late GBRs are persistent markers of cognitive reactivity, and may therefore be a useful index for evaluating the risk of depression recurrence. Nevertheless, additional research is needed to investigate the specific role of late GBRs in rMDD and compare it to that in other clinical conditions.

AUTHOR CONTRIBUTIONS

TY, NS, HK, and HS conceived and designed the experiments. TY and NS performed the experiments. TY, GS, and MT analyzed the data. TY, NS, GS, HK, HS, SM, EM-R, NR, AN, MT, YO, and SY wrote the paper, contributed to and have approved the final manuscript.

FUNDING

This work was supported by JSPS KAKENHI (grant number JP16H07011 and 18K13323); a grant-in-aid for JSPS Fellows (grant number 22-6038, 25-2106); Ministry of Education, Culture, Sports, Science and Technology, MEXT KIBANKEISEI (2010); and AMED (grant number JP17dm0107093).

ACKNOWLEDGMENTS

We wish to thank M. Kimura, A. Tamada, T. Sato, S. Maeda, and H. Ogishima for their contribution to the project. We also thank all of the subjects for participating in the study.

REFERENCES

1. Mueller TI, Leon AC, Keller MB, Solomon DA, Endicott J, Coryell W, et al. Recurrence after recovery from major depressive disorder during 15 years of observational follow-up. *Am J Psychiatry* (1999) 156:1000–6.
2. Mattisson C, Bogren M, Horstmann V, Munk-Jörgensen P, Nettelbladt P. The long-term course of depressive disorders in the Lundby Study. *Psychol Med.* (2007) 37:883–91. doi: 10.1017/S0033291707000074
3. Lau MA, Segal ZV, Williams JMG. Teasdale's differential activation hypothesis: implications for mechanisms of depressive relapse and suicidal behaviour. *Behav Res Ther.* (2004) 42:1001–17. doi: 10.1016/j.brat.2004.03.003
4. Figueroa CA, Ruhé HG, Koeter MW, Spinhoven P, Van Der Does W, Bockting CL, et al. Cognitive reactivity versus dysfunctional cognitions and the prediction of relapse in recurrent major depressive disorder. *J Clin Psychiatry* (2015) 76:e1306–12. doi: 10.4088/JCP.14m09268
5. Teasdale JD. Cognitive vulnerability to persistent depression. *Cogn Emot.* (1988) 2:247–74. doi: 10.1080/02699938808410927
6. Miranda J, Gross JJ, Persons JB, Hahn J. Mood matters: negative mood induction activates dysfunctional attitudes in women vulnerable to depression. *Cognit Ther Res.* (1998) 22:363–76. doi: 10.1023/A:1018709212986
7. Miranda J, Persons JB. Dysfunctional attitudes are mood-state dependent. *J Abnorm Psychol.* (1988) 97:76–9. doi: 10.1037/0021-843X.97.1.76
8. Ingram RE, Bernet CZ, McLaughlin SC. Attentional allocation processes in individuals at risk for depression. *Cognit Ther Res.* (1994) 18:317–32. doi: 10.1007/BF02357508
9. Ingram RE, Ritter J. Vulnerability to depression: cognitive reactivity and parental bonding in high-risk individuals. *J Abnorm Psychol.* (2000) 109:588–96. doi: 10.1037/0021-843X.109.4.588
10. Hedlund S, Rude SS. Evidence of latent depressive schemas in formerly depressed individuals. *J Abnorm Psychol.* (1995) 104:517–25. doi: 10.1037/0021-843X.104.3.517
11. Gemar MC, Segal Z V., Sagrati S, Kennedy SJ. Mood-induced changes on the implicit association test in recovered depressed patients. *J Abnorm Psychol.* (2001) 110:282–9. doi: 10.1037/0021-843X.110.2.282
12. Teasdale JD, Dent J. Cognitive vulnerability to depression: an investigation of two hypotheses. *Br J Clin Psychol.* (1987) 26:113–26. doi: 10.1111/j.2044-8260.1987.tb00737.x
13. Timbremont B, Braet C. Cognitive vulnerability in remitted depressed children and adolescents. *Behav Res Ther.* (2004) 42:423–37. doi: 10.1016/S0005-7967(03)00151-7
14. Scher CD, Ingram RE, Segal ZV. Cognitive reactivity and vulnerability: empirical evaluation of construct activation and cognitive diatheses in unipolar depression. *Clin Psychol Rev.* (2005) 25:487–510. doi: 10.1016/j.cpr.2005.01.005
15. Yamamoto T, Yamano M, Shimada H, Ichikawa K, Nakaya M. The specificity of cognitive reactivity in recurrent major depressive episodes. *Shinrigaku Kenkyu* (2014) 85:29–39. doi: 10.4992/jjpsy.85.29
16. Hooley JM, Gruber SA, Parker HA, Guillaumot J, Rogowska J, Yurgelun-Todd DA. Cortico-limbic response to personally challenging emotional stimuli after complete recovery from depression. *Psychiatry Res Neuroimag.* (2009) 172:106–19. doi: 10.1016/j.pscychresns.2008.04.001
17. Ramel W, Goldin PR, Eyler LT, Brown GG, Gotlib IH, McQuaid JR. Amygdala reactivity and mood-congruent memory in individuals at risk for depressive relapse. *Biol Psychiatry* (2007) 61:231–9. doi: 10.1016/j.biopsych.2006.05.004
18. Ingram RE, Atchley RA, Segal ZV. *Vulnerability to Depression: From Cognitive Neuroscience to Prevention and Treatment.* New York, NY: Guilford. (2011).
19. Foland-Ross LC, Gotlib IH. Cognitive and neural aspects of information processing in major depressive disorder: an integrative perspective. *Front Psychol.* (2012) 3:489. doi: 10.3389/fpsyg.2012.00489
20. Dawson G, Frey K, Panagiotides H, Yamada E, Hessl D, Osterling J. Infants of depressed mothers exhibit atypical frontal electrical brain activity during interactions with mother and with a familiar, nondepressed adult. *Child Dev.* (1999) 70:1058–66. doi: 10.1111/1467-8624.00078
21. Perez-Edgar K, Fox NA, Cohn JF, Kovacs M. Behavioral and electrophysiological markers of selective attention in children of parents with a history of depression. *Biol Psychiatry* (2006) 60:1131–8. doi: 10.1016/j.biopsych.2006.02.036
22. Stewart JL, Allen JJB. Resting frontal brain asymmetry is linked to future depressive symptoms in women. *Biol Psychol.* (2018) 136:161–7. doi: 10.1016/j.biopsycho.2018.06.004
23. Engel AK, Singer W. Temporal binding and the neural correlates of sensory awareness. *Trends Cogn Sci.* (2001) 5:16–25. doi: 10.1016/S1364-6613(00)01568-0
24. Gruber T, Müller MM, Keil A, Elbert T. Selective visual-spatial attention alters induced gamma band responses in the human EEG. *Clin Neurophysiol.* (1999) 110:2074–85.
25. Wyart V, Tallon-Baudry C. Neural dissociation between visual awareness and spatial attention. *J Neurosci.* (2008) 28:2667–79. doi: 10.1523/JNEUROSCI.4748-07.2008
26. Tallon-Baudry C, Bertrand O. Oscillatory gamma activity in humans and its role in object representation. *Trends Cogn Sci.* (1999) 3:151–62. doi: 10.1016/S1364-6613(99)01299-1
27. Herrmann CS, Lenz D, Junge S, Busch NA, Maess B. Memory-matches evoked human gamma-responses. *BMC Neurosci.* (2004) 5:13. doi: 10.1186/1471-2202-5-13
28. Gruber T, Tsivilis D, Montaldi D, Müller MM. Induced gamma band responses: an early marker of memory encoding and retrieval. *Neuroreport* (2004) 15:1837–41. doi: 10.1097/01.wnr.0000137077.26010.12
29. Jensen O, Kaiser J, Lachaux JP. Human gamma-frequency oscillations associated with attention and memory. *Trends Neurosci.* (2007) 30:317–24. doi: 10.1016/j.tins.2007.05.001
30. Fitzgerald PJ, Watson BO. Gamma oscillations as a biomarker for major depression: an emerging topic. *Transl Psychiatry* (2018) 8:177. doi: 10.1038/s41398-018-0239-y
31. Lenz D, Fischer S, Schadow J, Bogerts B, Herrmann CS. Altered evoked gamma-band responses as a neurophysiological marker of schizophrenia? *Int J Psychophysiol.* (2011) 79:25–31. doi: 10.1016/j.ijpsycho.2010.08.002
32. Siegle GJ, Condray R, Thase ME, Keshavan M, Steinhauer SR. Sustained gamma-band EEG following negative words in depression and schizophrenia. *Int J Psychophysiol.* (2010) 75:107–18. doi: 10.1016/j.ijpsycho.2008.04.008
33. American Psychiatric Association. *Diagnostic and Statistical Manual of Mental Disorders, 4th Edn.* Washington, DC:Text. (2000).
34. Oldfield RC. The assessment and analysis of handedness: the Edinburgh inventory. *Neuropsychologia* (1971) 9:97–113. doi: 10.1016/0028-3932(71)90067-4
35. Beck AT, Steer RA, Brown GK. *Manual for the Beck Depression Inventory-II.* San Antonio, TX: Psychological Corporation (1996).
36. Kojima M, Furukawa TA, Takahashi H, Kawai M, Nagaya T, Tokudome S. Cross-cultural validation of the Beck depression inventory-II in Japan. *Psychiatry Res.* (2002) 110:291–9. doi: 10.1016/S0165-1781(02)00106-3
37. Van der Does A, Williams J. *Leiden Index of Depression Sensitivity – Revised (LEIDS-R).* Leiden University (2003).
38. Oashi O, Aoyagi H, Hosoda K. Learned helplessness and attributional styles. *Japanese J Educ Psychol.* (1992) 40:287–94. doi: 10.5926/jjep1953.40.3_287
39. Mitterschiffthaler MT, Williams SCR, Walsh ND, Cleare AJ, Donaldson C, Scott J, et al. Neural basis of the emotional Stroop interference effect in major depression. *Psychol Med.* (2008) 38:247–56. doi: 10.1017/S0033291707001523
40. Stip E, Lecours AR, Chertkow H, Elie R, O'Connor K. Influence of affective words on lexical decision task in major depression. *J Psychiatry Neurosci.* (1994) 19:202–7.
41. Sheehan D V., Lecrubier Y, Sheehan KH, Amorim P, Janavs J, Weiller E, et al. The mini-international neuropsychiatric interview (M.I.N.I.): the development and validation of a structured diagnostic psychiatric interview for DSM-IV and ICD-10. *J Clin Psychiatry* (1998) 59(Suppl 20):22–33.
42. Gotoh F, Ohta N. Affective valence of two-compound kanji words. *Tsukuba Psychol Res.* (2001) 23:45–52.
43. Electrical Geodesics I. *Net Station Waveform Tools Technical Manual.* S-MAN-200-WFTR-001. EGI (2006)
44. Gratton G, Coles MGH, Donchin E. A new method for off-line removal of ocular artifact. *Electroencephalogr Clin Neurophysiol.* (1983) 55:468–84. doi: 10.1016/0013-4694(83)90135-9
45. Matthews G, Southall A. Depression and the processing of emotional stimuli: a study of semantic priming. *Cognit Ther Res.* (1991) 15:283–302. doi: 10.1007/BF01205174

46. Lenz D, Krauel K, Flechtner HH, Schadow J, Hinrichs H, Herrmann CS. Altered evoked gamma-band responses reveal impaired early visual processing in ADHD children. *Neuropsychologia* (2010) 48:1985–93. doi: 10.1016/j.neuropsychologia.2010.03.019
47. Hayes A. *Introduction to Mediation, Moderation, and Conditional Process Analysis: A Regression-Based Approach (2nd Edition)*. New York, NY: Guilford (2018).
48. Varela F, Lachaux JP, Rodriguez E, Martinerie J. The brainweb: phase synchronization and large-scale integration. *Nat Rev Neurosci.* (2001) 2:229–39. doi: 10.1038/35067550
49. Gupta R, Kar BR. Attention and memory biases as stable abnormalities among currently depressed and currently remitted individuals with unipolar depression. *Front Psychiatry* (2012) 3:99. doi: 10.3389/fpsyt.2012.00099
50. Park RJ, Goodyer IM, Teasdale JD. Categoric overgeneral autobiographical memory in adolescents with major depressive disorder. *Psychol Med.* (2002) 32:267–76. doi: 10.1017/S0033291701005189
51. Joormann J, Siemer M. Memory accessibility, mood regulation, and dysphoria: difficulties in repairing sad mood with happy memories? *J Abnorm Psychol.* (2004) 113:179–88. doi: 10.1037/0021-843X.113.2.179
52. Li M, Lu S, Wang G, Feng L, Fu B, Zhong N. Alleviated negative rather than positive attentional bias in patients with depression in remission: an eye-tracking study. *J Int Med Res.* (2016) 44:1072–86. doi: 10.1177/0300060516662134
53. McCabe C, Cowen PJ, Harmer CJ. Neural representation of reward in recovered depressed patients. *Psychopharmacology.* (2009) 205:667–77. doi: 10.1007/s00213-009-1573-9
54. Disner SG, Beevers CG, Haigh EAP, Beck AT. Neural mechanisms of the cognitive model of depression. *Nat Rev Neurosci.* (2011) 12:467–77. doi: 10.1038/nrn3027
55. Nakano Y, Baba H, Maeshima H, Kitajima A, Sakai Y, Baba K, et al. Executive dysfunction in medicated, remitted state of major depression. *J Affect Disord.* (2008) 111:46–51. doi: 10.1016/j.jad.2008.01.027
56. Yamamoto T, Shimada H. Cognitive dysfunctions after recovery from major depressive episodes. *Appl Neuropsychol.* (2012) 19:183–91. doi: 10.1080/09084282.2011.643959
57. Brown TA, Campbell LA, Lehman CL, Grisham JR, Mancill RB. Current and lifetime comorbidity of the DSM-IV anxiety and mood disorders in a large clinical sample. *J Abnorm Psychol.* (2001) 110:585–99. doi: 10.1037/0021-843X.110.4.585
58. Yamamoto T, Toki S, Siegle GJ, Takamura M, Takaishi Y, Yoshimura S, et al. Increased amygdala reactivity following early life stress: a potential resilience enhancer role. *BMC Psychiatry* (2017) 17:1–11. doi: 10.1186/s12888-017-1201-x

20

White Matter Microstructural Changes and Episodic Memory Disturbances in Late-Onset Bipolar Disorder

Gilberto Sousa Alves[1,2], Christian Knöchel[3], Michael Anton Paulitsch[1], Britta Reinke[3], André F. Carvalho[4,5], Richard Feddern[2], David Prvulovic[3], Felipe Kenji Sudo[6,7], Johannes Pantel[1], Andreas Reif[3] and Viola Oertel[3]*

[1] Institute of General Medicine, Goethe University, Frankfurt/Main, Germany, [2] Translational Psychiatry Group, Universidade Federal do Ceará, Fortaleza, Brazil, [3] Laboratory of Neuroscience, Department of Psychiatry, Psychosomatic Medicine and Psychotherapy, Goethe University, Frankfurt/Main, Germany, [4] Department of Psychiatry, University of Toronto, Toronto, ON, Canada, [5] Centre for Addiction and Mental Health, Toronto, ON, Canada, [6] Department of Psychology, Pontifical Catholic University of Rio de Janeiro, Rio de Janeiro, Brazil, [7] Memory Clinic, D' Or Institute for Research and Education, Rio de Janeiro, Brazil

***Correspondence:**
Gilberto Sousa Alves
gsalves123@hotmail.com

Background: Bipolar disorder (BD) has been associated with distributed network disruption, but little is known on how different clinical subtypes, particularly those with an earlier and later onset of disease, are related to connectivity changes in white matter (WM) tracts.

Methods: Diffusion tensor imaging (DTI) and volumetric measures were carried out in early-onset bipolar patients [(EOD) (n = 16)], late-onset bipolar disorder [(LOD)(n = 14)] and healthy controls (n = 32). We also computed ROI analysis of gray matter (GM) and white matter (WM) volumes using the regions with significant group differences in the DTI parameters. Cognitive and behavior measurements were analyzed between groups.

Results: Lower fraction of anisotropy (FA) in the right hemisphere comprising anterior thalamic radiation, fornix, posterior cingulate, internal capsule, splenium of corpus callosum was observed in the LOD in comparison with EOD; additionally, lower FA was also found in the LOD in comparison with healthy controls, mostly in the right hemisphere and comprising fibers of the splenium of the corpus callosum, cingulum, superior frontal gyrus and posterior thalamic radiation; LOD also showed worse episodic memory performance than EOD; no statistical significant differences between mood symptoms, WM and GM volumes were found between BD groups.

Conclusion: Even after correcting for age differences, LOD was associated with more extensive WM microstructural changes and worse episodic memory performance than EOD; these findings suggest that changes in the WM fiber integrity may be associated with a later presentation of BD, possibly due to mechanisms other than neuroprogression. However, these findings deserve replication in larger, prospective, studies.

Keywords: DTI, bipolar disorders, TBSS, white-matter, aging, cognition

INTRODUCTION

Bipolar Disorder (BD) is a chronic condition characterized by marked shifts in mood, energy, activity levels and ability to carry out everyday functions, which affects 1–1.5% of the general population (1, 2). Typically, the onset of the disorder occurs during young adult life, but cases with emergence in late-life have been increasingly reported (3). Compared to Early-onset BD (EOD), subjects with late-onset BD (LOD) were more likely to suffer from depressive symptoms and cognitive difficulties, namely processing speed, executive function and episodic memory impairments, according to observational researches (4, 5).

With the development of modern neuroimaging approaches to assess the neural circuitry in psychiatric disorders, especially the Diffusion Tensor Imaging (DTI), novel information about the microstructural integrity and the directional organization of white-matter (WM) tracts in this population could be obtained (5, 6). For instance, lower fractional anisotropy (FA) was identified in the posterior cingulate, fornix, thalamus, corpus callosum and cerebellum in subjects with BD (7–9). Although substantial evidence indicated that macro and microstructural abnormalities in those networks may be implicated in the pathophysiology of the disorder, current knowledge on structural and functional brain differences between groups with early and late disease-onsets is limited (10, 11). As suggested by a few studies, LOD may present more WM hyperintensities and gray matter (GM) reductions in anterior limbic areas, in comparison to EOD (12, 13), but the association between those features and the clinical manifestations in BD remains obscure (14).

In a previous study from this group, we used tract-based spatial statistics (TBSS) to investigate structural connections between BD and healthy controls. As main results, we have reported reduced fiber integrity and increased mean diffusivity in the fornix, the thalamus and the corpus callosum (both the splenium and the truncus) in BD patients in comparison with controls (10). In the present study, we aimed to explore differences between EOD and LOD through structural volumetry, DTI and clinical parameters using TBSS and voxel-based volumetry (VBM). Our objective was to examine whether cognitive performance in EOD and LOD groups was associated with cortical and WM abnormalities (either global or regional), particularly in the tracts that have been identified as compromised in BD. Based on previous reports (4, 5, 12, 13), we predict that LOD may be associated with more extensive neuronal disruption and higher cognitive impairment in comparison with EOD.

METHODS

Sample

Methods were described elsewhere (10). Thirty subjects diagnosed with BD type I according to the DSM-IV (15) criteria and thirty-two controls [mean age = 39.22 years [SD = 10.35]] were included in this study. BD group was classified as presenting EOD [age of onset < 27 years; $n = 16$; mean age = 31.12 years [SD = 8.06]] and LOD [age of onset ≥ 27 years; mean age = 48.50 years [SD = 9.63]]. We actually based our group definition on recent evidence presenting a two-component distribution of age of onset (and a sample of 515 BD subjects), with a peak in early adult life and a smaller peak in midlife (16). Parts of the sample have been analyzed in another work by our group [see (10)].

None of the participants were acutely depressed or manic during the procedures, according to the DSM-IV and their scores on the German version of the Beck Depression Inventory (BDI) (scores <18 corresponds to absence of major depression) (17) and the Bech-Rafaelsen Mania Rating Scale (BRMAS) (scores < 7 implies absence of maniac episode) (18). Other exclusion criteria were: (i) history of drug-related disorders; (ii) history of comorbid DSM-IV axis I or II disorder (controls presented no history of any psychiatric disorder); (iii) history of neurological disorder and (iv) inability to provide informed consent. In addition, controls had no family history of affective or psychotic disorder, as demonstrated through the Structured Clinical Interview for DSM-IV (SCID-I and SCID-II; German version) (19).

Clinical and Cognitive Assessment

All participants undertook the *Mehrfachwahl-Wortschatz-Intelligenz* test (MWT-B), a measure of general intelligence (20) and the Trail Making A and B, which assess executive function. Episodic memory was tested using the California Verbal Learning Test (CVLT) (21). The following parameters in this test were included: CVLT *discriminability* (CVLT DW), *delayed free recall I* (CVLT DFR 1) and *delayed free recall II* (CVLT DFR 2). Anxiety symptoms were assessed through Strait-Trait Anxiety Inventory (STAI-G) and the Symptom Checklist of Derogatis (SCL 90–R) was used to evaluate global measures of mental and physical health state (22, 23).

Data Acquisition and Image Processing

All participants undertook MRI using a Trio 3T scanner (Siemens, Erlangen, Germany) with a standard head coil for radiofrequency transmission and signal reception. DTI measures were acquired using an echo planar imaging (EPI) sequence [TR = 8760 ms; TE = 100 ms; bandwith = 1302 Hz/pixel, acquisition voxel size = $2 \times 2 \times 2$ mm^3; 60 axial adjacent slices; slice thickness = 2 mm (no gap); FOV = $192 \times 192 \times 120$ mm; acquisition matrix = 96×96; 10 images without diffusion weighting (b0)] with 60 diffusion-encoded images (b-values = 1000 s/mm^2 60 noncolinear directions). Both b0 b 1000 images were averaged three times (total acquisition time = 10 min 31 s). Parallel acquisition of independently constructed images using generalized auto-calibrating parallel acquisitions were used for this sequence (24). This was accompanied by an anatomical scan with each participant (MDEFT; voxel size: $1 \times 1 \times 1$ mm3, 176 slices) (25).

DTI Preprocessing

DTI data were preprocessed and analyzed using the standard procedure of the TBSS software with FSL 4.1 (Oxford Centre

Abbreviations: CVLT DFR I, CVLT-delayed free recall I; CVLT DFR II, CVLT-delayed free recall II; CVLT DW, CVLT discriminality; DTI, diffusion tensor imaging; EOD, early onset disorder; LOD, late onset disorder; VM, task performance of verbal episodic memory; STAI-G, Strait-Trait Anxiety Inventory; SCL-90 dep., SCL-90 d; TMT, Trail Making Test.

for Functional MRI of the Brain - FMRIB software library (FSL, http://www.fmrib.ox.ac.uk/fsl) (26). TBSS is a protocol that employs voxel-wise approach to analyze DTI sequences by projecting individual DTI sequences of each participant on a mean skeleton of a white matter mask (26). The following steps were performed using an in-house script pipeline (MRIST: MR Imaging and Spectroscopy Toolbox, Dept. of Neuroradiology, Oxford University). Each diffusion-weighted volume was affine-aligned to its corresponding b0 image, corrected for potential motion artifacts and eddy-current distortions by rigid transformation to the first image of the merged data set. Following that step, all files were averaged to one single e3D data set for every individual. Subsequently, brain masks of each b0 image with the following parameters were generated: fractional threshold $f = 0.1$, vertical gradient $g = 0$. This was done through FSL's Brain Extraction Tool (BET 2.1; http://www.fmrib.ox.ac.uk/analysis/research/bet/) (27). All subjects' maps were aligned with the most representative subject based on the calculation of the amount of warping needed for the images to be aligned, and further brought in the MNI (Montreal Neurological institute) space by nonlinear registration, using the TBSS routine (26). Finally, a fitting of all corrected images with a tensor model that generated the FA diffusion maps was provided for the TBSS analysis. To average the aligned FA images and create a mean FA image, a FA skeletonization program was used. The skeleton was thresholded at a FA value of 0.2 to limit the effects of poor alignment across subjects and ensure exclusion of CSF and GM voxels. The mean FA image was used to represent the center of all tracts common to the group and comprised all fiber pathways consistently across all participants.

ROI Analysis With VBM

A detailed description of the ROI analysis was published elsewhere (10). The VBM preprocessing and statistical analysis was carried out through the SPM8 (statistical parametric mapping [Wellcome Department of Imaging Neuroscience, London, UK]) and the MATLAB version 7.7.0. All images were assessed and reviewed for artifacts and structural abnormalities. Furtherly, customized T1 templates and prior images of GM, WMm and CSF were created for all participants and were used in the group analysis. Modulated data and prior probability maps (voxel intensity) were employed to guide segmentation in SPM. The segmentation included six different tissue types, light bias regularization (0.001), 60 mm bias FWHM cut-off, warping regularization of 4, affine regularization to the ICBM European brain template (linear registration) and a sampling distance of 3. Before further analysis, the segmentation process was checked for quality. Finally, all images were smoothed (28) with a Gaussian kernel of 8*8*8 mm^3 (FWHM), whereby the intensity of each voxel was replaced by the weighted average of the surrounding voxels, blurring the segmented image.

Statistical Analysis

FA maps were computed into general linear modeling (GLM), with covariates including age, education and gender. A global region of interest (ROI) was generated, representing the white matter skeleton and the mean values of FA were drawn. Thereafter, voxel-wise and ROI analysis using TBSS was performed (26). Voxel-wise cross-subject statistics was performed with permutation testing (randomize tool [FSL]). We set the number of permutation to 5,000 as recommended (29). Significance was tested at a $p < 0.05$ level, corrected for multiple comparisons [FWE, family wise error correction]). The voxel-wise analysis was followed by ROI analyses. For this, all significant clusters after voxel-wise analysis ($p < 0.001$) were located using the Jülich Histological [cyto- and myelo-architectonic] Atlas or Harvard-Oxford subcortical structural atlases recommended by FSL to define their topographical boundaries in MNI space. Based on these clusters, white matter masks have been created for each hemisphere. Absolute FA values of the ROIs were extracted from each participant. ANCOVA was applied to control for age differences between subjects in the socio-demographic group comparisons. Scheffe *post-hoc* contrasts were used for group comparisons. Bivariate correlation analysis of GM and WM volume with cognitive parameters and clinical scores was computed with Pearson Product Moment Correlation. Accordingly, bivariate correlation analysis (Pearson Product Moment correlation) between the volume and the medication doses were computed according to the method of Almeida and colleagues (30). The statistical package software SPSS 19.0 was employed for calculations;

Ethics

Participants were presented a full description of the study and provided written informed consent prior to the enrollment in the study. The protocol was approved by the ethical board of the medical department of the Goethe-University, Frankfurt am Main, Germany. All subjects gave written informed consent in accordance with the Declaration of Helsinki.

RESULTS

Sociodemographic Characteristics

The social-demographic characteristics of the sample are depicted in the **Table 1**. LOD subjects were older than controls and EOD (**Table 1**). Patients with EOD had a mean age of onset of 19 years, while LOD presented the first report of BD with mean age of 40 years. There were no significant differences in education scores between BD groups. Early BD tended to present longer duration of disease and more mood episodes than the LOD group; however, these differences did not reach statistical significance. The use of Lithium ($\chi^2 = 0.153$, $df = 1$, $p = 0.696$) or Valproate ($\chi^2 = 0.368$, $df = 1$, $p = 0.544$) was not statistically different between EOD and LOD. Furthermore, the dosage of lithium was neither associated with group ($r = -0.72$, $p = 0.707$) nor with age at disease onset ($r = -0.163$, $p = 0.388$).

Cognitive and Clinical Assessment

EOD vs. LOD

When compared to EOD, LOD subjects significantly performed worse in the CVLT, CVLT-VFW I, and CVLT-VFW-II. Regarding clinical measurements, no differences were found in the severity of current depressive, manic or psychotic symptoms between LOD and EOD groups.

Volumetric Measurement and Whole-Brain FA Maps

Interestingly, no significant differences in GM and WM volumes were found between LOD and EOD in the age-adjusted analysis. Both EOD and LOD exhibited lower WM volume than controls, but a significant statistical significant difference was found only for the EOD-control comparison (**Table 2**). All whole-brain group comparisons were shown on a mean FA skeleton, using the standard MNI152 1 × 1 × 1 mm brain template, on a $p \leq 0.001$ significance level (**Figure 1**, **Table 2**).

LOD vs. EOD

Voxelwise statistical analysis revealed significantly reduced FA in LOD in comparison with EOD, more extensively on the right hemisphere, in widespread areas comprising the following tracts: splenium of the corpus callosum, fornix (bilateral), cingulum fibers (bilateral), anterior thalamic radiation (right), nuclei of the internal medullary lamina (thalamus), ventroposterior medialis thalamus (right), ventromedial thalamic nucleus (right), pulvinar thalamus (right), anterior limb of the internal capsule (bilateral), retrolenticular part of the internal capsule (bilateral), cerebral penduncle (right), corticospinal tract (right), accumbens

TABLE 1 | Sociodemographic and clinical characteristics and cognitive performance of groups: LOD ($n = 14$), early onset BD ($n = 16$) and the control group (CON; $n = 32$). SD and range are in brackets.

Variable	CON ($n = 32$)	Early onset bipolar ($n = 16$)	Late onset bipolar ($n = 14$)	Significance
	Mean (SD)	Mean (SD)	Mean (SD)	
Gender	16 f/16 m	7 w/9 m	6 w/8 m	$\chi^2 = 0.28. p = 0.87$
Age	39.22 (10.36)	31.12 (8.06)	48.50 (9.63)	$F = 12.06. p < 0.01$
Years of education	14.86 (2.43)	15.85 (1.84)	15.50 (2.31)	$F = 1.44, p = 0.24$
Handedness (L: R)	All right handed	All right handed		
Duration of illness	–	11.31 (8.08)	8.86 (5.96)	$F = 2.43, p = 0.36$
Number of maniac episodes		10 (12.67)	7.64 (6.15)	$F = 0.40, p = 0.53$
Number of depressive episodes		13 (15.72)	6 (5.44)	$F = 2.50, p = 0.13$
Total episodes		23 (6.40)	13.71 (11.04)	$F = 1.58, p = 0.22$
Age at disease onset		19.6875 (4.14)	39.78 (7.83)	$F = 79.99, p < 0.001$
Age at first psychiatric admission		26.56 (9.47)	40.14 (7.65)	$F = 18.31, p < 0.001$
Duration of disease (years)		11.31 (8.08)	8.86 (5.96)	$F = 0.87, p = 0.36$
Number of admissions		2.37 (2.19)	4.57 (4.43)	$F = 3.08, p = 0.09$
Years of medication therapy		8.79 (8.35)	7.75 (6.41)	$F = 0.50, p = 0.71$

All comparisons by ANOVA, except for gender: χ^2 = Chi-Quadrat-Test.

TABLE 2 | Volumetric and clinical comparisons between groups—mean (SD) values expressed.

Test	Controls ($n = 32$)	EOD ($n = 16$)	LOD ($n = 14$)	F ratio	*P*-value**		
	Mean ± SD*	Mean ± SD*	Mean ± SD*		Con vs. LOD	LOD vs. EOD	EOD vs. Con
Gray matter volume	0.368 ± 0.005	0.373 ± 0.008	0.366 ± 0.009	1.68	0.565	0.364	0.568
White matter volume	0.338 ± 0.006	0.363 ± 0.009	0.363 ± 0.010	4.60	0.070	0.731	**0.044**
MWT	31.53 ± 2.58	29.37 ± 3.42	31.07 ± 2.84	3.05	0.883	0.280	0.057
CVLTIs	60.75 ± 1.44	58.05 ± 2.19	50.67 ± 2.44	6.20	**0.001**	**0.042**	0.460
CVLTvfw1	13.14 ± 0.42	12.43 ± 0.63	9.84 ± 0.71	7.85	**<0.001**	**0.014**	0.728
CVLTvfw2	13.56 ± 0.44	13.33 ± 0.66	10.69 ± 0.74	5.42	**0.002**	**0.017**	0.986
TMT A	27.16 ± 7.78	35.69 ± 12.98	38.14 ± 12.95	6.79	**0.007**	0.819	**0.035**
TMT B	56.65 ± 17.41	72.63 ± 28.89	86.64 ± 38.00	6.97	**0.003**	0.349	0.135
TMT total	83.75 ± 22.50	108.31 ± 39.28	119.07 ± 55.25	5.58	**0.013**	0.723	0.090
BDI II	2.48 ± 1.31	13.26 ± 2.08	7.76 ± 2.24	10.6	0.051	0.103	0.001
BRMAS	0.49 ± 0.27	1.17 ± 0.41	0.41 ± 0.46	1.044	0.890	0.258	0.687
SCL 90	0.20 ± 0.07	0.74 ± 0.11	0.469 ± 0.12	9.29	0.065	0.13	0.000
STAI_G	34.12 ± 2.16	35.38 ± 3.00	34.69 ± 3.40	2.782	0.891	0.89	0.116

CVLT, California Verbal Learning Task CVLTIs; BDI II, Beck depression Inventory; BRMAS, Bech Rafaelsen Mania Scale; MWT, Mehrfachwahl-Wortschatz-Test; SCL90, STAI-G: State-Trait Anxiety Inventory; SCL 90, Symptom checklist 90 items; EOD, Early Onset of Disease (<27 years); LOD, Late Onset of Disease (≥27 years) Estimate Mean. **P = significant on a ≤ 0.05-threshold. Values are highlighted in bold to show significant comparisons at p < 0.05 threshold.*

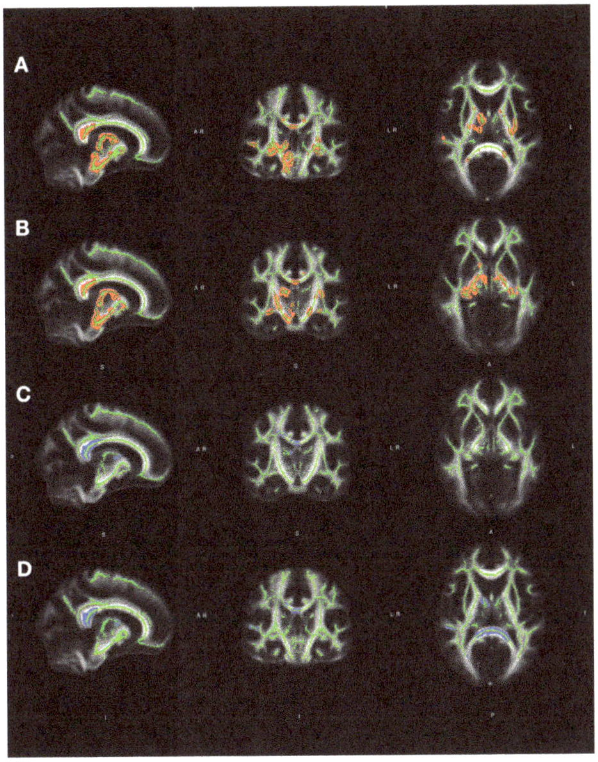

FIGURE 1 | (A, B) Significant group effect adjusted for age and gender (thresholded at p, $p \leq 0.001$) for voxel-wise statistics comparisons (late vs. early onset BD) with whole-brain FA in white matter areas of both hemispheres shown on skeletonised FA maps, using the standard MNI152 1 x 1 x 1 mm brain template; **(C, D)** Significant group effect adjusted for age and gender (thresholded at $p < 0.001$) for voxel-wise statistics comparisons (LOD vs. controls) with whole-brain FA in white matter areas of both hemispheres shown on skeletonised FA maps, using the standard MNI152 1 × 1 × 1 mm brain template. Color-code: red-yellow: early onset BD > LOD, blue-lightblue: controls > LOD. The FA skeleton is marked in green. All images are shown in radiological convention (left is right). Coordinates: **(A)** e **(D)**: X: 10, Y: −8, Z:10; **(B)** e **(C)**: X: 12, Y:−16, Z:4.

nucleus, external capsule (left), midbrain (right), precentral gyrus (right), posterior limb of the internal capsule (bilateral), cerebral peduncle (right), globus pallidus (bilateral).

LOD vs. Controls

LOD subjects exhibited significantly reduced FA in the posterior cingulate, proportionally distributed on both hemispheres, when compared to healthy controls, in the following tracts: splenium of the corpus callosum (right and left), cingulate (right), superior frontal gyrus (right), corpus callosum frontal (right), anterior thalamic radiation (right), ventroanterior thalamic nucleus (right), superior temporal gyrus (right), posterior thalamic radiation (right).

Controls vs. Early Onset BD

EOB did not show any statistically significant difference when compared to healthy controls.

Correlations Between Neuropsychological Measurements and FA Values

LOD vs. EOD

The mean correlations between neuropsychological tests and WM tracts are depicted in the **Table 3**, **Figure 2**. Among LOD participants, left inferior longitudinal fasciculus exhibited moderate positive correlations with CVLT1 ($r = 0.559, p = 0.010$) and CVLT2 ($r = 0.540$, $p = 0.010$); on the other hand, worse performance on CVLTdw was correlated with higher FA in the right inferior longitudinal fasciculus.

LOD vs. Healthy Controls

No statistical significant correlations were found. A trend toward significant negative correlation between CVLTdw and FA in the left cingulum hippocampus could be noted ($r = -489, p = 0.076$) and MWT showed a trend toward positive correlation with FA in the anterior thalamic radiation left hemisphere ($r = 0.521$, $p = 0.056$).

Correlations Between Clinical Symptoms and FA Values

LOD vs. EOD

For LOD individuals, GSI-SCL-90 global scores were moderately correlated with left cingulate hippocampus ($r = 0.564^*$, $p = 0.036$), right superior longitudinal fasciculus temporal part ($r = 0.593$, $p = 0.025$) and left cingulum fibers ($r = 0.617$, $p = 0.019$). Additionally, Gn-SCL-G90 was negatively correlated with right superior longitudinal fasciculus ($r = -0.603$, $p = 0.023$).

LOD vs. Healthy Controls

Manic symptoms rated by the BRMAS1 correlated positively with FA values in the Forceps Major ($r = 0.723$, $p = 0.004$) and GSI-SCL-90 correlated positively with right superior longitudinal fasciculus temporal part ($r = 0.571$, $p = 0.033$); STAI-G correlated with left cortical spinal tract ($r = 0.649, p = 0.042$).

DISCUSSION

The current study examined WM microstructural integrity in EOD and LOD patients in comparison with healthy controls. Our findings revealed widespread WM changes in the LOD when compared with EOD individuals, particularly in the right hemisphere. No significant abnormalities in diffusion parameters were observed between EOD and healthy controls. Our findings also demonstrated significant cognitive differences between EOD and LOD, particularly in the episodic memory, as observed with CVLT tasks. Contrasting with these results, EOD and LOD did not differ in terms of executive functioning performance. Overall, our study extended the current evidence by showing the presence of several WM abnormalities in late-onset presentation of BD.

The main WM alterations observed in the LOD group comprised the corpus callosum, fornix, cingulum fibers, nucleus accumbens, anterior thalamic radiation, and thalamus, all of them important structures associated with emotional regulation and memory functioning (31–34). The posterior cingulate, for instance, is a key component of the default mode network

TABLE 3 | Pearson rank correlations between FA values and cognitive variables.

FA	TMT A	TMT B	MWT	CVLT total	CVLT1	CVLT2	CVLT DW
INFERIOR LONGITUDINAL FASCICULUS (LEFT)							
Early onset	0.311	0.169	−0.282	−0.235	−0.199	−0.101	−0.215
Late onset	0.020	0.488	0.358	−0.205	**−0.559***	**−0.540***	0.062
INFERIOR LONGITUDINAL FASCICULUS (RIGHT)							
Early onset	0.130	0.270	0.073	**−0.557***	−0.460	−0.255	−0.488
Late onset	0.051	0.316	0.165	−0.508	−0.349	−0.432	**−0.596***
UNCINATE FASCICULUS LEFT							
Early onset	0.372	0.151	−0.145	−0.126	−0.157	−0.092	−0.214
Late onset	−0.114	0.463	0.312	−0.177	−0.421	−0.387	−0.328
UNCINATE FASCICULUS RIGHT							
Early onset	0.248	0.346	0.184	0.077	0.211	0.280	−0.214
Late onset	−0.516	−0.424	0.550	−0.059	0.039	0.083	−0.007
SUPERIOR LONGITUDINAL FASCICULUS -TEMPORAL PART (LEFT)							
Early onset	0.057	−0.034	−0.152	−0.514*	**−0.609***	−0.376	−0.291
Late onset	0.112	0.427	0.270	−0.017	−0.003	−0.005	0.071
SUPERIOR LONGITUDINAL FASCICULUS -TEMPORAL PART (RIGHT)							
Early onset	0.120	0.067	0.208	−0.115	−0.080	0.171	0.020
Late onset	0.094	0.453	0.394	−0.117	−0.437	−0.469	−0.426

FA, fractional anisotropy; MWT, Mehrfachwahl-Wortschatz-Test; CVLT, California Verbal Learning Test; CVLT1, CVLT delayed free recall 1; CVLT 2, CVLT delayed free recall 2; CVLT DW, CVLT discriminality; SLF, Superior Longitudinal Fasciculus; TMT, Trail Making Test.
*$p < 0.05$.

(DMN), a hub of WM tracts typically showing more activity during rest than in response to external stimulation, for example, during cognitive tasks (35, 36). Disturbances in DMN regions as a possible underlying pathophysiological mechanism in psychiatric diseases like schizophrenia, Alzheimer's disease (AD), and depression (36–38) have been reported more consistently by functional and structural MRI studies. On the other hand, the thalamus, nucleus accumbens and fornix comprise the limbic system, which is regarded as a consistent network associated with BD (39); Thalamic projections, mostly through the fornix, also connect with the hippocampus (40) and microstructural alterations in thalamic fibers have also been reported in several studies with BD (41–45), particularly in the right hemisphere (42, 43, 46). Our findings showing an absence of differences in executive function and worse performance on memory retrieval in the LOD group can also be supported by studies depicting a relatively sparing of working memory and executive functions in BD with later onset, in detriment of processing speed and episodic memory impairment (5, 9). In addition, only minor cognitive differences, particularly in the processing speed, were perceived between EOD and controls. The relatively higher average education of EOD subjects may account for these results, as supported by previous evidence showing higher education as one important moderator decreasing the extent of cognitive impairment between BD and controls (47).

The interpretation of our results in terms of putative mechanisms underlying DTI alterations and the clinical course of BD is puzzling. First, due to the cross-section nature, it remains unclear whether WM abnormalities are cause or consequence of late-onset BD. Secondly, whether WM microstructural changes are the result of primary or second pathological processes (i.e., WM primary degeneration, metabolic or endothelial changes affecting subcortical microvessels, WM degeneration due to GM atrophy) is largely unknown. Although a number of BD studies have linked cognitive decline to volumetric changes, particularly GM reductions (48), the effect these measurements on cognitive or mood variables was considered small in our study, and no significant differences in GM were observed between any group comparison. The absence of macrostructural reductions in LOD relatively to controls was described by Delaloye (5). Taken together, our results suggest that macroscopic volumes changes in WM or GM may not be the core of neurocognitive changes associated with the later onset of BD, as previously suggested (49).

Although we cannot draw any firm conclusions about the neurodegenerative, long-term nature of the observed anatomical changes, the lack of correlation between cognitive variables and age or years of illness speaks against purely progressive neurodegenerative changes due to BD. Indeed, BD itself is associated with complex alterations in cell signaling, neurotransmitters, calcium signaling, which may influence on a synergistic way the ability of cells to deal with extracellular stimuli the way patients respond to environmental events (50). Hence, we may find a better understanding of our findings through alternative hypotheses; the first is the Neuroplasticity model, which addresses the role of reduced connectivity between glial cells and neurons as a putative mechanism affecting synaptic transmission in distributive networks; these neurobiological changes have been reported in the hippocampus and could be associated with the onset and duration of the disease (50, 51) Furthermore, genetic, experimental and lifestyle factor have

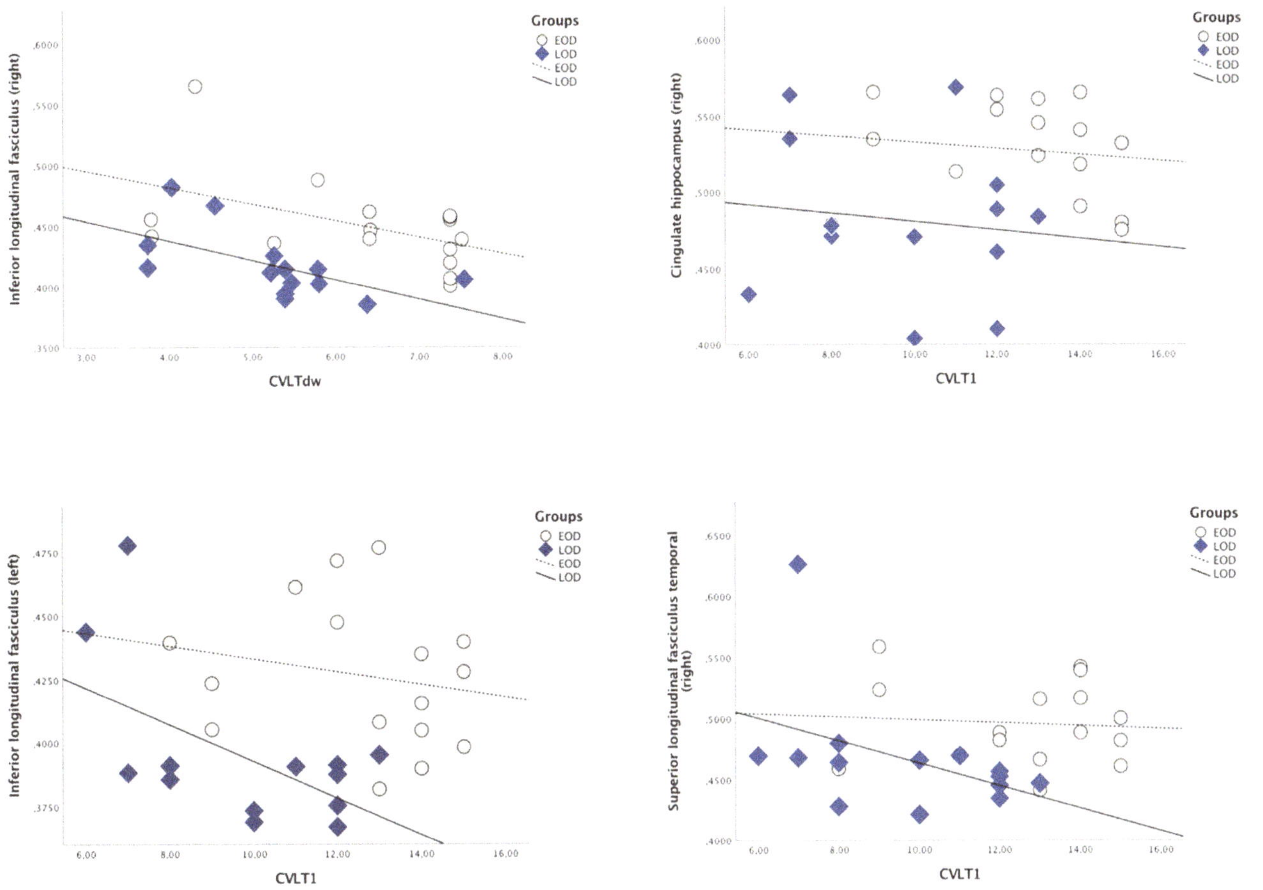

FIGURE 2 | Scatterplot depicting Pearson correlations between WM tracts and CVLT subtests (for correlation values, please refer to the **Table 3**).

cumulative effects throughout lifespan (52). Therefore, brain structure and cognitive and behavior changes found in the LOD may both result from poor succeeded compensatory mechanisms, as posited by the Scaffolding model (53). Finally, our findings may also be interpreted according to the Resource-Modulation hypothesis, which assumes that losses in brain structure resource in normal aging (like the case of WM microstructural abnormalities) modulate the effects of common genetic variations, magnifying its effect on cognitive and behavior performance (emotional imbalance) in late adulthood or even late life (54).

LIMITATIONS

As some of the strengths of the current investigation, we assessed a relatively high number of BD patients ($n = 30$) in a remitted state of illness through a multimodal approach, including voxel-based DTI, ROI DTI and VBM of GM; in addition, the high number of directions in the DTI sequence enhanced the validity of results, as suggested by previous studies on the field of BD (45). However, a few limitations need to be addressed. Firstly, all patients have been treated with psychiatric medication during the study investigation. However, we tested the potential influence of psychiatric medication on the structural brain changes and failed to show any associations DTI parameters and medication status or duration of medication. The absence of medication-related structural changes in BD subjects is in agreement with prior studies (8, 12). In despite of that, we were not able to fully control the effect of lithium over the years and thus complete rule out structural changes due to drug therapy. Finally, there is a lack of a consistent definition of EOD and LOD. Indeed, there is no consensual agreement on which age-point should reference the cut off line between EOD and LOD. Different criteria for defining age of onset among LOD, including cut off age of 38.8 (5) and earlier age, around 34.13 (9), have been reported. In despite of the inconsistences on the optimal cut off for defining younger and older subjects, our findings provided additional support on neuroimaging studies using age at onset to identify more homogeneous groups of BD, which may represent distinct subtypes of the disease.

CONCLUDING REMARKS

Our study found more widespread WM microstructural in LOD in comparison with early onset BD and controls, with differences being more pronounced in the right hemisphere and in neuronal circuits associated with episodic memory. The significance of such findings is still complex to interpret, but may suggest a closer association between WM microstructural alterations, cognitive impairment and the development of mood changes in older adults. Conversely, the early onset of BD was not associated with either micro or macrostructural age-related brain alterations; this finding represents an evidence against the neurodegeneration hypothesis among early onset BD. While the nature of WM pathological findings in the LOD remains largely unknown, there is a need to clarify whether these findings represent, in its nature, a result of complex pathological processes underpinning BD, particularly those involving the interplay of genetic predisposition, aging, cognitive resilience, regional tract degeneration, and neuronal circuitry depletion. One may also argue whether these WM changes represent a brain endophenotype pointing a higher risk to develop LOD. Future studies with larger samples, follow up measurement and a more universal accepted definition of late and early onset BD will help to clarify these issues.

AUTHOR CONTRIBUTIONS

GA, VO method design, systematic review of literature and results compilation (including creation of figures and tables), writing of the manuscript (abstract, introduction, methods, results, discussion, limitations and conclusions), selection and organization of bibliographic references; CK, discussion of the theory and method, critical review and text editing; AR, JP, discussion of the theory, critical review, and text editing; FS, discussion of theory, writing of the manuscript, and critical review; AC, discussion of the theory and method, writing of the manuscript, critical review, and text editing; MP, statistical analysis, writing of the manuscript; BR and RF data acquisition, patient selection, statistical analysis; DP, method design, critical review, text editing.

ACKNOWLEDGMENTS

MRI was performed at the Frankfurt Brain Imaging Centre, supported by the German Research Council (DFG) and the German Ministry for Education and Research (BMBF; Brain Imaging Center, Goethe-Universität, Frankfurt/Main, DLR 01GO0203). Thanks are also due to the Brazilian National Council of Research (CNPq) for funding Andre Férrer Carvalho (CNPq research fellowship awards level II) and GA, who received a post doctorate scholarship support from the CNPq (process 209981/2013-0) in an exchange cooperation program with the Goethe-Universität. The authors report no conflict of interest.

REFERENCES

1. National Institute of Mental Health. *Bipolar Disorder*. Bethesda, MD (Assessed May 24, 2018) (2018).
2. Clemente AS, Diniz BS, Nicolato R, Kapczinski FP, Soares JC, Firmo JO, et al. Bipolar disorder prevalence: a systematic review and meta-analysis of the literature. *Rev Bras Psiquiatr.* (2015) 37:155–61. doi: 10.1590/1516-4446-2012-1693
3. Prabhakar D, Balon, R. Late-onset bipolar disorder: a case for careful appraisal. *Psychiatry* (2010) 7:34–7.
4. Bora E, Yucel M, Pantelis, C. Cognitive endophenotypes of bipolar disorder: a meta-analysis of neuropsychological deficits in euthymic patients and their first-degree relatives. *J Affect Disord.* (2009) 113:1–20. doi: 10.1016/j.jad.2008.06.009
5. Delaloye C, Moy G, Baudois S, de Bilbao F, Remund CD, Hofer F, et al. Cognitive features in euthymic bipolar patients in old age. *Bipolar Disord.* (2009) 11:735–43. doi: 10.1111/j.1399-5618.2009.00741.x
6. Sexton CE, Mackay CE, Ebmeier, KP. A systematic review of diffusion tensor imaging studies in affective disorders. *Biol Psychiatry* (2009) 66:814–23. doi: 10.1016/j.biopsych.2009.05.024
7. Bellani M, Yeh, P-H, Tansella M, Balestrieri M, Soares JC, Brambilla, P. DTI studies of corpus callosum in bipolar disorder. *Biochem Soc Trans.* (2009) 37(Pt 5):1096–8. doi: 10.1042/BST0371096
8. Barnea-Goraly N, Chang KD, Karchemskiy A, Howe ME, Reiss AL. Limbic and corpus callosum aberrations in adolescents with bipolar disorder: a tract-based spatial statistics analysis. *Biol Psychiatry* (2009) 66:238–44. doi: 10.1016/j.biopsych.2009.02.025
9. Delaloye C, Moy G, de Bilbao F, Weber K, Baudois S, Haller S, et al. Longitudinal analysis of cognitive performances and structural brain changes in late-life bipolar disorder. *Int J Geriatr Psychiatry* (2011) 26:1309–18. doi: 10.1002/gps.268
10. Oertel-Knöchel V, Reuter J, Reinke B, Marbach K, Feddern R, Alves G, et al. Association between age of disease-onset, cognitive performance and cortical thickness in bipolar disorders. *J Affect Disord.* (2015) 174:627–35. doi: 10.1016/j.jad.2014.10.060
11. Torgerson CM, Irimia A, Leow AD, Bartzokis G, Moody TD, Jennings RG, et al. DTI tractography and white matter fiber tract characteristics in euthymic bipolar I patients and healthy control subjects. *Brain Imaging Behav.* (2013) 7:129-39. doi: 10.1007/s11682-012-9202-3
12. Tamashiro JH, Zung S, Zanetti MV, de Castro CC, Vallada H, Busatto GF, et al. Increased rates of white matter hyperintensities in late-onset bipolar disorder. *Bipolar Disord.* (2008) 10:765–75. doi: 10.1111/j.1399-5618.2008.00621.x
13. Bruno S, Cercignani M, Ron, MA. White matter abnormalities in bipolar disorder: a voxel-based diffusion tensor imaging study. *Bipolar Disord.* (2008) 10:460–8. doi: 10.1111/j.1399-5618.2007.00552.x
14. Berk M, Kapczinski F, Andreazza AC, Dean OM, Giorlando F, Maes M, et al. Pathways underlying neuroprogression in bipolar disorder: focus on inflammation, oxidative stress and neurotrophic factors. *Neurosci Biobehav Rev.* (2011) 35:804–17. doi: 10.1016/j.neubiorev.2010.10.001
15. American Psychiatric Association. *Diagnostic and Statistical Manual of Mental Disorders. 4th Edn.* Washington, DC: American Psychiatric Association (1994).
16. Manchia M, Maina G, Carpiniello B, Pinna F, Steardo L, D'Ambrosio V, et al. Clinical correlates of age at onset distribution in bipolar disorder: a comparison between diagnostic subgroups. *Int J Bipolar Disord.* (2017) 5:28. doi: 10.1186/s40345-017-0097-1
17. Hautzinger M, Keller F, Kühner C. *Das Beck Depressionsinventar, I. I. Deutsche Bearbeitung und Handbuch zum BDI II.* Frankfurt: Harcourt Test Services (2006).
18. Bech P, Rafaelsen O, Kramp P, Bolwig T. The mania rating scale: scale construction and inter-observer agreement. *Neuropharmacology* (1978) 17:430–1.
19. Wittchen HU, Wunderlich U, Gruschwitz S, Zaudig M. *Strukturiertes Klinisches Interview für DSM-IV (SKID).* Göttingen: Beltz-Test (1996).
20. Lehrl S. *Mehrfachwahl-Wortschatz-Intelligenztest M-W-T B.* Göttingen: Spitta Verlag GmbH (2005).
21. Delis DC, Kramer JH, Kaplan E, Ober, BA. *CVLT, California Verbal Learning Test: Adult Version: Manual.* Psychological Corporation (1987).

22. Krohne HW, Egloff B, Kohlmann C-W, Tausch A. *Positive and Negative Affect Schedule-German Version. American Psychological Association* (2016). Available online at: http://doi.apa.org/getdoi.cfm?doi=10.1037/t49650-000
23. Franke, GH. *Die Symptom-Checkliste von Derogatis (SCL-90-R) - Deutsche Version - Manual, 2nd Edn.* Göttingen: Beltz Test (2000).
24. Griswold MA, Jakob PM, Heidemann RM, Nittka M, Jellus V, Wang J, et al. Generalized autocalibrating partially parallel acquisitions (GRAPPA). *Magn Reson Med.* (2002) 47:1202–10. doi: 10.1002/mrm.10171
25. Deichmann R, Schwarzbauer C, Turner R. Optimisation of the 3D MDEFT sequence for anatomical brain imaging: technical implications at 1.5 and 3 T. *NeuroImage* (2004) 21:757–67. doi: 10.1016/j.neuroimage.2003.09.062
26. Smith SM, Jenkinson M, Johansen-Berg H, Rueckert D, Nichols TE, Mackay CE, et al. Tract-based spatial statistics: voxelwise analysis of multi-subject diffusion data. *NeuroImage* (2006) 31:1487–505. doi: 10.1016/j.neuroimage.2006.02.024
27. Donahue MJ, Hoogduin H, Smith SM, Siero JCW, Chappell M, Petridou N, et al. Spontaneous blood oxygenation level-dependent fMRI signal is modulated by behavioral state and correlates with evoked response in sensorimotor cortex: a 7.0-T fMRI study. *Hum Brain Mapp.* (2012) 33:511–22. doi: 10.1002/hbm.21228
28. Ashburner J, Friston KJ. Why voxel-based morphometry should be used. *NeuroImage* (2001) 14:1238–43. doi: 10.1006/nimg.2001.0961
29. Nichols TE, Holmes, AP. Nonparametric permutation tests for functional neuroimaging: a primer with examples. *Hum Brain Mapp.* (2002) 15:1–25. doi: 10.1002/hbm.1058
30. Almeida JRC, Mechelli A, Hassel S, Versace A, Kupfer DJ, Phillips, ML. Abnormally increased effective connectivity between parahippocampal gyrus and ventromedial prefrontal regions during emotion labeling in bipolar disorder. *Psychiatry Res Neuroimaging* (2009) 174:195–201. doi: 10.1016/j.pscychresns.2009.04.015
31. Choo IH, Lee DY, Oh JS, Lee JS, Lee DS, Song IC, et al. Posterior cingulate cortex atrophy and regional cingulum disruption in mild cognitive impairment and Alzheimer's disease. *Neurobiol Aging* (2010) 31:772–9. doi: 10.1016/j.neurobiolaging.2008.06.015
32. Torso M, Serra L, Giulietti G, Spanò B, Tuzzi E, Koch G, et al. Strategic lesions in the anterior thalamic radiation and apathy in early Alzheimer's disease. Ginsberg SD, editor. *PLoS ONE* (2015) 10:e0124998. doi: 10.1371/journal.pone.0124998
33. Mielke MM, Okonkwo OC, Oishi K, Mori S, Tighe S, Miller MI, et al. Fornix integrity and hippocampal volume predict memory decline and progression to Alzheimer's disease. Alzheimers *Dement J Alzheimers Assoc.* (2012) 8:105–13. doi: 10.1016/j.jalz.2011.05.2416
34. Cavallari M, Moscufo N, Meier D, Skudlarski P, Pearlson GD, White WB, et al. Thalamic fractional anisotropy predicts accrual of cerebral white matter damage in older subjects with small-vessel disease. *J Cereb Blood Flow Metab.* (2014) 34:1321–7. doi: 10.1038/jcbfm.2014.86
35. Raichle ME, MacLeod AM, Snyder AZ, Powers WJ, Gusnard DA, Shulman, GL. A default mode of brain function. *Proc Natl Acad Sci USA.* (2001) 98:676–82. doi: 10.1073/pnas.98.2.676
36. Greicius MD, Srivastava G, Reiss AL, Menon, V. Default-mode network activity distinguishes Alzheimer's disease from healthy aging: evidence from functional MRI. *Proc Natl Acad Sci USA.* (2004) 101:4637–42. doi: 10.1073/pnas.0308627101
37. Sheline YI, Barch DM, Price JL, Rundle MM, Vaishnavi SN, Snyder AZ, et al. The default mode network and self-referential processes in depression. *Proc Natl Acad Sci USA.* (2009) 106:1942–7. doi: 10.1073/pnas.08126 86106
38. Wu M, Andreescu C, Butters MA, Tamburo R, Reynolds CF III, Aizenstein, H. Default-mode network connectivity and white matter burden in late-life depression. *Psychiatry Res.* (2011) 194:39–46. doi: 10.1016/j.pscychresns.2011.04.003
39. Strakowski SM, editor. *The Bipolar Brain: Integrating Neuroimaging With Genetics.* New York, NY: Oxford University Press (2012). p. 272.
40. Oishi K, Faria AV, Zijl PCMV, Mori, S. *MRI Atlas of Human White Matter.* London, UK: Academic Press (2010). p. 267.
41. Heng S, Song AW, Sim, K. White matter abnormalities in bipolar disorder: insights from diffusion tensor imaging studies. *J Neural Transm.* (2010) 117:639–54. doi: 10.1007/s00702-010-0368-9
42. Chan W-Y, Yang G-L, Chia M-Y, Woon P-S, Lee J, Keefe R, et al. Cortical and subcortical white matter abnormalities in adults with remitted first-episode mania revealed by Tract-Based Spatial Statistics. *Bipolar Disord.* (2010) 12:383–9. doi: 10.1111/j.1399-5618.2010.00829.x.
43. Ha TH, Her JY, Kim JH, Chang JS, Cho HS, Ha, K. Similarities and differences of white matter connectivity and water diffusivity in bipolar I and II disorder. *Neurosci Lett.* (2011) 505:150–4. doi: 10.1016/j.neulet.2011.10.009
44. Lin F, Weng S, Xie B, Wu G, Lei H. Abnormal frontal cortex white matter connections in bipolar disorder: a DTI tractography study. *J Affect Disord.* (2011) 131:299–306. doi: 10.1016/j.jad.2010.12.018
45. Mahon K, Wu J, Malhotra AK, Burdick KE, DeRosse P, Ardekani BA, et al. A voxel-based diffusion tensor imaging study of white matter in bipolar disorder. *Neuropsychopharmacology* (2009) 34:1590–600. doi: 10.1038/npp.2008.216
46. Cui L, Chen Z, Deng W, Huang X, Li M, Ma X, et al. Assessment of white matter abnormalities in paranoid schizophrenia and bipolar mania patients. *Psychiatry Res.* (2011) 194:347–53. doi: 10.1016/j.pscychresns.2011.03.010
47. Mann-Wrobel MC, Carreno JT, Dickinson, D. Meta-analysis of neuropsychological functioning in euthymic bipolar disorder: an update and investigation of moderator variables: euthymic bipolar meta-analysis. *Bipolar Disorders.* (2011) 13:334–42. doi: 10.1111/j.1399-5618.2011.00935.x
48. Ekman CJ, Lind J, Rydén E, Ingvar M, Landén, M. Manic episodes are associated with grey matter volume reduction - a voxel-based morphometry brain analysis. *Acta Psychiatr Scand.* (2010) 122:507–15. doi: 10.1111/j.1600-0447.2010.01586.x
49. Rej S, Butters MA, Aizenstein HJ, Begley A, Tsay J, Reynolds CF, et al. Neuroimaging and neurocognitive abnormalities associated with bipolar disorder in old age: neuroimaging and neurocognitive abnormalities in BD. *Int J Geriatr Psychiatry* (2014) 29:421–7. doi: 10.1002/gps.4021
50. Fries GR, Magalhães PVS, Kapczinski F, Berk M. Neuroprogression and biological underpinnings of staging in bipolar disorder. In: da Silva Magalhães PV, Vieta E, Berk M, editors, *Neuroprogression and Staging in Bipolar Disorder. 1st Edn.* Cambridge: Oxford University Press (2015). p. 344.
51. Eastwood SL, Harrison PJ. Synaptic pathology in the anterior cingulate cortex in schizophrenia and mood disorders. a review and a Western blot study of synaptophysin, GAP-43 and the complexins. *Brain Res Bull.* (2001) 55:569–78. doi: 10.1016/S0361-9230(01)00530-5
52. Park DC, Festini SB. *The Middle-Aged Brain A Cognitive Neuroscience Perspective. In: Cognitive Neuroscience of Aging: Linking Cognitive and Cerebral Aging. 2 Edn.* Cambridge: Oxford University Press (2017). p. 606.
53. Reuter-Lorenz PA, Park DC. How does it stac up? Revisiting the scaffolding theory of aging and cognition. *Neuropsychol Rev.* (2014) 24:355–70. doi: 10.1007/s11065-014-9270-9
54. Papenberg G, Lindenberger U, Bäckman L. Aging-related magnification of genetic effects on cognitive and brain integrity. *Trends Cogn Sci.* (2015) 19:506–14. doi: 10.1016/j.tics.2015.06.008

21

Gene × Environment Interaction in Developmental Disorders: Where do we Stand and What's Next?

Gianluca Esposito[1,2], Atiqah Azhari[1] and Jessica L. Borelli[3]*

[1] *Psychology Program, Nanyang Technological University, Singapore, Singapore,* [2] *Department of Psychology and Cognitive Science, University of Trento, Trento, Italy,* [3] *Department of Psychological Science, University of California, Irvine, Irvine, CA, United States*

***Correspondence:**
Gianluca Esposito
gianluca.esposito@ntu.edu.sg;
gianluca.esposito@unitn.it

Although the field of psychiatry has witnessed the proliferation of studies on Gene × Environment (G×E) interactions, still limited is the knowledge we possess of G×E interactions regarding developmental disorders. In this perspective paper, we discuss why G×E interaction studies are needed to broaden our knowledge of developmental disorders. We also discuss the different roles of hazardous versus self-generated environmental factors and how these types of factors may differentially engage with an individual's genetic background in predicting a resulting phenotype. Then, we present examplar studies that highlight the role of G×E in predicting atypical developmental trajectories as well as provide insight regarding treatment outcomes. Supported by these examples, we explore the need to move beyond merely examining statistical interactions between genes and the environment, and the motivation to investigate specific genetic susceptibility and environmental contexts that drive developmental disorders. We propose that further parsing of genetic and environmental components is required to fully understand the unique contribution of each factor to the etiology of developmental disorders. Finally, with a greater appreciation of the complexities of G×E interaction, this discussion will converge upon the potential implications for clinical and translational research.

Keywords: gene × environment interaction, developmental disabilities, environmental hazards, genetic risk, self-generated environment, developmental trajectories, treatment outcomes

INTRODUCTION

Neurodevelopmental disorders emerge from numerous genetic and environmental sources, which begin to exert their effects at the embryological and early fetal stages of life (e.g., Brimacombe et al., 2007; Gardener et al., 2009; Esposito and Borelli, 2018). In the clinical setting, deciphering precise etiological pathways is not currently possible. Within the research context, newer screening technologies afford a continual shift from simplistic conventional nature-versus-nurture perspectives toward a nuanced framework of gene-by-environment interactions (G×E) – this shift promotes a more accurate understanding of the complexity of etiological pathways.

To illustrate the genetic complexity mired in the etiology of psychopathology, we must first develop an appreciation of the numerously intricate mechanisms of gene expression. At the level of the genetic structure, mutations in the DNA, such as a change in a single nucleotide base, may cause a significant alteration in the three-dimensional molecular structure of the expressed protein, potentially leading to drastic changes in the organism's traits. On other occasions, the extent to which such mutations affect the individual is dependent upon existing compensatory mechanisms of other interacting genes and gene products (i.e., RNA and proteins) within the same biological pathway, with similar overlapping functions and expression patterns (for a review, see Tautz, 1992). Furthermore, the nature of interaction between genes or gene products may differ according to the temporal (i.e., developmental period), biochemical (i.e., active or resting state of protein) and spatial (i.e., location of interaction within the body) parameters present during gene expression. Genes often do not possess a one-to-one relation with the characteristics that they contribute to (Morange, 2007), and this is the prevalent case for complex behavioral traits, and especially so for developmental disabilities.

In the quest to elucidate specific mechanisms that underpin psychological disorders, scientists have ventured beyond the scope of genetics, and mounting consideration has been paid to the interaction of genes with hazardous environmental factors. Specifically, grasping the concept of adaptation and developmental plasticity necessitates a deliberation of the impacts of genetic determinants, whether alone or in combination with environmental risk factors (i.e., maternal illnesses, maternal nutritional status and environmental toxins). Over the long term, appreciation of specific G×E mechanisms underlying neurodevelopmental disorders should result in more effective risk-mitigating or preventive interventions (Graf et al., 2013), but this promise has yet to be realized, in part because of the complexity of the relations among these factors. On one hand, studies have demonstrated that most cognitive traits as well as psychiatric disorders are moderately to highly heritable (Bishop, 2009); nevertheless, efforts by researchers to identify genes that account for significant portions of variance in these disorders have been fraught with difficulties and have yet to come to fruition. On the other hand, according to the hypothesis of differential susceptibility, the environment is full of potentially hazardous factors, but these factors only affect people with specific genetic predispositions that render them more susceptible to harmful environmental influences (Belsky and Pluess, 2009). Furthermore, many psychiatric disorders are neurodevelopmental in their origins: Human and animal studies point to the importance of a critical period during which neural circuits (that develop from genetic information) can be potentially affected by environmental hazards. In other words, there is a highly plastic critical period, which is a time of great responsiveness of the central nervous system to adverse events (Leonardo et al., 2007; Esposito et al., 2017b; Truzzi et al., 2017, 2018). Similarly, the expression of genetic factors may exert a specific effect in a time-dependent manner. An example of a neural structure that matures in the immediate postnatal period of infancy is the superior olivary complex (SOC), which is responsible for the onset of spatial hearing. Located in the brainstem, the development of this structure occurs over a critical time-window, during which extensive upregulation in the gene expression of serotonin-related genes and genes associated with the peripheral auditory system accompany this maturation (Friauf, 2004). Infants with an underdeveloped SOC may not be able to localize auditory cues from their surroundings, which in turn predispose them to auditory processing disorders and developmental disabilities, including dyslexia and autism spectrum disorder (ASD) (Tallal, 2012). Illustrations such as these lead us to consider G×E as a fluid model where the temporal dynamics play a very important role.

The great challenge in this field is related to how to conduct assessments of G×E relations, and to identify and subsequently set ideal standards for collecting, analyzing, and interpreting the data. When considering G×E interactions in research studies, the very first consideration is how to select the candidate gene/s to study. One pre-requisite of candidate gene selection is the availability of gene-disease databases from an array of past epidemiological and animal model research, as well as linkage and gene expression studies (Green and Moore, 2006). While web resources may expediate the selection of candidate genes, a robust understanding of genetics and neuropsychiatric pathogenesis is nonetheless necessary for optimal selection (Green and Moore, 2006). Which leads us to ask the question, *what can psychology and psychiatry contribute to the study of G×E interactions of developmental disorders?*

The goal we pursue in this perspective paper is to provide a framework that scientists can employ to design feasible theoretically driven studies assessing G×E interactions that have the potential to contribute to the field of developmental psychopathology. It is worth noting that in this paper, we refer to psychopathology as defined by DSM-5 criteria, but we believe that our recommendations are equally relevant for researchers interested in pursuing Research Domain Criteria (R-DoC) – informed projects pertaining to psychological dysfunction. Initiated by the National Institute of Mental Health[1], R-DoC is an unprecedented methodological approach which associates psychiatric problems with symptoms (e.g., low social functioning) instead of psychiatric categories (e.g., depression, borderline personality disorder) (Cuthbert, 2014, 2015). In theory, R-DoC should allow investigation into the causes of psychiatric problems to be liberated of the inaccuracies of diagnostic categorization. In this manner, R-DoC enables research into the basic mechanisms of psychiatric disorders, transcending traditional psychiatric classification (Insel and Cuthbert, 2009; Kozak and Cuthbert, 2016). Recently, studies on developmental disabilities, such as autism spectrum disorders (ASD), have begun to incorporate the R-DoC paradigm (e.g., Montalvo-Ortiz et al., 2015; Foss-Feig et al., 2016). However, to maintain consistency with the majority of the studies we cite in this review, we describe pathology in terms of psychiatric disorders. With the availability of more developed technological and statistical tools, researchers can move beyond employing singular methods examining psychological disorders, and can utilize our suggestions to inform their pursuit of G×E research. In the sections that follow, we provide our recommendations for such a research agenda.

TERMINOLOGY IN G×E

To facilitate comprehension, three key terms will be introduced in this section: single-nucleotide polymorphisms, heritability and

[1] https://www.nimh.nih.gov/research-priorities/rdoc/nimh-rdoc-publications.shtml

phenotypic variance. Firstly, single nucleotide polymorphism (SNP) is a DNA polymorphism that is most typically explored in numerous G×E studies. SNP is a variant in a DNA sequence that occurs commonly in the population (e.g., 1%) in which a single nucleotide base differs between members of the population (e.g., A versus G). Secondly, the term *heritability*, an important concept in G×E studies, refers to the extent to which genetic differences passed down from relatives, as compared to environmental factors, contribute to observed phenotypic differences between two or more individuals. Variations in a certain quality (e.g., height) within the population that are not accounted for by genetic factors could be due to environmental variables, a combination of both factors (such as in G×E interactions), or non-genetic contributions (i.e., residual effects). Lastly, a closely linked concept that is intuitive to the idea of G×E interaction is phenotypic variance. Phenotypic variance typically accounts for the combinatorial effects of genetic and environmental variance in explaining a specific presenting trait.

THEORETICAL FRAMEWORKS: DIATHESIS-STRESS VS. DIFFERENTIAL SUSCEPTIBILITY

Theoretical underpinnings within the G×E field usually fall into one of the two most prominent categories: the diathesis-stress or the differential-susceptibility model. The diathesis-stress model stipulates that an individual who possesses genetic vulnerability may be susceptible to a psychological disorder when exposed to an adverse environment, but the disorder does not manifest without the trigger of an environmental stressor. However, individuals without predisposing genetic susceptibility do not develop a psychological disorder even when faced with adverse environmental conditions. While this model has stimulated exciting research in this field, its disproportionate focus on negative life events, disregarding positive environments, render it myopic in its scope (Belsky and Pluess, 2009). An alternative theoretical framework, the differential-susceptibility perspective, was subsequently proposed (Belsky et al., 2007; Belsky and Pluess, 2009). Instead of suggesting that certain genotypes are intrinsically good or bad, this model proposes that individuals' susceptibility to environmental effects (both negative and positive) differ depending upon genes that are involved in responsivity to environmental states, coined as "plasticity genes." Specifically, plasticity genes can either aggravate the risk of psychopathology in negative environments, or alleviate the risk of psychopathology in positive environments, such that the most distressed individual in an undesirable environment is also the one who is most likely to be aided in a positive environment (Belsky and Pluess, 2009).

CHALLENGE ONE: SELECTING GENETIC VARIANT(S)

Perhaps the first step in beginning the process of designing a G×E study is to decide what gene(s) to study. This decision is greatly influenced by the method employed in conducting the G×E study, in which there are commonly two approaches from which to choose: candidate-gene studies or genome-wide association studies (GWAS). Candidate-gene studies typically focus on individual SNPs based on the argument that these variants have a high likelihood of being implicated in the biological mechanism through which the psychiatric disorder manifests. Some examples of established methods that have been adopted to investigate SNPs in G×E studies include the bivariate linear mixed model (Lee et al., 2015, 2017) and the random regression linear mixed model (Robinson et al., 2017). In the former, association analyses are conducted on SNPs and two environmental traits (e.g., winter-born, not winter-born) in cases and controls. The latter approach, by comparison, is more sophisticated and is based on an algorithm that allows for multivariate analysis of complex traits within the context of multi-trait models (Lee and van der Werf, 2016).

However, each genetic variant usually accounts for only a small slice of the genetic variation of the disorder (Duncan and Keller, 2011). Candidate-gene studies are usually conducted with small sample sizes and thus possess smaller statistical power as compared to GWAS studies. A large proportion of the existing G×E literature comprises of candidate-gene studies, possibly reflecting an increased interest in elucidating specific etiological pathways underlying psychiatric disorders with respect to the genetic polymorphisms under investigation. On the other hand, GWAS studies are conducted with large sample sizes (>1,000) and boast significantly higher statistical power, with no prior conception of specific genetic variants to target. Indeed, GWAS analyses usually scan entire genomes consisting of thousands of individuals to identify numerous associations of genetic variants with specific behavioral traits.

The past decade has witnessed a promising increase in the number of whole-genome screenings being conducted, set within the framework of G×E interactions (Aschard et al., 2012). To estimate the percentage of phenotypic variance from such GWAS studies, a conventional method compares the coefficients of determination across statistical models that either omit or include significantly related variants. The challenge in this approach is that it requires extensive genotypic and phenotypic data which is difficult to procure. Indeed, while genome-wide investigations of developmental disabilities represent the most complex and thorough method of understanding multiple etiological factors underlying developmental disabilities (Munafò and Flint, 2010; Cross-Disorder Group of the Psychiatric Genomics Consortium, 2013; Flint and Munafò, 2013), such designs necessitate larger samples than are typically enrolled in psychological studies.

These types of research projects may be possible if psychologists can collaborate across sites, first conducting genome-wide analyses of smaller samples (e.g., $N = 100$), before pooling these samples together for the purpose of genetic analyses. To facilitate this type of work, we have created a listserv for researchers interested in G×E research in developmental psychopathology (to subscribe, contact the first author). On this listserv, researchers can find colleagues with similar interests in collecting genetic data from participants in cross-sectional or longitudinal studies and can coordinate across studies (in terms of measure/outcome selection, method of collection of genetic material, etc.). Researchers can also forge collaborations with geneticists and assist them in using gold-standard psychiatric measures to assess children's psychopathology in their studies. We hope that this platform will facilitate greater collaborative work which will accelerate progress in this field.

In recent years, an alternative approach to genome-wide analyses has surfaced, utilizing only the summary statistics of GWAS G×E studies. In 2016, two groups of researchers, Pare et al. (2016) and Shi et al. (2016), formulated statistical methods to estimate marginal genetic variance, while simultaneously accounting for sample size limitations, linkage disequilibrium between variants of interest and correlation matrices of SNPs. This promising approach has been further extended by Laville et al. (2018), who implemented statistical packages that aid in the estimation of proportion accounted for by G×E interactions from GWAS summary statistics. In the absence of the ability to undertake a genome-wide analysis, it may be prudent to first understand which genes are most likely to have associations with psychopathology. A good place to start this investigation is with the genetic material that has been described as "generalist genes" (Kovas and Plomin, 2007). Generalist genes are a collection of genes which greatly account for genetic influence on a number of developmental disabilities (e.g., FOXP2, COMT, GABRB3, SHANK1-3, and DISC1). Studies have shown that alterations to this same group of genes exerts a fundamental genetic influence on a number of developmental disabilities, ranging from ASD to schizophrenia (Wang et al., 2016), to intellectual disability (Bhowmik et al., 2011) and attention deficit and hyperactivity disorder (ADHD) (Brinksma et al., 2017; Heinrich et al., 2017). However, the same alterations may also be found in the typical population - in other words, the presence of these genetic alterations alone is not sufficient to predict the resulting pathological phenotype. Indeed, what seems to precipitate the emergence of a typical or atypical phenotype is largely accounted for by the interaction of the environment with these genetic anomalies (Caspi et al., 2002, 2003). Broadly, environmental factors can be categorized into those that represent unwanted external hazards and those that are generated by the individuals (e.g., substance abuse). With this degree of environmental variables, investigators should work towards greater conceptual clarity under this dichotomous framework - either by more concise operationalization of terms or clearer categorization.

Having previously illustrated the complexity of genetic expression in manifesting a phenotype, whereby genes rarely have a one-to-one relation with a specific trait, a more holistic experimental design involves a polygenic approach. Polygenic inheritance refers to features and traits of an individual that develop due to the cumulative effect of several genes. Polygenic traits, such as skin color and behavioral characteristics, differ between individuals by such slight gradations that they are considered to be continuous in nature. While investigation of hypothesis-driven candidate genes has been recommended (Rutter et al., 2006), there is great likelihood that multiple genes function together to mold the genetic risk of developing a psychiatric disorder (Kraft and Aschard, 2015). This approach offers an exciting alternative to designing multigenic G×E studies as it simultaneously considers the contribution of multiple genetic variants commonly linked to a specific psychiatric disorder. Operationally, polygenic analyses are accomplished by tabulating the number of alleles for each SNP and weighting the sum by the effect size obtained from a GWAS, to generate a polygenic risk score (PRS). A higher PRS value indicates a greater genetic predisposition toward developing a psychiatric disorder. Thus, the PRS essentially is a numeric representation of the additive effect of several SNPs, reflecting an individual's genetic profile risk more accurately as compared to single candidate gene analyses. Recently, studies that employ a polygenic approach have elicited larger effect sizes and predictive power (Bulik-Sullivan et al., 2015; Maier et al., 2015). Alas, while the polygenic approach allows for a more complete impression of the genes it does so at the expense of finer genetic resolution, as it leaves investigators unable to identify specific genes associated with the disorder. However, complementary techniques at the level of singular genes can be conducted to supplement polygenic approaches, revealing the unique contribution of relevant variants.

CHALLENGE TWO: SELECTING THE DESIGN

The next step in designing G×E research involves identifying the ideal methodology for examining research questions. We discuss several types of research designs for assessing G×E interactions. The first type of design we consider here is case–control studies. Case–control studies employ correlational analysis to assess the difference in outcomes across two groups. The groups are determined based on genotype - participants who differ in one characteristic (e.g., a specific genotype) are distributed across groups. Investigators then compare participants in these two groups to determine whether this sole differentiating feature (group membership) is responsible for a significant percentage of the variance in the differences between these groups. Although gene–environment interactions may be investigated using case–control paradigms, an issue of concern is choosing of appropriate control subjects for these studies. In case-control studies, the control group (the group lacking the feature under consideration) needs to meet specific and rigid criteria to ensure that eventual differences in the outcomes are actually due to the investigated feature rather than to other spurious variables (for example, participants' age, cultural group, educational level, socio-economic status, or people's past, and current health). Therefore, a thorough consideration of control group characteristics should be performed and inclusion criteria should be tailored to each study to account for the specific characteristics of the considered population. To illustrate the complexity of identifying a case control group, consider the difficulty of finding a control group for a sample of depressed children - should this control group exclude children with anxiety-related symptoms or pathology given the extremely high rates of comorbidity between depression and anxiety (Unick et al., 2009)? Doing so will undoubtedly reduce the generalizability of the findings, yet the creation of four groups (depression only, depression plus anxiety, anxiety only, and no depression or anxiety) necessitates a significantly larger sample. Further, even if this fine-grained clinical distinction is made, there are undoubtedly numerous other variables on which these two groups differ that could be confounded with the variable of interest.

There are also non-traditional study designs, such as those that do not include a control group, which can prove useful to investigators who are interested in adopting a dimensional approach. As compared to a categorical paradigm that presumes distinctive typical and abnormal mental health states, a dimensional approach assumes that traits lie on a continuous spectrum, and one is only diagnosed with a disorder upon presenting symptoms that fall beyond the normative threshold. A dimensional perspective is consistent with the prevailing view of developmental psychopathology. Researchers working within this approach can utilize the following study designs: (a) the case-only study, (b) the case-parental control study, and (c) the affected relative-pair study. Case-only studies allow for the investigation of the association between a genotype and exposure to an environmental variable among case subjects only. For instance, this could involve recruiting a sample of youth with social anxiety disorder and examining the presence of the oxytocin receptor gene (OXTR) in combination with parental overcontrol, an environmental risk factor involved in the emergence of anxiety in children (Borelli et al., 2015). To calculate additive effects of psychopathological risk, due to simultaneous incidence of adverse environmental and genetic factors, odds ratios are interpreted as a synergy index, with the environment and the genotype assumed to be independent of each other (Rothman, 1986).

In the absence of a direct association between genotype and disease, case-parental control studies allow for the comparison of genotypic distribution of case subjects with the expected distribution based on parental genotypes. For instance, researchers may wish to examine the children of parents with and without autoimmune diseases for their risk for ASD (for a review, see Chen et al., 2016); information on case subjects' exposure status may be utilized to stratify the effect of a genotype.

In affected relative-pair studies, such as in twin-studies, comparison between allelic distribution, identical by descent between pairs of affected relatives, is made in contrast with the expected distribution in the case of an absence of genetic linkage between the locus and the disease; comparative analysis can be stratified according to extent of environmental exposure (i.e., exposure status). Twin-studies allow researchers to estimate the contributions and additive effects of genetic and environmental factors upon the emergence of the stipulated phenotype. An example of this can be observed in the study by Ivanov et al. (2017), where a twin-studies design was utilized to assess the influence of gene and environment on the emergence of hoarding symptoms.

Most of the methods above possess certain limitations, such as linkage disequilibrium (Slatkin, 2008), exceptions to the assumption of simple Mendelian transmission (e.g., polygenic traits), an inability to measure exposure effects accurately (Wong et al., 2004; Lobach et al., 2008; Holmans et al., 2009), the lack of availability of high-throughput environmental data (Patel et al., 2013) and imprecision of the type of G×E interaction being investigated: multiplicative scale (i.e., ratio measures of association) as compared to an additive scale (i.e., absolute difference measure of association). Despite these shortcomings, they serve as important tools to assess G×E etiology in disease states (Khoury and Flanders, 1996).

In the past decade, the advent of GWAS, which analyzed different individuals' genetic variants in order to associate a variant to a particular trait, has also driven the evolution of G×E research. Although GWAS did not characterize environmental factors, studies on G×E interactions nonetheless benefitted from drawing upon the vast body of data generated from GWAS. These studies have begun to complement findings from GWAS by integrating environmental data, including a substantial focus on exposure assessment, with relevant genetic variants that have been discovered (e.g., Thomas, 2010). Genetic variants commonly investigated in G×E research are SNPs.

However, as previously mentioned, etiological analyses of disorders based on a single genetic and environmental contributing factor represents a hasty oversimplification of G×E interactions. Recently, multigenic studies, which employ a polygenic approach that aggregate genetic markers across an array of SNPs, have emerged to reveal G×E signals which have previously gone undetected in individual SNP analyses. For instance, Guo et al. (2017) utilized PRSs to examine a combined GWAS study on common genetic markers underlying ASD and obsessive–compulsive disorder (OCD). Additionally, greater emphasis on characterizing environmental factors has led to more comprehensive G×E studies that employed a Multi-G–Multi-E framework (Dai et al., 2013; Naj et al., 2013; Patel et al., 2013; Velez Edwards et al., 2013). The continual progress of the field in recent years has also prompted the development of more advanced G×E statistical models using GWAS data, such as the mixed model for polygenic interactions (G×EMM) that aggregates minor G×E interactions distributed across various parts of the genome, thus possibly capturing "missing" heritability (Dahl et al., 2018). Another statistical model, which has emerged from the genomics era, is the structured linear mixed model (StructLMM), which efficiently computes the complex interaction of genetic loci with multiple different environments (Moore et al., 2018). With a growing interest in the G×E etiology of psychiatric disorders, a proposed model to address this need is the multivariate reaction norm model (RNM). The RNM allows for the joint modeling of genotype and covariate (i.e., environmental risk factor that affects complex trait). As the covariate is also modulated by genetic and environmental factors, a joint model approach allows for the simultaneous investigation of correlation and interaction effects (Ni et al., 2018).

The complexity of G×E findings in the field of developmental disabilities will be optimally captured from meta-analytic studies, which have the advantage of critically assessing the theoretical and statistical soundness of any given G×E study based on systematically pooled information. However, methods for the meta-analysis of studies investigating interactions are not well developed (Taylor and Kim-Cohen, 2007). In addition, procedures to determine the sample size needed to detect gene–environment interactions are still not well defined (Yang et al., 2003). We encourage researchers, particularly those without significant grant funding, to consider embracing meta-analysis as a design of choice – conducting a meta-analysis enables researchers to become acquainted with the field, to identify gaps in the literature, and to provide a useful empirical synthesis of the observed pattern of effects.

CHALLENGE THREE: SELECTING THE ENVIRONMENTAL FACTOR(S) OF INTEREST

In addition to identifying gene(s) of interest and the research design, it is also important to devote significant thought to identifying the environmental factor(s) of interest and having a clear conceptualization of what that environment, and the resulting G×E interaction, would represent. In the event in which the causal direction of the environmental variable in question is not unequivocally known, investigators may opt to apply a Mendelian Randomization (MR) method to first determine the direction of effect prior to the G×E investigation (Davey Smith et al., 2005). This method capitalizes on common genetic polymorphisms that have been found to modulate patterns of exposures (e.g., tendency to consume alcohol), which allows us to establish an association between a particular genotype and an intermediate phenotype. Such information may provide a more robust theoretical ground upon which G×E analysis can then be conducted.

Moving beyond this basic nature-nurture question, multivariate genetic analyses have revealed that genes serve as 'generalists' that broadly determine the range of one's learning capacity (especially in the domain of learning abilities and disabilities), while environments act as 'specialists' which fine-tune an individual's eventual aptitude.

Environmental Hazards

Environmental hazards are defined as substances or events which have the potential to threaten one's environment and, in so doing, adversely affect health. Recently, several epidemiological studies have demonstrated that environmental factors during the fetal phase, through early childhood, may modulate the risk of developmental disorders as well as diseases that will onset in adulthood (Brimacombe et al., 2007; Gardener et al., 2009). Numerous researchers around the world are interested in elucidating the long-term outcome of interactions between genes and early exposure to environmental hazards. Amongst them, there has also been a renewed focus in investigating medical and psychiatric conditions (Moffitt et al., 2005; Rutter, 2010). For example, in a recently published article (Sakurai et al., 2016) of a large cohort in Japan (Chiba study of Mother and Children's Health: C-MACH), the authors utilized multi-omics analysis, in which they evaluated multiple datasets from the genome, metabolome, DNA methylation in the umbilical cord (epigenome), gut microbiome and chemical (environmental) exposure. The authors sought to model the onset of a number of conditions, including obesity, allergies, metabolic, endocrine, and developmental disorders. Another example of a large-scale longitudinal study is the Twins' Early Development Study (TEDS). Using both multivariate quantitative and molecular genetic perspectives, TEDS investigated behavior problems and delayed development of linguistic, cognitive and academic capacities within the range of normal variation (Oliver and Plomin, 2007). TEDS data indicated that genetic and environmental factors have pertinent bearing in almost all areas of behavioral development. Moving beyond this basic nature-nurture question, multivariate genetic analyses have revealed that, especially in the domain of learning abilities and disabilities, genes serve as 'generalists' that broadly determine the range of one's learning capacity, while environments act as 'specialists' which fine-tune an individual's eventual aptitude. Consequently, while the environment influences differences in performance within and between learning abilities and disabilities, genes greatly impact similarities in performance across age (Oliver and Plomin, 2007).

Environmental hazards can be categorized into four types: (i) chemical, (ii) physical, (iii) biological, and (iv) psychosocial. An example of a chemical environmental hazard is exposure to pesticides, whereas an example of a physical environmental hazard is the presence of a strong electromagnetic field. A biological environmental hazard is something that alters the biological environment, producing a negative effect on health conditions, an example of which would be the presence of a pathogen (i.e., ebola). Finally, an example of psychosocial environmental hazard is extreme poverty.

One advantage of examining environmental hazards in G×E studies is that it is less likely that genetic variables contribute to the environmental factor, suggesting greater independence of influence on outcomes. For instance, while prenatal infections (e.g., rubella, herpes simplex virus, cytomegalovirus, and toxoplasmosis) disrupt fetal neurodevelopment, forming a possible etiological mechanism for psychopathology such as mental retardation, learning disabilities, and schizophrenia (Klein et al., 2006), there is a lower probability that gestational exposure to these infections is associated with individual differences that have genetic roots. However, we argue that even with respect to hazardous environmental factors, it is still important to account for the potential influence of genetics on environmental self-selection. Generally, individuals with psychiatric disorders are at an increased risk of engaging in sexual risk behaviors (Shrier et al., 2012), making them more likely to acquire these infections (Cunningham et al., 2017). Indeed, Clarke et al. (2009) reported that, on its own, prenatal exposure to pyelonephritis, a urinary tract infection (UTI) that is usually the result of sexually transmitted diseases, did not lead to a significant increase in risk of schizophrenia. However, the risk of developing schizophrenia increased fivefold in infants from families with a history of psychosis and who were gestationally exposed to this infection. Therefore, it is possible that children who have greater exposure to these prenatal infections also have stronger genetic loading for psychiatric disorders, which could render the examination of gestational exposure to infections as a genetically influenced environmental factor. To explicate yet another layer of complexity, it is critical that we address the possibility for hazardous environmental factors (e.g., substance use, smoking or alcohol) to exert epigenetic effects (mechanisms that modulate level of gene expression without changing the genetic code) (Rosen et al., 2018). Indeed, several researchers have discovered that the profile of DNA methylation and mechanisms of histone modification differ between heavy consumers of alcohol and healthy persons (Zhang et al., 2013; Lohoff et al., 2017). The modulation of gene expression by environmental exposure presents another mechanism, G–E correlation, to the complex phenomenon of G×E interaction, that should be further parsed apart.

Exemplar One: Autism Spectrum Disorder

Despite the issues related to methodological limitations, studies have reported useful results that have increased our knowledge on the G×E interaction in the ontogeny of developmental disorders. Among the early environmental factors, maternal lifestyle and prenatal factors play important roles and may trigger serious health consequences and diseases later in life (Barua and Junaid, 2015). Some of the factors that have been found to influence normal fetal development include stress, diet, gestational diabetes, and exposure to alcohol during pregnancy (e.g., Barker, 2006; Bose et al., 2017; Salihu et al., 2017; Thompson et al., 2017). Unhealthy lifestyles generate epigenetic changes, including DNA methylation alteration and chromatin modifications, which are believed to account for various types of developmental disabilities related to brain plasticity, including neural tube defects and ASD (Dunaway et al., 2016; Cataldo et al., 2017, 2018).

Autism spectrum disorder was initially thought to be a result of environmental factors. However, genetic factors have been increasingly considered to play a more pivotal role in the etiology of autism, a discovery which is largely owed to recent discoveries of genetic mutations that implicate the encoding of synaptic molecules which relay communication between neurons. Recent studies have explored the role of epigenetics in the development of ASD (e.g., Dunaway et al., 2016). Epigenetics is a mechanism that influences gene expression without changing DNA nucleotide sequence, but by modifying the expression of the gene by non-genetic influences (Berger et al., 2009). As epigenetic changes are, to some extent, affected by environmental factors such as nutrition, drugs and stress, autism is not only the sole product of congenital genetic alterations, but may also be elicited by environmental variables via epigenetic mechanisms (Miyake et al., 2012). An example of a hazardous environmental factor that has been linked to ASD (Costa e Silva, 2008) is pesticides (Pearson et al., 2016). *In vitro* studies have found that some pesticides (i.e., rotenone) as well as certain fungicides (i.e., trifloxystrobin, famoxadone, and pyraclostrobin) induce transcriptional modifications that are comparable to those found in brain samples from autistics. Other studies (Kaur et al., 2014; Chauhan and Chauhan, 2015) found that genetically linked mitochondrial dysfunction, associated to increased oxidative stress, (due for example to the exposure to bisphenol A-BPA) is a risk factor for ASD. These findings underscore the importance of uncovering G×E interactions that modulate the emergence of developmental disabilities, even amongst disorders which have been shown to be driven strongly by genetic factors, such as ASD.

Exemplar Two: Attention Deficit Hyperactivity Disorder

Besides the studies on ASD (Buchmayer et al., 2009; Maramara et al., 2014), investigations have examined G×E factors behind the etio-pathogenesis of ADHD (Thapar et al., 2012). Potential risk factors for autism span from genes, pre- and perinatal risks to psychosocial variables and environmental risk factors such as toxins (Sciberras et al., 2017; Kalkbrenner et al., 2014). As with ASD, it does not appear that there is a single risk factor underlying the etio-pathogenesis of ADHD. Both genetic and environmental factors interdependently contribute to the disorder, and genes implicated in ADHD overlap with other neurodevelopmental problems, notably, ASD (Lichtenstein et al., 2010; Rommelse et al., 2010; Lundström et al., 2011; Hartman et al., 2016). Several genetic factors, such as having a biological relative with ADHD or possessing minor allele variants have been associated with ASD. Environmental factors, including exposure to lead either pre- or postnatally, severe early childhood adversity, and lower than average birth weight, have been consistently related to autism risk, although none have been proven to be definitely causal. Perhaps unsurprisingly, there is also a large literature documenting association between ADHD and a diversity of putative environmental risk factors that can only be considered as correlates at present (Tarver et al., 2014).

Research paradigms that extend past mere assessments of statistical association have started to contest the robustness of some genetic components which have been previously regarded as ADHD risk factors. Generally, the genetic risks underlying ADHD, while rare, tend to possess small effect sizes and often increase the probability of other psychopathological conditions (Neale et al., 2010; Thapar et al., 2013). Importantly, genetic and environmental factors that modulate the onset of a particular disorder are not necessarily the same ones that shape its course and eventual outcome (Thapar et al., 2007), which, once again, highlights the significance of considering temporal dynamics when pursuing research on developmental disabilities. The influence of genes and the environment do not remain stagnant over the course of development and we have yet to elucidate how G×E interactions evolve over time to contribute to various developmental disabilities.

In sum, although research regarding G×E in developmental disorders has advanced our knowledge base, it has also uncovered a vast expanse of uncharted territory and opportunities for future research inquiries.

Pathological Self-Generated Environment

Recent articles have shown another potential way through which genetic and environmental factors interact and shape the manifestation of a specific pathological phenotype. Indeed, while environmental hazards represent environmental factors outside of the organism's control, it is possible for the organism to engage in specific behaviors that modify the environment. These are referred to as pathological self-generated environments, and can create, increase, or reduce the negative impact of the environment on the behavior.

Broadly speaking, each individual reacts differently to the same environment. This can come into play when determining consequences in the environment will trigger distinct responses in the individual. More specifically, this means that the same "starting environment" may trigger diverse outcomes (i.e., "precipitating environment") on different individuals according to their own responses to the environment. The active generation of environments unique to the individual is based, in part, on one's genetic propensities, which is a concept known as "active/selective G×E" (Jaffee and Price, 2008). For example, extroverted individuals pursue more socially stimulating environments as compared to individuals who are more withdrawn (Plomin and DeFries, 1979). Consequently, walking into a new office for the first time and saying hello to everyone will most likely generate a different work environment from one in which you walk in and quietly sit down without making eye contact with a soul. This is even truer in the case of pathological self-generated environments, where the pathological characteristics affect the environment in a deeper and potentially more lasting way.

Although at first glance the concept of self-generated environment may seem trivial, in truth, it highlights the strength of the interplay between genetic predispositions and environmental factors, since each interaction between genes and environmental factors precipitates a chain of events which will affect, either deeply or superficially, the subsequent G×E interactions. Therefore, taking into account self-generated characteristics in pathological disorders allows us to acquire a greater understanding of the etiological mechanisms of pathological behaviors and negative environmental situations, ultimately leading us toward the comprehension of the primary cause of the disorder.

However, since this interplay is astoundingly complex, there is a multitude of factors to consider and defining them may not be easy or straightforward. Research into pathological self-generated environments should clearly differentiate the "starting environment" from the "precipitating environment." Since these environments occur at different instances, it is also critical that researchers consider confounding factors, other than the variables of interest, that may change over time. Assessing a wide range of variables over time will undoubtedly be challenging. To enhance the feasibility of research paradigms investigating self-generated environments, researchers should first identify or shortlist the critical variables involved, either from existing literature or preliminary studies, before directing their efforts on obtaining detailed data on these aspects. Careful selection of experimental designs and operationalization of variables should be conducted prior to these empirical studies.

Exemplar One: Autism Spectrum Disorder

One such example has been recently shown in human and animal models of ASD. Clinically, ASD parents often state that interpreting their autistic infant's emotional signals is challenging, particularly during the infant's first year of life. Specifically, they report difficulties in perceiving the reasons for their infants' distress communications (Esposito and Venuti, 2010; Esposito et al., 2011, 2012; Bornstein et al., 2016). Deficits in understanding the causes behind their infant's distress vocalizations can trigger a vicious cycle – the mother is unable to recognize and sensitively respond to the infant's needs, which leads to inadequate feedback that is otherwise required to pacify the infant (Esposito et al., 2011, 2015); this lack of feedback for the infant could then lead to or further compound the child's regulatory difficulties. In other words, as a consequence of a genetically driven physiological deficit, which compromises the ability of the child to produce typical distress communication signals, caregivers are unable to understand the child's request and cannot provide adequate sensitive parenting responses to the child (see **Figure 1** extracted from Esposito et al., 2017a).

This finding has also been shown in a mouse model of ASD. Indeed, in mice, pups' vocalizations serve as distress cues for their mothers. Pups' calls alone are demonstrated to elicit maternal approach behaviors (Uematsu et al., 2007). Encoded in the 22q11.2 region (Hiramoto et al., 2011; Hiroi et al., 2013), *Tbx1* is a monogenic ASD risk gene (Paylor et al., 2006). Takahashi et al. (2015) demonstrated that ultrasound vocalizations (USVs) of pups with a heterozygous deletion of the gene *Tbx1* elicit diminished maternal approach as compared to the USVs of wild-type pups. Contrasted with wild-type littermate pups, the USVs of $Tbx1^{-}/Tbx1^{-}$ pups were also characterized by simpler call sequences and less complex call types. Upon randomized presentation of calls from wild-type and $Tbx1^{-}$ heterozygous pups, USVs from the former prompted less maternal approach behaviors. This suggests that a mutation of this ASD risk gene modifies neonatal vocalizations, which then renders the pup's social communication with their mothers ineffective, thus inducing less efficient maternal care (Takahashi et al., 2015; see also **Figure 1** extracted from Esposito et al., 2017a). While these findings present convincing evidence for a pathological self-generated environment in autism, another possible mechanism which may govern this phenomenon is pleiotropy, wherein a single gene manipulates the phenotypic expression of a number of disparate traits. In this case, a latent mechanism may stem from an inheritance of a single gene that controls for both reduced maternal sensitivity and atypical vocalizations; this hypothesis has yet to be empirically tested and remains a possible uncontested explanation.

Exemplar Two: Internalizing Symptoms

Another example derives from the literature on children's internalizing symptoms and children's interpersonal behaviors. Youth with more severe depressive symptoms, related to the expression of 5-HTT, are more likely to seek out for negative feedback and excessive reassurance, behaviors which are thought to serve a cognitive or emotional regulatory function (Caspi et al., 2002). For instance, youth who engage in negative feedback seeking, or the purposeful solicitation of confirmation of negative evaluations from others, are thought to gain a sense of cognitive consistency, which may enhance feelings of control. Ironically, however, both of these interpersonal behaviors are prospectively associated with worsening social relationships, in the form of exacerbating perceptions of

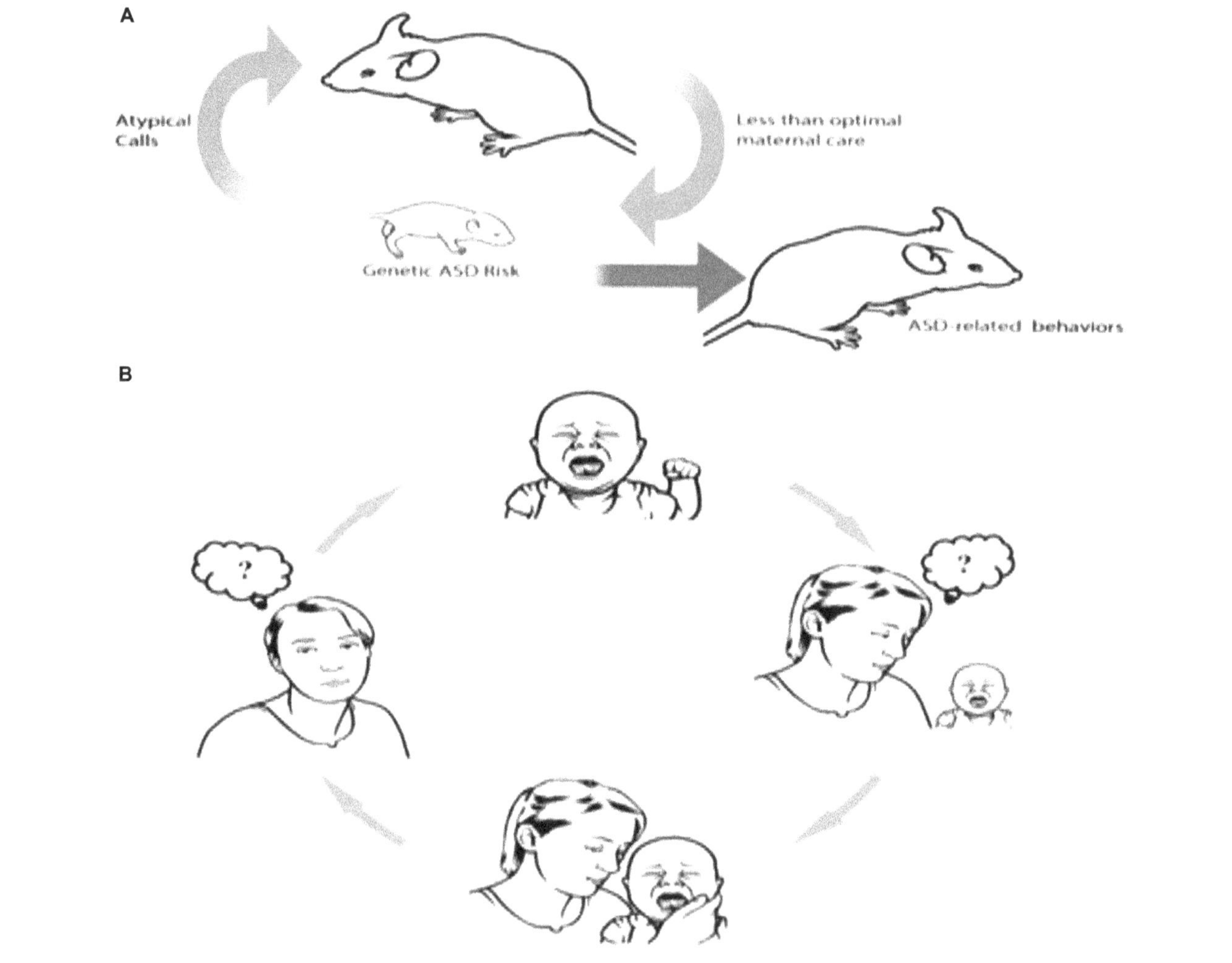

FIGURE 1 | A hypothetical causal chain of events involving atypical vocalizations in mice and humans. Human and mouse data suggest that some genes may lead to the production of atypical distress vocalizations, which in turn, jeopardize effective neonatal social communication between infants and mothers, which in turn worsens outcomes for infants. As illustrated in both rodents **(A)** and humans **(B)**, the cycle proceeds as follows: Atypical vocalization among infants with an ASD genetic risk factor evoke less maternal sensitivity, which in turn can lead to a vicious cycle of confusion and negative perception as to how to appropriately respond to baby's atypical cries (from Esposito et al., 2017a).

friends' criticism and decreased friendship quality. In addition, these interpersonal behaviors are associated with increased depressive symptoms over time (Prinstein et al., 2005; Borelli and Prinstein, 2006). Thus, youth at risk for higher depressive symptoms, such as carriers of the minor serotonin transporter allele, may have more vulnerable self-concepts and behave in ways that elicit from others the interpersonal reactions they fear – this self-fulfilling prophecy provides another instance of environmental effects that relate, at least in part, to genetic characteristics.

With only a handful of examples, we hope to have illustrated what we view as a central consideration within the field of studying G×E interactions – the fact that many of the environmental factors we examine are in fact partly dependent upon genetic factors. Thus, studying true G×E interactions becomes infinitely more challenging than examining statistical interactions between genes and environment.

CHALLENGE FOUR: CHOOSING A DEVELOPMENTAL PERIOD

The interaction of G×E plays a major role in determining developmental trajectories. As such, the timing of the measurement of individual difference factors is of key import.

Exemplar: G×E Informing Understanding of the *Development* of Psychopathology

Perhaps the most well-known example of how the study of G×E has impacted our understanding of developmental psychopathology hails from Caspi et al. (2003). These researchers showed that functional polymorphisms of a specific gene (MAOA) may modulate the likelihood of developing antisocial tendencies. Not only do these findings provide epidemiological evidence that support how genetic factors modulate children's sensitivity to environmental insults, they may also account for differences in developmental trajectories, and why not all victims of maltreatment victimize others later in life. In another study from the same group, Caspi et al. (2002) have shown how the impact of stressful life events (SLEs) on depression was moderated by a functional polymorphism in the promoter region of the serotonin transporter (5-HTT) gene. As compared to homozygotes who have two copies of the long allele, persons in possession of at least one copy of the short allele of the 5-HTT promoter polymorphism displayed higher levels of depressive symptoms and suicidality, and are more likely to be diagnosed with depression. In another study related to 5-HTT (Kochanska et al., 2011), researchers documented that an effect of developmental trajectories on children's social and cognitive development was due to interactions between children's serotonin transporter linked promoter region [5-HTTLPR] gene and maternal responsive care, observed at different time points during development (15, 25, 38, and 52 months). Specifically, children's genetic make-up moderated the impact of responsive maternal care on every domain of children's competence. Among children who have at least one short 5-HTTLPR allele (s/s, s/l), those with more responsive mothers were significantly more adept as compared to those with less responsive mothers. Interestingly, responsiveness had no discernible effect on children with two long alleles (l/l). The interaction of specific gene polymorphisms with early environmental factors (i.e., early caregiving experiences) has been reported in several other studies, suggesting how it plays a major role in differential developmental trajectories of responses to social stimuli (Esposito et al., 2016; Senese et al., 2016), conduct disorder (Brody et al., 2011), externalizing behavior (Brett et al., 2015), emotion regulation and depressive symptoms (Borelli et al., 2016).

Given the extensiveness of the human genome, it is only reasonable that another level of complexity, gene × gene (G×G) interaction, is at work as well. Some of the same genes (i.e., MAOA and COMT) involved in G×E interactions have been implicated in G×G studies. In a study on OCD, McGregor et al. (2016) revealed a G×G interaction of rs362204 (COMT) and rs1799836 (MAOB), and rs362204 (COMT) and rs6651806 (MAOB) in contributing to the pathology of OCD. Additionally, a G×E interaction of childhood severity with variants of COMT, MAOA, and MAOB was also found in relation to OCD. While G×G and G×E paradigms capture genetic and environmental contributions, a more intricate G×G×E study has recently been attempted by Wang et al. (2018). Indeed, they discovered a 3-way interaction of MAOA, COMT and SLEs on adolescents' aggressive behavior, demonstrating the complicated interplay of genetic and environmental interactions in shaping development.

Epigenetic Effects

Great interest has recently been given to studies on epigenetics, specifically, on DNA methylation. Epigenome-wide association studies (EWAS) is a technique that has been developed to further investigate G×E interactions. EWAS computes DNA methylation markers on the premise that epigenetic methylation is a phenomenon influenced by both extrinsic environmental factors and the genetic code (Ng et al., 2012; Murphy and Mill, 2014; Holbrook, 2015). Within the same chromosome (*cis*-acting), SNPs which are proximal to CpGs tend to produce methylation quantitative trait loci (methQTLs) (Gibbs et al., 2010; Zhang et al., 2010; Bell et al., 2011), which can be quantified using software suites such as the Gene, Environment, Methylation (GEM) toolkit (Pan et al., 2016). One startlingly comprehensive example is the methylation of FKBP5, which, among individuals with a risk allele, is reduced upon exposure to childhood trauma. The extent of methylation has also been evidenced to predict risk of psychopathology in adulthood (Klengel and Binder, 2013, 2015). Using methylation as a proxy of G×E interaction, Teh et al. (2014) showed that variations in the infant's methylation profile is most suitably explained by an interaction between the prenatal environment and a specific SNP.

Although assessment of methylation levels is still under debate, it has been suggested that saliva-derived samples for methylation analysis might present the field with tremendous opportunities for non-invasive epigenetic studies on typical and atypical developmental trajectories (van IJzendoorn et al., 2011). An example in this field is offered by the study of Schechter et al. (2016), which reported an association between serotonin receptor 3A methylation with maternal violence exposure, with the development of children's neural activity and antisocial behavior.

Response to Interventions

It is also within this domain of research on developmental trajectories that the onus for the creation of interventions lies. Identifying how gene–environment interaction modulates the mechanisms of disease development is paramount to identifying patients with an inherent vulnerability to certain conditions. This identification in turn may allow patients to be targeted with individualized treatment based on the knowledge of their inborn susceptibility to specific conditions (Harding, 2007). Certain developmental disabilities, such as ADHD (Huss et al., 2017) and intellectual disabilities (Tsiouris, 2010; Paton et al., 2011; McQuire et al., 2015), have been shown to benefit from pharmacological interventions. In the field of developmental disabilities, pharmacological treatments require development using animal models. However, not all symptoms of disorders, critical in the diagnosis of psychopathology in humans, is measurable in animal models. As a result, animal models of these disorders are as assorted as the disorders themselves, reconstructing some but not entire features of the disorder (Cope et al., 2016). This non-standardization of what constitutes a recreation of a specific disorder in an animal may partially explain why translational treatments derived from these models have yet to successfully cure the targeted patient populations. Besides the problem of transmuting findings from animal models to humans, further hurdles stem from inconsistencies in the environmental factors used in these models that may contribute to a myriad disorders. Moreover, these factors may influence specific psychological domains, cutting across various disorders. This limits translational efficacy since individual disorders are currently defined by diagnostic boundaries.

The next revolution in psychopathological intervention is geared toward tailoring treatment approaches to individuals based on one's characteristics and specific needs (Belsky and van Ijzendoorn, 2015). Taking a step further in this challenging direction, proponents of experimental-intervention research also assert the importance of considering differential genetic vulnerability to environmental stressors (e.g., Beach et al., 2010; Kegel et al., 2011), and others have made observations that support this (Belsky et al., 2007; Belsky and Pluess, 2009, 2013; Ellis et al., 2011). Knowing which individual traits modulate the impact of treatment allows therapists to adjust treatment programs accordingly so as to deliver maximum benefits. Without taking differences in susceptibility into account, treatment effects would appear larger for those who carry a greater genetic predisposition, and smaller for those who are less predisposed (Belsky and Pluess, 2009, 2013; van IJzendoorn et al., 2011). As a result, treatment might be misconstrued as ineffective, when in actuality, the success of intervention programs is influenced by the genetic basis of differential susceptibility in individuals. A paradigm shift that aims to understand the manner in which genetic variables interact with the environment will shed greater light on why treatment is rendered differentially efficacious (Meaney, 2010; van IJzendoorn et al., 2011). While ethical concerns such as stigma and discrimination must be addressed (Ellis et al., 2011), knowledge of individuals' genetic predisposition undoubtedly serves as invaluable information that informs therapists on how to best structure therapy intervention to further alleviate psychopathological distress.

The genes of serotonin transporter linked promoter region (5-HTTLPR) and dopamine receptor D4 (DRD4) have shown to have an impact on infant temperament and attachment style and to modulate the intervention efficacy (Cicchetti et al., 2011; Holmboe et al., 2011). In another study on intervention in depressive symptoms (Cicchetti et al., 2015), changes in symptomatology over time depended on genotypes (5-HTTLPR and CRHR1) and the type of psychological intervention they were receiving. Other studies focusing on dopamine D4 receptor polymorphism have found a G×E interaction in modulating intervention effects in literacy-delayed children (Plak et al., 2015), in toddlers' externalizing behavior (Bakermans-Kranenburg et al., 2008), and in preventive intervention on adolescent drug abuse (Brody et al., 2014, 2015).

Response to psychotherapy has also been related to level of DNA methylation. For instance, among individuals with borderline personality disorder, outcome of psychotherapy was related to methylation status of the BDNF gene, with the findings suggesting that, over time, variations in methylation status were considerably linked to changes in depression, hopelessness, and impulsivity scores (Perroud et al., 2013). In another study, responses of children with anxiety disorders to cognitive behavior therapy was associated with an increase in serotonin transporter methylation (Roberts et al., 2014).

G×E CHALLENGES

Although the number of G×E studies is rising with astounding alacrity, as with any other field, research in this area bears an indubitable set of challenges and limitations (Dick et al., 2015). In this section, we address the main challenges that beset this field and present suggestions on how to overcome them.

An issue that is of foremost concern from a methodological standpoint is the widespread implementation of candidate-gene studies. In such approaches, the mechanistic function of specific genes known to be linked to the psychiatric disorder of interest forms the basis of selecting them as genetic factors. Subsequently, researchers will investigate if there exists an interaction between variants in this gene (e.g., polymorphisms), and certain environmental conditions, in predicting the likelihood of the development of the psychiatric disorder. Despite numerous publications that have emerged from candidate-gene approaches, findings from these studies are often not consistently reported across multiple experiments. This lack of reproducibility seems to stem from the small sample sizes that often characterize candidate-gene studies (<1,000 participants), which consequently leads to low statistical power in detecting G×E interactions with small effect sizes. Since studies with larger sample sizes result in greater statistical power that can make this distinction, one might think that a straight-forward solution to this problem lies in advocating for larger sample sizes. However, in doing this, an unfortunate trade-off is the loss of a rich plethora of environmental information that could have otherwise been acquired in smaller sample sizes. To illustrate this point, consider a study that aims to investigate how specific genetic variants interact with the family environment to influence the development of psychiatric disorders: Should the study collect detailed environmental data (e.g., through numerous sessions of behavioral observations in a naturalistic home setting)? To answer this, we must consider that the likelihood of obtaining a massive number of participants in the thousands is small as only a handful of families would be agreeable to such arrangements and the research staffing necessary to complete this type of investigation is large. Conversely, a less complex method of obtaining data of the environment (e.g., by having a parent report on family environment using a self-report measure) may be an alternative solution, albeit generating less nuanced information would be more feasible and palatable to families. Researchers are hence faced with the difficulty of balancing these trade-offs of quality for quantity. A possible way of circumventing this obstacle is to increase collaborations across research groups, such that samples from numerous candidate-gene studies that are conducted in different locations are pooled to form a larger sample size. Another possible approach is to identify methods of collecting environmental data that is both convenient (i.e., short duration) and allows for retrieval of a rich amount of environmental information.

The discussion above primes us for the next issue to be addressed, which pertains to the lack of systematic examination of environmental variables in G×E studies. Despite an extensive psychiatric literature, it is uncommon for studies to consider both the positive and negative ends of the environmental spectrum (Bakermans-Kranenburg and van Ijzendoorn, 2006; Taylor et al., 2006), which leads to a restricted range of environments being investigated and an incomplete depiction of the development of psychiatric conditions (Belsky and Pluess, 2009). For example, studies which are interested in the effects of negative life events would categorize the absence of environmental stressors on the extreme end of the negative scale (e.g., Caspi et al., 2003), thus failing to consider the positive portion of the spectrum altogether. As a result, the nature of the G×E interaction under investigation can be incorrectly understood, with a risk of possibly identifying the presence of a G×E interaction when in fact, there is none. This leads to spurious associations of genetic and environmental variables and gives rise to high false discovery rates (Duncan and Keller, 2011). Researchers such as Patel et al. (2013), who have begun to address this gap in the literature, recommend generating high-throughput environmental data to distinguish key elements in the environment that contribute to shaping of psychiatric disorders. Broadening the scope and accuracy of critical environmental data being analyzed should ideally be accompanied by incorporation of a "differential susceptibility" and "plasticity" framework, such that positive and negative environmental influences are addressed in G×E studies at both the theoretical and methodological levels.

Since G×E research lies directly in the intersection of psychology and genetics, it is not surprising that increasing attention on this topic has been received from geneticists (Engelman et al., 2009). Despite ever increasing collaborations between these two fields, fundamental differences in the theoretical and practical approaches toward G×E studies continue to persist (Risch et al., 2009; Caspi et al., 2010). The challenges that have surfaced further cement the need for G×E studies to be validated beyond these specialties alone, with cross-disciplinary assessments ideally being replicated on a mechanistic level in the areas of neurobiology, neuroimaging, and other related disciplines. Indeed, to reduce high false discovery rates, Rutter et al. (2006) propose that hypotheses for these studies should stem from an understanding of potential biological pathways that integrate genetic and environmental influences, rather than searching for an interaction from open-ended statistical manipulations. For instance, since the discovery that individuals with two copies of the S-allele of 5-HTTLPR, who have been exposed to adverse environments, are at greater risk of suicide (Caspi et al., 2003), subsequent studies revealed that 5-HTTLPR also interacts with various environmental stressors to moderate the onset of a broad span of psychiatric disorders, such as depression, anxiety, ADHD, and eating disorders (Gibb et al., 2006; Kranzler et al., 2012; Stoltenberg et al., 2012; van der Meer et al., 2014; Liu et al., 2015). Likewise, in accordance with the differential susceptibility hypothesis, homozygotes of the S-allele who were exposed to supportive environments exhibited the fewest depressive symptoms (Eley et al., 2004; Taylor et al., 2006). Neuroimaging studies have also revealed promising findings that converge with those emerging from these G×E studies. Specifically, distinct patterns of activation in areas of the brain (e.g., amygdala) that are implicated in emotional processing have been observed for different genotypes of 5-HTTLPR (Canli et al., 2006; Munafò et al., 2008; Fortier et al., 2010; Alexander et al., 2012). Alteration in emotional processing based on different genotypes also manifest at the level of the autonomic nervous system. Congruent with brain imaging analyses, Mueller et al. (2012) reported that children who are carriers of the L-allele, as compared to those who are S-carriers, exhibited a greater increase in salivary α-amylase, which is suggestive of a faster recovery after exposure to stressors in individuals who are carriers of the L-allele. Each of these multi-level findings contribute a piece of information that stitches the pathway through which 5-HTTLPR exerts its effects. Findings from various fields point to a possible biological mechanism: differences in alleles of the serotonergic receptor dictates differences in reactivity of the brain toward stressors, and subsequently increases the risk of a dysregulated emotional processing and stress response system in S-allele carriers.

In the long-run, a comprehensive understanding of the biological mechanisms through which genetic differences lead to the development of psychiatric disorders allow for numerous possibilities in customization of individualized treatment. Individualized intervention aims to accurately profile a person's psychiatric diagnosis and verify the most effective mode of treatment (Ozomaro et al., 2013). In an effort to enhance treatment efficacy, extensive research into biological markers (Garriock et al., 2006; Ising et al., 2009; Keers and Aitchison, 2011) and sociodemographic indicators (Nanni et al., 2012; Nemeroff et al., 2003) have been utilized to predict treatment response but both approaches have elicited inconsistent findings. These findings suggest that neither genetic variants, nor environmental variables, can predict an accurate prognosis, whereas a consideration of the combination of both factors (i.e., G×E interaction) might possibly lead to more precise predictions that will be of invaluable assistance in treating psychiatric disorders.

CONCLUSION

Our hope is that this special issue raises interesting research questions and ideas that can be further explored in future investigations. We contend that the following goals are essential to pursue in the next decade of research. First, we are direly in need of more studies on G×E in developmental disabilities. Second, we must refine and articulate a clearer understanding of environmental hazards as opposed to self-generated dynamics, with the latter being more amenable targets of prevention and intervention efforts.

In sum, a multitude of developmental disorders emerge from the encounter of a generic genetic susceptibility and a specific environmental context (Kovas and Plomin, 2007). After the identification of this interaction, the first step to develop efficient treatments requires development using animal models (Cope et al., 2016). However, animal models of developmental disorders are as assorted as the conditions themselves, often unable to mimic all aspects of the disorder. For this limitation to be surmounted, greater accuracy in the replication of disorders in animal models needs to be obtained. A possible means of achieving this is through recognizing common endophenotypes that exist across both animal and human populations. The next frontier may be the stratification of developmental disorders based on both genetic and environmental markers. This would help to decrease the heterogeneity of the targeted population and will possibly identify specific endophenotypes that may be targeted in animal models, enhancing translational efficacy.

AUTHOR CONTRIBUTIONS

GE, AA, and JB have conceived, designed, and wrote the paper.

FUNDING

This research was supported by grants from the *FP7 PEOPLE-Marie Curie Career Integration Grants (GA-2013-630166)* and the NAP SUG of the Nanyang Technological University to GE.

REFERENCES

1. Alexander, N., Klucken, T., Koppe, G., Osinsky, R., Walter, B., Vaitl, D., et al. (2012). Interaction of the serotonin transporter-linked polymorphic region and environmental adversity: increased amygdala-hypothalamus connectivity as a potential mechanism linking neural and endocrine hyperreactivity. *Biol. Psychiatry* 72, 49–56. doi: 10.1016/j.biopsych.2012.01.030
2. Aschard, H., Chen, J., Cornelis, M. C., Chibnik, L. B., Karlson, E. W., and Kraft, P. (2012). Inclusion of gene-gene and gene-environment interactions unlikely to dramatically improve risk prediction for complex diseases. *Am. J. Hum. Genet.* 90, 962–972. doi: 10.1016/j.ajhg.2012.04.017
3. Bakermans-Kranenburg, M. J., and van Ijzendoorn, M. H. (2006). Gene- environment interaction of the dopamine D4 receptor (DRD4) and observed maternal insensitivity predicting externalizing behavior in preschoolers. *Dev. Psychobiol.* 48, 406–409. doi: 10.1002/dev.20152
4. Bakermans-Kranenburg, M. J., Van IJzendoorn, M. H., Pijlman, F. T. A., Mesman, J., and Juffer, F. (2008). Experimental evidence for differential susceptibility: dopamine D4 receptor polymorphism (DRD4 VNTR) moderates intervention effects on toddlers' externalizing behavior in a randomized controlled trial. *Dev. Psychol.* 44, 293–300. doi: 10.1037/0012-1649.44.1.293
5. Barker, D. J. P. (2006). Adult consequences of fetal growth restriction. *Clin. Obstet. Gynecol.* 49, 270–283. doi: 10.1097/00003081-200606000-00009
6. Barua, S., and Junaid, M. A. (2015). Lifestyle, pregnancy and epigenetic effects. *Epigenomics* 7, 85–102. doi: 10.2217/epi.14.71
7. Beach, S. R. H., Brody, G. H., Todorov, A. A., Gunter, T. D., and Philibert, R. A. (2010). Methylation at *SLC6A4* is linked to family history of child abuse: an examination of the Iowa Adoptee sample. *Am. J. Med. Genet. B Neuropsychiatr. Genet.* 153B, 710–713. doi: 10.1002/ajmg.b.31028
8. Bell, J. T., Pai, A. A., Pickrell, J. K., Gaffney, D. J., Pique-Regi, R., Degner, J. F., et al. (2011). DNA methylation patterns associate with genetic and gene expression variation in HapMap cell lines. *Genome Biol.* 12:R10. doi: 10.1186/gb-2011-12- 1-r10
9. Belsky, J., Bakermans-Kranenburg, M. J., and van IJzendoorn, M. H. (2007). For better and for worse. *Curr. Dir. Psychol. Sci.* 16, 300–304. doi: 10.1111/j.1467- 8721.2007.00525.x
10. Belsky, J., and Pluess, M. (2009). Beyond diathesis stress: differential susceptibility to environmental influences. *Psychol. Bull.* 135, 885–908. doi: 10.1037/a0017376 Belsky, J., and Pluess, M. (2013). Beyond risk, resilience, and dysregulation: phenotypic plasticity and human development. *Dev. Psychopathol.* 25, 1243– 1261. doi: 10.1017/S095457941300059X
11. Belsky, J., and van Ijzendoorn, M. H. (2015). What works for whom? Genetic Moderation of Intervention efficacy. *Dev. Psychopathol.* 27, 1–6. doi: 10.1017/ S0954579414001254
12. Berger, S. L., Kouzarides, T., Shiekhattar, R., and Shilatifard, A. (2009). An operational definition of epigenetics. *Genes Dev.* 23, 781–783. doi: 10.1101/gad. 1787609
13. Bhowmik, A. D., Chaudhury, S., Dutta, S., Shaw, J., Chatterjee, A., Choudhury, A., et al. (2011). Role of functional dopaminergic gene polymorphisms in the etiology of idiopathic intellectual disability. *Prog. NeuroPsychopharmacol. Biol. Psychiatry* 35, 1714–1722. doi: 10.1016/j.pnpbp.2011.05.005
14. Bishop, D. V. M. (2009). Genes, cognition, and communication: insights from neurodevelopmental disorders. *Ann. N. Y. Acad. Sci.* 1156, 1–18. doi: 10.1111/j. 1749-6632.2009.04419.x
15. Borelli, J. L., Margolin, G., and Rasmussen, H. F. (2015). Parental overcontrol as a mechanism explaining the longitudinal association between parent and child anxiety. *J. Child Fam. Stud.* 24, 1559–1574. doi: 10.1007/s10826-014-9960-1
16. Borelli, J. L., and Prinstein, M. J. (2006). Reciprocal, longitudinal associations among adolescents' negative feedback-seeking, depressive symptoms, and peer relations. *J. Abnorm. Child Psychol.* 34, 159–169. doi: 10.1007/s10802-005- 9010-y
17. Borelli, J. L., Smiley, P. A., Rasmussen, H. F., Gómez, A., Seaman, L. C., and Nurmi, E. L. (2016). Interactive effects of attachment and FKBP5 genotype on school- aged children's emotion regulation and depressive symptoms. *Behav. Brain Res.* 325(Pt B), 278–289.
18. Bornstein, M. H., Costlow, K., Truzzi, A., and Esposito, G. (2016). Categorizing the cries of infants with ASD versus typically developing infants: a study of adult accuracy and reaction time. *Res. Autism Spectr. Disord.* 31, 66–72. doi: 10.1016/j.rasd.2016.08.001
19. Bose, S., Chiu, Y.-H. M., Hsu, H.-H. L., Di, Q., Rosa, M. J., and Lee, A. (2017).
20. Prenatal nitrate exposure and childhood asthma: influence of maternal prenatal stress and fetal sex. *Am. J. Respir. Crit. Care Med.* 196, 1396–1403. doi: 10.1164/ rccm.201702-0421OC
21. Brett, Z. H., Humphreys, K. L., Smyke, A. T., Gleason, M. M., Nelson, C. A., Zeanah, C. H., et al. (2015). Serotonin transporter linked polymorphic region (5-HTTLPR) genotype moderates the longitudinal impact of early caregiving on externalizing behavior. *Dev. Psychopathol.* 27, 7–18. doi: 10.1017/ S0954579414001266
22. Brimacombe, M., Ming, X., and Lamendola, M. (2007). Prenatal and birth complications in autism. *Matern. Child Health J.* 11, 73–79. doi: 10.1007/ s10995-006-0142-7
23. Brinksma, D. M., Hoekstra, P. J., van den Hoofdakker, B., de Bildt, A., Buitelaar, J. K., Hartman, C. A., et al. (2017). Age-dependent role of pre- and perinatal factors in interaction with genes on ADHD symptoms across adolescence. *J. Psychiatr. Res.* 90, 110–117. doi: 10.1016/j.jpsychires.2017. 02.014
24. Brody, G. H., Beach, S. R. H., Chen, Y.-F., Obasi, E., Philibert, R. A., Kogan, S. M., et al. (2011). Perceived discrimination, serotonin transporter linked polymorphic region status, and the development of conduct problems. *Dev. Psychopathol.* 23, 617–627. doi: 10.1017/ S0954579411000046
25. Brody, G. H., Chen, Y.-F., Beach, S. R. H., Kogan, S. M., Yu, T., Diclemente,
26. R. J., et al. (2014). Differential sensitivity to prevention programming: a dopaminergic polymorphism-enhanced prevention effect on protective parenting and adolescent substance use. *Health Psychol.* 33, 182–191. doi: 10. 1037/a0031253
27. Brody, G. H., Yu, T., and Beach, S. R. H. (2015). A differential susceptibility analysis reveals the "who and how" about adolescents' responses to preventive interventions: tests of first- and second-generation Gene × Intervention hypotheses. *Dev. Psychopathol.* 27, 37–49. doi: 10.1017/ S095457941400128X

28. Buchmayer, S., Johansson, S., Johansson, A., Hultman, C. M., Sparen, P., and Cnattingius, S. (2009). Can association between preterm birth and autism be explained by maternal or neonatal morbidity? *Pediatrics* 124, e817–e825. doi: 10.1542/peds.2008-3582
29. Bulik-Sullivan, B. K., Loh, P.-R., Finucane, H. K., Ripke, S., Yang, J., Schizophrenia Working Group of the Psychiatric Genomics Consortium, et al. (2015). LD Score regression distinguishes confounding from polygenicity in genome-wide association studies. *Nat. Genet.* 47, 291–295. doi: 10.1038/ng.3211
30. Canli, T., Qiu, M., Omura, K., Congdon, E., Haas, B. W., Amin, Z., et al. (2006). Neural correlates of epigenesis. *Proc. Natl. Acad. Sci. U.S.A.* 103, 16033–16038. doi: 10.1073/pnas.0601674103
31. Caspi, A., Hariri, A. R., Holmes, A., Uher, R., and Moffitt, T. E. (2010). Genetic sensitivity to the environment: the case of the serotonin transporter gene and its implications for studying complex diseases and traits. *Am. J. Psychiatry* 167, 509–527. doi: 10.1176/appi.ajp.2010.09101452
32. Caspi, A., McClay, J., Moffitt, T. E., Mill, J., Martin, J., Craig, I. W., et al. (2002). Role of genotype in the cycle of violence in maltreated children. *Science* 297, 851–854. doi: 10.1126/science.1072290
33. Caspi, A., Sugden, K., Moffitt, T. E., Taylor, A., Craig, I. W., Harrington, H., et al. (2003). Influence of life stress on depression: moderation by a polymorphism in the 5-HTT gene. *Science* 301, 386–389. doi: 10.1126/science.1083968
34. Cataldo, I., Azhari, A., and Esposito, G. (2018). A review of oxytocin and arginine- vasopressin receptors and their modulation of autism spectrum disorder. *Front. Mol. Neurosci.* 11:27. doi: 10.3389/fnmol.2018.00027
35. Cataldo, I., Azhari, A., Lepri, B., and Esposito, G. (2017). Oxytocin receptors (OXTR) and early parental care: an interaction that modulates psychiatric disorders. *Res. Dev. Disabil.* doi: 10.1016/j.ridd.2017.10.007 [Epub ahead of print] doi: 10.1016/j.ridd.2017.10.007
36. Chauhan, A., and Chauhan, V. (2015). "Increased vulnerability to oxidative stress and mitochondrial dysfunction in autism," in *The Molecular Basis of Autism. Contemporary Clinical Neuroscience*, ed. S. Fatemi (New York, NY: Springer), 407–425.
37. Chen, S. W., Zhong, X. S., Jiang, L. N., Zheng, X. Y., Xiong, Y. Q., Ma, S. J., et al. (2016). Maternal autoimmune diseases and the risk of autism spectrum disorders in offspring: a systematic review and meta-analysis. *Behav. Brain Res.* 296, 61–69. doi: 10.1016/j.bbr.2015.08.035
38. Cicchetti, D., Rogosch, F. A., and Toth, S. L. (2011). The effects of child maltreatment and polymorphisms of the serotonin transporter and dopamine D4 receptor genes on infant attachment and intervention efficacy. *Dev. Psychopathol.* 23, 357–372. doi: 10.1017/S0954579411000113
39. Cicchetti, D., Toth, S. L., and Handley, E. D. (2015). Genetic moderation of interpersonal psychotherapy efficacy for low-income mothers with major depressive disorder: implications for differential susceptibility. *Dev. Psychopathol.* 27, 19–35. doi: 10.1017/S0954579414001278
40. Clarke, M. C., Tanskanen, A., Huttunen, M., Whittaker, J. C., and Cannon, M. (2009). Evidence for an interaction between familial liability and prenatal exposure to infection in the causation of schizophrenia. *Am. J. Psychiatry* 166, 1025–1030. doi: 10.1176/appi.ajp.2009.08010031
41. Cope, Z. A., Powell, S. B., and Young, J. W. (2016). Modeling neurodevelopmental cognitive deficits in tasks with cross-species translational validity. *Genes Brain Behav.* 15, 27–44. doi: 10.1111/gbb.12268
42. Costa e Silva, J. A. (2008). Autism, a brain developmental disorder: some new pathopysiologic and genetics findings. *Metab. Clin. Exp.* 57, S40–S43. doi: 10.1016/j.metabol.2008.07.005
43. Cross-Disorder Group of the Psychiatric Genomics Consortium. (2013). Identification of risk loci with shared effects on five major psychiatric disorders: a genome-wide analysis. *Lancet* 381, 1371–1379. doi: 10.1016/S0140-6736(12) 62129-1
44. Cunningham, K., Martinez, D. A., Scott-Sheldon, L. A. J., Carey, K. B., Carey, M. P., Mash Research, et al. (2017). Alcohol use and sexual risk behaviors among adolescents with psychiatric disorders: a systematic review and meta-analysis. *J. Child Adolesc. Subst. Abuse* 26, 353–366. doi: 10.1080/1067828X.2017.1305934
45. Cuthbert, B. N. (2014). The RDoC framework: facilitating transition from ICD/DSM to dimensional approaches that integrate neuroscience and psychopathology. *World Psychiatry* 13, 28–35. doi: 10.1002/wps.20087
46. Cuthbert, B. N. (2015). Research domain criteria: toward future psychiatric nosologies. *Dialogues Clin. Neurosci.* 17, 89–97.
47. Dahl, A., Cai, N., Flint, J., and Zaitlen, N. (2018). GxEMM: extending linear mixed models to general gene-environment interactions. bioRxiv doi: 10.1101/39 7638
48. Dai, X., Wu, C., He, Y., Gui, L., Zhou, L., Guo, H., et al. (2013). A genome-wide association study for serum bilirubin levels and gene-environment interaction in a Chinese population. *Genet. Epidemiol.* 37, 293–300. doi: 10.1002/gepi.21711
49. Davey Smith, G., Ebrahim, S., Lewis, S., Hansell, A. L., Palmer, L. J., and Burton, P. R. (2005). Genetic epidemiology and public health: hope, hype, and future prospects. *Lancet* 366, 1484–1498. doi: 10.1016/S0140-6736(05)67601-5
50. Dick, D. M., Agrawal, A., Keller, M. C., Adkins, A., Aliev, F., Monroe, S., et al. (2015). Candidate gene-environment interaction research: reflections and recommendations. *Perspect. Psychol. Sci.* 10, 37–59. doi: 10.1177/ 1745691614556682
51. Dunaway, K. W., Islam, M. S., Coulson, R. L., Lopez, S. J., Vogel Ciernia, A., Chu, R. G., et al. (2016). Cumulative impact of polychlorinated biphenyl and large chromosomal duplications on dna methylation, chromatin, and expression of autism candidate genes. *Cell Rep.* 17, 3035–3048. doi: 10.1016/j.celrep.2016. 11.058
52. Duncan, L. E., and Keller, M. C. (2011). A critical review of the first 10 years of candidate gene-by-environment interaction research in psychiatry. *Am. J. Psychiatry* 168, 1041–1049. doi: 10.1176/appi.ajp.2011.110 20191
53. Eley, T. C., Sugden, K., Corsico, A., Gregory, A. M., Sham, P., McGuffin, P., et al. (2004). Gene-environment interaction analysis of serotonin system markers with adolescent depression. *Mol. Psychiatry* 9, 908–915. doi: 10.1038/sj.mp. 4001546
54. Ellis, B. J., Boyce, W. T., Belsky, J., Bakermans-Kranenburg, M. J., and van Ijzendoorn, M. H. (2011). Differential susceptibility to the environment: an evolutionary–neurodevelopmental theory. *Dev. Psychopathol.* 23, 7–28. doi: 10. 1017/S0954579410000611
55. Engelman, C. D., Baurley, J. W., Chiu, Y.-F., Joubert, B. R., Lewinger, J. P., Maenner, M. J., et al. (2009). Detecting gene-environment interactions in genome-wide association data. *Genet. Epidemiol.* 33(Suppl. 1), S68–S73. doi: 10.1002/gepi. 20475
56. Esposito, G., and Borelli, J. L. (2018). Investigating genes, environments, and their interactions in the service of informing individualized diagnosis and treatment in developmental disabilities. *Res. Dev. Disabil.* doi: 10.1016/j.ridd.2018.07.008 [Epub ahead of print] doi: 10.1016/j.ridd.2018.07.008
57. Esposito, G., Hiroi, N., and Scattoni, M. L. (2017a). Cry, baby, cry: Expression of Distress as a Biomarker and Modulator in Autism Spectrum Disorder. *Int. J. Neuropsychopharmacol.* doi: 10.1093/ijnp/pyx014 [Epub ahead of print]. doi: 10.1093/ijnp/pyx014
58. Esposito, G., Nakazawa, J., Venuti, P., and Bornstein, M. H. (2012). Perceptions of distress in young children with autism compared to typically developing children: a cultural comparison between Japan and Italy. *Res. Dev. Disabil.* 33, 1059–1067. doi: 10.1016/j.ridd.2012.01.014
59. Esposito, G., Truzzi, A., Setoh, P., Putnick, D. L., Shinohara, K., and Bornstein, M. H. (2017b). Genetic predispositions and parental bonding interact to shape adults' physiological responses to social distress. *Behav. Brain Res.* 125, 156–162. doi: 10.1016/j.bbr.2016.06.042
60. Esposito, G., Truzzi, A., Setoh, P., Putnick, D. L., Shinohara, K., and Bornstein, M. H. (2016). Genetic predispositions and parental bonding interact to shape adults' physiological responses to social distress. *Behav. Brain Res.* 325(Pt B), 156–162.
61. Esposito, G., Valenzi, S., Islam, T., and Bornstein, M. H. (2015). Three physiological responses in fathers and non-fathers' to vocalizations of typically developing infants and infants with Autism Spectrum Disorder. *Res. Dev. Disabil.* 4, 43–50. doi: 10.1016/j.ridd.2015.06.007
62. Esposito, G., and Venuti, P. (2010). Understanding early communication signals in autism: a study of the perception of infants' cry. *J. Intellect. Disabil. Res.* 54, 216–223. doi: 10.1111/j.1365-2788.2010.01252.x
63. Esposito, G., Venuti, P., and Bornstein, M. H. (2011). Assessment of distress in young children: a comparison of autistic disorder, developmental delay

and typical development. *Res. Autism Spectr. Disord.* 5, 1510–1516. doi: 10.1016/j. rasd.2011.02.013

64. Flint, J., and Munafò, M. R. (2013). Candidate and non-candidate genes in behavior genetics. *Curr. Opin. Neurobiol* 23, 57–61. doi: 10.1016/j. conb.2012.07.005 Fortier, É, Noreau, A., Lepore, F., Boivin, M., Pérusse, D., Rouleau, G. A., et al. (2010). Early impact of 5-HTTLPR polymorphism on the neural correlates of sadness. *Neurosci. Lett.* 485, 261–265. doi: 10.1016/j.neulet.2010. 09.026
65. Foss-Feig, J. H., McPartland, J. C., Anticevic, A., and Wolf, J. (2016). Re- conceptualizing ASD Within a dimensional framework: positive, negative, and cognitive feature clusters. *J. Autism. Dev. Disord.* 46, 342–351. doi: 10.1007/ s10803-015-2539-x
66. Friauf, E. (2004). "Developmental changes and cellular plasticity in the superior olivary complex," in *Plasticity of the Auditory System. Springer Handbook of Auditory Research*, eds T. N. Parks, E. W. Rubel, A. N. Popper, and R. R. Fay (New York, NY: Springer), 49–95.
67. Gardener, H., Spiegelman, D., and Buka, S. L. (2009). Prenatal risk factors for autism: comprehensive meta-analysis. *Br. J. Psychiatry* 195, 7–14. doi: 10.1192/ bjp.bp.108.051672
68. Garriock, H. A., Kraft, J. B., Shyn, S. I., Peters, E. J., Yokoyama, J. S., Jenkins, G. D., et al. (2006). Serotonin transporter (5-HTTLPR) genotype, childhood abuse, and suicide attempts in adult psychiatric inpatients. *Suicide Life Threat. Behav.* 36, 687–693. doi: 10.1521/ suli.2006.36.6.687
69. Gibb, B. E., Alloy, L. B., Walshaw, P. D., Comer, J. S., Shen, G. H. C., and Villari, A. G. (2006). Predictors of attributional style change in children. *J. Abnorm. Child Psychol.* 34, 425–439. doi: 10.1007/s10802-006-9022-2
70. Gibbs, J. R., van der Brug, M. P., Hernandez, D. G., Traynor, B. J., Nalls, M. A., Lai, S.-L., et al. (2010). Abundant quantitative trait loci exist for DNA methylation and gene expression in human brain. *PLoS Genet.* 6:e1000952. doi: 10.1371/ journal.pgen.1000952
71. Graf, W. D., Kekatpure, M. V., and Kosofsky, B. E. (2013). Prenatal-onset neurodevelopmental disorders secondary to toxins, nutritional deficiencies, and maternal illness. *Handbook Clini. Neurol.* 111, 143–159. doi: 10.1016/B978-0- 444-52891-9.00014-2
72. Green, R. F., and Moore, C. (2006). Incorporating genetic analyses into birth defects cluster investigations: strategies for identifying candidate genes. *Birth Defects Res. A Clin. Mol. Teratol.* 76, 798–810. doi: 10.1002/ bdra.20280
73. Guo, W., Samuels, J. F., Wang, Y., Cao, H., Ritter, M., Nestadt, P. S., et al. (2017). Polygenic risk score and heritability estimates reveals a genetic relationship between ASD and OCD. *Eur. Neuropsychopharmacol.* 27, 657–666. doi: 10. 1016/j.euroneuro.2017.03.011
74. Harding, D. (2007). Impact of common genetic variation on neonatal disease and outcome. *Arch. Dis. Child. Fetal Neonatal Ed.* 92, F408–F413. doi: 10.1136/adc. 2006.108670
75. Hartman, C. A., Geurts, H. M., Franke, B., Buitelaar, J. K., and Rommelse, N. N. J. (2016). Changing ASD-ADHD symptom co-occurrence across the lifespan with adolescence as crucial time window: illustrating the need to go beyond childhood. *Neurosci. Biobehav. Rev.* 71, 529–541. doi: 10.1016/j.neubiorev.2016. 09.003
76. Heinrich, H., Grunitz, J., Stonawski, V., Frey, S., Wahl, S., Albrecht, B., et al. (2017). Attention, cognitive control and motivation in ADHD: linking event-related brain potentials and DNA methylation patterns in boys at early school age. *Sci. Rep.* 7:3823.
77. Hiramoto, T., Kang, G., Suzuki, G., Satoh, Y., Kucherlapati, R., Watanabe, Y., et al. (2011). Tbx1: identification of a 22q11.2 gene as a risk factor for autism spectrum disorder in a mouse model. *Hum. Mol. Genet.* 20, 4775–4785. doi: 10.1093/hmg/ddr404
78. Hiroi, N., Takahashi, T., Hishimoto, A., Izumi, T., Boku, S., and Hiramoto, T. (2013). Copy number variation at 22q11.2: from rare variants to common mechanisms of developmental neuropsychiatric disorders. *Mol. Psychiatry* 18, 1153–1165. doi: 10.1038/mp.2013.92
79. Holbrook, J. D. (2015). An epigenetic escape route. *Trends Genet.* 31, 2–4. doi: 10.1016/j.tig.2014.09.007
80. Holmans, P., Green, E. K., Pahwa, J. S., Ferreira, M. A. R., Purcell, S. M., Sklar, P., et al. (2009) Gene ontology analysis of GWA study data sets provides insights into the biology of bipolar disorder. *Am. J. Hum. Genet.* 85, 13–24.
81. Holmboe, K., Nemoda, Z., Fearon, R. M. P., Sasvari-Szekely, M., and Johnson, M. H. (2011). Dopamine D4 receptor and serotonin transporter gene effects on the longitudinal development of infant temperament. *Genes Brain Behav.* 10, 513–522. doi: 10.1111/j.1601-183X.2010.00669.x
82. Huss, M., Duhan, P., Gandhi, P., Chen, C.-W., Spannhuth, C., and Kumar, V. (2017). Methylphenidate dose optimization for ADHD treatment: review of safety, efficacy, and clinical necessity. *Neuropsychiatr. Dis. Treat.* 13, 1741–1751. doi: 10.2147/NDT.S130444
83. Insel, T. R., and Cuthbert, B. N. (2009). Endophenotypes: bridging genomic complexity and disorder heterogeneity. *Biol. Psychiatry* 66, 988–989. doi: 10. 1016/j.biopsych.2009.10.008
84. Ising, M., Lucae, S., Binder, E. B., Bettecken, T., Uhr, M., Ripke, S., et al. (2009). A genomewide association study points to multiple loci that predict antidepressant drug treatment outcome in depression. *Arch. Gen. Psychiatry* 66, 966–975. doi: 10.1001/archgenpsychiatry.2009.95
85. Ivanov, V. Z., Nordsletten, A., Mataix-Cols, D., Serlachius, E., Lichtenstein, P., Lundstro, M. S., et al. (2017). Heritability of hoarding symptoms across adolescence and young adulthood: A longitudinal twin study. *PLoS One* 12:e0179541. doi: 10.1371/journal.pone.0179541
86. Jaffee, S. R., and Price, T. S. (2008). Genotype–environment correlations: implications for determining the relationship between environmental exposures and psychiatric illness. *Psychiatry* 7, 496–499. doi: 10.1016/j. mppsy. 2008.10.002
87. Kalkbrenner, A. E., Schmidt, R. J., and Penlesky, A. C. (2014). Environmental chemical exposures and autism spectrum disorders: a review of the epidemiological evidence. *Curr. Probl. Pediatr. Adolesc. Health Care* 44, 277– 318. doi: 10.1016/j.cppeds.2014.06.001
88. Kaur, K., Chauhan, V., Gu, F., and Chauhan, A. (2014). Bisphenol A induces oxidative stress and mitochondrial dysfunction in lymphoblasts from children with autism and unaffected siblings. *Free Radic. Biol. Med.* 76, 25–33. doi: 10.1016/j.freeradbiomed.2014.07.030
89. Keers, R., and Aitchison, K. J. (2011). Pharmacogenetics of antidepressant response. *Expert Rev. Neurother.* 11, 101–125. doi: 10.1586/ern.10.186
90. Kegel, C. A. T., Bus, A. G., and van IJzendoorn, M. H. (2011). Differential susceptibility in early literacy instruction through computer games: the role of the dopamine D4 receptor gene (DRD4). *Mind Brain Educ.* 5, 71–78. doi: 10.1111/j.1751-228X.2011.01112.x
91. Khoury, M. J., and Flanders, W. D. (1996). Nontraditional epidemiologic approaches in the analysis of gene-environment interaction: case-control studies with no controls! American Journal of Epidemiology. 144, 207–213. doi: 10.1093/oxfordjournals.aje.a008915
92. Klein, J. O., Baker, C. J., Remington, J. S., and Wilson, C. B. eds (2006). "Current Concepts of Infections of the Fetus and Newborn Infant," in *Infectious Diseases of the Fetus and Newborn Infant*, (Philadelphia, PA: Elsevier saunders), 3–25. doi: 10.1016/B0-72-160537-0/50003-7
93. Klengel, T., and Binder, E. B. (2013). Allele-specific epigenetic modification: a molecular mechanism for gene–environment interactions in stress-related psychiatric disorders? *Epigenomics* 5, 109–112. doi: 10.2217/epi.13.11
94. Klengel, T., and Binder, E. B. (2015). FKBP5 allele-specific epigenetic modification in gene by environment interaction. *Neuropsychopharmacology* 40, 244–246. doi: 10.1038/npp.2014.208
95. Kochanska, G., Kim, S., Barry, R. A., and Philibert, R. A. (2011). Children's genotypes interact with maternal responsive care in predicting children's competence: diathesis–stress or differential susceptibility? *Dev. Psychopathol.* 23, 605–616. doi: 10.1017/S0954579411000071
96. Kovas, Y., and Plomin, R. (2007). Learning abilities and disabilities: generalist genes, Specialist Environments. *Curr. Dir. Psychol. Sci.* 16, 284–288. doi: 10. 1111/j.1467-8721.2007.00521.x
97. Kozak, M. J., and Cuthbert, B. N. (2016). The NIMH research domain criteria initiative: background, issues, and pragmatics. *Psychophysiology* 53, 286–297. doi: 10.1111/psyp.12518
98. Kraft, P., and Aschard, H. (2015). Finding the missing gene-environment interactions. *Eur. J. Epidemiol.* 30, 353–355. doi: 10.1007/ s10654-015-0046-1 Kranzler, H. R., Scott, D., Tennen, H., Feinn, R., Williams, C., Armeli, S., et al.
99. (2012). The 5-HTTLPR polymorphism moderates the effect of stressful life events on drinking behavior in college students of African descent. *Am. J. Med. Genet. B Neuropsychiatr. Genet.* 159B, 484–490. doi: 10.1002/ ajmg.b.32051
100. Laville, V., Bentley, A. R., Privé, F., Zhu, X., Gauderman, J., Winkler, T. W., et al. (2018). VarExp: estimating variance explained by genome-wide

GxE summary statistics. *Bioinformatics* 34, 3412–3414. doi: 10.1093/ bioinformatics/ bty379

101. Lee, S. H., Byrne, E. M., Hultman, C. M., Kähler, A., Vinkhuyzen, A. A. E., Ripke, S., et al. (2015). New data and an old puzzle: the negative association between schizophrenia and rheumatoid arthritis. *Int. J. Epidemiol.* 44, 1706–1721. doi: 10.1093/ije/dyv136
102. Lee, S. H., and van der Werf, J. H. J. (2016). MTG2: an efficient algorithm for multivariate linear mixed model analysis based on genomic information. *Bioinformatics* 32, 1420–1422. doi: 10.1093/ bioinformatics/btw012
103. Lee, S. H., Weerasinghe, W. M. S. P., and van der Werf, J. H. J. (2017). Genotype- environment interaction on human cognitive function conditioned on the status of breastfeeding and maternal smoking around birth. *Sci. Rep.* 7:6087. doi: 10.1038/s41598-017-06214-y
104. Leonardo, E. D., David Leonardo, E., and Hen, R. (2007). Anxiety as a developmental disorder. *Neuropsychopharmacology* 33, 134–140. doi: 10.1038/ sj.npp.1301569
105. Lichtenstein, P., Carlström, E., Råstam, M., Gillberg, C., and Anckarsäter, H. (2010). The genetics of autism spectrum disorders and related neuropsychiatric disorders in childhood. *Am. J. Psychiatry* 167, 1357–1363. doi: 10.1176/appi.ajp. 2010.10020223
106. Liu, Y., Garrett, M. E., Dennis, M. F., Green, K. T., Ashley-Koch, A. E., Hauser, M. A., et al. (2015). An Examination of the Association between 5-HTTLPR, Combat Exposure, and PTSD Diagnosis among U.S. Veterans. *PLoS One* 10:e0119998. doi: 10.1371/journal.pone.0119998
107. Lobach, I., Carroll, R. J., Spinka, C., Gail, M. H., and Chatterjee, N. (2008). Haplotype-based regression analysis and inference of case-control studies with unphased genotypes and measurement errors in environmental exposures. *Biometrics* 64, 673–684. doi: 10.1111/ j.1541-0420.2007. 00930.x
108. Lohoff, F. W., Sorcher, J. L., Rosen, A. D., Mauro, K. L., Fanelli, R. R., Momenan, R., et al. (2017). Methylomic profiling and replication implicates deregulation of PCSK9 in alcohol use disorder. *Mol. Psychiatry* doi: 10.1038/mp.2017.168 [Epub ahead of print] doi: 10.1038/mp.2017.168
109. Lundström, S., Chang, Z., Kerekes, N., Gumpert, C. H., Råstam, M., Gillberg, C., et al. (2011). Autistic-like traits and their association with mental health problems in two nationwide twin cohorts of children and adults. *Psychol. Med.* 41, 2423–2433. doi: 10.1017/S0033291711000377
110. Maier, R., Moser, G., Chen, G.-B., Ripke, S., Cross-Disorder Working Group of the Psychiatric Genomics Consortium, Coryell, W., et al. (2015). Joint analysis of psychiatric disorders increases accuracy of risk prediction for schizophrenia, bipolar disorder, and major depressive disorder. *Am. J. Hum. Genet.* 96, 283– 294. doi: 10.1016/j. ajhg.2014.12.006
111. Maramara, L. A., He, W., and Ming, X. (2014). Pre- and perinatal risk factors for autism spectrum disorder in a New Jersey cohort. *J. Child Neurol.* 29, 1645–1651. doi: 10.1177/0883073813512899
112. McGregor, N. W., Hemmings, S. M. J., Erdman, L., Calmarza-Font, I., Stein, D. J., and Lochner, C. (2016). Modification of the association between early adversity and obsessive-compulsive disorder by polymorphisms in the MAOA. MAOB and COMT genes. *Psychiatry Res.* 246, 527–532. doi: 10.1016/j.psychres.2016. 10.044
113. McQuire, C., Hassiotis, A., Harrison, B., and Pilling, S. (2015). Pharmacological interventions for challenging behaviour in children with intellectual disabilities: a systematic review and meta-analysis. *BMC Psychiatry* 15:303. doi: 10.1186/ s12888-015-0688-2
114. Meaney, M. J. (2010). Epigenetics and the biological definition of gene x environment interactions. *Child Dev.* 81, 41–79. doi: 10.1111/j.1467-8624.2009. 01381.x
115. Miyake, K., Hirasawa, T., Koide, T., and Kubota, T. (2012). Epigenetics in autism and other neurodevelopmental diseases. *Adv. Exp. Med. Biol.* 724, 91–98. doi: 10.1007/978-1-4614-0653-2_7
116. Moffitt, T. E., Caspi, A., and Rutter, M. (2005). Strategy for investigating interactions between measured genes and measured environments. *Arch. Gen. Psychiatry* 62, 473–481. doi: 10.1001/archpsyc.62.5.473
117. Montalvo-Ortiz, J. L., Gelernter, J., Hudziak, J., and Kaufman, J. (2015). RDoC and translational perspectives on the genetics of trauma-related psychiatric disorders. *Am. J. Med. Genet. B Neuropsychiatr. Genet.* 171, 81–91. doi: 10.1002/ ajmg.b.32395
118. Moore, R., Casale, F. P., Bonder, M. J., Horta, D., Franke, L., Barroso, I., et al. (2018). A linear mixed model approach to study multivariate gene-environment interactions. doi: 10.1101/270611
119. Morange, M. (2007). "Cancer Research (The History)," in *Van Nostrand's Scientific Encyclopedia*, ed. D. Considine (Berlin: Springer).
120. Mueller, A., Strahler, J., Armbruster, D., Lesch, K.-P., Brocke, B., and Kirschbaum, C. (2012). Genetic contributions to acute autonomic stress responsiveness in children. *Int. J. Psychophysiol.* 83, 302–308. doi: 10.1016/j. ijpsycho.2011.11.007
121. Munafò, M. R., Brown, S. M., and Hariri, A. R. (2008). Serotonin transporter (5- HTTLPR) genotype and amygdala activation: a meta-analysis. *Biol. Psychiatry* 63, 852–857. doi: 10.1016/j. biopsych.2007.08.016
122. Munafò, M. R., and Flint, J. (2010). How reliable are scientific studies? *Br. J. Psychiatry* 197, 257–258. doi: 10.1192/bjp.bp.109.069849
123. Murphy, T. M., and Mill, J. (2014). Epigenetics in health and disease: heralding the EWAS era. *Lancet* 383, 1952–1954. doi: 10.1016/S0140-6736(14)60269-5
124. Naj, A. C., Scott, W. K., Courtenay, M. D., Cade, W. H., Schwartz, S. G., Kovach, J. L., et al. (2013). Genetic factors in nonsmokers with age-related macular degeneration revealed through genome-wide gene-environment interaction analysis. *Ann. Hum. Genet* 77, 215–231. doi: 10.1111/ahg.12011
125. Nanni, V., Uher, R., and Danese, A. (2012). Childhood maltreatment predicts unfavorable course of illness and treatment outcome in depression: a meta- analysis. *Am. J. Psychiatry* 169, 141–151. doi: 10.1176/appi.ajp.2011.11020335
126. Neale, B. M., Medland, S. E., Ripke, S., Asherson, P., Franke, B., Lesch, K.-P., et al. (2010). Meta-analysis of genome-wide association studies of attention- deficit/hyperactivity disorder. *J. Am. Acad. Child Adolesc. Psychiatry* 49, 884– 897. doi: 10.1016/j.jaac.2010.06.008
127. Nemeroff, C. B., Heim, C. M., Thase, M. E., Klein, D. N., Rush, A. J., Schatzberg, A. F., et al. (2003). Differential responses to psychotherapy versus pharmacotherapy in patients with chronic forms of major depression and childhood trauma. *Proc. Natl. Acad. Sci. U.S.A.* 100, 14293–14296. doi: 10.1073/ pnas.2336126100
128. Ng, J. W. Y., Barrett, L. M., Wong, A., Kuh, D., Smith, G. D., and Relton, C. L. (2012). The role of longitudinal cohort studies in epigenetic epidemiology: challenges and opportunities. *Genome Biol.* 13:246. doi: 10.1186/ gb4029
129. Ni, G., van der Werf, J., Zhou, X., Hypponen, E., Wray, N. R., and Lee, S. H. (2018). Genotype-covariate correlation and interaction disentangled by a whole-genome multivariate reaction norm model. bioRxiv. doi: 10.1101/377796 Oliver, B. R., and Plomin, R. (2007). Twins' Early Development Study (TEDS): a multivariate, longitudinal genetic investigation of language, cognition and behavior problems from childhood through adolescence. *Twin Res. Hum. Genet.* 10, 96–105. doi: 10.1375/twin.10.1.96
130. Ozomaro, U., Wahlestedt, C., and Nemeroff, C. B. (2013). Personalized medicine in psychiatry: problems and promises. *BMC Medicine* 11:32. doi: 10.1186/1741- 7015-11-132
131. Pan, H., Holbrook, J. D., Karnani, N., and Kwoh, C. K. (2016). Gene, Environment and Methylation (GEM): a tool suite to efficiently navigate large scale epigenome wide association studies and integrate genotype and interaction between genotype and environment. *BMC Bioinformatics* 17:299. doi: 10.1186/ s12859-016-1161-z
132. Pare, G., Mao, S., and Deng, W. Q. (2016). A method to estimate the contribution of regional genetic associations to complex traits from summary association statistics. *Scientific Reports* 6, 27644. doi: 10.1038/ srep 27644
133. Patel, C. J., Chen, R., Kodama, K., Ioannidis, J. P. A., and Butte, A. J. (2013). Systematic identification of interaction effects between genome- and environment-wide associations in type 2 diabetes mellitus. *Hum. Genet.* 132, 495–508. doi: 10.1007/s00439-012-1258-z
134. Paton, C., Flynn, A., Shingleton-Smith, A., McIntyre, S., Bhaumik, S., Rasmussen, J., et al. (2011). Nature and quality of antipsychotic prescribing practice in UK psychiatry of intellectual disability services. *J. Intellect. Disabil. Res.* 55, 665–674. doi: 10.1111/j.1365-2788.2011.01421.x
135. Paylor, R., Glaser, B., Mupo, A., Ataliotis, P., Spencer, C., Sobotka, A., et al. (2006). Tbx1 haploinsufficiency is linked to behavioral disorders in mice and humans: implications for 22q11 deletion syndrome. *Proc. Natl. Acad. Sci. U.S.A.* 103, 7729–7734. doi: 10.1073/pnas.0600206103

136. Pearson, B. L., Simon, J. M., McCoy, E. S., Salazar, G., Fragola, G., and Zylka, M. J. (2016). Identification of chemicals that mimic transcriptional changes associated with autism, brain aging and neurodegeneration. *Nat. Commun.* 7:11173. doi: 10.1038/ncomms11173
137. Perroud, N., Salzmann, A., Prada, P., Nicastro, R., Hoeppli, M. E., Furrer, S., et al. (2013). Response to psychotherapy in borderline personality disorder and methylation status of the BDNF gene. *Transl. Psychiatry* 3:e207. doi: 10.1038/tp. 2012.140
138. Plak, R. D., Kegel, C. A. T., and Bus, A. G. (2015). Genetic differential susceptibility in literacy-delayed children: a randomized controlled trial on emergent literacy in kindergarten. *Dev. Psychopathol.* 27, 69–79. doi: 10.1017/S095457941400 1308
139. Plomin, R., and DeFries, J. C. (1979). Multivariate behavioral genetic analysis of twin data on scholastic abilities. *Behav. Genet.* 9, 505–517. doi: 10.1007/ BF01067347
140. Prinstein, M. J., Borelli, J. L., Cheah, C. S. L., Simon, V. A., and Aikins, J. W. (2005). Adolescent girls' interpersonal vulnerability to depressive symptoms: a longitudinal examination of reassurance-seeking and peer relationships. *J. Abnorm. Psychol.* 114, 676–688. doi: 10.1037/0021-843X.114. 4.676
141. Risch, N., Herrell, R., Lehner, T., Liang, K.-Y., Eaves, L., Hoh, J., et al. (2009). Interaction between the serotonin transporter gene (5-HTTLPR), stressful life events, and risk of depression: a meta-analysis. *JAMA* 301, 2462–2471. doi: 10.1001/jama.2009.878
142. Roberts, S., Lester, K. J., Hudson, J. L., Rapee, R. M., Creswell, C., Cooper, P. J., et al. (2014). Serotonin transporter [corrected] methylation and response to cognitive behaviour therapy in children with anxiety disorders. *Transl. Psychiatry* 4:e444. doi: 10.1038/tp.2014.83
143. Robinson, M. R., English, G., Moser, G., Lloyd-Jones, L. R., Triplett, M. A., Zhu, Z., et al. (2017). Genotype-covariate interaction effects and the heritability of adult body mass index. *Nat. Genet* 49, 1174–1181. doi: 10.1038/ng. 3912
144. Rommelse, N. N. J., Franke, B., Geurts, H. M., Hartman, C. A., and Buitelaar, J. K. (2010). Shared heritability of attention-deficit/hyperactivity disorder and autism spectrum disorder. *Eur. Child Adolesc. Psychiatry* 19, 281–295. doi: 10.1007/s00787-010-0092-x
145. Rosen, A. D., Robertson, K. D., Hlady, R. A., Muench, C., Lee, J., Philibert, R., et al. (2018). DNA methylation age is accelerated in alcohol dependence. *Transl. Psychiatry* 8:182. doi: 10.1038/s41398-018- 0233-4
146. Rothman, K. J. (1986). *Modern Epidemiology*, 1st Edn. Boston, MA: Little, Brown and Company.
147. Rutter, M. (2010). Gene-environment interplay. *Depress. Anxiety* 27, 1–4. doi: 10.1002/da.20641
148. Rutter, M., Moffitt, T. E., and Caspi, A. (2006). Gene-environment interplay and psychopathology: multiple varieties but real effects. *J. Child Psychol. Psychiatry* 47, 226–261. doi: 10.1111/j.1469-7610.2005. 01557.x
149. Sakurai, K., Miyaso, H., Eguchi, A., Matsuno, Y., Yamamoto, M., Todaka, E., et al. (2016). Chiba study of Mother and Children's Health (C-MACH): cohort study with omics analyses. *BMJ Open* 6:e010531. doi: 10.1136/ bmjopen-2015-01 0531
150. Salihu, H. M., Paothong, A., Das, R., King, L. M., Pradhan, A., Riggs, B., et al. (2017). Evidence of altered brain regulatory gene expression in tobacco- exposed fetuses. *J. Perinat. Med.* 45, 1045–1053. doi: 10.1515/ jpm-2016- 0279
151. Schechter, D. S., Moser, D. A., Pointet, V. C., Aue, T., Stenz, L., Paoloni-Giacobino, A., et al. (2016). The association of serotonin receptor 3A methylation with maternal violence exposure, neural activity, and child aggression. *Behav. Brain Res.* 325(Pt B), 268–277.
152. Sciberras, E., Mulraney, M., Silva, D., and Coghill, D. (2017). Prenatal risk factors and the etiology of ADHD—review of existing evidence. *Curr. Psychiatry Rep.* 19:1. doi: 10.1007/s11920-017-0753-2
153. Senese, V. P., Shinohara, K., Esposito, G., Doi, H., Venuti, P., and Bornstein, M. H. (2016). Implicit association to infant faces: Genetics, early care experiences, and cultural factors influence caregiving propensities. *Behav. Brain Res.* 325(Pt B), 163–172.
154. Shi, J., Park, J.-H., Duan, J., Berndt, S. T., Moy, W., and Yu, K. (2016). Winner's curse correction and variable thresholding improve performance of polygenic risk modeling based on genome-wide association study summary-level data. *PLoS Genet.* 12:e1006493. doi: 10.1371/journal.pgen.10 06493
155. Shrier, L. A., Walls, C., Lops, C., Kendall, A. D., and Blood, E. A. (2012). Substance use, sexual intercourse, and condom nonuse among depressed adolescents and young adults. *J. Adolesc. Health Care* 50, 264–270. doi: 10.1016/j.jadohealth. 2011.07.005
156. Slatkin, M. (2008). Linkage disequilibrium–understanding the evolutionary past and mapping the medical future. *Nat. Rev. Genet.* 9, 477–485. doi: 10.1038/ nrg2361
157. Stoltenberg, S. F., Anderson, C., Nag, P., and Anagnopoulos, C. (2012). Association between the serotonin transporter triallelic genotype and eating problems is moderated by the experience of childhood trauma in women. *Int. J. Eat. Disord.* 45, 492–500. doi: 10.1002/eat.20976
158. Takahashi, T., Okabe, S., Broin, P. Ó, Nishi, A., Ye, K., Beckert, M. V., et al. (2015). Structure and function of neonatal social communication in a genetic mouse model of autism. *Mol. Psychiatry* 21, 1208–1214. doi: 10.1038/mp. 2015.190
159. Tallal, P. (2012). Improving neural response to sound improves reading. *Proc. Natl. Acad. Sci. U.S.A.* 109, 16406–16407. doi: 10.1073/ pnas.12141 22109
160. Tarver, J., Daley, D., and Sayal, K. (2014). Attention-deficit hyperactivity disorder (ADHD): an updated review of the essential facts. *Child Care Health Dev.* 40, 762–774. doi: 10.1111/cch.12139
161. Tautz, D. (1992). Problems and paradigms: Redundancies, development and the flow of information. *BioEssays* 14, 263–266. doi: 10.1002/ bies.95014 0410
162. Taylor, A., and Kim-Cohen, J. (2007). Meta-analysis of gene-environment interactions in developmental psychopathology. *Dev. Psychopathol.* 19, 1029– 1037. doi: 10.1017/S095457940700051X
163. Taylor, S. E., Way, B. M., Welch, W. T., Hilmert, C. J., Lehman, B. J., and Eisenberger, N. I. (2006). Early family environment, current adversity, the serotonin transporter promoter polymorphism, and depressive symptomatology. *Biol. Psychiatry* 60, 671–676. doi: 10.1016/j.biopsych. 2006.04.019
164. Teh, A. L., Pan, H., Chen, L., Ong, M.-L., Dogra, S., and Wong, J. (2014). The effect of genotype and in utero environment on interindividual variation in neonate DNA methylomes. *Genome Res.* 24, 1064–1074. doi: 10.1101/gr.171439.113
165. Thapar, A., Cooper, M., Eyre, O., and Langley, K. (2012). Practitioner review: What have we learnt about the causes of ADHD? *J. Child Psychol. Psychiatry* 54, 3–16. doi: 10.1111/j.1469-7610.2012.02611.x
166. Thapar, A., Cooper, M., Eyre, O., and Langley, K. (2013). What have we learnt about the causes of ADHD? *J. Child Psychol. Psychiatry* 54, 3–16. doi: 10.1111/j.1469- 7610.2012.02611.x
167. Thapar, A., Langley, K., Asherson, P., and Gill, M. (2007). Gene-environment interplay in attention-deficit hyperactivity disorder and the importance of a developmental perspective. *Br. J. Psychiatry* 190, 1–3. doi: 10.1192/bjp.bp.106. 027003
168. Thomas, D. (2010). Gene–environment-wide association studies: emerging approaches. *Nat. Rev. Genet.* 11, 259–272. doi: 10.1038/ nrg2764
169. Thompson, L. A., Morgan, G., Unger, C. A., and Covey, L. A. (2017). Prenatal maternal cortisol measures predict learning and short-term memory performance in 3- but not 5-month-old infants. *Dev. Psychobiol.* 59, 723–737. doi: 10.1002/dev.21530
170. Truzzi, A., Bornstein, M. H., Senese, V. P., Shinohara, K., Setoh, P., and Esposito, G. (2017). Serotonin transporter gene polymorphisms and early parent-infant interactions are related to adult male heart rate response to female crying. *Front. Physiol.* 8:111. doi: 10.3389/fphys.2017. 00111
171. Truzzi, A., Poquérusse, J., Setoh, P., Shinohara, K., Bornstein, M. H., and Esposito, G. (2018). Oxytocin receptor gene polymorphisms (rs53576) and early paternal care sensitize males to distressing female vocalizations. *Dev. Psychobiol.* 60, 333–339. doi: 10.1002/dev. 21606
172. Tsiouris, J. A. (2010). Pharmacotherapy for aggressive behaviours in persons with intellectual disabilities: treatment or mistreatment? *J. Intellect. Disabil. Res.* 54, 1–16. doi: 10.1111/j.1365-2788.2009.0 1232.x
173. Uematsu, A., Kikusui, T., Kihara, T., Harada, T., Kato, M., Nakano, K., et al. (2007). Maternal approaches to pup ultrasonic vocalizations produced by a nanocrystalline silicon thermo-acoustic emitter. *Brain Res.* 1163, 91–99. doi: 10.1016/j.brainres.2007.05.056

174. Unick, G. J., Snowden, L., and Hastings, J. (2009). Heterogeneity in comorbidity between major depressive disorder and generalized anxiety disorder and its clinical consequences. *J. Nerv. Ment. Dis.* 197, 215–224. doi: 10.1097/NMD. 0b013e31819d954f

175. van der Meer, D., Hartman, C. A., Richards, J., Bralten, J. B., Franke, B., Oosterlaan, J., et al. (2014). The serotonin transporter gene polymorphism 5-HTTLPR moderates the effects of stress on attention-deficit/hyperactivity disorder. *J. Child Psychol. Psychiatry* 55, 1363–1371. doi: 10.1111/jcpp. 12240

176. van IJzendoorn, M. H., Bakermans-Kranenburg, M. J., and Ebstein, R. P. (2011). Methylation matters in child development: toward developmental behavioral epigenetics. *Child Dev. Perspect.* 5, 305–310. doi: 10.1111/ j.1750-8606.2011. 00202.x

177. Velez Edwards, D. R., Naj, A. C., Monda, K., North, K. E., Neuhouser, M., Magvanjav, O., et al. (2013). Gene-environment interactions and obesity traits among postmenopausal African-American and Hispanic women in the Women's Health Initiative SHARe Study. *Hum. Genet.* 132, 323–336. doi: 10.1007/s00439-012-1246-3

178. Wang, H. G., Jeffries, J. J., and Wang, T. F. (2016). Genetic and developmental perspective of language abnormality in autism and schizophrenia: one disease occurring at different ages in humans? *Neuroscientist* 22, 119–131. doi: 10.1177/ 1073858415572078

179. Wang, M., Li, H., Deater-Deckard, K., and Zhang, W. (2018). Interacting effect of Catechol-O-Methyltransferase (COMT) and Monoamine Oxidase A (MAOA) Gene Polymorphisms, and stressful life events on aggressive behavior in Chinese Male adolescents. *Front. Psychol.* 9:1079. doi: 10.3389/fpsyg.2018.01079 Wong, I. C. K., Besag, F. M. C., Santosh, P. J., and Murray, M. L. (2004). Use of selective serotonin reuptake inhibitors in children and adolescents. *Drug Saf.* 27, 991–1000.

180. Yang, Q., Khoury, M. J., Friedman, J. M., and Flanders, W. D. (2003). On the use of population attributable fraction to determine sample size for case-control studies of gene-environment interaction. *Epidemiology* 14, 161–167. doi: 10. 1097/01.EDE.0000040256.22618.12

181. Zhang, D., Cheng, L., Badner, J. A., Chen, C., Chen, Q., Luo, W., et al. (2010). Genetic control of individual differences in gene-specific methylation in human brain. *Am. J. Hum. Genet.* 86, 411–419. doi: 10.1016/j.ajhg.2010. 02.005

182. Zhang, H., Herman, A. I., Kranzler, H. R., Anton, R. F., Zhao, H., Zheng, W., et al. (2013). Array-based profiling of DNA methylation changes associated with alcohol dependence. *Alcohol. Clin. Exp. Res.* 37(Suppl. 1), E108–E115. doi: 10.1111/j.1530-0277.2012.01928.x

22

Early Trauma and Cognitive Functions of Patients with Schizophrenia

Carolina G. Carrilho[1], Simone S. Cougo[1], Tatiane Bombassaro[1], André Augusto B. Varella[2], Gilberto S. Alves[3], Sergio Machado[4,5,6], Eric Murillo-Rodriguez[5,7], Dolores Malaspina[8], Antonio E. Nardi[6] and André B. Veras[1,5,6,8]**

[1] Translational Research Group on Mental Health (GPTranSMe), Dom Bosco Catholic University, Campo Grande, Brazil,
[2] Research Laboratory on Autism and Behavior (LAPAC), Dom Bosco Catholic University, Campo Grande, Brazil,
[3] Department of Internal Medicine, Federal University of Maranhão (UFMA), São Luís, Brazil, [4] Physical Activity Neuroscience Laboratory, Physical Activity Sciences Postgraduate Program-Salgado de Oliveira University (UNIVERSO), São Gonçalo,
Brazil, [5] Intercontinental Neuroscience Research Group, Universidad Anáhuac Mayab, Mérida, Mexico, [6] Laboratory of Panic and Respiration (LabPR-UFRJ), Psychiatry Institute of Federal University of Rio de Janeiro (IPUB-UFRJ), Rio de Janeiro,
Brazil, [7] Laboratorio de Neurociencias Moleculares e Integrativas, Escuela de Medicina División Ciencias de la Salud, Universidad Anáhuac Mayab, Mérida, Mexico, [8] Departments of Psychiatry, Neuroscience and Genetics, Icahn School of Medicine at Mt. Sinai Medical Center, New York, NY, United States

***Correspondence:**
Carolina G. Carrilho
carolcarrilho1@hotmail.com
André B. Veras
barcielaveras@hotmail.com

Aim: The following work aims to investigate the putative correlation between early trauma and cognitive functions, as well as psychotic symptoms and cognitive functions, in individuals diagnosed with schizophrenia.

Methods: A quantitative assessment was performed with 20 individuals diagnosed with schizophrenia according to the 5th edition of the Diagnostic and Statistical Manual (DSM-5) criteria and who were in ongoing outpatient treatment in Psychosocial Care Centres in Brazil. Clinical measurements comprised a semistructured clinical interview, a screening questionnaire for common mental disorders, the Positive and Negative Syndrome Scale (PANSS), and the Early Trauma Inventory Self-Report—Short Form (ETISR-SF). Cognitive assessment included Beta III test, Concentrated Attention (CA) test, Color Trails Test (CTT), and Visual Face Memory (VFM) test.

Results: Age-adjusted analysis showed a negative correlation between early trauma and visual memory performance ($r = -0.585$, $p = 0.007$) and negative symptoms and attention performance ($r = -0.715$, $p = 0.000$).

Conclusion: Although a cause–effect relationship cannot be firmly stated, an association between early trauma experience and cognitive impairment such as visual memory, as well as a relationship between negative symptoms and attention domains, is suggested by our preliminary findings. Future studies with larger sample sizes and prospective design will clarify the long-term effects of early exposure to trauma and its clinical meaning in terms of developing psychotic-related illness.

Keywords: schizophrenia, early trauma, cognition, memory, attention

INTRODUCTION

More than 75% of patients with schizophrenia show some level of cognitive impairment, leading to poor functional status and impairments in social interaction. Therefore, when there is an improvement in cognition and executive function, there is also an improvement in quality of life, social interactions, and treatment outcomes (1).

Thus, cognitive performance in patients with schizophrenia may be related to the illness itself and to endophenotypes, with cognitive profiles indicating traits, which can be developed later on the course of the illness (2). This hypothesis has been supported by studies showing an overlap between cognitive deficits between SZ patients and their relatives. Patients with schizophrenia show a lower performance in neuropsychological tests when compared to both healthy controls and siblings. In addition, overlapping cognitive symptoms in patients with schizophrenia and their siblings seem to appear, with the latter exhibiting milder cognitive impairment, including memory, executive function, and attention.

Studies suggested that early trauma could be a risk factor associated with the development of schizophrenia. Environmental stimuli during childhood are crucial for the development of functional abilities in the human brain. Accordingly, physical or emotional trauma during childhood may cause cognitive impairment and increase the risk of developing schizophrenia or other mental disorders later in life (3). Early trauma is related to a reduced brain volume and reduced brain activity, therefore contributing to some of the neuropsychological impairments present in patients with schizophrenia. Moreover, patients with schizophrenia and an early trauma history show greater impairments in memory, attention, and social and executive functioning (4, 5).

Although previous studies suggest an association between early trauma and the risk to develop schizophrenia, there is still poor comprehension on how traumatic experiences may influence psychopathological and cognitive symptoms in those individuals. The current study is a preliminary investigation aiming to identify early trauma and their relationship with cognitive functions, and how cognitive functions can correlate to psychopathology in a clinical sample of patients with schizophrenia. We hypothesize that specific cognitive and psychopathological symptoms observed in schizophrenic individuals may be associated with early life exposure to sexual or psychological traumatic experience.

METHODS

All interviews and clinical assessments were conducted by one experienced psychiatrist (AV) and psychologists (SC and CC), no power analysis was carried out, and the recruitment was done by convenience with patients who were in ongoing outpatient treatment in Psychosocial Care Centres for mental health.

Participants

Twenty individuals with a diagnosis of schizophrenia according to the DSM-V criteria (6) were assessed. Of the 20 subjects, 15 were male and 5 were female, with ages ranging from 23 to 54 years old.

Inclusion criteria included subjects from both sexes (male/female), with an age ranging from 18 to 65 years old and a diagnosis of schizophrenia according to the DSM-V criteria, who were on outpatient treatment in a Psychosocial Care Centre in Brazil, were able to understand the instructions provided by the interviewer in the assessment process and able to understand and sign the informed consent form (ICF), and have formal authorization by their legal guardians to participate in the research.

Subjects who did not meet the inclusion criteria and individuals at psychotic states or any other acute condition (e.g., disorganized mental activity or psychomotor agitation), with neurodegenerative problems that have compromised cognitive functions, as well as any other primary condition rather than schizophrenia (alcohol or substance abuse, mood, or anxiety disorders), were excluded from the study. Of the 20 subjects initially approached, all agreed to participate in the study and met the inclusion criteria.

Materials

The research was approved by the local Ethics Committee. All patients answered sociodemographic data that were relevant to the research (age, ethnicity, education, occupational situation, family configuration, hospitalization history, and the development of schizophrenia). In addition, data were also supplemented with the information gathered from medical records of each patient or a complementary interview with the relatives.

Clinical and Psychiatric Measures

Clinical and psychiatric assessment comprised the following instruments: a) Screening Questionnaire [an instrument developed by the Psychiatry Genomics Consortium (PGC)—Centre of Genetic Psychiatry, from the University of Southern California and translated to Portuguese; the questionnaire screened for schizophrenia, mania, depression, use of substances, obsessive–compulsive behavior, post-traumatic stress symptoms (based on the DSM-5 criteria), and physical health history]; b) a Portuguese version of the Diagnostic Interview for Psychosis and Affective Disorder (DIPAD) (its objective is to use diagnostic criteria for schizophrenia and bipolar disorder through sociodemographic data and questions to identify depression, mania, and psychotic symptoms); c) Positive and Negative Syndrome Scale (PANSS) (7); and d) Early Trauma Inventory Self Report—Short Form (ETISR-SF) (8) composed of 27 items punctuated in dichotomous responses assessing the occurrence of trauma in childhood and adolescence. The assessment was subdivided into categories: general trauma (for example, occurrence of natural disasters, witnessing the death of close people, and separation of parents), physical abuse, emotional abuse, and sexual abuse.

Cognitive Assessment

Cognitive assessment included the following instruments: a) BETA III: Revised Beta Examination to assess intellectual abilities in low educated or illiterate subjects [nonverbal intellectual abilities through five subtests were explored: codes, complete figures, difference assessment, pictorial errors, and matrix reasoning (9)]; b) Visual Face Memory (VFM) [encompassing face memorization and other related information, e.g., names and surnames, profession, location, and employment (10)]; c) Concentrated Attention (CA; the test evaluates the ability to maintain focused attention by selecting a source of information among all that are available at a given time and manage to direct their attention to this stimulus during a certain time) (11); and d) Color Trails Test (CTT)—Forms A and B, which evaluates several functions, including the ability to maintain mental engagement, visual tracking, motor skills, mental flexibility, and inhibitory capacity. In Form A, the individual will draw lines by joining numbered circles consecutively, thus assessing sustained attention. In Form B, the individual will connect the circles with numbers consecutively, interspersing them with colors, thus assessing cognitive flexibility and divided attention (12).

Data Analysis

Continuous variables were evaluated for their mean and standard deviation (SD), and categorical variables were evaluated for absolute and relative frequencies. Correlations were assessed using Spearman's *r* test, considering statistically significant associations (those with a level of $p \leq 0.05$). Continuous variables were sorted by cognitive tests such as BETA III, VFM, CA, and CTT, and psychopathological assessment such as general trauma, physical trauma, sexual trauma, negative PANSS, and general symptoms PANSS. Categorical variables were divided into sex, marital status, occupational situation, education, and ethnicity. Data were analyzed using SPSS 20.0 version package.

Furthermore, because of the hypothesis-based proof-of-concept nature of this analysis, correction for multiple testing was not applied. This is a pilot study that aims at hypothesis testing for future protocols. Therefore, in a small sample, when there is a prior understanding of the correlations intended in order to make a pilot study (hypothesis testing), statistical tests that are used for larger samples in fully conclusive clinical trials are not needed.

RESULTS

Sociodemographic Characteristics

Research participants (n = 20) had a mean age of 37.4 years, were predominantly male (75%), were single (75%), were of African descent (60%), and were retired (80%). Most had a low education level (45% with incomplete primary education), with an average of 8.5 years in school (SD ± 3.14). Complete information on sociodemographic data is presented in **Table 1**.

The arithmetic mean of percentages with a positive response in the symptoms proceeded from the Screening Questionnaire, and 84% of the participants reported psychotic symptoms, 65% had obsessive symptoms, 63% had symptoms of post-traumatic stress, 54% had symptoms of mania, 45% presented compulsion, 41% had tobacco use, 25% had use of marijuana, 13% had use of alcohol, and 13% had dependence of other drugs. The data are shown in **Figure 1**.

In the assessment with the Diagnostic Interview for Psychoses and Affective Disorders (DIPAD), it was noted that the average age of individuals at the onset of schizophrenia was 20.8 years (SD = 8.35). Of the 20 participants in the study, 11 participants (55% of the sample) were employed/studied at the time of the onset and 16 (80%) had good social relationships (family/friends) before the first crisis. In the subscale with questions about depression, 12 participants (60%) presented symptoms of depression. In the questions about mania symptoms, most participants (65%) reported no symptoms. In the subscale with questions about delusions, 17 participants (85%) reported having strange or unusual experiences—beliefs that they later found to be untrue. All participants (100%) reported some level of positive response to neuroleptic medications to control the positive symptoms—delusions and hallucinations—after initiation of drug treatment.

TABLE 1 | Sociodemographic profile of the sample.

Sex	**N (%)**
Male	15 (75%)
Female	5 (15%)
Marital status	**N (%)**
Single	15 (75%)
Married	3 (15%)
Widower	1 (5%)
Divorced	1 (5%)
Occupational situation	**N (%)**
Retired	16 (80%)
In the process of retirement	2 (10%)
Withdrawn from work	2 (10%)
Education	**N (%)**
Elementary school incomplete	9 (45%)
Complete primary education	1 (5%)
Incomplete high school	3 (15%)
Complete high school	6 (30%)
Higher education	1 (5%)
Average education in years of study	8.5 (SD ± 3.14)
Ethnicity	**N (%)**
Indigenous	2 (10%)
Caucasian	2 (10%)
Black	4 (20%)
Mulatto	12 (60%)

The mean of the total score of the participants for this instrument was 61.1 (SD ± 11.69), and the subscales presented the following results: positive symptoms presented a mean of 14.6 (SD = 11.69), negative symptoms presented a mean of 12.4 (SD = 4.57), and overall psychopathology presented a mean of 33.55 (SD = 6.19).

Of the 20 people assessed, only 1 reported not remembering to have suffered any traumatic situation in childhood, and 1 reported a situation linked to the general trauma subscale (parental divorce). Thus, 90% of the sample reported suffering at least five traumatic situations (**Table 2**).

In this instrument, the average of different types of trauma experienced by the sample was calculated according to the subscales and total scale. In the general trauma subscale, with issues involving exposure to accidents, illness, and deaths of close associates, an average of 4.19 positive responses were identified among the 11 dichotomous issues that could be scored. Considering physical punishment, emotional abuse, and sexual abuse, it was possible to observe the higher

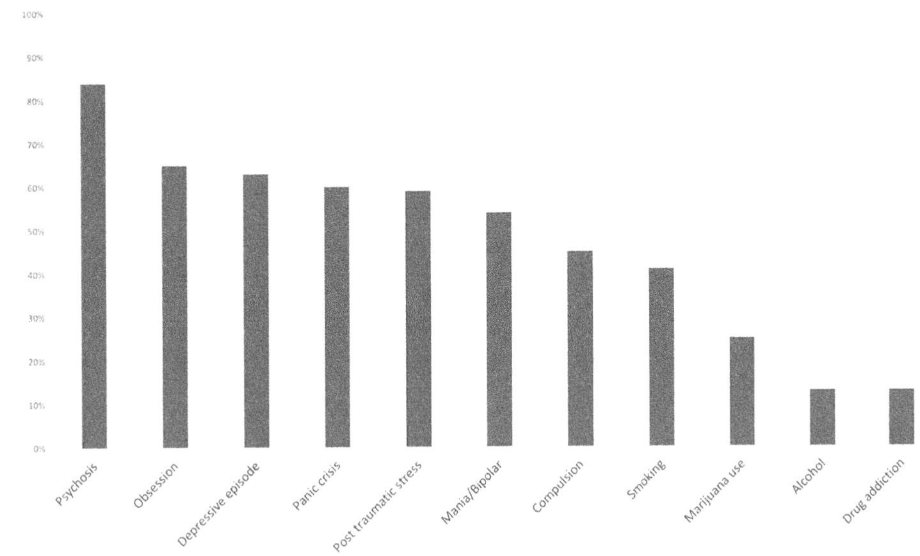

FIGURE 1 | Mean of the positive scores of the Screening Questionnaire.

TABLE 2 | Results of the early trauma scale.

Type of trauma	Statistics	Value
General trauma	Mean	4.19
	Standard deviation	2.65
	Minimum	0
	Maximum	10
Physical punishment	Mean	2.24
	Standard deviation	1.87
	Minimum	0
	Maximum	5
Emotional abuse	Mean	2.62
	Standard deviation	1.96
	Minimum	0
	Maximum	5
Sexual events	Mean	1.38
	Standard deviation	1.94
	Minimum	0
	Maximum	6
Fear and out of body feeling	Mean	1.0
	Standard deviation	0.80
	Minimum	0
	Maximum	2
Total of items	Mean	11.10
	Standard deviation	6.75
	Minimum	0
	Maximum	22

frequency of emotional abuse (mean of 2.62 out of five questions), physical punishment (2.24 of five questions), and sexual abuse (1.38 of six questions). The Fear and Out of Body Feeling subscales (altered state of consciousness) consist of trauma intensity markers.

Cognitive Performance

In the Matrix Reasoning (from BETA-III) subtest, the overall average was 18 (SD ± 8.8), corresponding to performance below the mean of the population assessed by the test, according to sex (average of 19%; median-inferior rating), age (29%; median-inferior rating), and level of education (37%; average rating; **Figure 2**). In the Codes—BETA III subtest, the overall mean was 15 (SD ± 10), corresponding to performance below the mean of the population assessed by the test, according to gender (average 15.25%; median-inferior rating), age (19%; lower rating), and level of education (16%; lower rating; **Figure 2**). The CA instrument presented an overall mean of 9.8 (SD ± 12), corresponding to performance below the average of the population evaluated according to the test references. Regarding gender, the result presented an average of 11% (medium-inferior rating), age 11.4% (medium-inferior rating), and level of education 15.6% (medium-inferior rating; **Figure 2**). The Visual Face Memory (VFM) test showed an average of 32.25 (SD ± 20.3), corresponding to performance within the average of the population, according to gender (average 46.25%; medium rating), age (28.25%; medium-inferior rating), and level of education (59%; medium rating; **Figure 2**). In the CTT—Form A, the result presented an average of 24.5 (SD ± 15.3), corresponding to performance below the average of the population, according to gender (average 21.75%; inferior rating), age (19.5%; inferior rating), and level of education (21.25%; inferior rating; **Figure 2**). In Form B of the CTT, the result presented an average of 24.5 (SD ± 11.7), corresponding to an inferior performance, according to gender (mean 21.75%; inferior rating), age (19.5%; inferior rating), and level of education (21.25%; inferior rating; **Figure 2**).

Correlations between early trauma (ETISR-SF) and VFM according to age and level of education, as well as a correlation between psychopathology (PANSS) and attention (AC and CTT),

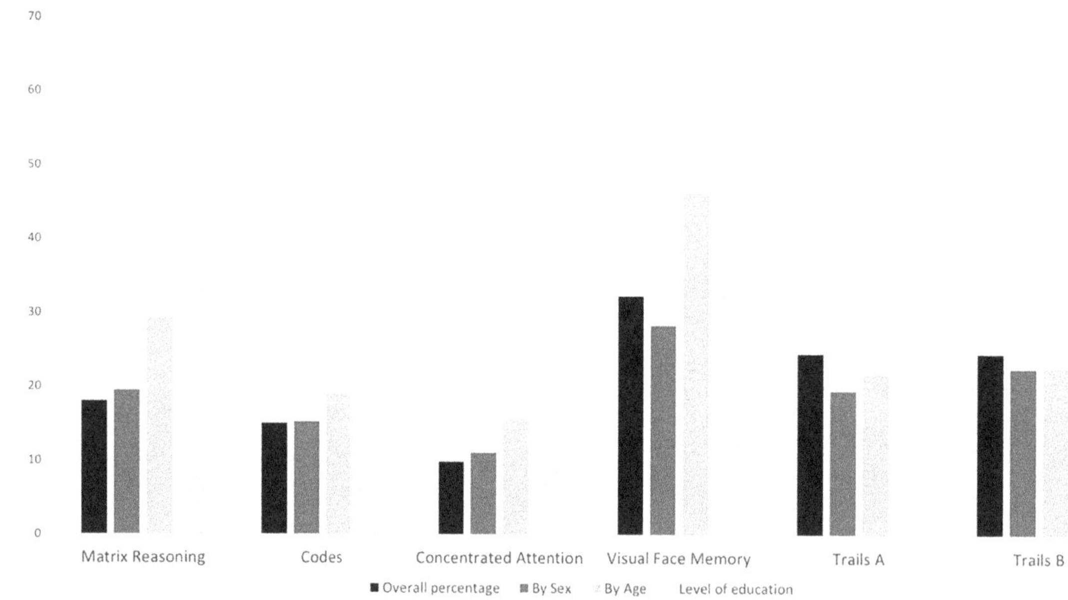

FIGURE 2 | Mean of cognitive tests scores.

were found. The correlations observed between variables that showed a trend towards statistical significance are shown in **Table 3**.

DISCUSSION

In this study, a negative correlation between general early trauma and visual memory (according to age and level of education) was found, that is, the higher the individual's early trauma score, the lower the visual memory performance. Studies show that individuals with schizophrenia and a history of early trauma show memory deficits when compared to schizophrenia patients with no history of early trauma, and that these traumatic experiences may lead to neurocognitive deficits (13). A neuroradiological and neuropathological study conducted by Suddath et al. (14) with twins with schizophrenia concluded that anatomical changes in the brain, such as a smaller left anterior hippocampus, are present in almost every twin with schizophrenia and not present in healthy twins. This finding indicates that hippocampal deficits are related to schizophrenia.

Within the sample assessed in the present study, 90% of the individuals reported suffering trauma during childhood, with emotional abuse being the most frequent, followed by physical abuse and sexual abuse. Gil (15) noted that there is a great relationship between early adversities and increased vulnerability to psychosis. With a sample of 100 individuals diagnosed with schizophrenia, the author observed that traumatic experiences increase or reduce the vulnerability to psychotic disorder. Besides, in addition to influencing the etiology of schizophrenia, these traumatic experiences also affect the functional and social performance of the patient. Considering the studies mentioned, and the correlation found in the present study, nongenetic exposure such as early trauma can be an aggravating factor for the differences found in hippocampal activity (hippocampal deficit) in schizophrenic patients (13).

According to Lardinois et al. (16), exposure to trauma can affect dopaminergic transmissions and contribute to a hyperactivity of the hypothalamic–adrenal–pituitary axis (HPA axis) during childhood, which also increases sensibility to stress events in adulthood. Both of these phenomena can be found in individuals with schizophrenia and were not found in control groups. A systematic review conducted by Read et al. (17) with articles between 1972 and 2004 on schizophrenia and early trauma present the Traumagenic Neurodevelopmental Model hypothesis that when the trauma is prolonged, severe or daily, it can increase vulnerability to stress and contribute to a hypersensitivity that may lead the individual to be more prone to psychotic experiences. This indicates that neurologic and biochemical alterations found in schizophrenia and seen as etiological biogenetic evidence can also be related to early trauma and not only to genetic factors.

A study conducted by Veras et al. (18) that assessed the role of oxytocin in the pathogenesis of 48 patients with schizophrenia showed that in 5 of those cases, patients who presented a variation in oxytocin receptor rare single-nucleotide variants also showed more severe cognitive deficits, despite the severity of psychopathology, and a history of early trauma. Considering schizophrenia as a neurodevelopmental disorder, and since it is not a single-cause disorder and most commonly emerges in adolescence, any abnormal brain changes during adolescence such as the exaggeration of typical synaptic elimination and other neural elements may contribute to both the development of psychosis and impairment of cognitive functions later on (19).

We also observed a negative correlation between attention and negative symptoms, that is, the greater the presence of negative symptoms, the poorer the performance in attention (sustained and divided). Negative symptoms are usually

TABLE 3 | Correlations between cognition and trauma with the Early Trauma Inventory Self Report—Short Form (ETISR-SF), and between cognitive tests and the Positive and Negative Syndrome Scale (PANSS).

Cognitive tests ↓	Psychopathological assessment →	Overall trauma	Physical trauma	Sexual trauma	Total trauma	Negative PANSS	General symptoms PANSS	Total
CA (Concentrated Attention)	r					−0.516		
(age)	Sig.					0.02		
VFM (Visual Face Memory)	r				−0.516			
(overall)	Sig.				0.02			
VFM (Visual Face Memory)	r	−0.446			−0.585			
(age)	Sig.	0.049			0.007			
VFM (Visual Face Memory)	r				−0.444			
(sex)	Sig.				0.05			
VFM (Visual Face Memory)	r			−0.597				
(level of education)	Sig.			0.005				
Trails A (Color Trails Test)	r						−0.455	
(overall)	Sig.						0.44	
Trails A (Color Trails Test)	r					−0.449	−0.542	−0.508
(level of education)	Sig.					0.047	0.014	0.022
Trails B (Color Trails Test)	r					−0.631	−0.474	−0.515
(overall)	Sig.					0.003	0.035	0.02
Trails B (Color Trails Test)	r					−0.715	−0.549	−0.604
(age)	Sig.					0.000	0.012	0.005
Trails B (Color Trails Test)	r		0.454			−0.596		
(sex)	Sig.		0.045			0.006		
Trails B (Color Trails Test)	r					−0.521	−0.622	−0.630
(level of education)	Sig.					0.018	0.003	0.003

related to attention impairments, and such impairments can cause disruption of the processing of social information. A study with 40 patients with schizophrenia and 40 healthy controls conducted by Sanz et al. (20) noted that patients with schizophrenia have severe attention deficits, and the lower the performance in attention assessment, the higher the score of negative symptoms in the PANSS scale. This indicates the patient's inability to gate and process incoming information properly and that an impairment in attention can cause difficulty in interpersonal interaction (21).

Post-traumatic symptoms (59%), depressive episodes (63%), and panic attacks (60%) are within the most observed comorbidity symptoms in the sample. Buckley et al. (22) observed that there is a significant relation between different groups of symptoms in schizophrenia, with depression, anxiety, and substance abuse being the most common. Anxiety is commonly present in patients with schizophrenia, varying from OCD, panic, PTSD, social phobia, specific phobias, GAD, and acute stress disorder. Studies show a high prevalence of post-traumatic comorbid symptoms in schizophrenia, which should bring greater clinical attention due to the higher risk of suicidality of those individuals (23), and there is also an indication that treating comorbid anxiety can help in the course of schizophrenia (24).

A review (25) with studies published from 2001 to 2014 about the relationship between childhood trauma and symptoms of psychosis showed that the etiology of schizophrenia is just as socially based as disorders such as depression and anxiety, and childhood trauma causes changes in the brain involving the hippocampus and HPA axis that are also found in depression and post-traumatic stress disorder. Also, a research conducted in 100 patients with early psychosis showed that over three-quarters of those patients reported exposure to childhood trauma, and the childhood trauma scores were positively correlated with emotional distress, such as increased depression, anxiety, and stress symptoms (26).

Childhood trauma can be an aggravating factor for psychosis, since exposure to early trauma increases the risk of psychosis (27). A study conducted in three different hospitals in Oslo (28) assessed 194 patients with schizophrenia and noted that 82% of the patients had experienced some kind of childhood trauma, having a higher prevalence of childhood trauma when compared to other groups, such as control groups. There is also a correlation between childhood trauma and psychosis, since siblings of patients with schizophrenia present lower scores of abuse and neglect compared to patients with schizophrenia, which can indicate that exposure to trauma may result in illness (29). Some limitations of our study deserve further comments. First, the small sample size limits the power of statistical analysis. Second, there is an absence of a control group. Finally, the cross-sectional basis of our data precludes any firm conclusion on the cause–effect relationship between trauma and clinical features. In spite of these constraints, the correlations may be considered clinically significant enough to show a trend towards statistical significance even in a heterogeneous and naturalistic sample.

CONCLUSIONS

This is the first study assessing a Brazilian sample on the relationship between early trauma, cognitive functions, and psychotic symptoms. Our preliminary findings, although limited by the small sample size, seem to validate the hypothesis of a specific association between memory deficits and childhood exposure to trauma. Our results thus shed light on the need to investigate the putative biological mechanisms related to the association of trauma and clinical characteristics in schizophrenia. Future studies encompassing larger samples and control groups are needed in order to address these questions with more details.

AUTHOR CONTRIBUTIONS

CC and SC contributed to data collection and analysis, text review, and editing. TB contributed to data analysis, text review and editing, and tables editing. ABV and GSA contributed to data analysis, text review and mentoring. SM, EM-R, DM, AN and AABV contributed to text review and mentoring. CLA contributed to data design and critical review.

ACKNOWLEDGEMENTS

Sergio Eduardo de Carvalho Machado, was supported by a grant from the Carlos Chagas Foundation for the Research Support in the State of Rio de Janeiro (FAPERJ), Young Scientists from the State of Rio de Janeiro, E -26/203.295/2017.

REFERENCES

1. Rispaud SG, Rose J, Kurtz MM. The relationship between change in cognition and change in functional ability in schizophrenia during cognitive and psychosocial rehabilitation. *Psychiatry Res* (2016) 244:145–50. doi: 10.1016/j.psychres.2016.07.033
2. Sitskoorn MM, Aleman A, Ebisch SJH, Appels MCM, Kahn RS. Cognitive deficits in relatives of patients with schizophrenia: a meta-analysis. *Schizophr Res* (2004) 71:285–95. doi: 10.1016/j.schres.2004.03.007
3. Van Os J, Kenis G, Rutten BP. The environment and schizophrenia. *Nature* (2010) 468:203–12. doi: 10.1038/nature09563
4. Xinbin L, Tian Q, Bo Q, Zhang G, Zheng W, Tag Y, et al. Impact of childhood trauma on sensorimotor gating in Chinese patients with chronic schizophrenia. *Psychiatry Res* (2018) 263:69–73. doi: 10.1016/j.psychres.2018.01.037
5. Shannon C, Douse K, McCusker C, Feeney L, Barrett S, Mulholland C. The association between childhood trauma and memory functioning in schizophrenia. *Schizophr Bull* (2011) 37:531–7. doi: 10.1093/schbul/sbp096
6. American Psychiatric Association. *DSM-5—Manual Diagnóstico e Estatístico de Transtornos Mentais*. Porto Alegre: Artmed (2014).
7. Kay SR, Fiszbein A, Opler LA. The Positive and Negative Syndrome Scale (PANSS) for schizophrenia. *Schizophr Bull* (1987) 13:261–75. doi: 10.1093/schbul/13.2.261
8. Bremner JD, Vermetten E, Mazure CM. Development and preliminary psychometric properties of an instrument for the measurement of childhood trauma: the Early Trauma Inventory. *Depress Anxiety* (2000) 12:1–12. doi: 10.1002/1520-6394(2000)12:1<1::AID-DA1>3.0.CO;2-W
9. Rabelo IS, Panacaro SV, Leme IFAS, Ambiel RAM, Alves GAS. *Teste não verbal de inteligência geral—BETA III—Subtestes raciocínio matricial e códigos*. Manual Técnico. São Paulo: Casa do Psicólogo (2011).
10. Seisdedos N. *Memoria Visual de Rostros (MVR)*. Madrid: TEA Ediciones (2002).
11. Cambraia SV. *O Teste de Atenção Concentrada AC*. Manual. São Paulo, SP: Vetor Editora (2009).
12. D'Elia LF, Satz P, Uchiyama CL, White T. *Color trails test: professional manual*. Odessa, FL: Psychological Assessment Resources (1996).
13. Ruby E, Polito S, McMahon K, Gorovitz M, Corcoran C, Malaspina D. Pathways associating childhood trauma to the neurobiology of schizophrenia. *Front Psychol Behav Sci* (2014) 3:1–17.
14. Suddath RL, Christison GW, Torrey EF, Casanova MF, Weinberger DR. Anatomical abnormalities in the brains of monozygotic twins discordant for schizophrenia. *N Eng J Med* (1990) 322:789–94. doi: 10.1056/NEJM199003223221201
15. Gil A. *A associação de abuso e negligência na infância com prejuízo da funcionalidade em esquizofrênicos [dissertation/master's thesis]*. Porto Alegre (RS): Universidade Federal do Rio Grande do Sul (2006).
16. Lardinois M, Lataster T, Mengelers R, Van Os J, Myin-Germeys I. Childhood trauma and increased stress sensitivity in psychosis. *Acta Psychiatr Scand* (2011) 123:28–35. doi: 10.1111/j.1600-0447.2010.01594.x
17. Read J, Van Os J, Morrison AP, Ross CA. Childhood trauma, psychosis and schizophrenia: a literature review with theoretical and clinical implications. *Acta Psychiatr Scand* (2005) 112:330–50. doi: 10.1111/j.1600-0447.2005.00634.x
18. Veras AB, Getz M, Froemke RC, Nardi AE, Alves GS, Walsh-Messinger J, et al. Rare missense coding variants in oxytocin receptor (OXTR) in schizophrenia cases are associated with early trauma exposure, cognition and emotional processing. *J Psychiatr Res* (2018) 97:58–64. doi: 10.1016/j.jpsychires.2017.11.011
19. Paus T, Keshavan M, Giedd JN. Why do many psychiatric disorders emerge during adolescence? *Nat Rev Neurosci* (2008) 9:947–57. doi: 10.1038/nrn2513
20. Sanz JC, Gomez V, Vargas ML, Marin JJ. Dimensions of attention impairment and negative symptoms in schizophrenia: a multidimensional approach using the conners continuous performance test in a Spanish population. *Cogn Behav Neurol* (2012) 25:63–71. doi: 10.1097/WNN.0b013e318255feaf
21. Tsai J, Lysaker PH, Vohs JL. Negative symptoms and concomitant attention deficits in schizophrenia: associations with prospective assessments of anxiety, social dysfunction, and avoidant coping. *J Ment Health* (2010) 19:184–92. doi: 10.3109/09638230903469277
22. Buckley PF, Miller BJ, Lehrer DS, Castle DJ. Psychiatric comorbidities and schizophrenia. *Schizophr Bull* (2009) 35:383–402. doi: 10.1093/schbul/sbn135
23. Seow LS, Ong C, Mahesh MV, Sagayadevan V, Shafie S, Chong SA, et al. A systematic review on comorbid post-traumatic stress disorder in schizophrenia. *Schizophr Res* (2016) 176:441–51. doi: 10.1016/j.schres.2016.05.004
24. Braga R, Reynolds GP, Siris SG. Anxiety and comorbidity in schizophrenia. *Psychiatry Res* (2013) 210:1–7. doi: 10.1016/j.psychres.2013.07.030
25. Read J, Fosse R, Moskowitz A, Perry B. The traumagenic neurodevelopmental model of psychosis revisited. *Neuropsychiatry* (2014) 4:65–79. doi: 10.2217/npy.13.89
26. Duhig M, Patterson S, Connell M, Foley S, Capra C, Dark F, et al. The prevalence and correlates of childhood trauma in patients with early psychosis. *Aust N Z J Psychiatry* (2015) 49:651–9. doi: 10.1177/0004867415575379
27. Varese F, Smeets F, Drukker M, Lieverse R, Lataster T, Viechtbauer W, et al. Childhood adversities increase the risk of psychosis: a meta-analysis of patient-control, prospective- and cross-sectional cohort studies. *Schizophr Bull* (2012) 38:661–71. doi: 10.1093/schbul/sbs050
28. Larsson S, Andreassen OA, Aas M, Røssberg JI, Mork E, Steen NE, et al. High prevalence of childhood trauma in patients with schizophrenia spectrum

and affective disorder. *Compr Psychiatry* (2013) 54:123–7. doi: 10.1016/j.comppsych.2012.06.009

29. Heins M, Simons C, Lataster T, Pfeifer S, Versmissen D, Lardinois M, et al. Childhood trauma and psychosis: a case-control and case-sibling comparison across different levels of genetic liability, psychopathology, and type of trauma. *Am J Psychiatry* (2011) 168:1286–94. doi: 10.1176/appi.ajp.2011.10101531

23

Disconnected – Impaired Interoceptive Accuracy and its Association to Self-Perception and Cardiac Vagal Tone in Patients with Dissociative Disorder

Eva Schäflein [1], Heribert C. Sattel [1], Olga Pollatos [2] and Martin Sack [1]*

[1] *Department of Psychosomatic Medicine and Psychotherapy, Klinikum Rechts der Isar, Technical University of Munich, Munich, Germany,* [2] *Department of Clinical and Health Psychology, Institute of Psychology and Education, Ulm University, Ulm, Germany*

Correspondence:
Eva Schäflein
e.schaeflein@tum.de

Patients suffering from dissociative disorders are characterized by an avoidance of aversive stimuli. This includes the avoidance of emotions and, in particular, bodily perceptions. In the present pilot study, we explored the potential interoceptive accuracy deficit of patients suffering from dissociative disorders in a heartbeat detection task. Moreover, we investigated the impact of facial mirror-confrontation on interoceptive accuracy and the potential association between cardiac vagal tone derived from heart rate variability and interoceptive accuracy. Eighteen patients suffering from dissociative disorders and 18 healthy controls were assessed with the Mental Tracking Paradigm by Schandry for heartbeat detection at baseline and after confrontations exposing them to their own faces in a mirror (2 min each, accompanied by a negative or positive cognition). During the experiment, cardiac vagal tone was assessed. We used Pearson correlations to calculate potential associations between cardiac vagal tone and interoceptive accuracy. Patients performed significantly worse than the healthy controls in the heartbeat detection task at baseline. They displayed no significant increase in interoceptive accuracy following facial mirror-confrontation. In the patient group, higher cardiac vagal tone was associated with a more precise heartbeat detection performance. Dissociative disorder patients showed a considerable deficit in interoceptive accuracy. Our results fit with the assumption that highly dissociative patients tend to tune out the perceiving of bodily signals. To the extent that bodily signal perception may play a causal role in these disorders, therapeutic approaches enhancing interoceptive accuracy and cardiac vagal tone may be considered important and practicable steps to improve the therapy outcome of this patient group.

Keywords: cardiac vagal tone, dissociation, facial mirror-confrontation, heartbeat detection, interoception, root mean square of successive differences, self-perception

INTRODUCTION

Even among experts, there is considerable disagreement about the definition of the concept of dissociation (Holmes et al., 2005; Dell, 2011; Nijenhuis and van der Hart, 2011). There are several diagnostic entities of dissociation. In the following, we present concepts and definitions of dissociation according to the Diagnostic and Statistical Manual of Mental Disorders (DSM) as well as some additional definitions of dissociation.

Dissociative Disorders (DD), as defined in the DSM-5, comprise a 'disruption of and/or discontinuity in the normal integration of consciousness, memory, identity, emotion, perception, body representation, motor control, and behavior' (American Psychiatric Association, 2013, p. 291). A Dissociative Disorder Not Otherwise Specified (DDNOS) is present in DD patients who suffer from all of the Dissociative Identity Disorder (DID) criteria except identity alteration or amnesia (American Psychiatric Association, 1994). Even though DDNOS is mentioned as a separate diagnostic category next to DID only in the DSM-IV (American Psychiatric Association, 1994) and not in the DSM-5 (American Psychiatric Association, 2013), it is clinically relevant, as DDNOS is frequent and the diagnostic criteria for 'full DID' are tightly defined (Sar, 2011). As the patients of the present investigation are patients that would match with the former diagnosis of DDNOS, we will use the term 'subthreshold DID' ('sDID') for them throughout the present article. According to the DSM-5 (American Psychiatric Association, 2013), DID is characterized by (A) identity alteration, (B) amnesia, (C) distress about the disorder, (D) the symptoms not corresponding to broadly accepted cultural or religious practice and (E) the symptoms not explained by substance abuse or another medical condition (American Psychiatric Association, 2013).

According to the concept of structural dissociation of the personality (van der Hart et al., 2004), sDID/DID patients have 'Apparently Normal Part(s) of the Personality' (responsible for coping with the demands of everyday life) and 'Emotional Part(s) of the Personality' (fixated in traumatic memories, which assure survival in situations of severe threat) (van der Hart et al., 2004, 2006). This is reflected psychophysiologically as well: Reinders et al. (2006) have shown that there are considerable differences in psychophysiological reaction (e.g., heart rate, heart rate variability) to a trauma script between 'neutral identity states' (i.e., 'Apparently Normal Parts of the Personality') that were characterized by a blunted psychophysiological reactivity to the trauma script and 'traumatic identity states' (i.e., 'Emotional Parts of the Personality') presenting a higher heart rate and lower heart rate variability during the trauma script (Reinders et al., 2006).

Dissociative symptoms are clinically relevant as they are very common in patients with several mental disorders, e.g., in post-traumatic stress disorder (PTSD) and in Borderline Personality Disorder (Sar, 2011) as well as in panic disorder (depersonalization/derealization), obsessive-compulsive disorder (absorption) or depression (depersonalization/derealization) (Soffer-Dudek, 2014). In addition, Levin and Spei (2004) found an association between dissociation and psychopathology in general. A recent meta-analysis by Lyssenko et al. (2017) further supports the notion that dissociative symptoms are prevalent in people with mental disorders.

Clinical experience has demonstrated that patients suffering from DID/sDID avoid self-perception, e.g., during personal hygiene or when seeing their faces in the mirror (see also Frewen et al., 2011). In particular, those patients tune out the perception of emotions and especially of bodily signals (van der Hart et al., 2006; Boon et al., 2011). According to Hayes et al. (2004), dissociation can be related to the construct of 'experiential avoidance,' a construct that is defined as 'the phenomenon that occurs when a person is unwilling to remain in contact with particular private experiences (e.g., bodily sensations, emotions, thoughts, memories, and behavioral predispositions) and takes steps to alter the form or frequency of these events and the context that occasion them' (Hayes et al., 1996, p. 1154). Dyer et al. (2015) found associations between specific areas of the body which were associated with trauma and highly aversive emotions in patients suffering from post-traumatic stress disorder. That is why the authors conclude that the perception of the patient's body might trigger traumatic memories (Dyer et al., 2015).

A construct describing the afferent information from the viscera, e.g., from the heart, is interoception (Herbert and Pollatos, 2008; Garfinkel et al., 2015). Craig (2003, p. 500) defines interoception as 'the sense of the physiological condition of the body,' e.g., hunger and thirst. Hoeschel et al. (2008) have shown that dissociative symptom severity is correlated to a compromised fluid intake, a fact that might be linked to impaired interoception in highly dissociative individuals. Numerous studies have investigated interoception in various mental disorders (see Schulz and Vögele, 2015, for a review). For instance, patients with panic disorders and anxiety disorders in general have shown heightened interoceptive accuracy (Domschke et al., 2010). In contrast, there is evidence for compromised interoceptive accuracy in patients suffering from personality disorders (Mussgay et al., 1999), conversion disorders (Ricciardi et al., 2016), or eating disorders (Pollatos et al., 2008; Herbert and Pollatos, 2014). Patients with Depersonalization-Derealization Disorder (Michal et al., 2014) or with Borderline Personality Disorder (Hart et al., 2013) did not exhibit compromised interoceptive accuracy when compared to healthy controls, contrary to the authors' hypotheses.

According to James (1884), bodily perceptions are crucial for the experience of emotion and precede the emotional experience. Experts distinguish between 'interoceptive accuracy' (IAc) meaning the accuracy of the perception of interoceptive signals that can be examined using heartbeat perception performance (also called 'cardiosensibility') and 'interoceptive sensibility' as the self-evaluation of subjective interoception (assessed by interviews or questionnaires) (Garfinkel et al., 2015). The 'Multidimensional Assessment of Interoceptive Awareness' (MAIA, Mehling et al., 2012), for instance, is a questionnaire that assesses interoceptive sensibility on eight subscales ('Noticing,' 'Not-Distracting,' 'Not-Worrying,' 'Attention Regulation,'

'Emotional Awareness,' 'Self-Regulation,' 'Body Listening,' and 'Trusting') using items such as 'I listen for information from my body about my emotional state' or 'I feel my body is a safe place'.

Self-perception and cardiac vagal tone have proven to be variables associated with IAc. In healthy participants, Weisz et al. (1988) and Ainley et al. (2012) have reported an improvement in interoception in the course of self-perception of participants' faces in a mirror, and Ainley et al. (2013) have further shown this IAc-improving effect for a paradigm including bodily as well as narrative self-aspects. Interestingly, Pollatos et al. (2016) found that in Anorexia Nervosa patients, interoceptive accuracy was higher when focusing on another person's face than when being confronted with their own faces, whereas the opposite was the case for healthy controls. We have recently shown altered self-perception in the sDID patient sample of the present investigation: mirror-confrontation with their own faces constituted a serious stressor for them regarding self-reported stress and state dissociation, whereas healthy controls did not exhibit these stress reactions (Schäflein et al., 2016, 2018). The effect of facial mirror-confrontation on IAc has not been experimentally reproduced in sDID/DID patients. Recent evidence has shown that, besides self-perception, cardiac vagal tone is linked to IAc (Pollatos et al., 2014). In healthy participants, Pollatos et al. (2014) have shown a correlation between higher IAc and higher vagal control of the heart ($r = 0.48$, $p < 0.05$). Thus far, there is no research replicating this finding in a clinical sample and especially not in sDID/DID patients.

Previous research has shown a correlation between dissociative symptoms and a poor psychotherapy outcome (Michelson et al., 1998; Rufer et al., 2006; Spitzer et al., 2007; Kleindienst et al., 2011). Angelovski et al. (2016) describe an association between a higher baseline heart rate variability and higher heart rate variability reactivity with a better clinical outcome for a psychotherapeutic intervention in patients with pain dominant somatoform disorders. The authors speculate that this might be linked to self-regulation and emotional learning capacities (Angelovski et al., 2016). Research on the potential reasons for the poor therapeutic outcome of highly dissociative patients is urgently needed (Lanius, 2015). There is ample evidence that interoception is correlated to emotional experience (Schandry, 1981; Wiens, 2005; Herbert and Pollatos, 2008, 2012; Füstös et al., 2012; Terasawa et al., 2013). Ebner-Priemer et al. (2009) have demonstrated that compromised emotional learning is associated with a high level of state dissociative experiences in Borderline Personality Disorder and speculate that a lack of emotional engagement might be responsible for the poor therapy outcome of highly dissociative patients. Another study by Jaycox et al. (1998) has shown that, besides habituation, emotional engagement is crucial for a good therapy outcome in PTSD exposure therapy.

We were interested to find out if IAc was impaired in sDID patients, a potential pathomechanism that might be associated with poor emotional engagement and thus a poor psychotherapy outcome in sDID/DID patients. Furthermore, we aimed to investigate whether the IAc of sDID patients might improve following facial mirror-confrontation. Moreover, it was of interest to us to see whether or not cardiac vagal tone derived from heart rate variability was linked to interoception in sDID patients.

We thus hypothesized a significant difference in baseline IAc (heartbeat detection score) between DD patients and healthy controls (HCs) (hypothesis 1). Furthermore, we assumed a significant increase in IAc in both patients (hypothesis 2a) and HCs (hypothesis 2b) when exposing them to their faces in a mirror. Additionally, we expected a significant association between cardiac vagal tone derived from heart rate variability and IAc in both patients (hypothesis 3a) and HCs (hypothesis 3b).

MATERIALS AND METHODS

Participants

The local ethics committee approved the investigation (proposal 1/14 S) in accordance with the Helsinki Declaration. All participants provided their written informed consent. The present study is a pilot study for the estimation of observed effect sizes. The results of the current study are based on the same sample as the findings of Schäflein et al. (2016) and of Schäflein et al. (2018). We sent invitations to 60 patients. Twenty-two of them did not reply or were not interested in participating. Eighteen patients did not meet the inclusion criteria. Inclusion and exclusion criteria will be specified below. Another two patients were not able to follow the instructions during the experiment. They repeatedly closed their eyes during the experiment and faded out due to severe and continuous detachment symptoms. Two hundred HCs replied to our notices and advertisements in the hospital and on the intranet. The two groups were matched for gender, age and body mass index, parameters that are known to influence psychophysiological measures. We chose 23 HC candidates that were suitable according to the matching criteria (age, gender, and body mass index) for matching. Four HC candidates were excluded because they suffered from a current mental disorder, and one of them was not able to participate due to language problems.

Exclusion criteria for all participants were a severe internal or neurological disorder or the taking of beta blockers or benzodiazepines. Patients with a current severe depressive episode, lifetime psychotic disorder or lifetime substance abuse were excluded. The inclusion criterion for patients was a score of 10 or more points on the Mini-SCID-D interview (Gast et al., 1999). We excluded HCs with a current mental disorder.

Eighteen (17 female) patients with sDID and 18 HCs (17 female) participated in the study. Patients were consecutive inpatients or outpatients at a center specialized in psychotraumatology at the Department of Psychosomatic Medicine and Psychotherapy, Klinikum rechts der Isar, Technical University of Munich, Germany. HCs were employees and medical students at Klinikum rechts der Isar, Technical University of Munich. Sociodemographic data and sample characteristics are shown in **Table 1**.

TABLE 1 | Sociodemographic data and sample characteristics.

	sDID	HCs	Group comparison
	$N = 18$	$N = 18$	p
Age (*M*; *SD*)	41.7 (8.3)	41.1 (10.0)	0.86
Education (% high-school diploma)	50.0	61.1	0.50
Gender (% female)	94.4	94.4	1.00
BMI (*M*; *SD*)	23.6 (4.1)	24.7 (2.9)	0.40

Between-group differences: t-tests for independent samples (continuous data)/χ^2-tests (nominal data). sDID, patients with subthreshold Dissociative Identity Disorder; HCs, healthy controls; M, mean; SD, standard deviation; BMI, body mass index.

There were no relevant differences in age, gender, percentage of high school diploma holders, or body mass index between the two groups (**Table 1**). Patients on average had had 5.1 ($SD = 5.0$) months of lifetime psychosomatic and 2.3 ($SD = 4.0$) months of lifetime psychiatric inpatient treatment. All but one patient had had outpatient psychotherapy treatment. Comorbidities were frequent and included major depression ($n = 9$, 50%) or major depression combined with an anxiety, obsessive-compulsive or eating disorder ($n = 6$, 33.3%). 44.4% of the sDID patients took antidepressant or neuroleptic drugs, and 27.8% of them took additional drugs other than psychopharmaceuticals. Only one of the HCs had had outpatient psychotherapy treatment. None of the HCs took psychopharmaceuticals, and 16.7% of them took additional drugs other than psychopharmaceuticals.

Instruments

We used the validated German translations of all instruments employed in this study.

Interviews

Subthreshold DID and PTSD diagnoses were assessed using the Mini-SCID-D interview (Gast et al., 1999; Steinberg et al., 1992, unpublished), which is the short form of the SCID-D interview (Steinberg et al., 1992, unpublished) and the SCID-PTSD interview (Wittchen et al., 1997; First et al., 2012) according to DSM-IV. The Mini-SCID-D and the SCID-D interview (Steinberg, 1994; Gast et al., 1999) consist of the subscales amnesia, depersonalization, derealization, identity disturbance, and identity alteration (Steinberg, 1994; Gast et al., 1999) and thus comprise fragmentation and detachment symptoms.

Self-Report Measures

Trait dissociation was assessed with the Dissociative Experiences Scale (DES, Bernstein and Putnam, 1986). The Impact of Event Scale (IES, Horowitz et al., 1979) was administered to measure the severity of trauma-related symptoms. We quantified child abuse and neglect using the Childhood Trauma Questionnaire CTQ and its five subscales (emotional abuse, physical abuse, sexual abuse, emotional neglect, and physical neglect) (Bernstein and Fink, 1998). The Multidimensional Assessment of Interoceptive Awareness (MAIA) (Mehling et al., 2012) is a 32-item questionnaire consisting of eight subscales ('Noticing,' 'Not-Distracting,' 'Not-Worrying,' 'Attention Regulation,' 'Emotional Awareness,' 'Self-Regulation,' 'Body Listening,' 'Trusting'). Items are categorized on a five point Likert scale from '0' = 'never' to '5' = 'always'. The MAIA total score is the mean of all items, some of them inversely coded. A higher MAIA score signifies better interoceptive sensibility. The Acceptance and Action Questionnaire (AAQ, Hayes et al., 2004) was used to measure experiential avoidance. We used the Subjective Units of Disturbance (SUD) Scale to quantify subjective distress on a scale of 0 ('no distress') to 10 ('maximum distress') (Wolpe, 1969).

Procedures

The entire experimental process and the different periods are depicted in **Figure 1**.

Participants were seated in a comfortable chair 1 m in front of a mirror (40 cm × 40 cm) that reflected their faces. The experiment comprised three mirror-confrontation phases (2 min each, **Figure 1**) during which participants were instructed to either look just at their faces or to silently think about a negative and then a positive cognition during facial mirror-confrontation. We assessed IAc (see section 'Heartbeat Detection Task') using heartbeat detection tasks at three points, at baseline, directly after facial mirror-confrontation accompanied by a negative cognition (2 min duration) and directly following facial mirror-confrontation accompanied by a positive cognition (2 min duration) (**Figure 1**). The mirror was covered during the whole experimental procedure (including the three heartbeat detection tasks, see section 'Heartbeat Detection Task') except for the mirror-confrontation phases.

Participants were asked to choose individual, pre-defined negative and positive cognitions about themselves from the Eye Movement Desensitization and Reprocessing Manual (Shapiro, 2001). They should report their most disturbing negative

NR 1	2 min
Relaxation	3 min
HDT baseline	2 min 45 s
NR 2	2 min
MC neutr	2 min
NR 3	2 min
MC neg	2 min
HDT after MC neg	2 min 45 s
NR 4	2 min
MC pos	2 min
HDT after MC pos	2 min 45 s
NR 5	2 min

FIGURE 1 | Course of the different measurement phases of the experiment. HDT, heartbeat detection task; MC, mirror-confrontation; NR, neutral reference (imagining washing the dishes); neutr, neutral (no cognitive accompaniment); neg, negative (with negative cognitive accompaniment); pos, positive (with positive cognitive accompaniment).

cognition which had to induce a Subjective Units of Disturbance (SUD, Wolpe, 1969) score of at least 7 to be eligible as an accompanying cognition. In HCs, a SUD score of 7 or more was not present since HCs reported they could not think about themselves in such a negative way. Before, between and after the mirror-confrontation periods and the heartbeat detection tasks, neutral reference conditions (2 min each, sitting and imagining washing the dishes) were performed (**Figure 1**). Before the baseline IAc measurement, participants performed a relaxation task (Wengenroth, 2012, p. 143) (adapted version) to limit anticipatory anxiety and for ethical reasons. During the whole experiment, electrocardiography (ECG) and impedance cardiography (ICG) data were collected continuously. For ethical reasons (mirror-confrontation with positive cognition should be at the end of the experiment), we did not permute the mirror conditions.

Heartbeat Detection Task

The Mental Tracking Task by Schandry (1981) served to assess heartbeat detection accuracy. The task is well-validated, reliable and widely used (Knoll and Hodapp, 1992; Mussgay et al., 1999; Pollatos et al., 2007). Participants were asked to mentally track (i.e., to count silently) their heartbeats in three time intervals of 25, 35, and 45 s without taking their pulse or facilitating heartbeat detection in any other way. Between these time intervals, there were short breaks of 30 s. Start and stop signals for each counting phase were given by the experimenter (ES). After each time interval, participants wrote down the number of heartbeats detected. As we asked participants to perform the heartbeat detection task three times, we permuted the order of the three time intervals in a balanced design.

During the Mental Tracking Task, we monitored heart rates by means of an ECG measured by the Vrije Universiteit Ambulatory Monitoring System (VU-AMS, Vrije Universiteit, Department of Psychophysiology, Amsterdam, Netherlands) Model 5 FS [see section 'Impedance Cardiography and Vrije Universiteit Ambulatory Monitoring System (VU-AMS)']. The Mental Tracking Task requires intervals of 25, 35, and 45 s. During these time periods, we assessed cardiac vagal tone [see section 'Impedance Cardiography and Vrije Universiteit Ambulatory Monitoring System (VU-AMS)'] and calculated a mean cardiac vagal tone score for each heartbeat detection task. For each of the three heartbeat detection tasks, we calculated a heartbeat detection score (HBDS) as the mean of the three intervals using the formula shown in **Figure 2**.

Using this transformation, the HBDS can vary between 0 and 1. Higher scores indicate smaller differences between recorded and perceived heartbeats and thus higher IAc.

$$\frac{1}{3}\sum\frac{(|\text{recorded heartbeats} - \text{counted heartbeats}|)}{\text{recorded heartbeats}}$$

FIGURE 2 | Formula used to calculate the heartbeat detection score.

Impedance Cardiography and Vrije Universiteit Ambulatory Monitoring System (VU-AMS)

The validated Vrije Universiteit Ambulatory Monitoring System (VU-AMS, Vrije Universiteit, Department of Psychophysiology, Amsterdam, Netherlands) served to assess peripheral psychophysiological activity by recording ECG and ICG using a sample rate of 1000 Hz (de Geus et al., 1995; de Geus and van Doornen, 1996; Willemsen et al., 1996; Riese et al., 2003). We used the Root Mean Square of Successive Differences (RMSSD) as a vagal index derived from heart rate variability to assess cardiac vagal tone (Malik et al., 1996). We employed the natural logarithm of RMSSD, lnRMSSD, for further analysis because of the skewed distribution of the RMSSD (Malik et al., 1996). An increase in lnRMSSD means an increase in cardiac vagal tone. We processed physiological data using the VU-DAMS 3.2 software. Suspicious beats were detected automatically by the VU-AMS. We visually inspected and manually corrected or deleted suspicious beats and artifacts using the procedures in the Vrije Universiteit Data Analysis and Management Software (VU-DAMS) manual (VU-DAMS, 2013). All files were processed.

Statistical Analyses

Statistical analyses were conducted using SPSS version 22.0, applying a statistical threshold for probability of $p < 0.05$ (two-sided). For group comparisons, *t*-tests for independent samples were computed. In the case of nominal data, χ^2 tests were used. To analyze data collected at different time points (within-group differences), we computed linear mixed models with the participant as a random effect and time and group as fixed effects (Singer, 1998). To assess the association between cardiac vagal tone and IAc, we used parametric correlations. We calculated between-group differences of subsequent experimental conditions using ANOVAs and controlled for the initial value of the dependent variable, respectively.

RESULTS

Psychometric Sample Characteristics

Table 2 shows the psychometric data of the sDID patients and the HCs. Mini-SCID-D interviewing to determine the severity of dissociative symptoms resulted in a score of 11.39 (SD = 1.09, range 5–15) points for the sDID group, indicating that all patients suffered from detachment symptoms (depersonalization/derealization) and, additionally, from compartmentalization symptoms (amnesia/identity disturbance/identity alteration). All of the patients had sDID (all DID criteria but amnesia or but identity alteration), but not a full DID. All patients met the criteria for a comorbid PTSD according to SCID-PTSD, but, as clinical expert interviews revealed, sDID was the main diagnosis and main complaint in every patient tested. All patients reported multiple traumatization (M = 3.2 traumatizations, SD = 1.3). In contrast to the HCs, sDID

TABLE 2 | Psychometric data.

		sDID	HCs	Group comparison
	Questionnaire (abbreviation) (range)	***M* (*SD*)**	***M* (*SD*)**	***p***
Dissociation	Mini-SCID-D total score (0–15)	11.39 (1.09)	0.00 (0.00)	<0.001*
	Mini-SCID-D amnesia (0–3)	2.44 (0.98)	0.00 (0.00)	<0.001*
	Mini-SCID-D depersonalization (0–3)	3.00 (0.00)	0.00 (0.00)	<0.001*
	Mini-SCID-D derealization (0–3)	2.11 (108)	0.00 (0.00)	<0.001*
	Mini-SCID-D identity disturbance (0–3)	2.33 (0.49)	0.00 (0.00)	<0.001*
	Mini-SCID-D identity alteration (0–3)	1.50 (0.92)	0.00 (0.00)	<0.001*
	Dissociative Experiences Scale (DES) (0–100%)	27.86 (9.28)	4.35 (2.79)	<0.001*
Trauma	PTSD (diagnosed with SCID-PTSD interview)	Yes	No	
	Impact of Event Scale (IES) (0–75)	54.28 (11.85)	–	–
	Childhood Trauma Questionnaire (CTQ) (25–125)	82.50 (15.75)	29.25 (3.25)	<0.001*
	CTQ emotional abuse (5–25)	18.90 (4.85)	6.20 (1.15)	<0.001*
	CTQ physical abuse (5–25)	12.90 (4.70)	5.15 (0.40)	<0.001*
	CTQ sexual abuse (5–25)	16.45 (5.60)	5.00 (0.00)	<0.001*
	CTQ emotional neglect (5–25)	21.45 (2.30)	7.55 (2.00)	<0.001*
	CTQ physical neglect (5–25)	12.80 (3.80)	5.30 (0.70)	<0.001*
Interoceptive sensibility	Multidimensional Assessment of Interoceptive Awareness (MAIA) (0–5)	1.70 (0.66)	3.25 (0.56)	<0.001*
Experiential avoidance	Acceptance and Action Questionnaire (AAQ) (9–63)	45.11 (6.72)	22.22 (3.46)	<0.001*

*Between-group differences: t-tests for independent samples. sDID, patients with subthreshold Dissociative Identity Disorder; HCs, healthy controls; M, mean; SD, standard deviation; SCID-D, Structural Clinical Interview for DSM-IV Dissociative Disorders; PTSD, post-traumatic stress disorder; DES, Dissociative Experiences Scale; IES, Impact of Event Scale; CTQ, Childhood Trauma Questionnaire; MAIA, Multidimensional Assessment of Interoceptive Awareness; AAQ, Acceptance and Action Questionnaire; *p < 0.05.*

patients exhibited more intense dissociative symptoms in the DES, severe PTSD symptomatology in the IES, reported considerably high childhood abuse and neglect intensity in the CTQ, remarkably compromised interoceptive sensibility in the MAIA and notably high experiential avoidance in the AAQ. The dissociation score according to the Mini-SCID-D interview was zero for each of the HCs. HCs comprised both traumatized and non-traumatized individuals. However, their average childhood traumatization scores were significantly lower than those of the patients. Their overall psychopathological symptoms were considerably lower than those of the patients (**Table 2**).

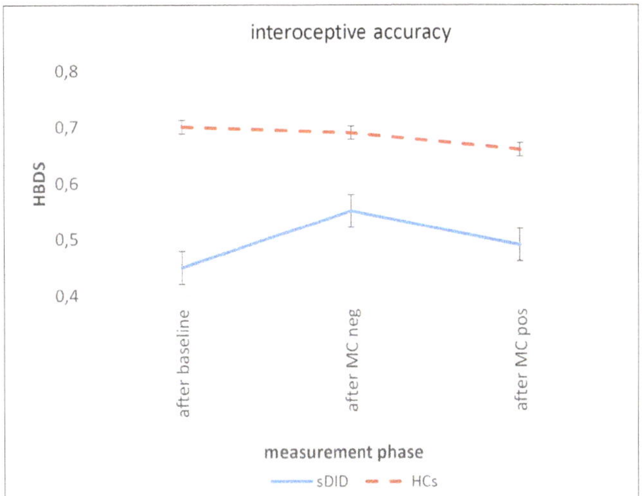

FIGURE 3 | Heartbeat detection score over the course of the experiment. Within-group differences: linear mixed models, between-group differences: ANOVAs controlling for initial value of HBDS. sDID, patients with subthreshold Dissociative Identity Disorder; HCs, healthy controls; MC, mirror-confrontation; neg, negative (negative cognitive accompaniment); pos, positive (positive cognitive accompaniment); HBDS, heartbeat detection score.

Interoceptive Accuracy Results at Baseline and in the Course of the Facial Mirror-Confrontation Paradigm

Figure 3 shows the courses of the heartbeat detection score for sDID patients (blue) and HCs (red) at the three measurement points: at the baseline assessment, after the facial mirror-confrontation with negative cognitive accompaniment and after the facial mirror-confrontation with positive cognitive accompaniment.

Table 3 depicts the baseline heartbeat detection scores (HBDS) of patients and HCs, the mean HBDS values and standard errors for each measurement period, the within-group changes in HBDS for the sDID patients and for the HCs in the course of the experiment and the between-group differences in the course of the experiment when controlling for the initial HBDS value. There was a significant difference in the HBDS between the sDID patients and the HCs at baseline [$T(\text{df}) = T(28.0) = -2.776$; $p = 0.010$]. For both groups, there were no significant changes from the HBDS at baseline to the HBDS after the facial mirror-confrontation with negative cognitive accompaniment [sDID: ES (CI) = 0.30 (−0.96 to 0.36), $p = 0.14$; HCs: ES (CI) = 0.05 (−0.60 to 0.70), $p = 0.77$]. Similarly, there were no significant changes going from the HBDS after the facial

TABLE 3 | Within-group courses of the heartbeat detection scores for sDID patients and HCs (left) and between-group differences calculated using ANOVAs, controlled for initial heartbeat detection score value (right).

	sDID				HCs				sDID compared to HCs[2]	
	M (SE)	*F*	ES (95% CI)	*p*[1]	*M* (*SE*)	*F*	ES (95% CI)	*p*[1]	*F*	*p*
HBDS at baseline	0.45 (0.03)				0.70 (0.09)					
HBDS after MC neg	0.55 (0.02)	2.36	0.30 (−0.96 to 0.36)	0.14	0.69 (0.08)	0.09	0.05 (−0.60 to 0.70)	0.77	0.13	0.72
HBDS after MC pos	0.49 (0.03)	2.45	0.18 (−0.48 to 0.83)	0.14	0.66 (0.09)	1.69	0.18 (−0.50 to 0.81)	0.21	0.16	0.70

[1]Mean within-group difference related to precedent measuring period calculated by linear mixed models; [2]between-group differences: ANOVAs controlling for initial value of the dependent variable. CI, confidence interval; sDID, patients with subthreshold Dissociative Identity Disorder; HCs, healthy controls; M, mean; SE, standard error; HBDS, heartbeat detection score; MC, mirror-confrontation; neg, negative (with negative cognitive accompaniment); pos, positive (with positive cognitive accompaniment); ES, effect size.

mirror-confrontation with negative cognitive accompaniment to the HBDS after the facial mirror-confrontation with positive cognitive accompaniment in both groups [sDID: ES (CI) = 0.18 (−0.48 to 0.83), p = 0.14; HCs: ES (CI) = 0.15 (−0.50 to 0.81), p = 0.21]. Controlling for the initial values of the HBDS, ANOVAs did not yield any significant between-group differences between sDID patients and HCs neither for the HBDS after the facial mirror-confrontation accompanied by the negative cognition (F = 0.13, p = 0.72) nor for the HBDS after the facial mirror-confrontation accompanied by the positive cognition (F = 0.16, p = 0.70) (**Table 3**).

Correlations Between Cardiac Vagal Tone and Interoceptive Accuracy

Table 4 depicts Pearson correlations between cardiac vagal tone (lnRMSSD) and IAc in the heartbeat detection tasks for sDID patients and healthy controls. In sDID patients, there were significant associations with high effect sizes at baseline and after mirror-confrontation with positive cognitive accompaniment (baseline: r = 0.55, p = 0.02; after mirror-confrontation with positive cognitive accompaniment: r = 0.54, p = 0.02). In the HCs, there were no substantial associations between cardiac vagal tone and IAc (baseline: r = −0.08, p = 0.74; after mirror-confrontation with negative cognitive accompaniment: r = −0.25, p = 0.33; after mirror-confrontation with positive cognitive accompaniment: r = −0.29, p = 0.25) (**Table 4**).

TABLE 4 | Correlation between cardiac vagal tone (lnRMSSD) and interoceptive accuracy (heartbeat detection score).

	sDID		HCs	
	r	*p*	*r*	*p*
HBDS at baseline	0.55	0.02*	−0.08	0.74
HBDS after MC neg	0.33	0.19	−0.25	0.33
HBDS after MC pos	0.54	0.02*	−0.29	0.25

ln, natural logarithm; RMSSD, root mean square of successive differences; sDID, patients with subthreshold Dissociative Identity Disorder; HCs, healthy controls; HBDS, heartbeat detection score; MC, mirror-confrontation; neg, negative (with negative cognitive accompaniment); pos, positive (with positive cognitive accompaniment); p < 0.05.

DISCUSSION

We compared IAc assessed by a heartbeat detection task between sDID patients suffering from both detachment and compartmentalization symptoms and HCs at baseline and in the course of a facial mirror-confrontation paradigm. Furthermore, we investigated potential correlations between IAc and cardiac vagal tone. In comparison to the HCs, we observed an IAc deficit in sDID patients at baseline. There was no substantial increase in IAc following facial mirror-confrontation for both patients and HCs. In sDID patients, higher cardiac vagal tone was correlated to a higher heartbeat detection accuracy.

In accordance with hypothesis 1, we found a significant IAc deficit in sDID patients compared to the HCs. Our outcome showing significantly attenuated IAc in sDID patients compared to HCs is in line with results from previous studies demonstrating IAc deficits in patients affected by personality disorders (Mussgay et al., 1999) or conversion disorders (Ricciardi et al., 2016). Moreover, a case study by Sedeño et al. (2014) showing an IAc deficit in a Depersonalization-Derealization Disorder patient compared to HCs fits with our results. Apart from this, results by Schaefer et al. (2012) reporting a correlation between lower IAc and higher symptom severity in somatoform disorder patients are also in accordance with our findings, as our sample showed severe general psychopathology (see section 'Psychometric Sample Characteristics,' **Table 2**).

In contrast, our results are not in line with research failing to show an IAc deficit in patients with Borderline Personality Disorder (Hart et al., 2013) or with Depersonalization-Derealization Disorder (Michal et al., 2014) compared to HCs. Dissociative symptoms are a diagnostic criterion for Borderline Personality Disorder (American Psychiatric Association, 2013). It is thus possible that including dissociative symptoms as a covariate in the study by Hart et al. (2013) might have shown an IAc deficit depending on dissociative symptom severity. Furthermore, our findings are not in line with the observation that patients suffering from panic disorder who often display depersonalization/derealization (Soffer-Dudek, 2014) have heightened IAc (Domschke et al., 2010). Compared to their findings and to the results of Michal et al. (2014), our data might be interpreted as related to fragmentation/compartmentalization symptoms such as amnesia or identity alteration that were present in our patients in addition to detachment symptoms

(Holmes et al., 2005). When interpreted in the light of the theory of structural dissociation of the personality (van der Hart et al., 2004, 2006), the role of fragmentation symptoms in the present study might imply that our patients have avoided their 'Emotional Parts of the Personality,' which are linked to trauma-associated emotions and thus most probably also to bodily signals. They might rather have been in their 'Apparently Normal Part of the Personality,' the personality state responsible for the demands of everyday life and detached from emotional experience linked to traumatic memories. Therefore, they might also have been detached from correspondent bodily signals, given the well-documented link between emotional experience and interoception/perception of signals arising from the body (Schandry, 1981; Wiens, 2005; Herbert and Pollatos, 2008, 2012; Füstös et al., 2012; Terasawa et al., 2013).

Contrary to hypotheses 2a and 2b, we did not observe a significant increase in IAc following facial mirror-confrontation in either sDID patients or HCs. Looking at the effect size, one may speculate that with a larger sample the small increase from the heartbeat detection task at baseline to the heartbeat detection task after the mirror-confrontation with negative cognitive accompaniment might have reached statistical significance in our patient sample. Our finding of no significant increase in IAc following facial mirror-confrontation in both sDID patients and HCs contradicts previous findings by Ainley et al. (2012). Those authors found a significant increase in IAc linked to facial mirror-confrontation in healthy participants. Since mirror-confrontation with their faces has proven to be associated with stress and state dissociation in the sDID patient sample of the present investigation (Schäflein et al., 2016, 2018), increased self-focus by facial mirror-confrontation might have resulted in an increase in IAc, whereas the simultaneous stress and state dissociation experience might have diminished IAc. Fairclough and Goodwin (2007), for instance, have shown an IAc decrease associated with stress in healthy women. Additionally, participants in our study underwent the heartbeat detection tasks following and not during facial mirror-confrontation. The effects of facial mirror-confrontation might already have diminished as the participants had executed the heartbeat detection tasks after the facial mirror-confrontations. Another potential reason why we were not able to detect the hypothesized IAc increase might be that sDID patients might have avoided self-perception. This interpretation is in line with Pollatos et al. (2016) demonstrating that IAc was enhanced when looking at another person's face and decreased when looking at their own faces in a sample of anorexia nervosa patients. The authors conclude that confronting anorexia nervosa patients with their faces might lead to increased body-related avoidance and thus a decrease in IAc (Pollatos et al., 2016).

In the HCs, there was also no significant increase in IAc associated with mirror-confrontation. At first sight, this finding contradicts three aforementioned investigations reporting a significant increase in IAc during mirror-confrontation with one's face (Weisz et al., 1988; Ainley et al., 2012) and during a task leading attention toward bodily or narrative self-aspects (Ainley et al., 2013) in healthy participants. Our finding concerning the HCs furthermore seems to be inconsistent with work by Pollatos et al. (2016) demonstrating an increase in IAc going along with explicit self-focus in healthy study participants. Again, a potential explanation might be that we performed the heartbeat detection tasks after and not during the mirror-confrontation intervals. Furthermore, the HCs exhibited high baseline IAc. The lack of an increase in IAc after HCs were exposed to their faces in the mirror might thus be associated with a ceiling effect.

In keeping with hypothesis 3a, we observed significant positive correlations between cardiac vagal tone and IAc at baseline and after mirror-confrontation accompanied by the positive cognition in sDID patients. There was no such correlation after mirror-confrontation accompanied by a negative cognition. Our results suggest that patients with a higher cardiac vagal tone detect a greater proportion of their heartbeats and that this effect might be attenuated by retrieving a negative cognition, i.e., that the negative cognition possibly leads to a decoupling of the association between cardiac vagal tone and interoceptive accuracy. The finding of a significant positive correlation between cardiac vagal tone and IAc in sDID patients is in line with Pollatos et al. (2014) reporting on an association between higher vagal control of the heart and higher IAc in healthy participants. To our knowledge, our study is the first to replicate this finding in a clinical population and especially in sDID patients. Cardiac vagal tone might be an important factor contributing to psychotherapy outcome in sDID patients as well, as shown by Angelovski et al. (2016) for patients with pain dominant somatoform disorders.

Herein, we show for the first time a link between cardiac vagal tone and IAc, a construct linked to emotional experience (Schandry, 1981; Wiens, 2005; Herbert and Pollatos, 2008, 2012; Füstös et al., 2012; Terasawa et al., 2013), in sDID patients. Evidence suggesting an association of impaired emotional experience with a poor psychotherapy outcome in post-traumatic disorders (Jaycox et al., 1998) and highly dissociative individuals (Ebner-Priemer et al., 2009) underlines that our findings might make an important contribution toward understanding the pathophysiology of poor emotional learning and thus compromised psychotherapy outcome in patients suffering from severe dissociative symptoms. When considering the pivotal role of interoception for emotional experience (Schandry, 1981; Wiens, 2005; Herbert and Pollatos, 2008, 2012; Füstös et al., 2012; Terasawa et al., 2013) and the herein-found link between cardiac vagal tone and interoception, one might speculate that deficiencies of both cardiac vagal tone and interoception might be psychophysiological correlates of poor emotional experience and thus might be pathways contributing to the thus far poor psychotherapy outcome of sDID/DID patients. The psychotherapy outcome of this severely disabled patient group might be improved if psychotherapeutic techniques focusing on the perception of the own body and bodily signals and aiming at heightening cardiac vagal tone were included into their psychotherapy.

In contrast to hypothesis 3b, we were not able to detect significant correlations between cardiac vagal tone and IAc in the HCs. This is most likely due to their relatively high baseline heartbeat detection score. Our HCs were mostly hospital employees and medical students, who probably have a better idea of a normal heart rate than the average population. Considering a ceiling effect, it is thus difficult to detect variables enhancing a high baseline heartbeat detection ability. Thus, our findings might not automatically contradict previous results by Pollatos et al. (2014) describing a positive correlation between vagal tone and interoceptive accuracy in a healthy population.

Our finding of impaired baseline IAc and of low interoceptive sensibility assessed by the MAIA questionnaire in sDID patients might be interpreted as fitting with the theory of experiential avoidance (Hayes et al., 2004). This theory implies that it is difficult for people high in experiential avoidance to 'remain in contact with particular private experiences (e.g., bodily sensations, emotions, [...])' (Hayes et al., 1996, p. 1154). Psychometrically, our sDID patient sample exhibited pronounced experiential avoidance in the Acceptance and Action Questionnaire (**Table 2**). However, it is not possible to conclude from our data whether impaired IAc is owed to avoidance, to inability, or both. Further studies including the subjective aversiveness of the heartbeat detection tasks could shed more light on this question. Considering data by Dyer et al. (2015) assuming the own body is a trigger in post-traumatic conditions, impaired IAc in our patients might be due to avoiding getting in touch with the trauma-associated own body.

Our data support the notion of the definition of dissociation, suggesting that a disruption in the normal integration of emotion, perception and body representation might be associated with impaired IAc in sDID patients. Given the differences between 'Apparently Normal Parts of the Personality' and 'Emotional Parts of the Personality' in DID patients concerning their reaction to a trauma script (Reinders et al., 2006), our patients might have been in their 'Apparently Normal Part of the Personality' state when performing the baseline heartbeat detection task. Avoidance of bodily signals and impaired IAc might thus be 'dissociative part'-dependent. Consequently, it would be interesting to replicate the experiment with DID patients in their 'Apparently Normal Part of the Personality' and 'Emotional Part of the Personality' states in order to differentiate systematically between these two conditions.

Considering our findings, it is possible that a good ability to regulate cardiac vagal tone might help sDID/DID patients to overcome their tuning-out of the perception of emotions and especially of bodily perceptions (van der Hart et al., 2006; Boon et al., 2011). Enhancing cardiac vagal tone and interoceptive abilities might thus counteract dissociation-specific feelings of disconnection from their bodies in sDID/DID. According to our findings, one might speculate that enhancing bodily perception, e.g., using body therapy or mindfulness exercises, as well as monitoring and influencing cardiac vagal tone, e.g., by biofeedback, might constitute psychotherapy targets for enhancing IAc in sDID/DID patients. Given the importance of bodily signals in general (e.g., James, 1884) and of interoceptive information in particular (Schandry, 1981; Wiens, 2005; Herbert and Pollatos, 2008, 2012; Füstös et al., 2012; Terasawa et al., 2013) for the experience of emotion, we suggest that impaired IAc might be a crucial factor associated with impaired emotional experience and thus emotional learning that most probably also occurs during psychotherapy in highly dissociative patients (Ebner-Priemer et al., 2009). This again might contribute to the poor psychotherapy outcome linked to dissociation described in previous research (Michelson et al., 1998; Rufer et al., 2006; Spitzer et al., 2007; Kleindienst et al., 2011, 2016). Another clinical implication of our results might be that impaired interoception most probably might be an explanation for clinically reported compromised fluid intake maintaining dissociation as reported by Hoeschel et al. (2008).

Limitations and Future Directions

Our study has several limitations. Due to the pilot character of our study, the sample size was relatively small. Another controversial issue might be that we conducted the heartbeat perception tasks after and not during the facial mirror-confrontations. Therefore, significant effects of the stimulation may have been missed. The task of heartbeat counting may have a distracting and relaxing effect by itself and may increase both IAc and cardiac vagal tone. Adding heartbeat detection tasks and also other ways to assess IAc, e.g., heartbeat discrimination tasks (Whitehead et al., 1977) during facial mirror-confrontations to the study protocol might shed more light on the acute self-focus effects on IAc in sDID patients. Moreover, we did not assess IAc after a neutral facial mirror-confrontation (without a negative or positive cognitive accompaniment). In addition, repeating the heartbeat detection task might have had a training effect, which might have confounded the results. The negative and positive conditions were not counterbalanced due to ethical reasons, i.e., we aimed at ending the experiment with a positive condition. However, there could have been a group receiving first a positive condition, then a negative condition and then again a positive condition which would not have been analyzed, but only inserted for ethical reasons. Furthermore, the relaxation task, which was performed before the baseline IAc assessment in order to minimize anticipatory anxiety, might have influenced the IAc baseline results. Heterogeneity in terms of comorbidities, psychotherapy experience and medication use might be considered another limitation of our study. This could not be ruled out since comorbidities are highly prevalent in patients suffering from sDID/DID (Freyberger and Spitzer, 2005). Our HCs sample might not be representative since all of them were hospital employees and medical students. Furthermore, we did not control for physical activity, a factor associated with improved IAc (Jones and Hollandsworth, 1981). Considering Kleckner et al. (2015) and Ring et al. (2015), it is necessary to take into account the methodological limitations of the Schandry task as well. Concerning the associations between cardiac vagal tone and IAc, our study design does not enable us to control for all possible confounders of heart rate variability in our sample, e.g., vigilance, emotional arousal, or physical activity. Analyzing heart rate variability dynamics and trait factors in general might have yielded interesting results in addition to the interindividual comparison.

Herein, we show for the first time substantially impaired IAc in sDID patients and first evidence that a higher cardiac vagal tone is correlated to better IAc in sDID patients. Consequently, it may be crucial to integrate therapy methods focusing on the perception of bodily signals into psychotherapy for sDID/DID patients, e.g., interoception training, body therapy or heart rate variability biofeedback. The body scan, an intervention from the Mindfulness Based Stress Reduction program (Fischer et al., 2017), and contemplative training (Bornemann and Singer, 2017), for instance, have proven to be potent interventions enhancing IAc in healthy participants.

CONCLUSION

We observed a considerable IAc deficit at baseline in sDID patients compared to HCs. In sDID patients, higher cardiac vagal tone was associated with a more precise IAc. Our data might be considered to psychophysiologically support previous findings linking dissociative symptoms to compromised emotional experience, to impaired emotional learning and to a poor psychotherapy outcome. To the extent that bodily signal perception may play a causal role in sDID/DID, integrating therapeutic approaches improving IAc and cardiac vagal tone like IAc training, body therapy, contemplative training, or heart rate variability biofeedback into psychotherapy for sDID/DID patients might contribute to improving the psychotherapy outcome of this severely affected patient group.

AUTHOR CONTRIBUTIONS

ES and MS designed the study. ES conducted the experiments and wrote the first version of the manuscript. All of the authors contributed substantially to data analysis, interpretation of the results, and critical revisions of the manuscript. The final version was approved by all authors. All authors agreed to be accountable for all aspects of the work in ensuring that questions related to the accuracy or integrity of any part of the work are appropriately investigated and resolved.

FUNDING

This work was supported by the German Research Foundation (DFG) and the Technical University of Munich within the funding programme Open Access Publishing.

ACKNOWLEDGMENTS

This study is part of the dissertation by ES. Parts of this work have been presented at the 19th Annual Meeting of the German-speaking Association of Psychotraumatology (Zurich, Switzerland, February 2017) and at the 25th Annual Meeting of the German Association of Psychosomatic Medicine and Psychotherapy (Berlin, Germany, March 2017). We are deeply indebted to the patients and HCs for agreeing to take part in this study and for sharing their experiences with us. Furthermore, we thank Christoph Prassler, Matthias Noertemann, and Michaela Baci for their help with patient recruitment.

REFERENCES

1. Ainley, V., Maister, L., Brokfeld, J., Farmer, H., and Tsakiris, M. (2013). More of myself: manipulating interoceptive awareness by heightened attention to bodily and narrative aspects of the self. *Conscious. Cogn.* 22, 1231–1238. doi: 10.1016/j.concog.2013.08.004
2. Ainley, V., Tajadura-Jiménez, A., Fotopoulou, A., and Tsakiris, M. (2012). Looking into myself: changes in interoceptive sensitivity during mirror self-observation: Looking into myself. *Psychophysiology* 49, 1672–1676. doi: 10.1111/j.1469-8986. 2012.01468.x
3. American Psychiatric Association (1994). *Diagnostic and Statistical Manual of Mental Disorders*, 4th Edn. Washington, DC: APA.
4. American Psychiatric Association (2013). *Diagnostic and Statistical Manual of Mental Disorders*, 5 Edn. Washington, DC: APA. doi: 10.1176/ appi.books. 9780890425596
5. Angelovski, A., Sattel, H., Henningsen, P., and Sack, M. (2016). Heart rate variability predicts therapy outcome in pain-predominant multisomatoform disorder. *J. Psychosom. Res.* 83, 16–21. doi: 10.1016/j. jpsychores.2016.02.003
6. Bernstein, D. P., and Fink, L. (1998). *Childhood Trauma Questionnaire: A Retrospective Self-Report.* San Antonio, TX: Pearson.
7. Bernstein, E. M., and Putnam, F. W. (1986). Development, reliability, and validity of a dissociation scale. *J. Nerv. Ment. Dis.* 174, 727–735. doi: 10.1097/00005053- 198612000-00004
8. Boon, S., Steele, K., and van der Hart, O. (eds). (2011). "Overcoming the phobia of inner experience," in *Coping with Trauma-Related Dissociation*, 1st Edn (New York, NY: W. W. Norton & Co).
9. Bornemann, B., and Singer, T. (2017). Taking time to feel our body: steady increases in heartbeat perception accuracy and decreases in alexithymia over 9 months of contemplative mental training: contemplative training improves interoception. *Psychophysiology* 54, 469–482. doi: 10.1111/ psyp.12790
10. Craig, A. (2003). Interoception: the sense of the physiological condition of the body. *Curr. Opin. Neurobiol.* 13, 500–505. doi: 10.1016/S0959-4388(03) 00090-4
11. de Geus, E. J., Willemsen, G. H., Klaver, C. H., and van Doornen, L. J. (1995). Ambulatory measurement of respiratory sinus arrhythmia and respiration rate.
12. *Biol. Psychol.* 41, 205–227. doi: 10.1016/0301-0511(95)05137-6
13. de Geus, E. J. C., and van Doornen, L. J. P. (1996). "Ambulatory assessment of parasympathetic/sympathetic balance by impedance cardiography," in *Ambulatory Assessment: Computer-Assisted Psychological and Psychophysiological Methods in Monitoring and Field Studies*, eds J. Fahrenberg and M. Myrtek (Göttingen: Hogrefe & Huber), 141–163.
14. Dell, P. F. (2011). An excellent definition of structural dissociation and a dogmatic rejection of all other models. *J. Trauma Dissociation* 12, 461–464. doi: 10.1080/ 15299732.2011.570236
15. Domschke, K., Stevens, S., Pfleiderer, B., and Gerlach, A. L. (2010). Interoceptive sensitivity in anxiety and anxiety disorders: an overview and integration of neurobiological findings. *Clin. Psychol. Rev.* 30, 1–11. doi: 10.1016/j.cpr.2009. 08.008
16. Dyer, A. S., Feldmann, R. E., and Borgmann, E. (2015). Body-related emotions in posttraumatic stress disorder following childhood sexual abuse. *J. Child Sex. Abus.* 24, 627–640. doi: 10.1080/10538712.2015.1057666
17. Ebner-Priemer, U. W., Mauchnik, J., Kleindienst, N., Schmahl, C., Peper, M., Rosenthal, M. Z., et al. (2009). Emotional learning during dissociative states in borderline personality disorder. *J. Psychiatry Neurosci.* 34, 214–222.
18. Fairclough, S. H., and Goodwin, L. (2007). The effect of psychological stress and relaxation on interoceptive accuracy: Implications for symptom perception. *J. Psychosom. Res.* 62, 289–295. doi: 10.1016/j. jpsychores.2006.10.017
19. First, M. B., Spitzer, R. L., Gibbon, M., and Williams, J. B. W. (2012). *Structured Clinical Interview for DSM-IV Axis I Disorders (SCID-I), Clinician Version, Administration Booklet*, 1st Edn. Washington, DC: American Psychiatric Publishing.
20. Fischer, D., Messner, M., and Pollatos, O. (2017). Improvement of interoceptive processes after an 8-week body scan intervention. *Front. Hum. Neurosci.* 11:452. doi: 10.3389/fnhum.2017.00452
21. Frewen, P. A., Dozois, D. J. A., Neufeld, R. W., Densmore, M., Stevens, T. K., and Lanius, R. A. (2011). Self-referential processing in women with PTSD:

22. Affective and neural response. *Psychol. Trauma* 3, 318–328. doi: 10.1037/a0021264
23. Freyberger, H. J., and Spitzer, C. (2005). Dissoziative Störungen [Dissociative disorders]. *Nervenarzt* 76, 893–900. doi: 10.1007/s00115-005-1956-z
24. Füstös, J., Gramann, K., Herbert, B. M., and Pollatos, O. (2012). On the embodiment of emotion regulation: interoceptive awareness facilitates reappraisal. *Soc. Cogn. Affect. Neurosci.* 8, 911–917. doi: 10.1093/scan/nss089
25. Garfinkel, S. N., Seth, A. K., Barrett, A. B., Suzuki, K., and Critchley, H. D. (2015). Knowing your own heart: distinguishing interoceptive accuracy from interoceptive awareness. *Biol. Psychol.* 104, 65–74. doi: 10.1016/j.biopsycho. 2014.11.004
26. Gast, U., Zündorf, F., and Hofmann, A. (1999). *Strukturiertes Klinisches Interview für DSM-IV - Dissoziative Störungen - Kurzform (Mini-SKID-D) [Structured Clinical Interview for DSM-IV - Dissociative Disorders - short form (Mini-SCID- D)]*. Göttingen: Hogrefe.
27. Hart, N., McGowan, J., Minati, L., and Critchley, H. D. (2013). Emotional regulation and bodily sensation: interoceptive awareness is intact in borderline personality disorder. *J. Pers. Disord.* 27, 506–518. doi: 10.1521/pedi_2012_ 26_049
28. Hayes, S. C., Strosahl, K., Wilson, K. G., Bissett, R. T., Pistorello, J., Toarmino, D., et al. (2004). Measuring experiential avoidance: a preliminary test of a working model. *Psychol. Rec.* 54, 553–578. doi: 10.1007/BF03395492
29. Hayes, S. C., Wilson, K. G., Gifford, E. V., Follette, V. M., and Strosahl, K. (1996). Experiential avoidance and behavioral disorders: a functional dimensional approach to diagnosis and treatment. *J. Consult. Clin. Psychol.* 64, 1152–1168. doi: 10.1037/0022-006X.64.6.1152
30. Herbert, B. M., and Pollatos, O. (2008). Interozeptive Sensitivität, Gefühle und Verhaltensregulation [Interoceptive sensitivity, feelings and behavioral control]. *Z. Neuropsychol.* 19, 125–137. doi: 10.1024/1016-264X.19.3.125
31. Herbert, B. M., and Pollatos, O. (2012). The body in the mind: on the relationship between interoception and embodiment. *Top. Cogn. Sci.* 4, 692–704. doi: 10. 1111/j.1756-8765.2012.01189.x
32. Herbert, B. M., and Pollatos, O. (2014). Attenuated interoceptive sensitivity in overweight and obese individuals. *Eat. Behav.* 15, 445–448. doi: 10.1016/j. eatbeh.2014.06.002
33. Hoeschel, K., Guba, K., Kleindienst, N., Limberger, M. F., Schmahl, C., and Bohus, M. (2008). Oligodipsia and dissociative experiences in borderline personality disorder. *Acta Psychiatr. Scand.* 117, 390–393. doi: 10.1111/j.1600- 0447.2008.01167.x
34. Holmes, E., Brown, R., Mansell, W., Fearon, R., Hunter, E., Frasquilho, F., et al. (2005). Are there two qualitatively distinct forms of dissociation? A review and some clinical implications. *Clin. Psychol. Rev.* 25, 1–23. doi: 10.1016/j.cpr.2004. 08.006
35. Horowitz, M., Wilner, N., and Alvarez, W. (1979). Impact of event scale: a measure of subjective stress. *Psychosom. Med.* 41, 209–218. doi: 10.1097/00006842- 197905000-00004
36. James, W. (1884). What is an emotion? *Mind* 9, 188–205. doi: 10.1093/mind/os-IX. 34.188
37. Jaycox, L. H., Foa, E. B., and Morral, A. R. (1998). Influence of emotional engagement and habituation on exposure therapy for PTSD. *J. Consult. Clin. Psychol.* 66, 185–192. doi: 10.1037/0022-006X.66.1.185
38. Jones, G. E., and Hollandsworth, J. G. (1981). Heart rate discrimination before and after exercise-induced augmented cardiac activity. *Psychophysiology* 18, 252–257. doi: 10.1111/j.1469-8986.1981.tb03029.x
39. Kleckner, I. R., Wormwood, J. B., Simmons, W. K., Barrett, L. F., and Quigley, K. S. (2015). Methodological recommendations for a heartbeat detection-based measure of interoceptive sensitivity: recommended methods for heartbeat detection. *Psychophysiology* 52, 1432–1440. doi: 10.1111/psyp.12503
40. Kleindienst, N., Limberger, M. F., Ebner-Priemer, U. W., Keibel-Mauchnik, J., Dyer, A., Berger, M., et al. (2011). Dissociation predicts poor response to dialectial behavioral therapy in female patients with borderline personality disorder. *J. Pers. Disord.* 25, 432–447. doi: 10.1521/pedi.2011. 25.4.432
41. Kleindienst, N., Priebe, K., Görg, N., Dyer, A., Steil, R., Lyssenko, L., et al. (2016). State dissociation moderates response to dialectical behavior therapy for posttraumatic stress disorder in women with and without borderline personality disorder. *Eur. J. Psychotraumatol.* 7:30375. doi: 10.3402/ejpt.v7. 30375
42. Knoll, J. F., and Hodapp, V. (1992). A comparison between two methods for assessing heartbeat perception. *Psychophysiology* 29, 218–222. doi: 10.1111/j. 1469-8986.1992.tb01689.x
43. Lanius, R. A. (2015). Trauma-related dissociation and altered states of consciousness: a call for clinical, treatment, and neuroscience research. *Eur. J. Psychotraumatol.* 6:27905. doi: 10.3402/ejpt.v6.27905
44. Levin, R., and Spei, E. (2004). Relationship of purported measures of pathological and nonpathological dissociation to self-reported psychological distress and fantasy immersion. *Assessment* 11, 160–168. doi: 10.1177/1073191103 256377
45. Lyssenko, L., Schmahl, C., Bockhacker, L., Vonderlin, R., Bohus, M., and Kleindienst, N. (2017). Dissociation in psychiatric disorders: a meta-analysis of studies using the dissociative experiences scale. *Am. J. Psychiatry* 175, 37–46. doi: 10.1176/appi.ajp.2017.17010025
46. Malik, M., Bigger, J. T., Camm, A. J., Kleiger, R. E., Malliani, A., Moss, A. J., et al. (1996). Heart rate variability: standards of measurement, physiological interpretation, and clinical use. *Eur. Heart J.* 17, 354–381. doi: 10.1093/oxfordjournals.eurheartj.a014868
47. Mehling, W. E., Price, C., Daubenmier, J. J., Acree, M., Bartmess, E., and Stewart, A. (2012). The multidimensional assessment of interoceptive awareness (MAIA). *PLoS One* 7:e48230. doi: 10.1371/journal.pone.0048230
48. Michal, M., Reuchlein, B., Adler, J., Reiner, I., Beutel, M. E., Vögele, C., et al. (2014). Striking discrepancy of anomalous body experiences with normal interoceptive accuracy in depersonalization-derealization disorder. *PLoS One* 9:e89823. doi: 10.1371/journal.pone.0089823
49. Michelson, L., June, K., Vives, A., Testa, S., and Marchione, N. (1998). The role of trauma and dissociation in cognitive-behavioral psychotherapy outcome and maintenance for panic disorder with agoraphobia. *Behav. Res. Ther.* 36, 1011–1050. doi: 10.1016/S0005-7967(98)00073-4
50. Mussgay, L., Klinkenberg, N., and Rüddel, H. (1999). Heart beat perception in patients with depressive, somatoform, and personality disorders. *J. Psychophysiol.* 13, 27–36. doi: 10.1027//0269-8803.13.1.27
51. Nijenhuis, E. R., and van der Hart, O. (2011). Dissociation in trauma: a new definition and comparison with previous formulations. *J. Trauma Dissociation* 12, 416–445. doi: 10.1080/15299732.2011.570592
52. Pollatos, O., Herbert, B. M., Berberich, G., Zaudig, M., Krauseneck, T., and Tsakiris, M. (2016). Atypical self-focus effect on interoceptive accuracy in anorexia nervosa. *Front. Hum. Neurosci.* 10:484 doi: 10.3389/fnhum.2016.00484
53. Pollatos, O., Kurz, A.-L., Albrecht, J., Schreder, T., Kleemann, A. M., Schöpf, V., et al. (2008). Reduced perception of bodily signals in anorexia nervosa. *Eat. Behav.* 9, 381–388. doi: 10.1016/j.eatbeh.2008.02.001
54. Pollatos, O., Traut-Mattausch, E., Schroeder, H., and Schandry, R. (2007). Interoceptive awareness mediates the relationship between anxiety and the intensity of unpleasant feelings. *J. Anxiety Disord.* 21, 931–943. doi: 10.1016/ j.janxdis.2006.12.004
55. Pollatos, O., Yeldesbay, A., Pikovsky, A., and Rosenblum, M. (2014). How much time has passed? Ask your heart. *Front. Neurorobot.* 8:15. doi: 10.3389/fnbot. 2014.00015
56. Reinders, A. A., Nijenhuis, E. R., Quak, J., Korf, J., Haaksma, J., Paans, A. M., et al. (2006). Psychobiological characteristics of dissociative identity disorder: a symptom provocation study. *Biol. Psychiatry* 60, 730–740. doi: 10.1016/j. biopsych.2005.12.019
57. Ricciardi, L., Demartini, B., Crucianelli, L., Krahé, C., Edwards, M. J., and Fotopoulou, A. (2016). Interoceptive awareness in patients with functional neurological symptoms. *Biol. Psychol.* 113, 68–74. doi: 10.1016/j.biopsycho. 2015.10.009
58. Riese, H., Groot, P. F., van den Berg, M., Kupper, N. H., Magnee, E. H., Rohaan, E. J., et al. (2003). Large-scale ensemble averaging of ambulatory impedance cardiograms. *Behav. Res. Methods Instrum. Comput.* 35, 467–477. doi: 10.3758/ BF03195525
59. Ring, C., Brener, J., Knapp, K., and Mailloux, J. (2015). Effects of heartbeat feedback on beliefs about heart rate and heartbeat counting: a cautionary tale about interoceptive awareness. *Biol. Psychol.* 104, 193–198. doi: 10.1016/j.biopsycho. 2014.12.010
60. Rufer, M., Held, D., Cremer, J., Fricke, S., Moritz, S., Peter, H., et al. (2006). Dissociation as a predictor of cognitive behavior therapy outcome in patients with obsessive-compulsive disorder. *Psychother. Psychosom.* 75, 40–46. doi: 10. 1159/000089225
61. Sar, V. (2011). Epidemiology of dissociative disorders: an overview. *Epidemiol. Res. Int.* 2011:404538. doi: 10.1155/2011/404538
62. Schaefer, M., Egloff, B., and Witthöft, M. (2012). Is interoceptive awareness really altered in somatoform disorders? Testing competing theories with

two paradigms of heartbeat perception. *J. Abnorm. Psychol.* 121, 719–724. doi: 10. 1037/a0028509

63. Schäflein, E., Sattel, H., and Sack, M. (2016). [Conference Abstract in German] Selbstwahrnehmung als Stressor bei Patienten mit dissoziativen Bewusstseinsstörungen [Self-perception as a stressor in patients with dissociative disorders of consciousness]. *Z. Psychosom. Med. Psychother.* 62, 84–85.
64. Schäflein, E., Sattel, H., Schmidt, U., and Sack, M. (2018). The enemy in the mirror: self-perception-induced stress results in dissociation of psychological and physiological responses in patients with dissociative disorder. *Eur. J. Psychotraumatol.* 9:1472991. doi: 10.1080/20008198.2018.1472991
65. Schandry, R. (1981). Heart beat perception and emotional experience. *Psychophysiology* 18, 483–488. doi: 10.1111/j.1469-8986.1981.tb02486.x
66. Schulz, A., and Vögele, C. (2015). Interoception and stress. *Front. Psychol.* 6:993. doi: 10.3389/fpsyg.2015.00993
67. Sedeño, L., Couto, B., Melloni, M., Canales-Johnson, A., Yoris, A., Baez, S., et al. (2014). How do you feel when you can't feel your body? Interoception, functional connectivity and emotional processing in depersonalization- derealization disorder. *PLoS One* 9:e98769. doi: 10.1371/journal.pone.0098769
68. Shapiro, F. (2001). *EMDR. Basic Principles, Protocols, and Procedures*, 2nd Edn. New York, NY: Guilford Publications.
69. Singer, J. D. (1998). Using SAS PROC MIXED to fit multilevel models, hierarchical models, and individual growth models. *J. Educ. Behav. Stat.* 24, 323–355. doi: 10.3102/10769986023004323
70. Soffer-Dudek, N. (2014). Dissociation and dissociative mechanisms in panic disorder, obsessive–compulsive disorder, and depression: a review and heuristic framework. *Psychol. Conscious.* 1, 243–270. doi: 10.1037/cns0000023
71. Spitzer, C., Barnow, S., Freyberger, H. J., and Grabe, H. J. (2007). Dissociation predicts symptom-related treatment outcome in short-term inpatient psychotherapy. *Aust. N. Z. J. Psychiatry* 41, 682–687. doi: 10.1080/00048670701449146
72. Steinberg, M. (1994). *Structured Clinical Interview for DSM-IV Dissociative Disorders (SCID-D) (revised).* Washington, DC: American Psychiatric Press.
73. Terasawa, Y., Shibata, M., Moriguchi, Y., and Umeda, S. (2013). Anterior insular cortex mediates bodily sensibility and social anxiety. *Soc. Cogn. Affect. Neurosci.* 8, 259–266. doi: 10.1093/scan/nss108
74. van der Hart, O., Nijenhuis, E., Steele, K., and Brown, D. (2004). Trauma-related dissociation: conceptual clarity lost and found. *Aust. N. Z. J. Psychiatry* 38, 906–914. doi: 10.1080/j.1440-1614.2004.01480.x
75. van der Hart, O., Nijenhuis, E. R. S., and Steele, K. (2006). *The Haunted Self: Structural Dissociation and the Treatment of Chronic Traumatization.* New York, NY: W.W. Norton.
76. VU-DAMS (2013). *Data Analysis and Management Software (DAMS) for the Vrije Universiteit Ambulatory Monitoring System (VU-AMS) - Manual version 1.1 2 January 2013 (written for VU-DAMS v 2.2).* Available at: http://www.vu-ams.nl/ fileadmin/user_upload/manuals/VU-DAMS_manual_v1.1.pdf
77. Weisz, J., Balázs, L., and Adám, G. (1988). The influence of self-focused attention on heartbeat perception. *Psychophysiology* 25, 193–199. doi: 10.1111/j.1469- 8986.1988.tb00987.x
78. Wengenroth, M. (2012). *Therapie-Tools Akzeptanz- und Commitmenttherapie: Mit Online-Materialien [Therapeutic tools Acceptance and Commitment Therapy: With Online Material.].* Weinheim: Beltz.
79. Whitehead, D. W., Drescher, V. M., Heiman, P., and Blackwell, B. (1977). Relation of heart rate control to heartbeat perception. *Biofeedback Self Regul.* 2, 371–392. doi: 10.1007/BF00998623
80. Wiens, S. (2005). Interoception in emotional experience. *Curr. Opin. Neurol.* 18, 442–447. doi: 10.1097/01.wco.0000168079.92106.99
81. Willemsen, G. H., De Geus, E. J., Klaver, C. H., Van Doornen, L. J., and Carroll, D. (1996). Ambulatory monitoring of the impedance cardiogram. *Psychophysiology* 33, 184–193. doi: 10.1111/j.1469-8986.1996.tb 02122.x
82. Wittchen, H. U., Zaudig, M., and Fydrich, T. (1997). *SKID- Strukturiertes Klinisches Interview für DSM-IV.* Göttingen: Hogrefe.
83. Wolpe, J. (1969). *The Practice of Behavior Therapy.* New York, NY: Pergamon Press.

24

ERP Evidence for Inhibitory Control Deficits in Test-Anxious Individuals

Wenpei Zhang[1,2], Alain De Beuckelaer[3,4], Lirong Chen[1] and Renlai Zhou[1,5]*

[1] Department of Psychology, Nanjing University, Nanjing, China, [2] Department of Business Administration, School of Business, Anhui University of Technology, Maanshan, China, [3] Institute for Management Research, Radboud University, Nijmegen, Netherlands, [4] Department of Personnel Management, Work and Organizational Psychology, Ghent University, Ghent, Belgium, [5] Key Laboratory for NeuroInformation of Ministry of Education, University of Electronic Science and Technology of China, Chengdu, China

***Correspondence:**
Renlai Zhou
rlzhou@nju.edu.cn*

Introduction: Individuals with test anxiety [i.e., high test anxiety (HTA)] always treat tests/examinations as a potential threat. This cognitive mode impairs these individuals' ability of inhibitory control and leads to a high level of anxiety. However, characterizing aspects of HTA's impaired inhibitory control ability are unclear and need to be studied.

Methods: Forty-six participants were recruited and divided into a HTA (N = 26) and low test anxiety (LTA; i.e., healthy control; N = 20) group. Self-reports (Test Anxiety Scale, State-Trait Anxiety Inventory for negative emotions) were obtained. An emotional Stroop (ES) task and a numerical Stroop (NS) task, causing different types of interferences, were used for assessing the emotional and cognitive aspects of attentional control ability (behavioral data). Event-related brain potentials (ERPs) were registered to further assess processing stages related to different aspects of attentional control ability.

Results: Compared with the LTA group, the HTA group has inhibitory control deficits of both emotional (see ERP components P1-P2-N2 and P3) and cognitive (see ERP component P3) interference. Compared with the LTA group, the HTA doesn't have lower accuracy in neither ES nor NS but displays longer reaction times only in ES. Additionally, the HTA group's ES results also show that (1) the degree of emotional interference indicates the level of an individual's anxiety, and (2) the ERP component P2 may serve as an index of the level of test anxiety.

Conclusion: HTA individuals have extensive inhibitory deficits for both emotional and cognitive aspects; however, impairment impacts more on emotional aspects than on cognitive aspects. Additionally, as compared to NS, the negative impact of more impaired processing stages on task performance is more substantial in ES.

Keywords: test anxiety, inhibitory control, emotional Stroop (ES), numerical Stroop (NS), ERPs

INTRODUCTION

Test anxiety is a situation-specific form of anxiety disorder; individuals who suffer from this anxiety disorder tend to appraise performance evaluative situations (e.g., taking an exam) as threatening, and continue to be in high anxiety (1). Test anxiety manifests itself at the individual level in cognitive, affective-physiological, and behavioral characteristics (2). If the individual expects exam results to have great impact (e.g., on the course of his/her life), the exam is perceived as "threatening," and the individual will display symptoms characterizing high anxiety (3). In most etiology models of anxiety disorders, cognitive evaluations of a (threatening) stimulus (i.e., a "cognitive pattern") affects the etiology and the maintenance of anxiety in the individual (4–6).

The cognitive pattern may cause and maintain anxiety through affecting an individual's ability of attentional inhibitory control. An individual who exerts inhibitory control is able to inhibit task-unrelated information or incorrect automatic responses when reacting to task-related information (7, 8). Worry caused by negative cognition stemming from an exam's appraisal leads to anxiety and elevates the individual's vulnerability to anxious cues. This vulnerability increases the degree of interference from exam/test-related information, which is unrelated to completing the task (i.e., task unrelated information), and decreases the ability of inhibitory control (9, 10). So, in comparison to low test anxiety (LTA) individuals, high test anxiety (HTA) individuals tend to show higher interference by test-related information than by neutral (i.e., including test-unrelated) information (11–13), an interference that may affect the allocation of attentional resources during the processing of task stimuli (13). More specifically, this interference may reduce the attentional resources used for the task at hand, impairing the individual's task performance and increasing the level of anxiety in the individual (14, 15).

Attentional control theory assumes that anxiety impacts two dimensions of task performance: (performance) "effectiveness" and (processing) "efficiency" (5). Effectiveness refers to an individual's "performance quality" usually measured as accuracy in task performance. Efficiency is conceptualized as the level of allocated resources used by an individual to process task stimuli, a conceptualization which is usually measured by the reaction time (RT) (5, 16). Most studies have shown that an inhibitory control deficit in HTA individuals led to detrimental efficiency, and sometimes even to detrimental effectiveness (13–15). Whether anxiety impairs the effectiveness may depend on cognitive load (17); when cognitive load is relatively low, anxious individuals apply some compensatory strategies, such as sacrificing on efficiency (causing the RTs to increase), to achieve equal effectiveness as non-anxious individuals [see, for instance, Refs. (18–21)].

However, previous evidence on these impairments all stem from emotion-activating experimental conditions in which participants needed to inhibit (test-related) threatening interference (11–13). In our view, it is necessary to make a conceptual distinction between (and also examine) different types of interference, namely, emotional and cognitive interference. Two reasons (explained below) make such distinctive conceptualization necessary.

Reason no. 1: Emotional and cognitive interference may reveal different cognitive aspects (i.e., the cognitive pattern) in HTA individuals. Two cognitive aspects are worthwhile mentioning. The first cognitive aspect concerns the impairment of emotional interference (such as test-related threatening interference), which is indicative of a negative cognitive mode related to test-related threatening information (13, 22, 23), including vigilance and further processing of threatening information (24); this first cognitive aspect manifests itself in both an early and a late stage of processing [e.g., Refs. (25, 26)]. The second cognitive aspect concerns the impairment of cognitive interference, which is indicative of an impaired cognitive function, attesting to a difficulty in inhibiting general interference (24); this second cognitive aspect manifests itself in a late stage of processing only (27, 28).

Reason no. 2: These two types of interference may lead to differential task performance. As impaired processing stages go hand in hand with a relatively high cognitive load (5), an impact on task performance is to be expected. The nature of the impact (on cognitive pattern, impaired processing stage, and task performance) is unclear at present. The differentially impaired processing stages involved in emotional and cognitive inhibition (as caused by different types of interference) may subsequently result in a differential impact on task performance.

In the present study, we relied on an emotional Stroop (ES) (29, 30) and a numerical Stroop (NS) (31, 32) paradigm to study the characteristics of inhibitory control ability when HTA individuals are exposed to test-related threatening interference and cognitive interference, respectively. In the Stroop paradigm, the stimulus, which is one word/number, reflects two dimensions at the time: (a) a task-related dimension, and (b) an interfering dimension. Consequently, one may systematically compare the time-course of an ongoing "competition" (for available attentional resources) between the two dimensions, and also assess how exactly different stages of processing are influenced by different types of interference (33). The ES paradigm is instrumental in studying vulnerability to threatening information, which is indicative of a negative mode of threats (34–36). Individuals are expected to display longer RTs and/or lower accuracy for threatening words, especially if they experience difficulties in inhibiting affective interference and, due to this inhibition, do not manage to recruit attentional resources (13, 37–39). The NS paradigm is instrumental in studying impairment of the cognitive inhibitory function. Individuals are expected to display longer RTs and/or lower accuracy for task-irrelevant aspects (for instance: the one-digit number that is larger in value is depicted in a smaller physical size), especially if they experience difficulties in inhibiting general interference (40–44).

Conventional Stroop studies are limited in that they only collect behavioral (i.e., mainly RT) data (45), while the use of event-related potentials (ERPs) in combination with behavioral data can provide many details on the stage in which the processing difficulties occur (46, 47). ERPs are known to have high temporal resolution, and therefore allow adequately "tracking" fast and temporal processing changes (48). Through the analysis of the "magnitude" of very specific ERP components (49), typically for different groups of stimuli (e.g., threatening and neutral stimuli), a researcher may collect clear indications of the nature of processing and processing difficulties encountered. For example, the magnitude of the ERP components P1, P2, and N2 are always examined when analyzing the automatic processing of emotional stimuli. The magnitudes of ERP components P1 and P2 indicate the allocation of attentional resources during the early (especially perceptual) stage of stimulus processing, an allocation that is indicative of the degree of hypervigilance of the stimulus (50–53). Additionally, the magnitude of ERP component N2 (especially when followed by perceptual components such as P1 and P2) indicates the automatic and facilitated processing following hypervigilance of the stimulus (50, 51). The magnitude of ERP component P3 is indicative of the cognitive processing of both emotional and cognitive stimuli; P3 is a component that reflects the allocation of attentional resources during a relatively late and cognitive stage of stimulus processing (44, 50–52). ERPs are known to change as a response to processing affective (i.e., emotional) stimulus content (rather than non-affective, that is, neutral stimulus content) (54–56). In addition, the magnitude and latency of ERP components adequately describe (processing) efficiency, and the activation of a (compensatory) strategy to reduce the effect of impaired efficiency on task performance (17, 28, 55). Therefore, ERPs offer very suitable descriptors of attention paid to stimuli/information in different processing stages, especially for HTA individuals as contrasted to LTA individuals (10, 48).

In sum, the purpose of the present study is to further examine how test-related threatening and cognitive interference impact inhibitory control deficits, processing efficiency, and task performance in HTA (as opposed to LTA) individuals. This examination is based on ES and NS paradigms, but relies, in addition to registering conventional behavioral outcomes (RTs), also on the registration and analysis of ERPs. As such, this study's design may offer useful insights in the nature of stimulus processing under different conditions of interference. Based on our reasoning presented above, we predict that (a) HTA individuals have both emotional and cognitive inhibitory control deficits; the emotional inhibitory control deficit manifests itself in both the early and late processing stages, while the cognitive inhibitory control deficit manifests itself in the late processing stage only, and (b) for HTA individuals, the different processing stages involved in emotional and cognitive control deficit attest to a more severe impairment of task performance in ES than in NS.

METHODS AND MATERIALS

Participants and Assignment to the LTA and the HTA Group

Individuals (from now on referred to as "participants") were recruited through posters or online advertisements. Eighty-two students from Nanjing University signed up for participating in the experiments, and 46 students got eventually selected for participation in the study. According to conventional criteria set for high statistical power (57), we must conclude that our actual sample size combined with the effect sizes as reported in this study leads to high levels of statistical power, that is, the statistical power for each significant difference reported in our (repeated-measures) ANOVA is consistently higher than 98% [$1-\beta > .98$, $\alpha = .05$, using the G-power software (58)]. Participants (aged from 18–26 years; all self-declared right handed) were chosen and assigned to a high test-anxious (HTA) group (n = 26; 12 males; 21.27 ± 1.89 years) and to a low test-anxious (LTA) group (n = 20; 9 males; 21.35 ± 2.96 years; not significantly different across groups: $t_{(1,44)} = .113, p = .910$) based on their score obtained with the (self-reported) Test Anxiety Scale survey instrument (TAS) (6). Thirty-six students were excluded because (a) they are neither HTA nor LTA, and/or (b) they appeared to have suffered or still suffer from currently known psychiatric disorders (e.g., depression, bipolar disorder, and substance abuse) as diagnosed (just before the start of this study) by a self-completed Structured Clinical Interview for DSM-IV (59). For descriptive purposes also the (self-reported) State-Trait Anxiety Inventory survey instrument (STAI) (60) was administered. STAI was used to unravel the effects of state and trait aspects of test anxiety on interference. Our study was carried out in accordance with a study protocol designed by ourselves, a study protocol that was approved by the Ethics Committee of Nanjing University, School of Social and Behavioral Sciences; the principles on the basis of which the Ethics Committee approves study protocols are described in a document entitled "Ethical Evaluation of Research Projects at the Department of Psychology, School for Social and Behavioral Sciences, Nanjing University." All study participants gave written informed consent in accordance with the Declaration of Helsinki. In the next paragraphs, details on both survey instruments are given.

Questionnaires

The Chinese version of TAS (6) was administered. The TAS contains 37 survey items reflecting symptoms of test anxiety, all of which are scored using the two true/false answer categories. A participant's total score ranges from 0 to 37. The higher the participant's total score, the more test anxiety symptoms are experienced. As documented in other studies (61), the Chinese version of TAS shows a Cronbach's alpha coefficient of .64 and a test-retest reliability coefficient of.61. Participants are assigned to (a) the HTA group if their TAS total score exceeds or equals 20, and (b) assigned to the LTA group if their TAS total score falls below or equals 12 (61, 62).

The Chinese version of the State-Trait Anxiety Inventory (STAI) was administered (60). The STAI contains 40 survey items, all of which are scored on a four-point, Likert type scale ranging from 1 (not at all) to 4 (very much so). Twenty survey items measure state anxiety (S-STAI) and the other 20 items measure trait anxiety (T-STAI). Obviously, the higher the S-STAI/T-STAI total score, the more symptoms of state-/trait- anxiety are observed, respectively. As documented by Li and Qian (60), the Chinese STAI scale shows a Cronbach's alpha coefficient of .91 for S-STAI and .88 for T-STAI (60). In contrast to TAS, no assessments of test-retest reliability have been published for STAI.

Stimuli, Behavioral Paradigm, and Test Procedure

Participants showed up in the laboratory to participate in the experiment within 1 week after completing TAS and STAI. Participants were connected to a 64-electrode head cap (technical details are given further on) and instructed to relax for 2 min. Then, they either started with the ES or the NS experiment (determined at random) and, after completion, went on with "the other" experiment. Both the ES and NS experiment consisted of a "practice block" (not providing data for analysis) and, subsequently, an "experimental block" (providing data for analysis). When participating in the ES and NS, participants were always asked to finish the tasks "as quickly and accurately as possible." After completion of both the ES and NS experiment, the electrode head cap was removed and participants got paid the equivalent of about 6 US dollars (i.e., 40 Renminbi).

Emotional Stroop (ES)

The ES task design was similar to that of Thomas et al. (52). Participants were asked to name the color of the word displayed (on screen) regardless of the word's meaning. The stimuli (words) chosen constitute two experimental conditions (or experimental groups): test-related threatening (e.g., "test paper" and "score") words and neutral (e.g., "garden" and "shoes") words. Each experimental condition includes 15 words that were selected based on scores (see **Table S1**) from a pool of 30 potential neutral/test-related threatening words that were scored by 40 individuals who did not participate in the present study. Words ranged in length from two to four Chinese characters. The words subtended a maximum of 3.81 degrees of visual angle in width. The words subtended 1.27 degrees in height.

Test-related threatening words and neutral words were picked out by following a procedure similar to that of Thomas et al. (52); in particular, they were picked out according to their threatening degree (by asking "How threatening is this word to you [including related unpleasant thoughts and feelings, such as worry or/and anxiety]?") and test-related degree (by asking "How relevant is this word to "test")?, and matched for frequency of usage (by asking "How often do you use or see this word?"). A seven point Likert-type scale ranging from 1 (not at all) to 7 (severely threatening/strongly relevant/always, respectively) was used. A significant difference exists in the threatening degree ($t_{(28)} = 30.190, p < .001$) and the test-related degree ($t_{(28)} = 38.166, p < .001$) between the two groups of words, of course in the expected direction, that is "threatening" words are relatively more threatening and test-related. As far as frequency of usage is concerned, no significant difference exists between the group of threatening words and the group of neutral words ($t_{(28)} = 1.436, p = .162$).

Two experimental blocks were offered: (a) a practice block, and, afterwards, (b) an experimental block. The practice block contained six trials; the set-up of the practice block is analogous to the experimental block, except for (a) the number of words offered (6 rather than 120 words), and (b) the fact that all words were neutral. All six words offered in the practice block were not used in the experimental block. To enable participants' learning in the practice block, the message "correct" or "false" was given after each trial (obviously, such message was not given in the experimental block). The experimental block contained 120 trials (every word was offered four times, picked randomly, and the word was displayed 50% of the times in red, and 50% of the times in blue). Each trial started with a fixation point "+" on a computer screen; that fixation point stayed on screen for 200 ms. Next, the screen turned blank and lasted for a time in-between 800 and 1200 ms (duration was randomly picked). Subsequently, the word (randomly picked) was presented in the center of the screen against a white background. This trial ended when (a) the participant reacted (i.e., pushed a button to indicate the color of the word) or (b) failed to react within 2000 ms. In-between consecutive trials, a screen with a white background was shown for a time in-between 1000 and 2000 ms (duration was randomly picked).

Numerical Stroop (NS)

The NS task design was similar to that of previous studies (63, 64). Participants were asked to compare the numerical value (i.e., indicate the larger value) of a pair of two white one-digit numbers positioned left and right against a gray background. In order to reduce the impact of distance in value, one digit was always three units larger in value than the other (1-4 or 4-1; 2-5 or 5-2; 3-6 or 6-3, etcetera) in each pair (65). Which position (left or right) was larger in value was determined at random. The pairs of one-digit numbers constituted three experimental conditions: (a) congruent, (b) incongruent, and (c) neutral. In a congruent pair, the one-digit number showing the larger numerical value was also the larger one in physical size (200 points in physical size and the other one-digit number 140 points in physical size). In an incongruent pair, the one-digit number showing the larger numerical value was the smaller one in physical size, that is, 140 points in physical size, whereas the other one-digit number was 200 points in physical size. In a neutral pair, two digits were of the same physical size (half of the times 140 points and half of the times 200 points). The words subtended almost 3.81 degrees of visual angle in width. The words subtended 1.59 degrees for larger physical size number in height and 0.5 degrees for smaller physical size number in height.

Two experimental blocks were offered: (a) a practice block afterwards, and (b) an experimental block. The practice block contained six trials; the set-up of the practice block is analogous to the experimental block, except for the fact that in the practice block only neutral pairs are offered. Just as in ES, participants were given feedback (correct/false) after each trial in the practice block (but not in the experimental block). The experimental block contained 108 trials (each experimental condition consisted of 36 trials). Each trial started with a fixation point "+" on a computer screen; that fixation point stayed on screen for 200 ms. Next, the screen turned blank and lasted for a time in-between 800 and 1200 ms (duration was randomly picked). Subsequently, the number pair (randomly picked) was presented in the center of the screen against a gray background. This trial ended when the participant gave a reaction (pushing a button to indicate which one-digit number was the larger one in value) or failed to react within 5000 ms. In-between consecutive trials, a screen with a gray background was shown for a time in-between 1000 and 2000 ms (duration was randomly picked).

Electrophysiological Recording and Analysis

A NeuroScan recording system and a 64-electrode head cap designed according to the International 10/20 system formed the technical equipment to collect electrophysiological (EEG) data. The electrode placed on the left mastoid served as a reference during recording. A horizontal electrooculogram (HEOG) was derived from EEG data collected by electrodes placed on the outer canthi of the eyes, and a vertical electrooculogram (VEOG) was derived from EEG data collected by an electrode placed above and below the left eye. The impedances were kept below 5 kOhm. EEG was recorded by a DC model with a sampling rate of 1000 Hz.

Offline analysis of EEG data was enabled through the software "Curry 7.0.8." EEG data was re-referenced to the average of the left and right mastoids, filtered using a 30 Hz bandwidth (24 dB/octave slope), and corrected for ocular artifacts. To retrieve ERPs from participants' responses to stimuli, data were epoched from 200 ms pre-stimulus to 1,000 ms post-stimulus, baseline-corrected by 200 ms pre-stimulus, and averaged for all experimental conditions. Interest areas were defined based on two steps. First, the interest areas of related ERP components from previous studies were identified to select specific ERP components for use in the present study; in ES: ERP components P1, P2, N2, and P3 components were selected (50–53); in NS: ERP component P3 was selected (44). Second, in the present study, the exact interest areas of each ERP component were identified based on the grand average latency (i.e., the average time intervals between stimulus onset and peak of each condition for each experimental group) determining the middle point of the interest area. Eventually, time windows of each ERP component were, in ES, P1 (120–170 ms), P2 (210–260 ms), N2 (240–290 ms), and P3 (320–370 ms) and, in NS, P3 (neutral: 300–400 ms; congruent: 300–350 ms; incongruent: 420–470 ms). ERP components' data were analyzed at five electrodes (Fz, FCz, Cz, CPz, and Pz). Mean amplitudes (i.e., mean amplitude of the peaks) and latency of each ERP component were calculated for each condition and for each participant. Per electrode (measuring a component) data on 60 trials in ES and 36 trials in NS were collected for each condition.

TABLE 1 | The TAS and STAI subscales scores in the HTA and LTA group (M ± SD).

	HTA (N = 26)	LTA (N = 20)	*t*	*p*
TAS	27.85 ± 4.78	8.65 ± 2.76	17.11	<.001
S-STAI	56.77 ± 9.28	31.55 ± 4.85	11.91	<.001
T-STAI	56.46 ± 9.19	31.95 ± 5.11	11.48	<.001

HTA, high test-anxious; LTA, low test-anxious; TAS, Test Anxiety Scale survey instrument; S-STAI, state subscale of State-Trait Anxiety Inventory; T-STAI, trait subscale of State-Trait Anxiety Inventory.

Statistical Analysis

TAS and STAI data (i.e., self-reported data) were analyzed using (standard) independent samples t-tests. In agreement with other ERP studies on attention [e.g., Refs. (8, 66)], ES and NS data from (a) erroneous trials (i.e., false answers) and (b) trials with RTs exceeding three standard deviations from the participant's mean RT (as calculated for the experimental condition) were removed prior to analysis. Also in agreement with previous studies (11, 67–69), statistical analyses mainly aimed at examining the statistical significance of between-group (i.e., HTA versus LTA) differences in attentional control ability as observed in given (experimental) conditions, rather than between-condition differences in attentional control ability for HTA individuals or, alternatively, LTA individuals. For behavioral and ERP data, in ES, RT (in milliseconds), accuracy (percent correct, %), and ERP amplitudes data were analyzed using a 2 group (HTA, LTA) × 2 condition (test-related threatening, neutral) repeated-measures ANOVA. In NS, RT, accuracy, and ERP amplitudes data were analyzed using a 2 group (HTA, LTA) × 3 condition (neutral, congruent, incongruent) repeated-measures ANOVA. Both behavioral and ERP data were corrected according to the Greenhouse–Geisser correction after running the ANOVAs. In our correlation analysis, we relied on the Pearson correlation. In all significance testing, we relied on the conventional criterion of $p < .05$. Significance is reported by reporting the exact significance (format used: "$p = \ldots$"), unless the p-value is less than.001 (format used: "$p < .001$").

RESULTS

TAS and STAI Results

In the present study, TAS shows a Cronbach's alpha coefficient of 0.87 and a test-retest reliability coefficient of 0.74, and STAI shows a Cronbach's alpha coefficient of 0.95 for S-STAI and 0.90 for T-STAI. Descriptive statistics (on TAS and STAI) for both HTA and LTA individuals are shown in **Table 1**. In line with the expectations, the HTA group displays a higher degree of test anxiety, state anxiety, and trait anxiety than the LTA group.

Behavioral Results

Behavioral Results in ES

Mean RTs, accuracy, and stimulus types are shown in **Table 2**. RT data show a significant condition main effect ($F_{(1,44)} = 6.005$, $p = .018$, $\eta^2 = .120$) and a significant group × condition interaction effect ($F_{(1,44)} =$

TABLE 2 | Emotional Stroop results on the HTA and LTA group: (1) reaction times (RTs, in ms) of test-related threatening words, neutral words, and test-related threatening interference, and (2) accuracy (in %) of test-related threatening and neutral words (M ± SD).

Condition	RT		Accuracy	
	HTA (N = 26)	LTA (N = 20)	HTA (N = 26)	LTA (N = 20)
Test-related threatening	502.78 ± 95.13***	453.90 ± 78.47	99.88 ± 1.45**	98.35 ± 1.63
Neutral	480.84 ± 89.91	452.25 ± 79.58	97.88 ± 2.17	99.25 ± 0.96*
Interference	21.94 ± 38.77	1.64 ± 21.14		

$^*p < .05$, $^{**}p < .01$, $^{***}p < .001$.

HTA, high test-anxious; LTA, low test-anxious; Interference: the RT as observed in the test-related threatening condition minus the RT as observed in the neutral condition.

4.447, $p = .041$, $\eta^2 = .092$). No significant group main effect was found ($F_{(1,44)} = 2.323$, $p = .135$, $\eta^2 = .050$). Additional simple effect analysis shows that, in contrast to the LTA group ($F_{(1,44)} = .052$, $p = .821$, $\eta^2 = .001$), the HTA group has a longer RT for test-related threatening words than for neutral words ($F_{(1,44)} = 11.953$, $p < .001$, $\eta^2 = .214$).

Accuracy data show a significant condition main effect ($F_{(1,44)} = .038$, $p = .846$, $\eta^2 = .001$) and a significant group × condition interaction effect ($F_{(1,44)} = 13.833$, $p < .001$, $\eta^2 = .239$). No significant group main effect was found ($F_{(1,44)} = .982$, $p = .327$, $\eta^2 = .022$). Additional simple effect analysis shows that the LTA group has higher accuracy for neutral words than for test-related threatening words ($F_{(1,44)} = 5.492$, $p = .024$, $\eta^2 = .111$); on the contrary, the HTA group has higher accuracy for test-related threatening words than for neutral words ($F_{(1,44)} = 8.814$, $p = .005$, $\eta^2 = .167$).

A substantial correlation between behavioral data and TAS or STAI scores was found; in particular, a higher accuracy for test-related threatening words is associated with a higher T-STAI total score ($r = .344$, $p = .019$).

Behavioral Results in NS

Mean RTs, accuracy, and stimulus types are shown in **Table 3**. RT data show a significant condition main effect ($F_{(1,43)} = 90.210$, $p < .001$, $\eta^2 = .672$) and a significant group × condition interaction effect ($F_{(1,43)} = 5.435$, $p = .011$, $\eta^2 = .110$). No significant group main effect was found ($F_{(1,43)} = 1.165$, $p = .286$, $\eta^2 = .026$). Additional simple effect analysis shows that (a) for each group, significant RT differences exist between the three conditions (HTA: $F_{(1,43)} = 24.225$, $p < .001$, $\eta^2 = .530$; LTA: $F_{(1,43)} = 39.288$, $p < .001$, $\eta^2 = .646$) and (b) for each condition, no significant RT difference is observed between the HTA and the LTA group (Neutral: $F_{(1,44)} = 1.776$, $p = .090$, $\eta^2 = .039$, Congruent: $F_{(1,44)} = 2.294$, $p = .137$, $\eta^2 = .050$, Incongruent: $F_{(1,44)} = .066$, $p = .799$, $\eta^2 = .001$).

Accuracy results show a significant condition main effect ($F_{(1,43)} = 31.054$, $p < .001$, $\eta^2 = .414$). No significant group × condition interaction effect ($F_{(1,43)} = .141$, $p = .729$, $\eta^2 = .003$) and group main effect ($F_{(1,43)} < .001$, $p = .996$, $\eta^2 < .001$) is reported.

No substantial correlations between behavioral data and TAS or STAI scores were found.

ERP Results

ERP Results in ES

Grand average ERP waveforms and scalp topographic maps for ES are shown in **Figure 1**.

The amplitude of ERP component P1 shows a significant condition main effect ($F_{(1,44)} = 4.989$, $p = .031$, $\eta^2 = .102$) and a significant group × condition interaction effect ($F_{(1,44)} = 4.928$, $p = .032$, $\eta^2 = .101$). No significant group main effect was found ($F_{(1,44)} = 2.74$, $p = .105$, $\eta^2 = .059$; at site Pz). Additional simple effect analysis shows that, in contrast to the LTA group ($F_{(1,44)} < .001$, $p = .993$, $\eta^2 < .001$), the HTA group has a larger P1 amplitude for test-related threatening words than for neutral words ($F_{(1,44)} = 11.405$, $p = .002$, $\eta^2 = .206$).

The amplitude of ERP component P2 shows a significant condition main effect ($F_{(1,44)} = 12.696$, $p = .001$, $\eta^2 = .224$) and a significant group × condition interaction effect ($F_{(1,44)} = 5.384$, $p = .025$, $\eta^2 = .109$). No significant group main effect was found ($F_{(1,44)} = .013$, $p = .909$, $\eta^2 < .001$; at site Cz, CPz, and Pz, and take site Pz as an example for presenting significant results). Additional simple effect analysis shows that, in contrast to the LTA group ($F_{(1,44)} = .683$, $p = .413$, $\eta^2 = .015$), the HTA group has a larger P2 amplitude for test-related threatening words than for neutral words ($F_{(1,44)} = 19.903$, $p < .001$, $\eta^2 = .311$).

The amplitude of ERP component N2 shows a significant condition main effect ($F_{(1,44)} = 24.378$, $p < .001$, $\eta^2 = .357$) and a significant group × condition interaction effect ($F_{(1,44)} = 15.989$, $p < .001$, $\eta^2 = .267$). No significant group main effect was found ($F_{(1,44)} = .817$, $p = .370$, $\eta^2 = .018$; at site Fz, FCz, and Cz, and take site Cz as an example for presenting significant results). Additional simple effect analysis shows that, in contrast to the LTA group ($F_{(1,44)} = .390$, $p = .536$, $\eta^2 = .009$), the HTA group has a smaller N2 amplitude for test-related threatening words than for neutral words ($F_{(1,44)} = 45.916$, $p < .001$, $\eta^2 = .511$).

The amplitude of ERP component P3 shows a significant condition main effect ($F_{(1,44)} = 64.656$, $p < .001$, $\eta^2 = .595$) and a significant group × condition interaction effect ($F_{(1,44)} = 27.817$, $p < .001$, $\eta^2 = .387$). No significant group main effect was found ($F_{(1,44)} = .320$, $p = .574$, $\eta^2 = .007$; at site Cz and Pz, and take site Pz as an example for presenting significant results). Additional simple effect analysis shows that, in contrast to the LTA group ($F_{(1,44)} = 3.386$, $p = .073$, $\eta^2 = .071$), the HTA group has a larger P3 amplitude for test-related threatening words than for neutral words ($F_{(1,44)} = 101.943$, $p < .001$, $\eta^2 = .699$).

No significant results are reported for the latency of the ERP components P1, P2, N2, and P3 (all *Fs* < 1.126, all *ps* > .335, all $\eta^2 s < .06$).

Significant correlations between ERP emotional interference (ERP amplitude as registered for the test-related threatening

TABLE 3 | Numerical Stroop results on the HTA and LTA group: (1) reaction times (RTs, in ms) and (2) accuracy (in %) in three experimental conditions (M ± SD).

Condition	RT		Accuracy	
	HTA (N = 26)	LTA (N = 20)	HTA (N = 26)	LTA (N = 20)
Neutral	504.43 ± 110.11	469.18 ± 48.60	99.54 ± 1.39	99.85 ± 0.67
Congruent	474.21 ± 99.55	437.62 ± 47.28	99.77 ± 0.81	99.85 ± 0.67
Incongruent	529.04 ± 99.27	522.97 ± 41.82	95.38 ± 5.73	95.00 ± 4.76
Congruent interference	−30.22 ± 26.42	−31.56 ± 25.99		
Incongruent interference	24.61 ± 41.82	53.79 ± 22.34		

HTA, high test-anxious; LTA, low test-anxious; Congruent interference: the RT as observed in the congruent condition minus the RT as observed in the neutral condition; Incongruent interference: the RT as observed in the incongruent condition minus the RT as observed in the neutral condition.

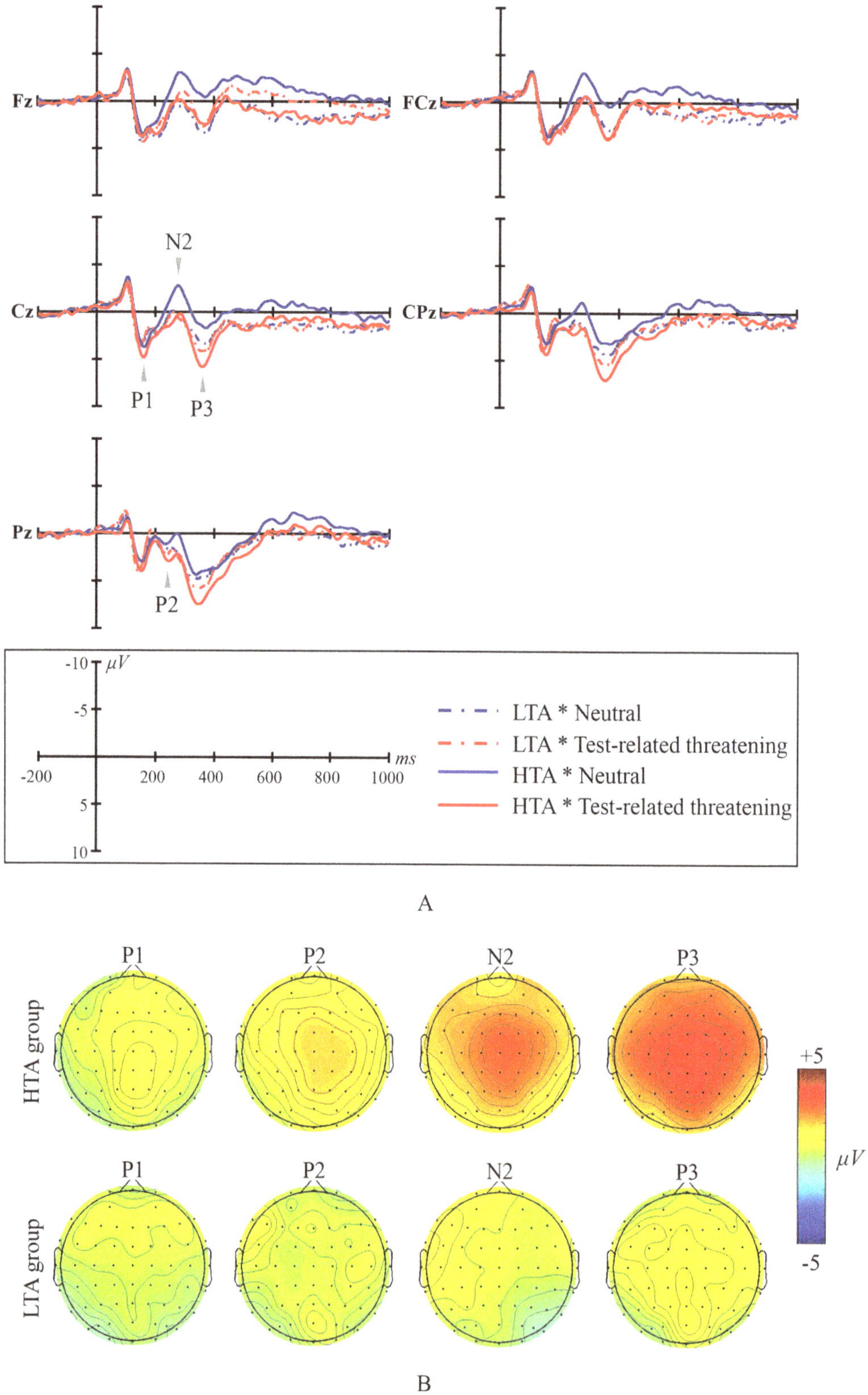

FIGURE 1 | Emotional Stroop ERP waveforms and scalp topographic maps for both the high test-anxious (HTA) and the low test-anxious (LTA) group: **(A)** grand average ERPs elicited by test-related threatening and neutral words for the HTA and the LTA group at Fz, FCz, Cz, CPz, and Pz sites; P1, P2, and P3 are all registered at site Cz, CPz, and Pz; N2 was registered at site Fz, FCz, and Cz; **(B)** topographic distribution of the amplitude at the peak latency of the P1, P2, N2, and P3 difference waveforms (i.e., the amplitude emerging from exposure to test-related threatening words minus the amplitude emerging from exposure to neutral words) for both the HTA and the LTA group.

condition minus ERP amplitude as registered for the neutral condition) and TAS or STAI subscales scores are reported (see scatter plots in **Figure 2**): (a) larger P2 emotional interference is associated with a higher TAS total score ($r = .377$, $p = .010$); (b) larger N2 emotional interference is associated with a higher TAS and a higher STAI subscale score (for TAS: $r = .366$, $p = .012$; for STAI: $r_{S\text{-}STAI} = .343$, $p_{S\text{-}STAI} = .020$; $r_{T\text{-}STAI} = .384$, $p_{T\text{-}STAI} = .008$); and (c) larger P3 emotional interference is associated with a higher TAS total score and a higher STAI subscale score (for TAS: $r = .550$, $p < .001$; for STAI: $r_{S\text{-}STAI} = .554$, $p_{S\text{-}STAI} < .001$; $r_{T\text{-}STAI} = .546$, $p_{T\text{-}STAI} = < .001$).

ERP Results in NS

Grand average ERP waveforms and scalp topographic maps for NS are shown in **Figure 3**.

The amplitude of ERP component P3 shows a significant condition main effect ($F_{(1,44)} = 57.740$, $p < .001$, $\eta^2 = .568$) and a significant group × condition interaction effect ($F_{(1,43)} = 3.702$, $p = .033$, $\eta^2 = .147$). No significant group main effect was found ($F_{(1,43)} = .673$, $p = .417$, $\eta^2 = .015$; site CPz). Additional simple effect analysis shows that (a) in contrast to the LTA group, the HTA group has a different P3 amplitude for three conditions ($F_{(1,43)} = 18.929$, $p < .001$, $\eta^2 = .468$), and (b) in contrast to the neutral condition, the

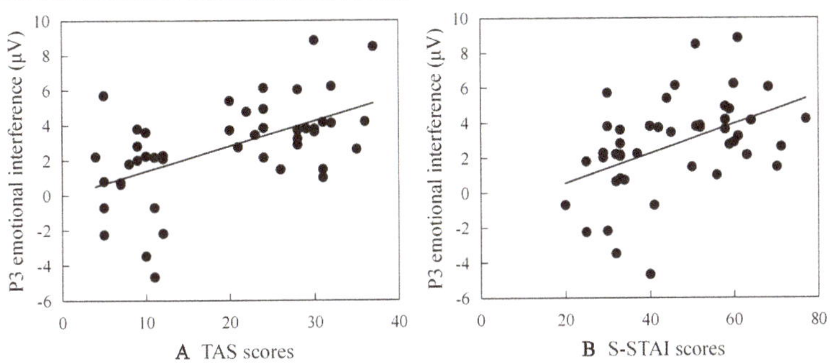

FIGURE 2 | Scatter plots (including the best fitting linear regression line) describing correlations between P3 emotional interference (ERP amplitude as registered for the test-related threatening condition minus ERP amplitude as registered for the neutral condition) and **(A)** scores on the Test Anxiety Scale survey instrument (TAS), **(B)** scores on the State subscale of State-Trait Anxiety Inventory (S-STAI), and **(C)** scores on the Trait subscale of State-Trait Anxiety Inventory (T-STAI), respectively.

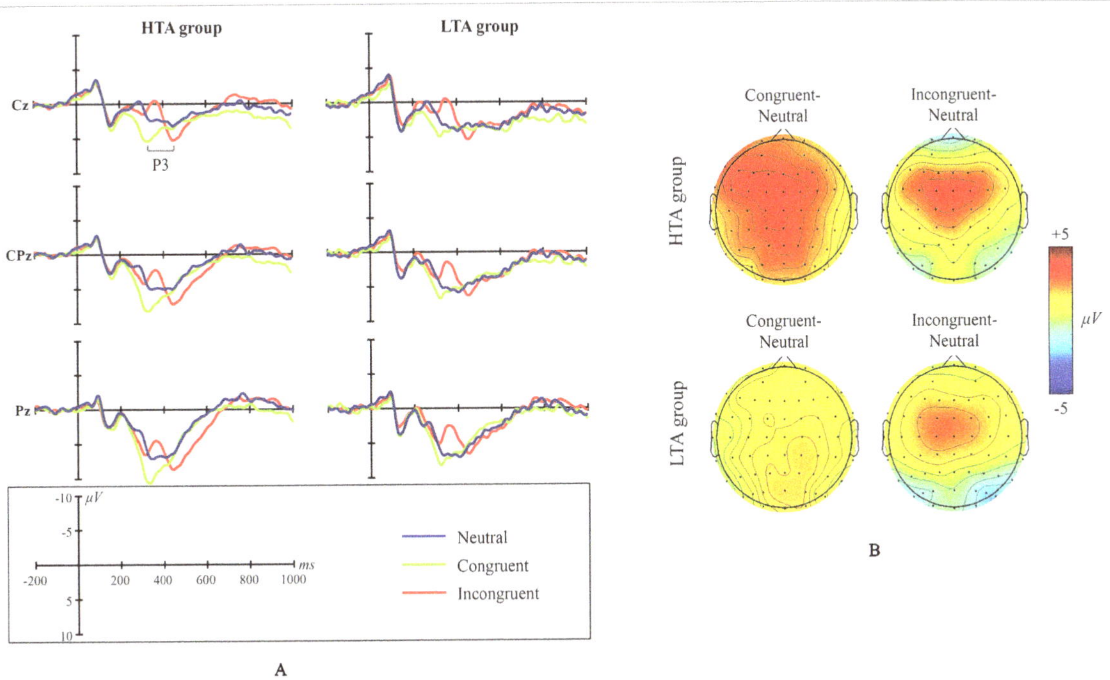

FIGURE 3 | Numerical Stroop ERP waveforms and scalp topographic maps for both the high test-anxious (HTA) and the low test-anxious (LTA) group: **(A)** grand average ERPs elicited by the three experimental conditions (neutral, congruent, and incongruent); the P3 component was registered at Cz, CPz, and Pz sites. **(B)** topographic distribution of the amplitude at the peak latency of the P3 difference waveforms (i.e., the amplitude emerging from exposure to the congruent condition minus the amplitude emerging from exposure to the neutral condition, and the amplitude emerging from exposure to the incongruent condition minus the amplitude emerging from exposure to the neutral condition) for both the HTA and the LTA group.

HTA group has a larger P3 amplitude for the congruent condition ($p < .001$) and the incongruent condition ($p = .004$).

The latency of ERP component P3 shows a significant condition main effect ($F_{(1,43)} = 86.342$, $p < .001$, $\eta^2 = .662$) and a significant group × condition interaction effect ($F_{(1,43)} = 3.784$, $p = .038$, $\eta^2 = .079$). No significant group main effect was found ($F_{(1,43)} = .142$, $p = .708$, $\eta^2 = .003$). Additional simple effect analysis shows that for each experimental condition, no significant ERP difference exists between the LTA and the HTA group (Neutral: $F_{(1,44)} = .433$, $p = .514$, $\eta^2 = .010$; Congruent: $F_{(1,44)} = .510$, $p = .479$, $\eta^2 = .011$; Incongruent: $F_{(1,44)} = .106$, $p = .746$, $\eta^2 = .002$).

DISCUSSION

Considering both the behavioral and ERP results we suggest that, compared to LTA individuals, HTA individuals show deficits in inhibitory control and show different behavioral and ERP characteristics for different aspects of attentional inhibitory control. For test-related threatening interference, inhibitory deficit is observed in HTA individuals in both the perceptual and the cognitive processing stage, while for cognitive interference, inhibitory deficit is observed in HTA individuals only in the cognitive processing stage. This stage-related difference between two types of interference attest to the existence of different task performance in HTA individuals; more specifically, HTA individuals show more aspects of impaired task performance with lower efficiency (i.e., longer RTs) for test-related threatening interference than that for cognitive interference. Also, having observed no impaired effectiveness of task performance (i.e., accuracy), we suggest that HTA individuals apply a cautious strategy to complete the task in situations in which task performance could be impaired by inhibitory control deficits. Additionally, because of meaningful correlations between questionnaire scales' scores and ES results, we present the results on questionnaire scales' scores after the presentation of ES results.

ES Results

In ES, longer RTs for test-related threatening words indicate that (a) HTA individuals show an inhibitory control deficit if they are exposed to a test-related threatening interference [see similar evidence, (11–13)] and (b) HTA individuals allocate extra attentional resources to process the threatening information instead of focusing on the task at hand. Additionally, ERP results further indicate that attentional resources are extra allocated in the early and late processing stages.

The Early/Perceptual Processing Stage

Through the study of characteristics of early/perceptual processing, one may appreciate the cognitive mode of emotional disorders. When individuals treat tests/examinations as threatening (i.e., are HTA individuals), emotionally congruent information is (i.e. test-related threatening words are) preferentially processed (70); preferential processing of information implies that the information is easily detected (in the perceptual stage) and processed prior to other information that is presented at the very same time. As the meaning of the word (i.e., the stimulus in ES Stroop) is irrelevant to the experimental task at hand, preferential processing of the emotional significance of the word should be conceived as an extra consumption of attentional resources of the central executive system and makes the nature of processing stimulus-driven rather than goal-driven (11, 18).

In our ERP results related to ES, the larger P1, P2, and smaller N2 amplitudes for test-related threatening words (in comparison to neutral words) in HTA individuals are indicative of a stimulus-driven processing in those individuals. Specifically, the ERP component P1 is known to be sensitive to (i.e., captures) emotional cues (71, 72), and the amplitudes of P1 may reveal hypervigilance (73) and one's orientation to the information (74). If the information has negative meaning to the individual, a situation may occur in which the individual could easily detect this negative information (i.e., hypervigilance) and allocate extra attentional resources to rapidly orient to this negative information in the perceptual stage; typical in such situation is that P1 amplitudes are increased. The ERP component P2 captures both attention towards stimuli with negative meaning as well as inhibition of the interference (53, 75). If the negative information activates hypervigilance and occupies additional resources of the individual, the individual may attempt to inhibit the interference caused by the processing of this negative information and focus on the task at hand. If making such attempt is too difficult or simply unsuccessful (e.g., because of an inhibitory control deficit), the individual will continue to pay extra attention on processing the negative information, as indicated by increasing P2 amplitudes (52, 76). The ERP component N2 captures changes in attention automatically paid to certain information content (77, 78). Previous studies claimed that early ERP components jointly (e.g., P1, P2, and N2) capture perceptual processing and low-level attentional allocation (79, 80). Relatively small N2 amplitudes followed by relatively large P1 and P2 amplitudes would indicate that both automatic and facilitated processing of negative information are manifest (81, 82). The automatic nature of stimulus-driven processing reflects the cognitive schemata of HTA individuals in which tests/examinations are automatically treated as threatening (Beck's theory) (83).

The Late/Cognitive Processing Stage

The larger P3 amplitudes for test-related threatening words (in comparison to neutral words) indicate that, in the late/cognitive processing stage, HTA individuals engage in top-down and elaborate processing of threatening stimulus content (78, 84, 85). The parallel distributed processing network model of ES by Mathews and Mackintosh (86) can provide a theoretical framework for understanding inhibitory deficits involved in early and late processing stages in HTA individuals. Information processed in the perceptual stage is monitored by the "threat assessment system." The threat assessment system works as follows: when relevant threatening information (i.e., test-related threatening word) is presented to an HTA individual, the threatening information is encoded and marked by the threat assessment system; subsequently, semantic content and/or feelings of threat are activated. The way of processing in the early, perceptual stage may affect the way of processing in late, cognitive stage (43, 44). Once stimuli are intense enough, the threat assessment system will recruit attentional resources to process/assess stimulus content and respond to the task at hand. Intense stimuli cause individuals to consume more top-down attentional resources to process stimulus content, and exert greater efforts to inhibit interference.

Additionally, the level of emotional inhibitory control deficit relates to the level of anxiety. Specifically, (a) test-anxiety correlates substantially and positively with the degree of difficulty in inhibiting test-related threatening interference (difference of P2, N2, and P3 amplitudes between the threatening condition and the neutral condition). This positive correlation is in line with our ERP results. Compared to individuals with less symptoms of test anxiety (i.e., LTA individuals), HTA individuals are more strongly affected by test-related threatening stimulus content; in addition, the higher the threat caused by the stimulus, the easier it becomes for HTA individuals to process and detect stimulus content in the early, perceptual stage, followed by the more elaborate processing in the late processing stage; in sum, there are more attentional resources allocated to process the threatening stimulus; (b) the level of trait anxiety correlates substantially and positively with the degree of difficulty in inhibition (see similar results) (21, 87). Not completely unexpected, our study results also demonstrate that HTA individuals have a higher level of state and trait anxiety than LTA individuals. However, the difficulty of inhibition to threat is higher with higher levels of trait anxiety (but not higher with higher levels of state anxiety). Reasoning in a causal way, one could (cautiously) state that especially the trait aspects of test anxiety may impact the impairment of inhibition, whereas the state aspects of test anxiety have far less impact (88); (c) test-related threatening interference of P2 amplitudes is only found to be substantially correlated with TAS, and the correlation is found to be positive. As expressed before, difficulty in inhibition of processing threatening information in the early stage of processing is evident from the P2 component, and is known to be a characteristic element of the cognitive pattern associated with test anxiety (89, 90). This characteristic element signifies that test-related threatening information can be detected and cannot be inhibited. So, the P2 component may serve as a diagnostic for identifying test anxiety.

NS Results

In NS, the behavioral results do not attest to an impairment of cognitive inhibitory control in HTA individuals. However, ERP results do provide evidence that HTA individuals display inhibitory control deficits for cognitive interference. Specifically, the larger P3 amplitudes for the congruent/incongruent condition (in comparison to the neutral condition) indicate that HTA individuals may have cognitive inhibitory control deficits, but such deficits were only encountered in the cognitive processing stage, a clear difference between the NS and ES results. This difference in impaired processing stages between ES and NS results may be an important reason for the difference in behavioral aspects of task performance (especially efficiency, that is, RT) between ES and NS results in HTA individuals. Specifically, the more impaired processing stages in ES (i.e., early and late processing stages), in comparison to NS (i.e., late processing stages only), the more cognitive load is involved in HTA individuals completing the tasks at hand (91). As indicated in the Introduction section, relative high cognitive load may lead to detrimental efficiency (13, 15), so the impaired behavioral aspect of task performance (i.e., longer RT) was observed in ES, but not in NS.

Additionally, in NS, the fact that no inhibitory control deficit was observed in the perceptual processing stage in HTA individuals may be because NS does not include emotional stimuli; as such, hypervigilance and related automatic processing were simply not activated. However, despite the fact that no inhibitory control deficit was observed in the perceptual processing stage, in NS, deficits in cognitive processing were still observed, indicating that HTA individuals may suffer from extensive inhibitory deficits (81). Particularly, HTA individuals were not only found to have difficulty in inhibiting the incongruent interference, an interference that negatively impacts task completion (see similar results) (92, 93), but were also found to have difficulty in inhibiting the congruent interference, an interference that facilitates a quick accomplishment of the task at hand. This difficulty in inhibiting the cognitive interference indicates that the extensive cognitive inhibitory deficits of HTA individuals are merely related to the appearance of interference rather than the exact nature (incongruent vs. congruent) of interference. Besides, we also observed a substantial difference in the latency of P3 among different conditions, a difference that is in line with RT differences observed across these different conditions. This difference in P3 latency may be due to varying difficulty in task completion across these different conditions, and this difference observed is also supported by previous studies (44, 94).

Strategy for Dealing With Deficits in HTA

In contrast to an impaired efficiency observed in ES and NS observed in HTA individuals, no impaired effectiveness (i.e., accuracy) in ES and NS was observed in these individuals. As explained in the Introduction, HTA individuals may apply a "cautious strategy" to achieve satisfactory effectiveness (equal or better accuracy than LTA individuals) by decreasing efficiency (more attentional resources consumed or/and longer RT) (95). Additionally, accuracy of inhibition is known to be associated with the trait referred to as "emotion-driven impulsivity" (96). Individuals who are impulsive, increase the frequency of inhibitory errors (i.e., low accuracy) when they are in an intense emotional state (97, 98). Our study results demonstrate that, during the experiment, HTA individuals do not show behavior that typically characterizes the emotionally driven impulsive trait. When inhibiting interference in an ES and a NS task, HTA individuals make a comparable number of mistakes as LTA individuals, and, when processing threatening words rather than neutral words in ES, HTA individuals make fewer mistakes (i.e., have a higher level of effectiveness, that is, accuracy) than LTA individuals; moreover, for the ES task, a higher level of trait anxiety was found to correspond with fewer mistakes (i.e., higher accuracy), indicating that emotionally driven impulsivity is not a characteristic of HTA individuals when it comes to explaining task performance (measured as accuracy). Instead, HTA individuals who are in an anxious state tend to be "cautious" in that they avoid mistakes in completing the task. Being cautious in such state may, at least partially, explain why test anxiety does not always lead to impaired task performance (especially when assessed in terms of effectiveness; in other words, accuracy).

The present study has some limitations. We got some indications of (possible study restrictions due to) the occurrence of "ceiling effects" in ES and NS. More specifically, accuracy was very high for each condition (above 95%). The occurrence of ceiling effects may be the consequence of two limitations of our present study: (a) low task pressure (or the absence of high task pressure); alternatively, high task pressure (e.g., great importance of task performance) would allow for a better differentiation of participants' task performance (e.g., accuracy) without imposing study restrictions due to the occurrence of ceiling effects (3). The participants in the present study were not subjected to high task pressure: given low task difficulty, participants could achieve high accuracy (99); and (b) highly educated participants: all HTA and LTA participants are highly educated, so these two groups may both have high accuracy, and this not being different in terms of accuracy (100). Future studies are required to further confirm (or partially disconfirm) our present study findings, for instance, by imposing higher task pressure and recruiting participants from a more heterogeneous (less highly educated) population.

In conclusion, HTA individuals show deficits of inhibitory control that can consume (additional) attentional resources without impairing accuracy. The inhibitory deficits reflect the etiological cognitive pattern of HTA individuals; during task completion and when confronted with interference (emotional or cognitive interference), HTA individuals recruit attentional resources to inhibit the interference. The deficits of inhibitory control can also appear in conditions (e.g., congruent interference) that are beneficial to accomplish the experimental task quickly. A crucial difference in the cognitive pattern of HTA individuals when confronted with emotional versus cognitive interference is that, in comparison to cognitive interference, emotional interference additionally affects the early processing stage and increases the required cognitive load. Thus, in comparison to LTA individuals, HTA individuals have lower behavioral efficiency of emotional interference as opposed to cognitive interference. Furthermore, considering the strong relationship between impaired attentional control ability and test anxiety, future studies aiming at diagnosing test anxiety could consider measuring attentional control ability by relying on the registration of important ERP components (such as P2 in this study) as an alternative method complementing or substituting the diagnosis of test anxiety through a (traditional) self-report questionnaire.

AUTHOR CONTRIBUTIONS

RZ and WZ contributed the study structure. WZ and LC collected the experimental data. WZ wrote the first draft of the manuscript. RZ and AB made critical revisions. All authors approved the submitted version of this manuscript.

FUNDING

This work was supported by grants from the Key Project of Philosophy and Social Science Research in Colleges and Universities in Jiangsu Province (2015JDXM001), the Research and Innovation Foundation of Academic Degree Graduate of Jiangsu Province (KYZZ16_0010), and the Humanity and Social Science Foundation of Education Committee of Anhui province (Key Program) (SK2017A0084).

REFERENCES

1. Spielberger C, Vagg P. Test anxiety: a transactional process model. In: *Series in clinical and community psychology. Test anxiety: theory, assessment, and treatment*. US: Taylor & Francis (1995). p. 3–14.
2. Rydell J. Behavioural variation in echolocation pulses of the northern bat, Eptesicus nilssoni. *Ethology* (1990) 85:103–13. doi: 10.1111/j.1439-0310.1990.tb00390.x
3. Lotz C, Sparfeldt JR. Does test anxiety increase as the exam draws near? – Students' state test anxiety recorded over the course of one semester. *Pers Individ Dif* (2017) 104:397–400. doi: 10.1016/j.paid.2016.08.032
4. Bar-Haim Y, Lamy D, Pergamin L, Bakermans-Kranenburg MJ, van IJzendoorn MH. Threat-related attentional bias in anxious and nonanxious individuals: a meta-analytic study. *Psychol Bull* (2007) 133:1–24. doi: 10.1037/0033-2909.133.1.1
5. Eysenck MW, Derakshan N, Santos R, Calvo MG. Anxiety and cognitive performance: attentional control theory. *Emotion* (2007) 7:336–53. doi: 10.1037/1528-3542.7.2.336
6. Sarason IG. Anxiety, self-preoccupation and attention. *Anxiety Res* (1988) 1:3–7. doi: 10.1080/10615808808248215
7. Brydges CR, Clunies-Ross K, Clohessy M, Lo ZL, Nguyen A, Rousset C, et al. Dissociable components of cognitive control: an event-related potential (ERP) study of response inhibition and interference suppression. *PLoS One* (2012) 7:3–7. doi: 10.1371/journal.pone.0034482
8. Friedman NP, Miyake A. The relations among inhibition and interference control functions: a latent-variable analysis. *J Exp Psychol Gen* (2004) 133:101–35. doi: 10.1037/0096-3445.133.1.101
9. Eysenck MW, Derakshan N. New perspectives in attentional control theory. *Pers Individ Dif* (2011) 50:955–60. doi: 10.1016/j.paid.2010.08.019
10. Pergamin-Hight L, Naim R, Bakermans-Kranenburg MJ, van IJzendoorn MH, Bar-Haim Y. Content specificity of attention bias to threat in anxiety disorders: a meta-analysis. *Clin Psychol Rev* (2015) 35:10–8. doi: 10.1016/j.cpr.2014.10.005
11. Kalanthroff E, Henik A, Derakshan N, Usher M. Anxiety, emotional distraction, and attentional control in the Stroop task. *Emotion* (2016) 16:293–300. doi: 10.1037/emo0000129

12. Lawson DJ. *Test anxiety: a test of attentional bias* [Doctoral dissertation] University of Maine (2006).
13. Putwain DW, Langdale HC, Woods KA, Nicholson LJ. Developing and piloting a dot-probe measure of attentional bias for test anxiety. *Learn Individ Differ* (2011) 21:478–82. doi: 10.1016/j.lindif.2011.02.002
14. Chapell MS, Blanding ZB, Silverstein ME, Takahashi M, Newman B, Gubi A, et al. Test anxiety and academic performance in undergraduate and graduate students. *J Educ Psychol* (2005) 97:268–74. doi: 10.1037/0022-0663.97.2.268
15. Szafranski DD, Barrera TL, Norton PJ. Test anxiety inventory: 30 years later. *Anxiety Stress Coping* (2012) 25:667–77. doi: 10.1080/10615806.2012.663490
16. Ansari TL, Derakshan N. The neural correlates of cognitive effort in anxiety: effects on processing efficiency. *Biol Psychol* (2011) 86:337–48. doi: 10.1016/j.biopsycho.2010.12.013
17. Ansari TL, Derakshan N. The neural correlates of impaired inhibitory control in anxiety. *Neuropsychologia* (2011) 49:1146–53. doi: 10.1016/j.neuropsychologia.2011.01.019
18. Berggren N, Derakshan N. Attentional control deficits in trait anxiety: why you see them and why you don't. *Biol Psychol* (2013) 92:440–6. doi: 10.1016/j.biopsycho.2012.03.007
19. Chamberlain SR, Blackwell AD, Fineberg NA, Robbins TW, Sahakian BJ. The neuropsychology of obsessive compulsive disorder: the importance of failures in cognitive and behavioural inhibition as candidate endophenotypic markers. *Neurosci Biobehav Rev* (2005) 29:399–419. doi: 10.1016/j.neubiorev.2004.11.006
20. Derakshan N, Smyth S, Eysenck MW. Effects of state anxiety on performance using a task-switching paradigm: an investigation of attentional control theory. *Psychon Bull Rev* (2009) 16:1112–7. doi: 10.3758/PBR.16.6.1112
21. Wieser MJ, Pauli P, Mühlberger A. Probing the attentional control theory in social anxiety: an emotional saccade task. *Cogn Affect Behav Neurosci* (2009) 9:314–22. doi: 10.3758/CABN.9.3.314
22. Gao X, Zhou RL. On the inhibition of selective attention by people with test anxiety. *Chin J Spec Educ* (2013) 151:85–91. doi: 10.3969/j.issn.1007-3728.2013.01.017
23. Liu Y, Zhang W, Zhou R. Cognitive and neural basis of attentional bias in test anxiety students. *Psychol Explor* (2015) 35:233–8. doi: 10.3969/j.issn.1003-5184.2015.03.008
24. Mincic AM. Neural substrate of the cognitive and emotional interference processing in healthy adolescents. *Acta Neurobiol Exp (Wars)* (2010) 70:406–22. doi: 7046 [pii]
25. Amir N, Elias J, Klumpp H, Przeworski A. Attentional bias to threat in social phobia: facilitated processing of threat or difficulty disengaging attention from threat? *Behav Res Ther* (2003) 41:1325–35. doi: 10.1016/S0005-7967(03)00039-1
26. Buckner JD, Maner JK, Schmidt NB. Difficulty disengaging attention from social threat in social anxiety. *Cognit Ther Res* (2010) 34:99–105. doi: 10.1007/s10608-008-9205-y
27. Basten U, Stelzel C, Fiebach CJ. Trait anxiety modulates the neural efficiency of inhibitory control. *J Cogn Neurosci* (2011) 23:3132–45. doi: 10.1162/jocn_a_00003
28. Righi S, Mecacci L, Viggiano MP. Anxiety, cognitive self-evaluation and performance: ERP correlates. *J Anxiety Disord* (2009) 23:1132–8. doi: 10.1016/j.janxdis.2009.07.018
29. Macleod CM. Haifa century of research on the Stroop effect: an integrative review. *Psychol Bull* (1991) 109:163–203. doi: 10.1037/0033-2909.109.2.163
30. MacLeod CM, MacDonald PA. Interdimensional interference in the Stroop effect: uncovering the cognitive and neural anatomy of attention. *Trends Cogn Sci* (2000) 4:383–91. doi: 10.1016/S1364-6613(00)01530-8
31. Besner D, Coltheart M. Ideographic and alphabetic processing in skilled reading of English. *Neuropsychologia* (1979) 17:467–72. doi: 10.1016/0028-3932(79)90053-8
32. Tzelgov J, Meyer J, Henik A. Automatic and intentional processing of numerical information. *J Exp Psychol Learn Mem Cogn* (1992) 18:166–79. doi: 10.1037/0278-7393.18.1.166
33. Bush G, Luu P, Posner MI. Cognitive and emotional influences in anterior cingulate cortex. *TrendsCogn Sci* (2000) 4:215–22. doi: 10.1016/S1364-6613(00)01483-2
34. Pury CLS. Information-processing predictors of emotional response to stress. *Cogn Emot* (2002) 16:667–83. doi: 10.1080/02699930143000400
35. Van Bockstaele B, Verschuere B, Tibboel H, De Houwer J, Crombez G. Koster EHW. A review of current evidence for the causal impact of attentional bias on fear and anxiety. *Psychol Bull* (2014) 140:682–721. doi: 10.1037/a0034834
36. Verhaak CM, Smeenk JMJ, van Minnen A, Kraaimaat FW. Neuroticism, preattentive and attentional biases towards threat, and anxiety before and after a severe stressor: a prospective study. *Pers Individ Dif* (2004) 36:767–778. doi: 10.1016/S0191-8869(03)00131-4
37. Cisler JM, Koster EHW. Mechanisms of attentional biases towards threat in anxiety disorders: an integrative review. *Clin Psychol Rev* (2010) 30:203–16. doi: 10.1016/j.cpr.2009.11.003
38. Hennessey NW, Dourado E, Beilby JM. Anxiety and speaking in people who stutter: an investigation using the emotional Stroop task. *J Fluency Disord* (2014) 40:44–57. doi: 10.1016/j.jfludis.2013.11.001
39. Rutherford EM, MacLeod C, Campbell LW. Negative selectivity effects and emotional selectivity effects in anxiety: differential attentional correlates of state and trait variables. *Cogn Emot* (2004) 18:711–20. doi: 10.1080/02699930341000121
40. Girelli L, Lucangeli D, Butterworth B. The development of automaticity in accessing number magnitude. *J Exp Child Psychol* (2000) 76:104–22. doi: 10.1006/jecp.2000.2564
41. Kaufmann L, Koppelstaetter F, Delazer M, Siedentopf C, Rhomberg P, Golaszewski S, et al. Neural correlates of distance and congruity effects in a numerical Stroop task: an event-related fMRI study. *Neuroimage* (2005) 25:888–98. doi: 10.1016/j.neuroimage.2004.12.041
42. Pinel P, Piazza M, Le Bihan D, Dehaene S. Distributed and overlapping cerebral representations of number, size, and luminance during comparative judgments. *Neuron* (2004) 41:983–93. doi: 10.1016/S0896-6273(04)00107-2
43. Szűcs D, Soltész F. Functional definition of the N450 event-related brain potential marker of conflict processing: a numerical stroop study. *BMC Neurosci* (2012) 13:35. doi: 10.1186/1471-2202-13-35
44. Szucs D, Soltész F. The interaction of task-relevant and task-irrelevant stimulus features in the number/size congruency paradigm: an ERP study. *Brain Res* (2008) 1190:143–58. doi: 10.1016/j.brainres.2007.11.010
45. Mama Y, Ben-Haim MS, Algom D. When emotion does and does not impair performance: a Garner theory of the emotional Stroop effect. *Cogn Emot* (2013) 27:589–602. doi: 10.1080/02699931.2012.726212
46. Edwards MS, Burt JS, Lipp OV. Selective attention for masked and unmasked threatening words in anxiety: effects of trait anxiety, state anxiety and awareness. *Behav Res Ther* (2010) 48:210–8. doi: 10.1016/j.brat.2009.11.003
47. Mangun GR, Hillyard SA. Mechanisms and models of selective attention. In: *electrophysiology of mind* (1995) 40–86. doi: 10.1093/acprof:oso/9780198524168.003.0003
48. Albert J, López-Martín S, Carretié L. Emotional context modulates response inhibition: neural and behavioral data. *Neuroimage* (2010) 49:914–21. doi: 10.1016/j.neuroimage.2009.08.045
49. Luck SJ, Woodman GF, Vogel EK. Event-related potential studies of attention. *Trends Cogn Sci* (2000) 4:432–40. doi: 10.1016/S1364-6613(00)01545-X
50. Fisher JE, Sass SM, Heller W, Silton RL, Edgar JC, Stewart JL, et al. Time course of processing emotional stimuli as a function of perceived emotional intelligence, anxiety, and depression. *Emotion* (2010) 10:486–97. doi: 10.1037/a0018691
51. Gootjes L, Coppens LC, Zwaan RA, Franken IHA, Van Strien JW. Effects of recent word exposure on emotion-word Stroop interference: an ERP study. *Int J Psychophysiol* (2011) 79:356–63. doi: 10.1016/j.ijpsycho.2010.12.003
52. Thomas SJ, Johnstone SJ, Gonsalvez CJ. Event-related potentials during an emotional Stroop task. *Int J Psychophysiol* (2007) 63:221–31. doi: 10.1016/j.ijpsycho.2006.10.002
53. van Peer JM, Spinhoven P, Roelofs K. Psychophysiological evidence for cortisol-induced reduction in early bias for implicit social threat in social phobia. *Psychoneuroendocrinology* (2010) 35:21–32. doi: 10.1016/j.psyneuen.2009.09.012
54. Carretié L, Martín-Loeches M, Hinojosa JA, Mercado F. Emotion and attention interaction studied through event-related potentials. *J Cogn Neurosci* (2001) 13:1109–28. doi: 10.1162/089892901753294400
55. Dennis TA, Chen CC. Trait anxiety and conflict monitoring following threat: an ERP study. *Psychophysiology* (2009) 46:122–31. doi: 10.1111/j.1469-8986.2008.00758.x

56. Gu R, Lei Z, Broster L, Wu T, Jiang Y, Luo Y. Beyond valence and magnitude: a flexible evaluative coding system in the brain. *Neuropsychologia* (2011) 49:3891–7. doi: 10.1016/j.neuropsychologia.2011.10.006
57. Cohen J. *Statistical power analysis for the behavioral sciences*. New York: Routledge (1988). doi: 10.4324/9780203771587
58. Faul F, Erdfelder E, Lang A-G, Buchner A. GPOWER: a general power analysis program. *Behav Res Methods* (2007) 39:175–91. doi: 10.3758/BF03193146
59. First MB, Gibbon M. The structured clinical interview for DSM-IV axis I disorders (SCID-I) and the structured clinical interview for DSM-IV axis II disorders (SCID-II). In: *Comprehensive handbook of psychological assessment, Vol. 2. Personality assessment*. John Wiley & Sons Inc. (2004). p. 134–43.
60. Li W, Qian M. Revision of the state-trait anxiety inventoty with sample of Chinese college students. *Acta Scicentiarum Nat Univ Pekinesis* (1995) 31:108–14. doi: 10.13209/j.0479-8023.1995.014
61. Wang C. Reliability and validity of test anxiety scale-Chinese version. *Chin Ment Heal J* (2001) 15:96–7. doi: 10.3321/j.issn:1000-6729.2001.02.011
62. Newman E. *No more test anxiety: Effective steps for taking tests and achieving better grades*. Los Angeles: Learning Skills Publications (1996)
63. Liu C, Yao R, Wang Z, Zhou R. N450 as a candidate neural marker for interference control deficits in children with learning disabilities. *Int J Psychophysiol* (2014) 93:70–7. doi: 10.1016/j.ijpsycho.2014.05.007
64. Soltész F, White S, Szucs D. Event-related brain potentials dissociate the developmental time-course of automatic numerical magnitude analysis and cognitive control functions during the first three years of primary school. *Dev Neuropsychol* (2011) 36:682–701. doi: 10.1080/87565641.2010.549982
65. Soltész F, Goswami U, White S, Szucs D. Executive function effects and numerical development in children: behavioural and ERP evidence from a numerical Stroop paradigm. *Learn Individ Differ* (2011) 21:662–71. doi: 10.1016/j.lindif.2010.10.004
66. Choi JM, Padmala S, Pessoa L. Impact of state anxiety on the interaction between threat monitoring and cognition. *Neuroimage* (2012) 59:1912–23. doi: 10.1016/j.neuroimage.2011.08.102
67. Dresler T, Attar CH, Spitzer C, Löwe B, Deckert J, Büchel C, et al. Neural correlates of the emotional Stroop task in panic disorder patients: an event-related fMRI study. *J Psychiatr Res* (2012) 46:1627–34. doi: 10.1016/j.jpsychires.2012.09.004
68. Dieter J, Hoffmann S, Mier D, Reinhard I, Beutel M, Vollstädt-Klein S, et al. The role of emotional inhibitory control in specific internet addiction – an fMRI study. *Behav Brain Res* (2017) 324:1–14. doi: 10.1016/j.bbr.2017.01.046
69. Ashley V, Honzel N, Larsen J, Justus T, Swick D. Attentional bias for trauma-related words: exaggerated emotional Stroop effect in Afghanistan and Iraq war veterans with PTSD. *BMC Psychiatry* (2013) 13:86. doi: 10.1186/1471-244X-13-86
70. Moriya J, Tanno Y. Relationships between negative emotionality and attentional control in effortful control. *Pers Individ Dif* (2008) 44:1348–55. doi: 10.1016/j.paid.2007.12.003
71. Eldar S, Bar-Haim Y. Neural plasticity in response to attention training in anxiety. *Psychol Med* (2010) 40:667. doi: 10.1017/S0033291709990766
72. Santesso DL, Meuret AE, Hofmann SG, Mueller EM, Ratner KG, Roesch EB, et al. Electrophysiological correlates of spatial orienting towards angry faces: a source localization study. *Neuropsychologia* (2008) 46:1338–48. doi: 10.1016/j.neuropsychologia.2007.12.013
73. Mueller EM, Hofmann SG, Santesso DL, Meuret AE, Bitran S, Pizzagalli DA. Electrophysiological evidence of attentional biases in social anxiety disorder. *Psychol Med* (2009) 39:1141. doi: 10.1017/S0033291708004820
74. Morel S, George N, Foucher A, Chammat M, Dubal S. ERP evidence for an early emotional bias towards happy faces in trait anxiety. *Biol Psychol* (2014) 99:183–92. doi: 10.1016/j.biopsycho.2014.03.011
75. Rossignol M, Campanella S, Bissot C, Philippot P. Fear of negative evaluation and attentional bias for facial expressions: an event-related study. *Brain Cogn* (2013) 82:344–52. doi: 10.1016/j.bandc.2013.05.008
76. Bar-Haim Y, Lamy D, Glickman S. Attentional bias in anxiety: a behavioral and ERP study. *Brain Cogn* (2005) 59:11–22. doi: 10.1016/j.bandc.2005.03.005
77. Yao Y, Du F, Wang C, Liu Y, Weng J, Chen F. Numerical processing efficiency improved in children using mental abacus: ERP evidence utilizing a numerical Stroop task. *Front Hum Neurosci* (2015) 9:245. doi: 10.3389/fnhum.2015.00245
78. Atchley R, Klee D, Memmott T, Goodrich E, Wahbeh H, Oken B. Event-related potential correlates of mindfulness meditation competence. *Neuroscience* (2016) 320:83–92. doi: 10.1016/j.neuroscience.2016.01.051
79. Telles S, Deepeshwar S, Naveen KV, Pailoor S. Long latency auditory evoked potentials during meditation. *Clin EEG Neurosci* (2015) 46:299–309. doi: 10.1177/1550059414544737
80. Pérez-Edgar K, Fox NA. Individual differences in children's performance during an emotional Stroop task: a behavioral and electrophysiological study. *Brain Cogn* (2003) 52:33–51. doi: 10.1016/S0278-2626(03)00007-1
81. Kóbor A, Takács Á, Bryce D, Szucs D, Honbolygó F, Nagy P, et al. Children with ADHD show impairments in multiple stages of information processing in a Stroop task: an ERP study. *Dev Neuropsychol* (2015) 40:329–47. doi: 10.1080/87565641.2015.1086770
82. O'Toole L, Dennis TA. Attention training and the threat bias: an ERP study. *Brain Cogn* (2012) 78:63–73. doi: 10.1016/j.bandc.2011.10.007
83. Beck AT, Clark DM. An information processing model of anxiey: automatic and strategic processes. *Behav Res Ther* (1997) 35:49–58. doi: 10.1016/S0005-7967(96)00069-1
84. Jo HG, Schmidt S, Inacker E, Markowiak M, Hinterberger T. Meditation and attention: a controlled study on long-term meditators in behavioral performance and event-related potentials of attentional control. *Int J Psychophysiol* (2016) 99:33–9. doi: 10.1016/j.ijpsycho.2015.11.016
85. Fan Y, Tang Y-Y, Tang R, Posner MI. Time course of conflict processing modulated by brief meditation training. *Front Psychol* (2015) 6:911. doi: 10.3389/fpsyg.2015.00911
86. Mathews A, Mackintosh B. A cognitive model of selective processing in anxiety. *Therapy* (1998) 22:539–60. doi: 10.1023/A:1018738019346
87. Savostyanov AN, Tsai AC, Liou M, Levin EA, Der Lee J, Yurganov AV, et al. EEG-correlates of trait anxiety in the stop-signal paradigm. *Neurosci Lett* (2009) 449:112–6. doi: 10.1016/j.neulet.2008.10.084
88. Osinsky R, Gebhardt H, Alexander N, Hennig J. Trait anxiety and the dynamics of attentional control. *Biol Psychol* (2012) 89:252–9. doi: 10.1016/j.biopsycho.2011.10.016
89. Calvo MG, Eysenck MW, Castillo MD. Interpretation bias in test anxiety: the time course of predictive inferences. *Cogn Emot* (1997) 11:43–64. doi: 10.1080/026999397380023
90. van den Heuvel OA, Veltman DJ, Groenewegen HJ, Witter MP, Merkelbach J, Cath DC, et al. Disorder-specific neuroanatomical correlates of attentional bias in obsessive-compulsive disorder, panic disorder, and hypochondriasis. *Arch Gen Psychiatry* (2005) 62:922. doi: 10.1001/archpsyc.62.8.922
91. Junhong H, Renlai Z, Senqi H. Effects on automatic attention due to exposure to pictures of emotional faces while performing Chinese word judgment tasks. *PLoS One* (2013) 8:e75386. doi: 10.1371/journal.pone.0075386
92. Grandjean J, D'Ostilio K, Fias W, Phillips C, Balteau E, Degueldre C, et al. Exploration of the mechanisms underlying the ISPC effect: evidence from behavioral and neuroimaging data. *Neuropsychologia* (2013) 51:1040–9. doi: 10.1016/j.neuropsychologia.2013.02.015
93. Tillman CM, Wiens S. Behavioral and ERP indices of response conflict in Stroop and flanker tasks. *Psychophysiology* (2011) 48:1405–11. doi: 10.1111/j.1469-8986.2011.01203.x
94. Osinsky R, Alexander N, Gebhardt H, Hennig J. Trait anxiety and dynamic adjustments in conflict processing. *Cogn Affect Behav Neurosci* (2010) 10:372–81. doi: 10.3758/CABN.10.3.372
95. Bettina O, Kingstone A, Olk B, Kingstone A. Why are antisaccades slower than prosaccades ? A novel ¢ nding using a new paradigm. *October* (2003) 14:1–5. doi: 10.1097/01.wnr.0000053062.88427
96. Fernández-Serrano MJ, Perales JC, Moreno-López L, Pérez-García M, Verdejo-García A. Neuropsychological profiling of impulsivity and compulsivity in cocaine dependent individuals. *Psychopharmacology (Berl)* (2012) 219:673–83. doi: 10.1007/s00213-011-2485-z
97. Lawrence AJ, Luty J, Bogdan NA, Sahakian BJ, Clark L. Impulsivity and response inhibition in alcohol dependence and problem gambling. *Psychopharmacology (Berl)* (2009) 207:163–72. doi: 10.1007/s00213-009-1645-x

98. Marczinski CA, Abroms BD, Van Selst M, Fillmore MT. Alcohol-induced impairment of behavioral control: differential effects on engaging vs. disengaging responses. *Psychopharmacology (Berl)* (2005) 182:452–9. doi: 10.1007/s00213-005-0116-2
99. Keng SL, Smoski MJ, Robins CJ. Effects of mindfulness on psychological health: a review of empirical studies. *Clin Psychol Rev* (2011) 31:1041–56. doi: 10.1016/j.cpr.2011.04.006
100. Kozasa EH, Sato JR, Lacerda SS, Barreiros MAM, Radvany J, Russell TA, et al. Meditation training increases brain efficiency in an attention task. *Neuroimage* (2012) 59:745–9. doi: 10.1016/j.neuroimage.2011.06.088

25

Psychopathology Assessment Methods Revisited: On Translational Cross-Validation of Clinical Self-Evaluation Scale and fMRI

Drozdstoy Stoyanov[1,2]*, *Sevdalina Kandilarova*[1,2], *Stefan Borgwardt*[3], *Rolf-Dieter Stieglitz*[3], *Kenneth Hugdahl*[4,5,6] *and Stefan Kostianev*[1,7]

[1] Research Complex for Translational Neuroscience, Medical University Plovdiv (MUP), Plovdiv, Bulgaria, [2] Department for Psychiatry and Medical Psychology, Medical University Plovdiv (MUP), Plovdiv, Bulgaria, [3] University of Basel, Basel, Switzerland, [4] Department of Biological and Medical Psychology, University of Bergen, Bergen, Norway, [5] Division of Psychiatry, Haukeland University Hospital, Bergen, Norway, [6] Department of Radiology, Haukeland University Hospital, Bergen, Norway, [7] Department of Pathophysiology, Medical University Plovdiv (MUP), Plovdiv, Bulgaria

***Correspondence:**
Drozdstoy Stoyanov
dstoyanov@meduniversity-plovdiv.bg

We present in this article a study design that combines clinical self-assessment scale, simultaneously administered with fMRI data acquisition. We have used a standard block-design with two different conditions. Each active block consisted of four text statements (items), alternating diagnostically specific (DS) blocks comprising items from von Zerssen depression scale and diagnostically neutral (DN) blocks with items from a questionnaire about general interests. All items were rated on four degree Likert scale, and patients provided responses with corresponding four buttons during the fMRI session. Our results demonstrated that in healthy controls, contrasting the two types of stimuli yielded no residual activations, e.g., the DS did not produce significantly different activations compared to the DN stimuli. Furthermore, the correlation analyses did not find a relationship between brain activations and the total score of the DS statements in this group. However, contrasting the DS stimuli to the DN stimuli in the patients produced significant residual activations in several brain regions: right pre- and postcentral gyrus (including right supramarginal gyrus), left middle frontal gyrus, triangular part of the left inferior frontal gyrus and middle temporal gyrus. The left precuneus demonstrated correlations with the patients' DS score. In the between-group comparisons, we found residual activations in the right pre- and postcentral gyrus, right supplementary motor area, medial segment of the right precentral gyrus, right superior parietal lobule, left middle frontal gyrus, left superior frontal gyrus, left occipital pole. Our results confirm the possibility of translational cross-validation of a clinical psychological test (von Zerssen's depression scale) and fMRI. At this stage, however, we can only confirm the sensitivity of the method (its ability to distinguish healthy controls from depressed patients), but we cannot conclude anything about its specificity (distinction from different psychopathology conditions).

Keywords: psychopathology, functional neuroimaging, translational medical research, neuroscience, depression

INTRODUCTION

Modern psychopathology has been in a long-term crisis from different perspectives (1). One critical issue which contributes to this is the problem of validity of diagnostic methods and current classifications, which is entailed to some extent from the methodological gap existing between psychopathology and neuroscience, and functional neuroimaging in particular (2–5).

The larger body of functional neuroimaging data was collected in fMRI studies using event-related or block designs where participants had to engage in different tasks. The most common task-related fMRI studies obtain sequential scans while subjects are doing/viewing either cognitive tasks (like Stroop's test) or emotionally valenced (sad, happy, angry, fearful) and neutral pictures. Common practice in clinical fMRI research is to perform a clinical assessment before and after the scanning that is subjected to a *post hoc* correlational analysis. This creates a temporal gap between the two measurements. In some cases, this may affect the consistency of such correlations (for example in bipolar patients with rapid cycling). Thus, the fMRI imaging and the clinical assessment may reflect different emotional states in such settings. Furthermore, the stimuli that are typically presented during an fMRI session are often diagnostically irrelevant, i.e., they cannot be incorporated directly into diagnostically valid operational procedures.

To this end unfortunately fMRI-techniques have provided rather controversial data on potential markers in psychopathology. It is difficult, if not impossible to attain universal agreement on what kind of procedures should be used in order to incorporate functional neuroimaging findings into diagnostic and treatment standards in psychiatry.

Having in mind the complexity of contemporary clinical practice, we have developed a novel study design that combines clinical assessment scales, simultaneously administered with fMRI data acquisition. For a broader explanation of the underlying arguments behind the concept of translational convergent cross-validation in psychiatry, see Ref. (2, 3, 6). In the following we will shortly present the background for the design.

In our design, clinical fMRI studies involve real-time ratings of the clinical state, using disorder-relevant self-evaluation scales administered during fMRI data acquisition. Several standardized clinical self-assessment scales are used by clinicians worldwide. For example, in the case of depression, the Beck Depression Inventory (7), Zung (8), and von Zerssen (9) are some commonly used self-report scales. Those scales are validated against observer-based interviews, such as the Montgomery-Åsberg Depression Rating Scale (10), or the Hamilton Depression Scale (11), which are basically composed of similar kind of statements (items), extracted from either patient's (first person) or professional's (third person) narratives (6, 12). We now suggest bringing together the narrative (subjective) perspective with its objective neurobiological correlates. The suggested simultaneous fMRI data acquisition and the standardized rating scales have the potential to overcome the described temporal gap.

By implementing this new design, we expect to find significant correlations between the psychological rating scale score (total score, or score on given items or groups of items) and the pattern of blood-oxygen-level dependent (BOLD) activity. This is a critical step forward to achieve *synchronization and concordance* of the applied measures and data bases in psychiatry as defined elsewhere (3, 13, 14). Ultimately, we can re-validate the clinical assessment tools according to the evidence from the simultaneous cross-validation with the neuroimaging methods. As a consequence, we will be able to rely on inexpensive instruments for clinical assessment. We consider such a convergent design with simultaneous clinical self-evaluation and fMRI data sampling, as having potential for revealing reliable constellations of biomarkers that could ultimately inform diagnosis and choice of treatment.

We have decided to focus on depressive episode on syndromal level as more consistent and homogenous clinical construct in comparison to schizophrenia, anxiety disorders and other psychopathological phenomena. We assume that the clear nosological approach as adopted from bio-medicine would not be appropriate for validation of psychiatric classification (15). Therefore, we have recruited subjects with current depressive episode in the context of either bipolar disorder or major depressive disorder compliant with the DSM-IV TR criteria.

Aim

The aim of the current study was thus to investigate the translational validity of von Zerssen's depression scale and its fMRI-correlates during their simultaneous implementation in patients with depression and healthy controls.

MATERIALS AND METHODS

Subjects

We recruited 18 adult subjects (mean age 44.3 ± 3.6 years, six males) complying with the DSM-IV-TR criteria for depressive episode (single or recurrent) in the context of major depressive disorder (12 subjects) or bipolar affective disorder (6 subjects), as assessed by the general clinical interview and the structured Mini International Neuropsychiatric Interview (M.I.N.I 6.0). Severity of current episode was assessed and only subjects with moderate to severe depression (e.g., a total score on the MADRS of at least 20 were included). Subjects were excluded if they had a second axis-I diagnosis (psychotic, anxiety, substance-related disorder), severe decompensated somatic disorder, neurological disorder, history of head trauma with loss of consciousness, severe suicidal risk (10th item of MADRS ≥ 2).

Eighteen age, sex, and education matched healthy controls (median age 39.1 ± 2.5 years, six males) were enrolled in the study as a control group. They were subjected to a general clinical interview and the structured M.I.N.I. and they were included if they did not comply with any of the DSM-IV-R diagnoses included, had no history of psychiatric disorder, neurological disorder, head trauma with loss of consciousness. All participants provided a written informed consent and the study was approved by the University's Ethics Committee.

MR Scanning

The scanning of the participants was done with a 3 T MRI system (GE Discovery 750w). The MR protocol included a structural scan [Sag 3D T1 FSPGR, slice thickness 1 mm, matrix 256 × 256, TR (relaxation time) −7.2 msec, TE (echo time) −2.3, flip angle 12°], and a functional scan (2D EPI, slice thickness 3 mm, matrix 64 × 64, TR −2,000 ms, TE −30, flip angle 90°). Before each functional scan, five dummy time series were acquired.

Experimental Procedure

We used a standard block-design with two different "ON" conditions and one "OFF" condition, with a total duration of 8 min and 32 s Each "ON" block consisted of four text statements presented for 8 s each on LCD screen. Diagnostically specific (DS) blocks consisted of 4 consecutive statements from the von Zerssen depression scale ("I cry easily," "I am more sensitive to criticism than I was before") and the diagnostically neutral (DN) blocks consisted of four statements from a questionnaire about genral interests and likes (such as "I like to write books or plays," "I like to repair household appliances," etc.). Under each statement four possible item responses were presented as well as the four buttons corresponding to the responses (completely true = upper left, mostly true = lower left, somewhat true = lower right, not true = upper right button). There were four blocks of each type, alternating between DS and DN conditions, and each ON block was followed by an "OFF" block with a fixation cross in the middle of the screen (DS_OFF_DN_OFF_DS_OFF...). The duration of ON and OFF blocks was 32 s. For the active conditions, the participants were instructed to read the statements carefully and to respond with a button press according to their level of agreement, and for the passive OFF condition, to focus on the fixation cross without thinking of anything in particular.

fMRI Data Analysis

Data were analyzed using the SPM 12 (Statistical Paramertic Mapping, http://www.fil.ion.ucl.ac.uk/spm/) software running on MATLAB R2015 for Windows. The preprocessing included the following steps: (i) realignment of the functional data for correction of head motion, (ii) coregistration between the high-resolution anatomical image and the functional scans, (iii) intra-individual estimation of spatial registration parameters based on the anatomical image and (iv) transformation of the coregistered functional data to standardized Montreal Neurological Institute (MNI) space, followed by (v) spatial smoothing with a 6 mm full-width-at-half-maximum Gaussian kernel.

The model for first-level analysis was then specified, parameters estimated and t-contrasts defined for the active vs. passive conditions, with the contrasts (DS > DN) and the (DN > DS), respectively. The resulting contrast maps from each comparison and for each subject were then used in a second-level random-effects analysis for between-group differences (patients > controls and controls > patients), and for the interaction of groups × conditions. The level of significance was set to $p > 0.05$ false discovery rate (FDR) corrected.

Behavioral Data Analysis

Correlations were tested for the total score from the DS statements and both the DS > DN and DN > DS contrast maps. Demographic and clinical characteristics of the subjects were analyzed by means of SPSS 22.0 for Windows. The level of significance for all tests was set to $p < 0.05$. Because of the small sample size, we used the Mann–Whitney test for comparison of continuous variables, Chi-square and Fisher's exact test for testing of categorical variables.

RESULTS

Demographic and Clinical Characteristics

There were no statistically significant differences in age, sex and education between the two groups. Expectedly, patients had significantly higher MADRS and von Zerssen score (**Table 1**).

TABLE 1 | Demographic and clinical characteristics.

	Healthy controls ($n = 18$)	Patients ($n = 18$)	*p*-Value
Age	39.1 ± 2.5	44.3 ± 3.6	0.308[a]
Sex (M:F)	6:12	6:12	1.0[b]
Education (secondary:higher)	8:10	8:10	1.0[b]
MADRS score	3 (2–3.5)	29.7 (25.7–33.7)	*0.001[a]
Von Zerssen score	6 (4–8)	25 (22–29)	*0.001[a]

[a]*Mann–Whitney U test.*
[b]*Fisher's exact test.*
$^*p < 0.005$.
IQR, interquartile range; MADRS, Montgomery–Åsberg Depression Rating Scale.

TABLE 2 | Patients > Controls for the DS > DN contrast maps.

Anatomical localization	Cluster size (number of voxels)	MNI coordinates			*p*-Value (FDR-corrected)
		x	*y*	*z*	
Right pre- and postcentral gyrus	734	48	−22	58	0.006
		32	−24	62	
Left middle frontal gyrus	58	−40	14	30	0.009
Medial segment of left superior frontal gyrus	23	−8	64	6	0.023
Right supplementary motor area	12	8	−12	72	0.026
Left occipital pole	16	−18	−98	2	0.027
Right superior parietal lobule	14	36	−46	60	0.027
Medial segment of the right precentral gyrus	11	10	−18	50	0.030

DS, diagnostically specific condition; DN, diagnostically neutral condition; FDR, false discovery rate; MNI, Montreal Neurological Institute.

fMRI Results

The first-level of analysis provided four contrast maps (DS > DN, DN > DS, DS > OFF, DN > OFF) for each subject, which were used in the second-level within- and between-group analyses. The *t*-contrast for the within-group DS vs. DN blocks yielded no residual activations in the healthy controls, while the patients showed higher activation in several clusters located in the right pre- and postcentral gyri (MNI coordinates 32, −14, 66 and 48, −22, 58), left middle frontal gyrus (−40, 16, 30), left middle temporal gyrus (−50, −38, 0), and the left inferior frontal gyrus triangular part (−50, 22, −4).

For the between-group analysis we performed first a two-sample t-test on the DS > DN contrast maps. The patients demonstrated significantly higher activations in the right pre- and postcentral regions, left middle frontal gyrus, medial segment of left superior frontal gyrus, right supplementary motor area, right superior parietal lobule (See **Table 2** and **Figure 1** for details).

On the group level, the DN > DS contrast yielded no significant residual activations neither in the patients nor in the control subjects. The between-group analysis resulted, as expected, in the same significant clusters as mentioned above (right pre- and

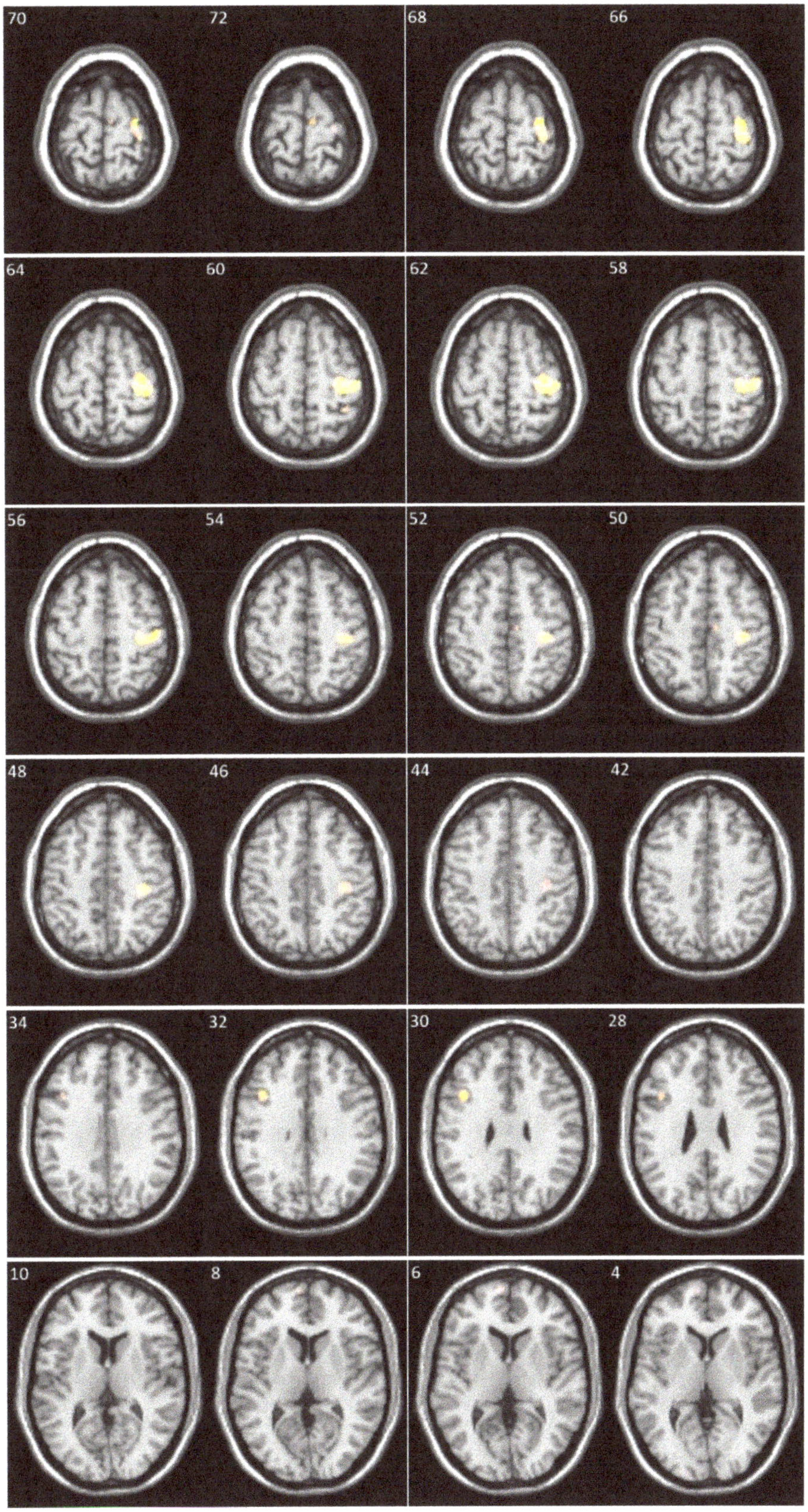

FIGURE 1 | Clusters significantly more activated in patients compared to controls (numbers in left upper corner represent x axis in Montreal Neurological Institute coordinates).

postcentral regions, left middle frontal gyrus, medial segment of left superior frontal gyrus, right supplementary motor area, right superior parietal lobule) now in control subjects > patients. While the opposite *t*-contrast, patients > controls, yielded no suprathreshold clusters.

The between-group analysis for the contrasts DS > OFF and DN > OFF, respectively, showed no statistically significant difference between the healthy controls and the patients although in each group both contrasts resulted in large clusters of activation in cortical and subcortical regions.

TABLE 3 | Positive correlations between the DS score and the DS > DN contrast in patients.

Anatomical localization	Cluster size (number of voxels)	MNI coordinates			*p*-Value (FDR-corrected)
		x	*y*	*z*	
Right pre- and postcentral gyrus	133	34	−14	66	0.044
		48	−22	58	
Left Precuneus	12	−2	−58	58	0.044
Right superior parietal lobule	9	34	−46	60	0.044

DS, diagnostically specific condition; DN, diagnostically neutral condition; FDR, false discovery rate; MNI, Montreal Neurological Institute.

Correlations between BOLD Signal and Behavioral Data

No significant correlations were found in the healthy controls between the total score of the von Zerssen scale statements and residual activations of the DS > DN contrast. For the patient group, however, there were significant positive correlations with activations in the right pre- and postcentral gyrus, as well as in left precuneus and right superior parietal lobule (**Table 3**; **Figure 2**).

DISCUSSION

Our results demonstrated that in healthy controls, contrasting the two types of stimuli yielded no residual activations, e.g., the diagnostically specific (DS) stimuli did not produce significantly different activations compared to the diagnostically neutral (DN) stimuli. Furthermore, the correlation analyses did not find a relationship between brain activations and the total score of the DS statements in this group.

However, contrasting the DS stimuli to the DN stimuli in the patients produced significant residual activations in several

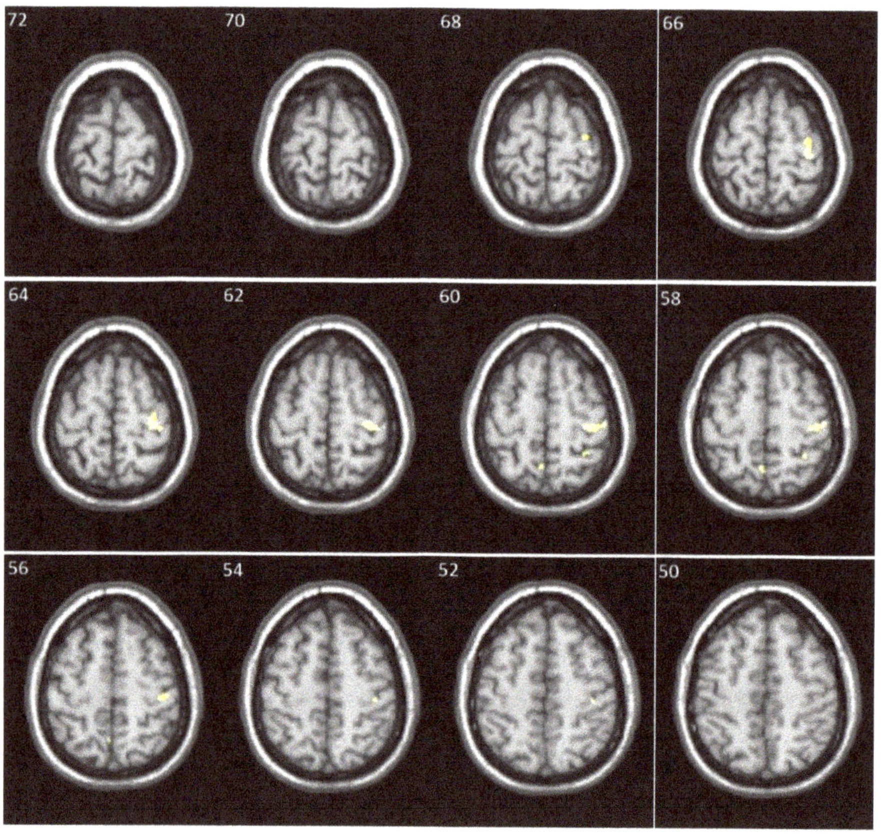

FIGURE 2 | Clusters showing significant positive correlation between the diagnostically specific (DS) score and the DS > DN contrast in patients (numbers in left upper corner represent *x*-axis in Montreal Neurological Institute coordinates).

brain regions (see **Table 2** and **Figure 1** for details). Positive correlations were also found between the DS > DN contrast and the DS score in several activation clusters (see **Table 3** and **Figure 2** for details).

Changes in brain activation, metabolism of glucose, neurotransmitters such as serotonin and its receptors and even gray matter volumes in various areas of the frontal cortex have previously been reported in patients with depression (16–21), and we will discuss our findings in light of current knowledge about the functional characteristics of the brain areas in which the significant clusters were located.

Residual activations in the depressed patients in the right pre- and postcentral gyrus can be explained by the demands for motor responses during the performance of the task (pressing the buttons). Since the patients in comparison to healthy controls were responding more frequently with the left hand buttons, i.e., positive answers (completely true, mostly true, see Methods), this means that they more often used their left hand in the DS condition. We cannot exclude the hypothesis that the observed motor cortex activations might be as well interpreted in terms of changes of psychomotor behavior (agitation or inhibition) regarded as fundamental symptoms of the depressive episode. Given the sample size it is difficult to justify to what extent and in which direction does this factor influence the results.

The remaining clusters (left middle frontal gyrus, triangular part of the left inferior frontal gyrus and middle temporal gyrus) were located in areas associated with language functions, semantic processing and memory (22–24). It is reasonable to assume that the patients probably would recruit these areas to a greater extent than controls when responding to the diagnostically relevant statements.

One of the statistically significant clusters that correlated with the DS total score items in the patients overlaps with the abovementioned cluster resulting from the DS > DN contrast with peaks in the right pre- and post-central gyrus. The explanation is that the more frequent motor response with the left buttons causes the activation of this area, and at the same time this leads to a higher DS score. Further, a significant area within the same cluster was identified to be the right supramarginal gyrus (rSMG), which is previously reported to be involved in empathy (25). The correlation with activations within the right superior parietal lobule is probably also, in addition, related to regulation of working memory, and motor function, assuming that this area is implicated in visual-motor coordination (26).

The left precuneus also demonstrated correlations with the patients' DS score, which can be explained by the variety of cognitive functions to which this area is related—visual-spatial imagery, reproduction of episodic and autobiographical memory, and self-processing operations, namely first-person perspective taking and experience of agency (27). We can assume that more frequent positive responses (higher DS scores) are accompanied by a higher degree of activation of processes related to autobiographical memory and a first-person perspective.

In the between-group comparisons, the more pronounced activations in the right pre- and postcentral gyrus are explained again by the more frequent left-handed motor response in the patients. The other clusters located in the right hemisphere—the right supplementary motor area and the medial segment of the right precentral gyrus (Brodmann area 6) and the right upper parietal lobule (Brodmann area 7) are also related to motor responses, and movement planning, and visual-motor coordination, respectively (26, 28).

The cluster with a peak in the left middle frontal gyrus (Brodmann area 8) falls into the functional area of the dorsolateral prefrontal cortex (DLPFC) associated with executive functions, such as attention, working memory, planning, and inhibition of response (29–32). Disturbances of the function of the DLPFC are associated with depression (33), and moreover, this area has been the target for transcranial magnetic stimulation (TMS) treatment in resistant depression patients (34). This result is also consistent with our preliminary pilot study findings (35).

Another of the significant clusters had a peak in the medial segment of the left superior frontal gyrus (Brodmann area 10), which is part of the ventromedial prefrontal cortex (VMPFC) associated with the regulation of emotions and decision making, including moral judgments (36–39). The role of the VMPFC in mood disorders is also well known (40).

The cluster of activation in the left occipital pole falls within the visual associative cortex (Brodmann area 18), which function is related to the awareness and understanding of visual signals. Since in our case, the stimuli were in the form of a written text, the localization of the activations on the left coincides with other data showing activation of the left associative visual cortex when reading a text (41). Probably, the patients generally retain their attention longer on the DS items than on the DN items.

Limitations of the study might be considered in the small sample size as well as its heterogeneity in terms of nosological diagnosis according to conventional diagnostic standards (bipolar disorder and major depressive disorder). The reported big size cluster (over 700 voxels) in the central cortical region encompasses various distinct functional areas but it is difficult to delineate the specific activations in the relevant subregions. The adopted block design approach in fMRI is more robust experimentally, however, it is relatively distant from clinical reality for application of self-evaluation tools.

In conclusion, we can say that the results confirm the possibility of translational cross-validation of a clinical psychological test (von Zerssen's depression scale). At this stage, however, we can only confirm the sensitivity of the method (its ability to distinguish healthy controls from depresed patients), but we cannot conclude anything about its specificity (distinction from different psychopathology conditions). For this purpose, it will be necessary in future studies to apply this paradigm to other clinical groups.

AUTHOR CONTRIBUTIONS

DS is author of the concept, major parts of the introduction and discussion SK: author of the empirical parts of the study. SB: contributed to the concept, the study design, pilot study and manuscript editing/revisions. R-DS contributed to the methodological framework, selection of the clinical assessment methods. KH contributed to the development of the study design, the pilot study, manuscript editing, and revisions. SK took part in the overall management/supervision of the project.

REFERENCES

1. Stoyanov D. *Towards New Philosophy of Mental Health, Perspectives from Neuroscience and Humanities*. New Castle: Cambridge Scholars Publishing (2015).
2. Stoyanov D, Borgwardt SJ, Varga S. The problem of translational validity across neuroscience and psychiatry. In: Zachar P, Stoyanov D, Aragona M, Jablenski A, editors. *Alternative Perspectives on Psychiatric Validation*. Oxford: Oxford University Press (2014). 128 p.
3. Stoyanov D, Stieglitz RD, Borgwardt SJ, Lenz C. The translational validation as novel approach to integration of neuroscience and psychiatry. In: Stoyanov D, Stieglitz R-D, editors. *New Developments in Clinical Psychology Research*. New York: Nova Science Publishers (2015). p. 195–209.
4. Borgwardt S, Schmidt A. Is neuroimaging clinically useful in subjects at high risk for psychosis? *World Psychiatry* (2016) 15(2):178–9. doi:10.1002/wps.20333
5. Fusar-Poli P, Broome MR. Conceptual issues in psychiatric neuroimaging. *Curr Opin Psychiatry* (2006) 19(6):608–12. doi:10.1097/01.yco.0000245750.98749.1b
6. Stoyanov D, Machamer PK, Schaffner KF. In quest for scientific psychiatry: towards bridging the explanatory gap. *Philos Psychiatry Psychol* (2013) 20(3):261–73. doi:10.1353/ppp.2013.0041
7. Beck AT, Steer RA. Internal consistencies of the original and revised Beck Depression Inventory. *J Clin Psychol* (1984) 40(6):1365–7. doi:10.1002/1097-4679(198411)40:6<1365::AID-JCLP2270400615>3.0.CO;2-D
8. Zung WW. A self-rating depression scale. *Arch Gen Psychiatry* (1965) 12:63–70. doi:10.1001/archpsyc.1965.01720310065008
9. von Zerssen D. Clinical self-rating scales (CSRS) of the Munich Psychiatric Information System (PSYCHIS München). In: Sartorius N, Ban TA, editors. *Assessment of Depression*. Berlin: Springer, Heidelberg (1986), 270–303.
10. Montgomery SA, Asberg M. A new depression scale designed to be sensitive to change. *Br J Psychiatry* (1979) 134:382–9. doi:10.1192/bjp.134.4.382
11. Hamilton M. A rating scale for depression. *J Neurol Neurosurg Psychiatry* (1960) 23:56–62. doi:10.1136/jnnp.23.1.56
12. Stoyanov D, Machamer PK, Schaffner KF, Hernández RR. The meta-language of psychiatry as cross-disciplinary effort: in response to Zachar (2012). *J Eval Clin Pract* (2012) 18(3):710–20. doi:10.1111/j.1365-2753.2012.01846.x
13. Borgwardt S, Fusar-Poli P. Third-generation neuroimaging in early schizophrenia: translating research evidence into clinical utility. *Br J Psychiatry* (2012) 200(4):270–2. doi:10.1192/bjp.bp.111.103234
14. McGuire P, Howes OD, Stone J, Fusar-Poli P. Functional neuroimaging in schizophrenia: diagnosis and drug discovery. *Trends Pharmacol Sci* (2008) 29(2):91–8. doi:10.1016/j.tips.2007.11.005
15. Telles Correia D. Different perspectives of validity in psychiatry. *J Eval Clin Pract* (2017) 23:988–93. doi:10.1111/jep.12766
16. Bhagwagar Z, Hinz R, Taylor M, Fancy S, Cowen P, Grasby P. Increased 5-HT(2A) receptor binding in euthymic, medication-free patients recovered from depression: a positron emission study with [(11)C]MDL 100,907. *Am J Psychiatry* (2006) 163(9):1580–7. doi:10.1176/ajp.2006.163.9.1580
17. Bora E, Harrison BJ, Davey CG, Yucel M, Pantelis C. Meta-analysis of volumetric abnormalities in cortico-striatal-pallidal-thalamic circuits in major depressive disorder. *Psychol Med* (2012) 42(4):671–81. doi:10.1017/s0033291711001668
18. Drevets WC, Frank E, Price JC, Kupfer DJ, Holt D, Greer PJ, et al. PET imaging of serotonin 1A receptor binding in depression. *Biol Psychiatry* (1999) 46(10):1375–87. doi:10.1016/S0006-3223(99)00189-4
19. Meyer JH, McMain S, Kennedy SH, Korman L, Brown GM, DaSilva JN, et al. Dysfunctional attitudes and 5-HT2 receptors during depression and self-harm. *Am J Psychiatry* (2003) 160(1):90–9. doi:10.1176/appi.ajp.160.1.90
20. Su L, Cai Y, Xu Y, Dutt A, Shi S, Bramon E. Cerebral metabolism in major depressive disorder: a voxel-based meta-analysis of positron emission tomography studies. *BMC Psychiatry* (2014) 14:321. doi:10.1186/s12888-014-0321-9
21. Drevets WC, Price JL, Furey ML. Brain structural and functional abnormalities in mood disorders: implications for neurocircuitry models of depression. *Brain Struct Funct* (2008) 213(1–2):93–118. doi:10.1007/s00429-008-0189-x
22. Binder JR, Desai RH, Graves WW, Conant LL. Where is the semantic system? A critical review and meta-analysis of 120 functional neuroimaging studies. *Cereb Cortex* (2009) 19(12):2767–96. doi:10.1093/cercor/bhp055
23. Linden DE. The working memory networks of the human brain. *Neuroscientist* (2007) 13(3):257–67. doi:10.1177/1073858406298480
24. Price CJ. A review and synthesis of the first 20 years of PET and fMRI studies of heard speech, spoken language and reading. *Neuroimage* (2012) 62(2):816–47. doi:10.1016/j.neuroimage.2012.04.062
25. Silani G, Lamm C, Ruff CC, Singer T. Right supramarginal gyrus is crucial to overcome emotional egocentricity bias in social judgments. *J Neurosci* (2013) 33(39):15466–76. doi:10.1523/jneurosci.1488-13.2013
26. Thakral PP, Slotnick SD. The role of parietal cortex during sustained visual spatial attention. *Brain Res* (2009) 1302:157–66. doi:10.1016/j.brainres.2009.09.031
27. Cavanna AE, Trimble MR. The precuneus: a review of its functional anatomy and behavioural correlates. *Brain* (2006) 129(Pt 3):564–83. doi:10.1093/brain/awl004
28. Nachev P, Kennard C, Husain M. Functional role of the supplementary and pre-supplementary motor areas. *Nat Rev Neurosci* (2008) 9(11):856–69. doi:10.1038/nrn2478
29. Johnson JA, Strafella AP, Zatorre RJ. The role of the dorsolateral prefrontal cortex in bimodal divided attention: two transcranial magnetic stimulation studies. *J Cogn Neurosci* (2007) 19(6):907–20. doi:10.1162/jocn.2007.19.6.907
30. Kaller CP, Rahm B, Spreer J, Weiller C, Unterrainer JM. Dissociable contributions of left and right dorsolateral prefrontal cortex in planning. *Cereb Cortex* (2011) 21(2):307–17. doi:10.1093/cercor/bhq096
31. Mars RB, Grol MJ. Dorsolateral prefrontal cortex, working memory, and prospective coding for action. *J Neurosci* (2007) 27(8):1801–2. doi:10.1523/JNEUROSCI.5344-06.2007
32. Ridderinkhof KR, van den Wildenberg WP, Segalowitz SJ, Carter CS. Neurocognitive mechanisms of cognitive control: the role of prefrontal cortex in action selection, response inhibition, performance monitoring, and reward-based learning. *Brain Cogn* (2004) 56(2):129–40. doi:10.1016/j.bandc.2004.09.016
33. Koenigs M, Grafman J. The functional neuroanatomy of depression: distinct roles for ventromedial and dorsolateral prefrontal cortex. *Behav Brain Res* (2009) 201(2):239–43. doi:10.1016/j.bbr.2009.03.004
34. Pascual-Leone A, Rubio B, Pallardó F, Catalá MD. Rapid-rate transcranial magnetic stimulation of left dorsolateral prefrontal cortex in drug-resistant depression. *Lancet* (1996) 348(9022):233–7. doi:10.1016/S0140-6736(96)01219-6
35. Stoyanov D, Kandilarova S, Sirakov N, Stoeva M, Velkova K, Kostianev S. Towards translational cross-validation of clinical psychological tests and fMRI: experimental implementation. *Comptes rendus de L'Academie bulgare des Sciences* (2017) 70(6):879–84.
36. Fellows LK, Farah MJ. The role of ventromedial prefrontal cortex in decision making: judgment under uncertainty or judgment per se? *Cereb Cortex* (2007) 17(11):2669–74. doi:10.1093/cercor/bhl176
37. Motzkin JC, Philippi CL, Wolf RC, Baskaya MK, Koenigs M. Ventromedial prefrontal cortex is critical for the regulation of amygdala activity in humans. *Biol Psychiatry* (2015) 77(3):276–84. doi:10.1016/j.biopsych.2014.02.014

38. Quirk GJ, Garcia R, Gonzalez-Lima F. Prefrontal mechanisms in extinction of conditioned fear. *Biol Psychiatry* (2006) 60(4):337–43. doi:10.1016/j.biopsych.2006.03.010
39. Young L, Bechara A, Tranel D, Damasio H, Hauser M, Damasio A. Damage to ventromedial prefrontal cortex impairs judgment of harmful intent. *Neuron* (2010) 65(6):845–51. doi:10.1016/j.neuron.2010.03.003
40. Myers-Schulz B, Koenigs M. Functional anatomy of ventromedial prefrontal cortex: implications for mood and anxiety disorders. *Mol Psychiatry* (2012) 17(2):132–41. doi:10.1038/mp.2011.88
41. Vorobyev VA, Alho K, Medvedev SV, Pakhomov SV, Roudas MS, Rutkovskaya JM, et al. Linguistic processing in visual and modality-nonspecific brain areas: PET recordings during selective attention. *Brain Res Cogn Brain Res* (2004) 20(2):309–22. doi:10.1016/j.cogbrainres.2004.03.011

Permissions

All chapters in this book were first published by Frontiers; hereby published with permission under the Creative Commons Attribution License or equivalent. Every chapter published in this book has been scrutinized by our experts. Their significance has been extensively debated. The topics covered herein carry significant findings which will fuel the growth of the discipline. They may even be implemented as practical applications or may be referred to as a beginning point for another development.

The contributors of this book come from diverse backgrounds, making this book a truly international effort. This book will bring forth new frontiers with its revolutionizing research information and detailed analysis of the nascent developments around the world.

We would like to thank all the contributing authors for lending their expertise to make the book truly unique. They have played a crucial role in the development of this book. Without their invaluable contributions this book wouldn't have been possible. They have made vital efforts to compile up to date information on the varied aspects of this subject to make this book a valuable addition to the collection of many professionals and students.

This book was conceptualized with the vision of imparting up-to-date information and advanced data in this field. To ensure the same, a matchless editorial board was set up. Every individual on the board went through rigorous rounds of assessment to prove their worth. After which they invested a large part of their time researching and compiling the most relevant data for our readers.

The editorial board has been involved in producing this book since its inception. They have spent rigorous hours researching and exploring the diverse topics which have resulted in the successful publishing of this book. They have passed on their knowledge of decades through this book. To expedite this challenging task, the publisher supported the team at every step. A small team of assistant editors was also appointed to further simplify the editing procedure and attain best results for the readers.

Apart from the editorial board, the designing team has also invested a significant amount of their time in understanding the subject and creating the most relevant covers. They scrutinized every image to scout for the most suitable representation of the subject and create an appropriate cover for the book.

The publishing team has been an ardent support to the editorial, designing and production team. Their endless efforts to recruit the best for this project, has resulted in the accomplishment of this book. They are a veteran in the field of academics and their pool of knowledge is as vast as their experience in printing. Their expertise and guidance has proved useful at every step. Their uncompromising quality standards have made this book an exceptional effort. Their encouragement from time to time has been an inspiration for everyone.

The publisher and the editorial board hope that this book will prove to be a valuable piece of knowledge for researchers, students, practitioners and scholars across the globe.

List of Contributors

Filipe Arantes-Gonçalves
CliniPinel, Lisbon, Portugal
Clínica de Saúde Mental do Porto, Porto, Portugal
CliniPinel - Clínica de Psiquiatria, Psicoterapia e Psicanálise, Lisbon, Portugal

João Gama Marques
Clínica Universitária de Psiquiatria e Psicologia Médica, Faculdade de Medicina, Universidade de Lisboa, Lisbon, Portugal
Consulta de Esquizofrenia Resistente, Centro Hospitalar Psiquiátrico de Lisboa, Lisbon, Portugal
Hospital Júlio de Matos, Centro Hospitalar Psiquiátrico de Lisboa, Lisbon, Portugal

Diogo Telles-Correia
Clínica Universitária de Psiquiatria e Psicologia Médica, Faculdade de Medicina, Universidade de Lisboa, Lisbon, Portugal
Serviço de Psiquiatria e Saúde Mental, Hospital de Santa Maria, Centro Hospitalar de Lisboa Norte, Lisbon, Portugal

Guilherme Messas
Department of Mental Health, Santa Casa de Sao Paulo School of Medical Sciences, São Paulo, Brazil

Melissa Tamelini
Institute of Psychiatry- Hospital das Clínicas de São Paulo, São Paulo, Brazil

Milena Mancini
Department of Psychological Sciences Humanities and Territory, University of Chieti, Chieti, Italy

Giovanni Stanghellini
Department of Psychological Sciences Humanities and Territory, University of Chieti, Chieti, Italy
Diego Portales University, Santiago, Chile

Drozdstoy Stoyanov and Sevdalina Kandilarova
Research Complex for Translational Neuroscience, Medical University Plovdiv (MUP), Plovdiv, Bulgaria
Department for Psychiatry and Medical Psychology, Medical University Plovdiv (MUP), Plovdiv, Bulgaria

Joana Jerónimo
Faculdade de Medicina da Universidade de Lisboa, Lisbon, Portugal
Hospital de Santa Maria, Centro Hospitalar Lisboa Norte, Lisbon, Portugal

Tiago Queirós
Hospital de Santa Maria, Centro Hospitalar Lisboa Norte, Lisbon, Portugal

Elie Cheniaux
Faculdade de Ciências Médicas da Universidade do Estado do Rio de Janeiro, Rio de Janeiro, Brazil
Instituto de Psiquiatria da Universidade Federal do Rio de Janeiro, Rio de Janeiro, Brazil

Maurício V. Daker
Departamento de Saúde Mental, Universidade Federal de Minas Gerais—UFMG, Belo Horizonte, Brazil

Ladislav Kesner
National Institute of Mental Health, Klecany, Czechia

Carla Moleiro
Instituto Universitário de Lisboa (ISCTE-IUL), CIS, Lisbon, Portugal

Camila Maria Severi Martins-Monteverde, Cristiane Von Werne Baes, Sandra Marcia de Carvalho Tofoli and Thalita Padovan
Stress and Affective Disorders Programme, University of São Paulo, São Paulo, Brazil

Emilene Reisdorfer
School of Community and Health Studies, Centennial College, Toronto, ON, Canada

Mario Francisco Juruena
Stress and Affective Disorders Programme, University of São Paulo, São Paulo, Brazil
Centre for Affective Disorders, Department Psychological Medicine, King's College London, London, United Kingdom

Diogo Telles-Correia and Sérgio Saraiva
Clinica Universitaria de Psiquiatria e Psicologia, Faculty of Medicine, Universidade de Lisboa, Lisbon, Portugal

Jorge Gonçalves
Faculty of Social and Human Sciences, IFILNOVA, Universidade Nova de Lisboa, Lisbon, Portugal

Helio Gomes Rocha Neto
Centro Universitario Lusíada, São Paulo, Brazil

Carlos Eduardo Estellita-Lins
Fundação Oswaldo Cruz (Fiocruz), Rio de Janeiro, Brazil

José Luiz Martins Lessa and Maria Tavares Cavalcanti
Instituto de Psiquiatria, Universidade Federal do Rio de Janeiro, Rio de Janeiro, Brazil

Petr Sojka
Department of Neurology, Faculty of Medicine, Masaryk University and St Anne's University Hospital Brno, Brno, Czechia

Martin Bareš and Tomáš Kašpárek
Department of Neurology, Faculty of Medicine, Masaryk University and St Anne's University Hospital Brno, Brno, Czechia
Department of Psychiatry, Faculty of Medicine, Masaryk University and University Hospital Brno, Brno, Czechia

Miroslav Světlák
Department of Neurology, Faculty of Medicine, Masaryk University and St Anne's University Hospital Brno, Brno, Czechia
Department of Psychology and Psychosomatics, Faculty of Medicine, Masaryk University and University Hospital Brno, Brno, Czechia

Bruno Palazzo Nazar
Institute of Psychiatry, Federal University of Rio de Janeiro, Rio de Janeiro, Brazil
Institute of Psychiatry, Psychology and Neuroscience, King's College London, London, United Kingdom

Amanda Pompeu Trindade
Institute of Psychiatry, Federal University of Rio de Janeiro, Rio de Janeiro, Brazil

Monica Leslie and Janet Treasure
Institute of Psychiatry, Psychology and Neuroscience, King's College London, London, United Kingdom

Leandro Fernandes Malloy-Diniz
Departamento de Saúde Mental, Universidade Federal de Minas Gerais, Belo Horizonte, Brazil

Joseph Sergeant
VU University Amsterdam, Amsterdam, Netherlands

Paulo Mattos
Institute of Psychiatry, Federal University of Rio de Janeiro, Rio de Janeiro, Brazil
D'Or Institute for Education and Research, Rio de Janeiro, Brazil

Sevdalina Kandilarova and Drozdstoy Stoyanov
Research Complex for Translational Neuroscience, Medical University of Plovdiv (MUP), Plovdiv, Bulgaria
Department of Psychiatry and Medical Psychology, Medical University of Plovdiv (MUP), Plovdiv, Bulgaria

Stefan Kostianev
Research Complex for Translational Neuroscience, Medical University of Plovdiv (MUP), Plovdiv, Bulgaria
Department of Pathophysiology, Medical University of Plovdiv (MUP), Plovdiv, Bulgaria

Karsten Specht
Department of Biological and Medical Psychology, University of Bergen, Bergen, Norway
Department of Education, The Arctic University of Norway (UiT), Tromsø, Norway

Aiko Sato, Atsushi Kimura, Tomihisa Niitsu and Masaomi Iyo
Department of Psychiatry, Chiba University Graduate School of Medicine, Chuo-ku, Japan

Tasuku Hashimoto
Department of Psychiatry, Chiba University Graduate School of Medicine, Chuo-ku, Japan
Department of Psychiatry, Sodegaura Satsukidai Hospital, Sodegaura, Japan

Seiji Muranaka and Jun Sasaki
Department of Clinical Psychology, Graduate School of Human Sciences, Osaka University, Suita, Japan

Pedro Castro-Rodrigues
Champalimaud Clinical Centre, Champalimaud Centre for the Unknown, Lisbon, Portugal
Champalimaud Research, Champalimaud Centre for the Unknown, Lisbon, Portugal
NOVA Medical School, Faculdade de Ciências Médicas, Universidade Nova de Lisboa, Lisbon, Portugal
Centro Hospitalar Psiquiátrico de Lisboa, Lisbon, Portugal

Marta Camacho
Champalimaud Clinical Centre, Champalimaud Centre for the Unknown, Lisbon, Portugal

Sílvia Almeida
Champalimaud Clinical Centre, Champalimaud Centre for the Unknown, Lisbon, Portugal
Champalimaud Research, Champalimaud Centre for the Unknown, Lisbon, Portugal

Mónica Marinho
Champalimaud Clinical Centre, Champalimaud Centre for the Unknown, Lisbon, Portugal
Centro Hospitalar Psiquiátrico de Lisboa, Lisbon, Portugal

Catarina Soares
NOVA Medical School, Faculdade de Ciências Médicas, Universidade Nova de Lisboa, Lisbon, Portugal

J. Bernardo Barahona-Corrêa and Albino J. Oliveira-Maia
Champalimaud Clinical Centre, Champalimaud Centre for the Unknown, Lisbon, Portugal
Champalimaud Research, Champalimaud Centre for the Unknown, Lisbon, Portugal
NOVA Medical School, Faculdade de Ciências Médicas, Universidade Nova de Lisboa, Lisbon, Portugal
Department of Psychiatry and Mental Health, Centro Hospitalar de Lisboa Ocidental, Lisbon, Portugal

David E. J. Linden
MRC Centre for Neuropsychiatric Genetics and Genomics, School of Medicine, Institute of Psychological Medicine and Clinical Neurosciences, Cardiff University, Cardiff, United Kingdom

Sílvia Almeida
Champalimaud Clinical Centre, Champalimaud Centre for the Unknown, Lisbon, Portugal
Champalimaud Research, Champalimaud Centre for the Unknown, Lisbon, Portugal

Ana Rita Moura
Champalimaud Clinical Centre, Champalimaud Centre for the Unknown, Lisbon, Portugal
Department of Psychiatry and Mental Health, Centro Hospitalar de Lisboa Ocidental, Lisbon, Portugal

Ana B. Fernandes and Joaquim Alves da Silva
Champalimaud Clinical Centre, Champalimaud Centre for the Unknown, Lisbon, Portugal
Champalimaud Research, Champalimaud Centre for the Unknown, Lisbon, Portugal
NOVA Medical School/Faculdade de Ciências Médicas, Universidade Nova de Lisboa, Lisbon, Portugal

Gabriela Ribeiro
Champalimaud Clinical Centre, Champalimaud Centre for the Unknown, Lisbon, Portugal
Champalimaud Research, Champalimaud Centre for the Unknown, Lisbon, Portugal
Lisbon Academic Medical Center PhD Program, Faculdade de Medicina, Universidade de Lisboa, Lisbon, Portugal

J. Bernardo Barahona-Corrêa
Department of Psychiatry and Mental Health, NOVA Medical School | Faculdade de Ciências Médicas, Centro Hospitalar de Lisboa Ocidental, Lisbon, Portugal
CADIN – Neurodevelopment, Cascais, Portugal
Champalimaud Clinical Centre, Champalimaud Centre for the Unkown, Lisbon, Portugal
Champalimaud Research, Champalimaud Centre for the Unknown, Lisbon, Portugal

Viola Oertel, Silke Matura, David Prvulovic, Robert A. Bittner, Andreas Reif, Michael Stäblein and Christian Knöchel
Laboratory for Neuroimaging, Department of Psychiatry, Psychosomatic Medicine and Psychotherapy, Goethe University, Frankfurt am Main, Germany

Dominik Kraft, Denisa Ghinea and Helena Storchak
Laboratory for Neuroimaging, Department of Psychiatry, Psychosomatic Medicine and Psychotherapy, Goethe University, Frankfurt am Main, Germany
Brain Imaging Centre, Goethe University, Frankfurt am Main, Germany

Gilberto Alves
Post Graduation in Psychiatry and Mental Health, Federal University of Rio de Janeiro, Rio de Janeiro, Brazil

Tetsuya Yamamoto
Graduate School of Technology, Industrial and Social Sciences, Tokushima University, Tokushima, Japan

Nagisa Sugaya
Unit of Public Health and Preventive Medicine, School of Medicine, Yokohama City University, Yokohama, Japan

Marta Camacho
Champalimaud Clinical Centre, Champalimaud Centre for the Unknown, Lisbon, Portugal

Greg J. Siegle
Department of Psychiatry, University of Pittsburgh School of Medicine, Pittsburgh, PA, United States

Hiroaki Kumano and Hironori Shimada
Faculty of Human Sciences, Waseda University, Tokorozawa, Japan

Sergio Machado
Physical Activity Neuroscience, Physical Activity Postgraduate Program, Salgado de Oliveira University, Niterói, Brazil

Eric Murillo-Rodriguez
Laboratorio de Neurociencias Moleculares e Integrativas, Escuela de Medicina, División Ciencias de la Salud, Universidad Anáhuac Mayab, Mérida, Mexico

Nuno B. Rocha
School of Health, Polytechnic Institute of Porto, Porto, Portugal

Antonio E. Nardi
Panic and Respiration Laboratory, Institute of Psychiatry, Federal University of Rio de Janeiro, Rio de Janeiro, Brazil

Masahiro Takamura, Yasumasa Okamoto and Shigeto Yamawaki
Department of Psychiatry and Neurosciences, Institute of Biomedical and Health Sciences, Hiroshima University, Hiroshima, Japan

Sousa Alves
Institute of General Medicine, Goethe University, Frankfurt/Main, Germany
Translational Psychiatry Group, Universidade Federal do Ceará, Fortaleza, Brazil

Christian Knöchel, Andreas Reif, Viola Oertel, David Prvulovic and Britta Reinke
Laboratory of Neuroscience, Department of Psychiatry, Psychosomatic Medicine and Psychotherapy, Goethe University, Frankfurt/Main, Germany

Michael Anton Paulitsch and Johannes Pantel
Institute of General Medicine, Goethe University, Frankfurt/Main, Germany

André F. Carvalho
Department of Psychiatry, University of Toronto, Toronto, ON, Canada
Centre for Addiction and Mental Health, Toronto, ON, Canada

Richard Feddern
Translational Psychiatry Group, Universidade Federal do Ceará, Fortaleza, Brazil

Felipe Kenji Sudo
Department of Psychology, Pontifical Catholic University of Rio de Janeiro, Rio de Janeiro, Brazil
Memory Clinic, D' Or Institute for Research and Education, Rio de Janeiro, Brazil

Gianluca Esposito and Atiqah Azhari
Psychology Program, Nanyang Technological University, Singapore, Singapore
Department of Psychology and Cognitive Science, University of Trento, Trento, Italy

Jessica L. Borelli
Department of Psychological Science, University of California, Irvine, Irvine, CA, United States

Carolina G. Carrilho, Simone S. Cougo and Tatiane Bombassaro
Translational Research Group on Mental Health (GPTranSMe), Dom Bosco Catholic University, Campo Grande, Brazil

André Augusto B. Varella
Research Laboratory on Autism and Behavior (LAPAC), Dom Bosco Catholic University, Campo Grande, Brazil

Gilberto S. Alves
Department of Internal Medicine, Federal University of Maranhão (UFMA), São Luís, Brazil

Sergio Machado
Physical Activity Neuroscience Laboratory, Physical Activity Sciences Postgraduate Program-Salgado de Oliveira University (UNIVERSO), São Gonçalo, Brazil
Intercontinental Neuroscience Research Group, Universidad Anáhuac Mayab, Mérida, Mexico
Laboratory of Panic and Respiration (LabPR-UFRJ), Psychiatry Institute of Federal University of Rio de Janeiro (IPUB-UFRJ), Rio de Janeiro, Brazil

Eric Murillo-Rodriguez
Intercontinental Neuroscience Research Group, Universidad Anáhuac Mayab, Mérida, Mexico
Laboratorio de Neurociencias Moleculares e Integrativas, Escuela de Medicina División Ciencias de la Salud, Universidad Anáhuac Mayab, Mérida, Mexico

Dolores Malaspina
Departments of Psychiatry, Neuroscience and Genetics, Icahn School of Medicine at Mt. Sinai
Medical Center, New York, NY, United States

Antonio E. Nardi
Laboratory of Panic and Respiration (LabPR-UFRJ), Psychiatry Institute of Federal University of Rio de Janeiro (IPUB-UFRJ), Rio de Janeiro, Brazil

André B. Veras
Translational Research Group on Mental Health (GPTranSMe), Dom Bosco Catholic University, Campo Grande, Brazil
Intercontinental Neuroscience Research Group, Universidad Anáhuac Mayab, Mérida, Mexico
Laboratory of Panic and Respiration (LabPR-UFRJ), Psychiatry Institute of Federal University of Rio de Janeiro (IPUB-UFRJ), Rio de Janeiro, Brazil
Departments of Psychiatry, Neuroscience and Genetics, Icahn School of Medicine at Mt. Sinai
Medical Center, New York, NY, United States

Eva Schäflein, Heribert C. Sattel and Martin Sack
Department of Psychosomatic Medicine and Psychotherapy, Klinikum Rechts der Isar, Technical University of Munich, Munich, Germany

Olga Pollatos
Department of Clinical and Health Psychology, Institute of Psychology and Education, Ulm University, Ulm, Germany

Lirong Chen
Department of Psychology, Nanjing University, Nanjing, China

Wenpei Zhang
Department of Psychology, Nanjing University, Nanjing, China
Department of Business Administration, School of Business, Anhui University of Technology, Maanshan, China

Alain De Beuckelaer
Institute for Management Research, Radboud University, Nijmegen, Netherlands
Department of Personnel Management, Work and Organizational Psychology, Ghent University, Ghent, Belgium

Renlai Zhou
Department of Psychology, Nanjing University, Nanjing, China
Key Laboratory for NeuroInformation of Ministry of Education, University of Electronic Science and Technology of China, Chengdu, China

Stefan Borgwardt and Rolf-Dieter Stieglitz
University of Basel, Basel, Switzerland

Kenneth Hugdahl
Department of Biological and Medical Psychology, University of Bergen, Bergen, Norway
Division of Psychiatry, Haukeland University Hospital, Bergen, Norway
Department of Radiology, Haukeland University Hospital, Bergen, Norway

Stefan Kostianev
Research Complex for Translational Neuroscience, Medical University Plovdiv (MUP), Plovdiv, Bulgaria
Department of Pathophysiology, Medical University Plovdiv (MUP), Plovdiv, Bulgaria

Index

www.ingramcontent.com/pod-product-compliance
Lightning Source LLC
LaVergne TN
LVHW082221200926
848484LV00008B/2283